Preparation Guide for the AP*
European History Exam to Accompany

THE MAKING OF THE WEST

PEOPLES AND CULTURES

SECOND EDITION

Preparation Guide for the AP*
European History Exam to Accompany

THE MAKING OF THE WEST

PEOPLES AND CULTURES

SECOND EDITION

ERIC JOHNSON
University of California, Los Angeles

VICTORIA THOMPSON
Arizona State University

BEDFORD/ST. MARTIN'S   Boston ◆ New York

For information, write: Bedford/St. Martin's, 75 Arlington Street, Boston, MA 02116
(617-399-4000)

ISBN: 0–312–44198–3
EAN: 978–0–312–44198–2

Preface

The AP European History course presents a bewildering catalog of names, dates, and places. European history considers cultures, places, and themes that high school students may encounter for the first time. Indeed, many of today's students come from parts of the world where knowledge of European or American history cannot be assumed, and even more students will be unfamiliar with the global cultures that have contributed to and shaped Western civilization. Following the guidelines of the College Board's *AP European History Course Description*, we have developed this *Prep Guide* to parallel *The Making of the West: Peoples and Cultures* beginning with Chapter 14, "Renaissance Europe, 1400–1500." This *Prep Guide* is intended to help AP students master content, review what happened and why, and develop skills of historical analysis and interpretation, all of which help prepare them for the AP European History exam.

Introducing Students to History

Two essays included in the *Prep Guide* introduce students to history as a discipline of study and describe what historians seek. Written by Timothy R. Mahoney, University of Nebraska–Lincoln, these essays use accessible language and examples that students can refer to as they study *The Making of the West: Peoples and Cultures*, work on exercises, and, hopefully, learn to appreciate history.

- "What Is History?" describes history as stories that take place at different times and in different places, and explains that there are many stories to study. This essay discusses four major themes of human activity: economic, social, political, and cultural, all of which are themes emphasized on the AP exam.
- "Why Study History?" explains how a historical narrative is similar to the stories we construct to describe our own lives.

Both essays aim to help high school students understand their lives and the world around them. Further, the study of history is useful for all students because it sharpens the ability to interpret evidence and articulate complicated ideas in a simple, straightforward way.

Content and Organization

To achieve the goals stated above, each chapter of the *Prep Guide* features three sections: Chapter Overview, Chapter Review, and Building Historical Skills. Students can use the ***Chapter Overview*** before they read the corresponding chapters in *The Making of the West* to help them focus on the narrative and on important events and individuals. Alternatively, they can use them as reinforcement afterward to retain and connect information. ***Chapter Review*** helps students test their memory and comprehension of key facts as well as their grasp of larger themes and chronology. The ***Building Historical Skills*** section contains exercises designed to develop skills of source analysis fundamental to historical investigation. These sections build students' skills for successfully responding to the Document-Based Essay Questions (the DBQ) on the AP exam. An answer key at the back of the *Prep Guide* provides the answers for all exercises or, in the case of essay responses, model answers are supplied. Most questions or answers refer students to the relevant text sections of the textbook.

Chapter Overview

To help students master the information presented in the chapter, the *Chapter Overview* asks them to read material and test their comprehension.

- *Chapter Overview Questions* prompt students to recall the major topics and themes of the chapter.
- The *Chapter Summary* follows the chapter section by section, highlighting the main events and concepts presented in the narrative.
- *Key Events* includes the chronology from the end of each chapter in the textbook, followed by a set of questions that reinforces students' grasp of causal relationships.
- *Key Terms* improves students' understanding of core concepts through a matching activity. Each term includes a page reference to the textbook to help students review the context of unfamiliar terms.
- *Identification* helps students review significant peoples, places, and events of each chapter with fill-in-the-blank exercises.

Chapter Review

The exercises in the *Chapter Review* section give students an opportunity to assess what they have learned and build their skills of historical analysis and interpretation.

- *Multiple Choice* questions allow students to determine how well they have mastered the material after studying the chapter. The correct answers are provided in the answer key.
- *Short Answer* questions are designed to focus students on analyzing the main issues covered in the chapter. Paragraph responses required for each question prepare students for writing essay exams. Model answers are provided in the answer key.

Building Historical Skills

A unique *Building Historical Skills* section guides students in analyzing three types of sources that appear in both *The Making of the West* and on the AP Exam: maps, illustrations, and documents.

- *Reading Maps* asks students to respond to questions based on an analysis of a key map found in each chapter.
- *Reading Illustrations* prompts students to think critically about an illustration from *The Making of the West* and to understand how visual documents inform historians about a particular time or audience.
- *Reading Historical Documents* poses questions to help students think critically about each of the primary source documents included in each chapter of *The Making of the West*.

Using the *Prep Guide*

There is no single, recommended way to use the *Prep Guide*. Each student can tailor use of the guide to his or her own style of studying and learning. Students who use the *Prep Guide* in conjunction with the textbook will deepen their reading and study skills, and also enhance their understanding of the development of European history. In this way, a successful student comes away with not only an understanding of some of the key themes in European history, but also a better appreciation of the distinctive nature of historical thought and the ability to analyze historical evidence and interpretation. These are some of the stated goals for the College Board's AP European course.

Contents

What Is History?

History is the story of the human past. Like all stories, whether told orally or written down, history is full of characters acting their parts within story lines in a wide range of settings. Given the vast diversity and range of human life over thousands of years since people have been recording their experiences, the varieties of history are almost infinite. Generally, however, histories vary according to four characteristics: time frame, setting, subjects, and themes.

The present is considered contemporary time. People record contemporary time by living through it. We mark the passing of time by our physical and mental development and our living each day as part of a story line of experiences. We create a meaningful story line by placing each experience in the context of our memories of past experiences. Historians consider past time from a broader perspective than we have on contemporary time. Some historians do examine the past over very short periods, telling the story of human activity over the course of a few months, days, even hours or minutes. But the pastness of that time fixes it in place, allowing a perspective that no one has on the present. Most historians take advantage of historical perspective to examine events or processes that occurred over longer periods, ranging from years to decades or generations. Still other histories follow patterns of human activity across centuries or millennia. By creating stories that encompass long passages of time, historians place human activity in a new perspective, giving it meaning that couldn't be appreciated as people lived through it.

Historians do more, however, than understand events within the context of the passage of time. They also examine and understand past events within a specific setting. Indeed, understanding events and developments within their specific time and place is what fundamentally defines the study of history. Moreover, the scope of the places historians study is as varied as the time frames they tackle. Some histories examine the activities of people in very precise places—a town or city, a village, a section of a town, a neighborhood, a house, or, in the most specific cases, a single room. But most analyze regions, nations, continents, and even the world, placing the events of specific places, including our own, in a broader perspective. Similarly, the number of subjects historians consider can be as diverse as the places they inhabit. Traditionally, historians have studied the people who make up a state, a region, a nation, groups of nations, a civilization, a culture, or even humanity as a whole. But historians also study people as individuals, as well as families, small groups, and large groups based on occupational, social, ethnic, racial, or gender identity.

Thematically, all histories focus on human activity within at least one of the four major themes or aspects of human life: economic, social, political, or cultural activity. Economic activity involves all human actions and behaviors directed toward or motivated by the human impulse to physically survive and maintain oneself. How people have done this, what returns or gains they made from it, and how they have employed those gains to alter their standard of living are all encompassed within economic activity. Social history focuses on the ways in which people have organized themselves in relation to one another in order to facilitate their chances of survival and maintenance. History written from a social perspective tells stories of how individuals, groups, or a mass of people in a past time and place went about the business of living their lives and influencing the lives of others. How people grew up, socially interacted with others, formed families, had and reared children, and assumed adult roles in families are central concerns. How people formed small and large social groups based on family ties, occupational status, level of wealth, cultural values, or ethnic, racial, or gender identity and employed these points of reference to achieve the social goals of survival, protection, socialization, and reproduction are questions at the center of most social history.

Such social agendas usually involve some effort to influence or interact with political activity and government. Thus political history studies the negotiation, competition, and struggle among people of various families, clans, groups, classes, parties or sections, and countries for power and control. Traditionally, political history has examined how leaders, politicians, and government officials acquired power and formulated both domestic and foreign policies. It also studies the various ways in which leaders implemented policy, executed laws, and exerted control through leadership over their own people. From another perspective, political history studies how people interacted with government. Sometimes people were removed from government, had little say in its operations, and did not try to exert any influence over it. At other times, people affected government by gaining a voice in choosing leaders, organizing groups, parties, or institutions to influence or change the nature or focus of government policy, or exerting personal influence to affect government. How people and social groups acted politically to influence or respond to their own government's policies or the policies of another country is a central theme of political history. War is the broadest, most violent activity in the national or international realm of politics.

Finally, cultural histories tell stories of how people in past times and places, as they pursued and acted upon their various economic, social, and political goals, interpreted their activities in oral, artistic, material, spiritual, or intellectual ways to themselves and to others. Stories of people in the past formulating a theory of the cosmos, founding or reinvigorating or reforming a religious theology or practice, expressing themselves in a certain language, celebrating an event or entertaining themselves or others in a particular behavioral or material way, presenting the human body — male or female — in a specific way and clothed in a specific style, producing art or literature in a certain style with certain subjects and themes, or building, designing, or decorating homes, public buildings, and places of work in certain ways are all stories of people acting and behaving culturally. Indeed, the capacity to express culture seems to be what primarily defines people as human beings and distinguishes them from more advanced species of animal life.

History, therefore, is as varied and diverse as the endless range of possible varieties of time frames, setting themes, and subjects about which one could write in studying people who lived in the past. One of the most powerful aspects of history is trying to discern some of the common patterns and themes in the infinite variety of stories within the human experience. By identifying patterns in history, we fit the many pieces into a comprehensive story or narrative that has relevance to us and thus gives meaning to our own lives. However various and diverse, all these stories are part of the broad canvas, or story of the human past, that is history.

Timothy R. Mahoney
University of Nebraska–Lincoln

Why Study History?

Many people live without any exposure to formal history. The dictum that those who do not understand the past are doomed to repeat it is generally true; but, at the same time many people live perfectly satisfying lives without giving much thought to history. Nevertheless, all people—merely by living in an economy, society, political system and culture—interact with and derive meaning from systems that people in the past helped to establish. All people are, therefore, implicitly historians.

People choose to study history formally, then, because it connects one's life to the lives of other human beings who lived in the past, thus enhancing the meaning of one's own life. History is a fundamental human endeavor that defines one's humanity. In going about everyday activity, every person constructs a story line to plot his or her life. Asking someone who he is means asking him where he has been, what he has done and experienced, where he is going, and what he wants to do. The basic questions we all face—"What do you want to be?" or "What do you do?"—are inextricably bound up with "Who are you?" The answers to all of these questions lie in how well we have formulated the narrative of our lives. Happiness in life could be defined as successfully acting as the protagonist of the plot one has written and directed oneself. This general process of personal development is analogous to the practice of history. As individuals pursue their own lives and create meaningful personal narratives, so, too, on a larger scale across time and space, do families, clans, groups, classes, and nations.

The study of history has practical value, too, in that it helps develop one's analytic ability. As written by historians, history makes use of intellectual methods that are employed by a wide variety of disciplines and uses them in distinctive ways that are shaped by the particular nature of history. By understanding the differences between the methods, assumptions, subjects, and practice of history and those of other disciplines, one sharpens one's intellectual and analytic skills in important, even essential, ways. The subject and methods of history, therefore make an understanding of some history a foundation for any education, whether its major focus is the liberal arts, the sciences, or professional, technical, or vocational training.

Historians use rational scientific methods as the study of statistics and data, but their ultimate goal is to tell stories that have a plot. The way they organize the information they gather into that plot is really an interpretation or a theory about how or why something happened the way it did. Many facts seem undisputed—the defenestration of Prague happened in May of 1618; World War I erupted in August of 1914—but the significance of those facts, or even the full story of what happened, is less evident than one might think. To understand and explain the past, the historian must develop a thesis, test that thesis, and then defend it, employing the evidence that he or she has gathered.

The type of evidence available to historians is what makes history distinctive. Historians have access only to the evidence that has physically survived over time. Historians of the recent past may have far more evidence than any one person could ever absorb, but even this is not a complete picture. Sometimes new evidence becomes available when a set of documents, letters, or papers previously believed to have been lost come to light. But in most cases historians find and use new evidence by developing new methods of analysis, asking new questions, or pursuing new story lines that give new relevance to evidence that was previously ignored. Often, historians have evidence—such as diaries, journals, personal letters, or secret documents—that contemporaries living through the events did not have or even know existed. Or they may have no more than fragments of evidence, such as a single statement or a partial list, that do more to obscure than to clarify an understanding of the event in question. Most of the time, historians have an intriguing mix of material that no contemporary would have had, combined with a loss of much material that contemporaries took for granted. Out of this surviving database, historians must develop a theory and try, as best they can, to demonstrate it. Add to these concerns the fact that most historical evidence is circumstantial, rather than the direct testimony of witnesses. Often, historians try to construct a story with little more than a scrap of evidence that places an individual or a group in a time and place but not address the historians' specific questions. Historians must be creative in searching the documents they have in ways that will help to answer their questions. In some ways, the database available to historians is analogous to our memories about events in our past, which we have broader perspective on now but find hard to re-create in total. Given the uniqueness of the database, no historian will ever achieve the finality of the scientist. No historical thesis can be indisputably "proved" because in any human activity there is room for interpretation in telling the story. Many historical theses would fail to convince most trial juries beyond a reasonable doubt. Interpretations of a historical event can vary as widely as the range of views it is possible to have about current events or people living today. History thus uses the scientific method, but within a broader interpretive framework often supported by evidence that is not definitive. Every time one tries to understand the past, therefore, one gains insight into the uncertainty, biases, and fluidity of any knowledge.

The fluidity of history sometimes makes it more like a detective story or a novel than an experiment in a laboratory, and the practice of history as written adds to that similarity. Historians generally try to present their theses in the colloquial, nontechnical language in which people speak and read in everyday life. As a rule, they present their stories in narrative form, though often with an analytic foundation. The fact that history tries to fuse an understanding of different areas of activity into a general narrative adds to its intellectual power. History is the art of understanding social, economic, political, and cultural activity, then connecting these elements and trying to explain how they interacted to shape the general course of human events. By studying history, we can develop the powerful skill of articulating complicated ideas in a simple, straightforward way. Acquiring the skill to rationally examine much of the complex real world around us, develop a thesis about it, and argue the evidence to sustain a thesis is, indeed, one of the primary goals of a college education. History adds to that skill an ability to recognize human complexity within the context of its time and place. While putting a powerful intellectual tool in our hands, history also cultivates and satisfies our deepest human impulses.

Timothy R. Mahoney
University of Nebraska–Lincoln

Renaissance Europe
1400–1500

CHAPTER OVERVIEW

Chapter Questions *Keep these questions in mind as you go through the study guide chapter.*

1. How did the revival of humanism and the revolution in printing make the Renaissance possible?

2. How did perspective and the new conception of artistic "genius" reveal a growing sense of human power over the world?

3. Were politics in Italy a model for political events in the rest of Europe?

4. How could the fall of Constantinople and the completion of the *reconquista* in Spain both be considered symbols of the Renaissance? How could they be considered its opposite?

5. What late fifteenth-century political, economic, and technological forces drove the extension of European power to other parts of the globe?

Chapter Summary

Widening Intellectual Horizons

During the fifteenth century a brilliant rebirth of the arts and learning expanded the intellectual horizons of Europeans, as new voices celebrating secular human achievement and ability were added to the voices glorifying God. The Renaissance thrived on a newfound human perspective on life, the intensified study of Greek and Latin writing, and revolutionary techniques in bookmaking.

The Humanist Renewal, p. 507

Europeans' rediscovery of Greek and Roman writers gave rise to humanism, the study of the liberal arts or the humanities. The fall of Constantinople in 1453 to the Ottoman Turks sent Greek scholars to Italy for refuge and gave extra impetus to the revival of interest in the Greek classics. Humanist scholars focused on classical history and literature in their eagerness to emulate the glories of the ancient world. They rejected the emphasis on logic and the abstract language of the scholastics, preferring instead the eloquence and style of the great Roman authors. Most humanists did not think that studying ancient texts conflicted with their religious beliefs. Rather, in "returning to the sources," scholars sought to harmonize Christian faith and ancient learning. The study of the humanities raised expectations regarding what it meant to be an educated person and influenced school curricula up to the middle of the nineteenth century and even beyond.

The Advent of Printing, pp. 509–510

In the 1440s, Johannes Gutenberg (c. 1400–1470), a German goldsmith, invented printing with movable type, which allowed printers to produce books and pamphlets on a scale and at a cost never before possible. A durable metal mold for each letter of the alphabet was used to cast multiple copies of a small block (a type) having the letter on its face. The type for the text of a page was set in a frame, then inked and pressed against a sheet of paper. Paper, which was much cheaper than parchment, had been introduced to Europe just before Gutenberg's invention. Movable type took bookmaking out of the hands of human copyists, allowing entire manuscripts to be printed with only a small amount of human labor. After the 1440s, printing spread rapidly from Germany to other European countries. The advent of printing was so important that it brought about a communications revolution.

Revolution in the Arts

The Renaissance was one of the most brilliant creative periods in the European arts. New techniques in painting, architecture, and music fostered original styles and new subjects. Artists' individual talents and genius were recognized; artists developed a more naturalistic style; and perspective brought a mathematical and scientific basis to the visual arts, architecture, and music.

From Artisan to Artist, pp. 511–512

During the fifteenth century, artists acquired a more prominent social status, as individual talent was recognized by society. Artists began to use a more naturalistic style, especially in representing the human body, and they used mathematics to depict images with realistic perspective. The concept of artistic "genius," sometimes fashioned by the artists themselves, convinced society of the unique and priceless nature of their works. However, the artists' imaginations were often tempered by their wealthy patrons, who did not always allow artists to work unrestricted. Renaissance artists worked under three possible arrangements: long-term service in princely courts, commissioned piecework, or production for the market. As the heads of workshops, where they trained apprentices and negotiated their own contracts, artists had a great degree of autonomy. Famous artists developed followings, and many gained greater contractual control over their work, so that specific directions from wealthy consumers became less common. A market system for the visual arts also began to emerge during the Renaissance; artists produced works without prior arrangement for sale—a development that became a major force in artistic creativity.

The Human Figure, pp. 512–514

In their works, Renaissance artists began to depict ever more expressively human movements and emotions. In paintings like *The Expulsion from Paradise*, Masaccio (1401–1428) shows Adam and Eve grieving in shame and despair. Many masterpieces represented feminine beauty, as in the classical pagan figures of Sandro Botticelli (c. 1445–1510), while many others, like the works of Raphael (1483–1520), depicted the Virgin Mary. Renaissance artists also painted images of their contemporaries, including a growing number of highly detailed and realistic portraits of the middle class, illustrating a new, elevated view of human existence. Painters from the Low Countries, such as Jan van Eyck (1390?–1441), distinguished themselves in portraiture, achieving a sense of detail and reality unsurpassed until the advent of photography. The ideal of a universal man found expression in the writing of Giovanni Pico della Mirandola (1463–1494), whose work *On the Dignity of Man* placed man at the center of the universe as the "molder and maker of himself" and as the measure of all things; the work stressed human responsibility in shaping society and a religious trust in God's divine plan. For the first time since classical antiquity, sculptors again cast the human figure in bronze in life-size or larger freestanding statues. One idealized depiction of the human body was Michelangelo Buonarroti's (1475–1564) eighteen-foot marble statue, *David*, posing free of fabric and armor.

Order through Perspective, pp. 514–516

Renaissance art was distinguished from earlier artistic trends by being more concerned with reality than symbolism. Renaissance artists used visual perspective—an illusory three-dimensional effect on a two-dimensional surface—to create realistic images as the eye would perceive them; to be described as an "imitator of nature" was the highest praise for a Renaissance artist. Implicit in the use of perspective to represent space was a new Renaissance worldview, in which humans asserted themselves over nature by controlling space itself. Artists like Lorenzo Ghiberti (c. 1378–1455), Andrea Mantegna (1431–1506), and Piero della Francesca (1420–1492) employed perspective in their work to create a sense of depth and space. Architects also exemplified the Renaissance ideal of uniting creativity with scientific knowledge. Florentine architect Filippo Brunelleschi (1377–1446) proved a master of engineering. The buildings of Leon Battista Alberti (1404–1472) reveal a strong classical influence; in his theoretical work *On Architecture* (1415), he argued the merits of large-scale urban planning and favored designs reminiscent of classical Rome. Pope Sixtus IV (r. 1471–1484) applied Alberti's architectural ideas to Rome, transforming the medieval city into one that recalled the grandeur of its ancient origins.

New Musical Harmonies, pp. 516–517

While Italy set the standard for Renaissance art and architecture, trends in northern Europe influenced musical styles. The leader of the polyphonic style of music was Guillaume Dufay (1400–1474) from the Low Countries. Dufay composed music with mathematical precision, traveling to all the cultural centers of the Renaissance, where nobles sponsored compositions and maintained corps of musicians at their courts. The new style of music was very popular among social elites. Renaissance polyphony consisted of three main genres: the canon (central texts) of the Catholic Mass; the motet, which used both sacred and secular texts; and the secular chanson, which often incorporated the tunes of folk dances. Composers frequently adapted folk melodies for sacred music, expressing religious sentiment through voices rather than instruments. The tambourine and lute, as well as small ensembles of wind and string instruments, became fashionable in the courts of Europe. Keyboard instruments, such as the harpsichord, which could play several sounds and melodies at once, were also in use by the fifteenth century.

The Intersection of Private and Public Lives

Beginning in the fourteenth century, the state attempted to shape private life through its institutions and laws. This process was most evident in Florence, where considerations of state power intruded into intimate personal concerns, such as sexuality, marriage, and childbirth.

Renaissance Social Hierarchy, pp. 517–518

In Florence, 1427, the center of Renaissance culture, the government compiled a comprehensive tax record of city households. Completed in 1430, this census provided important details about social relations and demographics. Florentines recognized class divisions, referring to the "little people" (workers, artisans, and small merchants; about 60 percent of the population) and the "fat people" (wealthier merchants and other professionals; about 30 percent of the population). At the bottom of the hierarchy were slaves and servants, largely women from the surrounding countryside employed in domestic service. At the top, a tiny one percent of patricians, bankers, and wool merchants controlled a quarter of the city's wealth. Based on the survey, men seem to have outnumbered women, an unusual statistic that can be explained by female infanticide and the underreporting of women. Most Florentines lived in households of six or more, although the family unit itself—whether nuclear or extended—varied depending on wealth. In rich patrician families and those of landowning peasants in the countryside, extended families and higher numbers of children were the norm. Poorer households could not afford additional mouths to feed.

Family Alliances, pp. 519–520

In a society where class clearly defined marriage patterns among the social elite, money, political status, and family standing all determined marriage alliances. The male head of the household typically orchestrated Italian Renaissance marriages, although widows working with male relatives could also play a role. Upper-class Florentine families traced their descent and determined inheritance through the male line. Daughters could claim inheritance only through a dowry. Fathers opened accounts for their daughters in the Dowry Fund, a public fund that provided handsome dowries to support a marriage market that ensured the social coherence of the ruling classes. Female subordination in marriage was often the result of young girls marrying significantly older men. This age disparity also left many women widowed in their twenties and thirties. Often pressed by their own families to remarry to make a new alliance, widows faced losing their children to their first husband's family if they did. Older widows, under less pressure to remarry, could hope to gain a greater degree of autonomy. By contrast, in northern Europe marriage partners were much closer in age and women enjoyed a more secure position. Women played a more active role in the northern economy, had more control over their dowries, and could represent themselves before the law—rights that appalled many Italian men who traveled to the north.

The Regulation of Sexuality, pp. 520–521

Class also manifested itself in child care. Middle- and upper-class families hired wet nurses to breast-feed their infants. Poor families sometimes could not afford to raise their children and abandoned them to strangers or public charity. In 1445, Florence opened the Ospedale degli Innocenti, a foundling hospital, to deal with children abandoned by poor families and unwed mothers, who were often servants impregnated by their masters. Over two-thirds of abandoned children were female, a further indication of gender inequity. Most upper-class men acknowledged and supported their illegitimate children as a sign of virility, and illegitimate children of noble lineage often rose to social and political prominence. Unwed mothers, however, were stigmatized and virtually lost their chances of marriage. The Florentine state's low tolerance for homosexuality led to the establishment of government brothels to "eliminate a worse evil by a lesser one." The Florentine state worked to uncover acts of sodomy, fining homosexuals and putting pederasts to death. European magistrates took the rape of women less seriously and the social class of the rapist and victim determined the punishments; noblemen who raped lower-class or slave women received light sentences or none at all.

The Renaissance State and the Art of Politics

During the Renaissance the state was seen as a work of art, a human creation to be shaped, conquered, and administered by princes according to the principles of power politics. Florentine political theorist Niccolò Machiavelli (1469–1527) laid out these principles in his work *The Prince*. During this time many states developed stronger and institutionally more complex central governments that paved the way for the nation-state in later centuries.

Republics and Principalities in Italy, pp. 522–524

Niccolò Machiavelli discussed politics without the slightest reference to ethical or moral goals. Although he believed states rested on republican virtue, his keen observations of Italian politics convinced him that power was necessary in founding a state. Italian states can be divided into two categories: republics such as Florence and Venice, which allowed a civic elite to govern, and principalities such as Milan and Naples, which were ruled by a single dynasty. In Rome, the popes' increased involvement in politics was meant to restore papal authority after the Great Schism. The popes curbed local power, expanded papal government, increased taxation, enlarged the papal army and navy, and extended papal diplomacy.

Renaissance Diplomacy, pp. 524–525

Many features characteristic of today's diplomacy were pioneered during the fifteenth century. Ceremonies, elegance, and eloquence formalized the new complex role of the diplomat, who was expected to keep a continuous stream of foreign political news flowing to the home government and not just conduct temporary missions as in the past. Milan led the way in the development of diplomacy: Francesco Sforza used his diplomatic corps to extend his political patronage, sending to his diplomats coded messages on individuals and events. As the center of Christendom, Rome became the diplomatic hub of Europe, with over two hundred diplomats stationed there by the 1490s. The papacy sent out far fewer diplomats than it received, establishing permanent nuncios (envoys) in every European state only at the end of the fifteenth century. The most outstanding achievement of Italy's diplomacy came when a general peace treaty settled decades of warfare engendered by Milanese expansion and civil war. The Treaty of Lodi (1454) established a delicate balance of power among the major Italian states that lasted until the more powerful northern European countries invaded in 1494.

Monarchies and Empires, pp. 525–531

With the exception of rulers in central Europe, political leaders expanded their empires and centralized their powers. In England, intermittent dynastic wars between the houses of Lancaster and York, later called the Wars of the Roses, continued until the coronation of Henry VII in 1485. In Spain, the marriage of Isabella of Castile and Ferdinand of Aragon ended decades of war between the two kingdoms. They ruled jointly over their territories, and their union represented the first step toward the creation of a unified Spain. Isabella and Ferdinand limited the privileges of the nobility and relied on the Hermandad, or civic militia, to enforce local justice and on lawyers to staff the royal council. Their reign ushered in an age when militant Catholicism became an instrument of state authority and shaped the Spanish national consciousness, in which the practice of Catholicism was seen as a sign of loyalty to the monarchy. After fourteen years of war, the last Muslim state in Spain, Granada, finally fell in 1492. Meanwhile, France had won the

Hundred Years' War but was overshadowed by the brilliant Burgundian court and its territorial holdings. Under Louis XI (r. 1461–1483), France seized large tracts of Burgundian territory after the death of Charles the Bold and inherited most of southern France after the Anjou dynasty died out. Louis strengthened royal power at home by promoting industry and commerce, imposing permanent salt and land taxes, and maintaining the standing army established by Charles VII. By contrast, in Hungary, Bohemia, and Poland the nobility maintained their right to elect kings, frustrating any attempts at state building. Sultan Mehmed II (r. 1451–1481) proclaimed a holy war and laid siege to Constantinople in 1453, taking the city after fifty-three days. North of the Black Sea and east of Poland-Lithuania, the princes of Muscovy began to assert their independence after the collapse of Mongol rule. Ivan III (r. 1462–1505) was the first Muscovite prince to claim the imperial title of *tsar*. The tsar enforced the Russian Orthodox faith and legitimized his rule by proclaiming Moscow the "Third Rome." The tsars divided the populace into land-holding elite in service to the tsar and a vast majority of taxpaying subjects, creating a state more in the despotic political tradition of the Ottoman Empire than of western Europe.

On the Threshold of World History: Widening Geographic Horizons

The fifteenth century ushered in the first era of world history, as European colonial expansion began to break down cultural frontiers. Before this period, Europe had remained at the periphery of world history, but European exploitation, conquest, and racism defined this era of transition from the medieval to the modern world.

The Divided Mediterranean, pp. 532–533

During the second half of the fifteenth century, the Mediterranean Sea began to lose its preeminence in trade to the Atlantic Ocean. Mediterranean states used the galley, a flat-bottomed vessel propelled by oars, dependent on human rowers, and incapable of open-ocean voyages. Although divided into Muslim and Christian zones, the Mediterranean still carried significant trade. Sugarcane from western Asia reached the western Mediterranean. Then, from the Balearic Islands off Spain, the crop traveled to the Canary Islands in the Atlantic, where the Spanish enslaved the natives to work sugar plantations. In this way, slavery was exported from the western Mediterranean to the Atlantic, and then on to the Americas. Different ethnic groups also crossed the Mediterranean. Muslims who had fled from Granada to North Africa continued to raid the Spanish coast. When Castile expelled the Jews, some of them settled in North Africa, more in Italy, and many in the Ottoman Empire.

Marked by these competing interests and religions, the divided Mediterranean prompted many Europeans to look for new opportunities across the unexplored oceans.

Portuguese Explorations, pp. 533–536

In 1433, Portugal began systematic exploration of the western coast of Africa. Using technologies such as the lateen sail, new types of ships, and better charts and instruments, and financed by the Portuguese monarchy, the explorers were motivated by a crusading zeal against Muslims and medieval adventure stories like those of Marco Polo. The Portuguese hoped to bypass the Ottoman Turks' overland routes and reach the spice-producing lands of South and Southeast Asia. In 1455, Pope Nicholas V (r. 1447–1455) granted King John II of Portugal and his successors a monopoly on trade with inhabitants of newly "discovered" regions. In 1499, Vasco da Gama led a Portuguese fleet around the southern tip of Africa and reached Calicut, India, the center of the spice trade. By 1517, a chain of Portuguese forts dotted the Indian Ocean, reaching from Mozambique to Malacca (modern Malaysia). After the voyages of Christopher Columbus, Portugal's interests clashed with those of Spain. Mediated by Pope Alexander VI, the 1494 Treaty of Tordesillas divided the Atlantic world between the two monarchies 370 leagues west of the Cape Verdes Islands, reserving the west African coast and the route to India for Portugal, and the oceans and lands to the west for Spain. Unintentionally, this agreement also allowed Portugal to claim Brazil in 1500.

The Voyages of Columbus, pp. 536–539

Born of Genoese parents, Christopher Columbus (1451–1506) gained valuable experience serving in Portuguese voyages down the west African coast and then settled in Spain. Inspired by *The Travels of Marco Polo*, Columbus proposed to sail west to Asia's gold and spices. Columbus found patrons in Isabella of Castile and Ferdinand of Aragon. In August 1492, with three ships and about ninety men, Columbus set sail with a contract to assert Castilian sovereignty over any new land and peoples and to share any profits with the crown. Reaching what is today the Bahamas, Columbus explored the Caribbean islands, encountered the peaceful Arawaks, and exchanged gifts of beads and glass for gold. Trusting natives notwithstanding, the Europeans' agenda was to find gold, subjugate the natives, and propagate Christianity. Columbus's second voyage in 1493 found no gold mines or spices and switched to kidnapping slaves, who were exported to Spain. The Spanish monarchs, eager for riches, sent officials and priests to the Americas (named after the Italian explorer Amerigo Vespucci). Columbus's career illustrated the changing

balance between the Mediterranean and the Atlantic. When the Ottomans drove Genoese merchants out of the eastern Mediterranean, the Genoese turned to the Iberian peninsula and the Atlantic.

A New Era in Slavery, p. 539

Although slavery had existed since antiquity, the European voyages of discovery expanded the economic scale of slave labor and attached race and color to slavery. During the Renaissance, nearly all slaves arrived in the Mediterranean ports of Barcelona, Marseille, Venice, and Genoa. Some were captured in war or piracy, others (black Africans) were sold by African and Bedouin traders to Christian buyers. In western Asia, impoverished families sold children into slavery, and many in the Balkans became slaves following the devastation of the Ottoman invasions. Slaves served as domestic servants in leading Mediterranean cities, as galley slaves in naval fleets, and as agricultural laborers. In the Ottoman army, slaves even formed an important elite contingent. After the Portuguese voyages, Africans increasingly filled the ranks of slaves. When traders exploited warfare in West Africa, the Portuguese trade in "pieces" (as slaves were called) drew criticism at home from some conscientious clergy. However, slavery's critics could not deny the enormous profits brought in by the slave trade. Most slaves worked in the sugar plantations in the Portuguese Atlantic islands and in Brazil. Some worked as domestic servants in Portugal, where Africans constituted 3 percent of the population in the sixteenth century. An institution of exploitation, slavery would truly begin to flourish in the Americas.

Europeans in the New World, pp. 539–541

In 1500, the native peoples of the Americas were divided into many different societies, with the Aztec and Inca civilizations of the Mexican and Peruvian highlands being the most organized. Spanish explorers Hernán Cortés (c. 1485–1547) and Francisco Pizarro (c. 1475–1541) organized gold-seeking expeditions from a base in the Caribbean. With the assistance of native peoples who had been subjugated by the Aztecs, Cortés captured the Aztec capital of Tenochtitlán in 1519, adding Mexico (then called New Spain) to the Spanish empire of King Charles V. In the south, Pizarro exploited civil war between Incan kings to seize the Andean highlands. Spain's American empire extended from Mexico to Chile. The Spaniards also subdued the Mayas on the Yucatan peninsula and discovered silver mines in what is today Bolivia. Not to be outdone, other Europeans joined in the scramble for gold and riches. The French began to search for a "northwest passage" to China. By 1504, French fishermen had appeared in Newfoundland, and French explorers were mapping the inland waterways of North America.

Because of harsh winters and native hostilities, however, permanent European settlements in Canada and the present-day United States would not succeed until the seventeenth century.

Key Events

For each question, select the most appropriate response from the choices provided.

1415 Portugal captures Ceuta, establishing foothold in Africa

1434 Medici establish influence in Florence

1438 Pragmatic Sanction of Bourges allows French kings to control church revenue and appoint bishops

1440s Printing press invented

1450 General Francesco Sforza seizes Milan

c. 1450–1500 Height of Florentine Renaissance

1453 Ottoman conquest of Constantinople; end of Byzantine Empire

1454 Treaty of Lodi balances power among major Italian states

1460–1485 Wars of the Roses; Tudor dynasty ascendant

1462 Ivan III becomes tsar

1471–1484 Pope Sixtus IV; Renaissance in Rome

1474–1516 Spain unified under Isabella and Ferdinand

1477 Death of Charles the Bold begins decline of Burgundy

1478 Inquisition carried out in Spain

1485 End of civil wars in England

1492 Spain conquers Granada; expels Jews; Columbus sails for Americas

1494 France invades Italy, beginning of more than fifty years of Habsburg-Valois conflict;

1519 Spain conquers Mexico

1530 Fall of Florentine Republic

1. Which kingdom established a foothold in Africa in 1415 and continued a systematic exploration of the west coast of Africa throughout the fifteenth century?
   a. England
   b. Portugal
   c. Spain
   d. France

2. What was the main result of the Pragmatic Sanction of Bourges?
   a. A balance of power was established among the various Italian states.
   b. German princes gained more autonomy from the Holy Roman Emperor.
   c. The Atlantic world was divided between Spain and Portugal.
   d. The king of France gained more control of the church in his realm.

3. Where was the printing press first introduced?
   a. Rome
   b. Germany
   c. Paris
   d. Florence

4. All of the following were consequences of the fall of Constantinople *except*
   a. a revival of the crusading movement.
   b. a new interest in Greek learning in Italy.
   c. a search for new trade routes to the east.
   d. the end of the Byzantine Empire.

5. What was the main result of the Treaty of Lodi?
   a. A balance of power was established among the various Italian states.
   b. German princes gained more autonomy from the Holy Roman Emperor.
   c. The Atlantic world was divided between Spain and Portugal.
   d. The king of France gained more control of the church in his realm.

6. Which dynasty came to power at the end of the Wars of the Roses?
   a. The Valois
   b. The Tudor
   c. The York
   d. The Lancastrian

7. Which was the last Muslim city to fall to Catholic Spain?
   a. Toledo
   b. Madrid
   c. Granada
   d. Seville

8. What was the main result of the Treaty of Tordesillas?
   a. A balance of power was established among the various Italian states.
   b. German princes gained more autonomy from the Holy Roman Emperor.
   c. The Atlantic world was divided between Spain and Portugal.
   d. The king of France gained more control of the church in his realm.

9. Which European power reached India by sailing around the southern tip of Africa?
   a. Spain
   b. France
   c. England
   d. Portugal

10. Which family seized control of Florence in 1530 and brought an end to its republic?
    a. The Sforza
    b. The Medici
    c. The Visconti
    d. The Borgia

Key Terms   *Match each key term to its definition.*

A. **auto a fé** (p. 528)
B. *conversos* (p. 528)
C. **duchy** (p. 523)
D. **Gallicanism** (p. 528)
E. **humanism** (p. 507)
F. **Renaissance** (p. 505)
G. **tsar** (p. 530)

1. _____ The rebirth of classical poetry, prose, and art in Europe that began in the fourteenth century; this word can also refer to other earlier cultural rebirths.

2. _____ A literary and intellectual movement that arose in the early fifteenth century to valorize the writings of Greco-Roman antiquity; it was so named because its practitioners studied and supported the liberal arts, or humanities.

3. _____ A state ruled by dukes; Florence, for example, became one in 1530.

4. _____ Jews in the Iberian peninsular who converted to Christianity in the fifteenth century.

5. _____ Literally "demonstration of faith"; the ritual of public confession that was one of the punishments given to heretics by the Inquisition in the fifteenth century.

6. _____ The higher loyalty of the French clergy to the interests of the French church and monarchy than to the papacy; established by the Pragmatic Sanction of Bourges in 1438.

7. _____ Russian imperial title first taken by Muscovite prince Ivan III (r. 1462–1505); alternative spelling derived from Caesar.

Identification   *This activity tests your recall of significant people, places, and events from this chapter. Fill in the blank with the correct answer.*

1. Under the intellectual leadership of _____, the Platonic Academy in Florence dedicated itself to the study and discussion of Plato.

2. The introduction of paper, first invented in _____, was an important precursor to the invention of the printing press.

3. In 1467 two German printers established the first press in Rome and produced twelve thousand volumes in five years, which in the past would have required _____ scribes working full time for the same number of years.

4. In the 1490s, the city of _____ became an international meeting place for printers and booksellers, and established a book fair that remains an unbroken tradition to this day.

5. Gutenberg's most famous printed work was _____.

6. In his painting *The Birth of Venus*, _____ presented feminine beauty in a pagan allegory.

7. One of the most distinguished painters of portraits was _____, who came from the Low Countries.

8. In his oration *On the Dignity of Man*, _____ expressed the optimism of Renaissance philosophy by his marveling at the human species.

9. In his book *On Architecture*, _____ argued for large-scale urban planning, with monumental buildings set on open squares that were harmonious and beautiful in their proportions.

10. To celebrate the completion of Brunelleschi's cathedral dome in Florence, _____ composed polyphonic music using harmonic ratios based on the dome's dimensions.

11. In 1430, the government of _____ completed a comprehensive tax survey of households that has become an important source of demographic information for Renaissance Italy.

12. Straddling the _____ River, Florence was a beautiful, thriving city with a defined social hierarchy.

13. The _____ supported the structure of the marriage market, in which the circulation of wealthy women consolidated the social coherence of the ruling classes.

14. In 1455, the government of Florence opened the Ospedale degli Innocenti to deal with the large number of _____ in the city.

15. Intended "to eliminate a worse evil by a lesser one," a 1415 statute established _____ in Florence.

16. Until 1447, when the last duke died without a male heir, the _____ ruled the duchy of Milan.

17. An illegitimate son of Pope Alexander VI, _____ became the model for the ruthless ruler in Machiavelli's *The Prince*.

18. After the death of _____ in 1477, Burgundian power declined.

19. The reign of _____ saw dramatic expansion of French territory, as southern France and much of the territories of Burgundy were added to the crown.

20. After ascending the throne in 1451, Sultan Mehmed II declared holy war on _____, conquering it two years later.

21. In a voyage lasting from 1497–1499, Vasco da Gama rounded the Cape of Good Hope and landed in _____, the center of the spice trade.

22. In _____, Ferdinand Magellan led the first expedition to circumnavigate the globe.

23. In 1500, _____ claimed Brazil for Portugal while on a voyage to India.

24. The capture of the _____ city of Tenochtitlán added Mexico to the Spanish Empire.

25. Looking for a northwest passage to China, _____ led three voyages that explored the St. Lawrence River as far as Montreal.

CHAPTER REVIEW

Self-Test and Analytical Exercises

Multiple Choice   *Select the best answer from the four choices provided.*

1. Which statement about humanists is *false*?
   a. Humanists studied and supported the liberal arts, or the humanities.
   b. Humanists used painstaking logic and abstract language in their discourses.
   c. Humanists were a heterogeneous group, although they were overwhelmingly wellborn.
   d. Most humanists did not consider their study of ancient cultures to be in conflict with their Christian faith.

2. What earlier innovation was an essential precondition to Johannes Gutenberg's invention of movable type in the 1440s?
   a. The public library
   b. The *quarto* and *octavo* books
   c. The mass production of paper
   d. Visual perspective

3. Who sponsored the Platonic Academy in Florence?
   a. Johannes Gutenberg
   b. Marsilio Ficino
   c. Matteo de Pasti
   d. Cosimo de Medici

4. What was Gutenberg's most famous book?
   a. The *Humanitas*, a collection of key classical texts on the liberal arts
   b. A two-volume edition of the Latin Bible
   c. An edition of the *Divine Comedy* by Dante
   d. *Augustus*, a history of the Roman Emperor Augustus

5. Where did a market system for the visual arts emerge during the Renaissance?
   a. Italy
   b. The Low Countries
   c. Germany
   d. France

6. Which man was *not* a distinguished painter of the Renaissance?
   a. Sandro Botticelli
   b. Raphael
   c. Guillaume Dufay
   d. Jan van Eyck

7. What was the highest accolade attributed to a Renaissance artist?
   a. To be blessed with "inspiration from God"
   b. To be described as an "imitator of nature"
   c. To be praised as an "artistic genius"
   d. To have possession of "a brilliant eye and talented hand"

8. Which statement regarding visual perspective is *false*?
   a. It was first practiced by the Chinese in the twelfth century.
   b. It involves the ordered arrangement of painted objects from one viewpoint.
   c. It creates an illusory, three-dimensional space on a two-dimensional surface.
   d. It became one of the distinguishing features of Western art.

9. In Florence, what percent of households belonged to the "fat people"?
   a. 15 percent
   b. 30 percent
   c. 45 percent
   d. 50 percent

10. Which of the following was *not* determined by wealth and class?
    a. Family structure
    b. The pattern of marriage
    c. The pattern of childbearing
    d. Religious commitment

11. What was the dilemma faced by Italian widows with children?
    a. They had a choice between the autonomy that came with living alone and the guarantee of security that came with moving back into their father's house with their children.
    b. Because children belonged to their father's family, widows had to decide whether to remain single and keep their children or to remarry and lose custody of the children from their first marriage.
    c. They were left to choose a new husband who would be good to their first husband's children.
    d. They could take over their husband's business and have less time with their children or contract the work out to a man in order to have more time for mothering.

12. Who tended to have more children in fifteenth-century Florence?
    a. Poor families
    b. Middle-class families
    c. Wealthy families
    d. Class did not affect the number of offspring

13. What Florentine political theorist wrote *The Prince*?
    a. Cosimo de Medici
    b. Niccolò Machiavelli
    c. Francesco Sforza
    d. Bernard du Rosier

14. What was the source of power of the Medici family?
    a. It headed the largest bank in Europe.
    b. It dominated the top political offices in Florence.
    c. It commanded a formidable personal army.
    d. The family was related by marriage to almost all the major European royal houses of the day.

15. What was accomplished by the Treaty of Lodi (1454)?
    a. It settled the Hundred Years' War.
    b. It established a complex balance of power among the major Italian states, settling decades of war.
    c. It reconfirmed peace following the Ottoman invasion of Constantinople.
    d. It reestablished French control over Burgundy.

16. Which statement about the end of the Byzantine Empire is *false*?
    a. The Turks invaded and sacked Constantinople in 1453.
    b. Greek Constantinople became Turkish Istanbul.
    c. The Turks carried off and enslaved over half the population of Constantinople.
    d. The Byzantine emperor fled the Turkish invasion and periodically led attacks against the Ottomans to recover his lands.

17. All of the following were motives for Portuguese exploration *except*
    a. profits and treasures.
    b. crusading zeal.
    c. glory.
    d. more farmland.

18. What was the 1494 Treaty of Tordesillas?
    a. It recognized French claims to the lands north of Mexico.
    b. It settled disputes between Portugal and Spain by dividing the Atlantic world between them.
    c. It divided the Mediterranean Sea into Muslim and Christian regions.
    d. It gave Portugal the monopoly on trade with the inhabitants of newly discovered lands.

19. On Columbus's second voyage, what became the main focus of the enterprise?
    a. Finding slaves
    b. Mapping a route to the Indies
    c. Acquiring goods for trading
    d. Exploring the newly discovered land

20. Who captured the Aztec capital Tenochtitlán in 1519?
    a. Hernán Cortés
    b. Francisco Pizarro
    c. Jacques Cartier
    d. Vasco da Gama

21. Which statement regarding the Renaissance is *false*?
    a. Latin and Greek classical rhetoric and eloquence appealed to writers.
    b. New focus on the beauty of nature appeared in painting, architecture, and music.
    c. Humanists drew from classical history and literature to emulate the glory of the ancient world.
    d. The revival of Greek learning in the West was opposed by the church.

22. How did the fall of Constantinople contribute to the development of the Renaissance?
    a. The celebration of Turkish military strength drove the west to assert its cultural superiority.
    b. Through increased contact and trade with the Turks, Islamic learning was brought to the west.
    c. It sent Greek scholars to Italy for refuge, reviving an interest in Greek learning in the west.
    d. The fall of Constantinople increased interest in that region and its history.

23. Who was the foremost Platonic scholar of the Renaissance?
    a. Matteo de Pasti
    b. Marsilio Ficino
    c. Cosimo de Medici
    d. Pico della Mirandola

24. What were *scriptoria*?
    a. Workshops where manuscripts were hand copied and sold
    b. Printing shops employing presses to produce books and pamphlets
    c. People who copied manuscripts for a living
    d. Sacred collections of writings and commentaries on the Scriptures

25. Which statement regarding fifteenth-century art is *false*?
    a. Artists gained greater control over their work.
    b. Portraiture of the middle classes became more widespread.
    c. The unique skills of individual artists were increasingly recognized.
    d. Artwork became more symbolic.

26. Who designed the bronze doors for the San Giovanni Baptistry in Florence?
    a. Andrea Mantegna
    b. Leonardo da Vinci
    c. Filippo Lippi
    d. Lorenzo Ghiberti

27. Each of the following was a main musical genre within Renaissance polyphony *except*
    a. the secular *chanson*.
    b. the canon of the Catholic Mass.
    c. the motet.
    d. the dance.

28. Fifteenth-century architects employed the Renaissance ideals by
    a. combining symbolism and realism.
    b. uniting artistic creativity and scientific knowledge.
    c. blending the functional with the whimsical.
    d. combining spiritual and secular subjects.

29. What percentage of Florence's wealth did the richest 1 percent of its households own?
    a. More than fifteen percent
    b. More than twenty-five percent
    c. More than forty percent
    d. More than seventy-five percent

30. All of the following were key considerations in marriage arrangements among upper-class Florentines *except*
    a. family standing.
    b. money.
    c. love.
    d. political status.

31. Typically, what was the age difference between northern European spouses?
    a. Husbands and wives were about the same age.
    b. Husbands were significantly older than their wives.
    c. Wives were significantly older than their husbands.
    d. Contemporary records are inadequate to make a determination.

32. Who generally orchestrated marriages during the Italian Renaissance?
    a. The parents of the couple
    b. The male head of a household
    c. The couple themselves
    d. The oldest women of the family

33. Who was the ultimate victor of the Wars of the Roses?
    a. Richard of York
    b. Henry VI
    c. Henry VII
    d. Edward IV

34. Which of the following *best* describes France in the fifteenth century?
    a. The French monarchy increased its power and dramatically expanded its territory.
    b. The French crown was repeatedly undermined by rebellious barons.
    c. After the Hundred Years' War, the French began another extended war against the duchy of Burgundy.
    d. Although France won the Hundred Years' War, it soon lost important territories to the Angevins.

35. Russian state building followed
    a. the same political trends as western Europe.
    b. the Polish and German patterns of fragmentation.
    c. the despotic political tradition of central Asia and the Ottoman Empire.
    d. the model of the early Roman empire.

36. Which of the following statements about Burgundy is *false*?
    a. To maintain one of the largest standing armies in Europe, Burgundian dukes sold political offices to raise funds.
    b. Following the death of Charles the Bold in battle in 1477, France seized the duchy of Burgundy.
    c. The Burgundian dukes ruled with a strong hand, alienating many of their subjects.
    d. The Burgundian dukes ruled over French-, Dutch-, and German-speaking subjects.

37. When did the first phase of European overseas expansion begin?
    a. In 1457 with the Italian invasion of North Africa
    b. In the 1490s with the Spanish voyages of exploration
    c. In 1433 with Portugal's systematic exploration of the west African coast
    d. In 1426 with the French discovery of Newfoundland

38. Who commanded the Portuguese fleet that rounded the Cape of Good Hope and reached India?
    a. Christopher Columbus
    b. Ferdinand Magellan
    c. Vasco da Gama
    d. Henry the Navigator

39. Who led the first expedition to successfully circumnavigate the globe?
    a. Amerigo Vespucci
    b. Ferdinand Magellan
    c. Vasco da Gama
    d. Henry the Navigator

40. All of the following enabled Atlantic exploration *except*
    a. the galley.
    b. the lateen sail.
    c. more exact charts.
    d. the caravel.

Short Answer   *Answer each question in three or four sentences.*

Widening Intellectual Horizons

1. Identify and briefly describe humanism and its practitioners.

2. Identify and briefly describe the two preconditions essential for the advent of printing.

3. Describe the technology of movable type, the fifteenth-century printing industry, and their immediate significance.

Revolution in the Arts

4. How were the artists of the fifteenth century different from—and the same as—those of previous centuries?

5. What new trends developed in art during the Renaissance?

6. What kinds of music were performed and who were some of the most influential figures in this field?

The Intersection of Private and Public Lives

7. What did the census taken between 1427 and 1430 reveal about the economics of Tuscany and the structure of Tuscan households?

8. Compare the rights and lifestyles of fifteenth-century Italian women with those of their northern counterparts.

9. Describe the social implications and remedies for sexual crimes and indiscretions in fifteenth-century Italy.

The Renaissance State and the Art of Politics

10. What were the four most powerful Italian republics and principalities, and what problems did each of them face during the fifteenth century?

11. What were the most important developments in the last half of the fifteenth century that changed the politics and affected the population on the Iberian peninsula?

12. What were the distinguishing characteristics of the state that rose when the Muscovite princes began to assert their independence in the fifteenth century?

On the Threshold of World History: Widening Geographic Horizons

13. Where did the Portuguese concentrate their efforts in exploration and expansion, and what was the papal attitude toward Portuguese expansion?

14. What relationships and precedents concerning the native peoples were established by Columbus's first two voyages across the Atlantic?

15. In the New World, what were the three most highly developed native societies encountered by the Spanish and what became of them?

BUILDING HISTORICAL SKILLS

Reading Maps   *Write a brief, paragraph-length response to each of the following questions based on Map 14.4: Early Voyages of World Exploration (p. 537).*

1. Which areas were known to Europeans before 1450?

2. Why would Ottoman control of the Middle East pose a problem for Europeans who wished to trade with Asia?

3. How did the goals of maritime exploration evolve during the Renaissance?

Reading Illustrations   *Write a brief, paragraph-length response to each of the following questions based on the painting Sacred and Social Body (p. 504).*

1. When you look at the picture, where is your eye drawn?

2. Why is your focus drawn there?

3. How does this composition illustrate the new approaches to visual representation that were characteristic of the Renaissance?

Reading Historical Documents   *Write a brief, paragraph-length response to each of the following questions based on the documents in your book.*

A Merchant's Advice to His Sons (p. 518)

1. How does Giovanni Rucellai implicitly criticize the Medici family in this passage?

2. How does Rucellai's view of power compare with Machiavelli's?

Christopher Columbus Describes His First Voyage, 1493 (p. 538)

3. What personal motivations does Columbus describe in his interaction with the Native Americans he encounters?

4. What possibilities for Europeans does Columbus describe in the lands he has encountered?

New Sources, New Perspectives: Portuguese Voyages of Discovery (pp. 534–536)

5. What do the nautical tide calendar and the nautical solar guide suggest were the sorts of hazards Portuguese sailors might have encountered in their maritime explorations?

6. In what ways have the Portuguese traditionally understood their country's maritime history, and why have scholars criticized this view?

7. In what new ways are historians examining the history and legacy of Portuguese colonialism?

The Struggle for Reformation Europe
1500–1560

CHAPTER OVERVIEW

Chapter Questions   *Keep these questions in mind as you go through the study guide chapter.*

1. What problems within the Catholic church made it unresponsive to the spiritual needs of Christians?

2. What kinds if solutions did reformers—before and during the Reformation, outside and within the Catholic church—propose?

3. How and why did the spread of religious reform challenge the social and political order?

4. How did religious and secular authorities seek to restore order and consolidate their power?

5. How did religious reform fuel political struggles throughout Europe?

Chapter Summary

A New Heaven and a New Earth

As the sixteenth century began, there was a predominant atmosphere of anxiety in Europe. The advance of Muslim Turks on Europe while Christian princes fought among themselves led many to believe that the Last Judgment was about to arrive. Consequently, many people intensified their search for religious comfort while intellectuals criticized the leadership of the church for failing to meet the needs of the people.

The Crisis of Faith, pp. 548–550

Some of the signs of mounting spiritual anxiety among the laity included the steady increase in the number of pilgrimages, the dedication of new shrines, and the brisk sale of prayer books in both Latin and the vernacular. Yet in this time of anxiety, the clergy seemed increasingly incapable of meeting the spiritual needs of the people.

Clerical privileges and deficiencies in their education or behavior sometimes offended the sensibilities of laypeople who yearned for a religion that fit their daily needs and for earnest, moral priests and edifying sermons. In addition, the church often placed more importance on external behavior than spiritual intent, and set forth numerous regulations to define sinful behavior. In the sacrament of penance, Christians confessed their sins to a priest in order to receive forgiveness. Yet confession did not always ease anxiety about salvation and, worse still, some priests demanded money or sexual favors in return for forgiveness. Although a sincere confession saved a sinner from hell, sinners still faced purgatory after death and, to shorten time spent in purgatory, a person could earn an indulgence by performing specific religious tasks. The church also sold indulgences, which suggested more interest in making money than saving souls. Dissatisfaction with the church's rules prompted several early reform attempts by bishops and leading clerics, but such movements were limited to individual monastic houses or dioceses.

Christian Humanism, pp. 550–552

Through scholarship and social reform, Christian humanists sought to adapt the ethical ideals of classical antiquity to a Christian society. Christian humanists like Desiderius Erasmus (c. 1466–1536) and Thomas More (1478–1535) emphasized Christian piety as defining true virtue. Erasmus used his sharp wit to criticize the corruption of the clergy and the bloody ambitions of the Christian princes. Erasmus believed that education could reform individuals and society. He dreamed of a unified, peaceful Christendom where learning would eclipse ignorance and charity, and good works would be valued over religious ceremonies devoid of meaning. In his *Handbook of the Militant Christian* (1503) and *The Praise of Folly* (1509), Erasmus satirized his contemporaries' love of power and wealth. A man of peace, Erasmus chose Christian unity over division as the Reformation swept Europe. He pleased neither the Protestants nor the

Catholics entirely and ended his career isolated from both. Thomas More, to whom Erasmus dedicated *The Praise of Folly*, was a lawyer and served as a member of Parliament and ambassador. In 1529, More became Henry VIII's lord chancellor, but he retired in 1532 in protest of Henry VIII's control of the clergy. More's best-known work, *Utopia* (1516), was inspired by the voyages of discovery. Describing an imaginary land, the book was a critique of his own society. The inhabitants of Utopia are equally dedicated to hard work and education, and do not suffer from crime, starvation, or poverty. More believed that politics, property, and war created human misery.

Protestant Reformers

Out of the predominant atmosphere of spiritual need and resentment grew a movement of explosive protests and reform. Martin Luther began the reform movement in Germany, while Huldrych Zwingli extended the Reformation to Switzerland. A generation later, John Calvin began another reform movement that extended throughout Europe.

Martin Luther and the German Nation, pp. 552–555

Martin Luther, a young German friar tormented by his own religious anxieties, triggered the first major religious reform. After abandoning the law for a monastery, Luther found little consolation in the sacraments. His sense of sinfulness and fear of damnation despite frequent penance deepened his unease with the church. Sent to study theology, Luther experienced grace and insight into salvation, realizing that faith alone saved him from sin. While teaching at the University of Wittenberg, Luther became disgusted when the archbishop of Mainz commissioned the sale of indulgences to raise money for building St. Peter's Basilica in Rome and to cover the expense of getting elected archbishop. In 1517, Luther posted ninety-five theses—propositions for academic debate—that questioned the sale of indulgences and church offices. Printed and spread rapidly, Luther's theses released a torrent of pent-up resentment among the laity, many of whom shared Luther's position. In *Freedom of a Christian*, Luther distinguished between teachings from the Gospels and invented church doctrines and laws, arguing that faith could be developed "by Scripture alone." He further argued that sinners were saved "by faith alone" rather than by good works. Finally, he argued that a "priesthood of all believers" should replace professional clerics. In *To the Nobility of the German Nation*, Luther appealed to nationalism, calling on German princes to defend their nation from corrupt Romans. In *On the Babylonian Captivity of the Church*,

he condemned the papacy as the Antichrist. The church misjudged Luther's influence when they ordered him to keep quiet. In 1521, Luther defended his faith before Charles V (r. 1520–1558) at the Imperial Diet of Worms, but was spared from the potential consequences of his actions because he enjoyed the protection of Frederick the Wise, the elector of Saxony. The early Reformation was essentially an urban movement, and anti-Roman evangelicals included German princes, city officials, professors, priests, and laypeople.

Huldrych Zwingli and the Swiss Confederation, pp. 556–557

The poor, mountainous country of Switzerland's chief source of income had been mercenary soldiers recruited for the papal, French, and imperial armies. In 1520, the chief preacher in Zurich, Huldrych Zwingli (1484–1531) criticized his superior, Cardinal Matthew Shinner, for sending the country's young men off to be killed or maimed while serving in the papal armies. Zwingli developed a reform movement independent from that of Luther. Zwingli was deeply influenced by Erasmus's ideas on education. He openly declared himself a reformer and attacked the corruption of the ecclesiastical hierarchy and church rules such as fasting and clerical celibacy. Under Zwingli's leadership, Zurich became the center of the Swiss reform movement. Zwingli brought together religion, politics, and morality, drawing no distinction between the ideal citizen and the perfect Christian—a stance that differed from Luther's position. The two also disagreed about the nature of the Eucharist. Luther believed that Christ was both truly and symbolically present in the bread and wine of this sacrament, whereas Zwingli believed that the Eucharist was only a symbol of Christ's union with believers. Troubled by these theological differences, evangelical princes and magistrates assembled the major reformers at Marburg in central Germany in 1529. Several days of intense discussions resolved some of the doctrinal differences, but Luther and Zwingli did not agree on the Eucharist; therefore, the German and Swiss movements continued along divergent paths.

John Calvin and Christian Discipline, pp. 557–559

John Calvin (1509–1564), a Frenchman who studied law, led another reform movement that took hold in France and Switzerland. Influenced by the humanists, Calvin gradually abandoned the Catholic church. The Reformation found many adherents in France, culminating in the Affair of the Placards in 1534 when church doors were posted with broadsheets denouncing the Mass. This affair provoked a national crackdown on Protestants, and Calvin fled abroad. He stopped in Geneva, which had renounced its allegiance to its Catholic bishop, and there took up leadership of the Genevan reform party with Guillaume Farel. After triumphing in 1541 over the old Genevan families who opposed his regime, Calvin made Geneva a tightly disciplined Christian republic. Calvin's 1536 publication *The Institutes of the Christian Religion* made him the first reformer to organize reformist doctrines, organization, history, and practices in a logical and systematic way. Calvin developed his own doctrine of predestination, according to which God had pre-destined every human to either salvation or damnation before the creation of the world. Fusing society and church into a "Reformed church," Calvin and his followers created a community that some praised for its lack of crime and low illegitimate birthrate. Intolerant of dissenters and advocating rigorous discipline, Calvin made Geneva the new center of the Reformation, the city in which missionaries trained and from which books of Calvinist doctrine were exported. Calvin's ideas spread throughout much of Europe and even to New England, his "Reformed Church" becoming the prevailing form of Protestantism in many of these countries.

Reshaping Society through Religion

The religious upheaval in the early years of the Reformation inspired many to challenge the social order in general. Radical movements such as the Anabaptists and the peasant rebels of the Holy Roman Empire challenged the foundations of the religious and political order. The brutal repression of these radicals ushered in a period of social disciplining, as the subversive potential of religious reforms alarmed authorities.

Challenging the Social Order, pp. 559–561

The message of Christian freedom proclaimed by Luther resonated with the oppressed, and popular demand pressured many local officials to appoint new clerics committed to reform. In 1525, a weakened church authority encouraged many peasants who resented the church's greed to rebel in a massive rural uprising in southern and central Germany that was brutally suppressed. Emerging as champions of an orderly religious reform, many German princes who had suppressed the peasant revolt confronted Emperor Charles V, who supported Rome. In 1529, Charles declared Catholicism the empire's only legitimate faith. The Lutheran German princes protested and thus came to be called Protestants. In Zurich, while Zwingli was challenging the Roman church, some laypeople secretly pursued their own religious path. Believing that only adults possessed the reason and free will to choose Christ, these men and women believed the baptism of infants was invalid; they came to be called Anabaptists, meaning "those who were rebaptized." Even though Zwingli condemned this movement, it spread quickly through southern Germany. One group of

Anabaptists seized control of the city of Münster. They abolished private property in imitation of the early Christian church and dissolved traditional marriages, allowing men to have multiple wives. Besieged by a combined Protestant and Catholic army in 1535, the city fell and the leaders of the Anabaptists were killed. Yet the Anabaptist movement survived in northwestern Europe under the Dutch reformer Menno Simons (1469–1561).

New Forms of Discipline, pp. 561–565

A new urban, middle-class culture in Protestant Europe dramatically altered European civilization and continued trends toward change begun during the Middle Ages. The Latin Bible—the Vulgate—was the only Bible authorized by the Catholic church. As reformers turned to the Scriptures, vernacular translations of the Bible appeared, making it more accessible to the laity. In the Holy Roman Empire, Luther encouraged princes and magistrates to establish new schools to educate children in the knowledge and fear of God, and medieval church schools were replaced by a state school system intended to train obedient, pious, and hardworking Christian citizens. Secular governments also began to take over public charity. The new Protestant work ethic linked hard work and prosperity with piety and consequently equated laziness and poverty with a lack of moral worth. In Catholic lands, poverty was still considered a Christian virtue, and collective charity persisted, although in a more regulated form. Different educational systems and different attitudes toward the poor widened the gulf between Protestants and Catholics. Protestants, in their quest for order and discipline in worship and in society, reaffirmed the ideal of the patriarchal family.

A Struggle for Mastery

The new patterns of conflict generated by the Reformation were superimposed on traditional dynastic strife. The ambitions of powerful princes combined with the passions of religious reformers fueled widespread violence that ultimately failed to settle religious differences. By 1560, an exhausted Europe found itself in a state of compromised peace that contained the seeds of future conflict.

The Court, p. 566

Throughout Europe, dynastic strife and religious zeal created political instability. A stabilizing center of the politics of dynasty and religion was the royal court, which was used to instill loyalty in nobles and awe in subjects. The court was the royal household, which included a community of servants, noble attendants, officials, artists, and soldiers. Court officials performed a myriad of other tasks. The French court of Francis I (r. 1515–1547) became the largest in Europe, numbering 1,622 members, excluding nonofficial courtiers. Courts were mobile at the time, and entourages of animals, people, furniture, and documents moved among a king's many palaces. Hunting and other warlike recreations were a passion for the men of the court. The literature of the time reveals much about this court culture. Two writers, Ludovico Ariosto (1474–1533) and Baldassare Castiglione (1478–1529) composed works that glorified this extravagant court culture. Ariosto's epic poem, *Orlando Furioso*, was modeled after Greek and Roman poetry and portrayed court culture as the highest synthesis of Christian and classical values; it tells a tale of combat and valor in the tradition of the medieval chivalric romance. Castiglione's equally popular *The Courtier* represented court culture as a perfect synthesis of military virtues and literary and artistic cultivation. In *The Courtier*, a man is defined in part by his service to his prince and his lady, but also by his outward appearance. The significance of proper clothing in court culture reflected the rigid distinctions between the classes and the sexes in sixteenth-century Europe.

Art and the Christian Knight, pp. 566–567

The idealized portraits, paintings, buildings, and other works commissioned by the Habsburg emperors and Catholic popes represented an undercurrent of hope and idealism in the charged atmosphere of the sixteenth century. Emperor Maximilian I (r. 1493–1519), for example, dreamed of restoring Christian chivalry and even hoped to rule as both emperor and pope. He appointed the Nuremburg artist Albrecht Dürer (1471–1528) as court painter. Dürer designed a triumphal carriage for the emperor that featured allegorical figures such as Prudence, Justice, Temperance, and Fortitude. For many Catholic artists and humanists, Emperor Charles V, Maximilian's grandson, represented the ideal Christian knight. The Venetian painter Titian (1477–1576) painted four images from the emperor's life: two portrayed the prince as victorious over Protestants, and one, *Gloria*, depicted the emperor in a white robe ascending to God amid a throng of the blessed. In Italy, Florentine artist Michelangelo Buonarroti (1475–1564) matured his talents in the service of the powerful Medici family. He became the favorite artist of the warrior-pope Julius II, painting for him the walls and ceiling of the Sistine Chapel. Later commissioned by Pope Paul III, he became the chief architect of St. Peter's Basilica in Rome. The work of Michelangelo exemplified the transition from the Renaissance to the age of religious conflicts; Michelangelo's creations glorified a papacy under siege, just as Titian's paintings helped defend the Habsburg dynasty against infidels and heretics.

Wars among Habsburgs, Valois, and Ottomans, pp. 568–570

French claims to Italian lands triggered wars between France and Spain for control of the continent. The Italian Wars (1494–1559) between the French Valois dynasty, led by Francis I, and the Habsburg dynasty, led by Charles V, eventually involved most Christian monarchs and the Ottoman sultan. England, for instance, acted out of power considerations, first siding with France and then with Spain. The Italian states fought for their independence, the Protestant princes of Germany used the conflict as leverage to obtain privileges from the emperor, whereas the Ottoman Turks saw the conflict as an opportunity for territorial expansion. Under Sultan Suleiman I "the Magnificent" (r. 1520–1566), the Ottoman Empire reached the height of its power, defeating Christian forces in Hungary and laying siege to Vienna. Desperate to overcome the forces of Charles V who had seized the French city of Nice and were campaigning to capture Tunis on the North African coast, Francis I formed an alliance with the Turks. The alliance between a Christian king and the Muslim sultan shocked many Christians and, although it was brief, the alliance demonstrated that religion was but one of many factors in power politics. Most battles between the Valois and Habsburgs were fought in Italy and the Low Countries. In 1525, the Spanish at Pavia captured Francis I. Francis was detained in Spain until he renounced his claims to Italy; but, he immediately resumed making these claims when he returned to France. In 1527, in retaliation for a papal alliance with France, Charles's troops, many of whom were German Protestant mercenaries, sacked Rome. Protestants and Catholics alike saw this as a punishment from God, prompting the Catholic church to turn toward reform. The Italian Wars dragged on through the 1540s, ending only when the French king, too bankrupt to keep fighting, acknowledged defeat by signing the Treaty of Cateau-Cambresis in 1559.

The Finance and Technologies of War, pp. 570–571

Western armies grew and armed themselves with new, more effective weapons. This trend was costly, as were new defensive measures. In England, war expenditures were more than double royal revenues in the 1540s. In response, the government devalued its coinage, which caused rapid inflation. Charles V boasted the largest army in Europe, but was sinking ever deeper into debt, as was his opponent Francis I. The European monarchs raised taxes, sold offices, and even confiscated property and goods to pay for their costly wars. When these efforts proved insufficient, both the Valois and Habsburg monarchs looked to their leading bankers for loans, but these loans carried high interest rates. The German Fugger Bank was the largest in sixteenth-century Europe. Begun by Jakob Fugger (1459–1525), it built an international financial empire that helped make kings. As personal banker to Charles's grandfather (Maximilian I) and the Habsburg dynasty, the Fugger family reaped handsome profits from the war. In 1519, Fugger assembled a consortium to secure the election of Charles V as Holy Roman Emperor, tightening the alliance between the bank and the imperial office. Between 1527 and 1547, the bank's assets more than doubled, the majority being loans to the Habsburgs. Charles, however, barely managed to stay one step ahead of his creditors, and his successor in Spain eventually lost control of state finances. To service debts, European monarchs sought revenues in tax increases and wars. But paying for wars took yet more money and more loans. The cycle of war and debt continued for years, draining the French and Spanish treasuries and forcing the monarchs to end sixty years of warfare with the Treaty of Cateau-Cambrésis in 1559.

Divided Realms, pp. 571–573

Throughout Europe, rulers viewed religious discord as a threat to the stability of their realms. In France, the Calvinist movement grew steadily despite a national crackdown on religious dissent in 1534, and some noble families became Huguenots, as French Protestants were called. Francis I and his successor Henry II maintained a balance between the Catholics and Huguenots but, after 1560, France plunged into decades of savage religious wars. English Protestants had been relatively few until the reign of Henry VIII (r. 1509–1547). When Pope Clement VII refused to grant the divorce Henry sought from Catherine of Aragon, the king broke away from Rome. The Act of Supremacy, passed by Parliament in 1529, made Henry the head of the Anglican Church (the Church of England). During the brief reigns of Edward VI (r. 1547–1553) and Mary (r. 1553–1558), official religious policies oscillated between Protestantism and Catholicism. Under Elizabeth I, Anglicanism was restored and came to define the English nation. In Scotland, as Protestantism gained adherents, powerful noble clans directly challenged the devoutly Catholic monarchy. In 1560, the Protestants seized control of the Scottish parliament and queen regent Mary of Guise (d. 1560), a Catholic, fled to England. In Germany, Protestant princes formed the Schmalkaldic League, which assailed the Catholic emperor Charles V, the bishops, and a few remaining Catholic princes. When Charles defeated the league in 1547, he proclaimed the "Interim," which restored Catholics' right to worship in Protestant lands. Protestants opposed the Interim, and the Protestant princes, now led by Duke Maurice of Saxony, once more raised arms against Charles and sent the surprised and bankrupt emperor fleeing to Italy where, in 1555, he agreed to the Peace of Augsburg. The settlement recognized the Evangelical (Lutheran) church and allowed the German princes—whether Catholic or Protestant—to determine the religion for their lands. The agreement omitted other groups, such as the Calvinists and Anabaptists, which would lead to conflict in the future.

A Continuing Reformation

In reaction to the Protestant challenge, the Catholic church mobilized itself for defense and renewal. The Council of Trent gave more clarity and definition to Catholic beliefs, while new religious orders campaigned to regain areas that had converted to Protestantism. Missionaries from Catholic Europe also began to travel to other parts of the world to win converts who might compensate for the millions of the faithful that were lost to the Protestant Reformation.

Catholic Renewal, pp. 574–575

Many Catholics had called for reform before Martin Luther, but the papacy had failed to respond. Under Pope Paul III (r. 1534–1549), the Catholic church finally pursued reform, a movement sometimes called the Catholic Reformation. Pope Paul III and Charles V convened the Council of Trent, which met sporadically from 1545 to 1563 and reached conclusions that would revitalize Catholicism for the following two centuries. The council reasserted clerical supremacy over the laity, required bishops to reside in their dioceses, and ordered the establishment of seminaries to train priests in each diocese. The council also reaffirmed the doctrine of transubstantiation, thus firmly rejecting the Protestant position on the Eucharist. It stipulated that all weddings take place in a church and be registered with the clergy. Finally, the council rejected the Protestants' permitting of divorce. The council's proclamations made permanent the divisions between the Catholics and Protestants and ended all hope for reconciliation. The Catholic Reformation also prompted the formation of new religious orders, most important the Society of Jesus (the Jesuits), who became the papacy's most vigorous defenders. Established by a Spanish nobleman, Ignatius of Loyola (1491–1556), the order was recognized by the church in 1540. Young men were attracted by Ignatius's austerity and piety and, by the time of Ignatius's death, Europe had more than one thousand Jesuits who established hundreds of colleges throughout Catholic Europe. In addition, Jesuit missionaries would help spread Roman Catholicism to Africans, Asians, and native Americans.

Missionary Zeal, pp. 575–577

To win new souls to replace those lost to Protestantism, and to convince Catholics and Protestants that the

Catholic church enjoyed divine favor, Catholic missionaries traveled throughout the globe. Different missionaries, however, brought differing messages to indigenous peoples. To some, Catholicism offered reason and faith; to others, it was a repressive and coercive alien religion. Some missionaries converted indigenous populations by force, despite criticism. Under the influence of critics such as Bartolome de Las Casas (1474–1566), the Spanish crown tried to protect native peoples from abuse, a policy weakened by the struggles among the missionaries, royal officials, and *conquistadores*. After an initial period of relatively little discrimination, the Catholic church began to adopt strict rules biased by color in Spanish America. In 1555, it forbade holy orders to Indians, mestizos (mixed European-Indians), mulattoes (mixed European-Africans), Moors, and Jews. The Portuguese, however, were more willing to train Africans and Asians as missionaries. Under Portuguese protection, Jesuit missionaries preached the Gospel to elite Confucian scholars in China and to the samurai (the warrior aristocracy) in Japan. Because European missionaries admired Chinese and Japanese civilizations, they relied on sermons rather than force to win converts. The Jesuit Francis Xavier pioneered missionary work in India and Japan, paving the way for future missionary success in Asia.

Key Events   *For each question, select the most appropriate response from the choices provided.*

1494 Italian Wars begin

1516 Erasmus publishes Greek edition of the New Testament; More writes *Utopia*

1517 Martin Luther composes ninety-five theses to challenge church profiteering

1520 Luther publishes three treatises; Zwingli breaks from Rome

1525 German Peasants' War

1527 Charles V's imperial troops sack Rome

1529 German Protestants; Colloquy of Marburg assembles to address disagreements between German and Swiss church reformers

1534 Act of Supremacy; Henry VIII breaks with Rome; Affair of the Placards in France

1536 Calvin publishes first edition of *Institutes*

1540 Jesuits established as new Catholic order

1541 Calvin installed in Geneva

1545–1563 Catholic Council of Trent condemns Protestant beliefs and confirms church doctrine and sacraments

1547 Charles V defeats Protestants at Mühlberg

1555 Peace of Augsburg ends religious wars in Germany and recognizes Lutherans

1559 Treaty of Cateau-Cambrésis ends conflict between Habsburg and Valois

1. Which of the following was written the same year that Erasmus published his Greek edition of the New Testament?
   a. Luther's *Freedom of a Christian*
   b. Calvin's *Institutes of the Christian Religion*
   c. More's *Utopia*
   d. Castiglione's *Book of the Courtier*

2. How long after Luther composed his ninety-five theses did the German Peasants' War begin?
   a. 1 year
   b. 5 years
   c. 7 years
   d. 8 years

3. How long after Luther composed his ninety-five theses did Calvin publish the *Institutes of the Christian Religion*?
   a. 5 years
   b. 18 years
   c. 29 years
   d. 33 years

4. How long after Luther composed his ninety-five theses did the Council of Trent begin?
   a. 18 years
   b. 23 years
   c. 28 years
   d. 33 years

5. How long did the Council of Trent last?
   a. 1 year
   b. 3 years
   c. 15 years
   d. 18 years

6. How long did the Italian Wars between the Habsburg and Valois last?
   a. 25 years
   b. 55 years
   c. 65 years
   d. 70 years

7. What was Luther's primary complaint in the ninety-five theses he composed in 1517?
   a. The treatment of the poor
   b. The overemphasis on power and wealth in European society
   c. Unfair taxation by the Holy Roman Emperor
   d. The sale of indulgences and church office

8. The Colloquy of Marburg in 1529 was an attempt to address doctrinal differences between which two religious movements?
   a. Luther's and Calvin's
   b. Luther's and the Anabaptists'
   c. Calvin's and Zwingli's
   d. Luther's and Zwingli's

9. Who established a Christian republic in Geneva in 1541?
   a. Thomas More
   b. John Calvin
   c. Huldrych Zwingli
   d. Martin Luther

10. What motivated Henry VIII of England to break with Rome in 1534?
    a. He was convinced by the teachings of Calvin.
    b. He was at war with Catholic Spain.
    c. The papacy was trying to collect taxes in England.
    d. The papacy would not allow him to divorce.

11. Which new Catholic order founded in 1540 played a leading role in the Catholic Reformation?
    a. The Franciscans
    b. The Dominicans
    c. The Cistercians
    d. The Jesuits

12. Which of the following was *not* an outcome of the Council of Trent (1545–1563)?
    a. The Catholic church reasserted the supremacy of the clergy over the laity.
    b. The doctrine of the Catholic church was clarified.
    c. The Catholic church reconciled itself with the Protestant church.
    d. The clergy became more disciplined and better trained.

13. The Treaty of Cateau-Cambrésis ended conflict between whom in 1559?
    a. The Habsburgs and Valois
    b. The Calvinists and the Lutherans
    c. The papacy and the Habsburgs
    d. The Tudors and the Valois

Key Terms   *Match each key term to its definition.*

A. **Anabaptists** (p. 561)
B. **Christian humanists** (p. 550)
C. **Evangelicals** (p. 548)
D. **indulgence** (p. 549)
E. **infidel** (p. 567)
F. **parish** (p. 563)
G. **predestination** (p. 558)
H. **Protestants** (p. 548)
I. **Vulgate** (p. 562)

1. _____ Supporters of Martin Luther and religious reform in the 1520s; the word refers to the Gospels.

2. _____ Members of the Christian branch that formed when Martin Luther and his followers broke from the Catholic church in 1517; the name was first used in 1529 in an imperial diet by German princes who protested Emperor Charles V's edict to repress religious dissent.

3. _____ In Roman Catholic doctrine, a remission of sin earned by performing certain religious tasks to avoid purgatory after death. In use by the 13th century, the Catholic clergy's practice of selling these came under fire during the Reformation.

4. _____ Thinkers who in the sixteenth century dreamed of ideal societies based on peace and morality, and who sought to realize the ethical ideals of the classical world. Desiderius Erasmus (c. 1466–1 536) and Thomas More (1478– 1535) are representative of these thinkers.

5. _____ John Calvin's doctrine that states that God preordained salvation or damnation for each person before creation; those chosen for salvation were considered the "elect."

6. _____ Sixteenth-century religious dissenters who believed that humans have free will and that people must knowingly select the Christian faith through rebaptism as adults. They advocated radical separation from society; though originally pacifist, some chose violent paths to religious renewal.

7. _____ The authoritative Latin version of the Catholic Bible, the only one authorized prior to the Protestant Reformation.

8. _____ The basic territorial organization of the Catholic and main Protestant churches.

9. _____ Someone outside of the particular faith.

Identification   *This activity tests your recall of significant people, places, and events from this chapter. Fill in the blank with the correct answer.*

1. _____ wrote about an imaginary land in his book *Utopia*, which was free from the miseries caused by politics, property, and war.

2. In *The Praise of Folly*, _____ argued that modesty, humility, and poverty represented true Christian virtues in a world that worshiped pomposity.

3. Erasmus tried to instruct the young _____ to rule as a just Christian prince.

4. One of the most notorious scandals prior to the Reformation occurred in the city of _____, where a group of Dominicans fabricated miracles that brought in crowds of pilgrims.

5. According to the church, a person through _____ could alleviate their suffering in purgatory after death by performing certain religious tasks or giving money to the church.

6. At the Imperial Diet of _____ in 1521, Martin Luther appeared before Emperor Charles V to defend his beliefs.

7. Huldrych Zwingli was the leader of a Protestant theocracy in _____.

8. At the Colloquy of _____ in 1529, Luther and Zwingli failed to agree on the meaning of the Eucharist; therefore, the German and Swiss reform movements continued on separate paths.

9. In *The Institutes of the Christian Religion*, _____ argued that God had ordained every man, woman, and child to salvation or damnation, even before the creation of the world.

10. The Affair of the Placards, which took place in Paris in the year _____, provoked a national crackdown on religious dissenters.

11. The ex-priest _____ led a peasant revolt in Thuringia in 1525.

12. In the year _____ Martin Luther translated Erasmus's Greek New Testament into German.

13. In his book *On the Support of the Poor*, _____ urged authorities to establish public poor relief.

14. In 1531, _____ asked justices of the peace to license the poor in his kingdom to differentiate between those capable of working and those who could not.

15. _____ reaffirmed Catholic tradition with his polyphonies that used themes from medieval Gregorian chants.

16. In his painting *Gloria*, _____ depicted the Holy Roman Emperor Charles V kneeling in a white death shroud worshiping the Trinity.

17. In 1529, the Ottoman Turks under Sultan Suleiman I laid siege to _____, which was unsuccessful but sent shock waves throughout Christian Europe.

18. _____, the personal banker to Maximilian I, began an international financial empire that became the largest in sixteenth century Europe.

19. King Henry VIII of England broke with papal authority after failing to obtain a divorce from his wife _____.

20. In the Peace of Augsburg in the year _____, Emperor Charles V agreed to the principle that all princes held the sole right to determine the religion of their lands and subjects.

21. In 1545, _____ and Charles V convened a general church council at Trent, which shaped the essential character of Catholicism for centuries.

22. The Council of Trent lasted from 1545 until _____.

23. The Society of Jesus, or Jesuit Order, was founded by _____.

24. The Jesuit Francis Xavier landed in _____ in 1549 and his missionary work eventually gained more than 100,000 converts.

25. At the _____ held in 1555, it was decided that the priesthood was not to be conferred on Indians, people of mixed European and Indian or African heritage, or the descendents of Moors and Jews.

CHAPTER REVIEW

Self-Test and Analytical Exercises

Multiple Choice   *Select the best answer from the four choices provided.*

1. People of the sixteenth century sought spiritual comfort in all of the following ways *except* by
   a. going on pilgrimages.
   b. building new shrines.
   c. using prayer books in the vernacular and Latin.
   d. joining crusades to the Holy Land.

2. Which of the following was *not* a reason why the sacrament of confession was unsatisfactory to many Christians?
   a. The demands of confession intensified their anxiety about salvation.
   b. Many worried about remembering to confess their sins and had doubts about God's mercy.
   c. A person was allowed to confess only once a year, leading to fears of dying in a state of sin.
   d. Some priests abused their authority and demanded favors in return for forgiveness.

3. Which of the following works was *not* written by Erasmus?
   a. *Adages*
   b. *The Book of the Courtier*
   c. *The Praise of Folly*
   d. *Handbook of the Militant Christian*

4. *Utopia* was *not*
   a. written by Thomas More in 1516.
   b. inspired by the recent voyages of discovery.
   c. a critique of English society.
   d. condemned by the church.

5. Which of the following *best* describes Luther's beliefs?
   a. He believed that no Christian could be certain of salvation without calling on the guidance of the clergy.
   b. He believed that there was no distinction between the Gospel teachings and church doctrine.
   c. He believed that faith, not good works, would save sinners.
   d. He believed that the church's doctrines were important, and was outraged that officials abused their offices.

6. Which of the following was *not* written by Martin Luther?
   a. *Freedom of a Christian*
   b. *To the Nobility of the German Nation*
   c. *On the Babylonian Captivity of the Church*
   d. *The Institutes of Christian Religion*

7. Who most influenced the thought of Huldrych Zwingli?
   a. John Calvin
   b. Martin Luther
   c. Erasmus
   d. Thomas More

8. Which of the following doctrines did John Calvin develop?
   a. Predestination
   b. Transubstantiation
   c. Christian humanism
   d. Institutionalism

9. What was Martin Luther's attitude toward the German peasants who revolted in 1525?
   a. He supported the peasants, but did not offer them any assistance.
   b. He did not take a position on the fighting because he did not want to involve his church reform movement in politics.
   c. He initially tried to mediate for them, but eventually condoned the use of violence against them.
   d. He actively supported the rebels and led them into battle.

10. Which of the following statements regarding the Anabaptists is *false*?
    a. They were pacifists, and rejected the authority of courts and magistrates.
    b. They considered themselves to be a community of true Christians modeled on the first Christian community.
    c. Theirs was primarily an upper-class movement.
    d. Though persecuted and condemned, the Anabaptist movement spread to many cities in southern Germany.

11. Which German city did a group of Anabaptists seize control of in 1534?
    a. Münster
    b. Augsburg
    c. Zurich
    d. Thurgia

12. Who was burned at the stake as a heretic for translating the Bible into English?
    a. Thomas More
    b. William Tyndale
    c. Thomas Cramner
    d. Thomas Cromwell

13. Which leading Italian composer used themes from Gregorian chants?
    a. Orlando de Lassus
    b. Thomas Muntzer
    c. Giovanni Pierluigi da Palestrina
    d. Guillaume Briconnet

14. Titian
    a. painted the Sistine Chapel, including the ceiling.
    b. designed palaces in Rome for Pope Paul III.
    c. painted Charles V four times, Charles's favorite being *Gloria*.
    d. was the chief architect of St. Peter's Basilica.

15. Which treaty established peace between the Valois and the Habsburgs?
    a. The Treaty of Fontainebleau
    b. The Peace of Augsburg
    c. The Treaty of Cateau-Cambrésis
    d. The Treaty of Mohács

16. What did the Act of Supremacy of 1529 promulgate in England?
    a. It declared the supremacy of the Roman church over the monarchy.
    b. It outlawed Protestantism.
    c. It strengthened royal control over the nobility.
    d. It made Henry VIII the head of the Church of England.

17. What was the most important new religious order of sixteenth-century Catholic Europe?
    a. The Augustinians
    b. The Dominicans
    c. The Jesuits
    d. The Franciscans

18. Which pope took the lead in church reform?
    a. Julius III
    b. Paul III
    c. Pius V
    d. Charles V

19. Which of the following was *not* a decision made at the Council of Trent?
    a. Bishops were required to reside in their dioceses.
    b. Seminaries should be established to train priests.
    c. Weddings must take place in churches and be registered by the clergy.
    d. The clergy and laity should share authority.

20. The first Mexican Ecclesiastical Provincial Council declared that
    a. holy orders should not be conferred on non-white, non-European ethnic peoples.
    b. the New World was the spiritual domain of the Catholic church.
    c. all Indians who adopted the Christian faith were guaranteed salvation.
    d. each Mexican province be a separate Catholic diocese and have its own bishop appointed by Rome.

21. All of the following contributed to the crisis of faith and a sense of dissatisfaction with the official church at the beginning of the sixteenth century *except* the
    a. belief that the Last Judgment was going to arrive soon.
    b. exploitation of gullible laypeople by an unscrupulous clergy.
    c. priests working in the countryside were too educated for the peasants to understand.
    d. sense that the church was more concerned with making money than saving souls.

22. All of the following are *true* about Desiderius Erasmus *except*
    a. he was very critical of the morals and customs of his time.
    b. he enthusiastically supported the Protestant Reformation.
    c. he emphasized charity and good works over the ceremonies of the church as a mark of true religion.
    d. his writings were condemned by many in the Catholic church.

23. Which of the following *best* describes Christian humanism?
    a. It combined a love of classical learning with an emphasis on Christian piety.
    b. It was uncritical of the church hierarchy, especially the pope.
    c. It was a militant movement that advocated the use of violence to protect religious orthodoxy.
    d. It rejected any learning that was not based directly on the Bible.

24. Which of the following *best* describes More's *Utopia*?
    a. It was a compilation of Latin dialogues.
    b. It was an eloquent plea for a simple religion devoid of greed and the lust for power.
    c. It was a critique of English society.
    d. It satirized values held dear by contemporaries.

25. Who most influenced the early Swiss reform movement?
    a. Thomas More
    b. Martin Luther
    c. Huldrych Zwingli
    d. John Calvin

26. Where did John Calvin develop his ministry and live most of his later life?
    a. Mainz
    b. Geneva
    c. Zurich
    d. Picardy

27. Which of the following *best* describes the doctrine of predestination?
    a. The belief that God had ordained everyone to salvation or damnation before the creation of the world
    b. The belief that a person's social standing was determined at birth
    c. The belief that a person could attain salvation through good works
    d. The belief that the clergy could forgive sins

28. Which of the following was a consequence of the Affair of the Placards?
    a. The French king became more sympathetic toward Protestants.
    b. John Calvin was invited to Paris to present his religious views.
    c. There was a national crackdown on religious dissent in France.
    d. The king confiscated church property.

29. When and where was the Peasants' War?
    a. 1525, in the Holy Roman Empire
    b. 1513, in England
    c. 1545, in France
    d. 1537, in the Papal States

30. What announcement concerning religion did Emperor Charles V make in 1529?
    a. He declared the Roman Catholic faith to be the empire's only legitimate religion.
    b. He proclaimed both Lutheranism and Catholicism the official religions of the empire.
    c. He announced that the Holy Roman Empire was now a Protestant land.
    d. He stated that, henceforth, the empire would have no official religion, making religious toleration the new imperial policy.

31. The vernacular Bible was condemned by the church because it was perceived as having the potential to
    a. dissuade literate women from the bonds of marriage.
    b. misrepresent the Gospels if poorly translated.
    c. distract literate peasants from their work.
    d. subvert the established order.

32. What new musical form emerged in sixteenth-century Protestant Europe?
    a. The chorale
    b. The motet
    c. Polyphony
    d. Vernacular polyphony

33. Which two dynasties fought for dominance of Europe in the sixteenth century?
    a. The Valois and the Habsburg
    b. The York and the Lancastrian
    c. The Tudor and the Anjou
    d. The Burgundian and the Castilian

34. Which French alliance scandalized many contemporaries?
    a. The Franco-Papal alliance
    b. The Franco-Spanish alliance
    c. The Franco-Turkish alliance
    d. The Franco-Russian alliance

35. What was the Schmalkaldic League?
    a. It was a group of German Protestant princes and cities opposed to Emperor Charles V.
    b. It was an English-Scottish Protestant group opposed to Mary of Guise.
    c. It was a French alliance with German Protestants to fight Emperor Charles V.
    d. It was an alliance of Catholic princes and bishops with Emperor Charles V.

36. Which of the following statements is *false*?
    a. Until 1527, Henry VIII firmly opposed the Reformation.
    b. In 1529, Henry VIII asked for a papal dispensation to divorce his wife, Anne Boleyn.
    c. Between 1529 and 1536, Parliament passed a number of acts that severed ties between the English church and Rome.
    d. Established in 1529, the principle of royal supremacy was a lasting feature of the Church of England.

37. The Peace of Augsburg
    a. allowed all princes of the Holy Roman Empire, whether Catholic or Lutheran, to determine the religion of their lands and subjects, but it excluded Calvinists and other dissenting groups.
    b. did not satisfy the claims of the French king, causing him to again take up arms as soon as he was able.
    c. allowed emperor Charles V to consolidate control over his Netherlandish-Burgundian territories, his Spanish dominions, and his Austrian lands.
    d. bankrupted the Spanish crown.

38. All of the following are *true* of the Council of Trent *except* it
    a. reasserted the supremacy of clerical authority over the laity.
    b. stipulated that bishops reside in their dioceses.
    c. decreed that seminaries be established in each diocese to train priests.
    d. asserted that Christ was only symbolically present in the Eucharist.

39. Who founded the Society of Jesus?
    a. Ignatius of Loyola
    b. Bartolome de Las Casas
    c. Gasparo Contarini
    d. Francis Xavier

40. Which pioneering missionary traveled to Asia, preaching in India and Japan?
    a. Bartolome de Las Casas
    b. Francis Xavier
    c. Gian Matteo Giberti
    d. Ignatius of Loyola

Short Answer *Answer each question in three or four sentences.*

A New Heaven and a New Earth

1. Prior to the Reformation, there was a mounting crisis of faith for many within the Christian community. What were some of the causes of this crisis, and how did people react?

2. Erasmus dominated the humanist world in the early sixteenth century. For what scholarly achievements is he known, and what was his fate during the Reformation?

3. One of the best-known Christian humanists, Thomas More, wrote *Utopia*, published in 1516. What kind of society did More depict in *Utopia*, and what message was he trying to convey?

Protestant Reformers

4. After writing his ninety-five theses in 1517, Martin Luther wrote and published three treatises in 1520. What were they, and what were their main themes?

5. What main issues and ideas compelled Huldrych Zwingli, and how did his reform movement differ from the German reform movement?

6. What were John Calvin's beliefs, and how did his government affect Geneva?

Reshaping Society Through Religion

7. What two radical movements mixed reformed religion and politics to challenge the social order in the Holy RomanEmpire in the 1520s and what was their fate?

8. What were the new attitudes toward poverty and the poor, and how did Protestant attitudes differ from Catholic attitudes?

9. How did the Reformation change marriage and sexual morality in Protestant and Catholic communities?

A Struggle for Mastery

10. As the Reformation was taking hold in Germany, Spain and France fought each other for domination of Europe. How did this conflict develop and why were other powers drawn into the fighting?

11. Which Reformation religious divisions threatened the unity and stability of England and Scotland, and how were they resolved?

12. How did Charles V resolve conflicts in the Holy Roman Empire inspired by religious issues, and how did these solutions plant the seeds for further conflict?

A Continuing Reformation

13. Which principles and policies did the Council of Trent confirm or establish that reformed the essential character of Catholicism?

14. How was the Society of Jesus formed and what activities did its members undertake?

15. What patterns emerged concerning the efforts of missionary groups throughout the world?

BUILDING HISTORICAL SKILLS

Reading Maps *Write a brief, paragraph-length response to each of the following questions based on* **Mapping the West: Reformation Europe, c. 1560 (p. 576).**

1. Which countries were affected by the Protestant Reformation c. 1560 and which were not?

2. Judging from the map, which other areas of Europe do you believe have the potential for conflict over the question of religion?

Reading Illustrations   *Write a brief, paragraph-length response to each of the following questions based on the illustration **Albrecht Dürer's The Knight, Death, and the Devil** (p. 550).*

1. What does this engraving depict?

2. Which figure in this illustration is meant to represent death?

3. How might this engraving support Erasmus's argument that greed and the lust for power served as obstacles to true religious faith?

Reading Historical Documents   *Write a brief, paragraph-length response to each of the following questions based on the documents in your book.*

Erasmus Writes to Martin Luther, 1519 (p. 556)

1. How does Erasmus view Martin Luther in this letter?

2. What are Erasmus's main concerns when he writes to Luther?

3. What solution does Erasmus propose to the controversy generated by Luther's work, and how does this reflect his view of learning?

Thomas More, Utopia, 1516 (p. 551)

4. What are some of the social values of More's imaginary island of Utopia?

5. How does More view the impact of society on human nature?

Contrasting Views: Martin Luther: Holy Man or Heretic? (pp. 554–555)

6. What served as propaganda in sixteenth-century Europe?

7. How did the invention of the printing press influence propaganda?

8. Why were images so important to propaganda?

A Century of Crisis
1560–1648

CHAPTER OVERVIEW

Chapter Questions *Keep these questions in mind as you go through the study guide chapter.*

1. What were the causes and results of the Wars of Religion in France?

2. What impact did the Thirty Years' War have on Europe?

3. Why did Spain's power decline in the seventeenth century?

4. How did economic decline affect ordinary people?

5. How and why did art, culture, and intellectual life change in the late sixteenth century and early seventeenth centuries?

Chapter Summary

Religious Conflicts and State Power, 1560–1618

The Peace of Augsburg of 1555 legally recognized Lutheranism, but did not offer the same recognition to Calvinists. Calvinism expanded rapidly after 1560 and threatened the religious balance of power in much of Europe, which inevitably had political consequences.

French Wars of Religion, 1562–1598, pp. 582–585

Following the Peace of Augsburg in 1555 Calvinism began to make inroads into France, where noble converts provided military protection for the newly established Huguenot church. The situation became volatile after King Henry II was accidentally killed in a jousting match in 1559, leaving his throne to his fifteen-year-old son Francis. Francis died soon after and ten-year-old Charles IX became king with his Florentine mother Catherine dé

Medici as regent. In 1562, a series of wars began in which two factions—the Catholics, led by the Guise family; and the Protestants, led by the Bourbon family—struggled for control and influence over the French throne tenuously held by the Catholic Valois. Catherine sought to play the Guise and Bourbon families against each other, but tensions continued, reaching a head in August 1572 when tens of thousands of Huguenots were massacred in Paris and in the provinces in a wave of violence known as the St. Bartholomew's Day Massacre. This led Huguenots to justify resistance by claiming that the Valois had violated a contract between ruler and ruled—an argument based on constitutionalism. The wars did not end until Henry of Navarre, head of the Bourbon faction, became king of France in 1589. To put an end to the fighting, Henry IV, as he was now known, converted to Catholicism and issued the Edict of Nantes, which allowed the Huguenots to worship freely in specified towns and maintain their own troops, fortresses, and courts. Henry IV reestablished monarchical authority by creating a new bureaucracy staffed by members of a new social elite, the "nobility of the robe," meant to act as a counterweight to the ancient nobility. Henry IV was assassinated in 1610.

Challenges to Spanish Power, pp. 586–589

At the time of his accession, Philip II of Spain (r. 1556–1598) controlled the western Habsburg lands in Spain and the Netherlands as well as the Spanish colonies in the Americas, making him the most powerful ruler in Europe. He made it his mission in life to restore Catholic unity to Europe and drive back the Muslims. In 1571, Philip defeated the Ottoman Turks in the battle of Lepanto, which gave him control of the Mediterranean. He also expelled the Moriscos, converts to Catholicism who practiced Islam in secret and rebelled when they lost hope of Turkish assistance. When Calvinists in the Netherlands attacked Catholic churches in 1566, Philip sent an army that sacked Antwerp in 1576, an atrocity known as the Spanish Fury. The Spanish Fury so shocked the largely Catholic southern provinces that they joined forces with the largely Protestant northern provinces to expel the Spanish. Whereas the southern provinces eventually returned to Spain, the northern provinces became the Dutch Republic, a federation controlled by the wealthiest families of each province. The economy of the Dutch Republic—based on shipping, commerce, and manufacturing—prospered, and Amsterdam became the main European money market for two centuries. The Dutch Republic tolerated religious diversity and became a haven for persecuted peoples, such as Jews who had been expelled from Spain and who helped to make the republic a leading intellectual and scientific center in the seventeenth and eighteenth centuries.

Elizabeth I's Defense of English Protestantism, pp. 589–590

When Elizabeth I (r. 1558–1603) succeeded her Catholic sister Mary as queen of England, she brought Protestantism back to England but refused to bow to Calvinist Puritans who wanted all traces of Catholicism removed from the ritual and governance of the Church of England. Puritans gained influence in English society and tried to have theaters and Sunday fairs closed down. In addition to internal tensions, Elizabeth faced foreign intrigues. In 1588, she beheaded her Catholic cousin, Mary, Queen of Scots, who was next in line for the English throne by offering Philip II of Spain her right to the Scottish throne. Frustrated for political and religious reasons, Philip sent his armada into the English Channel to fight the English navy and ferry an army of invasion from the Netherlands to England. When the Spanish Armada was virtually wiped out, Spain suffered a severe psychological blow. Triumphant, Elizabeth I consolidated her control as queen and left her successor, James I (r. 1603–1625), king of Scotland and England, a kingdom of expanding international importance.

The Clash of Faiths and Empires in Eastern Europe, pp. 590–591

The Battle of Lepanto was a setback for the Ottoman Turks but only a temporary one. Two years later—in 1573—they seized the island of Cyprus from the Venetians. The Ottoman Empire controlled the Balkans, where they allowed Orthodox Christians and Jews to practice their religions rather than forcing them to convert to Islam. Both Christians and Jews therefore had no reason to rebel. Orthodox Christians were also officially protected in Russian lands by the Muscovite tsars. Ivan IV (r. 1533–1584), named "the Terrible" for his ruthlessness, cruelty, and unpredictable fits of rage, brought the entire Volga valley under his control, expanded eastward into Siberia, and attempted to seize lands in the west to gain access to the Baltic Sea. Ivan's drive west was blocked by Sweden

and Poland-Lithuania. Poland-Lithuania maintained peace between the Catholic majority and Protestant nobles because its monarch had limited powers and was required to practice religious toleration. During the chaotic Time of Troubles that followed Ivan's death, the king of Poland-Lithuania tried to seize the Russian throne for his son, but was defeated in 1613. A Russian nobleman, Michael Romanov (r. 1613–1645) established a new dynasty that resumed state building.

The Thirty Years' War and the Balance of Power, 1618–1648

Although the eastern European states managed to avoid civil wars over religion, the rest of Europe was drawn into the final and most deadly wars of religion known today as the Thirty Years' War. Beginning in 1618 with conflicts between Catholics and Protestants in the Holy Roman Empire, it spread throughout most of Europe. By its end in 1648, the balance of power had shifted away from the Habsburgs toward France, England, and the Dutch Republic.

Origins and Course of the War, pp. 592–593

The fighting that devastated central Europe had its origins in a combination of political weakness, ethnic competition, and religious conflict. In 1617, Catholic Habsburg heir Archduke Ferdinand became king of Bohemia and curtailed Protestants' freedom. The Czechs, the region's largest ethnic group, began an anti-Habsburg, anti-Catholic resistance. When the unpopular king was elected Holy Roman emperor Ferdinand II (r. 1619–1637), the resistance deposed him and chose a new king. Imperial armies defeated the Czechs at the Battle of White Mountain. Ferdinand bought the services of Albrecht von Wallenstein (a Protestant Czech) to raise a mercenary army that plundered much of Protestant Germany with the emperor's approval. In response to Wallenstein, King Christian IV of Denmark (r. 1596–1648) invaded northern Germany to protect Protestants and to extend his own influence. Wallenstein defeated Christian IV, giving Ferdinand II reign over Denmark and the Protestants there. Ferdinand II issued the Edict of Restitution in 1629, which outlawed Calvinism in the empire and reclaimed Catholic church property confiscated by Lutherans. King Gustavus Adolphus of Sweden entered the war to protect Protestant interests (and Sweden's trade in northern Europe). Catholic France subsidized Sweden, glad to help any enemy of the Habsburgs. Gustavus Adolphus triumphed and occupied the Catholic parts of southern Germany until his death in 1632. In 1635, France entered the conflict openly by declaring war on Spain. Religion took a backseat as Catholic France and Catholic Spain fought for dominance of

Europe. By the early 1640s, exhaustion and internal conflicts brought all sides to the negotiating table.

The Effects of Constant Fighting, pp. 593–595

Ordinary people suffered horrors during the Thirty Years' War, as army after army plundered and destroyed cities and countryside alike. Peasant revolts and plague outbreaks added to the chaos. When warring governments neglected to pay their armies, soldiers then turned on the local population, looting, pillaging, raping, torturing, and murdering large numbers of civilians. War became increasingly expensive as rulers sought to build larger armies equipped with canons and warships. These huge expenses seriously strained state resources. The difficult economic conditions many people faced made it easier for rulers to recruit their own subjects into these armies, although mercenary armies still predominated.

The Peace of Westphalia, 1648, pp. 595–597

The Peace of Westphalia was the first time that all warring parties had been present during settlement negotiations and all agreed to a common treaty. This model is still used today. France and Sweden gained the most from this treaty. France acquired parts of Alsace and replaced Spain as the most powerful country in continental Europe, whereas Sweden acquired several northern territories from the Holy Roman Empire. The Habsburgs lost the most. The Dutch obtained their independence from Spain, and each German ruler gained the right to choose his state's religion and more autonomy from the Holy Roman Emperor. Within the Holy Roman Empire, Lutheranism would henceforth dominate in the north, Calvinism in the area of the Rhine River, and Catholicism in the south. The Thirty Years' War changed the political landscape of Europe forever. From this time onward, wars would be fought over political and economic problems not religious ones. States enlarged bureaucracies to raise the taxes necessary to support larger armies and lavish courts. As bureaucracies grew, monarchs started to rely on university-educated officials to manage them and advise on affairs of state. All ranks of society bitterly resented escalating demands for taxes. To mitigate the growth of the state, monarchs cultivated an image of power, requiring courtiers to follow precise rituals in splendid settings designed to showcase the vigor and prestige of the monarchy.

Economic Crisis and Realignment

The Thirty Years' War deepened a preexisting economic crisis. Massive imports of gold and silver had led to rising prices, but this leveled off in the early 1600s. In most of Europe, population growth slowed and agricultural yields declined just as states were trying to extract more revenues to pay for their expanding armies. The economic crisis and war were followed by famine, disease, and revolts.

From Growth to Recession, pp. 598–599

In the second half of the sixteenth century, population growth coincided with an influx of precious metals from the Americas into western Europe, resulting in dramatic inflation; in the early seventeenth century, however, a recession spread slowly across Europe. Both foreign trade and the population of Europe declined, in part because of the Thirty Years' War. The import of precious metals declined after 1625, largely because the native Americans who worked in Spanish colonial mines died off. Textile production declined as well due to a shrinking labor force and a decrease in demand. Grain prices fell as the population dropped, and many farmers used their land for pasture or vineyards. With the exception of the Dutch Republic, and to a lesser extent, England, western Europe entered a period of economic decline. Vulnerable populations succumbed to epidemic diseases and to famines caused by bad harvests.

Consequences for Daily Life, pp. 599–603

Food shortages were devastating, especially since most of the population depended on grain for survival. From 1594 to 1597, famine caused people across Europe to revolt in protest. England instituted the Poor Law of 1597, which required each community to support its poor. Many people ended up as vagabonds and bandits. Malnutrition made Europe's population less resistant to diseases such as typhus, and influenza, or, most feared of all, plague. The economic crisis heightened the contrast between rich and poor. Depending on where they lived in the seventeenth century, the peasantry either became better off due to increased landholdings and selling on the market, or continued to experience incredibly hard times losing land and working for others at low wages. Women were especially vulnerable to bad economic cycles because many job opportunities were restricted to men, and some who found jobs as servants were not allowed to leave them. Uncertain economic times led many to postpone marriage and have fewer children, especially the poor. Couples in all ranks of society began marrying later and limiting family size in the seventeenth century.

The Economic Balance of Power, pp. 603–605

The crisis of the seventeenth century led to a shift in the balance of power in Europe. The long-standing superiority of the Mediterranean economies of Italy and Spain came to an end. The northwestern countries of England, the Dutch Republic, and France became the new economic leaders. However, the difference between north and south in western Europe was soon overshadowed by the difference between east and west, as nobles east of the Elbe River increased their hold over the peasantry at the same time that peasants in western Europe were gaining greater autonomy. Eastern European economies depended exclusively on increased agricultural production, whereas those of Western Europe also expanded their trade with the new world. In Muscovy, peasants were forced into serfdom by the Code of Laws in 1649. Because of Spain and Portugal's hold on South America, the English, French, and Dutch turned to North America and the Caribbean. The English encouraged settlement in their colonies and attempted to convert to Christianity those native peoples whom they had not previously driven out through violent tactics. Religious groups on the margins of English society, such as the Pilgrims and Puritans, established new communities in North America. Because Huguenots were not permitted to emigrate, the French settlements in Canada were limited. Both England and France also gained control of territory in the Caribbean, where they cultivated tobacco and sugarcane.

A Clash of Worldviews

The countries that moved ahead during this period—England, the Dutch Republic, and to an extent France—all became receptive to new secular worldviews. In the long-term process known as secularization, religion became a matter of private conscience rather than public policy, and people sought nonreligious explanations for political authority and natural phenomena.

The Arts in an Age of Crisis, pp. 606–608

Traditional beliefs were increasingly challenged during the late sixteenth and early seventeenth centuries. The plays of William Shakespeare reflected the anxieties of the period, and in particular debates concerning the nature of power and the crisis of authority. Plays such as *Hamlet* (1601), *King Lear* (1605), and *Macbeth* (1606) particularly dramatize the uncertainty and chaos that result when authority is misappropriated or misused. These plays also link family relationships to questions about the legitimacy of government, just as they were for Elizabeth I herself. In painting, mannerism, noted for tricky use of perspective and bizarre effects often conveyed religious intensity. The most famous mannerist painter is El Greco. The baroque style (noted for its almost theatrical use of curves, exaggerated lighting, intense emotions, and release from restraint) broke with the Renaissance focus on perspective and harmony. The baroque was used to glorify the Catholic religion and the

power of monarchy in the Habsburgs' Catholic territories. One of the best-known baroque painters was Peter Paul Rubens. Painters in Protestant countries rejected the baroque in favor of greater realism, sometimes painting biblical scenes but more often painting subjects from everyday life. Opera, a new musical form that grew up parallel to the baroque style of the visual arts, combined music, drama, dance, and scenery in a grand sensuous display. It was often designed to be performed for aristocratic and royal audiences.

The Natural Laws of Politics, pp. 608–610

The conflicts over religion led some to develop a new set of principles upon which the authority of the state could be based. French essayist Michel de Montaigne revived the ancient doctrine of skepticism and argued that total certainty, in religion or in any other matter, was never attainable. This implied that religions were not worth fighting over. The French lawyer Jean Bodin promoted order as the most important quality for a state, and argued that only a strong monarch could ensure order. These ideas helped lay the foundation for absolutism, the idea that the monarch should be the sole and uncontested source of power. Dutch jurist Hugo Grotius argued that natural law, not religious authority, should govern politics. Natural law was designed to defend natural rights, which included the right to life, body, freedom, and honor, and Grotius said that it was the duty of government to uphold these rights. Grotius argued that torture, widespread during this time, infringed natural rights. All of these thinkers helped develop a more secular political theory in which authority was no longer based on religion.

Origins of the Scientific Revolution, pp. 610–615

By the early seventeenth century, a new scientific method based on systematic experiments and rational deduction was established. Previously, astronomy was based on Aristotle and Ptolemy, who had argued that the perfect planets revolved in perfect crystal spheres around the corrupted Earth. Nicolaus Copernicus began this revolution in astronomy by arguing that the Earth and other planets revolved around the sun. Tycho Brahe rejected this heliocentrist model, but his discovery of a new star in 1572 challenged the Aristotelian notion that the heavens were perfect and unchanging. Brahe's assistant Johannes Kepler continued Brahe's observations of planetary movement and was converted to the Copernican view. He provided mathematical proof for a heliocentric model and discovered that planetary motion was eliptic not circular. Galileo Galilei provided further evidence for heliocentrism and, using a telescope of his own design, discovered four moons around Jupiter, the phases of

Venus, sunspots, and hills on the moon, all of which proved that the heavens were no more perfect than the Earth. Better understanding of anatomy and pharmacology advanced medicine: the human body, like the universe, was now to be understood by experiment and rational deduction. Sir Francis Bacon championed inductive reasoning through observation and experimental research, and René Descartes promoted and deductive reasoning from self-evident principles. Scientific research and economic growth would come to be centered in the northern Protestant countries, where it was less constrained by church control.

Magic and Witchcraft, pp. 615–617

Despite the new emphasis on clear reasoning, observation, and independence from past authority, science had not yet become separate from magic. Many of the great scientists of the day also practiced alchemy and astrology. At a time when most people believed in astrology, magical healing, prophesy, and ghosts, it is not surprising that many people also believed in witchcraft, including magistrates such as Jean Bodin. Belief in witches was not new, but the official persecution of witches was. In a time of economic crisis, plague, constant warfare, and religious differences, witchcraft trials provided an outlet for social anxiety that was legitimated by state power. Witch trials peaked in Catholic and Protestant Europe between 1560 and 1640, ironically during the same time as the breakthroughs of the new science. Women accounted for an estimated 80 percent of accused witches. Targets were usually those who lived on the margins of society and were believed to harbor vengeful sentiments against those who were better off. Witchcraft trials declined when scientific thinking raised doubts about the quality of evidence being used in court and when the educated classes began to see witchcraft as nothing more than peasant superstition.

Key Events *For each question, select the most appropriate response from the choices provided.*

1562 French Wars of Religion begin

1566 Revolt of Calvinists in the Netherlands against Spain begins

1569 Formation of commonwealth of Poland-Lithuania

1571 Battle of Lepanto marks victory of West over Ottomans at sea

1572 St. Bartholomew's Day Massacre of French Protestants

1588 Defeat of the Spanish Armada by England

1598 French Wars of Religion end with Edict of Nantes

1601 William Shakespeare, *Hamlet*

1618 Thirty Years' War begins

1625 Hugo Grotius publishes *The Laws of War and Peace*

1629 English Puritans set up the Massachusetts Bay Co. and begin to colonize New England

1633 Galileo Galilei is forced to recant his support of heliocentrism

1635 French join the Thirty Years' War by declaring war on Spain

1648 Peace of Westphalia ends the Thirty Years' War

1. Which of the following marked the height of Spanish power in the sixteenth century?
   a. The Spanish Armada
   b. The revolt in the Netherlands
   c. The battle of Lepanto
   d. The Thirty Years' War

2. Who were the victims of the St. Bartholomew's Day Massacre in 1572?
   a. Catholics
   b. Huguenots
   c. Jews
   d. Muslims

3. What did the Edict of Nantes do in 1598?
   a. Outlaw Protestantism in France
   b. Establish peace between France and Spain
   c. Establish a French colony in the New World
   d. Allow limited religious freedoms to French Huguenots

4. Which of the following is *not true* of Hugo Grotius' *The Laws of War and Peace* (1625)?
   a. It was condemned by the Catholic church.
   b. It argued that politics should be governed by natural law, not religious authority or tradition.
   c. It condemned the use of torture because it violated rights that governments should defend.
   d. It encouraged rebellion against unjust governments.

5. What did the Catholic church force Galileo to recant in 1633?
   a. His support of Calvinism
   b. His belief that the earth revolved around the sun
   c. His belief that the heart worked like a pump
   d. His belief that natural law, not Scripture, should govern politics

6. Who set up the Massachusetts Bay Co. in 1629 and began to colonize New England?
   a. English Catholics
   b. English Puritans
   c. Dutch Calvinists
   d. French Huguenots

7. What agreement brought an end to the Thirty Years' War?
   a. The Peace of Paris
   b. The Edict of Nantes
   c. The Peace of Westphalia
   d. The Peace of Augsburg

Key Terms   *Match each key term to its definition.*

A. **baroque** (p. 607)
B. **heliocentrism** (p. 612)
C. **Huguenot** (p. 582)
D. **mannerism** (p. 607)
E. **Moriscos** (p. 587)
F. *politiques* (p. 585)
G. **Puritans** (p. 589)
H. *raison d'état* (p. 597)
I. **scientific method** (p. 611)
J. **secularization** (p. 606)
K. **tithe** (p. 601)

1. _____ Name given to Calvinists in France; its linguistic origin remains uncertain, but the label was applied to Calvinists in France after 1560.

2. _____ Political advisers during the French Wars of Religion who argued that compromise in matters of religion—limited toleration for the Calvinists—would strengthen the monarchy.

3. _____ Muslim converts to Christianity in Spain who remained secretly faithful to Islam; they were expelled from Spain in 1614.

4. _____ Strict Calvinists who opposed all vestiges of Catholic ritual in the Church of England.

5. _____ French for "reason of state." The political doctrine, first proposed by Cardinal Richelieu of France, which held that the state's interests should prevail over those of religion; Richelieu, for example, allied with the Lutheran king of Sweden even though he himself was a leading official of the Catholic Church.

6. _____ A tax equivalent to one tenth of the parishioner's annual income taken by both Catholic and Protestant churches; often the clergy took theirs in the form of crops and collected it directly during the harvest.

7. _____ The trend toward making religious faith a private domain rather than one directly connected to state power and science; it prompted a search for non-religious explanations for political authority and natural phenomena.

8. _____ A late sixteenth-century style of painting in which a distorted perspective created bizarre and theatrical effects that contrasted with the precise, harmonious lines of Renaissance painting.

9. _____ An artistic style of the seventeenth century that featured curves, exaggerated lighting, intense emotions, release from restraint, and even a kind of artistic sensationalism; like mannerism, it departed from the Renaissance emphasis on harmonious design, unity, and clarity.

10. _____ The view articulated by Polish clergyman Nicolaus Copernicus that the earth and planets revolve around the sun; Galileo Galilei was condemned by the Catholic church for supporting this view.

11. _____ A combination of experimental observation and mathematical deduction to determine the laws of nature; it became the secular standard of truth and as such challenged the hold of both the churches and popular beliefs.

Identification   *This activity tests your recall of significant people, places, and events from this chapter. Fill in the blank with the correct answer.*

1. The accidental death of _____ in a jousting match 1559 worsened the religious factionalism in France by leaving the monarchy in the hands of a fifteen-year-old.

2. The _____ family led the Catholic faction of the nobility in sixteenth-century France.

3. The botched assassination plot against _____ led to the St. Bartholomew's Day Massacre because the monarchy feared Huguenot revenge.

4. In 1588, _____ sent an armada of ships to England in a failed attempt to remove Protestant Queen Elizabeth from the throne.

5. The naval battle of _____ in which Philip II with his Venetian and papal allies defeated a Turkish fleet, was the greatest military victory of his reign.

6. The Thirty Years' War was sparked when a Protestant mob in _____ threw two Catholic deputies out of a castle window.

7. King _____ of Denmark responded to Albrecht von Wallenstein's occupation of Protestant Germany by invading it himself to protect the Protestants and extend his influence.

8. Louis XIII's chief minister _____ advocated a policy in which the interests of the state overrode all other concerns, including religion.

9. Hoping to block Spanish intervention in the Thirty Years' War and increase their influence in the Holy Roman Empire, the Catholic French monarchy subsidized Lutheran _____ of Sweden's invasion of Germany.

10. The _____ issued by Emperor Ferdinand II in 1629 outlawed Calvinism in the Holy Roman Empire and reclaimed Catholic church property that had been confiscated by the Lutherans.

11. African slaves were first imported to _____ in 1619.

12. The _____ were the only people to emerge from the economic downturn of the seventeenth century unscathed due to their innovative systems of field drainage, crop rotation, and animal husbandry.

13. The _____ government did not allow Protestants to emigrate to the New World, effectively denying itself a ready population for settling its colonies.

14. In _____ the complete enserfment of the peasantry was accomplished with the Code of Laws in 1649.

15. The crisis of the seventeenth century ended the dominance of the _____ economies, which had endured since the time of the Greeks and Romans.

16. The painter _____ epitomized the mannerist style, using larger-than-life figures and elongated figures to create an effect of religious intensity.

17. The ideas of _____ paved the way for absolutism by arguing that the monarch should be the sole and uncontested source of power.

18. In *The Laws of War and Peace*, _____ argued for a natural law that was more important than Scripture, religious authority, or tradition in politics.

19. The observation by _____ of a new star in 1572 and a comet in 1577 challenged the Aristotelian view that the universe was unchanging.

20. _____ helped establish the modern science of pharmacology by experimenting with new drugs, although he still pursued interests in magic, alchemy, and astrology.

CHAPTER REVIEW

Self-Test and Analytical Exercises

Multiple Choice *Select the best answer from the four choices provided.*

1. Calvinism in France
   a. was supported by the royal Valois family.
   b. did not receive support from noblewomen because it was too patriarchal.
   c. appealed to a much larger proportion of the nobility than the general population.
   d. had no relation to the political disputes among noble families.

2. What was the St. Bartholomew's Day Massacre?
   a. A mass killing of Catholics in Paris by Huguenots who saw them as "idol worshippers"
   b. A massacre of Huguenots in Paris and the provinces by the forces of King Charles IX and his mother Catherine dé Medici
   c. A massacre of Calvinist missionaries in Italy on orders of Pope Sixtus V, who then had church bells rung throughout Rome when the killing was accomplished
   d. A mass killing of Calvinists in the Navarre region by the forces of Philip II of Spain

3. The Edict of Nantes was significant because it
   a. gave full political and religious rights to the Huguenots throughout all of France.
   b. ran against the doctrine of the *politiques*, who advocated radical versions of both Calvinism and Catholicism.
   c. pacified a religious minority too large to ignore—the Huguenots—by giving them legal protection.
   d. passed the French crown from the Valois to the Bourbons, ending the French Wars of Religion.

4. Under Ottoman rule, Christians in the Balkans were
   a. mercilessly repressed, tortured, and imprisoned.
   b. forced to convert to Islam.
   c. allowed to retain their faith.
   d. constantly plotting with western powers to throw out the Ottomans.

5. Which of the following was the Protestant military commander who raised a mercenary army and offered its services to the Catholic Holy Roman Emperor?
   a. Gaspard Coligny
   b. Ferdinand II
   c. Hugo Grotius
   d. Albrecht von Wallenstein

6. All of the following are *true* of Gustavus Adolphus *except* he
   a. was a Lutheran.
   b. received support from Catholic powers.
   c. was Swedish.
   d. fought mainly against other Protestants.

7. Which two powers gained the most from the agreement that ended the Thirty Years' War?
   a. Sweden and Spain
   b. The Netherlands and the Holy Roman Empire
   c. Spain and France
   d. France and Sweden

8. All of the following were features of the growth of state authority *except* which of the following?
   a. The monarchs surrounded themselves with increasingly grand visible symbols of their power.
   b. States depended more on university-educated advisors who were well versed in law and politics.
   c. The royal courts became increasingly regulated and complex.
   d. There was a decrease in taxation because the Thirty Years' War had proved lucrative for the victorious powers.

9. All of the following contributed to economic recession at the beginning of the seventeenth century *except*
   a. climatic changes.
   b. a massive population boom throughout Europe.
   c. the decline in silver imports from the New World.
   d. the Thirty Years' War and the states' demand for more tax revenues.

10. The economic crisis affected women in all of the following ways *except* which of the following?
    a. They married earlier to help cope with the economic recession.
    b. Some female servants were unable to leave their jobs unless they could prove abuse by their employers.
    c. Women found their participation in guilds limited or prohibited.
    d. Many women had fewer children.

11. The economic recession of the seventeenth century caused the
    a. economies of southern Europe to become stronger and those of northern Europe to decline.
    b. Mediterranean economies to become the dominant force in Europe.
    c. states of northwestern Europe to become stronger and those in the south to decline.
    d. northern European states to fall behind in the mercantile opportunities provided by Atlantic trade.

12. Which of the following statements best describes the difference between peasants in western Europe and those in eastern Europe?
    a. In the west, nobles reinforced their control over peasants, while in the east, serfdom virtually ended.
    b. Peasants all over Europe suffered equally.
    c. In the west, labor shortages gave peasants some leverage to negotiate for more independence, while in the east, nobles reinforced their control over the peasantry.
    d. Western Europe's peasantry was nearly wiped out by starvation and the plague, whereas eastern European peasants shared in the new prosperity of their region's economic dominance.

13. Secularization could *best* be described as
    a. the loss of religious faith.
    b. the confiscation of church property.
    c. a search for nonreligious explanations for political authority and natural phenomena.
    d. the removal of clergymen from official government positions.

14. What was mannerism?
    a. A style of opera that mocked the merchant and peasant classes
    b. A style of church architecture
    c. A style of painting exhibiting distorted perspectives and allusions
    d. An austere style of painting based on mathematical proportions

15. Opera
    a. originated in Calvinist countries and involved the singing of songs in unison, thereby encouraging group participation.
    b. combined drama, dance, music, and scenery, and often explored themes pleasing to the aristocracy.
    c. avoided using traditional stories or subjects, as it was an innovative art form.
    d. found its origins in sacred music, where religious hymns were enhanced through harmony.

16. Who wrote the *Discourse on Method*?
    a. Sir Francis Bacon
    b. Michel de Montaigne
    c. René Descartes
    d. Paracelsus

17. The members of which French noble family were close relatives of the French king but became Huguenots?
    a. The Bourbon family
    b. The Medici family
    c. The Guise family
    d. The Valois family

18. Henry IV did all of the following *except*
    a. undermine the financial stability of the monarchy through overspending.
    b. create a new class of social elite through the sale of inheritable offices and the creation of a new bureaucracy.
    c. build the basis for a strong monarchy in France.
    d. use paintings, songs, court festivities, and royal processions to rally subjects around him.

19. Which of the following *best* describes the Dutch Republic?
    a. A wealthy trading republic that developed a highly democratic political system through the institution of the States-General
    b. A loose federation of wealthy towns that imposed a strict brand of Calvinism and traded only with other Protestant countries
    c. A federation of self-governing provinces that thrived on maritime commerce and tolerated religious diversity
    d. A republic composed of provinces that vested power in a strong centralized state in the face of Spanish threats.

20. All of the following are true of Philip II *except*
    a. he was uninterested in political events outside the lands over which he had direct rule.
    b. he took over Portugal when its king died without an heir, granting Spain an even vaster empire.
    c. his marriages opened the door to his involvement in the political affairs of England and France.
    d. he was an ardent Catholic who worked for Catholic unity against both Protestants and Muslims.

21. At the time of the Thirty Years' War, which dynasty ruled over the Holy Roman Empire?
    a. The Valois
    b. The House of Savoy
    c. The Austrian Habsburgs
    d. The Spanish Habsburgs

22. Which battle saw the defeat of the Czechs by the armies of the Habsburg emperor and became a symbol of the Czech desire for self-determination?
    a. White Mountain
    b. Lützen
    c. Prague
    d. Bohemia

23. Which two Catholic powers warred against each other during the Thirty Years' War?
    a. The Holy Roman Empire and Sweden
    b. Spain and France
    c. The Netherlands and Spain
    d. Bohemia and Spain

24. What was the name of the treaty that ended the Thirty Years' War?
    a. The Treaty of Augsburg
    b. The Thirty-Nine Articles
    c. The Peace of Westphalia
    d. The Edict of Nantes

25. In Europe in the 1600s, population growth
    a. stagnated or declined in most places, particularly in central Europe.
    b. grew dramatically, particularly in central Europe.
    c. declined in England, Wales, the Dutch Republic, and Scandinavia, but grew everywhere else.
    d. grew everywhere in Europe, especially in lands controlled by the Ottoman empire.

26. Outside England and the Dutch Republic, the essential staple of most Europeans' diets was
    a. vegetables.
    b. grain.
    c. meat.
    d. dairy products.

27. How did the economic crisis affect the status of the peasantry?
    a. The condition of prosperous and poor peasants leveled out.
    b. Most peasants prospered as populations declined and crop yields rose.
    c. The disparity between prosperous and poor peasants became more sharply divided.
    d. As male peasants died, female peasants gained economic opportunities.

28. All of the following are *true* of seventeenth-century colonization *except*
    a. a large number of colonists were religious refugees.
    b. Protestantism won more native American converts to Christianity than Catholicism.
    c. France denied its Protestants the right of emigration.
    d. English, French, and Dutch colonies dominated the commerce of North America and the Caribbean.

29. Who wrote *The Advancement of Learning*?
    a. Tycho Brahe
    b. Theophrastus Bombastus von Hohenheim
    c. Nicolaus Copernicus
    d. Sir Francis Bacon

30. Who developed the essay as a literary form and emphasized the doctrine of skepticism?
    a. Jean Bodin
    b. Hugo Grotius
    c. Machiavelli
    d. Michel de Montaigne

31. Who first published a book attacking the Ptolemaic account of the movement of the heavens and arguing that Earth revolved around the sun?
    a. Nicolaus Copernicus
    b. Giordano Bruno
    c. Galileo Galilei
    d. Tyco Brahe

32. In the sixteenth century, magic and science
    a. were closely linked, and many leading scientists also dabbled in alchemy and astrology.
    b. were openly practiced in Catholic countries but condemned in Protestant countries.
    c. were totally incompatible and led Jean Bodin to question the existence of true witchcraft.
    d. had little influence on religious beliefs, the long-standing explanation of the natural events.

Short Answer   *Answer each question in three or four sentences.*

Religious Conflicts and State Power, 1560–1618

1. Briefly describe the close connection between politics and religious conflict between 1550 and 1618.

2. What were some of the general political effects of the wars over religion throughout Europe between 1550 and 1618?

3. What effect did religious toleration have on politics between 1550 and 1618?

The Thirty Years' War and the Balance of Power, 1618–1648

4. How did the Thirty Years' War increase the size and power of national governments?

5. During the of Thirty Years' War, what shift took place in the motives of European nations for starting and conducting wars?

6. What was the effect of the Thirty Years' War on ordinary people?

Economic Crisis and Realignment

7. What were some of the main causes of the economic recession that hit Europe in the first half of the 1600s?

8. What was the impact of the economic crisis of the 1600s on the economic balance of power in Europe?

9. What were some of the effects of the recession on daily life?

A Clash of Worldviews

10. What was secularization? How was it expressed?

11. What happened to religion and the belief in magic as a result of new trends in scientific thought?

12. How did art reflect the trends in political and religious thought?

BUILDING HISTORICAL SKILLS

Reading Maps   *Write a brief, paragraph-length response to each of the following questions based on* **Map 16.2: The Empire of Philip II, r. 1556–1598 (p. 586).**

1. What was the extent of Philip II's empire?

2. How did the extent of Spanish power contribute to conflict in Europe between 1560 and 1648?

Reading Illustrations   *Write a brief, paragraph-length response to each of the following questions based on the illustration* **Queen Elizabeth I of England (p. 589).**

1. How does this picture emphasize the link between church and state in Elizabethan England?

2. What type of image of the monarchy does this picture present?

Reading Historical Documents   *Write a brief, paragraph-length response to each of the following questions based on the documents in your book.*

Galileo Galilei and Johannes Kepler, Correspondence (p. 613)

1. What does this letter reveal about scientific advancement at the end of the sixteenth century?

2. How were new ideas exchanged at the end of the sixteenth century?

The Horrors of the Thirty Years' War (p. 594)

3. How does Hans Grimmelshausen characterize the violence of the Thirty Years' War?

4. What does Hans Grimmelshausen's attitude toward religious war in general seem to be, and how is this reflected in the ultimate outcome of the Thirty Years' War?

New Sources, New Perspectives: Tree Rings and the Little Ice Age (pp. 600–601)

5. What evidence do historians have for the climate in the seventeenth century and what does this evidence suggest?

6. Which of this evidence is not typical of the evidence historians use, and why is it often helpful for historians to use atypical evidence?

State Building and the Search for Order
1648–1690

CHAPTER OVERVIEW

Chapter Questions   *Keep these questions in mind as you go through the study guide chapter.*

1. What was absolutism and what were its characteristics in France and in central and eastern Europe?

2. What was constitutionalism, and where and how did it flourish?

3. How did rulers impose order on their subjects?

4. Which new ideas and knowledge emerged in the second half of the seventeenth century?

5. How did the European emphasis on order and discipline manifest itself in culture and society?

Chapter Summary

Louis XIV: Model of Absolutism

Louis XIV of France personified the absolutist ruler who in theory shared power with no one. Yet the absoluteness of his power should not be exaggerated. Like all rulers of his time, he depended on the cooperation of many others such as local officials, the clergy, the nobility, the peasantry, and artisans. All of these played a role in making Louis' absolutism work, either by paying taxes, joining the armies, enforcing his will, or not causing trouble.

The Fronde, 1648–1653, pp. 623–624

Louis XIV came to the throne in 1643 at the age of five. His mother, Anne of Austria, and her advisor, Cardinal Mazarin, ruled in Louis's name. To raise money for the Thirty Years' War, Mazarin sold new offices, raised taxes, and forced creditors to lend money to the government. In 1648, a coalition of his opponents demanded that the parlements (high courts) have the right to approve new

taxes. When Mazarin refused and arrested the leaders of these parlements, a series of revolts broke out that at one time or another involved nearly every social group. These revolts are known as the Fronde. No one actually wanted to overthrow the king. Nobles wanted to reacquire the power and local influence they had lost after the religious wars ended in 1598, whereas the middle and lower classes opposed the government's taxation policies. Throughout France there was fighting among armies raised by diverse social and political groups. At one point, Louis and his mother were forced to flee Paris. The monarchy survived the rebellions, but they had a lasting influence on the young king.

Court Culture as an Element of Absolutism, pp. 624–626

In 1661, Mazarin died and Louis decided to conduct the government himself without appointing a first minister. Louis's first priority was controlling the nobility, which still possessed local armies and a great deal of local power and autonomy. Using a double-edged policy of bestowing honors and offices and threatening disfavor or punishment, Louis brought the nobility under control. He required their attendance at his court, which became the only route to power and influence. Life at court required careful attention, and the tiniest lapse in etiquette could lead to ruin. In this way, Louis made himself the center of French power and culture. Louis also used the arts to glorify his image, having himself represented as Apollo, the Sun King, a Roman emperor, and a great military leader. Artists, writers, and composers were employed and protected by the government to produce works that celebrated the monarchy. Louis also used massive public works projects and, in particular, the enlargement of the Palace of Versailles, to manifest and increase his prestige.

Enforcing Religious Orthodoxy, pp. 626–627

Louis believed that the defense of orthodox Catholicism was one of his most important tasks as king. Louis justified his actions by referring to the doctrine of divine right, which argued that kings were ordained by God to rule and had a duty to instruct their subjects in religion much like a father would his family. Louis first took action against the Jansenists, who, although Catholic, resembled the Protestants in their emphasis on God's grace, original sin, and in their austere religious practices that were similar to the English Puritans. Because Jansenists considered individual conscience to be more important than obeying church authority, Louis enforced decrees against Jansenists and closed their churches starting around 1660. In 1685, Louis revoked the Edict of Nantes, thereby depriving Huguenots of their rights. Louis wished to convert the Huguenots to Catholicism, but many instead immigrated to Protestant countries, whose citizens were shocked by the French king's actions.

Extending State Authority at Home and Abroad, pp. 627–630

Louis expanded the royal bureaucracy to consolidate his authority and run his kingdom more efficiently. Louis used his officials, who often held their positions directly from the king rather than owning their offices, to collect taxes, gather information regarding his subjects, and subordinate local interests to royal will. His most important minister was Jean-Baptiste Colbert, who helped Louis follow a mercantilist policy, meaning that the government intervened wherever possible to increase national wealth. By calling for government participation in the economy, by establishing trading companies or regulating standards of production, mercantilism resulted in an expanded bureaucracy. Also desiring to establish French dominance in Europe, Louis increased the size of the army and, between 1667 and 1713, was continually at war with other European powers. Even though Louis ultimately lost nearly all the territory he had won, France's many military victories conferred glory upon the French monarchy. Absolutism and war fed each other, as Louis' bureaucracy found new ways to raise money to support the army, and military success justified further expansion of state power. At the same time, however, these wars also eroded the state's resources and hindered administrative and legal reforms such as eliminating the buying of offices and lowering taxes.

Absolutism in Central and Eastern Europe

Rulers in central and eastern Europe viewed Louis XIV as a model of absolutist state building, but they did not directly emulate him because they were constrained by conditions peculiar to their regions. Much of the region was a mosaic of ethnic and religious groups that had been ravaged by the Thirty Years' War.

Brandenburg-Prussia and Sweden: Militaristic Absolutism, pp. 631–632

Frederick William of Hohenzollern, the Great Elector of Brandenburg-Prussia, welded the scattered lands that composed his territory into an absolutist state. Pressed by the expense of fighting the Thirty Years' War and then reconstructing after it, Frederick William struck a deal with his nobles that ensured him a dependable income. In exchange for allowing him to collect taxes, he granted the Junkers (nobles) complete control over their enserfed peasants and exempted the Junkers themselves from taxation. Avoiding the display of wealth and luxury of the French court, he used this revenue to create an efficient bureaucracy and enlarge the Prussian army to almost four times its original size. His army mirrored the rigid domination of the nobility over the peasantry—nobles were officers, peasants troops—in a militaristic society in which the army always had priority. He was so successful that, in 1701, his son Frederick I persuaded the Holy Roman Emperor to grant him the title "king in Prussia." Sweden, the most powerful country of northern Europe after the Thirty Years' War, also developed a form of absolutism in which the aristocratic estates gave the monarch power over war in exchange for a share of the spoils and offices in the bureaucracy. While Prussia would become an increasingly important power, the expense of constant war risked weakening Sweden's absolutist government.

An Uneasy Balance: Austrian Habsburgs and Ottoman Turks, pp. 632–634

To unite territories of different ethnicities, religions, and languages, Holy Roman Emperor Leopold I (r. 1658–1705) developed an absolutist government that chipped away at local powers, expanded the bureaucracy, and replaced the mercenaries hired to fight in the Thirty Years' War with a well-disciplined, permanent standing army. To the west, Leopold fought Louis XIV; to the east he fought Ottoman Turks. The Turks made it as far as Vienna in 1683, but with the help of the Polish cavalry Leopold repelled the siege. In the Treaty of Karlowitz the Turks surrendered Hungary to Leopold in 1699. To tighten his control in Hungary, Leopold revived the parliamentary diet, which was dominated by pro-Habsburg Hungarian aristocrats who buttressed the dynasty until its fall in 1918. Like Louis XIV of France, Leopold also engaged in public building projects to root out any remaining Turkish influence and assert Austrian superiority with the flamboyant Austrian baroque style. In Bohemia, Leopold replaced the Bohemian aristocracy, who had revolted against Austrian authority in 1618, with a new multi-ethnic aristocracy that was loyal to the emperor because it was dependent upon him for its position. The Ottoman Turks also consolidated state power but used different techniques. They settled large numbers of Turkish families in the Balkans. Rather than suppressing peasant armies, the Ottoman state hired them as mercenaries. To avoid a revolt by the elites, Ottoman leaders played them off against each other.

Russia: Foundations of Bureaucratic Absolutism, pp. 634–635

In 1648, Tsar Alexei (r. 1645–1676) set off a rebellion by attempting to change the administrative structure of the state. He responded to the rebellion by convoking the Assembly of the Land, which consisted of noble delegates from the provinces, and issuing a law code that assigned all subjects to a hereditary class. Slaves and free peasants were merged into a serf class, while nobles had to give absolute loyalty to the tsar and were required to serve in the military. In 1667, Stenka Razin led a rebellion that promised freedom from serfdom. Razin was captured four years later, and thousands of his followers met grisly deaths, but his memory lived on in folk songs and legends. To extend his power and emulate his western rivals, Alexei increased the size of his army to more than six times its original size, and imposed control over state policy and the Russian Orthodox church. This meant the obliteration of the Old Believers, who often chose martyrdom rather than adopt Russian Orthodox practices. The Assembly of the Land never met again after 1653, whereas the state bureaucracy continued to expand and intervene more and more in daily life.

Poland-Lithuania Overwhelmed, pp. 635–636

Poland-Lithuania did not merely reject the absolutist model. Through decades of war the monarchy had become weakened while its nobles became virtually autonomous warlords. In 1648, bands of runaway peasants and poor nobles in Ukraine formed bands and revolted against the king in a two-decades'-long uprising known as the Deluge. In 1654, they offered Ukraine to the Russian tsar, provoking a Russo-Polish war that ended with the tsar annexing eastern Ukraine and Kiev in 1667. Neighboring powers also took advantage of Poland-Lithuania's weakness and sent armies to seize territory. The fighting destroyed many towns and a third of the Polish population. Amidst the chaos, the country abandoned its policy of religious toleration of Jews and Protestants. Tens of thousands of Jews were slaughtered, and Protestants turned to Sweden for assistance. Poland-Lithuania elected Jan Sobieski to be king (r. 1674–1696); he attempted to rebuild the monarchy on the absolutist model, but was unsuccessful. The nobles put a stranglehold on monarchical authority. They dominated the parliament (or Sjem) and every member of the Sjem wielded an absolute veto power that deadlocked parliamentary government.

Constitutionalism in England

Although the English monarchy enjoyed many advantages over their continental rivals—they had stayed out of the expensive Thirty Years' War and ruled a relatively small and homogenous population—they failed to install absolutist policies. Two revolutions overturned two kings, confirmed the constitutional powers of an elected parliament, and laid the foundation for the idea that the government must guarantee certain rights under the law.

England Turned Upside Down, 1642–1660, pp. 637–643

When Parliament wanted Charles I (r. 1625–1649) to agree to the Petition of Right (a promise not to levy taxes without Parliament's consent), he closed Parliament for eleven years. He irritated Puritans by favoring church rituals similar to Catholic rites and when, with Charles's support, Archbishop Laud tried to impose the Anglican liturgy on Presbyterian Scots, the Scots invaded the north of England in 1640. This invasion forced Charles to summon Parliament to levy new taxes. Moderate elements within Parliament voted to undo some of the king's less-popular measures. Charles attempted to arrest them and, when opposition arose, left London to raise an army. The civil war began in 1642 and ended in 1646 when Oliver Cromwell's New Model Army defeated the royalists. Parliament then split into moderate Presbyterians and radical Independents. The Presbyterians made up the majority, but the Independents controlled the army and used it to purge the Presbyterians from Parliament. The remaining members, the Rump Parliament, then beheaded Charles, abolished the monarchy, and formed a republic led by Oliver Cromwell, who tolerated no opposition. He reconquered Scotland and brutally subdued Ireland, waged war on the Dutch, and enacted the first Navigation Act to protect English commerce. But Cromwell alienated supporters with taxes higher than the monarchy's and with his harsh tactics against dissent. In 1653, Cromwell abolished the Parliament, naming himself Lord Protector. In 1660, two years after Cromwell's death, a newly elected Parliament called Charles II to the throne.

The Glorious Revolution of 1688, pp. 643–644

Although most English welcomed the monarchy back in 1660, many soon came to fear that Charles II wished to establish absolutism on the French model. In 1670, Charles secretly agreed to convert to Catholicism in exchange for money from Louis XIV to fight the Dutch. Although Charles never pronounced himself a Catholic, he did ease restrictions on Catholics and Protestant dissenters, thereby coming into conflict with a Parliament intent on supporting the Church of England. In 1673, Parliament passed the Test Act, which required government officials to pledge allegiance to the Church of England. In 1678, Parliament tried to deny the throne to any Roman Catholic because they did not want the king's brother and heir James, a convert to Catholicism, to inherit the throne. Charles did not allow this law to pass, splitting Parliament into two factions: Tories, who supported a strong, hereditary monarchy and the Anglican church; and Whigs, who supported a strong Parliament and toleration for non-Anglicans. In 1685, James II became king and pursued absolutist and pro-Catholic policies. When his wife gave birth to a son that ensured a Catholic heir to the throne, Parliament offered the throne to James's older Protestant daughter Mary and her husband, the Dutch stadholder William, prince of Orange. In a "glorious revolution," James fled to France, and William and Mary granted a bill of rights that confirmed Parliament's rights in government. The propertied classes that controlled Parliament now focused on consolidating their power and preventing any future popular turmoil.

Constitutionalism in the Dutch Republic and the Overseas Colonies

When William and Mary came to the throne in England in 1689 the Dutch and English set aside rivalries that had brought them to war against each other on several previous occasions. Together they led a coalition that blocked Louis XIV's efforts to dominate continental Europe and the two were successful exceptions to absolutism in Europe. Many Dutch and English colonies developed constitutional governments, while simultaneously enslaving black Africans as a new labor force.

The Dutch Republic, pp. 645–648

By 1648, when it gained formal independence from Spain, the Dutch Republic was a decentralized state. Rich merchants called regents controlled local affairs and represented their province at the Estates General, which controlled foreign policy and appointed a stadholder, who was responsible for defense and represented the state at ceremonial functions. The Dutch Republic encouraged trade by importing products from all over the world and became Europe's finance capital. Dutch citizens became the most prosperous and best-educated middle class in Europe and supported the visual arts. Their relative wealth decreased the need for women to work outside the home and the Dutch made the family household the source of society's morality. The high levels of urbanization and literacy created a large readership and Dutch tolerance led to a freedom of publishing unknown elsewhere in Europe. By the late seventeenth century, the cost of repeated wars with England at sea and France on land contributed to a relative decline, and

French influence became more prominent in Dutch intellectual and artistic life.

Freedom and Slavery in the New World, pp. 648–649

After the Spanish and Portuguese demonstrated that using black Africans as slave labor in their colonies was profitable, the French and English purchased and brought African slaves to their Caribbean colonies. The highest church and government officials in Catholic and Protestant countries condoned the slave trade. The Dutch West India Company transported 36,000 Africans annually by 1700. The English instituted a slave code in Barbados in 1661 that stripped Africans of their legal rights and made slavery an inherited status. In 1685, Louis XIV similarly regulated Africans through a "black code." At the same time, English settlers in North America had representative legislatures that gave colonial elites control over local matters. Plentiful land made it possible for ordinary immigrants to become landowners and elites. Native Americans lost their lives and their homeland as they succumbed to disease and European force. Not recognizing private ownership of land, they frequently skirmished with settlers who claimed land rights.

The Search for Order in Elite and Popular Culture

With the early successes of constitutionalism in places like England, the Dutch Republic, and the colonies of North America came new debates about authority, freedom, and order. Most Europeans feared disorder above all else, especially after the chaos of the Thirty Years' War, the Fronde in France, and the English Civil War. European elites developed new codes of behavior to distinguish themselves, and sought to teach order and discipline to their social inferiors.

Social Contract Theory: Hobbes and Locke, pp. 650–651

Thomas Hobbes, an English royalist, believed that human beings were essentially self-centered and focused on survival. He also believed that only a strong authority (either a king or a parliament) that could assure stability would lead people to follow the laws. To obtain this strong authority, people had to give up some personal liberty. He outlined these thoughts in *Leviathan* (1651) and made his case by appealing to science instead of religion. Royalists opposed Hobbes because his ideas emphasized a social contract—instead of divine right—between ruler and ruled, whereas Parlimentarians objected to his emphasis on absolute authority. John Locke also believed in a contract between ruler and ruled, but Locke had a more optimistic view of human nature. He believed that human beings were essentially good and peaceful and that the purpose of government was to protect life, liberty, and property. If government failed in this task, or overstepped its bounds, the people had a right to resist. He articulated his anti-authoritarian position in *Two Treatises of Government* (1690). These views were central to American revolutionaries and abolitionists. In *Essay Concerning Human Understanding* (1690), Locke stated that each human was born with a mind that was a *tabula rasa* (blank slate). All knowledge came from sensory experience, not from anything innate, and education shaped personality by channeling sensory experience. These views indicated that "all men are created equal."

Newton and the Consolidation of the Scientific Revolution, pp. 651–653

New breakthroughs in science lent support to Locke's optimistic view of human potential. Building upon the earlier work of scientists, Sir Isaac Newton finally synthesized astronomy and physics with his law of universal gravitation. Far from seeing religion and science in conflict, Newton hoped that his discovery of universal laws would help demonstrate the existence of God and an orderly and rational creation. Absolutist rulers viewed science as a means for enhancing their prestige and supported scientific research through the patronage of scientific social organizations and government stipends for scientists. Some rulers supported scientific activity as another form of mercantilist intervention to enhance state wealth. Scientific research was encouraged in constitutional states as well, although not through direct governmental support. Science gained a broader audience among upper-class men and women, but women were rarely active in scientific research because they were excluded from most universities.

Freedom and Order in the Arts, pp. 653–656

Artists, writers, and architects explored the place of individuals within the universe. John Milton wrote about the benefits and dangers of individual liberty for human beings. The two dominant artistic styles of the era—baroque and classical—approached the individual differently. The baroque was favored by the Catholic church and patronized by Habsburg rulers because the emotional response it evoked proved to be especially suitable for inspiring awe in public displays of faith and of the power of the monarch and the Catholic church. The Habsburgs' enemy, Louis XIV rejected the baroque in favor of the classical, which reflected the ideals of antiquity, order, and harmony and was exemplified by the paintings of Nicolas Poussin and Claude Lorrain. Classicism placed the important individual firmly at the intersection of straight lines. Dutch painters who worked for a public, middle-class market tended to paint ordinary objects and people in a style neither baroque nor classical. Masters like Rembrandt and Vermeer created scenes in which ordinary individuals and activities looked precious and beautiful. Women artists like Merian and Ruysch excelled in documenting the natural world in vibrant still lifes and botanical paintings.

Women and Manners, pp. 656–658

Nobles developed individual self-discipline in the court, where they distinguished themselves from other groups in society through their dress, behavior, and activities. Noblemen, like noblewomen, learned the art of pleasing to gain favor with the king. The plays of Molière reassured aristocrats that this part of their identity was inimitable, yet they also implied that the middle class could learn manners, too. Treatises on etiquette were published. Elite women gained access to intellectual life through the salon, an informal gathering presided over by a socially eminent woman in her home. Salons encouraged conversations about love, philosophy, and literature, providing authors with an audience for their ideas. Some women also wrote; they were especially successful with a new literary genre, the novel. Aphra Behn, one of the first professional women writers, was a novelist and wrote the best-seller *Oroonoko*. As women became more important in taste, literature, and manners, they stirred the fear and resentment of many clergy, scientists, scholars, and playwrights, who warned of the dangers of their influence over men and ridiculed their literary and social ambitions.

Reforming Popular Culture, pp. 658–661

New developments in science, the arts, literature, and manners did not touch the majority of Europe's population: illiterate peasants. Protestant and Catholic churches extended their campaigns begun in the sixteenth centuries to root out "pagan" practices, reaching much of rural Europe in the seventeenth century. Royal officials worked with clergy to impose orthodox religious practices and to suppress activities they deemed incompatible with Christian doctrine and standards of behavior, such as maypoles, animal sacrifices, praying to the moon. In both Protestant and Catholic countries, the campaign against superstition helped to extend state power. At the same time, attitudes toward the poor changed: previously, poverty had been a Christian virtue and support of the poor a key part of Christian charity. Now the poor were seen as dangerous, lazy, and immoral. Local governments and organizations tried to reform the poor and to separate them from society by advocating discipline and putting them in hospitals built on government order.

Key Events *For each question, select the most appropriate response from the choices provided.*

1642–1646 Civil war between King Charles I and Parliament in England

1648 Peace of Westphalia ends Thirty Years' War; the Fronde revolt challenges royal authority in France; Ukrainian Cossack warriors rebel against the king of Poland-Lithuania; Spain formally recognizes independence of the Dutch Republic

1649 Execution of Charles I of England; new Russian legal code

1651 Thomas Hobbes publishes *Leviathan*

1660 Monarchy restored in England

1661 Slave code set up in Barbados

1667 Louis XIV begins first of many wars that continue throughout his reign

1670 Molière's play, *The Middle-Class Gentleman*

1678 Marie-Madeline de La Vergne (Madame de Lafayette) anonymously publishes her novel *The Princess of Clèves*

1683 Austrian Habsburgs break the Turkish siege of Vienna

1685 Louis XIV revokes toleration for French Protestants granted by the Edict of Nantes

1687 Isaac Newton publishes *Principia Mathematica*

1688 Parliament deposes James II and invites his daughter, Mary, and her husband, William of Orange, to take the throne

1690 John Locke's *Two Treatises of Government, Essay Concerning Human Understanding*

1. The Civil War in England between 1642 and 1646 was fought between Parliament and
   a. Charles I.
   b. Charles II.
   c. James II.
   d. Oliver Cromwell.

2. What was the rebellion against French royal authority in 1648 called?
   a. Thirty Years' War
   b. The Glorious Revolution
   c. The War of Devolution
   d. The Fronde

3. Which publication by Thomas Hobbes in 1651 argued that to maintain social order people needed to give up personal liberty to an absolutist state?
   a. *Two Treatises on Government*
   b. *Principia Mathematica*
   c. *Leviathan*
   d. *Essay Concerning Human Understanding*

4. Which of the following was established in Barbados in 1661?
   a. A democracy
   b. A slave code
   c. A religious colony
   d. Silver mining

5. Whose law code was established in 1649 assigning all Russians a place in a hereditary hierarchy?
   a. Stenka Razin's
   b. Tsar Alexei's
   c. Ivan the Terrible's
   d. Tsar Nicholas's

6. Which conflict did the Peace of Westphalia in 1648 bring an end to?
   a. The Fronde
   b. The Glorious Revolution
   c. The Thirty Years' War
   d. The War of Devolution

7. What did Louis XIV revoke in 1685 that eliminated religious toleration for Huguenots and led many of them to leave France?
   a. The Treaty of Aix-la-Chapelle
   b. The Treaty of Paris
   c. The Council of Trent
   d. The Edict of Nantes

8. Which publication by Sir Isaac Newton in 1687 explained the movement of bodies on earth and related them to planetary motion?
   a. *Leviathan*
   b. *Two Treatises on Government*
   c. *Principia Mathematica*
   d. *Areopagitica*

9. Where did the Glorious Revolution of 1688 occur?
   a. France
   b. The Netherlands
   c. England
   d. Spain

10. Which of the following authors wrote works supporting constitutionalism and suggesting that all knowledge comes from experience?
   a. John Locke
   b. Sir Isaac Newton
   c. Thomas Hobbes
   d. John Milton

Key Terms   *Match each key term to its definition.*

A. **Absolutism** (p. 621)
B. **bureaucracy** (p. 627)
C. **classicism** (p. 654)
D. **constitutionalism** (p. 622)
E. **Fronde** (p. 623)
F. **Glorious Revolution** (p. 644)
G. **law of universal gravitation** (p. 651)
H. **Levellers** (p. 639)
I. **mercantilism** (p. 628)
J. **Old Believers** (p. 635)
K. **parlements** (p. 623)
L. **social contract** (p. 650)

1. _____ A system of government in which the ruler claimed sole and uncontestable power.

2. _____ A system of government in which the ruler had to share power with parliaments made up of elected representatives.

3. _____ A series of revolts in France, 1648–1653, that challenged the authority of young Louis XIV and his minister Mazarin.

4. _____ High courts in France (the term comes from the French, to speak). Each region had its own; they could not propose laws, but they could review laws presented by the king and refuse to register them (the king could also insist on their registration).

5. _____ A network of state officials carrying out orders according to a regular and routine line of authority.

6. _____ The doctrine that governments must intervene to increase national wealth by whatever means possible.

7. _____ A Russian Orthodox religious group which rejected church efforts to bring Russian worship in line with Byzantine tradition.

8. _____ Disgruntled soldiers in Cromwell's New Model Army who wanted to "level" social differences and extend political participation to all male property owners.

9. _____ English Parliament overthrows King James II in 1688 and replaces him with William, Prince of Orange, and James's daughter, Mary.

10. _____ The doctrine found in the writings of Hobbes and Locke that all political authority derives not from divine right but from an implicit contract between citizens and their rulers.

11. _____ Newton's law uniting celestial and terrestrial mechanics held that every body in the universe exerts over every other body an attractive force directly proportional to the product of their masses and inversely proportional to the square of the distance between them.

12. _____ A style of painting and architecture that reflected the ideals of the art of antiquity; in this genre, geometric shapes, order, and harmony of lines took precedence over the sensuous, exuberant, and emotional forms of the baroque.

Identification   *This activity tests your recall of significant people, places, and events from this chapter. Fill in the blank with the correct answer.*

1. _____ was advisor to Louis XIV's mother, Anne of Austria, and helped rule France in the king's name during his infancy and adolescence.

2. Louis XIV modeled himself after the Greek god _____ as part of his campaign to enhance his image and prestige.

3. Louis XIV's favorite composer, _____, rose to become the virtual dictator of French musical taste.

4. After the death of his wife in 1683, Louis XIV secretly married his mistress, _____.

5. Between 1689 and 1697, a coalition known as the League of _____, fought Louis XIV to a stalemate that forced him to give up many of his previous conquests.

6. In 1701, _____ persuaded the Holy Roman Emperor to grant him the title "king of Prussia."

7. The Turkish siege of _____ in 1683 was the high-water mark of Ottoman westward expansion.

8. A Cossack named _____ led a peasant rebellion against the Russian tsar to resist enserfment.

9. Elected as king of Poland in 1674, _____ tried unsuccessfully to rebuild the Polish monarchy according to a French model.

10. The liberation of _____ in 1699, which had been the main battle zone between Austria and the Turks for over 150 years, devastated much of its countryside.

11. King _____ of England fell into confrontation with an increasingly aggressive Parliament that eventually cost him his head.

12. When _____ tried to impose increasingly elaborate ceremonies on the Anglican church, the Scots revolted, forcing the king to call Parliament into session.

13. When the English monarchy was restored to _____, some members of Parliament feared that the government would come to resemble French absolutism.

14. _____ sparked the Glorious Revolution by pursuing pro-Catholic and absolutist policies.

15. With the _____, William and Mary agreed not to raise a standing army or levy taxes without the consent of Parliament.

16. The stadholder of the Dutch Republic was usually a prince from the house of _____.

17. The philosophical work of _____ scandalized many Christians and Jews because he seemed to equate God and nature.

18. The _____ were the most successful traffickers of African slaves.

19. When William and Mary became king and queen of England, they led a coalition with the Dutch to block the efforts of _____.

20. Dutch tolerance extended to the work of _____, a Jewish philosopher and biblical scholar who was expelled from his synagogue for alleged atheism.

21. _____ rejected the arguments for absolute authority and argued for the notion of a social contract between ruler and subjects to provide a foundation for constitutionalism.

22. In his masterwork *Principia Mathematica*, _____ united celestial and terrestrial mechanics with his law of universal gravitation.

23. The poems of _____ gave attention to individual liberty, including his epic *Paradise Lost*.

24. The French playwright _____ wrote comedies of manners that revealed much about aristocratic behavior.

25. _____ wrote several books on domestic conduct, but published them under the name of her first husband.

CHAPTER REVIEW

Self-Test and Analytical Exercises

Multiple Choice   *Select the best answer from the four choices provided.*

1. The Fronde was
   a. an area of France in which some people still practiced paganism.
   b. a series of noble and popular revolts that seriously threatened the French crown from 1648–1653.
   c. the French term for the English called the Court of Star Chamber.
   d. the name taken by the Jansenists when they were driven underground beginning in 1660.

2. Louis XIV sought to reform the nobility and bring them under his control by
   a. giving them their own private armies and pitting them against each other.
   b. stripping them of their belongings and destroying their castles.
   c. gathering them at court, where they replaced violent disputes with court ritual.
   d. marrying his daughters to the sons of the nobility.

3. Under Louis XIV, the arts
   a. became less important because political power was the king's main goal.
   b. were repressed and many artists left France in search of royal patronage elsewhere.
   c. focused on monumental architecture and neglected other forms like drama and music.
   d. were treated as a branch of government and used to glorify the king.

4. Who were the Jansenists?
   a. Protestants that Louis XIV repressed ruthlessly through the revocation of the Edict of Nantes
   b. Catholics whose emphasis on grace and individual conscience resembled some aspects of Protestantism
   c. Dutch Protestants who spread doctrines of equality and endorsed constitutionalism
   d. Radical Catholics who ridiculed Louis XIV's lack of piety and religious knowledge

5. Absolutism in Sweden
   a. was a great success and the Swedish people prospered, free from the taxes needed to build an army.
   b. saw the nobles support the monarch because they benefited from lucrative foreign military campaigns led by the king.
   c. was ended forever when Queen Christina ceded her power to the estates and abdicated.
   d. was a failure, since the nobles refused to join a French-style court and remained at the head of their private armies.

6. The Ottomans pursued state consolidation by
   a. turning warlike nobles into courtiers for the sultan, the way Louis XIV tamed his aristocracy.
   b. brutally repressing the peasants, who frequently revolted.
   c. through a combination of settlement and military control.
   d. sending restless and ambitious nobles to the front lines in Hungary.

7. All of the following are ways that Tsar Alexei expanded his absolutist powers *except* he
   a. increased the size of the army.
   b. had the Russian Orthodox church declare him God's direct representative on Earth.
   c. met frequently with the nobles at the Assembly of the Land.
   d. expanded the state bureaucracy.

8. Poland-Lithuania
   a. was a model of absolutist state development under Jan Sobieski and his successors.
   b. peacefully evolved into a constitutionalist state.
   c. was weakened by the power of the nobles and twenty years of civil war and invasion.
   d. put itself under the rule of the Austrian Habsburgs to end internal divisions and deadlocks.

9. English kings enjoyed all of the following advantages over their continental rivals *except*
   a. they needed less money for their armies since they had stayed out of the Thirty Years' War.
   b. they ruled over an island kingdom that was easier and cheaper to defend.
   c. the English population was much larger than that of other continental countries, like France.
   d. England was relatively homogenous ethnically.

10. Which event forced Charles I to call Parliament into session in 1640?
    a. The attempted arrest of Puritan members of Parliament
    b. The calling of Charles's opponents before the Court of Star Chamber
    c. The revolt of Charles's nobility
    d. The Scottish invasion of northern England

11. The Rump Parliament did all of the following *except*
    a. create a high court to try Charles I for political crimes.
    b. outlaw Puritanism.
    c. abolish the House of Lords.
    d. abolish the monarchy.

12. The Glorious Revolution
    a. ended constitutionalism in England and saw William of Orange installed as an absolutist king.
    b. saw the triumph of constitutionalism in England with the institution of a Bill of Rights.
    c. was an unsuccessful revolt by the lower classes against the social inequalities of the times.
    d. restored the monarchy to England after the rule of Oliver Cromwell and his son.

13. Which of the following best characterizes most consumers of Dutch art?
    a. The Dutch nobility
    b. Merchants, artisans, and shopkeepers
    c. Foreign traders
    d. Schools and universities

14. Who was a stadholder?
    a. The absolutist ruler of the Dutch Republic
    b. A rich merchant who controlled the internal affairs of an individual province in the decentralized, constitutional Dutch Republic
    c. The executive officer of the Dutch Republic, responsible for defense and for representing the state at all ceremonial occasions
    d. A representative of the common people in the Netherlands

15. The slave trade was
    a. opposed by the church authorities of all the major Protestant and Catholic countries.
    b. condoned by Protestant church authorities, but not Catholic leaders.
    c. condoned by Catholic church authorities, but not Protestant leaders.
    d. condoned by nearly all Protestant and Catholic church authorities.

16. All of the following threatened Native Americans in the English colonies *except*
    a. disease and warfare
    b. loss of their homeland to Europeans
    c. forming alliances with other natives
    d. being sold into slavery

17. From which source(s) did Thomas Hobbes argue that rulers derived their power?
    a. Their proven ability to govern
    b. A social contract among citizens
    c. God and the Bible
    d. Their wealth and education

18. What does the term "tabula rasa" refer to in Locke's theory?
    a. A theory that asserted the rights of people to rebel against tyrannical rulers
    b. A justification for slavery on the grounds that Africans were an inferior people
    c. A theory that the human mind is blank at birth, and all knowledge comes from sensory experience
    d. A theory that are all born with inherent knowledge that forever shapes our worldview

19. Newtonian physics required an understanding of
    a. quantum mechanics.
    b. the speed of light and of sound.
    c. mass, inertia, force, velocity, and acceleration.
    d. the periodic table of elements.

20. Which of the following best describes a prominent theme of Milton's *Paradise Lost*?
    a. Personal liberty and the human condition
    b. The heroic nature of God
    c. The absolute control of the monarchy
    d. The history of the Christian church

21. All of the following are *true* about Louis XIV *except* he
    a. ascended to the throne when he was only five years old.
    b. created one of the most powerful absolutist states in Europe.
    c. did not depend on the cooperation of his subjects or their support.
    d. chose middle-class men as his ministers, manipulating their feelings of obligation.

22. Who wrote *Tartuffe*, a play that poked fun at religious hypocrites?
    a. Cardinal Mazarin
    b. Jean-Baptiste Lully
    c. Molière
    d. Pierre Corneille

23. What was the role of religion during Louis XIV's rule?
    a. Louis was indifferent to religion and took little action concerning it.
    b. Louis worked to extend religious toleration.
    c. Louis was a Catholic, but left religious matters up to local nobles or intendents.
    d. Louis saw Catholicism as a pillar of his rule.

24. Who was the government minister of Louis XIV who established a mercantilist economic policy?
    a. Cardinal Mazarin
    b. Bishop Jacques-Benigne Bossuet
    c. Jean-Baptiste Colbert
    d. Blaise Pascal

25. Which ruler established absolutist rule over Brandenburg-Prussia?
    a. Queen Christina
    b. Frederick William
    c. Leopold I
    d. William of Orange

26. Leopold I's priorities as an absolutist ruler were to
    a. modernize the army and reduce the independence of various ethnic provinces.
    b. revive Catholicism throughout Europe and undermine the power of Protestant states.
    c. negotiate with those who opposed him and respect the rights of ethnic minorities.
    d. hire a large mercenary army and defeat the Ottoman Turks.

27. Who were the Old Believers?
    a. A rebellious peasant group led by Stenka Razin
    b. A Russian religious group who refused to conform to the Byzantine Orthodox church
    c. The twelve noble delegates to the Assembly of the Land
    d. Russian constitutionalists executed for resisting Tsar Alexei's absolutist tendencies

28. The Jews in Poland-Lithuania
    a. were persecuted during the Deluge, and tens of thousands were killed.
    b. escaped persecution in the Deluge by assisting the Cossack warriors.
    c. became more powerful as Russian influence increased.
    d. were largely ignored during the long period of political discontent known as the Deluge.

29. In the Petition of Right of 1628, Charles I promised
    a. to reform the English church.
    b. not to levy taxes without the consent of Parliament.
    c. not to use the Court of Star Chamber against his rivals.
    d. to defer to Parliament in all matters of state.

30. The Parliament called in 1640 did all of the following *except*
    a. remove Archbishop Laud from office.
    b. abolish the Court of Star Chamber.
    c. abolish bishops and eliminate the Anglican prayer book.
    d. require a parliamentary assembly at least once every three years.

31. The victory of Parliament over Charles I led immediately to
    a. agreement among the parliamentary forces over the social reforms that were necessary.
    b. a decline in the political participation of the lower classes.
    c. the unquestioned dominance of the Independent faction.
    d. division among the victors over the extent of social and religious reform.

32. Cromwell faced growing opposition in the 1650s because he
    a. failed to pursue a vigorous mercantilist policy against the Dutch.
    b. was unable to control an Irish rebellion.
    c. grew fond of the trappings of royalty and lost his moral authority.
    d. raised taxes and gave himself too much power.

33. Which of the following *best* describes the government of the Dutch Republic?
    a. It was an absolutist state modeled after Louis XIV's France.
    b. It was a highly centralized state ruled by a parliament.
    c. It had a democratic government in which every citizen participated in politics.
    d. It was a decentralized constitutional state headed by an elected officer.

34. Which of the following best characterizes the beliefs of Benedict Spinoza?
    a. science and mathematics are not contrary to religion
    b. prayer is an agent of change
    c. Judaism is the only true faith
    d. God and nature are fundamentally separate

35. In 1700, approximately how many Africans were exported to the New World by the slave trade?
    a. Less than 1,000
    b. 8,000 to 10,000
    c. 25,000 to 26,000
    d. Over 35,000

36. Which of the following is *not* a historical explanation for the increase in the slave trade?
    a. Improvements in gun technology
    b. The use of native African slave traders
    c. The arming of African armies for the capture of slaves
    d. A shift from agriculture to manufacturing in the New World

37. Thomas Hobbes's book, *Leviathan*, argues for which type of governmental authority?
    a. Absolutist
    b. Constitutionalist
    c. Monarchical
    d. Democratic

38. Sir Isaac Newton
    a. came to believe that God was beyond the reach of human prayers or influence.
    b. believed a physical universe that followed rational principles proved the existence of God.
    c. saw the universe as a clockwork with no need for God's continuous intervention.
    d. was overshadowed by Leibniz in astronomy and physics, but was renowned for his experiments in optics.

39. John Milton did all of the following *except* write
    a. a treatise in favor of divorce.
    b. one of the first defenses of freedom of the press.
    c. *Paradise Lost*, which, among other things, considers the limits of human freedom.
    d. a defense of the divine rights of absolutist monarchies.

40. What was a salon?
    a. A French art gallery and school supported without state funding
    b. A scientific academy supported by state funding
    c. An informal gathering presided over by a socially prominent woman
    d. A room in a royal palace reserved for the king's favorite lover.

Short Answer   *Answer each question in three or four sentences.*

Louis XIV: Model of Absolutism

1. What was absolutism? What were some ways in which Louis XIV built absolutist rule?

2. What was Louis XIV's policy toward religion?

3. What was the relationship between war and the absolutism of Louis XIV?

Absolutism in Central and Eastern Europe

4. How did absolutism in central and eastern Europe differ from that built by Louis XIV in France?

5. Why did constitutionalism fail in Poland-Lithuania, and what were the consequences?

6. What do events in the seventeenth century tell us about the role of the nobility in absolutism?

Constitutionalism in England

7. What were Parliament's initial grievances against Charles I?

8. What were the differences between the various factions in the Parliament during and immediately following the English Civil War?

9. What led to the Glorious Revolution, and what did the revolution entail?

Constitutionalism in the Dutch Republic and the Overseas Colonies

10. What was the nature of the Dutch form of constitutionalism?

11. What were some of the most notable features of life in the Dutch Republic?

12. What effect did constitutionalism in this period have on freedom in North American colonies?

The Search for Order in Elite and Popular Culture

13. What were the differences between the ideas of Thomas Hobbes and John Locke?

14. How were the governments of absolutist and constitutional states involved in the sciences?

15. What was the significance of manners during this period?

BUILDING HISTORICAL SKILLS

Reading Maps   *Write a brief, paragraph-length response to each of the following questions based on* **Map 17.3: Dutch Commerce in the Seventeenth Century** *(p. 646).*

1. Where were some of the places that the Dutch Republic had commercial contact with?

2. Which commodities did the Dutch trade in, and how might some of these commodities have changed European society?

Reading Illustrations   *Write a brief, paragraph-length response to each of the following questions based on the illustration* **The Baker Arent Oostward and His Wife** *(p. 648).*

1. Who are the people in this painting and what are they doing?

2. What are the people in this painting wearing and what moods do their facial expressions and body postures suggest?

3. What does this painting tell us about Dutch attitudes toward daily life?

Reading Historical Documents   *Write a brief, paragraph-length response to each of the following questions based on the documents in your book.*

John Milton's Defense of Freedom of the Press (p. 654)

1. How does John Milton depict books in this passage?

2. Why is freedom of the press essential for maintaining virtue, even when published books are immoral?

Aphra Behn, Oroonoko (1688) (p. 659)

3. What in Aphra Behn's description sets Oroonoko apart from other Africans?

4. How does Aphra Behn's description of Oroonoko reflect European attitudes toward Africans in general?

Contrasting Views: The English Civil War
(pp. 640–641)

5. Who are the authors of the three documents, and what political, social, religious, personal, and so on, interests or concerns do they represent?

6. While the authors of the first two documents are arguing in defense of themselves or of someone close to them, Thomas Hobbes was writing a political treatise. Does this difference have an impact on the content and form of the argument being made?

The Atlantic System and Its Consequences
1690–1740

CHAPTER OVERVIEW

Chapter Questions   *Keep these questions in mind as you go through the study guide chapter.*

1. What was the Atlantic system and what impact did it have on Europe?

2. What new patterns emerged in rural and urban life?

3. How did the growth of a literate, middle-class public change European society?

4. How did international affairs and domestic policies change in the early eighteenth century?

5. What principles and issues characterized the early Enlightenment?

Chapter Summary

The Atlantic System and the World Economy

Although their ships had been circling the globe since the early 1500s, Europeans did not draw most of the world into their economic orbit until the 1700s. A three-part commercial network developed between western Europe, Africa, and America that involved the trade of slaves, raw materials, and manufactured goods. This system and the growth of international trade helped create a new consumer society.

Slavery and the Atlantic System, pp. 667–672

Realizing that plantations producing staples for Europeans could bring fabulous wealth, the European powers grew less interested in the dwindling supply of precious metals in the New World and more eager to colonize it. Western European trading nations sent ships loaded with goods to buy slaves from local rulers on the western coast of Africa, then transported the slaves to the colonies in North and South America and the Caribbean and sold them to the owners of plantations producing coffee, sugar, cotton, and tobacco. To complete the Atlantic trading cycle, they then shipped the raw commodities produced in the colonies back to Europe where these materials were refined or processed and then sold to other parts of Europe and the world. Beginning in the early eighteenth century, the African slave trade grew exponentially. While the institution of slavery in the Americas varied according to the crops they grew and the nationality of their enslavers, all slaves faced horrendous conditions on the journey from Africa and lived under harsh conditions on the plantations. Slavery disturbed many Europeans, but in the 1700s, slaveholders began to justify their actions by demeaning the mental and spiritual qualities of Africans, which originated modern racism.

World Trade and Settlement, pp. 673–675

The Atlantic system helped extend European trade relations across the globe. The textiles that Atlantic shippers exchanged for slaves in Africa, for example, were manufactured in India. To expand their trade, Europeans tried to establish permanent settlements throughout the globe. The most populous were in the Americas, where Spanish, British, and French settlers all competed for territory. Local economies shaped social relations. Trappers in Canada had little in common with the men and women of the plantation societies in Brazil. Intermarriage with the native population, particularly in Spanish colonies, helped spread Christianity. By contrast, European settlements in Africa and Asia remained small. Europeans had little contact with East Africa and none with Africa's vast interior. In China, Europeans were considered to be little more than barbarians and were limited to the city of Guangzhou where they could trade for spices, tea, and silk. In Java in the East Indies and in India, Europeans had more influence. By the 1740s England and France had become the leading rivals in India, where the local conflicts among Muslims, Hindus, and Sikhs allowed them to gain more power.

The Birth of Consumer Society, pp. 675–676

Population growth in Europe, especially in the cities, fueled demand for foreign goods. A number of factors caused a decline in the death rate, including an improvement in the climate, better agricultural techniques, and the disappearance of the plague after the 1720s. The combined effects of economic expansion and population growth brought about a consumer revolution. Items like tea, tobacco, chocolate, and coffee became virtual necessities. Coffeehouses appeared in all of Europe's major cities. Some writers criticized the new consumer culture, but this did not stop the fast growth of the market.

New Social and Cultural Patterns

The impact of the Atlantic system and world trade was most apparent in the cities, but rural changes also had long-term influence. An agricultural revolution made it possible to feed more people with a smaller agricultural workforce. More people moved to cities, where they engaged in new urban customs such as attending musical concerts and reading novels. However, these changes were not universal and depended on wealth and location.

Agricultural Revolution, pp. 676–678

Four major changes that revolutionized agriculture were pioneered by the Flemish and Dutch but matured in Britain and then spread throughout Europe. Farmers increased the amount of land under cultivation; consolidated small scattered plots into larger, more efficient units; linked livestock raising with crop growing, and began to selectively breed animals. Not everyone benefited equally. To take full advantage of the new techniques, some farmers sought to consolidate and enlarge their holdings by privatizing and enclosing in fences land previously held by peasants in common. In England, the "enclosure movement" often provoked conflict between villagers and landlords, and many small farmers were forced to sell their lands and become tenant farmers or salaried agricultural workers. As a result, in England and in other parts of northern and western Europe where a similar process occurred, the rural peasantry largely disappeared and was replaced by a more hierarchical society of big landlords, tenant farmers, and poor agricultural laborers. Subsistence agriculture still persisted throughout Europe, and attempts by landlords in eastern Europe to consolidate and improve their lands led to a worsening of conditions for the enserfed peasantry.

Social Life in the Cities, pp. 678–680

As the population increased, more people moved to the cities, which grew immensely after the second half of the seventeenth century. Along with the general growth of cities was a south-to-north shift. Whereas the greatest concentration of urbanization had previously been in the Italian states and the Iberian Peninsula, by 1700 northern urbanization had expanded enough to equal that of the south. In the city there were sharp class distinctions marked by clothing, housing, and diet. Many occupations could be recognized by how one dressed. Wealthier families hired servants from poorer families. Women especially worked as servants until they were married, and the majority of servants were female. Social status was not an abstract idea; it permeated every detail of daily life.

The Growth of a Literate Public, p. 680

The ability to read and write also reflected social differences. People in the upper classes were more literate than those from the lower classes; people in cities were more literate than those in the country. Protestant countries promoted literacy more successfully than Catholic countries, possibly because of the Protestant emphasis on reading the Bible. Although education remained inadequate, a new literate public arose, especially among the urban middle class. These new middle-class readers were the audience for new magazines and newspapers.

New Tastes in the Arts, pp. 680–683

The new literate public also interested itself in painting and concerts and was willing to support new writers and artists. For the first time, writers and artists had a source of income beyond the church, the aristocracy, and monarchs. Middle-class patrons enjoyed new artistic styles, forms, and content, such as the rococo style and the oratorio. Rococo painting, best exemplified by Antoine Watteau (1684–1721) and François Boucher (1703–1770) emphasized the intimately emotional and erotic. Public concerts also appeared for paying audiences. The oratorio combined the drama of opera with the majesty of religious and ceremonial music, and featured the chorus over the soloists. Novels also captured the imagination of the public, and new writers and booksellers appeared to meet the new demand for books. Many of these novels focused on contemporary social values.

Religious Revivals, p. 683

New religious movements that emphasized a more emotional, personal type of Christianity spread within the Protestant and Catholic churches and, like the arts, broke away from the authority of established leaders and institutions. In Protestant Europe, Pietism rocked the complacency of the established churches and emphasized a mystical religion of the heart. Pietists wanted a more deeply emotional, even ecstatic religion, and their emphasis on reading the Bible contributed to the increase in literacy. In Catholic France, Quietism and Jansenism had a common emphasis on mystical unions with God and an emotional form of religion. Despite the pressure of political persecution, adherents to these religious revival movements became influential, and joined the opposition to intolerant policies on religion.

Consolidation of the European State System

By the 1740s warfare had become less frequent in Europe, allowing states to spend more of their resources establishing and expanding control over their own populations at home and in their colonies. By this time the political dominance of France in Europe had been checked by a coalition of other countries, Great Britain had emerged as the preeminent maritime power, and Russia had defeated Sweden for supremacy in the Baltic region.

The Limits of French Absolutism, pp. 684–686

When Louis XIV died in 1714, many of his accomplishments had already begun to unravel. The War of Spanish Succession, which lasted from 1701–1713, brought about the downfall of French dominance in European power politics. The war began when the Spanish king Charles II died without an heir and named a relative of Louis XIV as his successor. In order to prevent the union of France and Spain, several other powers united against France. At the end of the war, Louis's second grandson was recognized as king of Spain, but he had to renounce any future claim to the French crown, thereby preventing the union of the two kingdoms. At home Louis XIV's absolutism fostered resentment from the nobility, and after his death the regents for his five-year-old great-grandson and successor tried to give the nobility and parliaments a greater say in political affairs. His regents also experimented with financial reforms, such as the creation of a state bank that could lend money to the state at low interests, thereby reducing the cost of financing the government's debts. The bank collapsed a few months later. France did benefit from peace at home, with large projects for canal and road construction, which contributed to a prolonged period of prosperity.

British Rise and Dutch Decline, pp. 686–688

With the death of William and Mary, the English crown passed to Mary's sister Anne, who died in 1714 without an heir. In order to prevent the crown from passing back to the Stuarts, who were sympathetic to Catholicism, Parliament provided for the elector of Hanover, a Protestant great-grandson of James I, to become king George I. The Catholic majority in Ireland, who had supported a rebellion against the Protestant monarchs of England, faced tighter legal and social restrictions. George I and George II relied heavily on Sir Robert Walpole, who strengthened the power of Parliament through his use of patronage and became the first "prime minister" responsible for guiding legislation through the House of Commons. While France's experiment with national banking failed, the Bank of England proved a great success and enabled the British government to raise considerable capital cheaply to finance its military operations abroad. During this period the Dutch Republic lost much of its influence in international politics as it lost much of its share in Baltic trade and its political grip in India, Ceylon, and Java.

Russia's Emergence as a European Power, pp. 688–690

In Russia, Peter the Great's (r. 1689–1725) attempt to transform Russia into a "western" nation with a consolidated and powerful central government had a great impact on the upper classes, but his reforms did not affect the mass of the population and the status of the serfs worsened under his rule. Peter recruited foreigners to Russia to build scientific academies and technical schools, and forced the nobility to adopt western language, culture, and manners. In 1703 he began construction of St. Petersburg, a new city on the Baltic coast that symbolized Russia's opening to the West. Through the Table of Ranks he made the social and economic privileges the nobles enjoyed depend on their service to the crown. His establishment of the Holy Synod, a bureaucracy of laymen under his supervision, brought the Russian Orthodox church under royal control. Following Peter's death in 1725, Russia went through a period of instability in which rapid turnover of the throne weakened the monarchy.

The Balance of Power in the East, pp. 690–692

Sweden had dominated the Baltic region since the Thirty Years' War, but lost its preeminence when Peter the Great joined an anti-Swedish coalition with Denmark, Saxony, and Poland. Charles XII of Sweden (r. 1697–1718) was initially successful against the coalition, but died in battle in 1718. After the Treaty of Nystad (1721) Sweden ceded its Baltic provinces to Russia and its territories on the north German coast to Prussia and its allied German states. An aristocratic reaction against the incessant demands for the war swept away Swedish absolutism. In Prussia King Frederick William I (r. 1713–1740) drew upon all state resources to support his army, which was the best equipped and best trained in Europe. Prussia sat on the sidelines during the War of Polish Succession (1733–1735), which pitted France, Spain, and Sardinia against Russia and Austria. After being driven out by the Russians, the French agreed to accept the Austrian candidate in exchange for the province of Lorraine. Austria remained busy with the Turks on its southeastern border. In the 1730s the Turks retook Belgrade, and in the meantime the Hungarians forced many political concessions from their Austrian rulers.

The Power of Diplomacy and the Importance of Numbers, pp. 692–693

No single power emerged from the wars of the first half of the eighteenth century clearly superior to the others, and the idea of maintaining a balance of power guided both military and diplomatic maneuvering. The diplomatic service developed a set of regular features, first in France and then in other European states. Despite the increase in professional diplomacy, rulers still employed secret agents. Nevertheless, the diplomatic system in the early eighteenth century proved successful enough to ensure that nations followed the model of the Peace of Westphalia (1648): in the midst of every crisis and war, the great powers would convene and work out a written agreement detailing the requirements for peace. Because each state's strength depended largely on the size of its army, the growth and health of the population became an increasing concern of government. William Petty's *Political Arithmetick* (1690) offered statistical estimates of human capital, such as population and wages, to determine Britain's national wealth. In 1727, Frederick William I of Prussia founded two university chairs to encourage population studies.

Public Hygiene and Health Care, pp. 693–695

Physicians used the new population statistics to explain the environmental causes of disease. Air quality became one of the key determinants of whether a place was considered healthy or unhealthy. Cities were the most unhealthy places due to poor sanitation and high population density. After studying specific cities, medical geographers urged government campaigns to improve public sanitation. As a result, local governments took such measures as draining low-lying areas, burying refuse, and cleaning wells, all of which helped lower the death rates from epidemic disease. Hospitals and medical care also underwent lasting transformations, although there was as yet no medical profession with nationwide organizations and licensing, so trained physicians had to compete with quacks. Physicians changed the practice of diagnosis by using specialized

Latin terms for illnesses and performing postmortem dissections to gain better knowledge of anatomy and disease.

The Birth of the Enlightenment

The Enlightenment was the intellectual corollary of eighteenth-century optimism toward the future that was generated by economic and political stability. The name *Enlightenment* refers to the work and ideas of a loosely knit group of writers and scholars who believed that humans could apply a critical, reasoning spirit to any problem they encountered in the world. These intellectuals and philosophers scrutinized everything, from the absolutism of Louis XIV to the traditional role of women in society.

Popularization of Science and Challenges to Religion, pp. 695–698

The writers of the Enlightenment glorified the geniuses of the new science and championed the scientific method as the solution for social problems. Works such as Bernard de Fontenelle's *Conversations on the Plurality of Worlds* (1686) made the Copernican heliocentric view of the universe accessible to the literate public. Soon mathematics and science became fashionable in high society. As the prestige of science increased, some developed a skeptical attitude toward enforced religious conformity. Pierre Bayle (1647–1706) was a Huguenot refugee from Louis XIV's persecutions. From the tolerant Dutch Republic, Bayle issued a series of books and essays that insisted that even religion must meet the test of reasonableness. Voltaire (François-Marie Arouet, 1694–1778) was inspired by Bayle's work, and launched a stellar career with his own attacks on Catholic bigotry and the French government. Voltaire also popularized Newtonian science with his *Elements of the Philosophy of Newton* (1738).

Travel Literature and the Challenge to Custom and Tradition, pp. 698–700

During the seventeenth century, travel accounts became more numerous, and travelers became more receptive to foreign and even non-European cultures. Montesquieu's fictional travel account *Persian Letters* suggested that French and Persian institutions were similarly despotic, and *The Spirit of the Laws*, inspired by Montesquieu's own travels to England, compared the governments of England and France. By the eighteenth century, a growing body of travel literature allowed Europeans to see that customs varied from place to place and to thus develop a more critical perspective on their own societies.

Raising the Woman Question, pp. 700–701

At the same time that ovism, a new scientific doctrine about the female reproductive system, challenged the established medical opinion that only the male seed carried spirit and individuality, women writers such as Mary Astell began to propose changes in women's status in society. In her book *A Serious Proposal to the Ladies* (1694), she advocated the founding of a private women's college to remedy women's lack of education. Later works such as *Reflections upon Marriage* (1706) criticized the unequal relationship between the sexes in marriage. Other women such as Elizabeth Elstob and Elizabeth Singer Rowe wrote in a similar vein.

Key Events
For each question, select the most appropriate response from the choices provided.

1690s Beginning of rapid development of plantations in Caribbean

1694 Bank of England established; Mary Astell's *A Serious Proposal to the Ladies* argues for the founding of a private women's college

1697 Pierre Bayle publishes *Historical and Critical Dictionary*, detailing errors of religious writers

1699 Turks forced to recognize Habsburg rule over Hungary and Transylvania

1703 Peter the Great of Russia begins construction of St. Petersburg, founds first Russian newspaper

1713–1714 Peace of Utrecht

1714 Elector of Hanover becomes King George I of England

1715 Death of Louis XIV

1719 Daniel Defoe publishes *Robinson Crusoe*

1720 Last outbreak of bubonic plague in western Europe

1721 Treaty of Nystad; Montesquieu publishes *Persian Letters* anonymously in the Dutch Republic

1733 War of the Polish Succession; Voltaire's *Letters Concerning the English Nation* attacks French intolerance and narrow-mindedness

1741 George Frederick Handel composes the *Messiah*

1. What was the main product of the Caribbean plantations that was developed rapidly after 1690?
   a. Sugar
   b. Cotton
   c. Tobacco
   d. Precious metals

2. Which of the following events *most* influenced Pierre Bayle in his *Historical and Critical Dictionary*?
   a. The mistreatment of slaves in European colonies
   b. The enclosure movement in England
   c. The Pietist movement in German Lutheran states
   d. Louis XIV's restrictions on French Protestants

3. Which of the following did *not* represent a break with the past in Peter the Great's new capital of St. Petersburg?
   a. The improvement in status for upper-class women
   b. The foundation of an Academy of Sciences
   c. The loosening of restrictions on serfs
   d. The use of French and German among the nobility

4. Which country lost much of its influence in European power politics as a result of the Peace of Utrecht (1713–1714)?
   a. France
   b. England
   c. The Dutch Republic
   d. Spain

5. Why did Parliament ensure that the German elector of Hanover become King George I of England in 1714?
   a. He was the closest relative of Queen Anne
   b. To block the succession of a Catholic, in particular the son of the deposed James II
   c. It was one of the terms of the Peace of Utrecht
   d. He had the support of the Scots and Irish, who welcomed a non-English king

6. Which country lost the most territory as a result of the Treaty of Nystad in 1721?
   a. Russia
   b. The Dutch Republic
   c. Prussia
   d. Sweden

7. What did France gain in return for recognizing the Austrian candidate for the Polish throne after the War of Polish Succession?
   a. The province of Lorraine
   b. The island of Sardinia
   c. Territories in North America
   d. The kingdom of Lithuania

Key Terms   *Match each key term to its definition.*

A. **agricultural revolution** (p. 676)
B. **Atlantic system** (p. 666)
C. **buccaneers** (p. 674)
D. **consumer revolution** (p. 676)
E. **enlightenment** (p. 696)
F. **Jacobitism** (p. 686)
G. **mestizo** (p. 674)
H. **Pietism** (p. 683)
I. **plantation** (p. 667)
J. **rococo** (p. 681)
K **Westernization** (p. 688)

1. _____ The triangular pattern of trade established in the 1700s that bound together western Europe, Africa, and the Americas. Europeans sold slaves from western Africa and bought commodities such as coffee and sugar that were produced by the new colonial plantations in North and South America and the Caribbean.

2. _____ Large tract of land producing staple crops such as sugar, coffee and tobacco; farmed by slave labor; and owned by a colonial settler who emigrated from western Europe.

3. _____ Person born to a Spanish father and native American mother.

4. _____ Pirates of the Caribbean who governed themselves and preyed on international shipping.

5. _____ Rapid increase in consumption of new staples produced in the Atlantic system as well as other items of daily life, such as mirrors, that were previously unavailable or beyond the reach of ordinary people.

6. _____ Increasingly aggressive attitudes toward investment and management of land that increased production of food in the 1700s; this revolution developed first in England and then spread to the continent.

7. _____ A style of painting that emphasized irregularity and asymmetry, movement and curvature, but on a smaller, more intimate scale than the baroque.

8. _____ Protestant revivalist movement that emphasized deeply emotional individual religious experience.

9. _____ Movement of support for deposed British king James II (from the Latin for "James") that had substantial support in Scotland and Ireland in the early eighteenth century.

10. _____ Effort, especially in Peter the Great's Russia, to make society and social customs resemble counterparts in western Europe, especially France, Britain and the Dutch Republic.

11. _____ Eighteenth-century intellectual movement whose proponents believed that human beings could apply a critical, reasoning spirit to every problem. Based on a popularization of scientific discoveries, the movement often challenged religious and secular authorities.

Identification   *This activity tests your recall of significant people, places, and events from this chapter. Fill in the blank with the correct answer.*

1. Before 1675 most black slaves taken from Africa were brought to _____.

2. After 1700, most black slaves taken from Africa were brought to _____.

3. The slave trade helped make

   _____ a standard food item during the eighteenth century.

4. Children of Spanish men and Indian women, called _____, came to account for a major segment of the population in Spanish colonies.

5. The staple of trade with India in the early 1700s was _____.

6. The first literary magazine, known as the _____, first appeared in 1709 and was devoted to the cultural improvement of the increasingly influential middle class.

7. _____ painting, which appeared in the eighteenth century, depicted scenes of intimate sensuality and took the place of heroic landscapes on grand, ceremonial canvases.

8. The oratorio was introduced to England by _____, who is most famous for his *Messiah*.

9. Well-known for novels that showed a concern for the proper place of women as models of virtue in a changing world, _____ began publishing a magazine that argued in favor

of higher education for women.

10. The _____ promoted an austere form of Catholicism and were very influential despite harassment from Louis XIV and the condemnation of the papacy.

11. The War of Spanish succession began when _____ died without an heir, leaving all of Europe to fight over the Spanish throne.

12. The financier _____ made a failed attempt in France to establish a state bank and issue paper money to help lower the government's cost of financing its debts in 1719.

13. Originally appointed by the king, _____ established an enduring pattern of parliamentary government in England in which a prime minister from the leading party guided legislation through the House of Commons.

14. In his book *Political Arithmetick*, _____ offered statistical estimates of population and wages to determine Britain's national wealth.

15. In 1796, _____ developed a serum to inoculate humans against smallpox based on a milder form of the disease called cowpox.

16. From his safe haven in the Dutch Republic, _____ launched an influential campaign against religious intolerance that inspired future thinkers of the Enlightenment.

17. In his *Letters Concerning the English Nation*, _____ criticized the Catholic bigotry and government rigidity in France.

18. Using satire to investigate the foundation of good government and morality, _____ compared France to Persia and suggested that the French monarchy might verge on despotism.

19. In the essay "Reflections on Marriage," _____ criticized the relationship between the sexes within marriage.

20. In 1709, _____ published a detailed account of the prominent role women played in promoting Christianity in English history.

CHAPTER REVIEW

Self-Test and Analytical Exercises

Multiple Choice   *Select the best answer from the four choices provided.*

1. Which of the following was *not* a commodity exchanged in the Atlantic system?
   a. Manufactured goods
   b. Slaves
   c. Spices
   d. Sugar

2. What became of the majority of the Caribbean islands' indigenous people?
   a. They migrated to Central America.
   b. They lived peacefully alongside white colonists.
   c. They moved into the forests and backwoods where white colonists could not reach them.
   d. They died off from warfare and disease.

3. The Spanish and Portuguese were more tolerant of intermarriage between Europeans and Native Americans than were the British or French; such tolerance often led to
   a. better treatment of slaves in Spanish and Portuguese colonies.
   b. a large number of natives becoming Catholic clergy.
   c. Native Americans siding with the Spanish and Portuguese in boundary disputes with Britain or France.
   d. mestizos composing over a quarter of the population in Spanish colonies.

4. All of the following products were part of the consumer revolution of the early eighteenth century *except*
   a. chocolate.
   b. tobacco.
   c. potatoes.
   d. coffee.

5. Which of the following was *not* an agricultural development that began in Britain and spread to other countries?
   a. An increase in the size of land parcels being cultivated
   b. The division of farmland into smaller, more easily managed holdings
   c. The linking of livestock raising to crop growing
   d. The selective breeding of animals

6. Which of the following *best* describes the trend of urbanization in the eighteenth century?
   a. Cities shrank as residents found opportunity in new farmlands that were being developed.
   b. Cities grew, with an important shift in urbanization from the south to the north of Europe.
   c. Urbanization in eastern Europe grew beyond urbanization in western Europe.
   d. Southern cities remained the same, while northern cities declined as people colonized America.

7. One likely reason countries like Scotland, parts of Switzerland, and the Scandinavian countries more successfully promoted education and literacy than countries like France is that they
   a. all had more trees than France, which allowed them to produce the paper for books more cheaply and efficiently.
   b. were all Protestant countries that emphasized the importance of personally reading the Bible, which most Catholic countries like France did not do.
   c. were so remote that reading was one of the only forms of entertainment for the population.
   d. taught English in their schools, which allowed their people to buy and read many of the numerous books published in London.

8. Although François Boucher's paintings and George Frederick Handel's oratorios are very different cultural art forms, one common aspect that links them is that
   a. both men produced their best work while living in Paris.
   b. they appealed to the middle class through their emphasis on emotion.
   c. their works were not very popular during their lifetimes.
   d. they influenced the working class because their works were so cheap that even the poorest laborer could afford to enjoy them.

9. Which conflict ended with the Peace of Utrecht (1713–1714)?
   a. The War of Polish Succession
   b. The War of Austrian Succession
   c. The War of Spanish Succession
   d. The Colonial Wars

10. In the early eighteenth century, Sir Robert Walpole increased the role of Parliament in the British government by
    a. creating the system in which the leader of the dominant Parliamentary party guided legislation through the House of Commons.
    b. introducing the concept of holding elections at set intervals, not simply at the whim of the monarch.
    c. limiting the powers of the House of Lords in order to give more power to the democratic House of Commons.
    d. creating a High Court that judged the constitutionality of legislation passed by Parliament.

11. In the eighteenth century the Dutch Republic
    a. annexed part of Poland-Lithuania.
    b. retained its status as chief commercial power.
    c. lost its status as a great power in European politics.
    d. was the country most innovative in agricultural techniques.

12. Which of the following was *not* an element of Peter the Great's westernization program?
    a. He ordered that English be the language of instruction in his new trade schools, since British traders were among the most successful in western Europe.
    b. He ordered his noblemen to shave their beards, dress in western clothes he prescribed, and learn western manners, dancing, and conversational styles.
    c. He decreed that noble women be freed from their traditionally secluded and denigrated status and participate in his conversational evenings and parties.
    d. He built a new capital city, St. Petersburg, which was intended to symbolize Russia's opening to the west.

13. In *Persian Letters* (1721), Baron de Montesquieu struck a chord with some European women when he had the wife of one of his Persian travelers
    a. journey to France alone and in disguise so that she could be with her beloved husband.
    b. denounce the tyranny in their marriage and proclaim that her mind had always been free and independent.
    c. die a lingering death following the birth of her only son and her husband's heir.
    d. consider having an affair with a servant because she was left alone by her husband for so long.

14. Travelers to the Americas or China often misinterpreted the native societies that they found, but some of them returned with the troubling lesson that
    a. Europe would have to conquer most other societies to bring them up to the level of civilization enjoyed by Europeans.
    b. Europeans in close contact with other civilizations were likely to be degraded by them and bring evil habits back home.
    c. European traditions and beliefs were neither universal nor superior to all others and that they were one of a number of options for humankind.
    d. European society had virtually no hope of redeeming itself from the corruption that civilization had brought upon it.

15. Some scientists in the eighteenth century changed their views about women's biology, conceding that
    a. women were biologically more capable than men of nurturing infant children.
    b. the female egg, and not just the male sperm, contained vital elements for creation of a fetus, a doctrine known as *ovism*.
    c. women had less strength but far more stamina than men, which made them more suited to certain types of labor than men.
    d. the structure of women's brains was different from that of men, but females were nevertheless capable of learning some of the same things as males.

16. Mary Astell's *A Serious Proposal to the Ladies* (1694) and the anonymous *Essay in Defense of the Female Sex* (1696) both argue that
    a. men and women should be completely equal partners in marriage.
    b. women should put off childbearing until they reach their late twenties.
    c. women should hide their intelligence because it hindered them in their efforts to get married.
    d. women should not be denied the opportunity to receive an education simply because of their gender.

17. Why were the number and size of European trading colonies in China limited?
    a. The journey was too far and dangerous to be profitable.
    b. Europeans succumbed too quickly to new diseases there.
    c. The Chinese government despised Europeans and allowed them to trade in only one location.
    d. There was little of interest to European merchants in China.

18. In the British colonies of New England, slavery
    a. was necessary for the functioning of the plantation system.
    b. was vigorously opposed by religious leaders.
    c. was uncommon since settlers did not own large agricultural estates.
    d. was less common than serfdom.

19. In the early eighteenth century, the "consumer revolution" occurred because
    a. new industrial methods created new products produced domestically in England and France.
    b. immigrants from eastern Europe and the colonies brought new tastes for new products to western Europe.
    c. a series of poor harvests caused farmers to raise more livestock, and the greater availability of meat changed European eating habits.
    d. new foreign goods such as calicoes and tea were available in greater quantities just as a growing European population emerged with enough disposable income to buy them.

20. Which of the following is *not* true about pirates in this period?
    a. They had once been authorized by the English and Dutch governments to prey on the Spanish and Portuguese.
    b. They formed associations in the late 1600s made up of deserters and crews from wrecked vessels.
    c. Pirate bands sometimes included women.
    d. The British government tolerated them because they attacked merchants of rival countries.

21. Which of the following *best* describes Pietism?
    a. An austere form of Catholicism that emphasized obedience to religious authority
    b. A rationalist form of Calvinism that sought to reconcile religion with new scientific discoveries
    c. A simplified form of Protestantism that placed less emphasis on Scripture than on prayer and meditation
    d. A deeply emotional form of Lutheranism that urged intense Bible study

22. The enclosure movement changed the social structure of the British countryside because
    a. small-scale farmers used it to gain land and become more independent of local landlords.
    b. it created a new class called the gentry, farmers who sold off their medium-size farms to be enclosed and lived off the profits.
    c. cottagers and small-scale farmers lost their independence when they lost their land to big landowners, who then employed them as farm laborers and tenant farmers.
    d. peasants were forced to become virtual serfs in some parts of England, and it took an Act of Parliament to force landlords to give them their freedom.

23. As the middle class became more literate,
    a. men and women read newspapers, novels, and religious tracts in coffeehouses.
    b. men read newspapers, novels, and religious tracts in coffeehouses while women read at home.
    c. men started attending salons hosted by men in social clubs.
    d. publishing regulations became much more stringent so that the government could reap more profits from permissions fees.

24. Which of the following *best* describes rococo painting?
    a. Ceremonial art that emphasized heroic subjects
    b. Portraits and pastoral paintings that often emphasized the erotic and emotional
    c. Religious painting that emphasized the glory of the church
    d. Popular painting that was meant to instruct the working class

25. Eighteenth-century Spain was
    a. a vibrant center of Enlightenment culture.
    b. in decline economically and culturally.
    c. a major player in European diplomacy.
    d. the center of a religious revolt.

26. Which country lost the most territory by the terms of the Treaty of Nystad?
    a. Russia
    b. Poland
    c. Prussia
    d. Sweden

27. The Table of Ranks, established by Peter the Great in 1722, was a pivotal element of his reform program because it
    a. provided incentives to peasants to work hard in order to obtain higher status.

    b. based noble status on service to the state, not on birth, which gave the tsar greater control over his nobles and a ready-made bureaucracy and officer corps.
    c. funded merchant ventures that helped bring foreign capital to Russia to pay for the tsar's wars and building projects.
    d. limited the power of the Russian Orthodox church.

28. Under King Frederick William I, Prussia became a formidable military power by
    a. seizing a large portion of Poland-Lithuania during the war of the Polish Succession.
    b. becoming the largest European supplier of mercenary soldiers.
    c. perfecting the smooth-bore musket, which made its army more deadly than others, even though it was much smaller.
    d. drawing on all the resources of the state to support and maintain the army.

29. Why were Pierre Bayle's books controversial when they appeared in the late 1600s?
    a. They opposed monarchical government in favor of democracy.
    b. They proposed allowing women access to higher education.
    c. They criticized the institution of slavery.
    d. They argued that religion must be subject to human reason.

30. Which of the following is *not* true about Voltaire?
    a. He was elected to the Royal Society in London.
    b. He suffered arrest, imprisonment, and exile over the course of his life.
    c. He was inspired by Bayle to attack religious bigotry.
    d. His work did not achieve any great success until after his death.

31. Authorities in France felt threatened by Voltaire's popularization of Sir Isaac Newton's discoveries in his *Elements of the Philosophy of Newton* (1738) because
    a. it glorified the human mind but seemed to reduce God to an abstract principle.
    b. it showed the British government in a much more favorable light than the French government and authorities thought this might incite rebellion.
    c. Voltaire simplified Newton's theories so much in order to make them intelligible to the working classes that they seemed to imply that no authority was valid.
    d. it criticized the harsh French legal system as inconsistent with reason and therefore invalid.

32. Mary Astell based her thoughts about educating women on
    a. Descartes's principles, in which reason took priority over tradition.
    b. Descartes's principles, in which women should be a part of mercantilist policies.
    c. Lady Mary Wortley Montagu's principles, in which reason took priority over tradition.
    d. Lady Mary Wortley Montagu's principles, in which everyone should be educated.

Short Answer   *Answer each question in three or four sentences.*

The Atlantic System and the World Economy

1. In what ways did aspects of the European coffee-house embody significant changes in the international economy as well as in domestic social relations?

2. What economic developments in the American colonies led to a dramatic increase in the number of slaves imported from Africa, followed by the rise of racism?

3. In the early eighteenth century, why did European influence in China differ from that in India?

New Social and Cultural Patterns

4. How did the Agricultural Revolution affect the lives of peasants in England differently from peasants in Prussia, Russia, and Poland?

5. How did novels reflect the values of the urban middle-class public?

6. What were some of the commonalities among the religious revival movements in the late seventeenth and early eighteenth centuries?

Consolidation of the European State System

7. What was the immediate cause of the War of the Spanish Succession, and how did the Peace of Utrecht reflect the changing balance of power in Europe?

8. How did Peter the Great bring the nobility and the Russian Orthodox church under his absolute control?

9. How did medicine change in the first half of the seventeenth century?

The Birth of the Enlightenment

10. How did the popularization of science contribute to the development of the Enlightenment?

11. How did Baron de Montesquieu's fictional *Persian Letters* reflect the impact of eighteenth-century travel literature on political commentary?

12. How did Mary Astell use political examples to support her call for more equal status within marriage?

BUILDING HISTORICAL SKILLS

Reading Maps   *Write a brief, paragraph-length response to each of the following questions based on* **Map 18.1: European Trading Patterns, c. 1740 (p. 668).**

1. What territories were primarily involved as exporters and importers in the slave trade at this time?

2. What products did Europeans import from colonies in the Americas?

3. Describe how the triangular trade network worked in the Atlantic system.

Reading Illustrations   *Write a brief, paragraph-length response to each of the following questions based on the illustration* **Africa (p. 676).**

1. What does this image tell us about eighteenth-century Europeans' perceptions of Africans and the African continent?

2. What impression of Africa do you think the artist wished to convey to her audience?

Reading Historical Documents   *Write a brief, paragraph-length response to each of the following questions based on the documents in your book.*

Voltaire, Letters Concerning the English Nation (p. 699)

1. How does Voltaire respond to those who might fear that philosophy is a danger to religious faith?

2. Does Voltaire's opinion of humanity as seen in this excerpt seem to be optimistic or pessimistic?

Lady Mary Wortley Montagu, Smallpox Inoculation in the Ottoman Empire (p. 694)

3. What attitudes toward non-European societies are evident in Lady Montagu's letter, and how do they compare with her attitude toward European culture?

4. How does this letter reflect the social and cultural changes occurring in Europe in the eighteenth century?

New Sources, New Perspectives: Oral History and the Life of Slaves (pp. 672–673)

5. What insights do the oral histories provide that historians would not otherwise have access to, and what possible problems accompany the insights?

6. What motivated the remembering and recounting of the oral descriptions of slaves and their lives?

The Promise of Enlightenment
1740–1789

CHAPTER OVERVIEW

Chapter Questions   *Keep these questions in mind as you go through the study guide chapter.*

1. What were the major ideas and themes developed in the Enlightenment?

2. Why were middle-class people interested in the Enlightenment?

3. How, and to what extent, did the lives of peasants and workers change?

4. What factors explained the shift in the European balance of power?

5. How did politics change in the second half of the eighteenth century?

Chapter Summary

The Enlightenment at Its Height

The Enlightenment emerged as an intellectual movement before 1740 and reached its peak in the second half of the eighteenth century. Writers of the Enlightenment called themselves *philosphes*, and concerned themselves with solving the real problems of the world.

Men and Women of the Republic of Letters, pp. 709–712

The Enlightenment was a cosmopolitan movement that stretched from the North American colonies to Russia. Although it was centered in France, Enlightened thinkers believed that they were part of a "republic of letters," which transcended political boundaries. They believed in the importance of reason, reform, and freedom—particularly, freedom of thought and of religion. The philosophes believed that education was essential to the eradication of superstition and bigotry, which they believed to be the chief obstacles to reform. Significantly, French, clergy-run universities were unreceptive to Enlightenment ideas. Philosophes argued that progress depended on the establishment of the "natural rights" of freedom of the press and freedom of religion, which they believed were rooted in "natural law." Although the philosophes were mostly from a mixed group of elite and middle-class men, women did participate in the movement. Upper-class women, although they rarely considered themselves philosophes, organized the salons that served as centers for the development and dissemination of Enlightenment ideas.

Conflicts with Church and State, pp. 712–713

Opposition to organized religion was a major propellant of the Enlightenment. Whereas most influential Europeans believed that religion was necessary for a good society and government, changes in attitude toward God and religion began to emerge in the eighteenth century. Both deism (the belief that God existed, but did not intervene in earthly affairs) and atheism (the belief that God did not exist) emerged as alternatives to the traditional belief that God constantly intervened in all aspects of human affairs. Deists like the philosophe Voltaire were influenced by Isaac Newton's vision of the universe as a clock set in motion by God, but then left to operate according to its own laws. Voltaire was adamantly opposed to religious intolerance, which he believed was a prime source of fanaticism and brutality among humans. Like other philosophes, Voltaire attacked the close ties between the church and the state and certain practices, such as torture, practiced by state governments. Philosophes also attacked both church and state for policies of colonization and for condoning slavery. Their belief in natural rights led many to argue that native Americans and Africans could not justifiably be deprived of their freedom. While some called on these grounds for the abolition of slavery, others condoned the institution; Hume argued that blacks were "naturally inferior to the whites." Even the most adamant critics of slavery, torture, and religious intolerance believed the answer to changing these institutions was reform, not revolution.

The Individual and Society, pp. 713–717

Governments were concerned with the philosophes' attacks on established religion because they viewed religion as necessary to good government and public order. Religion was thus considered to be a public concern. Enlightenment thinkers, however, argued that religion was essentially a private issue, a question of individual conscience. The philosophes argued that reason rather than religion should direct social and political life. At the same time, however, the philosophes disagreed about what reason revealed. For Adam Smith, reason's operation was most evident in the workings of the economy. Smith argued that in an economy left to follow its own natural laws and free of government intervention, individual interests would be harmonized with those of society as a whole, leading to increased wealth for society and individual improvement. Another philosophe, Jean-Jacques Rousseau, was less certain that individual interests and the welfare of the people as a whole could be reconciled. In works such as *The New Heloise* (1761) and *Emile* (1762) Rousseau explored the need for persons to deny their individual desires in order to become part of society. In *The Social Contract* (1762), Rousseau argued that giving up one's individual interests to the "general will" (the good of the community) could be a source of morality and freedom. Rousseau conceived of the general will as a contract that individuals entered into with each other, rather than with their rulers.

Spreading the Enlightenment, pp. 717–720

The Enlightenment flourished in places with an educated middle class and was thus centered in London, Amsterdam, and Paris. In those countries where constitutionalism and the guarantee of individual rights were most advanced (such as Adam Smith's England), Enlightenment thinkers tended to focus on economics, philosophy, and history. In countries with few middle class citizens (such as Spain), governments were more easily able to censor writings that didn't conform. Although France had fewer constitutional guarantees of individual freedom than Great Britain, it was not as autocratic as Spain or Russia. The French middle class was significant in size and well educated, and became increasingly adamant in calling for political reform. Feeding these calls for reform were the numerous Enlightenment works smuggled in from Switzerland and the Dutch Republic. From the 1760s on, the French government tended to ignore, rather than censor, the flood of philosophical treatises, as well as pornographic books and pamphlets that were undermining the authority of the monarchy. In the German states, on the other hand, intellectuals tended to avoid direct confrontation with the government. Thinkers such as Gotthold Lessing and Moses Mendelssohn promoted religious toleration, whereas Immanuel Kant laid the foundation for modern philosophy with his 1781 work, *The Critique of Pure Reason*. Kant argued that reason alone could not answer all philosophical questions.

The Limits of Reason: Roots of Romanticism and Religious Revival, pp. 720–721

Kant was not the only intellectual who believed that reason could not answer all of life's questions. A new artistic movement known as romanticism emphasized individual genius, emotion, and the joys of nature—aspects of life that could come into conflict with reason. Increased interest in the occult also revealed the limits of reason. The Austrian physician Franz Mesmer claimed to cure physical ailments by placing the afflicted in close proximity to a tub of water charged with a weak electrical current. The limitations of reason were popularized widely in a 1774 novel by Johann Wolfgang von Goethe, *The Sorrows of Young Werther*. In this novel, Werther's emotions get the better of his reason as his unrequited love leads to his suicide. Religious revivals also underlined the limits of reason. Pietism continued to spread in the German states, while the British North American colonies experienced a "Great Awakening." Israel ben Eliezer invented a new form of popular prayer for Jews that was meant to allow the supernatural to speak through the body of the person who prayed. Followers of ben Eliezer, known as the Hasidim, gathered outside the established synagogues throughout Poland and Lithuania. In Great Britain, John Wesley founded Methodism, which emphasized self-discipline and a methodical approach to religion. Like ben Eliezer and the Pietists, Wesley believed in an intensely personal and emotional faith. Wesley also advocated hard work, thrift, and abstinence.

Society and Culture in an Age of Enlightenment

Not all social and cultural developments manifested the influence of the Enlightenment. Many European nobles resisted the Enlightenment, which they saw as a threat to their traditional privileges, whereas the expanding middle classes saw it as an opportunity to join society's governing elite. The lower classes were more affected by the economic growth than by ideas that took place during this period.

The Nobility's Reassertion of Privilege, pp. 722–723

Although the standard of living of nobles varied, the wealthiest European nobles lived a lavish and luxurious lifestyle. In reaction to the commercialization of agriculture and inflation, and to sustain their increasingly expensive lifestyles, nobles converted their traditional legal rights into cash payments. In countries such as France, this added to the peasants' financial burden, which included government taxes, custom duties, and the tithe (one-tenth of the crop paid to the church). Nobles also protected exclusive rights, such as their right to hunt game. Despite Enlightenment writers' criticism of aristocratic privilege, nobles maintained their marks of distinction. Their dress, their exclusive right to wear a sword, their own pews in church, and their private quarters in the university all signified their superiority over other social groups. In many countries, most nobles cared little about Enlightenment ideas, but in France, Great Britain, and the western German states, nobles were more receptive.

The Middle Class and the Making of a New Elite, pp. 723–726

In western Europe, the Enlightenment helped break down boundaries between the aristocracy and the middle class. Through shared culture and common interest in reform, the middle class could aspire to mix with the nobles and to be like them. The middle class (or bourgeoisie) grew steadily in western Europe in the eighteenth century. Middle class persons did not possess legal titles like the nobility, but they also did not work with their hands like peasants, artisans, and workers. These individuals occupied the middle position on the social ladder; most lived in cities and worked as doctors, lawyers, or government officials, or earned a living through investment in trade, land, or manufacturing. Nobles and members of the middle class mingled in salons, Masonic lodges, and learned societies. Masonic lodges encouraged equality among their members (known as "freemasons"). Enlightenment ideas were also disseminated through learned societies, in which nobles and middle-class persons met to discuss new scientific innovations or methods to eliminate poverty. In learned societies, the emphasis was on practical reform. The intermingled elite of nobles and middle-class people also shared tastes in travel, architecture, and the arts. Travel to Italy among youths from both social groups inspired interest in a neoclassical style, which began pushing aside the baroque and rococo. This new emphasis on emotion and family inspired a growing taste for moralistic family scenes in paintings that evoked moral issues through the depiction of everyday life, and appealed to the middle class. Music was also affected by the rise of a new mixed elite, as it became more accessible to listeners. Professional orchestras in large concert halls began developing a repertoire of "classics," pieces performed repeatedly for paying audiences. A growing literate public read Enlightenment works at home. Publishing expanded rapidly, and books on secular subjects, as well as newspapers, proliferated. Lending libraries and book clubs facilitated reading. Women read as much as men, and a new genre of children's literature emerged.

Life on the Margins, pp. 726–728

Despite booming foreign trade, increased food production, and rising wages in many trades, at least 10 percent of Europe's urban population depended on some form of charity. Periodic food shortages and inflation caused economic difficulty for day laborers in the cities and peasants with small land holdings. The growing number of poor overwhelmed local governments. Workhouses in which the poor could be confined became more expensive to run; governments therefore developed new institutions to confine beggars and vagabonds that combined workshop, hospital, and prison. Both nobles and middle-class feared the increase in rural banditry and crimes against property that accompanied the growth of poverty. This fear was exacerbated by cultural differences. Although literacy had increased among the lower classes in western Europe, many still could not read. While the nobles and middle classes attended concerts and art exhibitions, peasants attended fairs and festivals, and workers relaxed in cafés or gambled at bullbaiting, bearbaiting, dogfighting, and cockfighting matches. Sexual behavior also changed, as out-of-wedlock births among the urban lower classes soared in the eighteenth century. Foundling hospitals were established to care for a growing number of abandoned babies, while other women attempted abortion or infanticide. Reformers criticized existing laws against fornication and infanticide as too harsh. Harsh punishments against male homosexuals (or "sodomites"), which could include imprisonment or execution, were retained.

The Roots of Industrialization, pp. 728–729

Industrialization began in England in the 1770s and 1780s. It consisted of four interlocking trends: (1) a dramatic increase in population, (2) the introduction of steam-driven machinery to increase output, (3) the establishment of factories to concentrate labor, and (4) the production of cotton goods. In response to a growing supply of raw cotton from the plantations of North America and the Caribbean, John Kay patented the flying shuttle. When it came into widespread use in the 1760s, weavers began to produce cloth more quickly than spinners could produce thread. The spinning jenny and the water frame, which was power driven, allowed spinners to overcome the shortage by spinning more rapidly. By the 1780s, a steam-driven mechanized loom sped the production of cloth. All the new machines brought workers into factories. England led the world in industrialization thanks to a large internal market, an increasing population, a supply of private investment capital, natural resources such as coal and iron, political stability, opportunities for social mobility, the pragmatism of inventors, and a culture of informal scientific education. Yet, even without mechanization, textile production expanded rapidly elsewhere in Europe. The "putting-out" system, in which peasant families manufactured cloth at home from raw materials supplied by manufacturers expanded immensely. The spread of the putting-out, or domestic manufacturing, system is sometimes called "proto-industrialization" to indicate that it paved the way for the full-scale Industrial Revolution.

State Power in an Era of Reform

While all rulers recognized that manufacturing created new sources of wealth, the diffusion of Enlightenment ideas of reform had a more immediate impact on how they exercised power than on industrialization. Historians label many of the sovereigns of the time as "enlightened despots" because they aimed to promote reform without giving up their absolutist powers. Reforms were affected directly by success or failure in the international competition for trade and territory.

War and Diplomacy, pp. 730–733

In contrast to the earlier religious wars that had killed thousands of civilians, wars in the eighteenth century were fought by professional armies. As military strategy became more cautious, wars became less frequent but could now be fought on a global scale. In the War of the Austrian Succession (1740–1748), Prussia and France fought Austria and Great Britain on the occasion of Maria Theresa's ascension to the imperial throne. Overseas, France and Great Britain fought for dominance in India. The peace treaty of 1748 established Maria Theresa as empress, but did not resolve the conflict in India. Unofficial fighting between Great Britain and France continued there, as well as in North America and the Caribbean. In 1756, a reversal of alliances—with Prussia and Great Britain allied against Austria, France, Russia, and Sweden—lay the foundation for the Seven Years' War (1756–1763). This war began when Prussia invaded Austria's ally Saxony and soon spread around the globe (in North America, this conflict was called the French and Indian War). Prussia emerged from the war a great power. The earlier militarization of Prussian society (through widespread noble participation in the military and the "canton system" that trained peasants and kept them on reserve) created one of the largest armies Europe had ever seen. While Prussia emerged strengthened from the war, France lost Canada and its position in India to Great Britain. In 1772, Prussia became even stronger when it, along with Austria and Russia, divided Poland-Lithuania, a large but weak state, among each other. The Polish-Lithuanian commonwealth effectively disappeared.

State-Sponsored Reform, pp. 733–735

In the aftermath of the Seven Years' War, Enlightened absolutists attempted to make increased taxes more acceptable by proposing social reforms designed to bring about greater equality and efficiency in justice and administration. In Austria and Prussia, monarchs insisted on greater attention to merit, hard work, and professionalism in the government bureaucracy. Frederick II of Prussia instituted a uniform civil justice system, Joseph II of Austria ordered the compilation of a uniform law code, and Catherine II of Russia drew up a document called the *Instruction* that represented her hopes for legal reform. Rulers used Enlightenment criticism of organized religion to gain greater control over church affairs. Catholic Spain, France, and Portugal expelled the Jesuits, the major Catholic teaching order that maintained close ties to the papacy. In 1773, Pope Clement XIV agreed under pressure to dissolve the order altogether. Enlightened absolutists also desired greater control over education: Joseph II issued a General School Ordinance in 1774 that ordered state subsidies for state-regulated, local schools; the Prussian school code of 1763 required all children between age five and thirteen to attend school; Catherine II also tried to expand education. Many rulers favored religious toleration, but Joseph II went furthest, granting freedom of religion in 1781 to Protestants, Orthodox Christians, and Jews. In 1787, Louis XVI restored the civil rights of Protestants, but still banned them from holding public office. Catholics could not worship freely or sit in Parliament in Great Britain, and most European states limited the rights and opportunities available to the Jews.

Limits of Reform, pp. 735–736

Groups threatened by reforms resisted government policy. Joseph II abolished the personal aspects of serfdom in 1781; he also removed the tithe to the church, shifted more tax burden to the nobles, and converted peasants' labor obligations into cash payments. These reforms were met with furious resistance from the nobility. When Joseph II died in 1790, his brother Leopold II was forced to revoke most of them. Reforms in France also met with resistance. The physiocrats, a group of economists, urged the deregulation of the grain trade and the abolition of the guilds because these prevented free entry into the trades. In 1763, the French government abolished price controls on grain, but was forced to reinstate these following a famine in 1770. Louis XV also wanted to decrease the power of the parlements, or high courts. When the government ruled that judges no longer owned their offices, they responded with charges of tyranny. In 1774, Louis XVI restored the old parlements.

Louis XVI had not, however, given up hope of reform. His chief minister Jacques Turgot (a contributor to the *Encyclopedia*) deregulated the grain trade, suppressed the guilds, converted peasants' forced labor into a cash tax payable by landowners, and reduced court expenses. He also began to introduce a system of elected local assemblies. Widespread resistance led by parlements and courtiers, as well as riots sparked by rising grain prices, forced the king to abandon his minister and his reforms.

Rebellions Against State Power

Enlightenment ideals and reforms changed the rules of the game in politics as governments became accountable for their actions to a much broader range of people than ever before. The growth of informed public opinion had its most dramatic consequences in the North American colonies, where a war for independence showed that Enlightenment ideals could have revolutionary implications when put into practice.

Food Riots and Peasant Uprisings, pp. 736–738

Population growth, inflation, and the extension of the market system placed added pressure on the indigent in the eighteenth century. As a result, citizens often rioted when they felt abandoned or threatened by the government. The food supply in particular became a focus of political and social conflict as the government's desire to deregulate the grain trade came in conflict with traditional beliefs that government should ensure an adequate food supply. With no political means to affect policy, the poor farmers, agricultural workers, and city wage workers rioted to enforce the sale of grain or flour at a "just" price. Riots were often led by women who could not feed their children. One of the most turbulent riots of the last half of the eighteenth century was the 1775 Flour War in France, prompted by a price increase caused by the 1774 deregulation of the grain trade. In Russia, frustrations with serfdom provoked the 1773 Pugachev rebellion. Emelian Pugachev, positioning himself as a "redeemer tsar," claimed he would save the people from oppression. The government finally captured and executed Pugachev, but only after the rebels had attacked and slain numerous noble families.

Public Opinion and Political Opposition, pp. 738–739

More enduring changes in government were caused by the rise of public opinion as a force independent of court society. This public opinion, expressed in the parlements of France, as well as in salons, Masonic lodges, newspapers, and pamphlets all over Europe, increasingly demanded broader political participation. It based its demand on the Enlightenment idea of individual rights. Monarchs such as Gustavus III of Sweden also appealed to public opinion in order to gain support for reforms. Public opinion could be mobilized to challenge a government, as the Wilkes affair in Great Britain demonstrated. John Wilkes, who was a member of Parliament, attacked the government in his newspaper and was arrested. Parliament denied Wilkes his rightful seat when he was reelected, and a major campaign against Parliamentary corruption was ignited. The devastation caused by the 1780 Gordon riots, which were organized by anti-Catholic crusader Lord George Gordon to protest limited toleration for Catholics, also demonstrated the new power of public opinion to make its voice heard on political matters.

Revolution in North America, pp. 739–742

In Great Britain's North American colonies, the public increasingly came to consider the British government corrupt and despotic. Reformers argued that the British government, by not allowing them representation in Parliament, did not recognize their traditional British liberties. When the furor over John Wilkes failed to produce concrete reforms, American reformers decided they would have to take a stand and, at the end of the Seven Years' War, when the British Parliament introduced new taxes to the colonies, they were met with violent rioting. These taxes were repealed, but the 1773 tax on tea revived opposition that culminated in the Boston Tea Party. Locally organized militias engaged British troops, and the First Continental Congress convened in 1774 and unsuccessfully petitioned the crown for redress. In 1775, the Second Continental Congress organized an army with George Washington at its head. The colonies declared their independence in 1776 in the Declaration of Independence, which was written in the language of the Enlightenment. In a radical departure from European models, the newly independent state created a Republic with a two-house legislature, an indirectly elected president, and an independent judiciary. Although women and slaves were excluded from political participation, the Constitution specified that the government drew its authority from the people. A 1791 Bill of Rights outlined essential individual rights that the government could never overturn.

Key Events
For each question, select the most appropriate response from the choices provided.

1740–1748 War of the Austrian Succession: France, Spain, and Prussia versus Austria and Great Britain

1751–1772 *Encyclopedia* published in France

1756–1763 Seven Years' War fought in Europe, India, and the American colonies

1762 Jean-Jacques Rousseau, *The Social Contract* and *Emile*

1764 Voltaire, *Philosophical Dictionary*

1770 Louis XV of France fails to break the power of the French law courts

1772 First partition of Poland

1773 Pugachev rebellion of Russian peasants

1776 American Declaration of Independence from Great Britain; James Watt improves the steam engine, making it suitable for new industrial projects; Adam Smith, *The Wealth of Nations*

1780 Joseph II of Austria undertakes a wide-reaching reform program

1781 Immanuel Kant, *The Critique of Pure Reason*

1785 Catherine the Great's Charter of the Nobility grants nobles exclusive control over their serfs in exchange for subservience to the state

1787 Delegates from the states draft a new United States Constitution

1. Who was the chief editor of the *Encyclopedia*?
   a. Denis Diderot
   b. Jean-Jacques Rousseau
   c. David Hume
   d. Voltaire

2. Which of the following countries allied itself with France during the Seven Years' War in a major reversal of alliances that historians call the "Diplomatic Revolution"?
   a. Prussia
   b. Great Britain
   c. Austria
   d. The Dutch Republic

3. In which book did Voltaire attack many of the claims of organized Christianity?
   a. *The Social Contract*
   b. *The Critique of Pure Reason*
   c. *Emile*
   d. The *Philosophical Dictionary*

4. In 1772, Poland was partitioned among all of the following powers *except*
   a. Russia.
   b. Sweden.
   c. Prussia.
   d. Austria.

5. Which of the following was a consequence of the Pugachev rebellion, which began in 1773?
   a. The monarchy in Russia was severely weakened, allowing the nobles to acquire more power.
   b. The peasantry in Russia gained several concessions and freedoms.
   c. The grain trade was deregulated, which led to more prosperity in the countryside.
   d. The rebellion was brutally suppressed and nobles tightened their control over their serfs.

6. What was James Watt's improved steam engine primarily used for when it was introduced in 1776?
   a. Weaving cloth
   b. Transportation
   c. Generating electricity
   d. Farm equipment

7. Which of the following was *not* part of Joseph II of Austria's reforms?
   a. The compilation of a unified law code
   b. Religious toleration for Jews and Protestants
   c. Elections for major state offices
   d. An improved educational system

8. Immanuel Kant argued in his book *The Critique of Pure Reason* that
   a. any social problem could be solved with the application of human reason.
   b. all humans had enough reason to act morally in society.
   c. philosophers should not concern themselves with worldly affairs.
   d. some philosophical questions were unanswerable by reason alone.

Key Terms
Match each key term to its definition.

A. **abolitionists** (p. 713)
B. **atheist** (p. 712)
C. **deist** (p. 712)
D. **enlightened despots** (p. 729)
E. **Freemasons** (p. 723)
F. **Hasidim** (p. 721)
G. **industrialization** (p. 728)
H. **laissez-faire** (p. 716)
I. **Methodism** (p. 721)
J. **philosophes** (p. 708)
K. **romanticism** (p. 720)
L. **salons** (p. 711)

1. _____ Public intellectuals of the Enlightenment who wrote on subjects ranging from current affairs to art criticism with the goal of furthering reform in society.

2. _____ Informal gatherings, usually sponsored by middle-class or aristocratic women, that provided a forum for new ideas and an opportunity to establish new intellectual contacts among supporters of the Enlightenment; works that could not be published officially were read aloud. (The word in French means "living rooms.")

3. _____ A person who does not believe in the existence of God.

4. _____ A person who believes in God but gives him no active role in human affairs, and during the Enlightenment believed that a benevolent, all-knowing God had designed the universe and set it in motion but no longer intervened in the functioning of the universe. This person might belong to no particular church (Catholic or Protestant).

5. _____ Advocates of the abolition of the slave trade and of slavery.

6. _____ An economic doctrine developed by Adam Smith based on his reading of the French physiocrats who advocated freeing the economy from government intervention and control. (The term is French for "to leave alone.")

7. _____ A view of art and literature that traced its emphasis on individual genius, deep emotion, and the joys of nature to thinkers like Rousseau who had scolded the Enlightenment writers for ignoring those aspects of life that escaped and even conflicted with the power of reason.

8. _____ A religious group within Judaism whose members pray in a highly emotional fashion and wear rustic clothing to emphasize their piety; founded by Ba'al Shem Tov in the 1740s and 1750s, and especially important in Poland-Lithuania. (The word is Hebrew for "most pious.")

9. _____ A religious movement founded by John Wesley that broke away from the Anglican church in Great Britain and insisted on strict self-discipline and a "methodical" approach to religious study and observance. Wesley emphasized an intense personal experience of salvation and a life of thrift, abstinence, and hard work.

10. _____ Members of Masonic lodges, which were based on the rituals of stonemasons' guilds and provided a place where nobles and middle-class professionals (and even some artisans) shared interest in the Enlightenment and reform; lodges drew up constitutions and voted in elections. The movement began in Great Britain and spread eastward across Europe.

11. _____ The process of economic transformation that began in Great Britain in the 1770s and 1780s; its most striking features were the introduction of steam engines to power machinery and the concentration of those machines in factories which mass-produced cotton cloth from cotton grown in the British colonies.

12. _____ A political term that refers to rulers who tried to promote reform without giving up their own supreme political power; the best examples were Catherine the Great of Russia, Frederick the Great of Prussia, and Joseph II of Austria. Also called enlightened absolutists.

Identification
This activity tests your recall of significant people, places, and events from this chapter. Fill in the blank with the correct answer.

1. _____ hosted the best-known salon in Paris.

2. An important example of female philosophes, _____, was Voltaire's lover and taught him much of what he knew about science.

3. In his book *The Natural History of Religion*, _____ argues that the belief in God rests on superstition and fear rather than on reason.

4. Believing that individual interests naturally harmonized with those of society as a whole, _____ advocated the concept of laissez-faire, in which the economy should be freed from government intervention and control.

5. Insisting on strict self-discipline and a methodical approach to religious study and observance, _____ preached a new brand of Protestantism in England that evolved into Methodism.

6. Employing neoclassical motifs, the English potter _____ created a mass market for domestic crockery that appealed to middle-class desires to emulate the rich and royal.

7. As an indication of how patterns of composing music had changed from occasional pieces for the court and noble patrons to works that could be performed repeatedly for paying audiences, _____ wrote only nine symphonies during his career.

8. Although neoclassical tastes were coming into fashion, other artistic styles were also supported, as seen in the palace _____ built in the rococo style and named Sans-souci.

9. The improved steam engine developed in 1776 by _____ became one of the cornerstones of the Industrial Revolution.

10. In the 1780s, Edmund Cartwright designed a _____, which allowed textiles to be manufactured by semiskilled laborers instead of skilled weavers.

11. The War of Austrian Succession began when a coalition of European sovereigns opposed _____ as heir to the Habsburg crown lands.

12. When the mentally unstable _____ came to the throne in 1762, Russia withdrew from the Seven Years' War.

13. With the Treaty of _____, signed in 1763, France ceded its territories in Canada to Great Britain in exchange for keeping its rich West Indian islands.

14. When _____ inherited the Habsburg throne from his brother in 1790, he was pressured by the nobility to overturn many of the reforms his brother had made in the 1780s.

15. A believer in the principles of the physiocrats, _____ was appointed as chief minister to Louis XVI and tried unsuccessfully to free the grain trade and suppress guilds.

16. The so-called _____ in France was caused by the deregulation of the grain trade in 1774.

17. Claiming to be the Tsar _____, the dead husband of Catherine II, Emelian Pugachev led a rebellion in Russia between 1773 and 1775.

18. Calling himself "the first citizen of a free people," _____ turned to public opinion to seek support against aristocratic opposition to reform.

19. In his play *The Marriage of Figaro*, _____ harshly criticized the privileges of the nobility.

20. In 1773, the _____ revived resistance to British governmental policy in its North American colonies.

CHAPTER REVIEW

Self-Test and Analytical Exercises

Multiple Choice   *Select the best answer from the four choices provided.*

1. Who wrote *The Natural History of Religion* (1755), which argued that belief in God rested on superstition and fear rather than on reason?
   a. Voltaire
   b. Jean-Jacques Rousseau
   c. Immanuel Kant
   d. David Hume

2. Who were deists?
   a. Individuals who believed in God, but rejected the idea that such a being took a role in earthly affairs
   b. Persons who denied the existence of God
   c. Those who defended religious traditions against atheism
   d. Church officials who persecuted Enlightenment thinkers

3. Who wrote the *Philosophical Dictionary* in 1764 and attacked most of the claims of organized Christianity, both Catholic and Protestant?
   a. Denis Diderot
   b. Abbé Guillaume Raynal
   c. Voltaire
   d. David Hume

4. What was the Enlightenment attitude toward slavery?
   a. All Enlightenment thinkers opposed slavery because they were committed to the freedom of all human beings.
   b. Although some Enlightenment thinkers denounced slavery as an infringement of natural human rights, others argued that blacks were "naturally inferior," and thus undeserving of the same consideration afforded whites.
   c. Enlightenment thinkers saw slavery as a necessary evil because slavery supported the European economic system that funded their reforms.
   d. Focused primarily on intellectual pursuits, Enlightenment thinkers had few opinions regarding slavery.

5. What were the general trends in reading and publishing during this period?
   a. Universities took the lead as the authorities on literary taste.
   b. There were fewer books being published on religion and the church-going public was shrinking.
   c. There was a vast increase in the publication of books aimed at working-class readers.
   d. There were more books being published on a wider variety of subjects and serving a mainly middle- and upper-class reading public.

6. What did European aristocrats do to transform their seigneurial dues in the face of rising prices and the commercialization of agriculture?
   a. They abolished all of their peasants' legal rights and demanded absolute obedience and 85 percent of surpluses.
   b. They converted them into cash payments.
   c. They reduced the amount of money that the peasants had to pay in order to prevent social disorder.
   d. They converted cash payments into other kinds of obligations and duties for the peasantry.

7. Among the elite classes, how did attitudes toward children change?
   a. As a result of religious awakenings in response to the Enlightenment, children were increasingly viewed as little sinners in need of harsh discipline.
   b. Children became less of a focus in elite families because they were incapable of the intellectual pursuits of utmost concern to adults.
   c. As Rousseau's ideas spread, children were left to develop entirely without supervision or limits.
   d. Children were no longer considered miniature adults, and books about and for children became popular.

8. What were the dominant trends in lower-class life during this time?
   a. All lower-class people lived in abject poverty, which local governments and charities did nothing to try to change.
   b. Peasants producing surpluses, shopkeepers, and artisans prospered during a period of rising prices and growing demand, but often destitute day laborers and peasants with insufficient land holdings were often forced to migrate to cities or wander the countryside in search of food and work.
   c. The poor took part in Enlightenment forms of culture and entertainment, as they were given free concerts and books by the upper classes as part of Enlightenment social reform.
   d. The disadvantaged were given generous and comprehensive benefits when they became sick or unable to work; workhouses were able to keep them healthy and well fed because enlightened governments made it a point to care for their people.

9. Which treaty ended the Seven Years' War and established British dominance in North America?
   a. The Treaty of Aix-la-Chapelle
   b. The Treaty of Paris
   c. The Pragmatic Sanction
   d. The Treaty of Austrian Succession

10. What was the "canton system"?
   a. A Russian system for imprisoning revolutionaries begun by Peter III, which helped slow the spread of Enlightenment ideals
   b. A system of Prussian military enrollment instituted by Frederick William I
   c. A new Swiss manner of diplomacy ushered in after the Treaty of Paris
   d. A new type of French military strategy involving long rows of infantrymen firing their weapons in turn

11. Which powers divided up Poland-Lithuania in 1772?
   a. Austria, the Ottoman Empire, and Prussia
   b. Prussia, Lithuania, and Russia
   c. Austria, Prussia, and Sweden
   d. Austria, Prussia, and Russia

12. During the eighteenth century, warfare was
   a. vicious, resulting in the mass murder of civilians and the implementation of terrorist tactics.
   b. conducted in small, localized battles that had little influence on the European balance of power.
   c. justified as necessary to preserve religion against rationalism.
   d. fought by professional armies according to more cautious and calculating strategies.

13. What was the Flour War?
    a. A turbulent series of food riots in France following a deregulation of the grain trade in 1774
    b. A Russian rebellion led by an Army deserter in 1773
    c. A Paris riot that began when the government forced grain merchants to sell grain at a cheap price
    d. A trade war between France and the Dutch Republic over the international trade in grain

14. Which monarch described herself/himself as "the first citizen of a free people"?
    a. Catherine the Great of Russia
    b. George III of England
    c. Louis XV of France
    d. Gustavus III of Sweden

15. During food riots,
    a. participants usually ransacked mills and stole grain as a way to gather private stockpiles of cereals.
    b. participants forced the sale of grain or flour at what they believed was a "just" price.
    c. participants usually attacked aristocratic landowners who were withholding grain from the market.
    d. men usually took the most active roles, while women avoided the danger of potential street violence and stayed at home.

16. Who wrote the original version of *The Marriage of Figaro*?
    a. Wolfgang Amadeus Mozart
    b. Pierre-Augustin Caron de Beaumarchais
    c. Cesare Beccaria
    d. Madame du Barry

17. Who were the philosophes?
    a. Opponents of reform who defended the prerogatives of religious doctrine
    b. European intellectuals who promoted the study of the abstract theories of Aristotle, Plato, and Socrates
    c. The intellectual writers of the Enlightenment who, disregarding abstract philosophical theories, dedicated themselves to solving the real problems of the world
    d. Constitutionalist politicians who advocated an end of monarchy and the establishment of democracy

18. Laissez-faire refers to an economic theory
    a. based on mercantilism, that argues governments should actively intervene in the economy to increase societal wealth.
    b. that societal wealth could reach its full potential only under a republican form of government.
    c. that argues governments should leave individual enterprises free from excessive interference.
    d. that called for hoarding gold and silver in order to stimulate the forces of supply and demand.

19. What argument did Jean-Jacques Rousseau make in his book, *The Social Contract*?
    a. Individual moral freedom could be achieved only by learning to subject one's individual will to the good of the community.
    b. Government should protect individual freedoms in obedience to natural social law.
    c. Members of society are free to rebel when governments break the social contract of justice.
    d. The social contract between monarch and subject must be modeled on the social contract between husband and wife.

20. Which statement *best* describes the "republic of letters"?
    a. This group of Enlightenment thinkers pushed for a republican political ideal; that is, representative government.
    b. The philosophes of the world saw themselves united in a cosmopolitan community that transcended national boundaries and was dedicated to intellectual pursuits and the ideals of reason, reform, and freedom.
    c. This underground group of political radicals, who opposed monarchy and absolutist rule, wrote letters to European leaders on behalf of the plight of the peasantry.
    d. As an exclusively French gathering of philosophical thinkers, the republic of letters organized political and social reforms in Paris in the decades following the death of Louis XIV.

21. Which of the following was *not* a change in European sexual mores during this period?
    a. The out-of-wedlock birthrate rose from 5 percent to nearly 20 percent by the end of the eighteenth century.
    b. There was an increase in the number of abandoned babies
    c. Greater toleration for homosexuality existed
    d. Parents became anxious about their children's sexuality

22. Which country led the Industrial Revolution?
    a. The Dutch Republic
    b. France
    c. England
    d. The American colonies

23. Which of the following was *not* a trend leading toward industrialization?
    a. Dramatic population increases
    b. A shift away from the production of cotton goods and toward woolens
    c. The introduction of steam-driven machinery
    d. The establishment of factories to concentrate the labor of workers

24. The new artistic and architectural style featuring an emphasis on Greek and Roman styles was called
    a. baroque.
    b. rococo.
    c. Sans-souci.
    d. neoclassicism.

25. Enlightenment ideas and absolutism
    a. were entirely incompatible.
    b. were united in their opposition to constitutionalism.
    c. were often combined as Europe's "enlightened despots" introduced reforms while maintaining their absolutist powers.
    d. were natural allies in the fight to abolish slavery.

26. Who were the Jesuits?
    a. A leading group of Protestant educators
    b. A group of Enlightenment thinkers who promoted secular ideas in European education
    c. The major Catholic teaching order and missionary network
    d. A group of law and prison reformers

27. Which enlightened absolutist leader had the most success in promoting religious toleration?
    a. Frederick William I
    b. Louis XVI
    c. Pope Clement XIV
    d. Joseph II

28. The implementation of Enlightenment reforms by rulers
    a. were often successfully resisted by groups that felt threatened by innovation, like the nobility.
    b. were always successful because absolutist rulers did not have to abide by the concerns of their people.
    c. were very popular with all members of the nobility, who knew that social reform could only be beneficial.
    d. frequently led to terrorist retaliation and even outright revolution.

29. Who were the "physiocrats"?
    a. A group of Enlightenment scientists who argued for educational reform
    b. A Catholic education society that ran a worldwide missionary network
    c. A new type of court in France, in which judges no longer owned their offices
    d. A group of economists who urged the French government to deregulate the grain trade and reform taxation

30. The American War of Independence was
    a. driven by ideas unique to the American colonies.
    b. a reaction to the fact that American colonists had always paid much higher taxes to Britain than did the residents of Britain.
    c. born of a common Atlantic culture of Enlightenment ideas and a belief in traditional British liberties.
    d. a reaction to the increased French threat in North America following the Seven Years' War.

31. American colonial resistance to British rule was largely driven by
    a. the imposition of new taxes.
    b. the brutality of British soldiers in suppressing the Boston Tea Party.
    c. fear of the French.
    d. the failure of the "Wilkes and Liberty" movement.

32. The American colonists
    a. had no interest in justifying their actions to Europeans still living in monarchies.
    b. received assistance from several European powers and the support of enlightened public opinion.
    c. created a social contract in which freedom was to be achieved by subjecting the individual will to the good of the community.
    d. abandoned application of Enlightenment principles to gain European assistance.

33. All of the following European powers assisted the American colonists *except*
    a. France.
    b. Austria.
    c. the Dutch Republic.
    d. Spain.

Short Answer   *Answer each question in three or four sentences.*

The Enlightenment at Its Height

1. Who were the philosophes and what did they advocate?

2. How were the ideas of the Enlightenment disseminated?

3. What were the contrasting Enlightenment views on the relationship between the individual and society?

Society and Culture in an Age of Enlightenment

4. Describe some of the new styles of travel, architecture, and the arts that appeared during this period.

5. What was the influence of the Enlightenment on the middle class?

6. What were some of the changes in sexual behavior and mores during this period?

State Power in an Era of Reform

7. How did absolutist rulers react to Enlightenment ideas?

8. How did a more literate public and a growing press affect governments?

9. What was the relationship between enlightened state reform and religion?

Rebellions Against State Power

10. What was the main focus of popular discontent and resistance during this period, and what form did popular resistance take?

11. How did the American Revolution demonstrate the extent to which the political "rules of the game" changed as a result of Enlightenment ideals?

12. What was the Wilkes affair and how did it move the American colonies toward a war for independence?

BUILDING HISTORICAL SKILLS

Reading Maps   *Write a brief, paragraph-length response to each of the following questions based on* **Map 19.3: The Seven Years' War, 1756–1763 (p. 732).**

1. What were the two main alliances during the Seven Years' War?

2. What were the main theaters of fighting during the Seven Years' War?

Reading Illustrations   *Write a brief, paragraph-length response to each of the following questions based on the illustration* **Broken Eggs (p. 725).**

1. What changes in artistic tastes does this painting represent?

2. What are some of the social changes of the time that might have influenced this painting?

Reading Historical Documents   *Write a brief, paragraph-length response to each of the following questions based on the documents in your book.*

Jean-Jacques Rousseau, The Social Contract, 1762 (p. 718)

1. How does Rousseau reconcile individual freedom with the need to live according to laws within a society?

2. How does this document represent a break from traditional notions of government?

Thomas Jefferson, Declaration of Independence, July 4, 1776 (p. 740)

3. In which ways is this document a product of the Enlightenment?

4. How does this document go beyond what original Enlightenment thinkers advocated?

Contrasting Views: Women and the Enlightenment (pp. 714–715)

5. What is the main issue at stake in these documents, and what differing opinion did each writer hold regarding it?

6. Why did the notion of the differences between the sexes become such a focus of debate among Enlightenment writers?

The Cataclysm of Revolution
1789–1800

CHAPTER OVERVIEW

Chapter Questions   *Keep these questions in mind as you go through the study guide chapter.*

1. What did the various movements of reform and revolution that occurred in the 1780s have in common?

2. What were the characteristics of the different stages of the French Revolution?

3. Why, and in what way, did the revolutionary government in France seek to effect a cultural revolution?

4. Why did various groups and individuals resist the French Revolution?

5. What impact did the French Revolution have on the rest of Europe?

Chapter Summary

The Revolutionary Wave, 1787–1789

Between 1787 and 1789, revolts in the name of liberty broke out in the Dutch Republic, the Austrian Netherlands, Poland, and France, while, at the same time, the United States of America prepared a new federal constitution. Historians sometimes refer to this series of revolts as the Atlantic revolutions. These were the product of long-term prosperity and high expectations, as Europeans in general were wealthier, healthier, more numerous, and better educated than they had ever been before.

Protesters in the Low Countries and Poland,
pp. 749–752

In the Dutch Republic, the Patriots wanted to reduce the powers of the *stadholder*, the Prince of Orange. Patriot

protest began among middle-class bankers, merchants, and writers but soon gained a wider audience by demanding political reforms and forming citizen militias called Free Corps. In 1787, a national assembly of the Free Corps joined with a group of Patriot Regents to demand a republic. Although the Free Corps overpowered the Prince of Orange's troops, Frederick II of Prussia sent troops to intervene, putting an end to the rebellion. The Patriots were then weakened by internal divisions between the Patriot Regents and the Free Corps, allowing the Prince of Orange to reestablish control. The Austrian Netherlands was another arena for rebellion. Joseph II's reforms, which included the reorganization of the administrative and judicial system, caused nobles and lawyers to organize to defend their traditional interests. Democrats were attracted to the movement as well and, by late 1789, each province had declared independence and announced the federation of the United States of Belgium. But when democrats demanded democracy, aristocratic leaders banded with the Catholic clergy and peasants, who opposed the urban democrats. This division opened the way for the new emperor Leopold II (r. 1790–1792) to reestablish control. A Patriot party emerged in Poland as well. Composed of a few aristocrats, middle-class professionals, clergy who espoused Enlightenment ideas, and the king, the Patriots sought to modernize Polish politics in order to avoid a further loss of territory like that which occurred in the 1772 partition. Austria and Prussia allowed the reform movement to proceed but, shortly after the new parliament enacted the constitution of 1791, Catherine II of Russia intervened to put down the rebellion.

Origins of the French Revolution, 1787–1789,
pp. 752–756

The French Revolution began with a fiscal crisis. With half the national budget going to pay interest on the debt that had accumulated during past wars, and unwilling to risk alienating an increasingly vocal public opinion by declaring bankruptcy, the French crown needed to overhaul the inequitable and inefficient tax system. The king was eventually forced to call a meeting of the Estates General, a representative body that had not met since 1614. Thousands of men and women (by proxy) met all over France to elect representatives to the three orders that made up the Estates General: the First Estate represented clergy, the Second Estate represented the nobility, and the Third Estate represented the commoners. Each group had grievances: the Third Estate denounced the traditional privileges of the nobility and called for voting by head rather than order, which would prevent the first two estates from overriding the voice of the Third Estate. The deputies arrived at Versailles in May 1789, but the actual meeting began only after weeks of stalemate over the question of whether to vote by head or by order. The Third Estate finally broke away from the meeting and declared itself the National Assembly on June 17, 1789. The clergy joined them two days later and, on June 20, when they were forced to meet in a nearby tennis court, the National Assembly swore they would not disband until they had written a constitution. Although Louis XVI publicly appeared to honor the new assembly, he had privately ordered thousands of soldiers to march on Paris. When the king fired his popular finance minister Jacques Necker on July 11, rumors spread quickly through Paris and the populace began to arm themselves. On July 14, Parisian crowds stormed the Bastille—a fortified prison that symbolized royal authority—in a fierce battle that left more than one hundred people dead. The fall of the Bastille set an important precedent by demonstrating that the common people were willing to intervene violently at a crucial political moment.

From Monarchy to Republic, 1789–1793

Unlike the Dutch and Belgian uprisings, the French Revolution did not come to a quick end. Revolutionaries first tried to establish a constitutional monarchy based on the Enlightenment principles of human rights and rational government. This failed when the king tried to raise a counterrevolutionary army. New tensions culminated in a second revolution on August 10, 1792, that deposed the king and established a republic.

The Revolution of Rights and Reason, pp. 757–761

Before drafting a constitution, the National Assembly had to confront growing violence in the countryside. Peasants in the French countryside, fearing that the presence of beggars and vagrants indicated an aristocratic plot, attacked their landlords in a movement historians refer to as the Great Fear. To restore order, the deputies of the new National Assembly abolished seigneurial dues, special legal privileges, and serfdom on August 4. Three weeks later, the assembly issued the Declaration of the Rights of Man and Citizen, which granted freedom of religion, freedom of the press, equality of taxation, and equality before the law. The document raised questions about the inclusion of blacks (free and enslaved), Jews, Protestants, and women. Protestants and Jews received the right to vote, and women were declared citizens but could not vote. In her 1791 *Declaration of the Rights of Women,* Olympe de Gouges pointed out that the revolutionaries' own language implied that women should be included. The Constitution of 1791, however, gave voting rights only to white men who passed a test of wealth. With this constitution, France became a constitutional monarchy with a one-house legislature, a new administrative system based on eighty-three departments, and a new tax system. In 1790, the deputies attempted to reform the hierarchy of the Catholic church by issuing the Civil Constitution of the Clergy. The government called for the election of parish priests and started paying clergy members a salary. Church property was used as a guarantee for a new currency, *assignats,* which were quickly rendered less valuable due to inflation. In November 1790, the National Assembly required the clergy to swear an oath of loyalty to the Civil Constitution of the Clergy, which about half the clergy refused. Resistance and even riots occasioned by this question of the oath then weakened the revolutionary government.

The End of Monarchy, pp. 761–763

In June of 1791, Louis XVI and his family attempted to flee France to Austria. When they were captured and brought back to Paris, some now regarded them traitors. Louis XVI was forced to endorse the Constitution, and a new Legislative Assembly was elected. Hoping that a war would overturn the Revolution, Louis declared war on Austria on April 21, 1792, an action that many deputies believed would reveal the king's treachery. Prussia immediately allied with Austria, and thousands of aristocrats joined the Austrian army. At first, the Austrians easily defeated the French and, as Prussian troops advanced toward Paris, the common people—also called the *sans-culottes*—discussed the news in newly organized political clubs, the most influential of which was known as the Jacobin Club. On August 10, 1792, the sans-culottes attacked the Tuileries palace. The Legislative Assembly agreed to new elections by universal male suffrage with no wealth qualifications, and became the National Convention. When the National Convention met on September 22, 1792, it abolished the monarchy and declared France a republic. Prussian troops continued their advance, and crowds of Parisians stormed the prisons and killed supposed traitors in the September massacres. In November and December, deputies debated the fate of the former king. The Girondins resented the growing power of the Parisian militants and favored reprimanding or exiling the king, but the Mountain, whose members were allied with the Parisian militants, favored execution. The Mountain won, and Louis XVI was executed on January 21, 1793.

Terror and Resistance

The execution of the king did not end the new regime's problems. The continuing war required money and soldiers, which provoked resistance in parts of France. In response to growing pressure, the National Convention named a Committee of Public Safety led by Maximilien Robespierre (1758–1794) to supervise the war effort and to root out counterrevolutionaries. Robespierre began a massive campaign of political reeducation combined with the brutal suppression of dissent known as the Terror.

Robespierre and the Committee of Public Safety, pp. 763–765

The conflict between the Girondins and the Mountain continued after the king's execution, when militants called for the expulsion of the Girondins. The Girondins responded by arresting several Parisian leaders. The militants organized a demonstration, invaded the National Convention on June 2, 1793, and forced the arrest of twenty-nine Girondins. The Convention agreed to establish paramilitary "revolutionary armies" to enforce the distribution of grain and agreed to speed up the revolutionary courts. The Convention created the Committee of Public Safety, which under Robespierre quickly acquired almost total control of the government. In September 1793, the Convention decided that emergency measures were needed and decreed the beginning of the Terror. Despite Robespierre's own belief in the importance of freedom and democracy, he became the chief proponent of the Terror, which aimed to eradicate dissent by purging unreliable officials, uncovering dissidents, and eliminating enemies of the Revolution. The Terror also organized the war effort to great success, establishing the first universal draft of men in history. The execution of the king had caused Prussia, Great Britain, Spain, Sardinia, and the Dutch Republic to join the war against France. However, with the entire country mobilized for war, the French armies stopped the advances of the allied powers by the end of 1793, and, in the summer of 1794, they invaded the Austrian Netherlands and crossed the Rhine River.

The Republic of Virtue, 1793–1794, pp. 765–768

In addition to fighting the war and eliminating domestic enemies, the Terror attempted a cultural revolution. Writings deemed counterrevolutionary were censored; whereas songs, paintings, books, posters, and even cham-

ber pots educated the population in the new revolutionary virtues. Festivals emerged with the spontaneous planting of "liberty trees" in villages and towns in 1789. Future festivals, such as the Festival of Unity, which celebrated the first anniversary of the overthrow of the monarchy, were organized by the government to destroy the mystique of monarchy and to create a sacred republic. The government also undertook a campaign of de-Christianization to break down the influence of Catholicism. Churches were closed and clergy were told to revoke their vows. Extremists attempted to establish a Cult of Reason to replace Christianity, but fear that devout rural populations would protest forced the government to offer an alternative: the Cult of Supreme Being. The Convention attempted to set up a system of free and compulsory primary schools for boys and girls but, without a clergy trained to teach, the effort failed, and school attendance dropped dramatically. Those who adhered to the Revolution were urged to manifest the Revolution in everything: by flying the tricolor flag of the republic, using republican language, and no longer naming children after biblical characters and saints. To create a people shaped by reason and revolutionary virtue, the government changed the method of measuring: from the various units of measurement used throughout France to the metric system. A new calendar—in which Year I dated from the beginning of the republic on September 22, 1792—marked the passage of time. The rules governing family organization also changed. Marriage became a civil contract and divorce was easy to obtain. Equal inheritance replaced the previous practice of passing all of one's possessions to the eldest son.

Resisting the Revolution, pp. 767–768

The magnitude of the changes instituted by the revolutionary government brought about resistance. Women expressed discontent concerning food shortages and high prices. Their complaints sometimes turned into demonstrations or riots. Individuals resisted as well: Charlotte Corday, a supporter of the more moderate Girondins, murdered Jean-Paul Marat, a fervent supporter of radical and violent revolution. Catholics rioted in places with large Protestant or Jewish populations (who tended to support the Revolution), and insurrection erupted in several areas when the Girondins were arrested in June 1793. Resistance was greatest in the Vendée, a region in western France, and, between March and December 1793, peasants, artisans, and weavers from the countryside joined under noble leadership to attack towns where the Revolution was firmly established. The peasants fought to defend Catholicism, to protest the draft, and to challenge the economic dominance of the towns. In the fighting that ensued, both sides committed horrible atrocities; many thousands of republican soldiers and civilians lost their lives; rebel deaths have been estimated at between 20,000 to 250,000 or perhaps even higher.

The Fall of Robespierre and the End of the Terror, 1794–1799, pp. 768–770

In the fall of 1793, the government began suppressing prorevolutionary groups. The first to go were women's political clubs, in particular the Society of Revolutionary Republican Women. Next, a group of "ultrarevolutionaries" was arrested; they were followed by the more moderate "indulgents," including the deputy Georges-Jacques Danton, a former member of the Committee of Public Safety. After these groups were eliminated, the Terror worsened. Although the military situation improved (with a French victory over the main Austrian army), the political situation deteriorated: those accused of crimes were no longer allowed counsel, fewer jurors were necessary for conviction, and judgments were now either acquittal or death. The number of executions rose alarmingly. Fearing for the safety of its members, in July 1794 (the revolutionary month of Thermidor), the Convention ended the Terror by arresting and executing Robespierre and his followers. The Convention then ordered new elections and drew up a new constitution that set up a two-house legislature and gave executive powers to a Directory headed by five directors. The new government released suspects and engineered a truce in the Vendée. Within a year, all the Jacobin Clubs were closed. Leading "Terrorists" were put to death and, during the White Terror in the southeast, paramilitary bands attacked those who had previously held power during the Jacobins' Red Terror. Churches reopened, and people sought escape from the atmosphere and anxiety of the Terror in a new pursuit of pleasure. The new government of the Directory lasted until 1799.

Revolution on the March

From 1792 until 1815, war raged throughout Europe almost constantly, and France proved to be an even more formidable opponent than it had been during the reign of Louis XIV. New means of mobilizing and organizing soldiers enabled the French to dominate Europe for a generation. The influence of the Revolution as a political model and the threat of French military conquest challenged the traditional order.

Arms and Conquests, pp. 770–772

In 1793, the French armies could have been easily defeated. Despite large numbers of new recruits, the army was plagued by disease, desertion, and the lack of food. But Prussia, Russia, and Austria were too preoccupied with Poland to engage France. By the summer of 1794, strengthened by a wish to defend the republic they had built, French soldiers fought hard. As they moved into the Austrian Netherlands, Mainz, Savoy, and Nice, French armies were welcomed, and officers organized Jacobin Clubs that petitioned for annexation to France. French legislation that abolished seigneurial dues was then introduced. When Prussia declared neutrality in 1795, French armies moved into the Dutch Republic, creating a new satellite called the Batavian Republic. In 1796–1797, young general Napoleon Bonaparte crossed into northern Italy to create the Cisalpine Republic; in 1798, the French turned the Swiss cantons into the Helvetic Republic; and, in 1798, they took over the papal states and renamed them the Roman Republic, forcing the pope to flee. Bonaparte also invaded Egypt in 1798. Although a military failure, the campaign allowed the French to introduce Enlightenment-inspired reforms into Egyptian law. All over Europe, constant war caused a rising death rate and the interruption of commerce and manufacturing.

European Reactions to Revolutionary Change, pp. 773–776

Even those countries not invaded by the French felt the force of the Revolution. In Great Britain, supporters of the Revolution joined constitutional and reform societies, the most important of which—the London Corresponding Society—corresponded with the Jacobin Club in Paris. Pro-French feeling was strong in Ireland, where Catholics and Presbyterians, both excluded from the vote, pressed for secession from England. In 1798, the Society of United Irishmen timed a rebellion to coincide with a French invasion, but it failed. While countries close to France with large middle classes generally sympathized with French ideas, other countries resisted French occupation. In the German Rhineland, gangs of bandits preyed upon the French and Jews (because the French emancipated Jews). After 1793, many intellectuals in the German states turned against the Revolution because of its record of violence and military aggression. These German intellectuals developed an anti-French nationalism followed by an artistic and intellectual regeneration. Countries farther from France were less affected, although there were exceptions. In Sweden, the assassination of King Gustavus III (r. 1771–1792) raised unfounded fears of a Jacobin plot. In Russia, 278 outbreaks of peasant unrest occurred between 1796 and 1798.

Poland Extinguished, 1793–1795, pp. 776–779

The spirit of revolt was especially strong in Poland, which had been deprived of one-third of its territory by the First Partition of Poland in 1772. While Prussia and Austria were fighting the French to the west, Catherine II sent Russian troops to quell Polish resistance. Prussia and Russia took possession of additional portions of Polish territory in the Second Partition of Poland in 1793. The Polish reform movement became more pro-French and, in the spring of 1794, Tadeusz Kosciuszko incited an uprising that spread from Cracow to Warsaw and the old Lithuanian capital, Vilnius. The uprising failed, in part because Kosciuszko could not offer serfs complete freedom without alienating the nobles. Russia, Prussia, and Austria combined wiped Poland off the map in the Third Partition of 1795.

Revolution in the Colonies, pp. 777–779

Revolution reached the French Caribbean colonies, the most important of which was St. Domingue. Most French revolutionaries had not considered slavery an important issue except for its importance to the French economy. In August 1791, slaves in northern St. Domingue organized a revolt. To restore authority over the slaves, the Legislative Assembly in Paris granted civil and political rights to free blacks. Angered white planters and merchants signed a treaty with Great Britain, while Spain offered freedom to slaves who joined the Spanish armies that controlled the rest of the island. In August 1793, the French commissioner freed all the slaves and, following his lead, the National Convention formally abolished slavery in February 1794. François Dominique Toussaint L'Ouverture (1743–1803), an ex-slave who served as a general in the Spanish army, changed sides and joined the French. The vicious fighting that continued in the colony left the economy in ruins. Toussaint, who had been named governor of the island, was arrested in 1802 by order of Napoleon Bonaparte, who attempted to restore slavery. Toussaint died in a French prison. In 1804, the remaining black generals defeated Napoleon's forces and proclaimed the Republic of Haiti.

The Rise of Napoleon Bonaparte, pp. 780–782

Napoleon Bonaparte (1769–1821) rose from a penniless artillery officer to the supreme ruler of France in four years. After his astounding military successes in the Italian campaigns of 1796–1797, he defeated the Piedmontese and the Austrians. He established client republics that were dependent upon him by negotiating directly with the Austrians and paying his army with the cash he received as tribute. Napoleon quieted any discontent in the Directory by sending confiscated Italian art back to France. While French soldiers were on earlier campaigns in Egypt, they uncovered the Rosetta stone, a slab of black basalt dating back to 196 B.C.E. that was inscribed with Egyptian hieroglyphics, Demotic, and Greek, allowing them to decipher hieroglyphs for the first time. Bonaparte returned to France in October 1799, when France was in the midst of a series of crises. Anti-Directory conspirators, including Bonaparte's brother,

arranged for the overthrow of the legislature, allowing a rump assembly to abolish the Directory and establish the Consulate, a three-man executive branch. Bonaparte became the First Consul, and a new constitution was written and submitted to the public for a vote. Many did not vote; the new government therefore falsified the results so as to make the Consulate appear legitimate.

Key Events   *For each question, select the most appropriate response from the choices provided.*

1787 Dutch Patriot revolt is stifled by Prussian invasion

1788 Beginning of resistance of Austrian Netherlands against reforms of Joseph II; opening of reform parliament in Poland

1789 French Revolution begins

1790 Internal divisions lead to collapse of resistance in Austrian Netherlands

1791 Beginning of slave revolt in St. Domingue (Haiti)

1792 Beginning of war between France and the rest of Europe; second revolution of August 10 overthrows monarchy

1793 Second Partition of Poland by Austria and Russia; Louis XVI of France executed for treason

1794 Abolition of slavery in French colonies; Robespierre's government by terror falls

1795 Third (final) Partition of Poland

1797–1798 Creation of "sister" republics in Italian states and Switzerland

1799 Bonaparte comes to power in a coup that effectively ends the French Revolution

1. What was the Dutch Patriot revolt in 1787 trying to accomplish?
   a. The overthrow of the House of Orange
   b. Universal voting rights
   c. Political reforms
   d. The abolition of slavery

2. Why did the resistance movement in the Austrian Netherlands collapse?
   a. It was stifled by a Prussian invasion
   b. There were too many internal divisions among its participants
   c. Its leader was assassinated
   d. The government launched a successful counterrevolutionary newspaper campaign

3. Which French colony experienced a slave revolt in 1791?
   a. Haiti
   b. Canada
   c. Louisiana
   d. India

4. What did the second revolution of August 1792 accomplish?
   a. The abolition of serfdom
   b. The abolition of Catholicism
   c. The restoration of the aristocracy
   d. The overthrow of the monarchy

5. On what charge was Louis XVI executed in 1793?
   a. Tyranny
   b. Treason
   c. Murder
   d. Attempting to escape France

6. What did the National Convention abolish in the French colonies in 1794?
   a. Catholicism
   b. Protestant rights
   c. Slavery
   d. Divorce

7. Who was the chief proponent of the Terror and unofficial head of the Committee of Public Safety?
   a. Georges-Jacques Danton
   b. Maximilien Robespierre
   c. Napoleon Bonaparte
   d. Jean-Paul Marat

8. Which country no longer existed in 1795, because its territory was taken by other powers?
   a. Germany
   b. Denmark
   c. Austria
   d. Poland

9. Which event effectively ended the French Revolution?
   a. Napoleon Bonaparte's coming to power
   b. The execution of Louis XVI
   c. The fall of Robespierre
   d. The adoption of the Constitution

Key Terms   *Match each key term to its definition.*

A. **Atlantic revolutions** (p. 749)
B. **de-Christianization** (p. 766)
C. **Declaration of the Rights of Man and Citizen** (p. 757)
D. **Estates General** (p. 753)
E. **First Consul** (p. 781)
F. **Great Fear** (p. 757)
G. **Jacobin Club** (p. 761)
H. **sans-culottes** (p. 761)
I. **Terror** (p. 763)
J. **Thermidorian Reaction** (p. 770)

1. _____ A term historians use to refer to protest movements that appeared on both sides of the Atlantic in the late 1780s: the new United States prepared a new constitution after winning its independence from Great Britain, while organized revolts occurred in the Dutch Republic, the Austrian Netherlands, and France.

2. _____ A body of deputies from the three estate, or orders, of France; the clergy (First Estate), the nobility (Second Estate), and everyone else (Third Estate); disputes about procedures of voting in this body in 1789 opened the way to the French Revolution.

3. _____ The term used by historians to describe the rural panic of 1789; fears of an aristocratic plot to pay beggars and vagrants to burn crops or barns sometimes turned into peasant attacks on aristocrats or on seigneurial records of peasants' dues kept in the lord's château.

4. _____ The preamble to the French constitution drafted in August 1789; it established the sovereignty of the nation and the equality of rights of citizens and granted freedom of religion, freedom of the press, equality of taxation, and equality before the law.

5. _____ The name given to politically active men from the lower classes (French for "without breeches"); they worked with their hands and wore the long trousers of workingmen rather than the knee breeches of the upper classes.

6. _____ The first and most influential of the political clubs formed during the French Revolution; this club inspired the formation of a national network of clubs whose members dominated the revolutionary government during the period known as the Terror.

7. _____ The emergency government established under the direction of the Committee of Public Safety during the French Revolution; the government aimed to establish a republic of virtue, but to do so it arrested hundreds of thousands of political suspects and executed thousands of ordinary people.

8. _____ Campaign of extremist republicans against organized churches; militants forced priests to give up their vocations and marry, sold off the buildings of the Catholic church, and set up festivals of reason to compete with Catholicism.

9. _____ Violent backlash against the rule of Robespierre that began with his arrest and execution; most of the instruments of the Terror were dismantled and supporters of the Jacobins were harassed or even murdered.

10. _____ The most important of the three consuls established by the French Constitution of 1800; the title, given to Napoleon Bonaparte, was taken from the ancient Roman republic.

Identification

This activity tests your recall of significant people, places, and events from this chapter. Fill in the blank with the correct answer.

1. Louis XVI of France was somewhat receptive to reform in France, as suggested by his granting civil rights to _____ in 1787.

2. Although royal support for the _____ against the British regained much of the prestige France had lost after the Seven Years' War, the debts incurred actually helped bring about the French Revolution and the downfall of the French monarchy.

3. Slandered increasingly by the underground press, the unpopularity of _____ helped undermine the French monarchy as an institution.

4. The calling of the Estates General in 1789 was a particularly momentous occasion in part because this institution had not met since _____.

5. In the midst of a deadlock with the nobility over voting procedure, the Third Estate unilaterally formed the _____ on June 17, 1789.

6. In July 1790, the National Assembly established the _____, by which the clergy would receive a standard salary according to a pay scale, and be elected by their parishioners.

7. On June 20, 1791, Louis XVI tried to escape from Paris with the royal family, but was stopped at _____.

8. Hoping that war might bring about the definitive defeat of the Revolution, Louis XVI declared war on _____ in April 1792.

9. Political clubs were very common in France, but the _____ was the first and most influential of them.

10. The _____ faction of the Convention pushed for the execution of the king and eventually violently suppressed its rivals.

11. Urging violent revolutionary measures in his newspaper *The Friend of the People*, _____ was assassinated by Charlotte Corday in July 1793.

12. In an effort to stabilize prices, the Convention established a _____ in September 1793 that set price limits on essential commodities and wages.

13. A former member of the Committee for Public Safety, _____ was executed on the Committee's instigation in 1794 for favoring a moderation of the Terror.

14. When a new revolutionary calendar was introduced in October 1793, _____ marked its beginning.

15. On the ninth of Thermidor, Year II of the revolutionary calendar, the National Convention arrested _____ and sent him to the guillotine the following day.

16. After the French attacked the Swiss cantons in 1798, they set up the _____ and curtailed many of the Catholic church's privileges.

17. Vowing to "fight Jacobinism," and defeat it in Poland, _____ abolished Poland's reform constitution of May 1791, and easily crushed Polish resistance.

18. Convinced that French Jacobins had been involved in his father's assassination in 1792, _____ insisted on avoiding "licentious liberty."

19. Originally a rebel leader, _____ was made governor of St. Domingue as a reward for his efforts.

20. Arriving in Egypt in 1798, Napoleon was stopped by _____, who destroyed the French fleet while it was anchored in Aboukir Bay.

CHAPTER REVIEW

Self-Test and Analytical Exercises

Multiple Choice   *Select the best answer from the four choices provided.*

1. The French Revolution
   a. was an unexpected political upheaval following a series of other protests in Europe in the 1780s stemming from popular unrest.
   b. followed several successful revolts in the Dutch Republic, the Austrian Netherlands, and Poland.
   c. was predicted by the foremost political analysts of the period, who proposed various preventative reforms but were ignored by the monarchy.
   d. was a direct result of the failed Dutch rebellion of 1787.

2. Which of the following did *not* contribute to the French fiscal crisis?
   a. Debt accumulated by the French in supporting the American War of Independence
   b. A taxation system that exempted the nobility and clergy from most taxes
   c. The lack of a national bank to help raise loans for the government
   d. The tax exemption of the Third Estate, which represented most of the people of France

3. The reforming efforts of Polish patriots sought to
   a. abolish serfdom and declare a democratic state.
   b. take Polish land back from the Prussians and Austrians.
   c. reduce Russian influence over their state and introduce modest, enlightened reforms.
   d. create a new constitutionalist state modeled after the American style of representative government.

4. What was one of the *most important* disputes dividing the Estates General?
   a. Their method of voting
   b. Their chosen meeting place
   c. Their chosen name
   d. Their allotted salaries

5. The tennis court oath was an oath taken by
   a. the clergy never to support the interests of the Third Estate and always to vote with the nobility.
   b. the deputies of the newly declared National Assembly that they would not disband before achieving constitutional reform.
   c. Louis XVI not to take military action against his own people.
   d. the nobility to defend the interests of the state against revolution.

6. Women
   a. accepted their exclusion from the Declaration of the Rights of Man and Citizen without protest.
   b. took few leadership roles in revolutionary activities.
   c. did not write any important revolutionary literature, but did facilitate the spread of information.
   d. joined demonstrations, wrote petitions and tracts, and organized political clubs.

7. The National Assembly granted the right to vote to
   a. all men.
   b. all men who served in the National Guard.
   c. all men and women who possessed a certain amount of wealth.
   d. white men who possessed a certain amount of wealth.

8. What was the new assembly established by the National Assembly and endorsed by Louis XVI in the Constitution of 1791?
   a. The Estates General
   b. The National Convention
   c. The Parlement of Paris
   d. The Legislative Assembly

9. Who abolished the monarchy?
   a. The people of Paris
   b. The Prussian army
   c. The National Convention
   d. The Legislative Assembly

10. The Terror refers to
   a. the period during which the Prussian army sacked Paris.
   b. a program instituted by Robespierre whereby political terror was used by the Committee of Public Safety to crush dissent and reorganize French society.
   c. a period of rural revolts caused by the peasants' refusal to cooperate with the dictates of the revolutionaries in Paris.
   d. the counterrevolutionary violence unleashed by the Girondins in their disputes with the Mountain.

11. The Republic of Virtue was
    a. the official name of the French state following the execution of Louis XVI.
    b. the name of the Constitution's bylaws established by the members of the Committee of Public Safety.
    c. the term used by the Prussian army when referring to the French revolutionary state.
    d. Robespierre's government, which aimed to instill republicanism in the populace via a program of political reeducation.

12. What was the basis of the new calendar instituted by the National Convention?
    a. An ancient calendar used by the Greeks
    b. Reason and republican principles
    c. The Christian calendar
    d. The movement of planet Earth and the sun as proved by scientists working with advanced telescopes

13. The Directory was
    a. a list of all the enemies of the revolution who were scheduled to be executed by the Committee of Public Safety.
    b. the governmental regime headed by five directors that followed the Terror.
    c. a series of directives issued by the Committee of Public Safety.
    d. the final thrust of the French army in its defeat of Austrian forces.

14. Why did the French invade Egypt?
    a. To strike the Ottoman Turks, who were the prime enemies of revolutionary France
    b. To begin a large-scale occupation of Africa and use African resources to fuel the French conquest of Europe
    c. To impede British trade by cutting off the route to India
    d. To confront the British navy anchored in Aboukir Bay under the command of Admiral Horatio Nelson

15. In 1798, the Society of United Irishmen
    a. began a rebellion against British occupying forces timed to coincide with a French invasion, but they were brutally repressed.
    b. joined the fight of the allied powers against France.
    c. succeeded in installing a revolutionary government in Ireland modeled on the French Republic of Virtue.
    d. supported the British government in fighting off a French invasion of England.

16. The Second and Third Partitions of Poland, between 1793 and 1795,
    a. forced Poland to take back land from Lithuania.
    b. made all of Poland a part of Russia.
    c. divided Poland between Austria and Prussia.
    d. completely abolished Poland as an independent country.

17. Napoleon Bonaparte's success was based on
    a. the part he played in running the Terror.
    b. military success and political connections.
    c. his charismatic speeches used to rally French troops.
    d. the booty acquired in his conquest of Egypt used to buy his way into politics.

18. On the eve of the French Revolution, in 1787, the French monarchy
    a. appeared to be secure in its power and had reestablished its prestige after its humiliating defeat in the Seven Years' War.
    b. was seriously disadvantaged, and most Enlightenment thinkers pointed to France as a country ripe for revolution.
    c. was actively resisting reform and was becoming less "enlightened" in its approach to state power.
    d. was clearly willing to replace absolutist power with a constitutionalist system.

19. The name of the citizen militias that pushed for the most radical change in the Dutch Republic was
    a. Free Corps.
    b. Patriot Regents.
    c. Orangists.
    d. stadholders.

20. The French Revolution began with a(an)
    a. fiscal crisis caused by a mounting deficit.
    b. attempt by the monarchy to crack down on dissent.
    c. foreign invasion.
    d. revolt by the lower classes in favor of democracy.

21. Which of the following did *not* lead to the attack on the Bastille?
    a. Louis XVI's firing of Jacques Necker, his finance minister
    b. The massacre by Louis XVI's troops of members of the National Assembly
    c. The marching of thousands of troops toward Paris by order of the king
    d. Fears of a plot by the king to arrest and disperse the members of the National Assembly

22. The National Assembly, on the night of August 4, 1789,
    a. abolished the monarchy and declared France a Republic.
    b. decreed the abolition of "the feudal regime," freeing the serfs and ending the special taxation privileges of the nobles.
    c. executed the king.
    d. declared war on the nobility.

23. Olympe de Gouges, in her *Declaration of the Rights of Women of 1791*, argued that
    a. women should be given all social and economic rights, but stopped short of demanding political rights.
    b. women should have new political and social rights as well as new social and economic responsibilities.
    c. women needed to postpone their demands for equal rights until after a constitutionalist government was implemented.
    d. men should have the leading role in government because they had taken the leading role in the Revolution.

24. The National Assembly did *not*
    a. assemble a legislature responsible for making laws.
    b. allow the king to veto any law he disapproved of.
    c. make all officials elected.
    d. reorganize the administrative division of the country into eighty-three departments.

25. Who were the sans-culottes?
    a. Leaders of the Revolution
    b. Ordinary citizens of Paris, mainly skilled artisans and their families
    c. Rural opponents of the Revolution who sided with the king
    d. The name for members of the new, revolutionary French army

26. The Committee of Public Safety was dominated by
    a. Maximilien Robespierre.
    b. George-Jacques Danton.
    c. Jean-Paul Marat.
    d. the Marquis de Lafayette.

27. What role did Jacques-Louis David play in the French Revolution?
    a. He led the movement that brought down the Committee of Public Safety.
    b. He was an important defender of the monarchy who voted against the execution of Louis XVI.
    c. He was an artist who planned revolutionary festivals.
    d. He edited a newspaper that called for the execution of the king.

28. Who were the "indulgents" during the Terror?
    a. Individuals who took advantage of the chaos to amass personal wealth
    b. Persons who favored a moderation of the Terror
    c. Citizens who favored a restoration of the monarchy
    d. A motley collection of local Parisian politicians

29. The Thermidorian reaction was the
    a. period of extreme violence in Vendée in which thousands of suspected dissenters were killed by supporters of Robespierre.
    b. revolt of the rural peasantry against the Revolution.
    c. period in which the Convention turned against Robespierre and his regime of Terror.
    d. abolition of the Convention by the Committee of Public Safety.

30. When French armies occupied an area, they
    a. brutally repressed the people living there according to the dictates of the Terror.
    b. introduced the laws of the French Republic, such as the abolition of seigneurial dues.
    c. allowed people to set up their own governments, entirely independent of France.
    d. were always regarded as liberators and welcomed by the native-born people.

31. The French revolutionary wars
    a. involved very few casualties because the armies fought primarily in small skirmishes rather than all-out battles.
    b. saw a great advance in medical techniques that reduced casualties through the use of hospitals.
    c. improved trade within France.
    d. disrupted international commerce and caused widespread shortages in France.

32. The German states
    a. were enraged by French religious toleration of the Jews and formed a defensive alliance against the French called the Allemagne League.
    b. experienced an artistic and intellectual revival influenced by anti-French nationalism.
    c. responded to the French Revolution by establishing their own reign of terror on government dissenters.
    d. took up French ideals and encouraged religious toleration of the Jews.

33. How did the French revolutionary government view slavery initially?
    a. It was seen as an insignificant issue and a necessary evil to support the French economy.
    b. The abolition of slavery was a primary objective of the Revolution and one of its first acts.
    c. Because there were no slaves in France, the French saw slavery as a British problem.
    d. French revolutionaries did not believe blacks were deserving of liberty because they were an inferior race.

Short Answer   *Answer each question in three or four sentences.*

The Revolutionary Wave, 1787–1789

1. What was the impetus for the so-called Atlantic revolutions, and what did they share in common?

2. What caused Louis XVI to call the Estates General?

3. Which circumstances transformed the calling of the Estates General into a revolution?

From Monarchy to Republic, 1789–1793

4. How did the National Assembly put Enlightenment principles into practice in the first two years after it came to power?

5. How did the National Assembly deal with the church?

6. Why did revolutionary and anti-monarchical sentiments intensify during the war with Austria and Prussia?

Terror and Resistance

7. What were the causes of the Terror?

8. What was the Republic of Virtue?

9. What ended the Terror?

Revolution on the March

10. What role did the French army play in spreading revolutionary ideals, and what were some of its results?

11. How did other countries react to revolution in France?

12. How did Napoleon Bonaparte come to power?

BUILDING HISTORICAL SKILLS

Reading Maps   *Write a brief, paragraph-length response to each of the following questions based on* **Map 20.3: French Expansion, 1791–1799 (p. 771).**

1. Which territories had France annexed or occupied by 1799?

2. Which states had revolutionary France established by 1799?

3. Which states would have felt threatened by the French expansion during the 1790s?

Reading Illustrations   *Write a brief, paragraph-length response to each of the following questions based on the illustration* **The Third State Awakens (p. 755).**

1. This print shows three figures interacting with each other: a noble, a clergyman, and a member of the Third Estate. Judging from the gestures of the figures, which two groups in society were shown as working for the same cause?

2. Artists use the gaze of the figures in their pictures to draw the viewer's eye in a certain direction. Although the noble and clergyman are looking at the member of the Third Estate, he is not looking at them. What effect does this have on the viewer?

3. Judging from your reading of this print, was it meant to gain support for the actions of the Third Estate or to oppose them?

Reading Historical Documents   *Write a brief, paragraph-length response to each of the following questions based on the documents in your book.*

The Rights of Minorities (p. 758)

1. What barriers does Clermont Tonnerre see to Jews being given French citizenship, and how does he propose to overcome them?

2. How does Clermont Tonnerre's speech represent some of the ideals of the Enlightenment?

Society of the Friends of Blacks, Address to the National Assembly in Favor of the Abolition of the Slave Trade, February 5, 1790 (p. 778)

3. What is the Society of the Friends of Blacks' position on slavery?

4. On what grounds does the society condemn slavery and the slave trade?

*Contrasting Views: Consequences of
the French Revolution (pp. 774–776)*

    5. What was the main point in the debate between
       Edmund Burke and Thomas Paine about the
       revolutions?

    6. When were Joseph de Maistre and Madame de
       Staël writing about the Revolution, and which
       events were they focusing on?

Napoleon and the Revolutionary Legacy
1800–1830

CHAPTER OVERVIEW

Chapter Questions *Keep these questions in mind as you go through the study guide chapter.*

1. How and why did Napoleon's reforms change European society?

2. What were the characteristics of the new ideologies and artistic movements that emerged as a result of the French and Industrial revolutions?

3. What impact did nationalism have on European politics in the 1820s and 1830s?

4. What explains the failure of some revolts in the 1820s and 1830s and the success of others?

5. How did the lives of women and workers change during this period?

Chapter Summary

Napoleon's Authoritarian State

When Napoleon Bonaparte came to power in 1799, his coup d'état appeared to be just the latest in a long line of upheavals in revolutionary France. Within a year, however, he had effectively ended the Revolution and set France on a new course toward an authoritarian state. To achieve his goals, Napoleon compromised with the Catholic church and with exiled aristocrats, tempered the principles of the Enlightenment and the Revolution, and patronized monumental architecture and the sciences.

From Republic to Empire, pp. 789–792

The Constitution of 1799 installed Napoleon Bonaparte as First Consul with the right to choose the Council of State, which drew up all the laws. The Council elimi-

nated direct elections for deputies and denied independent powers to the three houses of the legislature. Napoleon signed a concordat (agreement) with Pope Pius VII (r. 1800–1823) in 1801 to reconcile Catholics to the regime. Catholicism was recognized as the religion of "the great majority of French citizens," and the pope validated the sale of church lands that had occurred during the Revolution. Napoleon continued to centralize state power by creating the Bank of France and appointing prefects who supervised local affairs in each *département* (region). The government managed military-style education at the new lycées for boys but took little interest in educating girls. Napoleon used government censors and the police to limit opposition and censored newspapers, operas, and plays. In 1802, he named himself Consul for life and, in December of 1804, he crowned himself emperor. Napoleon worked hard to establish his authority and to cultivate his image, which was reproduced on coins, on public monuments, and in paintings. His ostentatious building projects, most of which were in the neoclassical style, included the Arc de Triomphe and the Stock Exchange. Napoleon's most trusted officials from past military campaigns helped him rule, and his bureaucracy was based on a patron–client relationship. He reinstituted a social hierarchy that rewarded merit and talent regardless of birth.

The New Paternalism: The Civil Code, pp. 792–793

One of Napoleon's first acts as emperor was the creation of the Civil, or Napoleonic Code: the first unified system of law for France. The code assured property rights, guaranteed religious liberty, and established a uniform system of law for all men that provided equal treatment for all adult males and affirmed the right of men to choose their professions. It also severely curtailed women's rights, making women responsible for private virtue because Napoleon believed a woman's place was in the home. The code was adopted in many European and Latin American countries, as well as in the French colony of Louisiana. Napoleon's familial model of power placed men firmly in charge: The Civil Code reasserted the Old Regime's system of male domination over women and insisted on a father's control over his children. The code also required fathers to provide for their children's welfare. Napoleon, as "father" of the French, encouraged the establishment of private charities for indigent mothers and made it easier for women to abandon their children anonymously so as to discourage abortion and infanticide. All workers were required to carry a card attesting to their good conduct, and workers' organizations were prohibited. Arbitration boards were established in 1806 to settle labor disputes, but they treated workers as minors and demanded that they be represented by foremen and shop superintendents. Limitations on workers' rights won Napoleon the support of French business.

Patronage of Science and Intellectual Life, pp. 793–795

Napoleon promoted scientific inquiry, especially if it served practical purposes. During his reign, experiments with balloons led to the discovery of laws about the expansion of gases, and research on fossil shells prepared the way for new theories of evolutionary change later in the century. Surgeon Dominique-Jean Larrey developed new techniques of battlefield amputation and medical care, winning appointment as an officer in the Legion of Honor and becoming a baron. While he encouraged scientists, Napoleon considered most writers useless or dangerous. Madame de Staël (1766–1817), like many of the country's talented writers, had to live in exile. Her novel *Corinne* (1807) criticized the regime by focusing on a brilliant woman thwarted by the French patriarchal system. Even though Napoleon restored the authority of the state and of religion, many Catholics and royalists criticized him. François-René de Chateaubriand (1768–1848) believed that Napoleon did not properly defend Christian values against the Enlightenment's emphasis on reason. In his *Genius of Christianity* (1802), Chateaubriand argued that Napoleon did not understand the mystical power of faith.

"Europe Was at My Feet": Napoleon's Conquests

Building on innovations introduced by the republican governments that preceded him, Napoleon revolutionized the art of war with tactics and strategy based on a highly mobile army. By 1812, he ruled an empire more extensive than any since Rome. One of the results was a great upsurge in nationalist feeling that has dominated European politics to the present day.

The Grand Army and Its Victories, 1800–1807, pp. 795–800

Less class-bound and more ready to reward merit than its enemies' armies, the French army enjoyed high morale that contributed to its success. Napoleon also inspired an almost fanatical loyalty, fighting next to his soldiers in some sixty battles. Napoleon's favorite tactic was to attack the main body of the opposing army in a lightning strike with the largest force possible. He served as his own operations officer, a style that worked only as long as Napoleon was present on the battlefield. A lack of coordination among his enemies' armies was one of his greatest advantages; he therefore maneuvered diplomatically and militarily to face them one at a time. Napoleon's victories in the battles of Marengo and Hohenlinden in 1800 forced the Austrians to agree to peace. This success was followed in 1802 by the Treaty of Amiens with the British, which lasted only until 1803. During this temporary truce, Napoleon sent forces to St. Domingue to retake the colony, but was forced to withdraw because of the organized resistance by the black population and an epidemic of yellow fever. As part of his retreat from the western hemisphere, and his especial need for funds, Napoleon sold Louisiana to the United States in 1803. When war resumed, the British navy defeated the French and their Spanish allies in the battle of Trafalgar (1805). That same year, Napoleon defeated the Austrians at Ulm, and the Austrians and Russians at Austerlitz. Prussia entered the war and was promptly defeated at Jena and Auerstadt in 1806. In 1807, Napoleon again defeated the Russians at Friedland. The ensuing treaties of Tilsit—negotiated between Napoleon and Russian tsar Alexander I (r. 1801–1825)—resulted in Prussia's suffering a significant loss of territory.

The Impact of French Victories, pp. 800–802

By annexing some territories and setting up others as satellite kingdoms with little autonomy, Napoleon attempted to unite Europe. He united the disparate German and Italian states to rule them more effectively and, in 1806, established the Confederation of the Rhine, which included all the German states except Austria and Prussia. Napoleon consolidated Italy by annexing the territories next to France and establishing the kingdoms of Italy and Naples. Annexed territories, ruled directly from France, and satellite kingdoms, usually ruled by one of Napoleon's relatives, were subject to French laws and French-style reforms. Napoleon abolished serfdom, eliminated seigneurial dues, introduced the Napoleonic Code, suppressed monasteries, subordinated church to state, and extended civil rights to Jews and other religious minorities. Reactions to these innovations were mixed: real improvements in roads, public works, law codes, education, and the economy were achieved, but increased taxes and conscription aggravated dissent. Republicans resented Napoleon for turning their sister republics into satellite kingdoms. Conflicts arose when Napoleon's desire to standardize and unify came up against local insistence on old customs and traditions. The one power standing between Napoleon and total domination of Europe was Great Britain. In 1806, Napoleon established the Continental System, which prohibited trade between Great Britain and France, its dependent states, and its allies. The system at first harmed Britain's trade, but because smuggling was rampant, British industrial growth continued. Resistance to the French encouraged the development of nationalism in other countries. In southern Italy, gangs of bandits and a network of secret societies, the *carbonari*, harassed the French army and local officials; German intellectuals wrote of German virtues and the superiority of German literature. Resistance was greatest in Spain and Portugal: the nobles feared revolutionary reforms, the Catholic church spread anti-French propaganda, and the peasants fought to defend their priests and resented French requisitions of food. Assisted by the British, Portuguese and Spanish rebels engaged Napoleon in a six-year war for national independence.

From Russian Winter to Final Defeat, 1812–1815, pp. 802–805

By 1812, only Great Britain and Russia remained independent of Napoleon. Great Britain sent aid to the Portuguese and Spanish rebels, while Tsar Alexander I made peace with the Ottoman Empire and allied himself with Great Britain and Sweden. In 1812, Napoleon invaded Russia, engaging the main Russian force at Borodino in September, which resulted in heavy casualties on both sides. Napoleon did manage to enter Moscow, but the departing Russians had set the city on fire, and the tsar refused to negotiate. With supplies running low, Napoleon began his retreat in October; in November, the bitter Russian winter began. By December, only one-sixth of Napoleon's original troops had returned to France. Napoleon replenished his armies by the spring of 1813, but a coalition of Russian, Austrian, Prussian, and Swedish armies—backed by British financial support—defeated him at the Battle of the Nations. In March 1814, the French Senate deposed and exiled Napoleon to the island of Elba off the coast of Italy. Louis XVIII (r. 1814–1824) was restored to the throne. The new king was caught between returning émigré nobles who demanded restoration of their lands and powers and those who had benefited from the Revolution or from Napoleon's reign. This chaos gave Napoleon the opportunity to escape exile and return to France, which he did during the so-called Hundred Days. Louis XVIII fled, and Napoleon reconstituted his army with former soldiers still loyal to him. Napoleon was once again defeated by a coalition of European powers at Waterloo. He abdicated and entered

permanent exile on the island of St. Helena off the coast of West Africa, where he died in 1821.

The "Restoration" of Europe

Even while Napoleon was making his last bid for power, his enemies were meeting in the Congress of Vienna (1814–1815) to decide the fate of postrevolutionary Europe. They settled the boundaries of European states, determined who should rule each nation, and established a new framework for international relations based on periodic meetings between the major powers. All these agreements helped to prevent another major European war until the 1850s, and it was not until 1914 that another conflict comparable to the Napoleonic wars occurred.

The Congress of Vienna, 1814–1815, pp. 805–808

The Congress of Vienna balanced post-Napoleonic Europe by relying on the major powers to cooperate while guaranteeing the status of smaller states. Boundaries were settled by representatives of the five major powers: Austria, Russia, Prussia, Britain, and France. The Austrian prince Klemens von Metternich (1773–1859) took the lead in the negotiations. He worked with British prime minister Robert Castlereagh (1769–1822) to check French aggression while preserving it as a great power to counter the ambitions of Prussia and Russia. Prince Charles Maurice de Talleyrand (1754–1838) represented France. Where possible, the congress restored traditional rulers, as in Spain and Italy. Elsewhere, it rearranged territorial boundaries to balance the competing interests of the great powers; the duchy of Warsaw thus became the kingdom of Poland ruled by the Russian tsar. The Dutch Republic and Austrian Netherlands united as the new kingdom of the Netherlands under the House of Orange. Sardinia was given Piedmont, Genoa, Nice, and part of Savoy. Sweden acquired Norway. The congress also condemned the slave trade in principle, but it continued until the 1840s. Alexander I of Russia proposed a Holy Alliance to ensure divine assistance in upholding religion, peace, and justice; Prussia and Austria agreed, but Great Britain declined. From that point on, the legitimacy of states depended on a treaty system, not divine right.

The Emergence of Conservatism, pp. 808–809

The French Revolution and Napoleon's domination of Europe had proved that the old order of government no longer had unquestionable authority. People needed justification to believe in restored governments, and conservatism provided that justification. Conservatives believed that the Enlightenment had led to the French Revolution, which produced both the Terror and the authoritarian

Napoleon. The most influential spokesman of conservatism was Britain's Edmund Burke (1729–1799), who believed that any change in government should be gradual and must respect national and historical traditions. Conservatives defended hereditary monarchy and the authority of the church, arguing that the "rights of man" must be balanced by the rights of the community; and that faith, sentiment, history, and tradition must fill the vacuum left over by the failure of reason and the excessive belief in individual rights. Not surprisingly, conservatism had its strongest appeal in ruling circles: the ascension of Louis XVIII tested conservative beliefs in France. He maintained the Civil Code, guaranteed rights of ownership to church lands sold during the Revolution, and created a parliament based on restricted suffrage. While the king tried to follow a moderate course of compromise, the Ultras (ultraroyalists) pushed for complete repudiation of the revolutionary past. In 1816, the Ultras insisted on abolishing divorce and set up special courts to punish opponents of the regime.

The Revival of Religion, pp. 809–810

Once peace returned to Europe, many renewed their religious faith. Revivalist movements, which had begun in Great Britain and Germany in the eighteenth century, sometimes challenged the status quo. In England, the Methodists, or Wesleyans, attracted thousands of shopkeepers, artisans, agricultural laborers, and workers in cottage industry. Although Methodism stressed obedience to the government, the group's hostility to rigid doctrine and encouragement of popular preaching promoted a sense of democratic community and even a rudimentary sexual equality. Women preachers traveled to sermonize in barns, town halls, and textile dye houses; and Sunday schools taught thousands of poor children to read and write. In the United States, the second Great Awakening began around 1790, bringing together thousands of worshipers in huge camp meetings. Protestant sects began missionary activity in other parts of the world in the late eighteenth century as well. In India, British missionaries succeeded in getting the practice of sati—the burning alive of widows on the funeral pyres of their husbands—abolished in 1829. Missionary activity by both Protestants and Catholics would become one of the arms of European imperialism and cultural influence later in the nineteenth century.

Forces for Social and Cultural Change

Rapid urban growth and the spread of industry created new social tensions in Europe and inspired new political doctrines to explain the meaning of economic and social changes. These doctrines soon galvanized opponents of the conservative Vienna settlement. Also, a new international movement in the arts and literature, called romanticism, began, which was a backlash to the Enlightenment.

Industrial and Urban Growth in Britain, pp. 810–811

Historians use the term Industrial Revolution to describe the set of changes that brought steam-driven machinery, large factories, and a new working class first to Britain and Europe and then to many other parts of the world. Unlike the French Revolution, the Industrial Revolution did not sweep across Europe; it had little effect on the continent outside of northern France, Belgium, and the Rhineland. Factories housing steam-driven machines quickly spread in urban areas, where there was a ready labor supply. Workers for the new factories came from farming families that could not provide land for their children, soldiers demobilized after the Napoleonic wars, artisans displaced by the new machinery, and children of earlier factory workers. As urban factories grew, workers came to constitute a new socioeconomic class holding common interests. This new working class organized societies for mutual aid and political reform. Because the factories threatened some individuals' livelihoods, Luddites reacted by wrecking factory machinery and burning mills; other workers focused on reform in Parliament. In August 1819, an open-air meeting of workers turned violent when the arrival of cavalry set off a panic, leaving six dead and hundreds injured. Following this Peterloo massacre, the government passed the Six Acts, which forbade large political meetings and restricted press criticism. British industrialization also affected other areas of the world, destroying the hand-manufacture of textiles in India and sustaining slavery in the southern United States, which produced and sold cotton to British factories. Industrialization also produced railroads, which were perfected as a mode of transport in the 1820s.

The New Ideologies, pp. 811–815

New ideologies—coherent sets of beliefs about the way a society's social and political order should be organized—responded to the French and Industrial revolutions. Liberalism traced its origins to John Locke and the Enlightenment. Liberals supported the Enlightenment ideals of constitutional guarantees of personal liberty and free trade in economics to promote social improvement and economic growth. Middle-class manufacturers, merchants, and professionals supported liberalism. On the one hand, they welcomed the changes of the Industrial Revolution; on the other, they opposed the violence and excessive state power of the French Revolution. Jeremy Bentham (1748–1832) argued that government was most useful when it promoted "the greatest good for the greatest number"—a clear rejection of policies that favored the aristocratic minority. Socialists advocated the total reorganization of society rather than reforming it. Many socialists were utopians who advocated the creation of ideal communities based on cooperation rather than competition. These socialists believed that society was divided into two classes: the middle-class factory owners, or capitalists; and the downtrodden working class. Socialist Robert Owen, a Welsh-born manufacturer, established a model factory town in New Lanark, Scotland, where working hours were curtailed, and children were sent to school rather than the factory. In France, Claude Henri de Saint-Simon (1760–1825) and Charles Fourier (1772–1837) were the most influential early socialist thinkers. Saint-Simon believed that work was the central element in the new society and that it should be controlled by scientists, artists, engineers, and industrialists (a term he coined, along with "industrialism"). Fourier also advocated the creation of utopian communities in which jobs would be rotated to maximize happiness, and in which women would be emancipated. Nationalism asserted that all persons derive their identities from the nations in which they reside, and are defined by common language, shared cultural traditions, and sometimes religion. Nationalism especially threatened the multi-ethnic Austrian Empire, which included Germans, Magyars, Slavs, and Italians. Metternich, a conservative, was willing to use secret police based on the Napoleonic model to restrain nationalist impulses. Metternich's policies provoked criticism in the writings of novelists, playwrights, and poets, and growing membership in groups such as the *carbonari*.

Romanticism, pp. 815–818

Romanticism was an artistic movement that glorified nature, emotion, genius, and imagination as antidotes to the Enlightenment's emphasis on reason, and classicism's emphasis on symmetry and ordered geometric space. Romantic poets such as George Gordon Byron (1788–1824) celebrated emotion and creative imagination. Byron also symbolized romanticism's idealism when he died fighting for Greek independence from the Turks. William Wordsworth (1770–1850) elevated the wonders of nature to a transcendent height. Mary Shelley (1797–1851) explored the nightmarish side of human genius in *Frankenstein* (1818). In the same mode as Shelley, Johann Wolfgang von Goethe (1749–1832) elaborated on the destructive potential of human nature in *Faust* (1832). In painting, romanticism idealized nature and often expressed anxiety about industrial changes. Caspar David Friedrich (1774–1840) depicted individual figures overwhelmed by an overpowering nature. Joseph M. W. Turner (1775–1851) anticipated later artists by blurring the outlines of objects in his misty seascapes. Like other romantics, French painter Eugène Delacroix (1798–1863) experimented with new techniques, emphasizing light and color in medieval and contemporary scenes. The German composer Ludwig van Beethoven (1770–1827) helped set the direction for romanticism in music when he transformed the symphony into a connected work with recurring and evolving musical themes, conveying the impression of organic growth. If any common political thread existed among the romantics, it was the support of nationalist aspirations—especially through the search for the historical origins of national identity. The enormously influential novels of Sir Walter Scott (1771–1832) were infused with romantic nationalism.

Political Challenges to the Conservative Order

The flood of discontent with the conservative Vienna settlement threatened to rise over its banks as liberals, nationalists, and socialists expressed their exasperation. Isolated revolts threatened the hold of some conservative governments in the 1820s, but most were put down. Then, in 1830, successive uprisings briefly overwhelmed the established order as protestors sought constitutional guarantees and national autonomy.

Political Revolts in the 1820s, pp. 819–823

Those who had hoped for constitutional government after Napoleon's fall were disappointed. In Spain, Ferdinand VII restored the prerevolutionary nobility, church, and monarchy, and established strict censorship. Members of the middle class, disturbed by repressive policies and army officers who had encountered and adopted French ideas, joined secret societies. A revolt by soldiers demanding that Ferdinand restore the constitution was put down by French troops, and Ferdinand's absolute power was restored. The Spanish revolt encouraged Italian rebellions in Naples, Piedmont, and Sardinia, all squashed by Austria in 1821. Great Britain opposed Austria's actions, but the other great powers supported it. In Russia, a brief revolt erupted in December 1825 over Alexander I's successor. His son Nicholas was to be crowned, but a faction of rebel officers preferred Nicholas's brother Constantine because he would favor reform and a constitution. When the officers called for Constantine to take the throne, soldiers loyal to Nicholas suppressed them in the so-called Decembrist Revolt; the rebels became heroes to later generations. Nicholas I (r. 1825–1855) dedicated his reign to preventing any further calls for reform. Serbia revolted and gained independence from the Turks in 1817. Prince Alexander Ypsilanti led a Greek revolt in 1820, but failed because he had not gained support from the great powers. A second Greek revolt, led by peasants, unleashed atrocities 1821 and 1822; public opinion in Europe supported the Greeks. In 1827, a combined British, French, and Russian force destroyed the Turkish fleet at Navarino Bay; and, in 1828, Russia declared war on Turkey and advanced close to Istanbul. The 1829 Treaty of Adrianople gave Russia a protectorate over the Danubian principalities in the Balkans and provided for an international congress that included Great Britain, Russia, and France. In 1830, Greece was declared an independent kingdom. This successful nationalist struggle was the first breach in Metternich's conservative system. Revolt spread across the Atlantic, when colonists from Mexico to Argentina took advantage of the upheaval in Spain and Portugal. These revolts were led by the son of a slave owner, Simon Bolívar, who had been educated in Europe and read Voltaire and Rousseau. Independent republics were formed in Latin America between 1821 and 1823. U.S. President James Monroe issued the foreign policy statement, the Monroe Doctrine in 1823, in opposition to European interference in the Americas.

Revolution and Reform, 1830–1832, pp. 823–825

In 1830, a new wave of liberal and nationalist revolts broke out throughout the European continent. In France, Charles X (r. 1824–1830) passed a Law of Indemnity that compensated those nobles who had lost estates during the Revolution, and a Law of Sacrilege that imposed the death penalty for offenses such as stealing religious objects from churches. Charles also dissolved the legislature, removed many wealthy and powerful voters from the rolls, and imposed strict censorship. A revolution began on July 26, 1830 and, after three days of street fighting and the flight of the king, a group of moderate liberals asked Charles X's cousin, the liberal Louis-Philippe, to take the throne. Although Louis-Philippe extended suffrage, only about 6 percent of the population could vote. Expressing their dissatisfaction, the indigent and working classes rebelled in Lyon in 1831. The revolt was quickly put down. Events in France inspired a revolt in Belgium, which had been annexed to the Netherlands in 1815. At a congress of the great powers, Belgium was granted its independence as a constitutional monarchy in exchange for neutrality in international affairs. In November 1830, Poland rebelled against Russia, and Polish aristocrats formed a provisional government. Without support from the British or French, the rebels were defeated by Russian forces. Nicholas I abolished the Polish constitution and ordered thousands of Poles executed or banished. Revolts in the Austrian Empire's Italian territories were also unsuccessful because of a lack of outside support. Great Britain pursued reform during the 1820s and 1830s. Controversy over George IV's (r. 1820–1830) attempt to divorce his wife Caroline tarnished the reputation of the monarchy, and sped the reform movement. In the 1820s,

Sir Robert Peel (1788–1850), the secretary for home affairs, revised the criminal code and established a municipal police force. In 1824, laws prohibiting unions were repealed (but the restrictions placed on strikes remained) and, in 1829, Catholics were allowed to sit in Parliament and hold most public offices. In 1832, Whigs in Parliament enacted the Reform Bill to extend voting rights. Mass demonstrations in favor of the bill had been held in many cities, but the bill granted the vote to only one-fifth of British voters, and still only male property-owners could vote. The bill did, however, grant representation to the new industrial centers in the north for the first time and set a precedent for widening suffrage without revolution.

Key Events   *For each question, select the most appropriate response from the choices provided.*

1799 Coup against Directory government in France; Napoleon Bonaparte named First Consul

1801 Napoleon signs a concordat with the pope

1804 Napoleon crowned as emperor of France; issues new Civil Code

1805 British naval forces defeat the French at the battle of Trafalgar; Napoleon wins his greatest victory at the battle of Austerlitz

1812 Napoleon invades Russia

1814–1815 Congress of Vienna

1815 Napoleon defeated at Waterloo and exiled to island of St. Helena, where he dies in 1821

1818 Mary Shelley, *Frankenstein*

1820 Robert Owen, *The Book of the New Moral World*; revolt of liberal army officers against the Spanish crown; the Karlsbad Decrees abolish German student societies and tighten press censorship

1824 Ludwig van Beethoven, Ninth Symphony

1825 Russian army officers demand constitutional reform in the Decembrist Revolt

1830 The Manchester and Liverpool Railway opens in England; Greece gains its independence from Ottoman Turks; rebels overthrow Charles X of France and install Louis-Philippe

1832 English Parliament passes Reform Bill; Johann Wolfgang von Goethe, *Faust*

1. Who came into power as a result of the coup against the Directory government of France in 1799?
   a. Maximilien Robespierre
   b. Napoleon Bonaparte
   c. Charles X
   d. Louis-Philippe

2. Which of the following resulted from Napoleon's concordat with the pope in 1801?
   a. Napoleon became a devout Catholic.
   b. Lands that had been sold during the Revolution were returned to the church.
   c. The pope became ruler of Italy.
   d. The decade-long conflict between the church and France came to an end.

3. Which of the following was *not* a result of the Civil Code of 1804?
   a. Religious liberty was guaranteed.
   b. Slavery was abolished.
   c. A uniform system of law provided equal treatment for all adult males.
   d. Men gained the right to choose their professions.

4. What were the results of Napoleon's invasion of Russia in 1812?
   a. Napoleon defeated the Russians at the battle of Moscow.
   b. The Prussians took advantage of the fact that Napoleon was busy in Russia and revolted against him.
   c. Supply problems and the weather forced Napoleon to withdraw, which began his eventual downfall.
   d. The Russians defeated Napoleon's army at the battle of Borodino.

5. What was the result of the revolt of liberal army officers against the Spanish crown in 1820?
   a. The monarchy was replaced with a military republic.
   b. A truce between King Ferdinand VII and the rebels introduced liberal reforms.
   c. King Ferdinand VII was replaced by his more popular cousin.
   d. The rebellion was crushed by an invading French army.

6. From which country did the new king of Greece come after it won its independence from the Turks in 1830?
   a. Bavaria
   b. Greece
   c. Russia
   d. Turkey

Key Terms   *Match each key term to its definition.*

A. **Civil Code** (p. 792)
B. **conservatism** (p. 808)
C. **consuls** (p. 789)
D. **Continental System** (p. 801)
E. **ideology** (p. 812)
F. **liberalism** (p. 812)
G. **nationalism** (p. 814)
H. **restoration** (p. 808)
I. **romanticism** (p. 815)
J. **socialism** (p. 813)
K. **working class** (p. 811)

1. _____ Title given to the three leaders of the new French government installed in 1799; in fact, Napoleon as First Consul held the reins of power.

2. _____ New French legal code formulated by Napoleon in 1804 (hence also called the Napoleonic Code); it assured equal treatment under the law to all classes of men and guaranteed religious liberty but curtailed many of the rights of women.

3. _____ System inaugurated by Napoleon's order in 1806 that France and its satellites boycott British goods; after some early successes in blocking British trade, the system was undermined by smuggling.

4. _____ The Congress of Vienna's policy, after the fall of Napoleon, to "restore" as many regimes as possible to their former rulers.

5. _____ A political doctrine that emerged after 1815 and rejected much of the Enlightenment and the French Revolution, preferring monarchies over republics, tradition over revolution, and established religion over Enlightenment skepticism.

6. _____ Term introduced in the early nineteenth century for those who worked in the new factories of industrial production.

7. _____ A coherent set of beliefs (conservatism, liberalism, socialism, etc.) about the way the social and political order should be organized and changed; the word was coined during the French Revolution.

8. _____ An economic and political doctrine that emphasized free trade and the constitutional guarantees of individual rights such as freedom of speech and religion; liberals were favorable to the Enlightenment but critical of the violence of the French Revolution.

9. _____ A social and political doctrine that advocated the reorganization of society to overcome the new tensions created by industrialization; early socialists emphasized the need to restore social harmony through communities based on cooperation rather than competition.

10. _____ A political doctrine that holds that all peoples derive their identities from their nations and should have states to express their common language and shared cultural traditions.

11. _____ An artistic movement of the early nineteenth century that glorified nature, emotion, genius, and imagination.

Identification

This activity tests your recall of significant people, places, and events from this chapter. Fill in the blank with the correct answer.

1. Formerly a leading figure in the Terror of 1793–1794, _____ became Napoleon's minister of police.

2. Napoleon favored the _____ style for his many architectural projects.

3. Wanting to establish an imperial succession, Napoleon divorced his wife _____ in 1809 and married an eighteen-year-old Austrian princess the following year.

4. In 1802, Napoleon took the first step toward creating a new nobility by founding the _____.

5. Although he admired Napoleon, _____ believed that he had not properly understood the need to defend Christian values against the Enlightenment's excessive reliance on reason.

6. In 1803, Napoleon sold _____ to the United States.

7. Often considered his greatest victory, Napoleon fought the battle of _____ on December 2, 1805, the first anniversary of his coronation.

8. After a crushing defeat at the hands of Napoleon in 1806, _____ appointed a reform commission that recommended the abolition of serfdom and an overhaul of the army.

9. Although Napoleon defeated the Russians at the battle of _____ in 1812, it proved to be a hollow victory when the Russians employed a scorched-earth strategy of defeat.

10. After his final defeat in 1815, Napoleon was exiled to _____.

11. At the Congress of Vienna, Austria's chief negotiator _____ took the lead in devising a settlement for post-Napoleonic Europe.

12. _____, an aristocrat and former bishop who had embraced the French Revolution, served as Napoleon's foreign minister, then helped engineer the emperor's overthrow, and undertook the task of ensuring the status of France at the Congress of Vienna.

13. To impart spiritual substance to the calculated settlement of political affairs at the Congress of Vienna, _____ proposed a Holy Alliance that called on divine assistance in upholding religion, peace, and justice.

14. The original British critic of the French Revolution, _____, inspired many of the conservatives who followed.

15. In the 1820s, _____ perfected an engine to pull wagons along tracks, which revolutionized transportation.

16. A romantic poet, _____ acted upon his emotions by fighting and dying in the Greek war for independence.

17. In "Tintern Abbey," one of the most beloved exemplars of romantic poetry, _____ endowed nature with human emotions.

18. The French painter _____ chose contemporary as well as medieval scenes of great turbulence to emphasize light and color.

19. The paintings by the German artist _____ captured the romantic fascination with the sublime power of nature with melancholic figures that looked lost in its vastness.

20. In Russia, _____ formed a new political police called the Third Section to spy on potential opponents and stamp out rebelliousness.

21. In 1833, the son of King Ludwig of Bavaria was crowned _____ of Greece.

22. Educated in Europe, _____ fancied himself a Latin American Napoleon and rebelled against Spanish rule.

23. In the wake of the July Revolution of 1830, _____ became the new king of France.

24. In 1820, domestic quarrels between the new king _____ and his German wife seemed to threaten the future of the British monarchy.

CHAPTER REVIEW

Self-Test and Analytical Exercises

Multiple Choice   *Select the best answer from the four choices provided.*

1. The lycées were
   a. government censors who limited the literature and artistic works under Napoleon.
   b. prefects that Napoleon appointed to run local affairs in every region of France.
   c. salaries paid to the Catholic bishops and priests.
   d. state-run secondary schools for boys.

2. Which of the following is *not* true regarding the Civil Code of 1804?
   a. Assured property rights
   b. Guaranteed religious liberty
   c. Provided freedom of the press and of expression
   d. Established a uniform system of law that provided equal treatment for adult males

3. In order to maintain social control, Napoleon did all of the following *except*
   a. put the educational system into the hands of the state.
   b. rely on a steady stream of mass executions.
   c. repair the state's relationship with the Catholic church.
   d. censor artistic works and ban his opponents from political participation.

4. What impact did the Civil Code have on women?
   a. It established equal rights for women in all aspects of civil life.
   b. Although it denied women political rights, women's equality in social and economic spheres was assured.
   c. For the first time, it allowed women to have full control over their property.
   d. It curtailed women's political and economic rights, even revoking some rights they had had under the monarchy.

5. The Treaty of Amiens in 1802
   a. granted the Louisiana Territory to the United States.
   b. caused Napoleon to lose control of St. Dominigue.
   c. allowed Napoleon time to reorganize the French armies following a long series of French defeats.
   d. was a short-lived truce between Napoleon and Great Britain.

6. What was the Continental System?
   a. The network of Napoleon's family members installed to rule various subject kingdoms throughout Europe
   b. Napoleon's new method of warfare, involving conscription and large-scale battles
   c. A prohibition of trade with Great Britain by France and its dependent states and allies
   d. A French legal code that reformed the feudal laws of all territories captured by the French

7. The alliance between which two European states successfully challenged Napoleon's domination of the European continent?
   a. Austria and Russia
   b. Great Britain and Russia
   c. Spain and Portugal
   d. Great Britain and Spain

8. Which battle is considered Napoleon's final defeat?
   a. Elba
   b. Austerlitz
   c. Waterloo
   d. Trafalgar

9. The major European powers met to decide the fate of post-Napoleonic Europe at the
   a. Concert of Europe.
   b. Hundred Days' council.
   c. Congress of Vienna.
   d. Peterloo congress.

10. Which British prime minister helped arrange the post-Napoleonic settlement?
    a. Jeremy Bentham
    b. Arthur Wellesley
    c. Robert Castlereagh
    d. Robert Peel

11. Which political doctrine justified the restoration of traditional rulers?
    a. Nationalism
    b. Liberalism
    c. Radicalism
    d. Conservatism

12. Who were the Luddites?
    a. Workers who believed that machinery improved their working lives
    b. Soldiers who put down people rioting against machinery
    c. Factory owners who introduced machine manufacturing
    d. Hand-loom weavers who broke machinery and burned factories because they feared they would be displaced by machines

13. Religious revivalism
    a. had little impact outside of Europe.
    b. led to an increase in global missionary activity.
    c. was mainly a trend in Catholic countries.
    d. was confined to the United States.

14. A coherent tenet of beliefs about the way society's social and political order should be organized is
    a. social constructionism.
    b. an ideology.
    c. socialism.
    d. political determinism.

15. Which of the following is *not* true of socialism?
    a. It argues that the liberties advocated by liberals only benefit the middle class
    b. It seeks to reorganize society totally rather than to reform it piecemeal
    c. It criticizes the class divisions of industrial society
    d. It wholeheartedly advocates the violent overthrow of existing society

16. What were the *Burschenschaften*?
    a. Antinationalist spies sent by Metternich to monitor student groups and international travelers
    b. Nationalist student societies in the Germanic Confederation
    c. Decrees that ended the student societies and censored the press in the Germanic Confederation
    d. A series of plays by August Kotzebue that advocated German nationalism

17. Which Spanish king's repressive policies caused resistance after his restoration to the throne in 1814?
    a. Joseph I
    b. Francisco IX
    c. Charles IV
    d. Ferdinand VII

18. European nationalist movements proved most successful against which power?
    a. The Ottoman Turks
    b. Austria
    c. Russia
    d. Great Britain

19. Which country gained independence from the Dutch in 1831?
    a. Bolivia
    b. Belgium
    c. Prussia
    d. Holland

20. Who revised the British criminal code, introduced a municipal police force in London, and passed laws allowing trade union organization?
    a. The Duke of Wellington
    b. Sir Robert Peel
    c. King William IV
    d. Lord Castlereagh

21. Napoleon
    a. alienated the Catholic church by confiscating church lands and denying Catholics government posts.
    b. recognized Catholicism as the religion of the great majority of French citizens in exchange for the pope's support of his regime.
    c. refused to pay the salaries of Catholic bishops and priests.
    d. was a devout Catholic and welcomed the guidance of the pope in state matters.

22. The "new paternalism" of the Napoleonic state saw
    a. the government take a smaller role in the lives of citizens to allow families greater autonomy.
    b. employer–employee relationships regulated and workers' organizations prohibited.
    c. prostitution outlawed as a force destructive to the purity of the French nuclear family.
    d. that it became more difficult for women to abandon their children.

23. What was Napoleon's opinion of scientific inquiry?
    a. He viewed it with distrust, believing it a threat to his personal power.
    b. Napoleon could not fathom how scientific inquiry would ever serve the interests of the state.
    c. He did everything he could to promote French scientific inquiry, particularly when it showed practical applications.
    d. He believed scientific inquiry was useful, but also that scientific developments would advance more quickly without state funding or involvement.

24. François-René de Chateaubriand's book, *Genius of Christianity*,
    a. argued that the values espoused by Christianity and the Enlightenment were united perfectly in the Napoleonic state.
    b. deemed the Enlightenment's focus on reason as destructive to Christianity.
    c. was sponsored by Madame de Staël and was critical of the excessive paternalism of the new French state.
    d. saw Napoleon as the champion of Christianity following the atheistic fervor of the Revolution.

25. Napoleon
    a. spent little time on the battlefield, choosing instead to direct the war from Paris.
    b. avoided large-scale battles and concentrated on small raids using guerrilla tactics.
    c. had a very personal and highly centralized military command.
    d. trained his subordinates to be independent commanders in his absence.

26. Which battle prevented a French invasion of Britain and was a huge defeat for the French and Spanish navies?
    a. Ulm
    b. Trafalgar
    c. Marengo
    d. Austerlitz

27. What impact did Napoleon's victories have in Prussia?
    a. Prussian rulers tightened their grip on the peasantry by increasing the legal restrictions of serfdom.
    b. Prussian rulers introduced democracy in order to counter Napoleon's absolutist rule.
    c. In awe of Napoleon's successes, the Prussian government tried to emulate the French Empire; Frederick William III declared himself emperor in 1806.
    d. In order to emulate the French, Prussia instituted reforms: serfdom was abolished and the army was made more efficient.

28. Who were the *carbonari*?
    a. Napoleon's supporters in Italy
    b. A series of nationalist secret societies that resisted Napoleon's rule in Italy
    c. The fleet of French ships that attempted to enforce the Continental System
    d. The Italian equivalents of the Jacobins

29. The Vienna settlement
    a. asserted British dominance over European affairs.
    b. required the cooperation of the major powers and guaranteed recognition of smaller states.
    c. ignored the status of smaller states, which were all taken over by major powers.
    d. eliminated France as a major power in Europe.

30. As part of the post-Napoleonic settlement, France
    a. lost all the territory it had gained since 1790.
    b. was eliminated as a great power and denied an army of any sort.
    c. was restored to a republic.
    d. became a satellite state of Great Britain.

31. After his restoration, Louis XVIII
    a. desired complete repudiation of the revolutionary past.
    b. made concessions and maintained the Napoleonic Code.
    c. distanced himself from the church in an effort to quell Protestant dissenters.
    d. immediately introduced policies to reestablish absolutist rule.

32. Methodism
    a. was founded as a movement against the government.
    b. stressed reason as the true path to moral and social reform.
    c. was mainly a religion of the upper classes.
    d. was conservative, but fostered a sense of democratic community.

33. The development of industrialized cloth production in Britain
    a. destroyed hand textile manufacture in India.
    b. increased the importation of Indian wool, cotton, and silk.
    c. eliminated the need for cotton produced by U.S. slaves.
    d. led to high tariffs on British cloth entering India.

34. What were the Six Acts?
    a. Legislation passed by the British Parliament that forced workers to accept machine production
    b. Legislation passed by the British Parliament that forbade large political meetings and restricted the press's criticism of the government
    c. Legislation that raised the tariffs on imported Indian cloth
    d. Legislation that restricted the importation of cotton produced by slave labor

35. Who developed the theory of utilitarianism?
    a. Jeremy Bentham
    b. George Stephenson
    c. John Locke
    d. Robert Owen

36. All of the following were socialists *except*
    a. Robert Owen.
    b. Jeremy Bentham.
    c. Claude Henri de Saint-Simon.
    d. Charles Fourier.

37. Which of the following is *not* true about romantics?
    a. They glorified nature, emotion, genius, and imagination.
    b. They challenged classicism's reliance on reason, symmetry, and orderly geometric spaces.
    c. Their influence was most apparent in architectural designs of the period.
    d. They sought out all that was wild, fevered, and disorderly.

38. Which king's increasingly repressive policies sparked another revolution in France in 1830?
    a. Louis XVIII
    b. Ferdinand VII
    c. Charles X
    d. Louis-Philippe

39. The constitutional uprising in which country was suppressed by Tsar Nicholas I after it failed to receive support from other European powers?
    a. France
    b. Spain
    c. Naples
    d. Poland

40. The Duke of Wellington's government passed a law in 1829 allowing what group to sit in Parliament and hold most public offices?
    a. Catholics
    b. Protestants
    c. Socialists
    d. Jews

Short Answer   *Answer each question in three or four sentences.*

Napoleon's Authoritarian State

1. Which policy did Napoleon pursue regarding the Catholic church? Why?

2. What impact did the Civil Code have on women?

"Europe Was at my Feet": Napoleon's Conquests

3. Which factors contributed to Napoleon's military successes in Europe?

4. What impact did Napoleon have on territories he conquered?

5. How was Napoleon defeated?

The "Restoration" of Europe

6. Define and describe the "restoration" of Europe after the Congress of Vienna.

7. What was Conservatism?

8. What spawned religious revivals in post-Napoleonic Europe? How did they influence society?

Forces for Social and Cultural Change

9. What was the Industrial Revolution?

10. Describe the ideology known as liberalism.

11. What influence did nationalism have during this period?

Political Challenges to the Conservative Order

12. Which factors influenced the success or failure of liberal and nationalist revolts?

13. What was the cause and result of the French Revolution of 1830?

14. What was the significance of the British Reform Bill of 1832?

15. What was the "new paternalism"?

BUILDING HISTORICAL SKILLS

Reading Maps   *Write a brief, paragraph-length response to each of the following questions based on* **Map 21.2: Europe after the Congress of Vienna, 1815** *(p. 807).*

1. How was Europe in 1815 "restored," and in which ways was the Congress of Vienna not a restoration?

2. Compare this map to Map 21.1: Napoleon's Empire at Its Height, 1812 on page 798 of your textbook. Which territories did France lose as a result of the Congress of Vienna, and what became of the French satellite states?

Reading Illustrations   *Write a brief, paragraph-length response to each of the following questions based on the painting* **The Coronation of Napoleon and Josephine** *(p. 791).*

1. Is the scene depicted in *The Coronation of Napoleon and Josephine* one of grandeur and respectfulness, or one of disorganization and lawlessness? What in the picture leads you to describe it this way?

2. In his diary and in the history of his reign, Napoleon argued that his rule was legitimate because it was based on popular sovereignty. Does this painting send the same message?

3. Why did David choose to paint Napoleon crowning Josephine, instead of showing him crowning himself?

Reading Historical Documents   *Write a brief, paragraph-length response to each of the following questions based on the documents in your book.*

An Ordinary Soldier on Campaign with Napoleon (p. 804)

1. What are some of the obstacles that Napoleon's army faced when it invaded Russia?

2. How did the Russian campaign differ from Napoleon's preferred strategy?

Wordsworth Poem (p. 816)

3. What are the main themes or images of this poem?

4. How does Romanticism as exemplified here differ from Enlightenment thought?

Contrasting Views: Napoleon: For and Against (pp. 796–797)

5. What, according to his critics, were Napoleon's greatest faults or crimes?

6. How does Napoleon defend his actions?

Industrialism, Urbanization, and Revolution
1830–1850

CHAPTER OVERVIEW

Chapter Questions   *Keep these questions in mind as you go through the study guide chapter.*

1. What changes did industrialization and urbanization produce in the lives of ordinary people?

2. To what extent, and in what which ways, was life changing in European rural areas in Europe?

3. How did persons of the middle and upper classes react to problems of poverty among workers?

4. Which new ideologies emerged in response to the changes European society was experiencing?

5. What were the causes and consequences of the revolutions of 1848?

Chapter Summary

The Advance of Industrialization and Urbanization

Industrialism and urbanization transformed Europe and eventually most of the world in the nineteenth and twentieth centuries. States exercised little control over the consequences of industrial and urban growth, and many worried that unchecked growth would destroy social relationships and create disorder. Some held out the constancy of rural life as an antidote to the problems of industrialization and urbanization, but population growth in the countryside produced its own tensions.

Engines of Change, pp. 831–835

During the late eighteenth century, Great Britain led the way in the development of factories and railroads. In the 1830s and 1840s, industrialization began to spread throughout continental Europe, moving from west to east and north to south. Railroad construction was a leading sector of industrialization. Governments backed railroads, realizing that railroad construction with its demand for iron and coal pushed further industrial development. The steam engine that powered the railroads was also used by steamboats, mining operations, and textile factories. Although industrialization increased steadily in western Europe, its advance in eastern Europe was slow, in large part because serfdom still survived there. Serfs could not move to the towns to work in factories, and landlords with large estates had little incentive to invest in manufacturing. Over decades, factories gradually replaced the households of preindustrial artisans. Many peasants continued to alternate seasonally between manufacturing and agriculture. Workers also continued putting-out work, an option especially attractive to women. In time, even the putting-out system changed, due to the division of labor into simpler, lower-paid tasks known as piecework. Factories drew criticism for the pollution they created and for the growing income gap between owners and workers. As industrialism and its consequences grew, local and national governments collected information about workers' health, their living conditions, and their families. Government inquiries often focused on women and children and, in Great Britain, inquiries led to the Factory Act of 1833, which outlawed the employment of children under age nine in textile mills and limited the hours of children under age eighteen; and the 1842 Mines Act, which prohibited the employment of women and girls underground. The continental countries eventually followed the British lead, but most did not insist on inspection; enforcement was therefore lax.

Urbanization and Its Consequences, pp. 835–839

Industrialization was linked with rapid urban growth. Great Britain was the leader in this case also: by 1850, half the population of England and Wales lived in towns. Urban populations soared all over Europe because of massive rural out-migration. Agricultural improvements had increased the food supply and therefore the rural population. As it grew, farm work became scarce, and people went to the cities in search of employment. As the cities grew, they dismantled their medieval walls and incorporated parks, zoos, cemeteries, and greenways. Housing, however, was neglected, and overcrowding severe. Overcrowding fostered disease as garbage and refuse littered the streets, smog and smoke obscured the atmosphere, and water was scarce and unclean. Without sewage removal, human waste collected in cesspools and ended up in the rivers that supplied drinking water. Cities with populations of fifty thousand or more had twice the death rates of rural areas. From 1830 to 1832, and again from 1847 to 1852, cholera swept through Europe. Epidemics shocked governments into concern for public health and, in Great Britain, reports on sanitary conditions among workers led to new public health laws. Middle-class persons lived in more spacious and cleaner neighborhoods, but the nearby poor were a source of anxiety. Middle-class reformers, pointing to the living conditions of the poor as a cause of moral degeneracy, collected statistics on illegitimacy and infanticide. Reformers also addressed prostitution, alcoholism, and crime. At the same time that they drew attention to public health issues, reformers unfortunately stereotyped workers as helpless and out of control.

Agricultural Perils and Prosperity, pp. 839–840

Burgeoning populations created rising demands for food and altered rural life. Peasants and farmers planted fallow land, chopped down forests, and drained marshes. Railroads and canals improved food distribution, but much of Europe remained isolated from markets and thus vulnerable to local famines. Most still lived on the land, and the upper classes still dominated rural society, although businessmen and peasants were sometimes able to buy land. In France, almost two million independent peasants tended their own small properties. But in England, southern Italy, Prussia, and eastern Europe, large landowners expanded their estates. The survival of independent peasant families was threatened as men often migrated seasonally to earn cash in factories while women stayed behind to tend the crops. To avoid further subdivision of their land to potential heirs, peasants practiced rudimentary forms of birth control. Unpropertied individuals in cities began marrying earlier, and they, too, practiced birth control. Rural population pressure also caused people to emigrate, often to the United States. Between 1816 and 1850, five million Europeans left their home countries and traveled overseas. Despite the challenges of rural life in Europe, political power remained in the hands of traditional elites. The biggest property owners controlled political assemblies and often personally selected clergy and local officials. The old rural order

seemed most impregnable in Russia, where troops easily suppressed serfs' uprisings in 1831 and 1842.

Reforming the Social Order

In the 1830s and 1840s, Europeans organized to reform the social evils created by industrialization and urbanization. Middle-class women often took the lead in charitable organizations that sought to uplift the poor through religion, education, and reforming their manners. Many hoped to apply the same zeal for reform to the native peoples of colonies administered by Europeans.

Cultural Responses to the Social Question, pp. 840–844

The social question reflected concern about social changes—a concern that pervaded all forms of art and literature. The dominant artistic movement of the time, Romanticism, tended to glorify nature and deplore industrial and urban growth. The English poet Elizabeth Barrett Browning decried child labor, and architects used the Gothic style, reminiscent of the Middle Ages, to glorify the preindustrial world. Although romantic painters glorified the landscape as a way of calling attention to the wonders of nature, some painted landscapes reflected the power of new technologies. Attention to social problems reached its greatest audience via the novel thanks to increasing literacy, the spread of reading rooms and lending libraries, and serials published in newspapers and journals. Unlike the novels of the eighteenth century, which focused on individual personalities, the great novels of the 1830s and 1840s tended to portray individuals in the context of social life. French novelist Honoré de Balzac (1799–1850) cataloged the social types of French society, whereas English writer Charles Dickens (1812–1870) drew attention to the negative effects of industrialization and urbanization. Novels by women (usually published under a male pseudonym) often revealed the bleaker side of women's situations. In *Jane Eyre* (1847), Charlotte Brontë (1816–1855) explored the difficulties that unmarried middle-class women faced when trying to earn a living. French novelist George Sand (Amandine-Aurore Lucie Dupin, 1804–1876) scandalized Europe with her love affairs, her masculine dress, and her novels such as *Indiana* (1832), a narrative of an unhappily married woman. Just as an audience for novels grew, so too did a public for cultural events. Popular theaters drew large crowds of lower- and middle-class spectators. Museums opened to the public, and middle-class persons began to collect art. In 1839, daguerreotypes (early photographs) offered artists a new medium for expression. Whether in painting or photography, visual images heightened the public's awareness of the effects of industrialization and urbanization.

The Varieties of Social Reform, pp. 844–847

Religious convictions inspired many reformers, as many clergy and religious groups tried to raise working-class peoples' interest in religion and undertook secular reforms as well. In Great Britain, the Sunday school movement taught working-class children to read at a time when few could attend to school. Women assumed a prominent role in charitable works. Catholic religious orders enrolled women to run schools, hospitals, leper colonies, insane asylums, and old-age homes. Protestant women established Bible, missionary, and reform societies. One of their chief concerns was prostitution. Women could be activists in such areas because charity was seen as an extension of their domestic role. Both Catholics and Protestants promoted temperance. Temperance advocates viewed drunkenness as immoral and a threat to social order. Social reformers stressed education for the poor and working classes. British churches organized to promote education and, in 1833, the French government passed a law that required every town to maintain a primary school, pay a teacher, and provide free education to poor boys. Girls' schools were optional, but hundreds of women taught at the primary level. Prussia had 75 percent of its children in primary school by 1835. By contrast, Russian tsar Nicholas I (r. 1825–1855) blamed the Decembrist Revolt on education, and thus excluded peasants from primary schools. In Great Britain, the Society for the Prevention of Cruelty to Animals attempted to eliminate lower-class sports such as cockfighting and bearbaiting. According to the ideals of domesticity, women were to devote their lives to home and family. Many believed that men and women had to act according to distinct roles in order to ensure social order. The notion of separate spheres for women and men left most women economically dependent, preventing them from pursuing higher education, careers, or politics. Gender distinctions were most noticeable among elites. Boys attended school while girls lived at home; men wore practical clothing while women dressed for decorative effect. Lower-class women may have considered domesticity an ideal; however, because they had to work to support their families, staying at home was rarely a reality.

Abuses and Reforms Overseas, pp. 847–849

In the first half of the nineteenth century, colonialism became imperialism. This meant, first, a shift from direct to indirect rule by European nations; and, second, a shift in focus from the Caribbean to Asia and Africa. One sign of the decline of colonialism was the decline of the slave trade. In 1807, the British withdrew from the slave trade, and abolished slavery in 1833, whereas the French government suppressed the clandestine slave trade in the 1830s, and abolished slavery in its colonies in 1848. Brazil, Cuba, and the United States continued slavery,

and the slave trade in those countries reached its peak in the early 1840s. In 1830, France invaded Algeria, taking control by 1850. France also took over Tahiti. The British granted Canada greater self-determination in 1839, but annexed Singapore in 1819, and New Zealand in 1840. In addition, the British extended their control over India via the East India Company and educated a native elite as colonial administrators. The East India Company pushed opium trade with China. The Chinese government tried but failed to keep opium out of its country. When the Chinese tried to expel British merchants for importing the drug, the British bombarded Chinese coastal cities and imposed the Treaty of Nanking in 1842, which ended the first opium war. This treaty forced the Chinese to open four more ports to Europeans, and to cede the British Hong Kong with the guarantee that British merchants could continue the opium trade.

The Ferment of Ideologies

Despite the rapid growth of reform movements, many Europeans found them insufficient to resolve the problems created by industrialization and urbanization, and turned to movements inspired by new political ideologies that had taken shape in the aftermath of the French Revolution. Liberals and socialists sought their own solutions, but the most potent ideology was nationalism, which looked past social problems to concentrate on achieving political autonomy and self-determination for groups identified by common ethnicity rather than by class.

The Spell of Nationalism, pp. 849–853

Nationalists sought political autonomy for their ethnic groups of individuals linked by language and shared traditions. Nationalist leaders called for cultural revival, scholars compiled dictionaries, and writers glorified vernacular languages. After the failed revolt against the Russians in 1830, ten thousand Poles fled Poland, primarily to western Europe. The poet Adam Mickiewicz (1798–1855) became a hero by portraying Polish exiles as martyrs and by forming a Polish Legion to fight for restoration of Poland, but conflicts among the nationalists prevented action until 1846. Galicia's revolt against the Austrian Empire collapsed when peasants slaughtered not the Austrians but their Polish masters. Giuseppe Mazzini (1805–1872) was inspired by Mickiewicz to found Young Italy, a secret society dedicated to Italian-led, European-wide revolution. Nationalism made the Austrian Empire especially volatile because it comprised so many ethnic groups. In 1834, the German states moved toward economic unification by creating a customs union, the *Zollverein*, to help Germans compete economically with the rest of Europe. German nationalists desired political union as well, but the question of whether to include both Prussia and Austria was difficult to resolve. Russian nationalism defined itself as opposition to western ideas. Slavophiles ("lovers of the Slavs") argued that only a return to non-Westernized religious traditions and historical principles could protect the country against the corrosive effects of rationalization and materialism. Irish nationalists developed strong organizations in the 1840s. The Young Ireland movement, formed in 1842, aimed to recover history and preserve the Gaelic language. Irish landowner and representative to Parliament Daniel O'Connell attracted huge crowds with his call to repeal the 1801 Act of Union, which had made Ireland part of Great Britain. O'Connell was arrested, convicted of conspiracy and, thereafter, withdrew from politics.

Liberalism in Economics and Politics, pp. 853–854

Nationalism was strongest in eastern Europe, whereas liberalism had a strong base of support in the west. British liberals advocated free markets, arguing that governments should limit their economic role in maintaining the currency, enforcing contracts, and financing major enterprises like the military and the railroads. Liberals sought to repeal tariffs such as the Corn Laws, which kept the price of grain artificially high to the benefit of landowners and the detriment of the poor. When their efforts to lower grain tariffs were thwarted by landowners, liberals established an Anti-Corn Law League, which published newspapers and journals, campaigned in elections, and eventually won the support of the Tory prime minister Sir Robert Peel, whose government repealed the Corn Laws in 1846. On the continent, liberals, craving more political control, gave priority to constitutional reform. Fearing competition from Great Britain, they did not support international free trade, although they did seek to abolish internal tariffs. The failure of liberals to win political reforms in the 1830s and 1840s opened the door to more radical groups. In France and elsewhere, governments used repression and censorship to stifle the reformers. Reform organizations emerged where industrialization was most developed, as industrialists called for greater political clout. In Austria, Metternich allowed some of these organizations to form; their members looked to Great Britain as a model. In Hungary, the nationalist Lajos Kossuth (1802–1894) publicized American democracy and British political liberalism, and a boycott of all non-Hungarian (and especially Austrian) goods. Despite state opposition, reformers emerged even in Russia, where they discussed western ideas in informal "circles." Nicholas I banned all western liberal writings and all books about the United States and exiled tens of thousands of political activists to Siberia.

Socialism and the Early Labor Movement, pp. 854–857

Socialism had many variants in the 1830s and 1840s, but all socialists considered liberalism inadequate to deal with the class inequalities caused and perpetuated by industrialization. Given their interest in reconstructing social relationships, women were attracted to socialist movements. In Great Britain, many women joined Robert Owen's movement and helped to form cooperative societies and trade unions. Women's influence turned Owenism toward community experimentation and to issues of religious thought, women's rights, marriage reform, and popular education. Although most socialist groups did not welcome women, they did believe in working-class associations. French socialists Louis Blanc (1811–1882) and Pierre-Joseph Proudhon (1809–1865) both argued for the importance of associations; their arguments shaped the French labor movement. After 1840, some socialists, such as Étienne Cabet (1788–1856), began to call themselves communists to indicate their plan to replace private property with communal ownership. French socialist ideas circulated throughout Europe, evoking a response in areas undergoing industrialization. Karl Marx (1818–1883) and Friedrich Engels (1820–1895)—both sons of prosperous German-Jewish, middle-class families—developed a form of "scientific" socialism. Marx established the Communist League and, with Engels, published *The Communist Manifesto* (1848). Marx and Engels embraced industrialization, believing it would bring about the inevitable proletarian revolution and thus the abolition of exploitation, private property, and social class. Socialist doctrines led to working-class organizations: cooperative societies, local trade unions, and societies for mutual aid. Workers became more involved in politics as well. In Great Britain, workers joined the Chartist movement, which called for universal manhood suffrage, vote by secret ballot, equal electoral districts, and the payment of stipends to members of Parliament. Although many women took part in the movement, leaders feared that advocating women's suffrage would alienate potential supporters. The Chartists organized massive petition campaigns in 1838 and 1839, presenting the House of Commons with the People's Charter (as their list of demands was called), signed by over a million people. Because the House of Commons repeatedly refused to act, Chartists allied themselves with working-class strike movements and distanced themselves from women workers. The last wave of Chartist demonstrations came in 1848. Trade unions and strikes were illegal on the continent, so workers there were less organized.

The New Historical Imagination, pp. 857–858

Nationalism fostered an enthusiasm for history because history legitimized claims for a common national identity. Friedrich C. Schlosser's eighteen-volume *General History for the German People* was read by many German nationalists, while British writer Thomas Macaulay glorified the British past. This focus on history was felt in the arts as well. Romanticism cloaked history in special glamour; readers loved the historical novels of Alexandre Dumas, whereas governments valued historical paintings that could be used to support their claims to rule. Opera also incorporated history; instead of drawing on classical mythology or contemporary social satires, opera turned to passionate tragedy set in the historical past. In the writing of history itself, professional training came to be valued over literary skill. The German professor Leopold von Ranke (1795–1886) was at the forefront of this new trend. He sought to understand the past objectively, and organized small seminars for young men for the close study of documents. This reliance on source materials rather than legend or tradition had an impact on the history of religion, as scholars like David Friedrich Strauss argued that the Gospels were not history but imaginative stories. The study of geology also prompted the reconsideration of religious doctrine. In 1830–1833, Charles Lyell argued that the earth was much older than the dating of the Bible's story of creation. Lyell's argument influenced Charles Darwin (1809–1882), who began to work on his theory of evolution by natural selection.

The Revolutions of 1848

Food shortage, overpopulation, and unemployment all helped turn ideological turmoil into revolution. In 1848, demonstrations and uprisings toppled governments, forced rulers and ministers to flee, and offered revolutionaries an opportunity to put liberal, socialist, and nationalist ideals into practice. All these revolutions failed in the end because the various political movements quarreled with one another, leaving an opening for rulers and their armies to return to power.

The Hungry Forties, pp. 859–860

In 1845, an airborne blight destroyed the potato crop, a staple of peasant diets, especially in Ireland. During the following year, drought in southern Europe and excessive rain in northern Europe destroyed other crops. Those farmers who did produce enough to sell sold their goods at inflated prices. Marginal cultivators and farm laborers starved, while urban workers, thrown out of work by a lack of demand for manufactured goods in rural areas, faced higher food prices. The population growth of the 1830s and 1840s exacerbated the food shortage. In Ireland alone, as many as one-eighth of the population died horribly of starvation and disease. Hundreds of thousands emigrated from Ireland to England, the United States, and Canada. Across Europe, famine led village crowds to attack bakeries, markets, and officials to prevent rumored hoarding. By 1848, when harvests improved, many in rural areas had lost their land or become hopelessly indebted. In the cities, unemployment and higher costs of living rendered workers' lives even more difficult.

Another French Revolution, pp. 860–862

Everywhere, hunger gave rise to voices that were critical of the government. In France, opposition leaders began in 1847 to host banquets where they demanded liberalization of Louis-Philippe's regime. On February 22, 1848, demonstrations began in Paris, and students, workers, and the unemployed began to build barricades. The following day, fighting broke out between the crowds and soldiers and, on February 24, Louis-Philippe abdicated and fled to England. Alphonse de Lamartine (1790–1869) was among the leaders of the new republic, which issued liberal reforms and established universal manhood suffrage. To further appease the lower classes, Lamartine's government set up national workshops to provide construction work for minimal wages to unemployed men (later to women as well). To pay for the workshops, not popular with the middle-class to begin with, the government levied a surtax on property taxes, alienating the peasants and landowners. Simultaneously, many supported the reforms and the workshops with enthusiasm; priests blessed liberty trees, while new newspapers praised the republic, and political clubs sought to give men and women an opportunity to debate political issues. This outburst of activism alarmed middle-class liberals and conservatives, and prompted the government to enlist unemployed youths in a mobile guard. Concern about demonstrations such as that led by the communist Étienne Cabet resulted in the election of a largely conservative National Assembly in April 1848, which closed the national workshops. In response to the closure of the workshops, workers took to the streets on June 23 by the tens of thousands. During the June Days, as the following week came to be called, the army, the National Guard, and the mobile guard were joined by provincial volunteers to put down the uprising. More than ten thousand demonstrators were killed and twelve thousand were arrested. Later that year, Louis-Napoleon Bonaparte, nephew of the dead emperor, won the presidential election. In 1852, he declared himself Emperor Napoleon III.

Nationalist Revolution in Italy, pp. 862–863

In January 1848, a revolt against the Bourbons broke out in Palermo, Sicily. When news of the revolution in Paris arrived, mass demonstrations took place throughout the Italian peninsula. Nationalists hoped to unite the diverse territories of Italy, but class divisions and regional differences barred the way; nationalists found themselves in conflict with the Bourbon rulers in the south, as well as the pope and the Austrian emperor. In central Italy, peasants and artisans turned against local rulers, demanding land reform and higher wages. Property owners and business leaders supported liberal reforms and a conservative government, while workers and intellectuals envisioned a social democracy. Charles Albert, king of Piedmont-Sardinia, the most powerful Italian state, led a military campaign against Austria that failed largely because of tactics and goals' disagreements. Austria defeated the rebels in the north during the summer of 1848. In the fall, the Romans drove the pope from the city and declared a republic, but Louis-Napoleon Bonaparte intervened to restore Pius IX to the papal throne. Republican leaders Mazzini and Garibaldi fled; the revolution was over in Italy.

Revolt and Reaction in Central Europe, pp. 863–866

As in Italy, news of the revolt in Paris touched off demonstrations in Austria, Prussia, and the many German states of central Europe. In March, revolutions in the German states brought together different social groups demanding political liberalization. The Prussian king agreed to call an assembly to draft a constitution, but the goal of German unification soon took precedence among the rebels. In March and April, most of the German states agreed to elect delegates to a federal parliament at Frankfurt that would attempt to unite Germany. But the delegates had little political experience, no access to an army, and feared demands for social reforms made by the lower classes. The Prussian king Frederick William IV (r. 1840–1860) soon recovered his confidence and crushed the revolution in Berlin in the fall of 1848. His troops intervened to put down revolts in other German states during the spring of 1849. In Austria, the empire seemed in a state of collapse in the summer of 1848. In addition to the revolts in Italy, the Austrians faced Magyar nationalists who demanded autonomy for Hungary, and revolution for political reform in Vienna itself. The beleaguered Austrians granted Hungary home rule, but the Magyars alienated other ethnic groups in Hungary who preferred the Austrians. Social conflicts and ethnic divisions like these would doom the diverse nationalist revolutionaries within the Austrian Empire. The Austrians took advantage of these divisions and abolished serfdom to put an end to peasant discontent. The continued fragmentation of revolutionary groups enabled military forces, in June 1848, to begin a counteroffensive, crushing the revolt in Prague, then Vienna, and eventually Hungary, which was placed under martial law. Eighteen-year-old Francis Joseph (r. 1848–1916) ascended to the throne as the new Habsburg ruler.

Aftermath to 1848, pp. 866–869

The revolutionaries of 1848 failed to achieve most of their goals, but the revolutions did have an impact on Europe. After 1848, no French government, even Louis-Napoleon's empire, could rule without extensive popular consultation. Likewise, after 1850, almost all the German states had a constitution and a parliament. In Italy and Germany, calls for national unity had been given widespread publicity and came to be seen as a practical reality, not just an ideal. No revolution occurred in Great Britain, despite massive demonstrations organized by the Chartists. But the middle classes, encouraged by the 1832 Reform Bill, did not support revolution as they had in other countries. Russia, where Nicholas I kept a tight grip on education and the expression of ideas, also escaped revolution. Everywhere in Europe, governments continued to expand their bureaucracies, increasingly intruding into the lives of ordinary people. Almost everywhere, the aristocracy remained the dominant power. Women's participation in revolutionary activity led to a conservative reaction against women's public roles. The feminist movement in France, the most advanced in Europe, disintegrated after the conservative Republican government forbade women to form political clubs and arrested feminist leaders. Gender definitions hardened. The revolutions of 1848 brought to the fore the profound tensions within a European society moving toward industrialization and modernization, but revolution had done little to resolve these tensions. Confronted with the threat of further revolts on the scale and scope of 1848, political leaders began to search for alternatives.

Key Events   *For each question, select the most appropriate response from the choices provided.*

1830–1832 Cholera epidemic sweeps across Europe

1830 France invades and begins conquest of Algeria

1831 British and Foreign Temperance Society established

1832 George Sand, *Indiana*

1833 Factory Act regulates work of children in Great Britain; abolition of slavery in the British Empire

1834 German customs union (*Zollverein*) established under Prussian leadership

1835 Belgium opens first continental railway built with state funds

1839 Beginning of Opium War between Britain and China; invention of photography

1841 Charles Dickens, *The Old Curiosity Shop*

1846 Famine strikes Ireland; Corn Laws repealed in England; peasant insurrection in Austrian province of Galicia

1847 Charlotte Brontë, *Jane Eyre*

1848 Revolutions of 1848 throughout Europe; last great wave of Chartist demonstration in Britain; Karl Marx and Friedrich Engels, *The Communist Manifesto*; abolition of slavery in French colonies; end of serfdom in Austrian Empire

1851 Crystal Palace exhibition in London

1. What causes cholera, which swept across Europe between 1830 and 1832?
   a. Polluted air from factories
   b. Sexual contact
   c. Polluted water
   d. Fleas from infected rats

2. What did the British and Foreign Temperance Society campaign against when it was founded in 1831?
   a. Slavery
   b. Domestic violence
   c. Industrial pollution
   d. Alcohol abuse

3. What was the immediate impact of the abolition of slavery in the British Empire in 1833 on slavery worldwide?
   a. A revolt among plantation owners who depended on slave labor
   b. There was little immediate effect, and the slave trade continued, peaking in the early 1840s
   c. France followed the example of Great Britain and abolished slavery the following year
   d. The slave trade came to an abrupt end

4. What was the *Zollverein*?
   a. A revolutionary student association in Prussia
   b. A conservative newspaper in Austria
   c. An economic alliance in the German Confederation
   d. A special parliament that met in Frankfurt in 1848

5. The 1846 famine in Ireland caused hundreds of thousands of Irish to emigrate to which country?
   a. France
   b. Algeria
   c. The United States
   d. China

6. Which two countries were *not* affected by the wave of revolutions in Europe in 1848?
   a. France and Belgium
   b. Great Britain and Italy
   c. Prussia and France
   d. Great Britain and Russia

7. What was the Crystal Palace?
   a. An exhibition hall for displays of modern industry
   b. A romantic novel by George Sand
   c. A resort for the European aristocracy
   d. A palace in colonial India

Key Terms   *Match each key term to its definition.*

A. **Chartism** (p. 855)
B. **cholera** (p. 829)
C. **communists** (p. 855)
D. **Corn Laws** (p. 853)
E. **daguerreotype** (p. 843)
F. **domesticity** (p. 847)
G. **imperialism** (p. 848)
H. **lithograph** (p. 829)
I. **opium** (p. 830)
J. **social question** (p. 840)
K. **temperance movement** (p. 845)

1. _____ An epidemic, usually fatal disease that appeared in the 1830s in Europe; it is caused by a waterborne bacterium that induces violent vomiting and diarrhea and leaves the skin blue, eyes sunken and dull, and hands and feet ice cold.

2. _____ A mass-produced print using an inked stone (the Greek *lithos* means "stone"); these items played a key role in social commentary and political discussion in the 1830s–1850s.

3. _____ An addictive drug derived from the heads of poppy plants; it was imported to Europe from the Ottoman Empire and India, available in various forms, and often used by ordinary people until restricted in 1868.

4. _____ An expression common in the 1830s–1850s that reflected a widely shared concern about the effects of industrialization and urbanization on the fabric of social life.

5. _____ A form of photography named after its inventor Jacques Daguerre.

6. _____ A movement in the United States and Europe begun in the early nineteenth century to discourage consumption of alcohol.

7. _____ The set of beliefs, prevailing in the early to mid-nineteenth century, purporting that women should live their lives within the domestic sphere and devote themselves to their families and the home.

8. _____ European dominance of the non-West through economic exploitation and political rule (as distinct from the word *colonialism*, which usually implied establishment of settler colonies, often with slavery as the labor system); the word was coined in the mid-nineteenth century.

9. _____ Tariffs on grain in Great Britain that benefited landowners by preventing the import of cheap foreign grain; after much agitation, these tariffs were repealed by British government in 1846.

10. _____ Those socialists who after 1840 (when the word was first used) advocated the abolition of private property in favor of communal, collective ownership.

11. _____ The movement of supporters of the People's Charter (drawn up in Britain in 1838), which demanded universal manhood suffrage, vote by secret ballot, equal electoral districts, annual elections, and the elimination of property qualifications for and the payment of stipends to members of Parliament. This movement attracted many working-class adherents.

Identification   *This activity tests your recall of significant people, places, and events from this chapter. Fill in the blank with the correct answer.*

1. Although it was still far behind Great Britain, _____ was the fastest growing industrial power on the continent in the early 1800s.

2. Although it was the largest industrial power, England's factories still employed a small minority of workers, only _____ percent in the 1840s.

3. One of several worker reform acts, the Mines Act of 1842 prohibited the employment of _____ underground.

4. Although it had less social impact because it did not kill large numbers in a single outbreak, _____ was still the number-one deadly disease in nineteenth-century Europe.

5. In 1847, the _____ successfully pressured Parliament to limit the workday of women and children to ten hours.

6. One of many romantic painters who took a dim view of industrialization, _____ traveled to the United States where he painted landscapes untouched by machinery.

7. When the British Houses of Parliament were rebuilt in the 1830s, they were built in a _____ style reminiscent of the Middle Ages.

8. One of many women social reformers, _____, an English Quaker minister, helped establish institutions for female prisoners modeled on the school and manufacturing shop she had organized at Newgate Prison in London.

9. After a brief war ending in 1842, the Treaty of Nanking reaffirmed the right of the British East India Company to import _____ into China.

10. Blaming the Decembrist Revolt of 1825 on education, _____ restricted peasant access to education.

11. Inspired by the nationalist vision of _____, Giuseppe Mazzini founded Young Italy, a secret society that attracted thousands.

12. The most significant nationalist movement in western Europe could be found in _____.

13. Until repealed in 1846, the _____ protected the interests of wealthy landowners to the detriment of the poor by outlawing the import of low-cost foreign grain.

14. In France, _____ devoted herself to reconciling the interests of male and female workers by arguing that the emancipation of male workers would not be possible while women remained in a degraded state.

15. _____ writings aimed to broaden history by including everyday life, politics, war, diplomacy, and to promote a sense of British nationalism; his histories of Great Britain became famous.

16. A romantic poet and eloquent orator, _____ became the most noteworthy leader of the February Revolution of 1848 in France.

17. In _____, on the forty-eighth anniversary of Napoleon I as emperor, Louis-Napoleon Bonaparte declared himself Emperor Napoleon III.

18. Under pressure from popular demonstrations, King Frederick William IV of Prussia was forced to call a parliament that met in _____ in an attempt to unify Germany.

19. In one of many examples of the breakdown of unity within nationalist movements, the new _____ government alienated other nationalities when it tried to impose the Magyar language on them.

20. Creating an aura of fantasy with its nine hundred tons of glass, the _____ opened in May 1851 as a government-sponsored spectacle of what industry, hard work, and technological imagination could produce.

CHAPTER REVIEW

Self-Test and Analytical Exercises

Multiple Choice   *Select the best answer from the four choices provided.*

1. Which country had achieved industrial supremacy by the early nineteenth century?
   a. France
   b. Prussia
   c. Belgium
   d. Great Britain

2. Why did industrialization advance slowly in eastern Europe?
   a. There was limited labor mobility due to the continuing existence of serfdom, and wealthy landlords had little incentive to invest in manufacturing.
   b. Anxiety over urban growth and an expanding criminal element slowed the building of factories.
   c. There was a shortage of coal in that region.
   d. Frequent wars sapped government funds.

3. In Great Britain, the Factory Act of 1833
   a. outlawed the employment of children under age nine in the textile industry.
   b. forced employers to reduce the amount of pollution emitted by their factories.
   c. required a minimum wage for employees of the textile industry.
   d. outlawed the exportation of machinery and the emigration of artisans.

4. Which of the following was *not* a feature of rural European life?
   a. Rising child mortality rates
   b. An expanding birthrate, as couples married earlier in life
   c. The steady emigration of rural inhabitants to other parts of Europe or to the United States
   d. The continued dominance of traditional elites

5. Which of the following was *not* a feature of the artistic movement known as romanticism?
   a. Glorification of nature
   b. Desire of its practitioners to recapture the pre-industrial world
   c. Vivid expression of anxiety over economic and social change
   d. Portraits of middle-class families

6. Which of the following pairs depicted social conditions in their novels?
   a. Elizabeth Barrett Browning and Thomas Cole
   b. Thomas Cole and Charles Dickens
   c. Honoré de Balzac and Charles Dickens
   d. Joseph M. W. Turner and Charlotte Brontë

7. Which statement *best* expresses middle-class attitudes toward the education of the lower classes?
   a. Education would create a docile working class that would accept grueling hours of factory labor.
   b. Education would improve the lives of the working classes, and possibly lead to social mobility.
   c. Education would lead directly to revolution.
   d. Education should only be undertaken by religious societies, never by the state.

8. Imperialism was usually characterized by
   a. the direct rule and wholesale destruction of indigenous peoples by Europeans.
   b. a booming trade in African slaves.
   c. indirect forms of economic exploitation and political rule.
   d. religious motives and Christianizing missions.

9. The Chartists advocated
   a. the redistribution of wealth along socialist lines.
   b. democratic government, annual parliaments, secret ballots, and universal manhood suffrage.
   c. free trade, including abolition of the Corn Laws.
   d. the overthrow of the British state.

10. Which statement *best* expresses the goals of British liberals?
    a. They desired free markets and limited government.
    b. They recommended high tariffs designed to protect British industry.
    c. They aimed at constitutional reform in order to limit the expanding power of the monarchy.
    d. They saw the need for an expansion of the role of government in English society.

11. Pierre-Joseph Proudhon defined property as
    a. the cornerstone for civilization.
    b. something that the state should monopolize.
    c. theft.
    d. the rightful desire of all productive laborers working in earnest.

12. New attitudes toward history and its interpretation
    a. were used by all the competing ideologies to advocate their causes.
    b. were ignored by socialists because they rejected established societal norms of Europe.
    c. emphasized the role of women and promised female European citizens a bright future.
    d. were largely ignored by the general populace, who were uneducated and largely illiterate.

13. Which statement regarding famines in the 1840s is *false*?
    a. High food prices drove workers toward socialist politics.
    b. Famine was exacerbated in some places by overpopulation.
    c. The threat of starvation saw citizens overcome class differences to face food shortages together.
    d. The inability of many to afford industrial goods saw factories close or reduce production and urban workers lose their jobs.

14. The provisional government formed after the February Revolution in France did all of the following *except*
    a. abolish the death penalty for political crimes.
    b. put an end to slavery in French colonies.
    c. introduce freedom of the press.
    d. advocate socialist economic policies.

15. What were the June Days?
    a. The violent suppression of French workers by the National Guard and provincial volunteers
    b. Political meetings disguised as banquets at which the opposition leaders plotted against Louis-Philippe

c. The week of celebration following the election of Louis-Napoleon Bonaparte
    d. The relative calm following the establishment of the French national workshops

16. Italian revolutionaries fought the armies of which two nations?
    a. France and Austria
    b. France and Prussia
    c. Austria and Britain
    d. Austria and Spain

17. Despite industrialization, by the 1840s most workers were employed in
    a. coal mining.
    b. nonfactory work.
    c. steel manufacturing.
    d. railroad building.

18. Which disease swept across Europe during 1830–1832 and 1847–1851, devastating urban populations?
    a. Bubonic plague
    b. Cholera
    c. Malaria
    d. Typhus

19. Which of the following was the *primary* cause of rapid urban population growth?
    a. Increased fertility of urban women
    b. Rising life expectancy of urban inhabitants
    c. Large-scale emigration from rural areas to cities and towns
    d. Expanding birthrate, a result of couples marrying earlier in life

20. All of the following were features of urban life *except*
    a. overcrowding.
    b. poor sanitation.
    c. the limited availability of safe, drinkable water.
    d. rising life expectancy.

21. The dominant artistic movement of the 1830s and 1840s was
    a. Neoclassicism.
    b. Romanticism.
    c. Utilitarianism.
    d. Impressionism.

22. Which female French writer dressed like a man, became a socialist, and created novels emphasizing romantic love and moral idealism?
    a. Charlotte Brontë
    b. Elizabeth Barrett Browning
    c. George Sand
    d. Jane Eyre

23. Which of the following is *not* a feature of middle- and upper-class women's lives in the 1830s and 1840s?
    a. In the aristocracy and middle classes, women's education differed from that of men, and emphasized religion, obedience, and the arts.
    b. Their fashions became more practical, reflecting their expanding public role.
    c. Scientists argued that women were morally superior because they were largely uninterested in sex.
    d. Most women had little hope of economic independence.

24. The Treaty of Nanking
    a. forced an expanded British opium trade on the Chinese.
    b. incorporated Algeria into France.
    c. saw the British Empire annex Singapore.
    d. ended the Atlantic slave trade.

25. The *Zollverein* was a
    a. failed uprising by Austrian peasants in 1839.
    b. customs union that included most German states.
    c. play that glorified Germany's national past.
    d. tariff placed on all non-German goods.

26. The Corn Laws
    a. prevented the import of low-cost grain into Britain.
    b. promoted better nutrition among the working classes.
    c. were designed by nationalists to promote British trade abroad.
    d. harmed landlords by raising the price of food.

27. Which statement *best* describes socialism and women in the 1830s and 1840s?
    a. Women participated in socialist organizations and male workers welcomed their support.
    b. Women did not participate in socialist politics; socialists believed woman's place was in the home.
    c. Women had to create separate socialist societies in defiance of male socialists.
    d. Women attempted to broaden socialist politics to further women's rights and issues.

28. With history and nationalism influencing the arts, which Polish composer incorporated his country's folk music into his compositions?
    a. Alexandre Dumas
    b. Adam Mickiewicz
    c. Frédéric Chopin
    d. Lajos Kossuth

29. Famine in the 1840s
    a. strengthened the bond between citizens and governments, who blamed foreigners for the high price of food.
    b. aroused social and political unrest as citizens blamed government officials for not ensuring fair prices and merchants for reaping benefits from high prices.
    c. had little impact on politics.
    d. was so devastating that all revolutionary actions were quelled in the face of impending death.

30. All of the following resulted from the revolutions of 1848 *except* the
    a. reassertion of conservative rule.
    b. hardening of gender distinctions.
    c. end of aristocratic dominance.
    d. increase of nationalism.

31. Revolutions occurred in 1848 in all of the following regions *except*
    a. the Italian states.
    b. Prussia.
    c. Great Britain.
    d. France.

32. Which major feature of the rebellions in the Austrian Empire was a minor part of other national revolutions of 1848?
    a. Defeat of the revolutionaries by military force
    b. Ethnic divisions
    c. Class conflict
    d. Widespread demonstrations

Short Answer *Answer each question in three or four sentences.*

The Advance of Industrialization and Urbanization

1. Which technological developments effected the greatest changes during the Industrial Revolution?

2. What effect did the factory system have on European society and its laborers?

3. Which social problems resulted from rapid urbanization?

Reforming the Social Order

4. What was the social question and what were some of the cultural responses to it?

5. What influence did religion have on social reform?

6. How did Europe's approach to its colonies change during the first half of the nineteenth century?

The Ferment of Ideologies

7. What were the goals of nationalism? What influence did it have?

8. For what did European liberals lobby?

9. How did socialists view the problems of the Industrial Revolution?

The Revolutions of 1848

10. What contributed to the outbreak of revolutions in 1848?

11. What caused the 1848 revolution in France, and why did it fail?

12. What was accomplished by the revolutions of 1848?

BUILDING HISTORICAL SKILLS

Reading Maps   *Write a brief, paragraph-length response to each of the following questions based on* **Map 22.1: Industrialization in Europe, c. 1850** *(p. 833).*

1. Where were the most industrialized regions in Europe by 1850?

2. Where were the least industrialized areas in Europe in 1850?

3. In what ways were nonindustrialized countries still important to the Industrial Revolution?

Reading Illustrations   *Write a brief, paragraph-length response to each of the following questions based on the illustration* **The Fighting *Téméraire* Tugged to Her Last Berth to Be Broken Up** *(p. 842).*

1. What does this painting symbolize?

2. What elements of this painting are typical of romanticism?

Reading Historical Documents   *Write a brief, paragraph-length response to each of the following questions based on the documents in your book.*

A Romantic Poet Mourns the Fate of the Workers (p. 841)

1. Why does Heinrich Heine say that Germany is doomed?

2. How does this poem mark a shift in romanticism?

Communist Manifesto (p. 856)

3. How do Marx and Engels fit into the "new historical imagination" that was prevalent around the same time?

4. Why did Marx and Engels believe that industrialization was a positive development?

New Sources, New Perspectives: Statistics and the Standard of Living of the Working Class (pp. 836–837)

5. What are some of the positive and negative effects that scholars emphasize in the debate over industrialization?

6. What do the numbers in the table on page 837 indicate? What is meant by the gap in wages between those who work on farms and those who don't?

7. What evidence could one look for to argue that higher wages did not necessarily lead to a higher standard of living?

Politics and Culture of the Nation-State
c. 1850–1870

CHAPTER OVERVIEW

Chapter Questions *Keep these questions in mind as you go through the study guide chapter.*

1. How did the balance of power shift in the 1850s and 1860s?

2. What were the motivations and results of state unification?

3. What types of reforms did governments sponsor and why?

4. Which trend characterized developments in literature, the visual arts, and science?

5. How did Marxism present itself as a challenge to the modern state?

Chapter Summary

The End of the Concert of Europe

The revolutions of 1848 had weakened the concert of Europe, driving out Metternich and allowing the forces of nationalism to flourish. It became more difficult for countries to control their competing ambitions and act together. The resurgence of Bonapartism in the person of Napoleon III added to the volatility of international politics as France sought to reassert itself.

Napoleon III and the Quest for French Glory, pp. 875–876

In France, Louis-Napoleon encouraged French grandeur and the cult of his famous uncle. As emperor, Napoleon III maintained a lavish court while his wife, the Empress Eugénie, fulfilled the role of devoted mother and philanthropist. Napoleon III also supported economic modernization, which promoted economic growth, free trade,

and innovative investment banking. Following an economic downturn in the late 1850s, Napoleon III sought liberal support by allowing working-class organizations and admitting some democratic features to his government. Napoleon III broke the Congress of Vienna's containment of France by realigning foreign powers and engaging Russia, Austria, and Prussia in a series of wars including the disastrously bloody Crimean War (1853–1856). Outside of Europe, he enforced French rule in Algeria and southeast Asia, and attempted to install Habsburg Maximilian as ruler of Mexico, a plan that ended in rebellion and Maximilian's execution in 1867. He also encouraged such projects as the Suez Canal, which connected the Mediterranean and Red seas.

The Crimean War, 1853–1856: Turning Point in European Affairs, pp. 877–879

Russian tsar Nicholas I had wanted to absorb as much of the ailing Ottoman Empire as possible, and Napoleon III encouraged his aggressiveness. Because Britain feared Russia would control British routes through the Mediterranean to East Asia, the British supported the Ottomans. The Austrians, who still harbored resentment over Russia's help to put down a Hungarian revolt in 1849, remained neutral—again with encouragement from Napoleon III. In alliance, France and Great Britain declared war on Russia in 1854. The Russian naval base at Sevastopol in the Crimea on the Black Sea was besieged for a year; both sides suffered high casualties. Lacking adequate sanitation and medical care and led by incompetent generals, three-quarters of a million men died, more than two-thirds of them from disease and starvation. Alexander II (r. 1855–1881) became tsar on his father's death and sued for peace. The 1856 Peace of Paris deprived Russia of its naval bases in the Dardanelles Straits and the Black Sea. Moldavia and Walachia (which soon merged to form Romania) became autonomous Turkish provinces. The Crimean War introduced new technologies such as the railroad, the shell-firing cannon, the breech-loading rifle, the telegraph, and the steam-powered ship. It was also the first war subjected to extensive public scrutiny, as increased press coverage, the use of the telegraph, and the advent of photography brought the war home to Europeans in a way never before possible. Individual civilians went to the front lines to help.

Spirit of Reform in Russia, pp. 879–881

In the decade preceding the Crimean War, peasant insurrection was common in Russia. Defeat in the war confronted the educated public with the poor performance of serf-conscripted armies and the intolerable liability of serf labor. Tsar Alexander II realized that, to avoid revolution, he had to heed reformers. Alexander II launched a series of "Great Reforms," beginning with the emancipation of nearly 50 million people. The former serfs were given land, but not as private landowners. Rather, they and the land they farmed were organized into a community (*mir*) controlled by male village elders. Although no individual peasants actually owned land, all were required to repay the original landowners via payments to the government. Emancipated but chained to enormous debts, the serfs still could not form the pool of free labor Russia needed. Military reform followed in 1874 when the government replaced the twenty-five-year period of conscription with a six-year term. Attention to education, efficiency, and humane treatment of recruits created a Russian army more competitive with other European forces. Reaction to the reforms often differed along generational lines. Young aristocrats emphasized the importance of practical activity over leisure and identified with workers and peasants. Traditionalists pessimistically labeled these radical young people "nihilists"—those who believed that nothing exists, is knowable, or can be communicated, and who rejected all moral values. The reforms also sparked resistance in Russian-dominated nations, including Poland, which sought full independence in 1863. As in the past, the Russian government responded to unrest in Poland, the Caucasus, and elsewhere with military force, but also with a policy of Russification—an intense campaign to force minorities to adopt Russian language and culture. Despite the Great Reforms, Alexander II only partially developed the institutions that buttressed other nation-states. The reins of government were still tightly held by the tsar and his inner circle. The persistence of autocracy and the abuse of large population groups suffocated the shared national identity felt so strongly elsewhere.

War and Nation Building

Politicians in the German and Italian states used the opportunity provided by the weakened concert of Europe to unify their countries quickly and violently by means of war. Historians sometimes treat the rise of powerful nation-states such as Italy, Germany, and the United States and the accompanying sense of national identity among their peoples as part of an inevitable process. However, millions of individuals maintained a regional or local sense of identity rather than a national one.

Cavour, Garibaldi, and the Process of Italian Unification, pp. 881–883

The disintegrating of the Concert of Europe allowed Italy to make its bid for freedom from the Austrian empire. Despite failed revolutions in 1848, the idea of political unification had not disappeared. The obvious leader for this Risorgimento was Piedmont-Sardinia, the most economically and militarily advanced of the Italian states. Its prime minister, Camillo di Cavour (1810–1861) attempted to liberate Austrian-held regions by allying with Napoleon III. In exchange for military aid, France was promised the city of Nice and the province of Savoy. Cavour provoked the Austrians to invade northern Italy in April 1859. With the help of the French and the newly built Piedmontese railroad, the forces of Piedmont-Sardinia won stunning victories over Austria at Solferino and Magenta. To Cavour's dismay, Napoleon III then signed a treaty granting Lombardy to Piedmont-Sardinia, but leaving Venetia in Austrian hands. Nevertheless, the Piedmontese victories had created a groundswell of nationalism, and Parma, Modena, Tuscany, and the Papal States (except Rome, which was occupied by French troops) elected to join Piedmont-Sardinia. In May 1860, Giuseppe Garibaldi (1807–1882), a committed republican and inspired guerrilla fighter, raised a volunteer army, liberated Sicily from overbearing landlords and a corrupt government, and then crossed to the mainland and headed north. Cavour, who feared the influence of the radical republican Garibaldi, sent his troops south to stop him. But, when the two men met in Naples in the autumn of 1860, Garibaldi gave way to Cavour and, in 1861, the kingdom of Italy was proclaimed. Former Piedmont-Sardinian king Victor Emmanuel was at its head. Cavour died shortly thereafter, and divisions among successive political leaders and differences between the wealthy commercial north and the impoverished agricultural south kept Italy relatively weak.

Bismarck and the Realpolitik of German Unification, pp. 883–887

Called by William I of Prussia (r. 1861–1871) to take the position of prime minister in 1862, Otto von Bismarck (1815–1898) overrode liberals in parliament and rammed through programs to build up the army. He then embarked on a series of wars: with Denmark in 1864, Austria in 1866, and France in 1870. In the course of these wars, Bismarck united the smaller German states behind Prussia rather than Austria, thus excluding that great power from German unification. This exclusion was confirmed when Austria, laden with debt and plagued by its restless national minorities, was provoked by Bismarck into declaring war on Prussia. Within seven weeks, Prussia won a decisive victory. To bring in the remaining German holdouts, Bismarck goaded France into declaring war over the choice of a new king for Spain. Bismarck's diplomacy with Great Britain, Austria, and Russia had isolated France from potential allies. France quickly fell to the Prussian forces, ending Napoleon III's Second Empire, on September 4, 1870. France had to give Alsace and Lorraine to Germany. As the crowning blow, the Germans crowned King William of Prussia kaiser of the new German Empire at the Palace of Versailles in January 1871. The kaiser also remained the king of Prussia, henceforth one of the new empire's states. He controlled the military and appointed Bismarck chancellor of the empire. The adult male population of all the states elected representatives to a new assembly, the Reichstag, which ratified budgets. To maintain the social hierarchy, votes from the upper classes counted more than those from the lower classes. The liberals, giddy with military success, supported Bismarck's blend of economic progress, constitutionalism, and militaristic nationalism. Bismarck, filled with national pride, was now poised to dominate continental politics.

Francis Joseph and the Creation of the Austro-Hungarian Monarchy, pp. 887–888

Losses to Cavour and Bismarck confronted Austria with the need to make some changes. Emperor Francis Joseph (r. 1848–1916) attempted to enhance his authority through elaborate and formal court ceremony, but he resisted change. Nonetheless, in the 1850s and 1860s, standards of honesty and efficiency improved within the government, and the state promoted local education and respected the rights of minorities to be educated—and to communicate with officials—in their native language. Most internal customs barriers were abolished, free trade with Germany was established, and much of the state railway system was sold, creating a boom in private railway construction and foreign investment. Eventually, Vienna underwent extensive renovation, and more jobs opened up as industrialization progressed. When money for military modernization and warfare dried up, Francis Joseph was forced to modify his absolutism by creating a more modern Parliament (the Reichsrat), but German liberals imposed financial constraints on the military. In 1866, the Hungarian agrarian elites requested Magyar home rule, which was granted, creating a "dual monarchy." Although Francis Joseph was crowned king of Hungary and was in charge of coordinating Austro-Hungarian foreign policy, Hungary largely ruled itself after 1867 through the restored Hungarian parliament. Following the establishment of this dual monarchy, other ethnic groups within the empire increased their demands for self-rule. Some turned to Russia, hoping to form a Pan-Slavism movement (a transnational alliance of all Slavic peoples) that would allow them to break away from Austria's influence.

Political Stability Through Gradual Reform in Great Britain, pp. 888–889

In contrast to the upheaval in continental Europe, Great Britain, ruled by Queen Victoria (r. 1837–1901) with the aid of her husband, Prince Albert, basked in domestic tranquility, morality, and middle-class virtues. Parliament, dominated by the Conservatives (formerly the Tory party) and the Liberals (formerly the Whigs), enjoyed smooth decision making and liberal progress. In 1867, the Conservative party, led by Benjamin Disraeli (1804–1881), passed the Second Reform Bill, which enfranchised a million new male voters. As the electorate expanded, differing groups encouraged both parties to support reform. Under pressure from women's groups, the government addressed family and marital issues, passing the Matrimonial Causes Act of 1857, which facilitated divorce; and the Married Women's Property Act of 1870, which allowed married women to own property and keep the wages they earned. In addition to accepting the necessity of reform within the political system, the government created plush ceremonies that united supporters and opponents, as well as members of all social classes, in national unity. Architects adopted building styles that glorified the English past, while celebrations of royal family events created loyalty to the monarchy and the state in this "Victorian" age, a term used to refer to anything from manners to political institutions during Victoria's reign. All was not peaceful, however: Britain's politicians were as devoted to Realpolitik as Bismarck, and used violence to expand their overseas empire and to control an always suffering Ireland. But the violence was far removed from the sights and minds of most British citizens.

Civil War and Nation Building in the United States and Canada, pp. 889–891

The United States continued to expand westward; Texas was annexed in 1845, and an 1848 victory over Mexico brought in California and large portions of the southwest. Although politicians and citizens agreed that native American peoples should be banned from these lands, they disagreed over whether slavery should be allowed. As the issue came to polarize the country, the election in 1860 of Abraham Lincoln to the presidency created fears that his Republican administration would ban slavery in the west. Most of the slaveholding states seceded to form the Confederate States of America following his election. Between 1861 and 1865, the United States was torn apart by a civil war fought over the dual issues of secession and slavery. In January 1863, Lincoln issued the Emancipation Proclamation, which freed slaves in the Confederate states, as a wartime measure. By April 1865, despite the assassination of Lincoln, the North, stronger economically and militarily, had prevailed. Slavery was abolished, but the constitutional guarantee of full political rights to African American men was effectively nullified once Southern whites regained control of state politics after 1877. In retribution for Great Britain's partiality to the Confederacy, the United States demanded the annexation of Canada. To avoid this, Great Britain granted Canada the status of self-governing dominion.

Establishing Social Order

This age of nation building disturbed everyday life, often bringing chaos and sometimes dramatic public protest. Government officials developed mechanisms to forge internal social unity and order. Confronted with exploding population growth and crowded cities, governments intervened to guard social peace by attending to public health and safety. Greater confidence in European institutions in general helped drive an expansion of European influence across the globe.

Bringing Order to the Cities, pp. 891–893

European cities became the backdrop for displays of state power and national solidarity, thus efforts to improve sanitation revitalized the state's credit. In 1857, Austrian emperor Francis Joseph ordered the destruction of Vienna's medieval city walls and replaced them with boulevards lined with public buildings such as the Opera House and the Reichsrat. Napoleon III of France ordered broad boulevards that allowed crowds to observe royal pageantry and troops faster access to the city and its inhabitants. These renovated cities highlighted class differences: poor neighborhoods were razed, and boulevards separated the rich from the poor. In London, renovation replaced slums and lower-class neighborhoods with large commercial streets. Despite such renovation, disease still remained a problem. The stench, diseases, and "morbid air" in cities indicated such a degree of failure, disorder, and danger that sanitation became a government priority. Louis Pasteur provided the key when he discovered that bacteria and parasites were responsible for many illnesses. He demonstrated that heating foods such as wine and milk—pasteurization—could kill these organisms. Joseph Lister applied Pasteur's discovery to medical care and developed antiseptics for treating wounds. At the same time, governments improved drainage and water supplies. In Paris, Haussmann devised a system to pipe in water from less-contaminated sources in the countryside, a system imitated throughout Europe. On the lookout for disease and sanitary dangers, people became more aware of foul odors and air that had been an accepted part of life for thousands of years. Now aware of the importance of hygiene, the middle and lower classes began to bathe more often, a refinement in harmony with government concern for order.

Expanding the Reach of Bureaucracy, pp. 893–894

Enacting new programs to build social order and safety and enhance the nation expanded state bureaucracies. Government authority reached further into the realm of everyday life, in part through regular census taking. Details of people's lives—their ages, occupations, and marital status, for example—could be used to set quotas for military conscription or to predict the need for new prisons. Sweden, in 1860, introduced an income tax, exposing its citizens' earnings to governmental scrutiny. Reformers like Florence Nightingale believed that the gathering of quantitative information made government less susceptible to corruption and inefficiency. Decisions would be based on facts rather than influence-peddling or ill-informed guesses. Another "intrusion" was the increase in government regulation of prostitution, designed to limit the spread of venereal disease. As government increased such functions, new departments and agencies were established, providing new sources of employment. To open jobs in the civil service to themselves, the middle classes successfully lobbied to make civil-service jobs merit-based rather than rewards for political loyalty or high birth. In Austria-Hungary, Britain, Sweden and other countries, legislation required that these positions be earned through competitive examinations. Citizens thus ordered the state to conform with their ideas of fairness, competence, and opportunity.

Schooling and Professionalizing Society, pp. 894–895

Increased requirements for empirical knowledge and objective standards of evaluation elevated and altered certain professions: doctors, lawyers, managers, professors, and journalists began to influence state policy and regulate admission to their fields. Nation building required major improvements in the education of all citizens, professional or not. Governments introduced compulsory schooling to reduce illiteracy and educate their growing electorates. Among the working poor, education became a shared value and made traveling lecturers, public forums, reading groups, and debating societies popular. Traditionally, primary education had been religious, but the 1850s and 1860s introduced secular and scientific instruction. Nationalists also saw that to cohere as a nation, the young had to be educated in its language, literature, and history. Secondary and university education remained elite luxuries, but now secondary education developed along different tracks. In Prussia, the *gymnasia* offered a liberal arts education, but in the 1860s added the Realschulen to prepare students for business or technical careers. Reformers pushed for more advanced and complex courses for young women than they had been offered in the past. Alexander II and Napoleon III, as part of their campaigns of controlled modernization, both sponsored secondary and university-level courses for women. Some young women took advantage of new opportunities in medicine. These women saw the need to protect the modesty of female patients and to bring feminine values to health care. Women also entered teaching in large numbers, as primary education expanded. Yet, because this work took them outside the domestic sphere, it raised a storm of controversy.

Spreading Western Order Beyond the West, pp. 895–899

In an age of nation building and industrial development, colonies took on new political dimension. Once the Suez Canal was opened in 1869, it offered a shorter trade route to Asia. After mid century, Great Britain, France, and Russia revised their colonial policy by instituting direct rule, expanding colonial bureaucracies, and providing a wide array of social and cultural services. The French government pushed its dominion over Cochin China (in modern Vietnam) in the 1860s and occupied all of Algeria by 1870. Local leaders in Algeria were attracted to services such as schools and to French goods, technology, and institutions, and thus cooperated in building railroads and borrowing money from French banks. Although British colonialism in the first half of the century had been laissez-faire, British institutions and power nonetheless gradually spread through India. In 1857, Hindu and Muslim troops rebelled against regulations that violated their religious beliefs. This Indian mutiny coincided with a revolt in Jhansi, sparked when the East India Company tried to seize the kingdom from the late rajah's widow. After putting down the revolt, the British government took direct control with the 1858 Government of India Act. China had eluded complete takeover, but Christian missionaries and traders disturbed a society already unsteady from an exploding population, defeat in the Opium Wars, and other trade pressures from Europe. Contact with the West touched off the Taiping (Heavenly Kingdom) movement, which attracted millions of followers. The leader, Hung Hsui-ch'uan (Hong Xinquan), preached the end of the ruling Qing dynasty, reform, and the expulsion of foreigners. By the mid 1850s, the Taiping controlled half of China. A bloody civil war broke out between Taiping followers and the Qing regime. When peace finally came, the Europeans had profited, gaining virtually unlimited access to the country. Japan alone was able to escape domination. By 1853, when Americans claimed to open Japan to trade, Dutch traders at Nagasaki had already made the Japanese keenly aware of western industrial, military, and commercial innovations. Trade agreements with the United States and others followed, leading to concerted effort for reform. In 1867, Japanese reformers, after a brief civil war, pressured the ruling Tokugawa shogun to abdicate and restored the emperor to full power in 1868. The goal of this Meiji Restoration was to establish Japan as a modern, technologically powerful state free from western control.

The Culture of Social Order

After 1848, many artists and writers expressed profound grievances, especially about political repression, economic growth, and the effects of enfranchising working-class men. Infused with commercial values and organized by governmental officials, daily life seemed tawdry and hardly bearable to many artists. Such disenchantment promoted the literary and artistic style called realism. In contrast, intellectuals proposed theories called positivism and Darwinism.

The Arts Confront Social Reality, pp. 900–903

The reading public devoured biographies of political leaders, and the general public attended an increasing number of artistic, scientific, and natural history exhibitions. Realism dominated the novel. The hugely popular novels of Charles Dickens (1812–1870) appeared in serial form in magazines and periodicals. His characters came from contemporary English society and ranged from starving orphans to ruthless opportunists that drew attention to the impact on society of industrialization and civil law. The widely read novels of George Eliot (Mary Ann Evans, 1819–1880) explored contemporary personal problems. French writer Gustave Flaubert (1821–1880) scandalized French society with *Madame Bovary* (1857), the tale of an unhappy wife whose longing for possessions she could ill afford, and illicit affairs, ultimately lead her to commit suicide. The poet Charles-Pierre Baudelaire (1821–1867) also shocked the public by writing explicitly about sex, as well as drug- and wine-induced fantasies, in *Les Fleurs du mal* (Flowers of Evil [1857]). Russian writers during this era of Great Reforms debated whether or not western European values were insidiously transforming their societies. Ivan Turgenev (1818–1883) captured generational conflict in *Fathers and Sons* (1862), a story of nihilistic children rejecting the older generation's Romantic spiritual values. Fyodor Dostoevsky (1821–1881) created antiheroes in works such as *Notes from Underground* (1864) and *Crime and Punishment* (1866). After 1848, painters turned away from idealized portraits of workers and peasants and adopted the realist style. French painter Gustave Courbet (1819–1877) depicted how backbreaking physical labor could be. Édouard Manet (1823–1883) abandoned romanticism in his portrayals of women and sexuality in paintings such as *Déjeuner sur l'herbe* (*Luncheon on the Grass* [1863]) and *Olympia* (1865). Opera was a commercially profitable enterprise and accessible to most classes of society. Giuseppe Verdi (1813–1901) used the genre to contrast the noble ideals of honor, love, and patriotism with the corrosive effects of power. He explored social issues as well, as in *La Traviata* (1853). Richard Wagner (1813–1883), the era's most flamboyant and musically innovative composer, revolutionized opera by fusing music and drama to arouse an audience's fear, awe, and engagement with his vision. His cycle of four operas—*Der Ring des Nibelungen*—exploring the destructiveness of materialism and the pursuit of power, concluded that only unselfish love could redeem society. Although oftentimes controversial, writers, visual artists, and composers helped create a unified cultural community.

Religion and Secular Order, pp. 903–905

Although organized religion provided a source of stability after 1848, liberals and nationalists came to reject a religious worldview. Rationalism replaced religious faith for many. Additionally, rulers of new nation-states in Italy and Germany found that loyalty to the church weakened nationalistic feeling. In 1864, Pope Pius IX (r. 1846–1878) issued *The Syllabus of Errors*, which put the church explicitly at odds with liberalism and progress. In 1870, the First Vatican Council approved the doctrine of papal infallibility. Despite such pronouncements, church attendance declined among workers and artisans, although many in the upper and middle classes and most of the peasantry remained faithful. This period saw an outburst of religious fervor, among women in particular. In 1858, a peasant girl in Lourdes in southern France, Bernadette Soubirous (1844–1879), began having visions of the Virgin Mary. Less than ten years later, railroad track had to be laid to Lourdes to enable millions of pilgrims to visit the shrine. At the same time, Charles Darwin (1809–1882) published *On the Origin of Species* (1859), in which he stated that human beings had evolved over the course of millions of years. Darwin argued that only the strongest or best adapted to the environment would find sexual partners and reproduce. Darwin's theories challenged the biblical creation story and the view that nature was noble and humans essentially rational. Darwin tried to explain the social hierarchy by maintaining that white European men naturally dominated the world because they were more highly evolved than men of color and all women.

From Natural Science to Social Science, pp. 905–906

Darwin's theories accelerated the search for alternatives to the religious explanation of social order. Auguste Comte (1798–1857) originated the ideas for positivism, a social science that called for the careful study of facts so as to generate accurate or "positive" laws of society. Because Comte promoted women's participation in reform, his ideas opened the fields of the social sciences to them. English philosopher John Stuart Mill (1806–1873) was initially an enthusiastic supporter of Comte and argued for mass education and the complete enfranchisement of women. His treatise *On Liberty* (1859) argued for individual liberty protected from state intrusion. Mill's promotion of women's rights—an argument he developed with the help of his wife, Harriet Taylor Mill (1808–1858)—inspired him to write *The Subjection of Women* (1869), in which he stated that a woman's assigned role of love and obedience in marriage masked gross marital inequality. Mill's thought, however, was submerged in a flood of Social Darwinism, theories that incorporated Darwin's ideas about evolution to justify the existing social hierarchy. In particular, Herbert Spencer's promotion of laissez-faire and unadulterated competition seemed to be justified by Darwin's theories, and found admirers in the middle and upper classes.

Contesting the Growing Power of the Nation-State

By the close of the 1860s, the unchecked growth of the state and the ongoing process of economic change had led to palpable tensions in European society. New theories of work life and politics appeared to counter nationalism and capitalism, most notably those of Karl Marx. From the 1870s onward, Marxism and the fury of the working class renewed fear among the middle cases that the nation-state and the entire social order might be violently destroyed.

The Rise of Marxism, pp. 906–908

After repression in the 1850s, workers' organizations reemerged as a political force in the West. In the 1850s, governments often outlawed unions; workers therefore came together in secret but poorly organized groups. Among the various leaders of these groups was French printer and utopian socialist Pierre-Joseph Proudhon (1809–1865), who argued that the private ownership of property robbed those without property of their share of the planet's benefits; he advocated the organization of artisans into mutualist social organizations that would bring about the end of government. Russian nobleman Mikhail Bakhunin (1814–1876) gained prominence with the 1864 establishment of the International Workingmen's Association. Bakhunin argued that the state should not in any way infringe upon individual freedom. His ideas formed the basis of anarchism, a doctrine that advocated the destruction of all state power. Author of *The Communist Manifesto* (written with Friedrich Engels [1848]) and *Das Kapital* (1867–1894), Karl Marx (1818–1883) also supported the International, as this organization was called, but he developed the theories of historical and dialectical materialism, which argued that human existence was defined by work and that society was organized by relationships arising from work. Marx believed that capitalism would give way to socialism, that a proletariat revolution would eradicate private ownership and bring about a classless society. The radical change that Marx and others envisioned inspired many during the 1860s, when conditions of working-class life remained harsh. Hoping for change, workers organized a wave of strikes that focused on economic issues such as wages. Some governments accepted unions because these structured protest and made it more manageable.

The Paris Commune Versus the French State, pp. 908–911

In the winter of 1870–1871, Paris was suffering from a harsh winter and the Prussian siege that deprived them of food. Parisians demanded a local elected government to deal with the crisis. Following Napoleon III's surrender and abdication in mid March 1871, Parisians declared themselves a self-governing commune, an act that was imitated by other French cities. The Paris Commune lasted for two months; during that time, Parisians set up political clubs, local ceremonies, and cooperative workshops. The Communards (members of the Commune) were inspired by mutualist and socialist ideas and agreed to bring about a social revolution, one that would include women. But they frequently disagreed on the path to a changed society: mutualism, anticlericalism, feminism, international socialism, and anarchism were proposed. Meanwhile, the provisional government at Versailles quickly stamped out communes in other cities. On May 21 of that year, the army entered the capital. In a week of fighting, both the Communards and the army executed hostages and set fire to the city. The Commune was put down, and the army shot down tens of thousands citizens in the streets. Many more were arrested and either executed or sent to penal colonies. The French establishment saw all Parisians as traitors, but gradually a new "history" of the Commune was promulgated: it was the fault of women—a case of women run mad, crowding the streets in a frenzy of destruction and wanton sexuality. Both feminism and socialism suffered a set back as a result of the Commune.

Key Events
For each question, select the most appropriate response from the choices provided.

1850s–1860s Positivism, Darwinism become influential

1850s–1870s Realism in the arts

1854–1856 Crimean War

1857 British-led forces suppress Indian Rebellion

1861 Victor Emmanuel declared king of a unified Italy; abolition of serfdom in Russia

1861–1865 United States Civil War

1867 Second Reform Bill in England; Austro-Hungarian monarchy

1868 Meiji Restoration begins in Japan

1869–1871 Women's colleges founded at Cambridge University

1870 Franco-Prussian War

1871 German Empire proclaimed at Versailles; self-governing Paris Commune established

1. What did the ideology of positivism entail?
   a. A sense of optimism about the future of society
   b. The idea that careful study of facts would generate accurate laws of society
   c. A sense of absolute certainty about religious issues
   d. The idea that persons of color were inferior to whites in intelligence and civilization

2. Which conditions led to the development of the literary and artistic movement known as realism?
   a. The need for artists and writers to compete with new technologies in photography
   b. The relaxation of censorship laws that allowed writers and artists to describe things as they really were
   c. New techniques and a new market for realistic portrayals of nature and the technological progress
   d. A sense of disillusionment with commercial values and the expanding reach of the nation-state

3. What was the most important consequence of the Crimean War?
   a. Russia achieved political dominance over the former Ottoman Empire.
   b. The horrors of the war made the European public more pacifist.
   c. The concert of Europe, which had lasted since 1815, came to an end.
   d. France regained many of the territories it had conquered under Napoleon I.

4. What was the result of the Indian mutiny in 1857?
   a. The British government began to rule India directly.
   b. Large areas of India regained independence.
   c. The East India Company strengthened its control over the Indian colonies.
   d. Most English colonials left India because they considered it too dangerous.

5. What led Russia to abolish serfdom in 1861?
   a. The ascent of the liberal tsar Nicholas I to the throne
   b. A massive peasant revolt
   c. Russia's defeat in the Crimean War
   d. The election of a reform-minded majority to the Russian parliament

6. Which of the following characterized the Meiji restoration that began in Japan in 1868?
   a. The restoration of the Tokugawa shogun to the imperial throne
   b. A conservative reaction to western influence
   c. A move to turn Japan into a modern, technologically powerful state
   d. The establishment of a British colonial government

7. For women, what was a consequence of the Paris Commune in 1871?
   a. They gained the right to vote.
   b. They gained access to university education.
   c. They were honored as heroes in the new republic.
   d. They were blamed for causing violence and disorder in the Commune.

Key Terms   *Match each key term to its definition.*

A. **anarchism** (p. 907)
B. **dual monarchy** (p. 887)
C. **Haussmannization** (p. 891)
D. **Kulturkampf** (p. 903)
E. **Marxism** (p. 907)
F. **Meiji Restoration** (p. 898)
G. **mir** (p. 880)
H. **nation-state** (p. 881)
I. **Pan-Slavism** (p. 888)
J. **positivism** (p. 905)
K. **proletariat** (p. 907)
L. **realism** (p. 899)
M. **Realpolitik** (p. 873)
N. **Russification** (p. 881)
O. **zemstvos** (p. 880)

1. _____ Policies associated initially with nation building that are said to be based on hard-headed realities rather than the romantic notions of earlier nationalists. The term has come to mean any policy based on considerations of power alone.

2. _____ A Russian farm community fortified by the emancipation of the serfs in 1861, that provided for holding the land in common and regulating the movements of any individual by the group. The mir hindered the free movement of labor and individual agricultural enterprise, including modernization.

3. _____ Regional councils of the Russian nobility established after the emancipation of the Serfs in 1861 to deal with education and local welfare issues.

4. _____ A program for the integration of Russia's many nationality groups involving the forced acquisition of Russian language and the practice of Russian orthodoxy as well as the settlement of ethnic Russians among other nationality groups.

5. _____ A sovereign political entity of modern times based on representing a united people.

6. _____ A shared power arrangement between the Habsburg Empire and Hungary after Prussian defeat of the Austrian Empire in 1867.

7. _____ A movement in the nineteenth century for the unity of all Slavs across national and regional boundaries.

8. _____ The process of urban renewal followed by many governments after the middle of the nineteenth century, and named after its prime practitioner, Georges-Eugène Haussmann.

9. _____ A change in the Japanese government in 1867 that reinstalled the emperor as legitimate ruler in place of the military leader, or shogun.

10. _____ A style in the arts that arose in the mid-nineteenth century and was dedicated to depicting society realistically without romantic or idealistic overtones.

11. _____ Literally, a "culture war," but in the 1870s the word indicated German chancellor Otto von Bismarck's attempt to fight the cultural power of the church through a series of injurious policies.

12. _____ A theory, developed in the mid-nineteenth century, at the foundation of the social sciences that study of facts would generate accurate, or "positive," laws of society; these laws can, in turn, help in the formulation of policy and legislation.

13. _____ The belief that people should not have government; it was popular among peasants and workers in the last half of the nineteenth century and the first decades of the twentieth.

14. _____ A body of thought about the organization of production, social inequality, and the processes of revolutionary change as devised by the philosopher and economist Karl Marx.

15. _____ The working class, or, in Marxist terms, those who do not control the means of production such as factories, tools, workshops, and machines.

Identification
This activity tests your recall of significant people, places, and events from this chapter. Fill in the blank with the correct answer.

1. As part of his authoritarian rule, Napoleon III established a rubber-stamp legislature called the _____, which reduced representative government to a façade.

2. While Napoleon III cultivated an image of masculinity, his wife _____ followed the middle-class convention of separate spheres for men and women.

3. One of Napoleon III's most visionary accomplishments was his support of the _____, which connected the Mediterranean and the Red seas.

4. Traditional enemies for more than a century, _____ and Great Britain allied against Russia during the Crimean War.

5. In the aftermath of the Crimean War, Moldavia and Walachia became autonomous provinces that soon merged to form _____.

6. The clear leader of the movement for Italian unification was the kingdom of _____ in the economically modernizing north of Italy.

7. In _____, the kingdom of Italy was proclaimed with Victor Emmanuel at its head.

8. As the minister-president under _____ of Prussia, Otto von Bismarck was instrumental in achieving German unification.

9. After Austria's loss to the Prussians in 1866, the elites of _____ forced Francis Joseph to accept a dual monarchy that gave the Hungarian parliament control of internal policy.

10. In 1867, the Conservatives in the English Parliament, led by _____, passed the Second Reform Bill, which made a million more men eligible to vote.

11. Under the supervision of the Prefect of Paris _____, Paris underwent an enormous renovation that widened city streets but displaced many of the poor.

12. Beginning his work by studying fermentation, _____ advanced the germ theory of disease and its widespread implementation to protect food and increase sanitation.

13. In 1860, _____ became the first country to introduce taxation based on income, which opened yet another area of private life to government scrutiny.

14. In _____, a system of technical schools called Realschulen provided an education that emphasized math, science, and modern languages.

15. The Taiping (Heavenly Kingdom) movement in _____ sought the elimination of foreigners, equal treatment of women, and land reform.

16. In works like *The Mill on the Floss* and *Middlemarch*, _____ examined contemporary moral values and deeply probed private, "real life" dilemmas.

17. Called "satanic" by his critics, _____ wrote scandalous poems that explicitly described sexual passion, and drug-induced fantasies.

18. In books like *The Possessed*, _____ showed the dark, ridiculous, neurotic side of nihilists.

19. Rejecting romantic conventions idealizing ordinary folk, painters like _____ portrayed groaning laborers at backbreaking work.

20. In his operatic cycle _____, Richard Wagner reshaped ancient German myths into a modern, nightmarish allegory of a world doomed by its obsessive pursuit of money and power.

21. In the 1840s, _____, a former printer, coined the explosive phrase "Property is theft."

22. Believing that the slightest infringement on freedom was unacceptable, the political theory of _____ advocated the destruction of all state power.

23. In *Das Kapital*, _____ adopted the liberal idea that human existence was defined by the necessity of working as a way of fulfilling basic needs.

24. At a meeting in _____ in 1864, workers from Italy, Germany, Britain, and France accepted anarchism and mutualism as guiding ideas for the labor movement.

25. After the _____ besieged their city in 1870, Parisians declared themselves a self-governing commune in March 1871.

CHAPTER REVIEW

Self-Test and Analytical Exercises

Multiple Choice *Select the best answer from the four choices provided.*

1. Napoleon III's foreign policy
   a. sought to overcome the containment of France imposed by the Congress of Vienna.
   b. struggled to maintain the diplomatic concert of Europe.
   c. undermined the power of Great Britain through a series of wars.
   d. abandoned costly colonial ambitions in northern Africa.

2. Which two powers allied to fight against Russia in the Crimean War?
   a. France and Austria
   b. France and Britain
   c. France and Prussia
   d. Britain and Austria

3. Which of the following was *not* a consequence of the Crimean War?
   a. Railroads, telegraphs, and steam-powered ships had military applications for the first time.
   b. The telegraph and increased press coverage brought the war closer to the civilians at home.
   c. The alliance between Russia and Austria was strengthened.
   d. Defeat in the war forced reforms in Russian society.

4. Which of the following reforms was *not* introduced by Alexander II?
   a. Eliminating serfdom
   b. Reforming the judicial system on a principle of equality before the law

   c. Shifting political power from the nobility to the peasants
   d. Reducing the period of military conscription and improving the treatment of recruits

5. To what does the term Risorgimento refer?
   a. Italian determination to join imperial powers
   b. The movement in favor of Italian unification
   c. A secret system of Italian nationalist groups
   d. A nationalist opera by Giuseppe Verdi

6. Which ruler's intervention was a key part of Italian unification?
   a. Queen Victoria
   b. Napoleon III
   c. Alexander II
   d. William I

7. Who was the main architect of German unification?
   a. William I
   b. Richard Wagner
   c. Georges-Eugène Haussmann
   d. Otto von Bismarck

8. In Great Britain, politics came to be dominated by the
   a. Whig and Tory parties.
   b. Reform and Conservative parties.
   c. Conservative and Liberal parties.
   d. Tory and Reform parties.

9. Which of the following was *not* a result of urban renewal?
   a. Widening of streets to allow for pageantry and improved troop movement
   b. New buildings, like museums and opera houses, to display national wealth and power
   c. Public gardens, which suggested state control of nature and orderly, leisure pursuits
   d. Reduction of class distinctions in architecture, location, and amenities

10. Who discovered the heating process to make food safe?
    a. Joseph Lister
    b. Louis Pasteur
    c. Gregor Mendel
    d. Georges-Eugène Haussmann

11. What did the civil service law passed in Britain in 1870 accomplish?
    a. It required that a minimum number of government posts be filled by persons from the working class.
    b. It opened government posts to women.
    c. It required competitive examinations to assure competency in government posts.
    d. It required all able-bodied males to serve in the military for eighteen months.

12. The Indian mutiny was the result of the British
    a. teaching Indian children European culture and values.
    b. expanding their presence and the erosion of local Indian autonomy.
    c. favoring Hindu over Muslim soldiers for promotions and salaries.
    d. interfering with traditions and customs such as child marriages and sati.

13. Artists' responses to mid-century social issues affected the literary and artistic style known as
    a. romanticism.
    b. positivism.
    c. nihilism.
    d. realism.

14. Which two writers were prosecuted for obscenity?
    a. Dostoevsky and Turgenev
    b. Flaubert and Baudelaire
    c. Comte and Courbet
    d. Mendel and Soubirous

15. Which painter argued that an artist should "never permit sentiment to overthrow logic," and thus portrayed laborers at backbreaking work?
    a. Auguste Comte
    b. George Eliot
    c. Gustave Courbet
    d. Pierre-Joseph Proudhon

16. What is positivism?
    a. Tough-minded realism aimed at strengthening the state and tightening social order
    b. A theory that the careful study of facts will generate accurate laws of society
    c. An offshoot of social Darwinism that argues for white, male, middle-class superiority
    d. A political theory of social progress through gradual reform

17. What are "horizontal allegiances"?
    a. A pattern of loyalties that reflects hierarchy and subordination
    b. Socialist organizations for the working classes
    c. Old feudal organization of European society
    d. A pattern of loyalty and equality among persons possessing similar backgrounds

18. Who coined the phrase, "Property is theft"?
    a. Karl Marx
    b. Mikhail Bakhunin
    c. Pierre-Joseph Proudhon
    d. Auguste Comte

19. Karl Marx
    a. synthesized mutualism and anarchism into Marxism.
    b. laid out a detailed plan for the operation of the socialist state.
    c. attacked mutualism and anarchism as emotional, wrongheaded, and unscientific.
    d. derided the Paris Commune as bourgeois and far too moderate.

20. Which of the following was one of the founders of the political theory of anarchism?
    a. Mikhail Bakhunin
    b. Fyodor Dostoevsky
    c. Giuseppe Garibaldi
    d. Pierre-Joseph Proudhon

21. Napoleon III's rule of France
    a. combined democratic rule and economic nationalism.
    b. combined economic liberalism, nationalism, and authoritarian rule.
    c. opposed all economic reforms and diminished nationalism.
    d. expanded political liberties and authoritarian economic planning.

22. The main factor leading to the fall of Napoleon III was
    a. hyperinflation and unemployment.
    b. failed imperialist projects in Algeria and Egypt.
    c. violent resistance to his intended "Haussmannization" of Paris.
    d. defeat in the Franco-Prussian War.

23. The person who organized a battlefield nursing service during the Crimean War was
    a. Mary Ann Evans.
    b. Florence Nightingale.
    c. Bernadette Soubirous.
    d. Mikhail Bakhunin.

24. Who did Ivan Turgenev label nihilists?
    a. Incompetent generals of the Crimean War
    b. Corrupt members of the *zemstvos*
    c. Young nobles who repudiated traditional behavior and values
    d. Those who most rigidly opposed emancipating the serfs

25. Who was the main architect of the Italian unification movement?
    a. Giuseppe Verdi
    b. Giuseppe Garibaldi
    c. Victor Emmanuel II
    d. Camillo di Cavour

26. Which major power stood between Italy and Italian independence and unification?
    a. The Ottoman Empire
    b. France
    c. Prussia
    d. Austria

27. An example of resistance to British colonial rule was the
    a. building of the Suez Canal.
    b. Algerian insurrection.
    c. Indian mutiny.
    d. Taiping rebellion.

28. Who invaded southern Italy with a volunteer army, thereby including it in Italian unification?
    a. Napoleon III
    b. Giuseppe Garibaldi
    c. Victor Emmanuel
    d. Camillo di Cavour

29. Who carried out the renovation of Paris?
    a. Napoleon III
    b. Georges-Eugène Haussmann
    c. Louis Pasteur
    d. Joseph Lister

30. Which part of the Austrian Empire negotiated a dual monarchy and relative independence?
    a. Czechoslovakia
    b. Hungary
    c. Bohemia
    d. Poland

31. After mid century, Great Britain, France, and Russia changed their colonial policies in all of the following ways *except*
    a. granting more independence to colonized peoples.
    b. expanding colonial bureaucracies.
    c. instituting direct rule.
    d. providing a wider array of social and cultural services.

32. Taiping was a
    a. civil war in China that killed between 600,000 and 700,000 Chinese.
    b. Chinese rebellion seeking expulsion of foreigners, equality for women, and land reform.
    c. Chinese anti-European movement secretly backed by the ruling Qing dynasty.
    d. quasi-Christian cult that advocated rapid westernization of China and the end of Qing rule.

33. Which of the following was *not* an accomplishment of the dominant literary style of this period?
    a. Depiction of characters from all levels of society
    b. Idealization of characters and arguments for political utopias
    c. Profess to present ordinary reality accurately
    d. Question or attack social conventions

34. Which composer wrote operas set in a world doomed by the pursuit of power and redeemable only through unselfish love?
    a. Giacomo Puccini
    b. Georges Bizet
    c. Giuseppe Verdi
    d. Richard Wagner

35. Who published *On the Origin of Species* in 1859?
    a. Charles Lyell
    b. Thomas Malthus
    c. Charles Darwin
    d. Gregor Mendel

36. Who was the founder of positivist thought?
    a. John Stuart Mill
    b. Herbert Spencer
    c. Charles Darwin
    d. Auguste Comte

37. Pierre-Joseph Proudhon
    a. advocated political equality of the sexes.
    b. believed that a strong centralized state was needed to achieve socialist goals.
    c. saw property ownership as the key to social harmony.
    d. proposed organizing society around natural groupings of artisans in workshops.

38. How did Marx define materialism?
    a. The fundamental problem of bourgeois society is greed.
    b. The fundamental organization of societies arises from relationships of work or production.
    c. Nothing exists beyond the material world.
    d. In a socialist society, materials and political power is shared communally.

39. Which event sparked the Paris Commune?
    a. Formation of the International Working Men's Association
    b. Translation and publication of Karl Marx's *Das Kapital* in French
    c. Siege of Paris at the end of the Franco-Prussian War
    d. Assassination of Pierre-Joseph Proudhon

40. What was a *pétroleuse*?
    a. One of the shameless, sex-crazed women created by propagandists to be blamed for inciting the Paris Commune and torching the city
    b. The name given by the Communards to the women who set fire to sections of Paris to hold off the French army
    c. An insulting word used by the French army when addressing the Communard leaders
    d. A gasoline bomb used by the Communards during street fighting

Short Answer   *Answer each question in three or four sentences.*

The End of the Concert of Europe

1. What were the state policies of Louis-Napoleon Bonaparte?

2. What were the consequences, innovations, and results of the Crimean War?

3. What were the Great Reforms of Alexander II in Russia?

War and Nation Building

4. Describe the process of Italian unification.

5. Describe the process of German unification.

6. How did Britain manage to maintain political stability during this period?

Establishing Social Order

7. Describe the causes and effects of urban change during this period.

8. How did nation building change the relationship between the state and the individual citizen?

9. How did the treatment of colonies by European powers change?

The Culture of Social Order

10. Describe the artistic movement known as realism.

11. How did established religions mesh with the social changes transpiring during this period?

12. What were the most significant discoveries in the natural sciences, and how did they affect society?

Contesting the Growing Power of the Nation-State

13. Describe some of the important developments in workers' organizations in the 1850s and 1860s.

14. What were the theories of Karl Marx?

15. What was the Paris Commune?

BUILDING HISTORICAL SKILLS

Reading Maps   *Write a brief, paragraph-length response to each of the following questions based on* **Map 23.1: The Crimean War, 1853–1856 (p. 877)**.

1. What strategic interests were at stake during the Crimean War?

2. Why were France and Great Britain drawn into the Crimean War, even though it did not affect their borders?

Reading Illustrations   *Write a brief, paragraph-length response to each of the following questions based on the illustration* **Darwin Ridiculed** *(p. 905)*.

1. Why did this illustrator picture Darwin with a monkey? In what ways are Darwin and the monkey similar?

2. In which ways do Darwin and the monkey differ?

3. Are Darwin and the monkey depicted as equals in the illustration? Which has more authority, and what is used to indicate that? How does this reflect Social Darwinism?

Reading Historical Documents   *Write a brief, paragraph-length response to each of the following questions based on the documents in your book.*

Mrs. Seacole (p. 879)

1. How does Mary Seacole's career reflect nineteenth-century attitudes about the roles of women?

2. What was unconventional about Mary Seacole's career?

Bismarck Tricks the Public to Get His War (p. 886)

3. How does Bismarck justify doctoring this document to trick the public into war?

4. What were some of the social conditions in nineteenth-century Prussia that allowed Bismarck to pull this deception off?

New Sources, New Perspectives: Photographs and Their Messages (pp. 898–899)

5. How was the new innovation of photography used by different people and institutions?

6. What are some of the advantages and disadvantages of using photographs as historical documentation?

Industry, Empire, and Everyday Life
1870–1890

CHAPTER OVERVIEW

Chapter Questions *Keep these questions in mind as you go through the study guide chapter.*

1. How did governments, businesses, and individuals respond to economic instability?

2. What were the consequences of imperialism in Africa and Asia?

3. How did relations change between workers and employers, and between male and female workers?

4. In which activities did each class participate?

5. How did Social Darwinism shape Europeans' view of their society and their response to perceived problems in it?

Chapter Summary

The Advance of Industry

The end of the Franco-Prussian War and the Paris Commune in 1871 saw an initial burst of prosperity. Beginning in 1873, however, a series of business downturns threatened both entrepreneurs and the working class. Businesspersons sought remedies in new technology, financial innovations, and managerial techniques, while governments changed business law and supported the drive for global profits.

Industrial Innovation, pp. 917–920

Industrial, technological, and commercial innovation characterized the late nineteenth century. New products—from the telephone to the internal-combustion engine—provided proof of industrial progress. Leading industrial nations mined massive quantities of coal, iron, and produced steel during the 1870s and 1880s, all neces-

sary for the growth of industry. For Great Britain, this second Industrial Revolution—founded this time not on steam and textiles but on the advent of steel, iron, and electricity—affirmed their preeminence in industrial development. On the continent, these two industrial revolutions arrived simultaneously in many countries. Industrialization transformed agriculture in the late nineteenth century, as chemical fertilizers boosted crop yields and reapers and threshers mechanized harvesting. The development of refrigeration accommodated the transport of fruit and meat, diversifying and increasing the urban food supply, while the importation of tin from the colonies facilitated the large-scale commercial canning of foods. Great Britain began to lose its industrial predominance to Germany and the United States, both of which rapidly industrialized during this period. French industry grew, but French business establishments remained smaller than those in Germany and the United States. In Spain, Austria-Hungary, and Italy, industry developed in highly concentrated areas, but the rest of these countries remained tied to nonmechanized agriculture. Electricity allowed the Scandinavian countries, poor in coal and ore, to industrialize, and Sweden and Norway became leaders in the use of hydroelectric power and the development of electrical products. Russian industrialization continued to lag behind. Russian peasants, still tied to the *mir*, only worked in small numbers in industry when they were not needed to work the land.

Facing Economic Crisis, pp. 920–921

Before 1850, economic crises were usually caused by an agricultural crisis. In 1873, however, a crisis of industry and finance developed on its own because entrepreneurs were facing more and more obstacles. First, industry had become "capital intensive" because entrepreneurs had to invest heavily in expensive machinery to start a business. Second, the distribution and consumption of goods were both inadequate to sustain growth. Governments responded to this crisis with new laws that limited personal liability in cases of bankruptcy, thereby increasing investor confidence. Governments also encouraged new sources of capital, particularly in stock markets where individuals with modest means could invest in industries. Businesses began to band together into cartels (favored in Germany) and trusts (predominant in the United States) in order to control prices and competition. Trusts and cartels also vertically integrated companies thereby enabling them to control the entire process of manufacturing from raw material to finished product. Trusts and cartels reflected a lack of faith in free trade, a cornerstone of liberal economics; this lack of faith was shared by many governments, which set tariffs to protect domestic industry from foreign competition. By the early 1890s, all but Belgium, Britain, and the Netherlands had ended free trade.

Revolution in Business Practices, pp. 921–924

To minimize the effects of the economic crises, industrialists revolutionized the everyday conduct of their businesses by hiring managers to run their complex operations. At the upper levels, managers specialized in finance, sales and distribution, and the purchase of raw materials. At the lower levels, they oversaw worker productivity. A white-collar service sector emerged simultaneously, consisting of office workers employed as secretaries, file clerks, typists, and bank tellers, all educated in state-run primary schools. Many women, including middle-class women, worked in service-sector jobs. Employers saved money by designating certain types of jobs as "female" and then paying women lower wages than they would have had to pay men. Consumption changed along with the workplace. The department store, developed after the mid century, sought to stimulate consumer desires, especially among female shoppers. Such stores brought women out of the domestic sphere into the public, either as shoppers or as salesclerks. Mail-order catalogs and the extension of the railroad system gave rural populations access to the variety of goods department stores had to offer, many of which (coffee, tea, or soap made from palm oil) were imported from the colonies.

The New Imperialism

In the last third of the nineteenth century, industrial demand and rampant business rivalry added fuel to the contest for territory in Africa and Asia. A new imperialism, unlike the trader-based domination of earlier centuries, brought direct European rule to many regions of these two continents. Champions of nation building came to connect industrial prosperity and imperial expansion with national identity. Their aim to advance Western religions and culture also increased the subjugation of local peoples and radically altered their lives.

Taming the Mediterranean, pp. 924–925

The European countries eyed the African and Asian shores of the Mediterranean for the chance to profit from trade. Great Britain and France, which were especially eager to do business with Egypt, were able to do so via the Suez Canal. In 1879, the French and British took over the Egyptian treasury to secure their investments, and Britain used the nationalist resistance that ensued as an excuse to invade Egypt in 1882. The British began to run the government from behind the scenes, reshaping the Egyptian economy to meet British needs. In place of a diversified and self-sufficient agricultural system, for example, British officials, working with local landowners and moneylenders, limited agricultural production to a few crops destined for export. In Algeria, the French continued to extend their presence and occupied neighboring Tunisia in 1881. Businessmen from Britain, France, and Germany flooded Asia Minor with cheap goods, driving artisans out from their trades and into low-paying work building railroads or processing tobacco.

Scramble for Africa, pp. 925–928

After the British takeover of the Egyptian government, Europeans became more involved in sub-Saharan Africa, seeking to expand trade in raw materials such as palm oil, rubber, and diamonds. In the 1880s, one African territory after another fell to the French, Belgians, Portuguese, Italians, and Germans. The chaos that ensued prompted German chancellor Otto von Bismarck to call a conference in Berlin. During a series of meetings in 1884 and 1885, the European powers agreed that settlements along the African coast guaranteed rights to internal territory, an agreement that divided Africa into territories along straight lines that cut across indigenous boundaries. Western domination in Africa was easily accomplished using railroads, steamships, breech-loading rifles, and the machine gun. The discovery of quinine in South America and its use in Africa allowed Europeans to survive in areas where malaria flourished. Social Darwinism justified the domination of territories and peoples. Europeans destroyed African economic and political systems to ensure their own profit and domination. Ignoring evidence to the contrary, most Europeans considered Africans barely civilized, unlike the Chinese and Indians, whom Europeans credited with a scientific and artistic heritage, deeming Africans good only for manual labor.

Acquiring Territory in Asia, pp. 928–930

In India, close to a half a million Indians governed the country supervised by a few thousand British men. In 1876, the British Parliament declared Queen Victoria the Empress of India. Closing down the Indian production of cotton textiles among other goods, the British altered

India's economy to serve British needs and treated Indians as a lower class. This discrimination drove educated elite Indians to found the Indian National Congress in 1885, and challenge Britain's right to rule. To the east, Britain took control of the Malay peninsula in 1874, and the interior of Burma in 1885, territories that provided natural resources and a trade route to China. The British viewed with mistrust Russian annexations in central Asia and France's creation (in 1887) of the Union of Indochina from Cambodia, Tonkin, Annam, and Cochin China. (Laos was added in 1893.) In Indochina, the French introduced Western programs and increased the amount of cultivated land in the Mekong Delta, thus increasing the food supply. The resulting rapid population growth, however, strained other resources. The French, like the British, imported their culture to their colonies; the upper classes of the Indochinese were exposed to French art and literature, and urban building programs were designed to make Saigon emulate Paris. Western models were taken up by Indochinese nationalists.

Japan's Imperial Agenda, pp. 930–931

Under the Meiji Restoration, the Japanese embraced foreign trade and industry. In the 1870s, Japanese officials traveled to Europe and the United States to study industry and technology; Western dress was adopted at the imperial court, and Western architecture was introduced in Tokyo. The government tolerated no opposition to these changes. In 1889, legal scholars drafted a constitution on the German model that emphasized state power rather than individual rights. The state also invested in economic development by building railroads and shipyards and establishing financial institutions. In the 1880s, with the costs of modernization draining resources, these businesses were auctioned off to private entrepreneurs. The adoption of Western-style enterprises became a patriotic goal. Japan also adopted the imperialist mentality of the West and began intervening in struggles elsewhere in Asia.

The Paradoxes of Imperialism, pp. 931–933

Although imperialism was intended to stabilize greatpower status, international distrust intensified as countries vied for world influence. Politicians began to question the value of colonies whose costs exceeded their profits. Yet, for certain businesses, such as French metallurgy, colonies provided crucial markets. They also provided jobs for people in European port cities, but all taxpayers shared the burden of paying for them. Many believed that colonies meant national strength, but others worried that they might be a source of weakness and conflict. Europeans agreed, however, in the belief that they were superior in culture and religion to the people they colonized and also that the imperialist venture was a noble and worthwhile cause in that it converted indigenous peoples to Christianity or generally "civilized" them. Western scholars and travelers added to this notion of Western superiority, despite their claims of objectivity. Although a few believed that conquered peoples were better off than Europeans because they were less "civilized," this romantic notion ignored the realities of imperialist rule.

The Transformation of Culture and Society

Advancing industrialization and empire building transformed everyday culture and society. Success in manufacturing and foreign ventures created new millionaires, and the expansion of the middle class allowed more people to own property, travel, and provide their children with a more cosmopolitan education. These changes affected the lower classes, in many cases replacing their labor with machinery while giving them opportunities for mobility as European expansion opened up the globe. Artists captured the imperial and industrial spectacle in increasingly iconoclastic works influence by non-Western styles.

The "Best" Circles and the Expanding Middle Class, pp. 933–936

The profits from industry and empire building added new members to the upper classes, or "best" circles, as they were called. Persons in these circles often came from the aristocracy, but new millionaires from the ranks of the bourgeoisie joined, and some intermarried. The ranks of aristocrats and rich bourgeois became increasingly blurred, and millionaires without aristocratic connections made conspicuous displays of wealth and segregated themselves in suburbs or new urban areas away from the bourgeois and the indigent. Upper-class men popularized big-game hunting expeditions in Asia and Africa, which replaced the more modest fox and bird hunting as the fashionable masculine sport of the highest class. Members of the best circles maintained exclusivity by controlling their children's social lives, especially their marriages. Upper-class men were engaging in sexual liaisons with lower-class women, but upper-class women of marriageable age were closely supervised. Once married, upper-class women devoted themselves to having children, directing staffs of servants, and maintaining standards of etiquette and social conduct. A solid middle class was expanding in western and central Europe. The lives of these professionals remained modest; most households employed at least one servant. In place of the conspicuous consumption of the very rich, the middle class proudly maintained a high level of cleanliness and polish.

Professional Sports and Organized Leisure, pp. 936–937

Organized team sports replaced village games, integrating migrants as well as the lower and higher classes in a common pastime. Newspapers reported the results of sporting contests such as the Tour de France, and competitive sports began to be viewed as a sign of national strength and spirit. Team sports for women emerged, such as soccer, field hockey, and rowing; but individual sports, such as horseback riding, were considered more feminine. Men were encouraged to embrace team sports, fostering a sense of national unity and preparing them for cooperation in the governments and militaries of empire. Demonstrating the increased belief in physical health and strength for both sexes, schools for girls introduced gymnastics and exercise. The middle classes wanted their leisure sports to be educational as well as fun. Working-class persons adopted middle-class habits by joining clubs for pursuits such as bicycling, touring, and hiking. The new emphasis on healthy recreation afforded individuals a greater sense of individual freedom and power and thereby contributed to a developing sense of citizenship based less on constitutions and rights than on an individual nation's exercise of raw power.

Working People's Strategies, pp. 937–939

Empire and industry were powerful factors in migration. Parts of Europe simply could not produce enough or provide enough employment to support a growing population, so hundreds of thousands left their native lands to find work elsewhere in Europe or the United States. Millions of rural Jews, especially those of eastern Europe, left their villages for economic reasons. Russian Jews fled in the face of violent pogroms that destroyed Jewish homes, businesses, and lives. Most emigrated to North and South America, Australia, and New Zealand to seek out new opportunities. The development of railroads and steamships made the trip faster, cheaper, and more comfortable. Once established in their new countries, immigrants frequently sent money home. Male immigrants had to learn new languages and new civic practices in order to obtain employment, as did some female immigrants. Immigrant women who stayed at home were insulated from their new environments and often preserved traditional ways and languages. Urbanization accelerated, although most still resided in rural areas; many urban dwellers returned to rural areas at harvest time. In cities, changes in technology and management meant that workers had to adapt to an insecure job market and changing work conditions. Stepped-up productivity demanded more physical exertion, but wages were not increased accordingly. Men and women resented managers, and women were often sexually harassed. Many women worked at home doing outwork for which they were paid extremely low wages, forcing them to

work long hours to make ends meet. Notwithstanding, the working classes grew more informed, more visible, and more connected to the progress of industry and empire.

Reform Efforts for Working-Class People, pp. 939–942

The social problems caused by economic instability, the uneven prosperity of industrialization, and the upheaval of migration were addressed through reform organizations and charities formed by the middle and upper classes. Motivated by a Social Darwinist fear that the working classes lacked the fitness to survive in a competitive world, reformers and philanthropists focused on improving worker health. Young men and women of the middle and upper classes, some motivated by religion, turned to scientific study to find solutions to social problems, establishing and moving into settlement houses in poor neighborhoods, so they could live near the poor and thereby better understand and help them. Philanthropists, industrialists, schools, and governmental agencies intervened in workers' lives to teach mothers child-care techniques and to provide health care for children. They expected working-class mothers to conform to middle-class standards of housekeeping and child-rearing. Dutch physician Aletta Jacobs, began to make birth control available. Working-class women sought out these clinics, and knowledge of birth control spread by word of mouth among workers. Governments took a different approach, sponsoring laws that barred women from "unhealthy" night work and from trades such as pottery that were considered dangerous. Laws also limited women's access to higher-paying jobs.

Artistic Responses to Industrial and Imperial Change, pp. 942–945

Darwin had theorized that strong civilizations that failed to keep up with changing conditions would perish, an idea that influenced many writers. Émile Zola (1840–1902) produced a series of novels that described the effects of industrial society on individuals through the portrayal of a family plagued by alcoholism and madness. Spanish writer Emilia Pardo Bazán (1859–1921) and English writer Thomas Hardy (1840–1928) depicted a fatalistic world in which men and women faced personal deterioration and forces beyond their control. Norwegian playwright Henrik Ibsen (1828–1906) and South African novelist Olive Schreiner (1855–1920) criticized the oppressive aspects of marriage on women. Country people used mass-produced textiles to design "traditional" costumes and concocted ceremonies based on a mythical past. Thought to be old and authentic, these quaint "traditions" attracted tourists and caught the eye of architects and industrial designers, who turned to rural styles for models. English designers William Morris (1834–1896) and his daughter Mary Morris (1862–1938) designed fabrics, wallpaper, and household items with motifs found in nature, such as the silhouettes of plants, and Asian art. New photographers' depictions of places and people were accessible to a wider public. In response, painters altered their styles, while still maintaining their focus on the depiction of contemporary society. Georges Seurat (1859–1891) depicted white-collar workers at leisure in newly created parks; Edgar Degas (1834–1917) painted women hard at work, as dancers or laundresses. Artists, trying to capture a fleeting moment by focusing on the ever-changing light and color of everyday vision, experimented with a new style labeled impressionism. Impressionists Claude Monet and Vincent Van Gogh experimented with color and brush strokes. Many impressionists, like the American expatriate Mary Cassatt (1845–1926), were influenced by Japanese art.

The Birth of Mass Politics

Struggles for political voice, especially via the vote, accompanied imperial and economic expansion. The growth of industry and urban development strengthened networks of political communication. As national consciousness grew among workers, western European governments continued to allow more men to vote. Without the vote, women still participated in a range of political activism.

Workers, Politics, and Protest, pp. 945–947

Struggling for a political voice, workers came together in unions to exert pressure on governments and businesses, marking the beginning of mass politics. Despite fears of revolution, some industrialists found unions appealing because they made strikes more predictable (or even preventable) and also provided a liaison for labor-management relations. From the 1880s on, the pace of collective action for more pay, lower prices, and better working conditions accelerated. Housewives carried out their own protests against high food prices, confiscating merchants' goods and selling them at what they considered a just price. Although strikes were not about politics, governments increasingly responded with force. Unions continued to attract skilled artisans, but a new unionism also attracted transport workers, miners, matchgirls, and dockworkers. These new unions were nationwide groups that could plan massive general strikes affecting a number of trades simultaneously. Like cartels and trusts, these unions increasingly influenced business practices and society's views of workers. New political parties, such as the Labour Party in England, also addressed working-class issues. In 1889, some four hundred socialists from across Europe formed the Second International. This organization adopted a Marxist revolutionary program, but also advocated suffrage. Members wanted to rid the organization of anarchists; such extremists, for whom Marxist ideology was not as applicable, flourished in less industrial parts of Europe, notably in Italy, Spain, and Russia. During the 1880s, anarchists bombed stock exchanges, parliaments, and businesses. Politics were also incorporated more informally into everyday life through a range of organizations designed to forge worker solidarity through leisure activities—gymnastic and choral societies, for example.

Expanding Political Participation in Western Europe, pp. 947–950

The rise of mass journalism after 1880 gave Europeans access to information about politics and world events. Journalism created a community of up-to-date citizens, but elites grumbled about its predilection for the sensational and the scandalous. William Gladstone used journalism to his advantage when he waged a campaign for a seat in the British Parliament in 1879; newspapers reported his tour of northern England and Scotland, highlighting his speeches to thousands of working men and women. This campaign exemplified the trend toward expanded participation in Britain's political life, a process begun with the Reform Act of 1832—an extension of the franchise to middle-class men—and continued with the Ballot Act of 1872, which made voting secret. Then, with the Reform Act of 1884, the electorate was doubled, enfranchising many urban workers and artisans. As many British men entered politics for the first time, both Liberals and Conservatives established political clubs to gain party loyalty. British political reforms weakened the control of the landed aristocracy, a change that was especially revolutionary in Ireland, where Irish tenant farmers gained the right to vote and could use that vote against absentee English landlords. In France, the Third Republic (established in 1874) was unstable, due to scandal and political struggle among competing factions. This instability was diminished somewhat when a new constitution strengthening the Chamber of Deputies was elected in 1875, by universal manhood suffrage, at the expense of the presidency. However, newspaper stories of financial scandals involving members of the Chamber of Deputies eroded confidence in the government; an aborted coup by General Georges Boulanger might have succeeded had he not bowed out at the last minute. Republican leaders sought to create national unity by instituting a system of compulsory and free public education in the 1880s. Spain and Belgium established universal manhood suffrage in 1890 and 1893, respectively, whereas Denmark, Sweden, Italy, and the Netherlands continued to limit political participation.

Power Politics in Central and Eastern Europe, pp. 950–954

In Germany, Austria-Hungary, and Russia, agrarian political forces remained powerful, often working to block political, social, and economic change. Once Bismarck succeeded in uniting the German states, he sought stability and a respite from war. In 1873, he forged an alliance called the Three Emperors' League with Austria-Hungary and Russia, both of which shared Germany's commitment to maintain the political status quo. Bismarck joined with liberals at home to create financial institutions destined to further German commerce and industry. He opposed the Catholic church as an obstacle to the creation of national sentiment, and began a culture war, or Kulturkampf, against it. This culture war ended during the pontificate of Leo XIII (r. 1878–1903), whose encyclical Rerum novarum ("On the Condition of the Working Classes" [1891]) urged Catholics to develop a social conscience and to work in their countries for religious and political unity among the classes. In Austria-Hungary, the liberals held power for a time in the 1870s, and the government enacted free-trade provisions, but the country remained monarchist and authoritarian. In the Balkans, Slavs of Bulgaria and Bosnia-Herzegovina rebelled against Ottoman control in 1876; they were followed by Serbia and Montenegro. Russian Pan-Slavic organizations sent relief to the rebels, and Russia declared war on Turkey in 1877. The 1878 Treaty of San Stefano created a large, pro-Russian Bulgaria. Austria-Hungary and Great Britain feared that it would become a Russian satellite enabling the tsar to dominate the Balkans. An international congress held in Berlin staved off the threat of war, and rolled back the Russian victory by partitioning Bulgaria. Following this congress, the European powers attempted to ensure stability through a series of alliances and treaties. Germany and Austria-Hungary formed a defensive alliance in 1879 against Russia. In 1882, Italy joined, turning the Dual Alliance into the Triple Alliance. At the same time, Germany, Austria-Hungary, and Russia joined a revived Three Emperors' League that lasted from 1881 to 1887. Although Russia achieved some international success, its internal affairs were in disarray; the era of Great Reforms had come to an end, and a dissatisfied, reform-minded youth increasingly turned to revolutionary groups for solutions to political and social problems. Writers participated in the debate over Russia's future. Leo Tolstoy and Fyodor Dostoevsky both opposed revolution, believing that Russia required spiritual regeneration. The more radical revolutionary groups, however, saw a need for violent action. In 1881, one of these groups—the People's Will—murdered tsar Alexander II in a bomb attack. In response, Alexander III (r. 1881–1894) rejected any calls for further reform, gave the secret police virtually unchecked power, and embarked on a campaign of intense Russification. The five million Jews who were confined to the Pale of Settlement, an area to which they had been restricted since the eighteenth century, suffered especially severe oppression in the form of government-instigated pogroms. As Russia's internal politics became more chaotic and repressive, its international alliances were altered by the decision of the new German kaiser William II (r. 1888–1918) to dismiss Bismarck and allow the alliance with Russia to lapse in favor of closer ties with Austria-Hungary. The international scene was growing ever more dangerous and unpredictable.

Key Events

For each question, select the most appropriate response from the choices provided.

1860s–1890s Impressionism flourishes in the arts; absorption of Asian influences

1870s–1890s Vast emigration from Europe continues; the new imperialism

1873 Extended economic recession begins with global impact

1876 Invention of the telephone

1879 Dual Alliance formed between Germany and Austria-Hungary

1882 Triple Alliance formed between Germany, Austria-Hungary, and Italy; Britain invades Egypt

1882–1884 Bismarck sponsors social welfare legislation

1884 British Parliament passes the Reform Act, doubling the size of the male electorate

1884–1885 European nations carve up Africa at the Berlin conference

1889 Japan adopts constitution based on European models; Socialists meet in Paris and establish the Second International

1. Which of the following motivated impressionist painters to seek out new techniques of artistic representation in the 1860s–1890s?
   a. Gasoline engine
   b. Typewriter
   c. Camera
   d. Telegraph

2. Which of the following *best* describes the aftermath of the economic crisis of 1873?
   a. A continued period of economic depression that only ended with the beginning of World War I in 1914
   b. A thirty-year period of economic fluctuations that featured sharp downturns, the severity of which varied from country to country
   c. A period of rapid recovery because the crisis led to radical changes in business practices
   d. The beginning of the third Industrial Revolution as jobs in the service sector boomed.

3. The Dual Alliance was formed between Germany and Austria-Hungary to offer mutual protection against which power?
   a. Great Britain
   b. The Ottoman Empire
   c. Russia
   d. France

4. What prompted Italy to join the alliance between Germany and Austria-Hungary in 1882, which was henceforth called the Triple Alliance?
   a. Its economic interests with German industry
   b. The need to protect its colonies in Africa
   c. King Humbert I of Italy was married to a daughter of Kaiser William I
   d. Italy had an imperial rivalry with France

5. Which of the following was a consequence of the Second Reform Act in Britain in 1884?
   a. Small numbers of upper-class women were allowed to vote
   b. Middle-class industrialists were admitted into the aristocracy
   c. The aristocracy lost its traditional influence in the countryside
   d. All British males were granted the vote

6. After it was established in 1889, which group did the Second International try to rid itself of?
   a. Anarchists
   b. Marxists
   c. Communists
   d. Socialists

Key Terms   *Match each key term to its definition.*

A. **capital-intensive industry** (p. 920)
B. **Dual Alliance** (p. 953)
C. **home rule** (p. 948)
D. **impressionism** (p. 944)
E. **limited liability corporation** (p. 921)
F. **new unionism** (p. 946)
G. **outwork** (p. 918)
H. **Reform Act of 1884** (p. 948)

I. **Second International** (p. 946)
J. **Third Republic** (p. 949)

1. _____ The process of having some aspects of industrial work done outside factories in individual homes.

2. _____ A mid- to late-nineteenth-century development in industry that required great investments of money for machinery and infrastructure to make a profit; it contrasts with labor-intensive industry.

3. _____ A legal entity developed in the mid to late nineteenth century in which the amount that owners of a factory or other enterprise owed creditors was restricted (limited) in case of financial failure.

4. _____ A mid- to late-nineteenth-century artistic style that captured the sensation of light in images, derived from Japanese influences and from an opposition to the realism of photographs.

5. _____ A mid- to late-nineteenth-century development in working-class organizing that entailed nationwide unions with bureaucracies and a membership of all kinds of workers, including unskilled ones and replacing local, craft-based unions.

6. _____ A transnational organization of workers established in 1889, mostly committed to Marxian socialism.

7. _____ British act that granted the right to vote to a mass male citizenry.

8. _____ The right to an independent parliament demanded by the Irish from the second half of the nineteenth century on and resisted by the British.

9. _____ The government that succeeded Napoleon III's Second Empire after its defeat in the Franco-Prussian War of 1870–1871 and lasted until France's defeat in World War II (1940).

10. _____ A defensive alliance forged by German chancellor Otto von Bismarck between Germany and Austria-Hungary in 1879 as part of his system of alliances to prevent or limit war, joined by Italy in 1882 as a third partner and then called the Triple Alliance.

Identification *This activity tests your recall of significant people, places, and events from this chapter. Fill in the blank with the correct answer.*

1. In 1885, _____ designed a workable gasoline engine that was used in the first automobile constructed six years later.

2. An example of the new breed of entrepreneurs in America that appeared after 1880, _____ earned a fortune in the iron and steel industry.

3. As the Russian minister of finance, _____ attracted foreign capital, entrepreneurs, and engineers to build the Trans-Siberian Railroad.

4. The economic crisis of _____, which showed that agriculture was no longer the dominant force in the economy, initiated nearly three decades of economic fluctuations.

5. Signaling a new trend in which department stores replaced single-item stores that consumers entered knowing what they wanted to purchase, _____ opened a department store in Philadelphia.

6. In 1882, the British invaded _____, claiming that it was necessary to put down a nationalist uprising.

7. Leopold II claimed the _____ region of central Africa, which resulted in increased colonial competition with the French and unparalleled acts of cruelty perpetrated on its indigenous peoples.

8. Sent to South Africa for his health, British businessman and politician _____ cornered the diamond market and claimed a vast amount of African territory.

9. In _____, the Indian elite founded the Indian National Congress.

10. After a fire in 1872, the Japanese city of _____ was rebuilt in a western style.

11. First held in _____, the Tour de France is an example of the growing interest in group competitions that eventually replaced village games.

12. Established in 1884, the _____ sought to reform society through state planning rather than revolution.

13. Moved by the plight of women in Amsterdam slums, _____ opened the first birth-control clinic in the 1880s.

14. A fatalistic author whose characters battle forces beyond their control, _____ novel *The Mayor of Casterbridge* is about a man who rises to power but is unable to escape his murky past.

15. Profiting on the enthusiasm for "craft" goods of an earlier preindustrial age, _____ began the "arts and crafts" style of design.

16. The Second International was founded in _____ to combat the growing nationalism that separated workers rather than binding them to a common cause.

17. An example of sensationalism in mass journalism, the _____ reported on the "white slave trade" in a series of articles in 1885.

18. Recognizing the power of journalism and taking advantage of ballot reforms, _____ won office by touring England in a widely reported election campaign.

19. Irish leader _____ demanded British support for home rule, but his political career came to an early end when news broke of his affair with a married woman.

20. An aborted coup by the highly popular general _____ in the late 1880s showed the fragility of the Third Republic in France.

CHAPTER REVIEW

Self-Test and Analytical Exercises

Multiple Choice *Select the best answer from the four choices provided.*

1. All of the following were key technological innovations in the nineteenth century *except*
   a. refrigeration.
   b. motion pictures.
   c. typewriters.
   d. the use of electricity in everyday life.

2. Which of the following protected business owners from personal responsibility for their business's debts?
   a. Cartels
   b. Industrial trust accounts
   c. Municipal bonds
   d. Limited liability corporations

3. In which type of employment did women predominate late in the nineteenth century?
   a. Manufacturing
   b. Transportation
   c. Management
   d. Service

4. Historians now believe that any distinction made between a first and a second Industrial Revolution applies mainly to which country?
   a. Germany
   b. France
   c. Great Britain
   d. Spain

5. Which countries took the greatest interest in trade with Egypt?
   a. Germany and Great Britain
   b. Italy and France
   c. Italy and Great Britain
   d. Great Britain and France

6. Which European country claimed the Congo region of central Africa?
   a. France
   b. Germany
   c. Great Britain
   d. Belgium

7. The death rates among missionaries, adventurers, traders, and bureaucrats plummeted because medicinal quinine was developed as a defense against
   a. yellow fever.
   b. typhus.
   c. cholera.
   d. malaria.

8. Which European country colonized the region called Indochina?
   a. Great Britain
   b. France
   c. Germany
   d. Russia

9. How did profits from industry and empire building affect the distinction between aristocrats and the upper middle class?

   a. The distinction between the rich and the aristocratic blurred.
   b. Old families closed themselves off from the newly wealthy.
   c. Families with "new money" avoided "old money" families, whom they saw as stuffy and weak.
   d. The old aristocracy disappeared and was replaced by members of the new bourgeois elite.

10. Which region sent forth one-third of all European emigrants between 1840 and 1920?
    a. Southern Italy
    b. Western France
    c. The British Isles
    d. Southern France

11. The Fabian Society was
    a. committed to socialism based on reform and state planning, rather than revolution.
    b. focused on promoting birth control, beginning in the Netherlands.
    c. a French organization committed to "protecting" women from certain types of work.
    d. an English religious charitable organization.

12. Who produced a series of novels set in industrializing France that explored social degeneration?
    a. William Morris
    b. Henrik Ibsen
    c. Émile Zola
    d. Georges Seurat

13. Which country had the largest Socialist Party in Europe after 1890?
    a. Great Britain
    b. France
    c. Russia
    d. Germany

14. Which British Liberal politician successfully focused a Parliamentary campaign on mass participation?
    a. Charles Parnell
    b. William Gladstone
    c. David Lloyd George
    d. Benjamin Disraeli

15. Georges Boulanger
    a. imposed a national draft in France and instituted free public education.
    b. refused to accept the tricolor flag, thereby preventing the monarchists from taking power.
    c. led an abortive coup against the Third Republic.
    d. ruined his political career by selling memberships in the Legion of Honor.

16. Which group was responsible for the assassination of tsar Alexander II in 1881?
    a. Pale of Settlement
    b. Populists
    c. Dual Alliance
    d. People's Will

17. Who built a gasoline-powered automobile in 1891 and tested it by chasing a bicycle race?
    a. Karl Benz
    b. Andrew Carnegie
    c. John D. Rockefeller
    d. Armand Peugeot

18. Industrialization became increasingly _____, making entrepreneurial activity more difficult.
    a. labor intensive
    b. consumer oriented
    c. capital intensive
    d. globally oriented

19. *Cartel* or *trust* both refer to
    a. the banding together of firms in the same industry to control prices and competition.
    b. the establishment of limited liability for a company's debt.
    c. the sale of a company's stock on a public exchange.
    d. tariffs set on the importation of goods.

20. A company that acquired control over all stages of production from raw materials to distribution was utilizing
    a. international cartels.
    b. vertical integration.
    c. limited liability.
    d. industrial trusts.

21. One of the main European economic interests in sub-Saharan Africa was access to
    a. cinchona bark.
    b. raw materials.
    c. a market for European goods.
    d. cheap labor.

22. What did the Berlin conference of 1884 and 1885 accomplish?
    a. It intervened in the inhuman abuses by King Leopold of Belgium in his colonies.
    b. It made it a crime to sell arms and alcohol to native peoples and effectively restricted land ownership to white Europeans.

    c. It banned the sale of alcohol to native peoples and controlled the sale of arms to them, and led to the division of the African continent along lines of latitude and longitude.
    d. It engineered a compromise between France and Great Britain, giving France uncontested control of Morocco in exchange for withdrawing French troops from Egypt and Tunisia.

23. Descendants of Dutch farmers in southern Africa were known as
    a. Boers.
    b. *Pied noirs.*
    c. Rhodesians.
    d. Afrikaaners.

24. Which non-European country adopted western architecture, industrialization, and military organization, thereby escaping western imperial domination?
    a. Sudan
    b. Egypt
    c. China
    d. Japan

25. Nineteenth-century women
    a. were encouraged to join team sports and compete for national glory.
    b. never participated in sporting activities; such events belonged to men.
    c. were generally encouraged to participate in individual sports and exercise in order to better prepare them for the rigors of motherhood.
    d. competed against men in noncontact sports such as bicycle racing.

26. Violent, government-approved anti-Semitism during the nineteenth century forced large numbers of Jews to flee
    a. Germany.
    b. France.
    c. Great Britain.
    d. Russia.

27. Which of the following was *not* involved in industrialized work?
    a. The replacement of skilled workers by unskilled workers, often women who were paid less
    b. The continuing of outwork performed by women in their homes
    c. A decline in work intensity and work hours demanded from working people
    d. A proliferation of managers, foremen, and supervisors in the industrial workplace

28. Which of the following is *not true* about the impressionists?
    a. They attempted to capture a single moment by focusing on the interplay of color and light.
    b. They borrowed from Asian art and architecture.
    c. They increased the realism of their art in response to the growing popularity of the camera and photography.
    d. Members of the public viewed the painters' style as outrageous.

29. Which of the following is *false* regarding the Second International?
    a. It was a federation of socialist working-class organizations.
    b. It adopted a revolutionary Marxist program.
    c. It welcomed the participation of anarchists.
    d. It advocated the extension of suffrage and improvements in working conditions.

30. Which of the following allowed voters to cast their ballot in secret in Great Britain, thereby limiting the influence of landlords and employers?
    a. Ballot Act of 1872
    b. Reform Act of 1884
    c. Reform Bill of 1832
    d. Home Rule Bill of 1868

31. In which three countries did powerful agrarian conservatives frequently block political, social, and economic change?
    a. Great Britain, France, and Russia
    b. Russia, Germany, and Austria-Hungary
    c. Russia, Germany, and France
    d. Italy, Russia, and France

32. "Jingoism" is a derogatory term for
    a. Pan-Slavism.
    b. religious conservatism.
    c. socialist propaganda.
    d. militant sloganeering.

Short Answer
Answer each question in three or four sentences.

The Advance of Industry

1. What were some of the dominant trends in late-nineteenth-century industry?

2. How were European economies challenged in the 1870s and 1880s?

3. How did industrial production affect consumerism in the 1870s and 1880s?

The New Imperialism

4. Describe the new imperialism of the 1870s and 1880s and some of the ways in which it differed from previous forms of imperialism.

5. What was Japan's reaction to European industrialization?

6. What were the paradoxes of imperialism in the late nineteenth century?

The Transformation of Culture and Society

7. How did leisure-time activities change during this period?

8. What was the importance of migration to working-class life?

9. How did the nature of work change in this period?

The Birth of Mass Politics

10. Which new forms of working-class political activism were common in the 1870s and 1880s?

11. Which factors led to the beginnings of mass politics in western Europe?

12. Compared to western Europe, what made trends in political participation different in central and eastern Europe?

BUILDING HISTORICAL SKILLS

Reading Maps *Write a brief, paragraph-length response to each of the following questions based on* **Map 24.1: Africa, c. 1890 (p. 926).**

1. What were the major routes of colonial expansion into Africa?

2. How did the borders of the Congo Free State correspond with political and geographic boundaries?

Reading Illustrations *Write a brief, paragraph-length response to each of the following questions based on the illustration* **The Letter (p. 944).**

1. How does this painting compare with earlier portraits such as that of Germaine de Staël on page 795 of your textbook?

2. Which contemporary social and cultural trends are evident in this painting?

Reading Historical Documents
Write a brief, paragraph-length response to each of the following questions based on the documents in your book.

Imperialism's Popularity among the People (p. 929)

1. How is European imperialism portrayed in this song?

2. What does this song reveal about European attitudes toward imperialism?

Henrik Ibsen, A Doll House (p. 943)

3. What is the central conflict in this excerpt?

4. Which contemporary social tensions are reflected in this excerpt?

Contrasting Views: Experiences of Migration (pp. 940–941)

5. Who was emigrating, and why?

6. What were the positive consequences of emigration? What were its negative consequences?

7. Why was emigration so hotly debated?

Modernity and the Road to War
c. 1890–1914

CHAPTER OVERVIEW

Chapter Questions   *Keep these questions in mind as you go through the study guide chapter.*

1. What were the major trends in population and identity in the late nineteenth century?

2. How did changes in science, philosophy, and art reflect an age of new thinking?

3. What did women, minorities, and labor groups do to protest their conditions?

4. Which factors brought about the shift toward independence in the colonies?

5. Why did alliances lead the world toward war?

Chapter Summary

Private Life in the Modern Age

Western ideals of a comfortable family life flourished because of Europe's improved standard of living, yet the prosperity brought by industrialization and empire-building challenged traditional social norms. A falling birthrate, a rising divorce rate, and growing activism for marriage reform provoked intense debate by the turn of the century. New discussions of gender roles and private life demonstrated the close connection of private and public concerns.

Population Pressure, pp. 961–964

The staggering population increase of the eighteenth century continued through the nineteenth century due to improvements in sanitation and public health that extended longevity and reduced infant mortality. However, despite an absolute rise in the population in much of the West, the birthrate (births per thousand people), which had been decreasing in France since the eighteenth century, began declining in other countries as well. Traditionally, limiting births was a community decision; responding to food shortages, agrarian communities forced couples to marry later thereby limiting their reproductive years. As society industrialized, individuals began making the decision to limit births on their own, often practicing coitus interruptus (withdrawing before ejaculation). In the 1840s, the development of the vulcanization process for rubber made diaphragms and condoms fairly reliable methods of birth control. Abortion was also practiced in cities. Government officials and concerned citizens worried that declining birthrates would result in an inability to compete militarily with other European powers. Nationalism and racism also played a role because many feared that the declining birthrate would cause Western European populations to be absorbed by foreigners such as Slavs and Jews.

Reforming Marriage, pp. 964–965

Those who adhered to Social Darwinist ideas feared that a declining birthrate among the middle and upper classes would lead to social decay as those from the "worst" classes would outnumber those from the "better." The pseudoscience of eugenics grew in popularity as eugenicists advocated increasing the fertility of the "fittest" and limiting the fertility of, or even sterilizing, "degenerates." Some believed that the answer to the population problem resided in marriage reform. The inability of women to control their wages and property, the complications and costs of divorce where permitted, and women's lack of legal control over their children were cited as reasons why women limited their fertility. In response to such complaints, women gained legal rights to their wages and their property in much of Europe. Some countries legalized divorce and made it easier and cheaper to obtain. By the early twentieth century, several countries had passed legislation that provided government subsidies to improve motherhood among the lower classes. The concern for population laid the foundations for the modern welfare state, concerned not just with war and diplomacy, but with the everyday life of its citizens.

New Women, New Men, and the Politics of Sexual Identity, pp. 965–966

The increasing availability of white-collar employment meant that more European women could live independently. These so-called new women dressed with fewer petticoats and looser corsets, biked and hiked, lived on their own in women's clubs or apartments, and supported themselves financially. They also adopted new attitudes toward sexuality and reproduction. Sexual identity was generally a topic of great discussion as the new field of sexology emerged. Havelock Ellis (1859–1939), a British medical doctor who wanted to study sex scientifically, argued in his book *Sexual Inversion* (1894) for the existence of a new personality type: the homosexual, or "third sex." Self-identified homosexuals called for recognition, while the press reported on homosexual scandals such as the trial of British playwright Oscar Wilde (1854–1900) for indecency, or the court-martials of men in German kaiser William II's entourage for transvestitism and homosexuality. In the context of concern over falling birthrates, sexual identity and sexuality came to be viewed through the light of nationalism, and patriotism and sexual issues became weapons regularly employed in politics.

Sciences of the Modern Self, pp. 966–970

Social Darwinists also believed that nervous illness was a cause of national decline. In one of the most influential of the many books written on this subject in the 1890s, Hungarian-born physician Max Nordau (1849–1923) blamed overstimulation of the senses for individual and national degeneration in a world characterized by rapid change. The cure for such overstimulation, Social Darwinists claimed, was imperial adventure, renewed virility, and increased childbearing. The Viennese physician Sigmund Freud (1856–1939) sought a means to understand and remedy a variety of nervous ailments. In works such as *The Interpretation of Dreams* (1900), Freud argued that repressed parts of a person's personality are located in the "unconscious" and surface only indirectly via dreams, symptoms of physical illness, and abnormal behavior. He also argued that the psyche was composed of three parts—the id, the superego, and the ego—and that psychic development (or the creation of a healthy ego) entailed a constant attempt on the part of the superego (the conscience) to repress the sexual urges (seated in the id) that all children possess from birth. Freud, a meticulous scientist who believed in the rational examination of detailed evidence, believed that human beings were motivated by irrational drives toward death and destruction and that these drives shaped society's collective mentality.

Modernity and the Revolt in Ideas

The rejection of accepted beliefs and artistic forms by the intellectuals and artists who participated in the turmoil and triumph of turn-of-the-century society announced a new era. New scientific theories rocked established truths about time, space, matter, and energy, while artists and musicians created deliberately shocking and lurid works. The disorienting revolution in ideas and creative expression is now collectively identified as "modernism."

The Challenge to Positivism, pp. 970–971

Late in the nineteenth century, many philosophers and social thinkers rejected positivism: the belief that in science one could discover social laws based on rationally determined principles. German philosopher Wilhelm Dilthey (1833–1911) and American philosopher John Dewey (1859–1952) declared instead that human understanding was founded on one's ever-changing, day-to-day existence. Therefore, social theories and practices, relativists and pragmatists argued, cannot be constant or enduring, and persons must react pragmatically to the immediate conditions at hand. German sociologist and political theorist Max Weber (1864–1920) began to question the dependability of bureaucracy, maintaining that, as the numbers of persons involved in policymaking expanded, decisive action would become impossible, especially in times of crisis. In this situation, Weber argued, a charismatic leader might usurp power. German philosopher Friedrich Nietzsche (1844–1900) stated that all assertions of scientific fact and theory were illusions that people clung to because they could not face the primal, irrational side of human existence. Nietzsche wrote much of his work in aphorisms—short, disconnected statements of truth or opinion—a form that broke with the logical rigor of traditional philosophy and that presented his ideas as statements of individual perspective and not as universal truths. One aphorism declared that "God is dead," meaning that dogmatic truth was on the decline, freeing people to search for new "poetries of life."

Revolutionizing Science, pp. 971–972

New scientific discoveries challenged accepted knowledge about the nature of the universe, undermining the principles of time, space, matter, and energy. These challenges shook the foundations of traditional scientific certainty. In 1896, Antoine Becquerel (1852–1908) discovered radioactivity and suggested the mutability of elements by a rearrangement of their atoms. French chemist Marie Curie (1867–1934) and her husband Pierre (1859–1906) isolated the elements polonium and radium. Building on these and other discoveries, scientists concluded that atoms are largely empty space acting as an intangible electromagnetic field. German physicist Max Planck (1858–1947) announced his quantum theorem in 1900, which demonstrated that energy is emitted in irregular packets, not in a steady stream. In 1905, physicist Albert Einstein (1879–1955) published his Special Theory of Relativity, which argued that space and time are not absolutes, but rather vary according to the vantage point of the observer. Only the speed of light is constant. Einstein also transformed Planck's quantum theorem by suggesting that light travels in little packets and as waves. Later, Einstein proposed the blurring of mass and energy, expressed as $E = mc^2$, and postulated a fourth mathematical dimension to the universe. These theories often faced resistance from the scientific community but eventually transformed the foundations of science.

Modern Art, pp. 972–974

The same conflicts between traditional values and new ideas raged in the arts, as artists distanced themselves still farther from classical Western styles and from the conventions of polite society. A group of Parisian artists who decided to abandon the soft colors of impressionism for intense blues, greens, reds, and oranges came to be known as the fauves (wild beasts). One of the movement's leaders, Henri Matisse (1869–1954), soon struck out in a new direction, seeking to create soothing art designed for white-collar workers. Paul Cézanne (1839–1906) adopted a geometric vision in his paintings, accentuating the lines and planes found in nature. Spanish artist Pablo Picasso (1881–1973) followed in Cézanne's footsteps and invented cubism—a style of painting where a radical emphasis is placed on planes and surfaces that made people and objects almost unrecognizable. Picasso was influenced by African, Asian, and South American art, as well as by the anarchist sentiments that flourished in his native Barcelona. In 1912, he and French painter Georges Braque (1882–1963) devised a new kind of collage that incorporated newspaper clippings (which often described battles and murders), bits of string, and other artifacts, effectively creating a canvas covered in refuse. Expressionism, another artistic style, broke with middle-class optimism, as is evident in Norwegian painter Edvard Munch's (1863–1944) attempt to convey the horror of modern life in *The Scream* (1895). With styles changing so rapidly, the works of the "old masters" gained status and increased in value, and trade in art became increasingly professionalized. One innovative style that was a commercial success was art nouveau ("new style"). Designers working in this new style created an array of beautiful things for the general public—from posters to street lamps to dishes—drawing inspiration from organic and natural elements and from Asian art.

Musical Iconoclasm, pp. 974–975

Modern dance and music shocked audiences. American dancer Isadora Duncan (1877–1927) drew on Japanese practices to develop the first performance of modern dance. Like Duncan, the Russian ballet experimented with bodily expression in the 1913 performance of Igor Stravinsky's (1882–1971) *The Rite of Spring*. French composers like Claude Debussy (1862–1918) transformed their style to reflect the influence of non-European musical patterns and themes. Composers also experimented with tonality, creating sounds that jarred the listeners. Richard Strauss (1864–1949) used several keys simultaneously to distort familiar harmonic patterns. Hungarian pianist and composer Béla Bartók (1881–1945) incorporated folk melodies, but played two at the same time in different keys. Austrian composer Arnold Schoenberg (1874–1951) proposed eliminating tonality altogether. Modernists in music, like those in the other arts, felt that they were shattering old norms and values. But new aesthetic models distanced these artists from their audiences, separating high and low culture, and creating a distinction between the artistic elite and the social elite.

Growing Tensions in Mass Politics

Alongside modernist disturbances in cultural and intellectual life, the political atmosphere grew more charged. Networks of communication—especially the development of journalism—enhanced the impact of expanded male suffrage in Europe, leading to the creation of mass politics. Not all political activists were satisfied with the liberal reforms sought a century earlier, and some, such as militant nationalists, anti-Semites, and socialists, vigorously opposed them. Mass politics soon threatened social unity, especially in Central and Eastern Europe.

Labor's Expanding Power, pp. 976–977

European leaders watched with dismay as working-class political power increased in the late nineteenth century. In many countries such as Germany, England, and France, socialists gained seats in the government. Yet, some socialists felt uncomfortable sitting in parliament with members of the upper classes, whereas others worried that electoral victories might compromise the goal of revolution. Between 1900 and 1904, the Second International debated the issue of revisionism, which proposed that socialism be achieved by evolutionary rather than revolutionary means. Russian socialists had little power, and most operated in exile. V. I. Lenin (1870–1924) emigrated to western Europe after serving a jail term in Siberia, where he became involved with exiled Russian Marxists and advanced the theory that a highly disciplined party elite would lead a lightly industrialized Russia into socialism. His faction of Bolsheviks constantly struggled with the dominant Mensheviks. Neither group, however, had as large a constituency as the Socialist Revolutionaries, whose goal was to politicize peasants rather than workers. During this period, anarchists and some trade union members, known as syndicalists, resorted to terrorist acts and assassinated prominent political figures. The power of working people's voices caused the upper and middle classes grave anxiety.

Rights for Women and the Battle for Suffrage, pp. 977–978

Throughout the nineteenth century, the women's movement had been committed to gaining rights for women and had worked for various causes, including women's education, the monitoring of the regulation of prostitution, and pacifism. By the 1890s, however, many activists concluded that the right to vote should be the primary goal. Women's rights activists were predominantly from the middle class; their education exposed them to feminist ideas, and their greater leisure time gave them the opportunity to organize. Most working-class women distrusted middle-class men and women, and believed that economic reform was more important than suffrage. Influential women such as Millicent Garrett Fawcett (1847–1929) in England and Susan B. Anthony (1820–1906) in the United States emerged as leaders of the movement. In 1906, suffragists achieved their first major victory when women were granted the vote in Finland. But failure elsewhere prompted some women to more radical tactics. The Women's Social and Political Union founded in England by Emmeline Pankhurst (1858–1928) and her daughters began a campaign of violence, property destruction and hunger strikes in 1909.

Liberalism Modified, pp. 979–980

In 1905, the British Liberal Party won a majority in the House of Commons and seemed determined to enact legislation designed to gain working-class support. They passed the National Insurance Act of 1911 and, when Conservatives in the House of Lords resisted raising taxes to pay for this and other social programs, they threatened to create more peers (lords) so as to dilute the power of the nobility. Under this threat, the House of Lords approved the Parliament Bill of 1911, which eliminated their veto power. One of the series of bills the Lords had blocked repeatedly was home rule for Ireland, but yet, in 1913, the British Parliament approved home rule for Ireland. The outbreak of World War I prevented this legislation from taking effect. In Italy, corruption plagued the constitutional monarchy. In the 1890s, prime ministers used patriotic rhetoric; bribes to the

press; and imperial adventure, which culminated in the failed attempt to conquer Ethiopia (1896), to forge a national consensus. These policies failed and led to riots and strikes that were repressed by armed government troops. A new prime minister, Giovanni Giolitti (1842–1928), followed a policy known as *trasformismo* (Italian for "transform"), using bribes, public works programs, and other benefits to localities to influence their deputies in parliament in the absence of well-developed political parties. Giolitti's policies met with unrest in the rapidly industrializing cities of Turin and Milan and in the depressed agrarian south. Urban and rural workers demanded change, especially a widening of the suffrage. Giolitti appeased the protesters by instituting social welfare programs and, in 1912, virtually complete male suffrage.

Anti-Semitism, Nationalism, and Zionism in Mass Politics, pp. 980–985

Anti-Semitism and nationalism offered pat answers to complex questions, and leaders invoked these concepts to maintain interest-group support, to direct hostility away from themselves, and to win elections. Russian tsar Nicholas II used anti-Semitism to direct attention away from the government. Pogroms became a regular feature of the Easter holiday, and Nicholas II increasingly limited where Jews could live and how they could earn a living. In France, a Jewish army officer, Alfred Dreyfus (1859–1935), was convicted of spying for Germany in 1894. As evidence came to light regarding his innocence, novelist Émile Zola (1840–1902) accused governmental officials of a list of lies and cover-ups in the affair, and Dreyfus was eventually pardoned in 1899. In Germany, ruling elites used anti-Semitism as a political weapon to gain support from those who feared the consequences of Germany's rapid industrialization. These elites based their power and wealth on agriculture. As agriculture came to comprise a smaller percentage of the gross national product, these elites came to loathe industry and the working class. In Austria-Hungary, nationalism played a different role. While Hungarians demanded more autonomy for themselves, they forcibly imposed their own language and culture on other, smaller ethnic groups (a policy called Magyarization). Unrest in Hungary fueled unrest elsewhere in the empire, as Croats, Serbs, and other Slavic groups in the south called for equality with the Hungarians. The central government granted the Czechs more privileges because the heightened development of industry in their region gave them more influence. This increase in Czech influence outraged ethnic Germans and politicians in Vienna, like mayor Karl Lueger (1844–1910), who linked the growing power of Hungarian and Czech politicians with the Jews. The rise of nationalism and anti-Semitism further destabilized politics in the Dual Monarchy. Jews in western Europe had responded to legal emancipation with assimilation, adopting liberal political and cultural values, intermarrying with Christians, and sometimes converting to Christianity. By contrast, Jews in Russia and Romania were increasingly singled out for persecution, legally disadvantaged, and forced to live in ghettos. In the 1880s, Ukrainian physician Leon Pinsker (1821–1891) advocated the migration of Jews to Palestine. In 1896, Hungarian journalist Theodor Herzl (1860–1904) published "The Jewish State", which called for the creation of a Jewish nation-state. With the support of poor eastern European Jews, Herzl succeeded in calling the first International Zionist Congress in 1897, which endorsed settlement in Palestine and gained financial backing from the Rothschild banking family. By 1914, some eighty-five thousand Jews had resettled in Palestine.

European Imperialism Contested

Inflamed nationalism throughout the west made it difficult for nations to calm domestic politics and the traumas of modern, industrial life. Imperialism aggravated relations among the European powers while, at the same time, colonized peoples challenged European control. Nationalist movements for independence gained strength, which led to new rebellions against European rule.

The Trials of Empire, pp. 985–990

As the twentieth century opened, imperial adventure soured for Britain and France, while Italy and Germany found it difficult to establish themselves as imperial powers. In 1896, the British experienced a bloody defeat when Cecil Rhodes (1853–1902), prime minister of the Cape Colony in southern Africa, ordered a raid into Boer territory. Not willing to accept defeat, Britain went to war with the Boers and succeeded in annexing the Transvaal and the Orange Free State in 1902. The brutality of the war horrified Britons. At almost the same time, Spain lost Cuba, Puerto Rico, and the Philippines as a result of a defeat in the Spanish-American war of 1898. Subsequently, the United States waged a bloody war against the Filipinos who were demanding independence, further disillusioning the European public about the "civilizing" aspect of imperialism. European confidence fell further as Japan emerged as a power. In 1874, Japan invaded the Chinese island of Formosa (Taiwan) and, in 1894, Japan sparked the Sino-Japanese War, which forced China to end its domination of Korea. As Russia expanded east and south into Asia, the Japanese became anxious, and attacked Russian forces (1904). The complete destruction of Russia's Baltic fleet in the battle of Tsushima Straits (1905) was the first victory of a non-European power over a European power in modern history.

The Russian Empire Threatened, pp. 988–990

Although the Russian Empire had expanded during the nineteenth century, internally the threat of revolution was constant. In January 1905, a crowd gathered outside the tsar's palace in St. Petersburg to make Nicholas II aware of industry's brutal working conditions. Soldiers fired on the crowd, killing hundreds and wounding thousands, an event that came to be known as Bloody Sunday. The quashing of this demonstration spurred other workers to rebel. During the following year, workers struck over wages, hours, and working conditions, and demanded political representation. In response to the continuing violence, Nicholas II created a representative body: the Duma. The Duma convened in 1907, and revolutionary activity abated. Although very few citizens had voting privileges, the Duma's existence—coupled with the right of public political debate—liberalized government. However, when the tsar disliked its recommendations, he disbanded the Duma. Prime Minister Pyotr Stolypin (1863–1911) resolved to eliminate sources of discontent by ending the mir system, canceling land redemption payments, and making governmental loans available to peasants. These reforms allowed more persons to move to the cities and created a larger group of independent peasants. At the same time, Stolypin clamped down on revolutionary organizations, urged more pogroms, and stepped up Russification. Despite these measures, rebels continued to assassinate government officials, including Stolypin himself, who was killed in 1911. Without curbing unrest, the reforms created a larger industrial workforce and a more assertive peasantry.

Growing Resistance to Colonial Domination, pp. 990–992

China's 1895 defeat by Japan forced the ruling Qing dynasty to grant economic concessions to the Western powers. Consequently, peasants organized into secret societies to restore Chinese integrity. One such group, the Society of the Righteous and Harmonious Fists (or Boxers) rebelled in 1900, and colonial powers, after putting down the rebellion, forced the Chinese government to pay a huge indemnity and to allow more extensive foreign military occupation. In 1911, the Qing dynasty was overthrown, and the following year China was declared a republic. Sun Yat-Sen (1866–1925), the leader of the revolutionaries, used Western concepts to promote Chinese values while pursuing a cluster of Western programs. In India, the Japanese victory over Russia and the Russian Revolution of 1905 stimulated politicians to take a more radical course than that offered by the Indian National Congress. A Hindu leader, B. G. Tilak (1856–1920), preached complete noncooperation with the British and promoted Hindu customs, while inspiring violent rebellion in his followers. In an attempt to stop Tilak, the British sponsored the Muslim League, a rival nationalist group. Nationalism was also weakening the Ottoman Empire. When Sultan Abdul Hamid II (r. 1876–1909) attempted to promote a pan-Islamic solution to nationalist discontent, he provoked Turkish nationalism in Constantinople. Turkish nationalists emphasized their distinct history, culture, and language. In 1908, a group of nationalists, called the Young Turks, took control of Constantinople. Their victory motivated other groups in the Middle East and the Balkans to assert their independence from the Ottomans. In German East Africa, colonial forces responded to native rebellion with a scorched-earth policy, while in Indochina the French closed the University of Hanoi, executed Indo-Chinese intellectuals, and deported thousands of suspected nationalists.

Roads to War

International developments simultaneously aggravated competition among the great powers and caused Western nationalism to swell. Governments spent great amounts on an "arms race" and many contemporaries feared that the increasingly hostile atmosphere would make physical combat inevitable.

Competing Alliances and Clashing Ambitions, pp. 993–994

At the beginning of the twentieth century, the Triple Alliance between Germany, Austria-Hungary, and Italy faced the alliance forged by France and Russia in the 1890s. France and Great Britain also strengthened ties with a series of secret agreements concerning French claims in Morocco and British claims in Egypt. These agreements became a British-French alliance called the "Entente Cordiale." Germany unwittingly strengthened this alliance in a series of challenges to French predominance in Morocco in 1905 and 1911 known respectively as the first and second Moroccan Crises. However, they were disappointed in their expectations for more colonial power. Frustrated in the colonies, German statesmen turned their hopes to the creation of a Mitteleuropa that would include central Europe, the Balkans, and Turkey. The Habsburgs, backed by Germany, wished to expand into the Balkans, believing the resulting addition of more ethnic groups would weaken those already present in the Dual Monarchy. Promoting itself as protector of the Slavs, Russia was outraged at Austria-Hungary's 1908 annexation of Bosnia-Hungary, where many Serbian Slavs resided. Among the Balkan states themselves, Greece, Serbia, Bulgaria, Romania, and Montenegro all wanted to incorporate territories in Austria-Hungary and the Ottoman Empire in which members of their ethnic groups lived. In 1912, the First Balkan War broke out.

Greece, Serbia, Bulgaria, and Montenegro joined forces to take Macedonia and Albania from the Ottomans. In a second war in 1913, Greece, Serbia, and Montenegro won a quick victory over Bulgaria. In the peace negotiations, Austria-Hungary managed to prevent Serbia from annexing parts of Albania. The peace conditions did not demilitarize the region, however, and strategists began to think that a quick war in the Balkans could resolve the multiple tensions that existed.

The Race to Arms, pp. 994–997

Technology, nationalism, and imperialism had transformed the practice and rationale for war. During the nineteenth century, governments began to conscript ordinary citizens for periods of two to six years in large standing armies. Between 1890 and 1914, as competition in the colonies and in Europe increased the threat of war, the rates of conscripts and military expenditure rose. At the same time, the modernization of weaponry had a huge impact. Swedish arms manufacturer Alfred Nobel (1833–1896) patented dynamite and developed a type of gunpowder that improved the accuracy of firearms. Military leaders began to devise strategies to protect their armies, such as the trenches used by Russia during the Russo-Japanese War. Arms manufacturers throughout Europe increased production as governments stockpiled weapons. The modernization of weaponry also affected navies; battleships began to be constructed out of metal rather than wood. German grand admiral Alfred von Tirpitz (1849–1930) encouraged Germany to increase and modernize its fleet. German ambitions caused France and Great Britain to draw even closer together in the Entente Cordiale. Military buildup was a response to a possible threat of war; however, it also added to economic and social stability by creating jobs. Public-relations campaigns created support for an arms race that had external and internal benefits. By 1914, most of the general public believed that war was imminent and necessary to settle lingering international tensions.

1914: War Erupts, pp. 997–999

On June 28, 1914, Archduke Francis Ferdinand (1863–1914), heir to the Habsburg throne, and his wife, Sophie, were on a state visit to Bosnia when they were assassinated by Bosnian nationalist Gavrilo Princip (1895–1918). Evidence showed that Princip had received arms and information from Serbian officials who hoped, like Princip, to join Bosnia to Serbia. Austria, backed by Germany, presented Serbia with a harsh ultimatum. Serbia agreed to every condition except Austrian participation in the investigation. Austria-Hungary, confident of Germany's backing, declared war on Serbia on July 28. As the tsar and the kaiser corresponded, each asked the other to avoid starting a European war; British foreign secretary Sir Edward Grey (1862–1933) unsuccessfully proposed an international conference. The German military leadership was fixed on fighting a short war that could provide territorial gains leading toward the goal of Mitteleuropa, and hoped that martial law would justify arresting the leaders of the Social Democratic Party. While the press fanned war fever, military leaders prepared for an attack. The Austrians mobilized on July 31. In response, Nicholas II ordered Russian mobilization to aid her ally, Serbia. The Germans mobilized on August 1. German military strategy was based on the plan drawn up by Alfred von Schlieffen, which anticipated a two-front war and thus called for a rapid strike through Belgium against France and a subsequent campaign against Russia. When Belgium refused Germany uncontested passage, and the Germans entered anyway, Britain and France entered the war. As war broke out, celebrations erupted throughout Europe. Europeans believed the conflict would be short, and that it would resolve tensions ranging from the rise of the working class to imperial competition.

Key Events   *For each question, select the most appropriate response from the choices provided.*

1894–1895 Japan defeats China in the Sino-Japanese War

1894–1899 Dreyfus Affair lays bare anti-Semitism in France

1899–1902 Boer War fought between Dutch descendants and the British in South African states

1900 Sigmund Freud publishes *The Interpretation of Dreams*

1901 Irish National Theater established by Maud Gonne and William Butler Yeats; death of Queen Victoria

1903 Emmeline Pankhurst founds the Women's Social and Political Union to fight for woman suffrage in Great Britain

1904–1905 Japan defeats Russia in the Russo-Japanese War

1905 Revolution erupts in Russia; violence forces Nicholas II to establish an elected body, the Duma; Albert Einstein publishes his "Special Theory of Relativity"

1906 Women receive the vote in Finland

1907 Pablo Picasso launches cubist painting with *Les Demoiselles d'Avignon*

1908 Young Turks revolt against rule by the sultan in the Ottoman Empire

1911–1912 Revolutionaries overthrow the Qing dynasty and declare China a republic

1914 Assassination of the Austrian archduke Francis Ferdinand and his wife by a Serbian nationalist precipitates World War I

1. How did the European powers react to the Japanese victory in the Sino-Japanese War?
   a. Supported the Japanese because the Chinese resisted European imperialism
   b. Were unconcerned with the Japanese because they had more immediate concerns in Europe
   c. Were alarmed at Japan's victory and forced it to relinquish other imperial gains it made
   d. Took the side of the Chinese and sent several gunboats to Japan to defend China

2. Which of the following was a result of the Boer War?
   a. Britain took over the Transvaal and the Orange Free State.
   b. An uprising among the indigenous population forced the Dutch to withdraw from Africa.
   c. Cecil Rhodes was forced to resign in disgrace.
   d. The war ended with a repartitioning of all of Africa.

3. Which of the following was argued by Freud in his *The Interpretation of Dreams*?
   a. There is a repressed part of the human psyche where all sorts of desires are more or less hidden.
   b. There is a personality type—homosexual—that can be identified by traits such as effeminate behavior in males.
   c. Overstimulation causes both individual and national deterioration.
   d. There is a rational side of human existence and a "Dionysian" side that is expressed by primal urges.

4. Which of the following was used by Emmeline Pankhurst's Women's Social and Political Union to fight for woman's suffrage?
   a. Intense lobbying of members of Parliament
   b. Establishing alliances with labor unions
   c. Waging campaigns through mass journalism and public speeches
   d. Violent attacks on public and private property

5. In Russia, what resulted from the establishment of the Duma?
   a. Aristocrats returned to power because they controlled the most important seats.
   b. Soviets rose to power and eventually overthrew the tsar.
   c. Little changed because the tsar could dismiss the Duma and force new elections.
   d. The Duma and the tsar worked closely together to implement reform in Russia.

6. Which of the following *did not* contribute to the discrediting and overthrow of the Qing dynasty?
   a. China's defeat to the Japanese in the Sino-Japanese War
   b. The Boxer Rebellion
   c. Russia's victory in the Russo-Japanese War
   d. An increased foreign military presence

7. Which of the following country's declaration of war on Serbia in 1914 sparked World War I?
   a. Great Britain
   b. Russia
   c. Germany
   d. Austria-Hungary

Key Terms   *Match each key term to its definition.*

A. **art nouveau** (p. 974)
B. **Boer War** (p. 985)
C. **Duma** (p. 989)
D. **Entente Cordíale** (p. 993)
E. **Mitteleuropa** (p. 993)
F. **Modernism** (p. 970)
G. **new woman** (p. 965)
H. **psychoanalysis** (p. 967)
I. **suffragists** (p. 977)
J. **Zionism** (p. 984)

1. _____ A woman of the turn of the twentieth century, often from the middle class, who dressed practically, moved about freely, lived apart from her family, and supported herself.

2. _____ Freud's theory of human mental processes and his method for treating their malfunctioning.

3. _____ Changes in the arts at the end of the nineteenth century that featured a break with realism in art and literature and with lyricism in music.

4. _____ A successful style in the arts, household and fashion design, and graphics that featured flowing, sinuous lines that contrasted with the mechanical influence of the early twentieth century. It borrowed many of its motifs from Asian and African art and was internationally popular.

5. _____ Women around the turn of the twentieth century who worked actively for the right to vote.

6. _____ A movement that began in the late nineteenth century among European Jews to found a Jewish state.

7. _____ The war between Britain and Boer (originally Dutch) inhabitants of South Africa for control of the region. Lasting between 1899 and 1902, the war convinced many British people that empire was wrong or at least too costly to maintain.

8. _____ The Russian parliament set up in the aftermath of the outbreak of the Revolution of 1905. Few Russians could actually vote for representatives, but it held out promise to those of all classes.

9. _____ An alliance between Britain and France that began with an agreement in 1904 to honor colonial holdings.

10. _____ Literally "central Europe," but used by influential military leaders in Germany before World War I to refer to land in both central and eastern Europe that they hoped to acquire as a substitute for vast colonial empires in Africa and Asia. This territory ultimately formed a war aim in World War I and for Hitler thereafter.

Identification   *This activity tests your recall of significant people, places, and events from this chapter. Fill in the blank with the correct answer.*

1. In his book *Sexual Inversion*, _____ postulated a new personality type: the homosexual.

2. The new "science" of _____ advocated the improvement of the human species through the elimination of members that were seen as unfit.

3. In the spring of 1895, _____ was sentenced to two years in prison for indecency, a charge that referred to his homosexual affairs with younger men.

4. A pioneer in approaches to mental health problems, _____ proposed that causing a subject to associate a desired response with a previously unrelated stimulus, or a conditioning mental reflex, could modify behavior.

5. Believing that the human psyche was far from rational, _____ postulated that innate sexual impulses had to be repressed in order for a person to attain maturity and for society to remain civilized.

6. Challenging the positivist notion that fundamental laws governed human behavior, _____ argued that the sheer numbers involved in policymaking would often make decisive action by bureaucrats impossible.

7. Claiming that knowledge of nature had to be expressed in mathematical, linguistic, or artistic representations, _____ argued that all assertions of scientific fact and theory were mere illusions.

8. In 1900, _____ introduced his quantum theorem, which demonstrated that a flow of energy is emitted in irregular packets, not in a steady stream.

9. American dancer _____ took Europe by storm with a primitivist style that drew on Japanese practices and featured wearing flowing garments and dancing barefoot.

10. In Stravinsky's *Rite of Spring*, a tale of an orgiastic dance to the death, the choreography of its star _____ stirred enormous controversy in Paris.

11. Between 1900 and 1904, the Second International wrestled with the issue of _____; that is, whether socialists should accept incremental gains in power for workers rather than promoting a revolution to overthrow the government.

12. Until Lenin outmaneuvered them in 1903, the _____ had been the dominant voice in Russian Marxism.

13. British suffrage leader _____ pressured members of Parliament for women's right to vote and participated in national and international congresses on behalf of suffrage.

14. Confronting modern life with an unswerving belief in religious orthodoxy, Russian tsar _____ incorporated anti-Semitism into state politics thereby blaming any failures in Russian policy on the Jews.

15. In his scathing newspaper article *J'accuse*, _____ exposed a list of lies and cover-ups perpetrated by high governmental officials to create an illusion of Alfred Dreyfus's guilt of spying for the Germans.

16. In _____, the United States gained Cuba, Puerto Rico, and the Philippines as a result of its victory over Spain in the Spanish-American War.

17. In the Sino-Japanese War of _____, the Chinese lost control of Korea to the Japanese.

18. Although delegates from revolutionary parties such as the Social Democrats encouraged direct blows against the central government in Russia, workers rejected their leadership and organized their own councils called _____.

19. In a rebellion in 1900, the _____ fought against what they perceived as a growing foreign influence in China.

20. In _____, B. G. Tilak opposed the moderation subscribed to by other reformers and preached blatant noncooperation against the British.

21. In 1911, Germany triggered the Second Moroccan Crisis by sending a gunboat into the port of _____ and demanding concessions from the French.

22. In the First Balkan War of _____, Serbia, Bulgaria, Greece, and Montenegro joined forces to wrest Macedonia and Albania from the Ottomans.

23. _____ patented dynamite and developed a type of gunpowder that improved the accuracy of and reduced the smoke from firearms, thereby modernizing and transforming warfare.

24. Influential American naval theorist _____ argued that command of the seas determined superior international power.

25. On June 28, 1914, a radical nationalist, _____, assassinated Austrian Archduke Francis Ferdinand, giving the spark that ignited World War I.

CHAPTER REVIEW

Self-Test and Analytical Exercises

Multiple Choice *Select the best answer from the four choices provided.*

1. In the late nineteenth and early twentieth centuries, population levels
   a. stayed about the same.
   b. increased dramatically.
   c. declined slightly.
   d. increased in only a few countries, such as Great Britain and Germany.

2. The phrase "new women" referred to
   a. wives who adopted more traditional behaviors in reaction to the uncertainties of urban living.
   b. women who gave birth to larger numbers of children in response to social concerns about falling birthrates.
   c. women who adopted a more private way of life away from the trends that were shaping modern existence.
   d. women who took advantage of modern trends to live more independent, public, and assertive lives than had been traditionally available to them.

3. Who wrote the book *Degeneration* in which it was suggested that the "overstimulation" of modern life was the cause of individual and national deterioration?
   a. Sigmund Freud
   b. Max Nordau
   c. Cesare Lombroso
   d. Alfred Binet

4. Sigmund Freud's approach to modern anxieties emphasized the role of which of the following in shaping human behavior?
   a. Rationality
   b. The unconscious
   c. Self-interest
   d. Conditioned mental reflexes

5. Which of the following, no longer popular beliefs held that in science one could discover enduring social laws based on rationally determined principles?
   a. Pragmatism
   b. Relativism
   c. Positivism
   d. Fundamentalism

6. The Special Theory of Relativity argued that
   a. the speed of light varies with the motion of the earth.
   b. energy is emitted in irregular packets rather than in a steady stream.
   c. space and time vary according to the vantage point of the observer, but that the speed of light is constant.
   d. atoms are composed of subatomic particles moving about a core and are largely empty spaces acting as intangible electromagnetic fields.

7. Which of the following artists initiated the style known as "cubism"?
   a. Pablo Picasso
   b. Georges Braque
   c. Edvard Munch
   d. Wassily Kandinsky

8. The artistic style that won wide approval and was an immediate commercial success was
   a. expressionism.
   b. art nouveau.
   c. cubism.
   d. collage.

9. Advocates of which political theory assassinated political leaders and committed terrorist acts?
   a. Syndicalism
   b. Revisionism
   c. Anarchism
   d. Bolshevism

10. What did pogroms involve?
    a. Attacks upon Jews in Russia
    b. Forced conversion of Jews to the Russian Orthodox religion
    c. Reeducation policies of the Russian government that taught Jews to speak Russian (Russification)
    d. A series political scandals that accused high-ranking Jewish military officers of treason

11. The Dreyfus Affair involved
    a. a series of pogroms on Jewish-owned businesses.
    b. the wrongful conviction of a Jewish officer in the French military for treason.
    c. the refusal of the École Polytechnique in Paris to admit Jews.
    d. the forced conversion of French Jews to Catholicism.

12. What was Magyarization?
    a. The demand by the Magyar majority in Hungary for greater Hungarian influence over other ethnic groups in their nation
    b. The exclusion of the Magyars, who were Hungarian Jews, from conducting business in Austria
    c. The formation of anti-Semitic organizations in Austria under the leadership of Karl Lueger
    d. The decree of the Austro-Hungarian government in 1897 that governmental officials, overseeing the Czech region of the empire, would have to know the Czech language as well as German

13. Which country was foremost among the new competitors for acquiring an empire?
    a. France
    b. The United States
    c. Germany
    d. Japan

14. The revolution of 1905 in Russia began with
    a. the killing and injuring of peaceful demonstrators outside the tsar's palace in St. Petersburg.
    b. demonstrations protesting Russia's defeat in the Russo-Japanese War.
    c. an attempted coup led by Marxist revolutionaries.
    d. the invasion of Russia by Japanese troops.

15. What was the name of the tsarist prime minister who instituted both a series of land reforms *and* repressive measures against revolutionary organizations?
    a. Leon Trotsky
    b. V. I. Lenin
    c. Pyotr Stolypin
    d. Grand Duke Sergei

16. Which of the following was the policy advocated by B. G. Tilak?
    a. Tilak encouraged an increase in British influence in India in order to disempower his country's Muslim inhabitants.
    b. As leader of the Indian National Congress, Tilak wanted to achieve Indian independence gradually, through evolutionary rather than revolutionary means.
    c. He led the Muslim League, which garnered British support because of its moderate demands.
    d. Completely anti-British, Tilak promoted Hindu customs and preached noncompliance with British rule, inspiring violent rebellion against British imperialism in his followers.

17. Which countries comprised the Triple Alliance?
    a. Germany, Austria-Hungary, and Italy
    b. Great Britain, Russia, and Austria-Hungary
    c. France, Russia, and Great Britain
    d. Germany, France, and Great Britain

18. In the years leading up to World War I, Germany was
    a. weak economically and strong diplomatically.
    b. interested in forming an alliance with France.
    c. fully confident in its empire-building ability.
    d. strong economically and weak diplomatically.

19. Which countries stationed an increasing number of troops on Balkan borders following the First and Second Balkan Wars, raising tensions in south-central Europe?
    a. Austria-Hungary and Russia
    b. Germany and Austria-Hungary
    c. France and Russia
    d. the Ottoman Empire and Austria-Hungary

20. Who was the architect of the buildup of German naval power?
    a. Alfred Nobel
    b. Alfred Thayer Mahan
    c. Alfred von Tirpitz
    d. Alfred von Schlieffen

21. The dramatic rise in population in the nineteenth century was due to
    a. improvements in sanitation and public health.
    b. an increasing birthrate.
    c. passage of tax breaks for growing families.
    d. the outlawing of contraception.

22. In the majority of European countries, how did the legal rights of married women change during this period?
    a. Women lost more control to their husbands, as states sought to reinforce the bonds of marriage and reverse trends that resulted in a declining birthrate.
    b. Women's rights changed little because governments were preoccupied with other issues during the late nineteenth century.
    c. Women's rights improved somewhat as states attempted to make marriage more appealing to women in order to counter a declining birthrate.
    d. States tried to limit women's rights and make marriage unappealing, all to combat a rapidly escalating birthrate.

23. Who postulated the existence of a new personality type —the homosexual—in the 1890s?
    a. Oscar Wilde
    b. Havelock Ellis
    c. Friedrich Nietzsche
    d. Sigmund Freud

24. Which of the following was *not* asserted by Sigmund Freud?
    a. Children have sexual drives that need to be repressed in order for them to achieve maturity
    b. Adult sexual identity depends on the repression of infantile urges, like incest and bisexuality
    c. Gender identity is entirely dependent upon biology
    d. The human psyche is made up of three competing parts: the id, the ego, and the superego

25. Which of the following are applied to the theories of turn-of-the-century thinkers who declared that human understanding could never be constant, but was instead founded on the conditions of day-to-day existence?
    a. Positivism and pragmatism
    b. Pragmatism and relativism
    c. Postmodernism and relativism
    d. Apollonianism and Dionysianism

26. Who discovered radioactivity in 1896?
    a. Marie Curie
    b. Max Planck
    c. Albert Einstein
    d. Antoine Becquerel

27. The artistic style known as "expressionism"
    a. aimed at representing the shifting quality of light and fleeting moments of perception.
    b. placed a radical emphasis on planes and surfaces, presenting people in unrecognizable forms.
    c. sought to portray the anguish of modern life and humankind's inner reality.
    d. emphasized the creation of beautiful objects for mass, commercial consumption.

28. Which American dancer took Europe by storm in the first modern dance performance with a primitive style that drew on Japanese practices?
    a. Isadora Duncan
    b. Ellen Key
    c. Maud Gonne
    d. Emmeline Pankhurst

29. Which British woman founded the Women's Social and Political Union, began a campaign of violence on male property, and used confrontational tactics to demonstrate for the right to vote?
    a. Emmeline Pankhurst
    b. Susan B. Anthony
    c. Millicent Garrett Fawcett
    d. Bertha von Süttner

30. The Italian government's policy of *trasformismo* involved
    a. uniting the Italian people through imperialism, as was the case with the successful invasion of Ethiopia.
    b. bribes and public works programs distributed by the central government to localities in order to influence members of parliament.
    c. a comprehensive program of economic development that met with support among Italian socialists.
    d. widespread repression that rejected liberal reforms in an effort to maintain political stability.

31. Which of the following was *not* a significant argument supporting the women's suffrage movement?
    a. Male chivalry was supposed to protect women, but had led to abuse and exploitation.
    b. Gaining the vote might help women improve their working conditions.
    c. Women possessed qualities needed to counterbalance men's nature in the running of society.
    d. Women were superior to men and should take over the administration of politics and society.

32. Which of the following *best describes* how Jews fared in Europe at the turn of the century?
    a. Jews thrived in turn-of-the-century Europe, despite widespread urban anti-Semitism.
    b. Jews were often prominent in cultural and economic affairs in cities, but suffered discrimination and persecution elsewhere.
    c. Jews were discriminated against and persecuted throughout Europe and could only participate in culture as second-class citizens.
    d. As a result of persecution, Jews resisted conversion, intermarriage, and participation in cosmopolitan European culture.

33. Which country won the first victory by a non-European nation over a European great power in the modern age?
    a. China
    b. Korea
    c. Japan
    d. Cuba

34. Which of the following *best* defines *soviets*?
    a. Secret underground cells of Marxist revolutionaries
    b. Russian word for well-educated elites
    c. Political councils organized by discontented workers in the Russian Revolution (1905)
    d. Councils within the Liberal Party of Russia that pressed for Western-style political reforms

35. Who were the Boxers?
    a. Chinese dockworkers and cargo haulers who undertook a general strike by refusing to load British cargo in protest against poor working conditions
    b. Members of a secret Chinese fighting society opposed to Western influences
    c. Chinese enthusiasts who encouraged Western influences, particularly sports, in China
    d. Members of a Chinese secret society opposed to the Qing dynasty

36. Who were the Young Turks?
    a. Nationalist supporters of Sultan Abdul Hamid II who promoted Islam against the influence of Serbs and Bulgarians
    b. A Turkish organization that advocated pan-Islamic unity in order to strengthen the Ottoman Empire
    c. A group of Turkish nationalists who rejected pan-Islamism in favor of celebrating the uniqueness of Turkish culture, and took control of the government in Constantinople (1908)
    d. Anti-western revolutionaries who sought to liberate all territories in the Ottoman Empire from European influence

37. Mitteleuropa refers to
    a. Austria-Hungary's decision to avoid gaining any more territory in the Balkans, which would only add to the number of ethnic groups under their control.
    b. the territorial aspirations of German statesmen, who envisioned central Europe, the Balkans, and Turkey under their control.
    c. the Russian conviction that it was the protector of Slavic peoples in central Europe.
    d. the Serbian resistance to increased German influence.

38. The First and Second Moroccan crises were colonial disputes between which two countries?
    a. Great Britain and France
    b. Germany and France
    c. Russia and France
    d. Germany and Italy

39. The treaty between Britain and France was known as the
    a. Triple Alliance.
    b. Naval Entente.
    c. Entente Cordiale.
    d. Nationalist Alliance.

40. The violation of which country's neutrality caused Great Britain to enter into World War I?
    a. The Netherlands
    b. Luxembourg
    c. Denmark
    d. Belgium

Short Answer   *Answer each question in three or four sentences.*

Private Life in the Modern Age

1. What were the reactions to the declining birthrate of the late nineteenth and early twentieth centuries?

2. Describe the "new women" of the nineteenth century.

3. What were some important contributions of Sigmund Freud's psychological theories?

Modernity and the Revolt in Ideas

4. What was *positivism*, and why was it rejected by late-nineteenth-century philosophers?

5. Describe the paradigm shift that took place in the sciences of the late nineteenth century.

6. What were the responses of artists to the issues raised by modernity?

Growing Tensions in Mass Politics

7. How did the Labor and Socialist parties' politics change in this period?

8. Why and how did women pursue expanded political rights during this period?

9. How was anti-Semitism used as a tool during this period?

European Imperialism Contested

10. How was European imperialism challenged at the turn of the century?

11. What were the causes and effects of the Russian Revolution of 1905?

12. Which forms did nationalism take in Asia, and what was gained by colonized territories that experimented with nationalistic activism?

Roads to War

13. How did imperialistic ambitions contribute to the tensions that instigated World War I?

14. What changes took place in the conduct of war in the decades leading up to World War I?

15. What was the chain of events that led to the beginning of World War I?

BUILDING HISTORICAL SKILLS

Reading Maps
Write a brief, paragraph-length response to each of the following questions based on **Map 25.2: Africa in 1914 (p. 986)**.

1. Look at the territory controlled by Great Britain and France. What might be Britain's goals for expansion? France's goals for expansion?

2. Judging from the map of Africa, why might Germany have felt insecure about its position as an imperial power?

3. Which patterns are evident in the uprisings against Europeans, and what might explain the timing of the uprisings?

Reading Illustrations
Write a brief, paragraph-length response to each of the following questions based on the illustration **The "Foreign Pig" Is Put to Death (p. 991)**.

1. How are foreigners and those who adopt foreign ways portrayed in this image?

2. How does this image legitimize the Boxers' actions?

Reading Historical Documents
Write a brief, paragraph-length response to each of the following questions based on the documents in your book.

Leon Pinsker Calls for a Jewish State (p. 984)

1. What arguments does Leon Pinsker present for why European Jews should have their own nation?

2. What contemporary social trends are evident in this excerpt?

An Historian Promotes Militant Nationalism (p. 996)

3. Why, according to Heinrich von Treitschke, was war a necessity?

4. What scientific and historical evidence does he use to support his claims?

Psychohistory and Its Lessons (pp. 968–969)

5. How does psychohistory differ from history as it was practiced in the nineteenth century?

6. What are the advantages of psychohistory as a historical method?

7. What are some of the criticisms of psychohistory?

War, Revolution, and Reconstruction
1914–1929

CHAPTER OVERVIEW

Chapter Questions   *Keep these questions in mind as you go through the study guide chapter.*

1. Where did the major battles of the war take place?

2. How did protests bring about the war's end?

3. What did the allies do to attempt peace at the war's end?

4. Why was democracy considered so important in postwar society?

5. What factors led to the rise of dictators during the 1920s?

Chapter Summary

The Great War, 1914–1918

When war erupted in August 1914, the ground had been prepared with long-standing alliances, the development of strategies for war, and the buildup of military technologies such as heavy artillery, machine guns, and the airplane. Most were expecting a short, decisive conflict, but it unexpectedly dragged on for more than four years. It was a total war, mobilizing entire societies and producing unprecedented horror.

Blueprints for War, pp. 1004–1006

World War I pitted the Central Powers—Germany, Austria-Hungary, and Turkey, against the Allies—Great Britain, France, and Russia. In late August 1914, Japan joined the Allies and, in the fall, Turkey joined the Central Powers. Italy joined the Allies in 1915 in exchange for a promise of territorial gains after the war (agreed to in the Treaty of London). Other, smaller countries also entered the war on one side or the other. Germany's goal in

entering the war was to create a Central European empire formed by annexing Russian territory and parts of Belgium, France, and Luxembourg. Austria-Hungary wanted to retain its great power status, whereas Russia wanted to reassert its status as a great power *and* as the protector of the Slavs by annexing a reunified Poland, the Austro-Hungarian territory peopled by Ukrainians, and reorganizing Austria-Hungary into a Triple Monarchy that would recognize the Slavs. Those powers possessing colonies enlisted or conscripted tens of thousands of colonized men. All the powers used recently developed, more powerful weaponry; and the new technologies that had emerged: chlorine gas, bombs, and tanks. On both sides of the conflict, officers originally believed in a "cult of the offensive," which called for spirited attacks and a reliance on old-fashioned weaponry—sabers, lances, and bayonets—because, at the opening of the war, such Napoleonic weaponry and strategy seemed crucial to victory.

The Battlefronts, pp. 1006–1011

The major armies mobilized rapidly and, by August 4, the Germans had reached Belgium. The neutral Belgians unexpectedly resisted, which afforded the British and French forces time to reach the northern front. In September, they engaged Germany along the Marne River. Casualties were shocking; in the first three months of the war, 1.5 million men fell on the western front alone. During the following four years, the two sides faced off along a line that stretched from the North Sea in Belgium and northern France to Switzerland. Soldiers on both sides dug in, excavating parallel lines of trenches up to thirty feet deep. On the eastern front, the Russians advanced more quickly than expected, driving into East Prussia and parts of Austria-Hungary by mid-August, but Germany crushed the invading Russian forces. War at sea proved equally indecisive. The Allies blockaded the entries to the Mediterranean and North seas to prevent supplies from reaching Germany and Austria-Hungary. William II retaliated with a massive U-boat (submarine) campaign against Allied and neutral shipping around Britain and France. In May 1915, the Germans sank a British passenger ship, the *Lusitania*, killing 1,198 people, including 124 Americans. Not wanting to provoke U.S. president Woodrow Wilson further, the Germans called off unrestricted submarine warfare. In May 1916, the navies of Germany and Great Britain clashed in the battle of Jutland which, although inconclusive, proved that the German fleet could not defeat the British. On both sides, governments rejected the idea of a negotiated peace, and maintained the cult of the offensive. Each attack opened with troops going "over the top" to charge the enemy's trenches, usually to be confronted with round upon round of machine-gun fire. In 1916, the Germans assaulted the forts of Verdun, hoping to crush French morale by its loss. Although French and German losses were close to a million men, the French held Verdun. In June 1916, the British launched an offensive in the Somme region; over several months of battle, 1.25 million men were killed or wounded, with no decisive victory won by either side. The Russians then struck again, with the Germans stopping the advance. Whereas governments and officers saw the war as a "kill or be killed" situation, some battalions on the front lines often went long stretches with hardly a casualty as both sides' troops mutually agreed to avoid battles. Soldiers on both fronts fraternized, and sometimes came to feel more warmly toward their "enemies" in the trenches than toward civilians back home who did not share their experiences. Male camaraderie alleviated some of the misery of trench life and aided survival. Living, fighting, and dying together weakened traditional class distinctions, and sometimes even racial barriers. Most troops of colonized soldiers, however, experienced the front differently from that experienced by their European comrades. Colonials were often placed in the immediate front ranks where the risks were greatest, and endured unfamiliar climates and strange foods. Apart from their suffering, colonial troops gained a new perspective on Europeans, whom they observed exhibiting completely "uncivilized" behavior.

The Home Front, pp. 1011–1014

World War I was a "total war," meaning that civilian involvement was indispensable to the war effort. Civilians were needed to manufacture the weapons that were the backbone of technological warfare, as well as the crutches, wheelchairs, and coffins needed to attend to the wounded after an assault. The war effort depended as well on consensus regarding the war itself. When hostilities broke out in 1914, most of the population—including the socialists—put aside their differences to support the war, and political parties coalesced in a *burgfriede* ("domestic peace") in Germany and a *union sacre* ("sacred union") in France. Feminists were divided over whether or not to support the war, but many did participate in war work and philanthropic efforts. After the first, heavy losses occurred, all involved countries were caught without troop replacements, and backup weapons and military equipment. This was a result of the general opinion that it would be a short war.

War ministries were established to allocate labor on the home and military fronts, and to ensure the steady production of armaments and other necessities. Industrialists were offered incentives to encourage productivity, and all citizens—both men and women—were increasingly expected to perform some sort of war work. Governments mobilized the home front with varying degrees of success: some passed laws that made it a crime to criticize official policies, and created propaganda agencies that presented the war as a patriotic mission. Open opposition to the war did, however, exist. In 1915, activists in the international women's movement met in The Hague, determined to end the war. Others indirectly hampered the war effort, such as nationalist groups in Austria-Hungary, whose agitation for independence detracted from an all-out focus on the war. The Allies encouraged independence movements as part of their strategy to defeat the Habsburgs. In addition to increasing nationalist agitation, the war restructured the workforce: women took over higher paying jobs vacated by men who left for the trenches. The press praised women's patriotism, and some women demonstrated uncustomary strength and enthusiasm for war. Others were concerned that the war would destroy women's femininity and that, once the war was over, women would refuse to give up their jobs to men.

Class conflict was also exacerbated. While workers endured longer hours on less food (because rationing had begun), the wealthier classes were able to afford food and fashionable clothing, paying large amounts of money for products only available on the black market that operated outside the official system of rationing. Governments also allowed many businesses to reap high profits, a policy that brought about increases in the cost of living as shortages of staples like bread and meat worsened during the brutal winter of 1916–1917 (called the turnip winter because turnips were often the only food available). Civilians in occupied areas and the colonies suffered the worst conditions. Combatants deported from or conscripted able-bodied persons in territories they occupied, and inhabitants of the colonies were forced to work for the war effort at home or in Europe. Colonized peoples also experienced increased taxes and elevated prices.

Protest, Revolution, and War's End, 1917–1918

By 1917, the situation was becoming desperate for politicians, the military, and civilians alike, and discontent on the home front began to shape the course of the war.

Neither patriotic slogans before the war, nor propaganda during it had prepared people for wartime suffering. Civilians in cities across Europe revolted, soldiers mutinied, nationalist struggles continued to plague Britain and Austria-Hungary, and revolutions swept Europe, toppling the Russian dynasty forever.

War Protest, p. 1014

On February 1, 1917, hard-pressed by public clamor over mounting casualties, the German government resumed unrestricted submarine warfare. The British responded by mining harbors and the seas and by developing depth charges—antisubmarine weapons dropped or catapulted from ships' decks, that exploded underwater. Unrestricted submarine warfare brought the United States into the war in April 1917 after the Germans had sunk several American ships. As living conditions deteriorated, political opposition took the form of outright revolt by civilians. Food shortages in Italy, Russia, Germany, and Austria-Hungary provoked women to riot and, as inflation mounted, tenants conducted rent strikes and factory and white-collar workers went on strike. By 1917, the war had also strengthened nationalist movements, and the new emperor of Austria-Hungary secretly asked the Allies for a negotiated peace. The German Reichstag also announced its desire for peace, and American president Woodrow Wilson issued his Fourteen Points in January 1918, promising a nonvindictive peace settlement.

Revolution in Russia, pp. 1014–1018

Of all the warring nations, Russia had sustained the greatest number of casualties: 7.5 million by 1917. The politicization that had evolved since the Revolution of 1905, combined with the government's incompetence during the war, created a highly unstable situation. When the riots erupted in March 1917, Nicholas II abdicated and politicians from the old Duma formed a new Provisional Government. However, continuing hardships made governing difficult. Spontaneously elected soviets —councils of workers and soldiers—competed with the government for political support and often challenged its policies. The peasantry began to confiscate the gentry's estates and withheld produce from the market, which intensified urban food shortages. In April 1917, the Germans provided safe rail transportation for Lenin and other prominent Bolsheviks to return from exile to Petrograd. Upon his return, Lenin issued the April Theses, a radical document that called for Russia to withdraw from the war, for the soviets to seize power on behalf of workers and poor peasants, and for all private lands to be nationalized. After another Russian defeat to the Austrians, groups of workers, soldiers, and sailors agitated for the soviets to replace the Provisional Government. As Bolshevik popularity rose, the Provisional

Government led by Aleksandr Kerensky (1881–1970) was thoroughly discredited. In November 1917, the Bolshevik leadership, urged on by Lenin, staged an uprising against Kerensky to prevent him from holding elections. The Bolsheviks took over key facilities and seized power, which they placed in the hands of a congress of soviets while claiming the right to form a government. In January 1918, elections were finally held and, when the Bolsheviks did not fare well, they forcibly took control of the government. Soon after, the Bolsheviks sued Germany for peace. The resulting Treaty of Brest-Litovsk (March 1918) placed vast regions of the old Russian Empire under German occupation, thus partially realizing the goal of a Mitteleuropa. Because the loss of territory placed Petrograd at risk, the Bolsheviks relocated the capital to Moscow. Lenin had agreed to this catastrophic treaty because he had promised to bring peace, but also because he believed that the rest of Europe would soon rebel and overthrow the capitalist order.

Civil War in Russia, p. 1019

Resistance to Bolshevik policies, especially those that nationalized private property, soon mushroomed into full-fledged civil war between the pro-Bolshevik "Reds" and antirevolutionary "Whites." Some fought to restore the old government, but others—especially non-Russian nationality groups—fought for independence. However, without a common goal, the counterrevolutionaries could not win. The civil war shaped communism; Leon Trotsky (1879–1940), Bolshevik commissar of war, built a highly disciplined army by ending democratic procedures that had originally attracted soldiers to Bolshevism. Lenin and Trotsky also introduced war communism, whereby urban workers and troops confiscated grain from the peasantry. The Cheka (secret police) set up detention camps for political opponents and black marketers and often shot them without trial. The Bolsheviks also founded the Third International, known as the Comintern (Communist International) to distinguish it from its predecessors. By mid-1921, the Red Army had successfully consolidated Bolshevism in Russia and secured the Crimea, the Caucasus, and the Muslim borderlands. When the Japanese withdrew from Siberia in 1922, the civil war ended in Central and East Asia. Although revolution had removed the tsar and the privileged aristocracy, the brutal oppression meted out by the Bolsheviks ushered in a political style far different from that which had been hoped for by earlier socialists.

Ending the War, 1918, pp. 1019–1020

In the spring of 1918, the Germans made a final attempt to smash through Allied lines but, by then, the British and French had begun to make effective use of tanks supported by airplanes. The fighting halted and, in the summer of 1918, the Allies—fortified with American troops—pushed back the Germans all along the western front. By October 1918, the German high command helped create a new civilian government, saddling it with the responsibility for defeat; the military insisted that it was not losing the war and that, by suing for peace, the civilian government had "stabbed Germany in the back." On November 9, 1918, Kaiser William II fled. By the fall of 1918, unrest had reached unmanageable proportions in Austria-Hungary as well, where Czechs and Slovaks declared an independent state, as did Croatians. Finally, on November 11, 1918, at 5 A.M., an armistice was signed. Conservative figures put the battlefield toll at a minimum of ten million dead and thirty million wounded, some of whom would eventually die from their wounds. In Europe, food supplies for civilians had often fallen below subsistence levels, and the impact of Europe's declining production was felt worldwide. From 1918 to 1919, the weakened global population was hit by an influenza epidemic that killed at least twenty million more. In addition to the physical costs, war provoked tremendous moral questioning, as soldiers returning home published memoirs in order to try to come to terms with their experiences. While some maintained that the Great War had been a heroic endeavor, others insisted that the fighting had been absolutely meaningless.

The Search for Peace in an Era of Revolution

Amidst the quest for peace, revolutionary fervor swept the continent, especially in the former empires of Germany and Austria-Hungary, while others hoped for a political order based on military authority. Faced with a volatile mix of revolution and counterrevolution, diplomats from around the world arrived in Paris in January 1919 to negotiate the terms of peace. The terms arrived at often failed to recognize the magnitude of the changes brought about by war, and shocked many Europeans.

Europe in Turmoil, p. 1021

Until 1921, the triumph of socialism seemed plausible because the newly independent peoples of Eastern and Central Europe supported socialist principles, and workers and peasants in Germany were in a revolutionary frame of mind. The red flag of socialist revolution even flew from city hall in Glasgow, Scotland, in January 1919. Germany was particularly unstable in November 1918, partly because of the shock of defeat in World War I. By December, independent socialist groups and workers' councils were vying with the dominant Social Democrats for control of the government. Demonstrators demanded economic policies that would assuage workers' misery and remit the veterans' back pay. Some were inspired by one of the most radical socialist factions—the Spartacists—

led by cofounders Karl Liebknecht (1871–1919) and Rosa Luxemburg (1870–1919). The Spartacists favored direct worker control of institutions. Social Democratic leader Friedrich Ebert (1871–1925) who headed the new government, believed that parliamentary politics would best realize his party's objectives. He called on the German army and the Freikorps—a paramilitary band of students, demobilized soldiers, and others—to suppress the workers' councils and demonstrators. Members of the Freikorps hunted down and killed Luxemburg and Liebknecht, and a measure of calm returned to Berlin and other cities. In February 1919, a constituent assembly met in the city of Weimar, where it approved a constitution and founded a parliamentary republic. Contempt for republican institutions motivated Freikorps' officers to attempt a *putsch* (coup), known as the Kapp Putsch after one of its leaders, in the spring of 1920. When the military command refused to crush the coup, Ebert called for a general strike. Although coups from the right and left failed, the Weimar Republic's grip on power was tenuous, and it had set the precedent of relying on extraparliamentary means to resolve political conflict. In Bavaria and Hungary, leftists proclaimed Soviet republics in late winter 1919, both of which were overthrown. The Bolsheviks attempted to establish a Marxist regime in Poland, but the Poles resisted and the Allies rushed supplies and advisers to Moscow.

The Paris Peace Conference, 1919–1920, pp. 1021–1026

The Paris Peace Conference opened in January 1919, with fears of communism spreading westward. But the desperation of war-ravaged citizens, the status of Germany, and the reconstruction of a secure Europe topped the agenda. French premier Georges Clemenceau (1841–1929) had to satisfy angry French citizens who demanded revenge, or at least compensation. British prime minister David Lloyd George (1863–1945) also supported the harsh treatment of Germany, whereas Italy wanted the territory promised to it in the Treaty of London. The presence of Woodrow Wilson (1856–1924) indicated a realignment of power away from any single European country. Wilson hoped for a conciliatory peace, one that would incorporate his Fourteen Points, which called for open diplomacy, arms reduction, and the self-determination of peoples. However, while the Germans refused to admit that their army had lost the war, the Allies campaigned to make Wilson appear naive and deluded. In fact, Wilson's commitment to settlement as opposed to surrender contained some tough provisions because he recognized Germany's strength; he wished to balance the various European powers. After six months, the statesmen produced the Peace of Paris, composed of a cluster of individual treaties. The treaties shocked the countries that had to accept them. Austria and Hungary were separated, Hungary was enormously reduced, and the Ottoman Empire was broken up. A series of small, weak states were created as a result: Czechoslovakia; Poland; and the Kingdom of the Serbs, Croats, and Slovenes, later renamed Yugoslavia. Many Austrians wanted to join Germany, but that was forbidden. Poland was reconstructed from parts of Russia, Germany, and Austria-Hungary, with one-third of its population ethnically non-Polish. The treaties also called for a Polish corridor that connected Poland to the Baltic Sea and separated East Prussia from the rest of Germany. The Treaty of Versailles with Germany returned Alsace and Lorraine to France, which would also temporarily occupy the western bank of the Rhine and the coal-bearing Saar basin. Germany was to pay reparations set in 1921 in the amount of 132 billion gold marks. Additionally, Germany was to surrender the largest ships of its merchant marine, reduce its army, almost eliminate its navy, cease manufacturing offensive weapons, deliver a large amount of free coal each year to Belgium and France, and give up its colonies. Finally, Germany was forbidden to have an air force. The Peace of Paris also set up a League of Nations, which was henceforth to be responsible for maintaining peace, a principle called "collective security." The effectiveness of the league was limited, however, when the United States Senate failed to ratify the peace settlement and refused to join. Further, Germany and Russia were initially excluded from the league. The charter of the league called for Germany's former colonies to be ruled through a system of mandates in which European powers would exercise political control over mandated territory, but local leaders would retain limited authority. However, the war had depleted the financial resources and mental resolve of the European powers, and colonized peoples began to challenge the claims of their European masters.

Economic and Diplomatic Consequences of the Peace, pp. 1026–1028

In the aftermath of World War I, Western leaders were deeply concerned about economic recovery and an enduring peace. France, the hardest hit by wartime destruction, was billions of dollars in debt to the United States and therefore in dire need of collecting German reparations. The British worried about maintaining their empire and restoring trade with Germany, but still wanted some form of financial redress to pay war debts back to the United States. Germany claimed that the demand for reparations further strained its already unstable political system. As early as 1919, British economist John Maynard Keynes (1883–1946) predicted that placing a heavy financial burden on Germany would have disastrous repercussions. Because the kaiser had refused to increase taxes to pay for the war, inflation was a serious problem; this, along with war debt and reparations, created a

serious economic situation in Germany. Only after France occupied several cities in the Ruhr did Germany agree to a payment plan. Embroiled in conflict in the west, Germany turned east and reached an agreement to foster economic ties with Russia in the Treaty of Rapallo (1922), which was renewed in the Treaty of Berlin (1926).

Even before the economic question was settled, statesmen concluded that ensuring a lasting peace meant disarmament. At the 1921 Washington Conference, Great Britain, Japan, France, and Italy agreed to reduce the number of their existing battleships and cease constructing new ones for ten years. In 1923, after Germany defaulted on coal deliveries, the French and Belgians sent troops into the Ruhr basin. Ruhr citizens fought back by not reporting for work, and the German government issued trillions of worthless marks to support them. Germany was soon suffering from a staggering inflation that wiped out people's savings and ruined those individuals living on fixed incomes. The Dawes Plan (1924) and Young Plan (1929) restored economic stability by reducing reparation payments, restoring the value of German currency, and balancing Germany's trade between east and west. In 1925, at a meeting of the great powers in Locarno, Switzerland, German diplomat Gustav Stresemann (1878–1929) negotiated a treaty that provided Germany a seat in the League of Nations (as of 1926) in return for a promise not to violate the borders of France and Belgium and to keep troops out of the Rhineland.

To prevent German expansion to the east, Czechoslovakia, Yugoslavia, and Romania formed the "Little Entente" in 1920–1921. Between 1924 and 1927, France allied itself with the Little Entente and with Poland. In 1928, the major European powers, Japan, and the United States signed the Kellogg-Briand Pact, which formally condemned international violence. The nations did not, however, commit themselves to concrete action to prevent its outbreak. The new openness among the great powers suggested a diplomatic revolution and promised a peaceful age. However, open diplomacy also exposed the negotiating process to nationalist demagogues who could rekindle political hatreds.

A Decade of Recovery: Europe in the 1920s

The 1920s were devoted to coming to terms with the sociopolitical legacy of the war. Although people referred to the 1920s as the Roaring Twenties, the Jazz Age, and the Crazy Years, the sense of cultural release evident during this decade masked the serious problems of restoring social stability and implementing democracy. The creation of the League of Nations, the emergence of new nations, the formation of a constitutional German republic, the extension of the vote to women to reward them for their war work, and to make revolution less tempting all contributed to a sense of democratic rebirth. Governments also continued to build welfare states by expanding insurance programs for workers and payments to families with dependent children. New governments believed that economic democracy—more evenly distributed wealth—would contribute to maintaining social stability. War had blurred class divisions in European society, giving rise to expectations that life would be fairer afterward. Massive casualties had allowed ordinary soldiers to enter the ranks of officers, and members of all classes had served together in the trenches. On the home front, middle-class daughters had worked outside the home and mothers did their own housework as servants moved into higher-paying factory work. The Bolshevik refusal to honor prewar Russian bonds also harmed tens of thousands of European investors, adding to the social leveling. Despite these changes, the reemergence of cycles of boom and bust made it difficult to maintain the trend toward economic democracy. A short postwar boom gave way to a severe economic downturn in 1920. Skyrocketing unemployment led some to question governmental policies. Women in particular lost many of the economic opportunities they had gained by the mid-1920s.

Changes in the Political Landscape, pp. 1028–1031

Hard times corroded the new republics of Eastern Europe, especially because none but Czechoslovakia had a mature industrial sector. The development of Poland exemplified the postwar political landscape in eastern Europe. Polish reunification occurred without a common currency, political structure, or language, and with virtually no support from the Allies, economic or otherwise. Notwithstanding, a government *was* formed under a constitution that professed equal rights for all ethnic and religious groups. Economic conditions made it difficult for the Sejm (parliament) to redistribute large estates to the peasantry, and urban workers were worse off than other laborers across Europe.

Strikes and violence began in 1922, and the inability of coalition governments to bring about economic prosperity led to a coup in Poland (1926) by Jozef Pilsudski (1867–1935). In Germany, although the economy had improved, political life remained precarious because so many people felt nostalgia for the empire and loathed the restrictions imposed by the Treaty of Versailles. Contempt for parliamentary politics was widespread, and right-wing parties favored violence rather than consensus building. Support for the far right came from wealthy landowners and businessmen, white-collar workers whose standard of living had declined during the war; and members of the lower and middle classes hurt by inflation. Bands of disaffected youths and veterans proliferated. One group, the Brown Shirts, led by Adolf Hitler (1889–1945), participated in a failed coup in Munich in 1923. Hitler spent less than a year in jail, while his coconspirator, Erich Ludendorff (1865–1937), was acquitted. After the mid-1920s, however, the economy improved and extreme political movements lost some of their appeal. In France and Britain, right-wing parties had less of an effect because parliamentary politics were better established and the upper classes were not plotting to restore an authoritarian monarchy. Politicians in France formed coalitions to rally support for reconstruction and the pursuit of reparations. The French parliament also focused on increasing the birthrate, making the distribution of birth-control information illegal and abortion a severely punished crime.

In Britain, the election of the first Labour prime minister Ramsay MacDonald (1924) was a sign of the growing political ambitions of the working class. Much of British industry was obsolete or in poor condition, as in the ailing coal industry when, in May 1926, workers conducted a nine-day general strike against wage cuts and dangerous conditions in the mines. The strike provoked unprecedented middle-class resistance, with individuals from all walks of life stepping in to drive trains, work on docks, and replace workers in other sorts of jobs. Ireland also continued to be a problem. Irish republicans had attacked government buildings in Dublin on Easter Monday 1916, and the British had retaliated with force. In January 1919, republican leaders announced Ireland's independence from Britain and established a separate parliament. The British refused to recognize the parliament, and sent in a volunteer army—the Black and Tans—who waged guerrilla warfare in Ireland. By 1921, public outrage forced the British to negotiate. A treaty created the Irish Free State, a self-governing dominion owing an oath of allegiance to the British crown. Ulster, a group of six northern counties, was self-governing but had representation in the British Parliament.

European powers also encountered rebellion in overseas colonies, as colonized peoples who had served in the war expected increased rights, if not outright independence. The British massacred protesters at Amritsar in India in 1919, and put down revolts against the mandate system in Egypt and Iran in the early 1920s. The Dutch jailed political leaders in Indonesia, while the French punished Indochinese nationalists. Europeans wanted to hold on to their empires because any hint of declining prestige abroad would feed antidemocratic forces at home.

Reconstructing the Economy, pp. 1031–1032

Although the European economy had lost many of its international markets to other countries, the war had forced manufacturing to become more efficient. Mergers and the formation of cartels continued after the war, and owners of large manufacturing conglomerates came to wield extensive financial and political power. By the late 1920s, Europe was enjoying economic prosperity. The

United States was the trendsetter in modernization, and Europeans visited Henry Ford's auto plant to study his high productivity. Scientific management also aimed to increase productivity by ridding the work process of superfluous movements. European industrialists balanced this focus on Frederick Taylor's management methods with a belief that workers also needed time for leisure. However, although union leaders promoted these benefits of the "cult of efficiency," many workers felt that the emphasis on efficiency turned them into human automatons. Management expanded during the war and continued to do so afterward, but workers were perceived as uncreative and lacking in innovation, and women received lower wages to stem male competition. Union bureaucracy also continued to expand after the war, with unions mobilizing masses of people and playing a key role in mass politics.

Restoring Society, pp. 1032–1034

Many returning veterans were hostile toward civilians who, they believed, had overly complained about wartime conditions instead of patriotically and stoically enduring them. Veterans returned to a world that was markedly different from the one they left to serve in the war. Veterans felt particularly alienated from women who had bobbed their hair and now smoked, held jobs, and sometimes found other men to replace them while they were overseas performing their patriotic duty. Women, in turn, felt estranged from the returning soldiers who had survived different and brutalizing experiences. Many suffragists embraced the gender segregation that they had fought so hard to dismantle before the war, and focused their attention now on aiding women and their families. These changes caused some to proclaim that feminism was dead.

Governments wanted to reintegrate veterans so as to avoid the spread of Bolshevism. They created programs granting pension plans for veterans, stipends for war widows, benefits for unemployed men, and housing for veterans. These housing developments included all the modern conveniences, but in most cases, benefited the more highly paid, skilled workers.

Despite governmental efforts to restore traditional family values, war had dissolved many middle-class conventions. Freer, more open discussions of sex and sexuality occurred. Unmarried men and women now socialized without chaperones. Still, most discussions of sexuality placed it within the context of marriage, where greater attention to sexual pleasure was advocated by authors such as Theodoor van de Velde (1873–1937) in his 1927 *Ideal Marriage: Its Physiology and Technique.* Among the working classes, the flapper—a sexually liberated, working woman—became a new symbol of womanhood. Male sexual prowess was examined by authors such as D. H. Lawrence (1885–1930) in *Women in*

Love (1920) and Ernest Hemingway (1899–1961) in *The Sun Also Rises* (1926). As images of men and women changed, greater attention was paid to physical appearance and hygiene. Ordinary women began "painting" their faces—something only prostitutes had done previously, and a multibillion-dollar cosmetics industry emerged. Exercise also became more important because the consumer focus on personal health coincided with modern industry's need for a physically fit workforce. As prosperity returned, people could buy more consumer goods. Modern conveniences became standard household items, sometimes purchased on the new installment plans that were popularized in the 1920s. Housework became more mechanized, and family intimacy came to revolve around radios, phonographs, and automobiles.

Mass Culture and the Rise of Modern Dictators

The aim of wartime propaganda had been to unite all classes against a common enemy. In the 1920s, the process of incorporating diverse groups into a homogenous, Western culture continued. The instruments of mass culture—primarily radio, film, and newspapers—expanded their sphere of influence during the 1920s. Mass media had, on the one hand, the potential for creating an informed citizenry and thus enhancing democracy. On the other hand, it provided tools for dictators to use in the troubled postwar climate.

Culture for the Masses, pp. 1034–1035

The instruments of mass culture—primarily radio, film, and newspapers—expanded their influence in the 1920s. Media had received a big boost from the war. Bulletins from the battlefront whetted the public's appetite for new, real-life stories and sales of nonfiction books soared. In the 1920s, filmmaking became an international business, with a star system that turned film personalities into international celebrities. Stars and directors worked within a "studio": a large, corporate structure that created the films, set up theater chains to exhibit them, and marketed their films. Fan magazines and paraphernalia made movies a part of everyday life. Films incorporated familiar elements from other genre: the piano accompaniment for silent films was derived from music halls and familiar classical compositions; while comic characters, farcical plots, and slapstick humor had their origins in street or burlesque shows. Movies attracted some one hundred million weekly viewers, most of whom were women, and crossed national borders easily. Filmmakers touched upon postwar fantasies and fears. The German film *The Cabinet of Dr. Caligari* (1919) depicted events and inmates in an insane asylum as symbols of state power; Fritz Lang's *Metropolis* (1926) depicted technological forces as destructive and out of control. English comedian Charlie Chaplin (1889–1977) won international popularity with his character of the Little Tramp, the anonymous modern man. Radio broadcasts also gained in popularity. In the first half of the 1920s, mass audiences listened to radio broadcasts in public halls but, when radio receivers became inexpensive, people could listen to the broadcasts in their homes. By the 1930s, radio was used as a powerful tool for politicians.

Cultural Debates over the Future, pp. 1035–1039

Many cultural leaders were obsessed by the horrendous experiences of war. German artist Kathe Kollwitz (1867–1945) portrayed heart-wrenching, antiwar images of bereaved parents and starving children. George Grosz (1893–1959) joined Dada, an artistic and literary movement that had emerged during World War I. His paintings and political cartoons depicted maimed soldiers and brutally murdered women. Dadaists produced works punctuated by nonsense, incongruity, and shrieking expressions of alienation; whereas avant-garde art, in general, portrayed seedy scenes from everyday life, to show civilian decadence.

A controversy erupted in postwar Germany over what the proper attitude should be toward the war, as popular writers such as Ernst Jünger (1895–1998) glorified life in the trenches and called for the militarization of society. On the side of the controversy, Erich Maria Remarque's (1898–1970) *All Quiet on the Western Front* was a powerful antiwar statement. Poets throughout Europe also reflected on postwar conditions, often using innovative styles. T. S. Eliot (1888–1965) portrayed postwar life as petty and futile in "The Waste Land" (1922) and "The Hollow Men" (1925), while William Butler Yeats (1865–1939) bemoaned the end of traditional society in "Sailing to Byzantium" (1928). In the arts, dystopia, a utopian fantasy turned upside down, became an important theme. Franz Kafka (1883–1924) depicted the world as a vast, impersonal machine in novels such as *The Trial* (1925) and *The Castle* (1926). Marcel Proust (1871–1922) continued the prewar predilection with psychology in his multivolume *Remembrance of Things Past* (1913–1927), which explored the haunted inner life of the narrator/author. James Joyce (1882–1941) and Virginia Woolf (1882–1941) also focused on the interior life and the power of memories and sensations in *Ulysses* (1922) and *Mrs. Dalloway* (1925), respectively. Other artists looked to the future and celebrated the promise of technology. Many worked in large collectives, such as the Bauhaus led by Walter Gropius (1883–1969). This group of German artists created streamlined office buildings and designed functional furniture, utensils, and decorative objects. Russian artists optimistically wrote novels about cement factories and created ballets about steel. Artists, fascinated by technology and machinery, were drawn to the United States, the most modern of all countries, and were especially attracted to jazz. American performers like Josephine Baker (1906–1975) and Louis Armstrong (1901–1971) became international sensations.

The Communist Utopia, pp. 1039–1041

Communism promised a modern, technological culture and a shining future. But Bolsheviks encountered significant obstacles to consolidating their rule. In the early 1920s, peasant bands, called "Green Armies" revolted against war communism. Further, industrial production stood at only 13 percent of its prewar output. The civil war had produced massive casualties, housing shortages that affected the entire population, and refugees who clogged the cities and roamed the countryside.

In the early spring of 1921, workers in Petrograd and seamen at the naval base at Kronstadt revolted, calling for "soviets without Communists." Lenin was enraged by the rebels, and Trotsky had many of them shot, but the rebellion did force Lenin to realize that reform was needed. He instituted the New Economic Policy (NEP), which imposed a tax on grain rather than confiscating it. He also returned portions of the economy to the free market; consumer goods and more food soon became available. This change led to the rise of "NEPmen" who lived in splendid homes and practiced conspicuous consumption. Protest over this change erupted among the Communists, and Lenin responded by setting up procedures for purging dissidents. Bolshevik leaders also attempted to create a cultural revolution, setting up classes in the countryside on various social and political subjects. They also made birth control, abortion, and divorce readily available, and Alexandra Kollontai (1872–1952) promoted birth-control education and day-care programs. The Zhenotdel (Women's Bureau) sought to educate the masses about the changes taking place. Officials promoted "Americanization" (use of Henry Ford and Frederick Taylor's methods) in the factories, the army, the arts, and everyday life. Also occurring during 1920s, Bolshevik culture retained the rebelliousness of the prewar period, and artists experimented with blending high art, technology, and mass culture. The government's agency, Proletkult, aimed at developing proletarian culture; the Bolsheviks confiscated mansions and imperial buildings and turned them into workers' clubs and galleries that displayed art to the masses. As with war communism, many resisted the reshaping of culture to "modern" or "Western" standards, as Bolshevik policies undermined traditional ways of life and belief systems.

Lenin suffered a debilitating stroke in 1922 and died in 1924. The party congress declared the day of his death a permanent holiday, his funeral was celebrated with elaborate pomp, and no one was allowed to criticize anything associated with his name. The general secretary of the Communist Party, Joseph Stalin (1879–1953) led the deification of Lenin. He also discredited his chief rival, Trotsky, and was able to achieve virtually complete dictatorship by 1928–1929.

Fascism on the March in Italy, pp. 1041–1043

Postwar discontent in Italy began when the Allies refused to honor the promises made in the Treaty of London (1915). To make matters worse, peasants, who had made great sacrifices during the war, protested their serflike status, and workers seized factories to draw attention to their economic plight. Many Italians blamed parliament for their problems. In the midst of this chaos, Benito Mussolini (1883–1945), a socialist journalist who joined the radical right, built a personal army of veterans and unemployed men called the "Black Shirts." In 1922, Mussolini's supporters, known as Fascists, marched to Rome and threatened a coup. To save his throne, King Victor Emmanuel III (r. 1900–1946) "invited" Mussolini to become prime minister. The Fascist movement attracted many who opposed socialism and parliament, and who felt cheated by the postwar settlement. Mussolini placed himself at the head of governmental departments, made criticism of the state a criminal offense, and used force—even murder—to silence his opponents. Despite this brutality, many considered the sight of the Black Shirts marching through the streets a sign that order had been restored. Large landowners and businessmen approved the tough tactics the Fascists had taken against socialists, and supported them financially. Mussolini used mass propaganda and the media to gain support for his government. He also hired the unemployed to work on his staff and to complete the massive building projects launched by his government.

Mussolini eschewed intellectual debate, promoting instead action and avant-garde culture. He also recognized the importance of maintaining traditional values, signing the Lateran Agreement with the Vatican (1929). This agreement made the Vatican a state under papal sovereignty and recognized the church's right to determine family doctrine and to assume a role in education. Mussolini also introduced the "corporate" state that denied individual rights in favor of duty to the state. He organized employers, workers, and professionals into groups that could settle grievances through state-controlled channels. Mussolini also gained favor by reducing women's wages and barring them from certain professions.

Mussolini had many admirers, including Adolf Hitler, who had been occupied during the 1920s with building a paramilitary group and a political organization called the National Socialist German Workers' Party (Nazis). But, to Hitler's chagrin, the austere conditions that had allowed Mussolini's rise to power in 1922 no longer existed in Germany by the late 1920s. During his brief imprisonment, Hitler wrote *Mein Kampf* (1925), a political plan based on racial annihilation.

Key Events   *For each question, select the most appropriate response from the choices provided.*

1914 August World War I begins

1914–1925 Suffrage for women expands in much of Europe

1916 Irish nationalists stage Easter Uprising against British rule

1917 March Revolution in Russia overturns tsarist autocracy

1917 April The United States enters World War I

1917 November Bolshevik Revolution in Russia

1918 November Armistice ends fighting of World War I; revolutionary turmoil throughout Germany; the kaiser abdicates

1918–1922 Civil war in Russia

1919 The Weimar Republic Established

1919–1920 Paris Peace Conference redraws the map of Europe

1922 Ireland is split in two: the independent Irish Free State in the south and British-affiliated Ulster in the north; Fascists march on Rome; Mussolini becomes Italy's prime minister; T. S. Eliot publishes "The Waste Land"; James Joyce publishes *Ulysses*

1924 Lenin dies; Stalin and Trotsky contend for power

1924–1929 Period of general economic prosperity and stability

1929 October Stock market crash in United States

1. Which of the following countries steadfastly refused to grant women the vote, even though several other European nations granted women's suffrage between 1914 and 1925?
   a. France
   b. Great Britain
   c. Germany
   d. Finland

2. What were the immediate results of the Easter Uprising in Ireland in 1916?
   a. Great Britain was forced to withdraw from the war so it could focus its attention on home.
   b. Irish Republicans established their own parliament.
   c. The uprising was quickly defeated.
   d. The British negotiated a treaty and created a self-governing Irish Free State.

3. Who succeeded tsar Nicholas II when the Revolution of 1917 overturned his government?
   a. Bolsheviks
   b. Soviets
   c. Provisional Government
   d. Cheka

4. The civil war in Russia between 1918 and 1922 brought which of the following to power?
   a. V. I. Lenin
   b. Joseph Stalin
   c. Leon Trotsky
   d. Grigori Rasputin

5. At the Peace of Paris, which empire was divided into a series of small, internally divided, and relatively weak states?
   a. Austria-Hungary
   b. Russia
   c. The Ottoman Empire
   d. Germany

6. Who made Benito Mussolini his prime minister in 1922?
   a. V. I. Lenin
   b. Adolf Hitler
   c. King Victor Emmanuel III
   d. Nicholas II

7. What were the effects of the United States stock market crash in 1929?
   a. There were no effects outside the United States, which recovered within a year.
   b. Germany and Great Britain were able to regain their position at the forefront of worldwide industry.
   c. Economic disaster circled the globe making militarism and authoritarianism seem appealing to many.
   d. The American Socialism Movement was able to gain power briefly.

Key Terms   *Match each key term to its definition.*

A. **Bolshevik Revolution** (p. 1017)
B. **cult of the offensive** (p. 1006)
C. **Fascism** (p. 1041)
D. **Fourteen Points** (p. 1022)
E. **League of Nations** (p. 1023)
F. **mandate system** (p. 1026)
G. **march on Rome** (p. 1041)
H. **Peace of Paris** (p. 1022)
I. **Provisional Government** (p. 1016)
J. **Schlieffen Plan** (p. 1006)
K. **soviets** (p. 1016)
L. **total war** (p. 1003)
M. **war guilt clause** (p. 1022)
N. **Weimar Republic** (p.1021)

1. _____ A war built on full mobilization of soldiers, civilians, and the technological capacities of the nations involved. The term also refers to a highly destructive war and one that is both a physical war and a war for ideas and ideologies.

2. _____ A military strategy of constantly attacking the enemy, believed to be the key to winning World War I. Given the firepower of both sides, however, this strategy boosted casualties and failed to bring victory to either side.

3. _____ Strategy in World War I named for former chief of the German general staff, that called for attacks on two fronts concentrating first on France to the west and then turning east to attack Russia.

4. _____ The initial government to take control in Russia after the overthrow of the Romanov empire in 1917. The government was composed of aristocrats and members of the middle class, often deputies in the Duma, the assembly created after the Revolution of 1905.

5. _____ Councils of workers and soldiers first formed in Russia in the Revolution of 1905; they took shape to represent the people in the early days of the 1917 Russian Revolution. These groups saw themselves as a more legitimate political force than the Provisional Government

6. _____ The overthrow of Russia's Provisional Government in the fall of 1917 by V. I. Lenin and his forces because of continuing defeat in the war, failure to bring political reform, and a continuing decline in the conditions of everyday life.

7. _____ The parliamentary republic established in 1919 in Germany to replace the imperial form of government.

8. _____ A proposal by U.S. President Woodrow Wilson for peace during World War I. This proposal called for a peace based on settlement rather than on victory or a definitive conquest and thus helped bring about the surrender of the Central Powers.

9. _____ The series of peace treaties that provided the settlement of World War I. These treaties were resented, especially by Germany, Hungary, and states of the Middle East in which England and France took over the government.

10. _____ The part of the Treaty of Versailles that assigned blame for World War I to Germany.

11. _____ International organization set up following World War I to maintain peace by arbitrating disputes and promoting collective security.

12. _____ League of Nations covenant that granted the victors of World War I political control over Germany's former colonies.

13. _____ The threat by Benito Mussolini and his followers in 1922 to take over the Italian government in a military convergence on Rome; this event forced King Victor Emmanuel II to make Mussolini prime minister.

14. _____ A doctrine advocated by Benito Mussolini that glorified the state over the people and their individual or civil rights. Politically grounded in instinctual male violence and opposed to the so-called antinationalist socialist movement and parliamentary rule, this regime began in the 1920s.

Identification

This activity tests your recall of significant people, places, and events from this chapter. Fill in the blank with the correct answer.

1. The German war plan, designed by _____, outlined a way to combat the enemy on two fronts by concentrating on one foe at a time, striking a heavy blow on France while holding back the Russians to the east.

2. Wanting to show support for Great Britain during the war, suffragist leader Emmeline Pankhurst changed the name of her newspaper to _____.

3. After the sinking of the _____ in 1915, the Germans temporarily stopped unrestricted naval warfare for fear of bringing America on the side of the Allies.

4. After being promised territory in Africa, Asia Minor, and the Balkans in return for joining the Allies, _____ joined the war in 1915.

5. The clash between the German and British navies at the battle of _____, in 1916, demonstrated that the Germans could not overtake British seapower.

6. The Provisional Government of Russia, led by Socialist revolutionary _____, attempted to continue the war but was unable to counter the Bolsheviks.

7. A military coup, led by General _____, exposed the weakness of the Provisional Government of Russia in 1917.

8. In March 1919, the Bolsheviks founded the Third International, or _____.

9. As Bolshevik commissar of war, _____ introduced a policy of war communism, whereby the government confiscated grain from the peasantry to feed the army and workforce.

10. On the morning of _____, delegates from the Allies and the Central Powers signed an armistice, essentially ending over four years of combat.

11. As leader of the new German government after 1918, Social Democrat _____ shunned revolution and backed the creation of a paramilitary republic.

12. The _____, a roving band of disaffected students and veterans, were employed to suppress workers' councils and demonstrations in the Weimar Republic.

13. British Prime Minister _____ used the mood of the British public to win his 1918 campaign with such slogans as "Hang the Kaiser."

14. In the Treaty of _____ in 1922, Germany reached an agreement to foster economic ties with Russia.

15. The _____ of 1929 reduced German payments to the victors of World War I, and restored the value of German currency.

16. In the wake of the Ruhr occupation of 1923, political newcomer Adolf Hitler and war hero _____ led the Beer Hall Putsch in Munich in an attempt to take over the government.

17. Fearful of losing India to native nationalists, British forces massacred protesters at _____ in 1919.

18. The best-seller *Married Love* (1918) by _____ described sex in rhapsodic terms and offered precise information about birth control and sexual physiology.

19. In *The Sun Also Rises*, _____ deals with impotence and male sexual vigor.

20. One of the key figures of the "cult of efficiency," American efficiency expert _____ developed methods to streamline workers' tasks for maximum productivity.

21. Receiving government support for his film *Ten Days that Shook the World*, director _____ used the new medium of motion pictures to present a Bolshevik view of history to domestic and international audiences.

22. One of the leaders of the Dada movement in art and literature, _____ produced drawings and paintings of maimed soldiers and brutally murdered women.

23. In his international best-seller *All Quiet on the Western Front*, _____ depicted the conditions shared by enemies at the front of World War I.

24. The multivolume *Remembrance of Things Past*, by _____, explored the workings of memory, the passage of time, and sexual modernity through the life of a narrator.

25. An example of Europe's fascination with modern culture in America, African American jazz singer-dancer _____ became an international sensation after a tour of Europe's capital cities.

Chapter Review

Self-Test and Analytical Exercises

Multiple Choice *Select the best answer from the four choices provided.*

1. An alliance between which of the following was known as the Central Powers?
   a. Great Britain, France, and Italy
   b. Germany, Austria-Hungary, and Turkey
   c. Russia, Turkey, and Italy
   d. Germany and Russia

2. Which country made the greatest use of submarine warfare?
   a. Great Britain
   b. Germany
   c. France
   d. The United States

3. Soldiers in the trenches
   a. became more warlike and supportive of the war as they lost friends to enemy forces.
   b. developed close bonds with their comrades as well as with opposing troops in order to cope with the terrible conditions on the fronts.
   c. blindly followed orders, relying more and more on military discipline as conditions in the trenches worsened.
   d. became divided among themselves as their concern for personal survival replaced feelings of fraternal camaraderie.

4. Which of the following is *true* regarding women during World War I?
   a. Women tended to oppose the war because, by nature, they were less militaristic than men.
   b. Women were divided as to how to respond to the war, but most opted to patriotically support the war effort.
   c. Women definitely supported the war.
   d. Women refused to support the war because they had not been granted the vote.

5. What triggered the entry of the United States into World War I on the side of the Allies?
   a. Determination to prevent a German victory and German expansion in Europe
   b. Fears of British dominance in any postwar settlement
   c. Threats to American colonies by the German military
   d. Unrestricted submarine warfare, which led to the sinking of American ships

6. Which country sustained the greatest number of war casualties?
   a. Great Britain
   b. France
   c. Germany
   d. Russia

7. The Provisional Government of Russia (1917)
   a. was composed of radical Marxist revolutionaries, who withdrew Russia from the war.
   b. was primarily composed of political moderates.
   c. was dominated by representatives from the soviets.
   d. removed wealthy officials in an attempt to establish a classless society.

8. Who issued the Fourteen Points, a blueprint for a new international order and a nonvindictive peace settlement?
   a. Woodrow Wilson
   b. Kaiser Wilhelm
   c. David Lloyd George
   d. V. I. Lenin

9. Which of the following is *true* regarding the Spartacists?
   a. The name given the Social Democratic Party by the German military
   b. A radical socialist faction that favored Leninist policies of control by a small number of leaders
   c. A conservative, paramilitary organization that opposed ending the war
   d. A radical, socialist faction that favored direct worker control of institutions

10. Which of the following describes the Freikorps?
    a. Armed revolutionary units of the Sparticists
    b. German army units that supported socialist revolution
    c. Roving paramilitary band of students and demobilized soldiers that helped the Social Democratic Party suppress workers' councils and demonstrators in Germany
    d. New name for the German army after the war

11. Which of the following was *not* accomplished by the Treaty of Versailles?
    a. Ascribed to Germany the responsibility for starting the war
    b. Returned the territories of Alsace and Lorraine to France
    c. Limited the size and scope of the German military
    d. Confirmed Germany's claims to its colonies and reincorporated Germany into the community of nations

12. In 1923, in response to the failure of Germany to make coal payments to France and Belgium,
    a. the United States intervened and reduced German payments.
    b. France permitted the Germans to pay the debts in cash instead.
    c. the two countries sent troops to occupy the resource-rich Ruhr basin in Germany.
    d. Great Britain offered to supply the coal instead in order to maintain peaceful relations in Europe.

13. In the 1920s, Poland
    a. was ethnically homogenous because the post-war reunification of Poland had drawn the borders to exclude other ethnic groups.
    b. was weakened by ethnic division and the lack of common cultural and social institutions.
    c. disintegrated in the face of ethnic divisiveness and was subsequently usurped by Russia.
    d. developed a stable, constitutional government that genuinely addressed the needs of the peasantry.

14. In Britain, the general strike of union miners in 1926
    a. effectively shut down the country and forced the government to follow the leadership of the unions.
    b. provoked unprecedented middle-class resistance and failed to help the unions.
    c. was brutally repressed by British soldiers and hundreds were killed.
    d. was broken up by gangs of right-wing extremists who forced workers to go back to their jobs.

15. In the 1920s, which country was considered as the trendsetter in economic modernization?
    a. Great Britain
    b. Germany
    c. Russia
    d. The United States

16. Which of the following statements is *true* regarding sexuality and family during the 1920s?
    a. Sexuality was addressed more openly, and relationships between young men and women were freer; however, the dominant context for sexuality remained marriage.
    b. Governments made strides toward repressing sexuality in an effort to reconstruct prewar, middle-class, social conventions and restore family values.
    c. Authors who published sexually frank books were persecuted by the state and their books disseminated only on the black market.
    d. The institution of marriage was perceived as outdated and most ceased to regard it as the dominant context for sexuality.

17. Which of the following brought entertainment and information into individuals' private living spaces?
    a. Telephone
    b. Radio
    c. Television
    d. Newspapers

18. Who wrote the poems "The Waste Land" and "The Hollow Men," which portrayed postwar life as petty and futile?
    a. Erich Maria Remarque
    b. T. S. Eliot
    c. William Butler Yeats
    d. Franz Kafka

19. Artists from which artistic movement created streamlined office buildings and designed functional objects for everyday use, expressing optimism about the promise of technology?
    a. Dada
    b. Bauhaus
    c. Dystopianism
    d. Primitivism

20. By the end of the 1920s, who had achieved virtually complete dictatorship in the Soviet Union?
    a. Leon Trotsky
    b. V. I. Lenin
    c. Joseph Stalin
    d. Vladimir Mayakovsky

21. By 1915, which countries were known collectively as the Allies?
    a. Germany, Austria-Hungary, Turkey, and Italy
    b. Turkey, Russia, Great Britain, and France
    c. Great Britain, France, Russia, and Italy
    d. Great Britain, France, and Austria Hungary

22. The Russian army
    a. depended primarily on its superior military technology.
    b. was by far the best organized of the European armies.
    c. believed that its superior numbers would outweigh its poor training and outdated equipment.
    d. acted according to the Schlieffen Plan and devised a foolproof defense against Germany.

23. Which of the following was *not* involved in "total war"?
    a. Reorganization of civilian society in order to support the war effort
    b. Suspension of normal politics and the willingness of most political parties and citizens to support the war
    c. Expanding freedoms of speech and increased democratic participation in government in order to rally public support for the war effort
    d. Widespread conscription and increased governmental intervention in the daily lives of the civilian population.

24. Women's role in the civilian workforce
    a. diminished because they were required to stay at home to care for their children.
    b. was prohibited by governments that feared an expanded role for women would mean social disorder.
    c. focused on work they could do in the privacy of their homes.
    d. expanded as women took over jobs traditionally unavailable to them in order to replace the working men sent to the front.

25. Which of the following soured civilians toward the war effort?
    a. Revocation of free speech
    b. War's violence, which undermined civilian patriotism
    c. Mounting inflation caused by wartime shortages
    d. Domestic upheaval and social disorder, brought about as women established themselves as the primary, civilian workforce

26. Which of the following was a prime minister of the Russian Provisional Government and a member of the Socialist Revolutionary political party?
    a. V. I. Lenin
    b. Leon Trotsky
    c. Aleksandr Kerensky
    d. Lavr Kornilov

27. The policies of war communism did all of the following *except*
    a. introduce democratic procedures into the army to increase support among workers for the Bolsheviks.
    b. confiscate grain from the peasantry to feed urban workers and soldiers.
    c. set up detention camps for political opponents and black marketers.
    d. increase the power of the secret police.

28. In 1918 the German military
    a. admitted it could not win the war and signed an armistice.
    b. continued to fight the Allies until all of Germany was occupied.
    c. helped to create a civilian government and tricked inexperienced politicians into taking the blame for defeat in the war.
    d. refused to give power to a civilian government until forced into submission by widespread mutinies.

29. The postwar German Republic was founded in
    a. Berlin.
    b. Kiel.
    c. Munich.
    d. Weimar.

30. Which of the following was *not* proposed by Woodrow Wilson's Fourteen Points?
    a. Open diplomacy
    b. Arms reduction
    c. Self-determination of peoples
    d. Crushing reparations from Germany

31. Which of the following is *true* regarding the League of Nations?
    a. Vigorously supported by the American government, but received little interest in Europe
    b. An attempt to replace secretive power politics with collective security
    c. Immediately accepted Germany and Russia as full members in an effort to reconcile opposing powers in Europe
    d. Freed colonial peoples from European domination

32. What was the main economic problem that created chaos in 1920s Germany?
    a. The high value of German currency, which made it difficult for Germany to export goods
    b. A lack of natural resources, which had been used up during the war
    c. Runaway inflation
    d. Labor strikes and the unwillingness of individuals to work under the new republican form of government

33. World War I
    a. heightened distinctions among the social classes.
    b. increased social mobility, provided new economic opportunities for women, and sparked tendencies toward social leveling.
    c. increased the number of servants in middle-class homes.
    d. diminished economic and social opportunities for women.

34. The Easter Uprising was a(n)
    a. attempted seizure of power by right-wing extremists in the city of Munich, Germany, led by Adolf Hitler.
    b. general strike in Britain in which the country's industry was brought to a standstill by widespread working-class protest.
    c. successful coup by Catholic extremists in Poland, which replaced parliamentary government with a powerful, authoritarian leader.
    d. attack on government buildings in Dublin, Ireland, by Irish republicans seeking independence from Britain.

35. Who developed the practice of scientific management by timing and studying the motions workers used to accomplish tasks?
    a. Ramsay MacDonald
    b. Frederick Taylor
    c. Henry Ford
    d. Theodoor van de Velde

36. To whom did the word *flapper* refer in the 1920s?
    a. An idealized version of postwar femininity that involved a woman staying at home to fill traditional domestic roles
    b. A sexually liberated workingwoman
    c. A veteran who returned from the war injured or shell-shocked
    d. A new style of revealing clothing that became popular in the 1920s

37. Which of the following characterized the artistic movement known as Dada?
    a. Violent, stark, heart-wrenching antiwar images
    b. Bright, sweeping, confident, utopian visions of postwar possibilities and success
    c. Geometric order and conformity
    d. Nonsense, incongruity, and alienation

38. Who wrote the novels *The Trial* and *The Castle*, which depicted modern life as a vast, impersonal machine?
    a. George Grosz
    b. T. S. Eliot
    c. Franz Kafka
    d. James Joyce

39. In which city did Europeans find a potent example of avant-garde expression that rejected a terrifying past and boldly shaped the future?
    a. Berlin
    b. London
    c. Paris
    d. New York

40. In which country did the movement known as Fascism begin?
    a. Italy
    b. Germany
    c. Russia
    d. France

Short Answer   *Answer each question in three or four sentences.*

The Great War, 1914–1918

1. The main alliances that opposed each other in the World War I consisted of which nations?

2. What was life like for soldiers on the front?

3. What did total war mean for civilian life on the home front?

Protest, Revolution, and War's End, 1917–1918

4. How did domestic discontent on the home front shape the conduct of World War I?

5. How did the Bolsheviks seize power in Russia?

6. How did the civil war in Russia influence Bolshevik rule and their original socialist goals?

The Search for Peace in an Era of Revolution

7. What was the Weimar Republic and how did it come into being?

8. What were the main provisions of the postwar settlement negotiated by the victorious powers?

9. What were the main political issues and developments of the 1920s in Europe?

A Decade of Recovery: Europe in the 1920s

10. Which social and political tensions undermined European peace and security in the 1920s?

11. What characterized European economic reconstruction in the 1920s?

12. What effect did the return of veterans to civilian life have on European society?

Mass Culture and the Rise of Modern Dictators

13. What were the instruments of "mass culture" and how were they developed in the 1920s?

14. What were some of the dominant trends in art in the 1920s?

15. Which factors led to the rise of Fascism in Italy?

BUILDING HISTORICAL SKILLS

Reading Maps   *Write a brief, paragraph-length response to each of the following questions based on* **Map 26.4: Europe and the Middle East after the Peace Settlements of 1919–1920** *(p. 1023).*

1. Look at the territory ceded by Austria-Hungary. Why was it broken down into so many small countries?

2. Why did Germany lose so little territory compared to Austria-Hungary, and why were demilitarized zones established in western Germany?

3. Does the map suggest that the territorial settlement was likely to create stability in Europe?

Reading Illustrations   *Write a brief, paragraph-length response to each of the following questions based on the illustration* **Inflation in Germany** *(p. 1026).*

1. What does this image say about the state of the German economy in 1923?

2. What type of response might images such as this have solicited from the German people?

Reading Historical Documents   *Write a brief, paragraph-length response to each of the following questions based on the documents in your book.*

Virginia Woolf's Orlando (1928) (p. 1038)

1. Which artistic or literary trends of the 1920s are apparent in this excerpt from *Orlando*?

2. Which social trends of the 1920s are expressed in this story?

Outbreak of the Russian Revolution (p. 1018)

3. What was the mood of the crowd on this first day of the revolution?

Contrasting Views: Arguing with the Victors (pp. 1024–1025)

4. What do documents 1 and 2 tell us about the attitude of colonized peoples toward Europeans after the war?

5. What do the various demands in these documents tell us about attitudes toward change after the war?

6. What do these documents tell us about the conflicts and tensions in the postwar world?

An Age of Catastrophes
1929–1945

CHAPTER OVERVIEW

Chapter Questions *Keep these questions in mind as you go through the study guide chapter.*

1. What were the major results of the Great Depression?

2. Why did dictators succeed in the 1930s?

3. What progress was made toward social equality in the West during the 1930s?

4. Why did the United States enter World War II?

5. What impact did World War II have on European society?

Chapter Summary

The Great Depression

The Great Depression threw tens of millions out of work and brought suffering to rural and urban folk alike. The impact was felt worldwide as commerce and investment in industry declined. The depression had social effects as well, as gender roles were upset and the birthrate plummeted.

Economic Disaster Strikes, pp. 1050–1051

In the 1920s, U.S. corporations, banks, and millions of individuals borrowed money on margin to invest in the stock market, which had experienced a long, upward trend. In order to stabilize the market, the nation's central bank—the Federal Reserve Bank—tightened the availability of credit. This action forced anxious brokerage firms to send margin calls demanding that clients immediately pay back the money they had borrowed to buy stock. As more and more individuals and institutions sold their stocks to pay back their margin debts to

brokers, the market collapsed between October and mid-November 1929. In response to the crisis, the United States cut back on loans to Europe and called in short-term, international debts, which caused a financial crisis in Europe. This worldwide crisis was worsened by a long-term decline in consumer buying, overproduction, and stagnant wages relative to the rising, inflated, cost of living. This worldwide economic crisis is called the Great Depression. Governmental actions taken to alleviate the crisis—cutting budgets and enacting huge tariffs levied on foreign goods—made the depression even worse and longer lasting.

Social Effects of the Depression, pp. 1051–1053

The situation was not, however, uniformly bleak, and modernization proceeded during the 1930s. Municipal and national governments continued road construction and sanitation projects and running water, electricity, and sewage pipes were installed in many homes for the first time. Despite high rates of unemployment, the majority of Europeans and Americans were employed throughout the 1930s, and some even enjoyed considerable prosperity. Even those who held jobs, however, felt the threat of unemployment, which created a mood of fear and resentment throughout the West. Economic catastrophe upset social life and strained gender relations. Sometimes, unemployed men stayed at home all day, increasing the tension in small apartments. Women accepted low-paying jobs, like housecleaning or doing laundry, to make ends meet, and men often had to assume housekeeping chores at home. Men could be observed on street corners begging while women worked to support their families. As the percentage of farm workers decreased, patriarchal authority continued to decline in rural areas. The falling birthrate also concerned politicians. Tough economic times led couples to have fewer children, and mandatory education caused parents extra expense and prevented children of working-class families from bringing in wages. The population crisis reinvigorated racist politics and rhetoric with the argument that, while "superior" peoples were failing to breed, "inferior" peoples were ready to take their place.

The Great Depression Beyond the West, pp. 1053–1055

The effects of declining purchasing power and unavailability of ready credit extended beyond the West, reducing the demand for copper, tin, and other raw materials and for the finished products manufactured in urban factories. The depression also drove down the price of foodstuffs like rice and coffee, which proved disastrous to those persons who had been forced to grow a single, cash crop. The economic picture was also uneven in the colonies; established industrial sectors of the Indian economy, like textiles, gained strength, with India achieving virtual independence from British cloth. Economic distress added to smoldering grievances and contributed to colonial independence movements. In India, Mohandas (Mahatma or "great-souled") Gandhi (1869–1948) emerged as the charismatic leader for Indian independence by advocating civil disobedience: the peaceful but deliberate breaking of the law. In the Middle East, westernizer Mustafa Kemal (1881–1938) or Atatürk ("first among Turks"), took advantage of Europe's vulnerability both after World War I and during the depression to found an independent Turkish republic (1923). Persia also loosened Europe's grip by forcing the negotiation of oil contracts and, in 1935, changed its name to Iran. Persistent uprisings compelled Britain to end its mandate in Iraq in 1930 and, in 1936, Britain agreed to end its military occupation of Egypt (but *not* the Suez Canal). The French made fewer concessions because their trade with the colonies increased as trade with Europe lagged; they viewed the population growth in Africa and Asia in an optimistic light. When, in 1930, Western-educated leader Ho Chi Minh (1890–1969) the founder of the Indochinese Communist Party, led a peasant uprising against French rule, the French responded with force.

Totalitarian Triumph

In many countries, representative government collapsed under the sheer weight of social and economic crises. Totalitarian leaders were able to mobilize vast support for their violent regimes because they appeared to bring order and discipline to social and economic life. Many were willing to overlook violent political tactics because they were perceived as a sign of restored power.

The Rise of Stalinism, pp. 1055–1060

When Joseph Stalin (1879–1953) took control of the Soviet Union, he ended the New Economic Policy (NEP) and announced (spring of 1929) the first of several five-year plans to radically transform the Soviet economy. This first plan called for massive increases in the output of coal, iron ore, steel, and industrial goods as an emergency measure to end Soviet backwardness. Such central planning, which had its precedent in World War I, helped create a new elite of bureaucrats and industrial officials, especially managers who dominated the workers by limiting their ability to change jobs or move from place to place. Workers often lacked the technical education and the tools necessary to accomplish the goals set out in the five-year plan, so almost everyone falsified records to protect their jobs. To feed this workforce, Stalin demanded more grain from peasants, grain that could also be exported so as to finance this forced industrialization. When peasants resisted these demands by reducing production or withholding produce from the market, Stalin called for the liquidation of the kulaks ("prosperous peasants"). Kulaks and their associates were evicted, imprisoned, exiled, or murdered. Confiscated kulak land formed the basis of the c*kolkhoz* ("collective farm"). Collectivization was a disaster, and Soviet citizens starved as the grain harvest declined. Because work life was politicized, economic failure took on political meaning; Stalin blamed the failure on "wreckers," saboteurs of communism. He instituted purges—state violence in the form of widespread arrests, imprisonment in labor camps, and executions—to rid society of these traitors. To accommodate detaining those caught in the purges, Stalin's government developed an extensive system of prison camps, known as the Gulag, that stretched from Moscow to Siberia. In the midst of the anxiety caused by the purges, cultural and social life retreated from its earlier emphasis on experimentation. Modernism in the arts and creativity in urban planning were curtailed; the falling birthrate led to a restriction of birth-control information and the encouragement of marriage, and the criminalization of homosexuality. Propaganda now referred to the family unit as a "school for socialism"—a miniature Soviet state.

Hitler's Rise to Power, pp. 1060–1062

When the Great Depression hit Germany, the National Socialist German Workers' Party (Nazi Party), led by Adolf Hitler, began to outstrip its rivals in elections. The Nazi Party gained the support of prominent businessmen who viewed it as a preferable alternative to communism, which also enjoyed widespread support. As parliamentary government was virtually halted over their inability to reach an accord on economic measures, Hitler's followers made the government appear even less effective by rampaging through the streets, wrecking stores owned by Jews, and beating up Social Democrats and Communists. The Nazis' attack on the left won them the approval of the middle classes who feared Russian-style revolution and the loss of their property. Most of

Hitler's strongest supporters were young and idealistic, the vast majority of Nazi Party members being under age forty, but the party also found support in every class. Effective propaganda in the media garnered further support for Hitler. In the elections of 1930 and 1932, both the Nazis and the Communists made gains. To stop the Communists, the political and social elite persuaded President Paul von Hindenburg (1847–1934) to invite Hitler to become chancellor in January 1933.

The Nazification of German Politics, pp. 1062–1063

When the Reichstag building was destroyed by fire in February 1933, Hitler blamed the Communists and suspended civil rights, declared censorship of the press, prohibited meetings of opposition writers and artists, and disrupted the work of other political parties. Intimidated delegates of the Reichstag passed the Enabling Act the following March, which suspended the constitution for four years and allowed subsequent Nazi law to take effect without parliamentary approval. The Nazis then began suppressing individual rights in the name of what they called a *Volksgemeinschaft* ("people's community") composed of like-minded, racially pure Germans ("Aryans," in Nazi terminology), and organizations with vast powers to arrest, execute, or imprison people in the newly built concentration camps. The Nazis filled these camps with socialists, homosexuals, Jews, and other so-called non-Aryans. Hitler continued his drastic reform of Germany via social and economic programs. Needing to reduce the rate of unemployment, he stimulated the economy through government spending. Hitler also announced a four-year plan in 1936, with the secret aim of preparing Germany for war by 1940. Defense spending soared to 50 percent of Germany's budget but, although huge trade deficits were created, Hitler believed the spoils of future conquest would eliminate these. Hitler also enacted legislation designed to increase the birthrate and reinforce traditional gender roles.

Nazi Racism, pp. 1063–1064

The Nazis defined Jews as an "inferior" race and held them responsible for most of Germany's problems. The 1935 Nuremberg Laws deprived Jews of citizenship, assigned "Jewishness" according to a person's ancestry, ended special consideration for Jewish war veterans, and prohibited marriage between Jews and other "Aryan" Germans. Nazi doctors helped organize the T4 project, which used carbon monoxide and other means to exterminate large numbers of elderly and handicapped persons. By the outbreak of World War II in 1939, more than 50 percent of Germany's half a million Jews had emigrated, often leaving behind all their possessions and paying huge fees to the government for exit visas.

Democracies on the Defensive

Nazism, communism, and fascism offered bold new approaches to modern politics with new economic and social policies. The energetic, militaristic style of mobilizing the masses made representative government and democratic values seem useless. Many ordinary people found aspects of totalitarianism appealing.

Confronting the Economic Crisis, pp. 1065–1068

As the rate of unemployment in the United States rose to fifteen million persons, Franklin Delano Roosevelt (FDR [1882–1945]) defeated Herbert Hoover (1874–1964) in the 1932 presidential election. Roosevelt pushed through legislation known as the "New Deal," which was partially inspired by the central control of the economy during World War I. It included relief for businesses and instructions for how firms could cooperate in stabilizing prices, price supports for farmers, and public works projects. The Social Security Act of 1935 established a fund for retirement, unemployment, and payments to mothers with dependent children and the disabled. Sweden likewise developed a coherent program for resolving economic and population problems. Under Sweden's program, central planning of the economy and social welfare programs were instituted, and its currency was devalued to make exports appear more attractive to international buyers. Sweden used pump-priming programs of public works to maintain consumer spending and encourage modernization.

Britain and France also sought ways to escape economic crisis. In 1933, the British government took effective steps: a massive program of slum clearance and new housing projects provided employment and infused money into the economy. By 1938, an extension of the National Insurance Act was providing minimal health benefits to twenty million workers and their families. Shocked into action by the force of fascism, French members of the Liberal, Socialist, and Communist parties rallied in support of democracy and established a coalition known as the Popular Front, which established Socialist leader Léon Blum (1872–1950) as premier. Blum extended family subsidies, state services, and welfare benefits, and appointed women to his government. In June 1936, the government of France guaranteed workers two-weeks' paid vacations, a forty-hour work week, and the right to collective bargaining.

Cultural Visions in Hard Times, pp. 1068–1069

Instead of turning away from public life, writers, filmmakers, and artists of the 1930s responded vigorously to the depression. In 1931, French director René Clair's (1898–1981) *À nous la liberté* (Give Us Liberty) depicted prison life as an analogy to work on a factory assembly line. Charlie Chaplin's film *Modern Times* (1936) showed his character, the Little Tramp, as a worker in a modern factory, his job so ingrained that he assumed everything he could see needed mechanical adjustment. Women were portrayed alternately as the cause of or the cure for society's problems. *The Blue Angel* (1930), a German film starring Marlene Dietrich (1901–1992), showed how a modern woman could destroy civilization. In comedies and musicals, however, women pulled men out of debt and set things right, smiling all the while. While new techniques were used during the 1930s, like montage, which overlaid two or more images to create a heightened visual impact, some intellectuals turned away from experimentation with nonrepresentational forms. Art became increasingly politicized because some writers found it crucial to reaffirm their belief in Western values such as rationalism, rights, and concern for the poor. German writer Thomas Mann (1875–1955) went into self-imposed exile when Hitler came to power and began a series of novels based on the Old Testament that commented on the struggle between humanist values and barbarism. In her nonfiction work *Three Guineas* (1938), Virginia Woolf (1882–1941) also rejected experimental forms for a direct attack on militarism, poverty, and the oppression of women.

Scientists continued to point out limits to human understanding and turn away from the certainties that science and technology once boasted of. In California, astronomer Edwin Hubble (1889–1953) determined, in the early 1930s, that the universe is an expanding entity. German physicist Werner Heisenberg (1901–1976) developed the "uncertainty" or "indeterminancy" principle in physics. Scientific observation of atomic behavior, according to this theory, actually disturbs the atom, thereby making precise formulations impossible. The Swiss theologian Karl Barth (1886–1968) encouraged rebellion against the Nazis. In his 1931 social encyclical, a letter addressed to the world on social issues, Pope Pius XI (1922–1939) condemned the failure of modern societies to provide their citizens with a decent life and supported governmental intervention to create better moral and material conditions.

The Road to Global War

The economic crash intensified global competition for wealth and influence among the major powers, as politicians sought to solidify their control over peoples and resources. The importance of possessing colonies rose to even greater importance because these softened some of the effects of the depression. Seeking relief from economic catastrophe and a path to boost their economies and power, Hitler, Mussolini, and Japan's military leadership marched the world toward another war by aggressively acquiring new territories.

A Surge in Global Imperialism, pp. 1070–1073

The 1930s set the last surge of global imperialism in a trend that led to global war and is still shaping international politics to the present day. European Jews continued to go to Palestine and claim the area as theirs; pan-Arabism intensified; and Japan, Germany, and Italy entered into competition with other nations for land and resources. Japan's military leaders desired greater control of Asia and saw China, Russia, and other powers as obstacles to their empire's prosperity and the fulfillment of its destiny. In September 1931, Japan invaded Manchuria and set up a puppet government. China asked the League of Nations to adjudicate the question of Manchuria. The league formally condemned the invasion, but imposed no sanctions. The condemnation nonetheless outraged the Japanese public and goaded the government into an alliance with Hitler and Mussolini. In 1937, Japan again attacked China, justifying its offensive as the first step in a "new order" that would liberate East Asia from Western imperialism. Hundreds of thousands of Chinese were massacred in the "Rape of Nanjing." President Roosevelt immediately announced an embargo on the U.S. export of airplane parts to Japan and later enforced stringent economic sanctions on the crucial raw materials that drove Japanese industry. However, the actions by Western powers and the Soviet Union did not effectively curtail Japan's territorial expansion in Asia and the Pacific.

Hitler's agenda included reestablishing control over the Rhineland, breaking free from the Versailles Treaty's military restrictions, and bringing Germans living in other nations into the Third Reich's orbit. Superior "Aryans," Hitler believed, needed more Lebensraum ("living space") to thrive, space that would be taken from "inferior" Slavic peoples and Bolsheviks. In March 1936, Hitler ordered his troops into the demilitarized Rhineland. Instead of countering with an invasion as they had in the Ruhr in 1923, the French protested to the League of Nations.

In 1935, Mussolini invaded Ethiopia, taking the capital, Addis Ababa, in the spring of 1936. The League of Nations voted in favor of imposing sanctions against Italy, but British and French opposition to a serious oil embargo kept the sanctions from having an effect. The imposition of sanctions, notwithstanding, drove Mussolini into Hitler's camp. Hitler and Mussolini formed a Rome-Berlin Axis, which appeared powerful next to the seemingly timid democracies of France and Great Britain.

The Spanish Civil War, 1936–1939, pp. 1073–1075

In what seemed like an exception to the trend toward authoritarian government, Spanish republicans overthrew their king in 1931. Although the republicans hoped to modernize Spain's economy, they failed to enact land redistribution, which would have won them popular endorsement and loyalty. Antimonarchist forces included an array of competing and thus divided groups, whereas large landowners and clergy acted in unison and drew on their substantial, collective, financial resources. In 1936, pro-republican forces temporarily banded together in a Popular Front coalition to win elections and to prevent the republic from collapsing under the weight of growing monarchist opposition. The right-wingers, however, revolted under the leadership of General Francisco Franco (1892–1975). This military uprising led to the Spanish Civil War, which pitted the republicans, or Loyalists, against the fascist Falangists and the authoritarian right. The struggle became a rehearsal for World War II when Hitler and Mussolini sent military personnel in support of Franco and the right to test new weapons and to practice new tactics, particularly terror bombing civilians. The Spanish republican government appealed everywhere for assistance, but only the Soviet Union answered. Stalin sent troops and tanks, but withdrew in 1938 as the government's ranks floundered. Despite the outpouring of popular support for the cause of democracy, Britain and France refused to send aid. Instead, a few thousand volunteers from several countries fought for the republic. Franco defeated the republicans in 1939 and established a dictatorship that would last until 1975.

Hitler's Conquest of Central Europe, 1938–1939, pp. 1075–1077

In March 1938, Austrian chancellor Kurt von Schuschnigg (1897–1977) called for a referendum on Anschluss—a unification between his country and Germany. Fearing a negative result, Hitler ordered an invasion and annexed Austria. This action was the first step in Germany's taking over the resources of Central and Eastern Europe. Hitler next turned his focus toward Czechoslovakia. His task was more difficult here because Czechoslovakia had a large army, formidable border defenses, and armament factories, and most Czechs were prepared to defend their country. German propaganda accused Czechoslovakia of persecuting its German minority and demanded that it grant autonomy to the German-populated region of the Sudetenland. British prime minister Neville Chamberlain (1869–1940), French premier Edouard Daladier (1884–1970), and Mussolini met with Hitler in Munich and agreed not to oppose Hitler's claim to the Sudetenland. The strategy of preventing war by making concessions was, at that time, perceived as a positive act. Despite the decision taken at the conference, Hitler, in March 1939, invaded Czechoslovakia anyway.

World War II, 1939–1945

World War II began when Hitler launched an all-out attack on Poland on September 1, 1939, and France and Germany declared war on Germany two days later. Other powers such as Japan, Italy, and the United States joined the war later, which spread the fighting all over the world. By the time the war ended in 1945, millions of Europeans were dead, and much of the continent lay in ruins.

The German Onslaught, pp. 1077–1078

Hitler's Blitzkrieg ("lightning war") tactics in which airplanes, tanks, and motorized infantry encircled defenders, assured Germans that the human cost of conquest would be light. After successfully using this strategy first in Poland, then in Denmark and Norway, the Germans attacked Belgium, the Netherlands, and France in May and June 1940. When the French surrendered on June 22, 1940, Germany ruled the northern half of the country. The southern part was named Vichy France, after the spa town where the government sat, and the aged World War I hero Henri Philippe Pétain (1856–1951) was allowed to govern. Stalin used the diversion of war in the west to annex the Baltic States and to seize Bessarabia and Bukovina from Romania. Britain, now alone in its fight against Hitler's Germany, elected Winston Churchill (1874–1965) as prime minister. In the battle of Britain, which the British called the Blitz, the German air force (Luftwaffe) bombed public buildings and monuments, harbors, weapons depots, military bases, and industry. The British government poured its resources into antiaircraft weapons, its code-breaking group Ultra, and the development of radar. By the fall of 1940, German air losses over England forced Hitler to abandon his plan for a naval invasion of that country. In June 1941, Hitler began the invasion of the Soviet Union. Although German troops quickly penetrated Soviet territory, they were slowed down by Hitler's insistence on attacking several regions simultaneously. This strategy cost the Germans time because they got bogged down by the autumnal Soviet rains. In the winter, the Soviets began to fight back, and Hitler's ill-supplied troops succumbed to weather and disease.

War Expands: The Pacific and Beyond, pp. 1078–1079

With the outbreak of war in Europe, Japan took control of parts of the British Empire, bullied the Dutch in Indonesia, and invaded parts of Indochina. In December 1941, Japanese launched airplanes from aircraft carriers and bombed American naval and air bases at Pearl Harbor in Hawaii, then decimated a fleet of U.S. airplanes based in the Philippines. The U.S. Congress declared war on Japan. By spring 1942, as the United States prepared to intervene actively in the war, Japan had conquered Guam, the Philippines, Malaya, Burma, Indonesia, Singapore, and much of the southwestern Pacific. Hitler declared war on the United States, and Mussolini followed suit.

The War Against Civilians, pp. 1079–1082

Everyone was a target in World War II, and the war killed far more civilians than soldiers. Both sides bombed cities to destroy the civilian will to survive; conversely, this tactic often seemed to inspire defiance. As the German army moved through Eastern Europe, it murdered all racial "inferiors," including Jews, Communists, and Slavs. In Poland, the SS (Hitler's elite military force) murdered nobility, clergy, and intellectuals, and transported, like cattle, hundreds of thousands of Polish citizens to forced labor camps. The extermination of Jews during the war became a special mission of the Nazis. As German troops gained control of much of Europe, vast numbers of Jews were confined to ghettoes, or massacred en masse. In addition to the massacres, a bureaucratically organized and efficient technological system for rounding up Jews and sending them to extermination camps had taken shape by the fall of 1941. Six camps in Poland were developed specifically for the singular purpose of mass murder. About 60 percent of new arrivals—particularly children, women, and the elderly—were directly selected to be mass murdered in Nazi gas chambers. The remaining 40 percent labored until they too were sent to their deaths. Effective resistance was nearly impossible; starvation and disease weakened Jews in the ghettos and, because men and young women had emigrated, ghettos were more likely to be populated by middle-aged women and the elderly. Resistance, as in the uprising at the Warsaw ghetto in 1943, meant certain death. The Nazis went to great lengths to hide what they were doing in the extermination camps. They had bands playing when the trains arrived at the camps, and sometimes gave people cheery postcards to send home. Those not immediately killed in the camps experienced harsh conditions of forced labor and that killed most of the internees more slowly. By the end of the war, six million Jews—the vast majority from Eastern Europe—along with an estimated five to six million gypsies, homosexuals, Slavs, and others were murdered by the Nazis.

Societies at War, pp. 1082–1085

Even more than World War I, World War II depended on industrial productivity geared totally toward war and mass murder. Neither Japan nor Germany took the resources and morale of its enemies into full account. Allied governments were overwhelmingly successful in generating civilian participation, especially among women. In the Axis, women followed the fascist doctrine of separate spheres, even though they were desperately needed in offices and factories. In the Soviet Union, women constituted more than half the workforce by war's end. Stalin encouraged a revival of Russian nationalism, whereas the democracies used propaganda to mobilize participation. People were glued to their radios for war news; and films, monitored by governmental agencies, depicted aviation heroes, infantry men, and the working women and wives left behind. Anti-Semitic, anti-Slav, and antigypsy sentiment was a hallmark of Nazism, whereas Allied propaganda depicted Germans as sadists and perverts and Japanese as uncivilized, insect-like fanatics.

From Resistance to Allied Victory, pp. 1085–1090

The combined efforts of the military ultimately defeated the Axis powers, but civilian resistance in Nazi-occupied areas, such as the *maquis* in France also contributed to the Allied victory. A major turning point came for the Allied forces in August 1942, when the German army began its siege on Stalingrad, a Russian city that would provide access to Soviet oil. Stalin's successful defense of Stalingrad marked the beginning of the Soviet's drive westward. Meanwhile, the British army in North Africa stood firm against the Germans in Egypt and Libya and, together with U.S. forces, invaded Morocco and Algeria in the autumn of 1942. The Allies invaded North Africa and Europe and pounded German cities with strategic bombing to demoralize civilians and destroy the enemy's war industry. On June 6, 1944, the combined Allied forces under the command of U.S. General Dwight D. Eisenhower (1890–1969) invaded the Normandy coast of France. In late July, Allied forces broke through German defenses and, in August, helped liberate Paris, where rebellion had erupted against the occupiers. British, Canadian, U.S., and other Allied forces then fought their way eastward to join the Soviets. When the Soviet army entered and took the city of Berlin, Hitler and his wife, Eva Braun, committed suicide. Germany surrendered on May 8, 1945. The German surrender allowed the Allies to shift their focus on Japan.

Three years earlier, in May 1942, the U.S. forces had stopped the Japanese in the battle of the Coral Sea. In battles at Midway Island and Guadalcanal later that year, the Allies turned the tide, destroying some of Japan's formidable naval power. The Allies, at great personnel loss, took one Pacific island after another, but the Japanese refused to surrender. Instead, they adopted *kamikaze* tactics, in which pilots deliberately crashed their planes into American ships, killing themselves in the process. More than one hundred thousand scientists, technicians, and others were, meanwhile, developing the atomic bomb. Fearing that defeating Japan might take too long, cost too many lives, and allow the Soviet Union the opportunity to seize territory in the East, the United States dropped atomic bombs on Hiroshima and Nagasaki on August 6 and 9, 1945. One hundred forty thousand people were killed instantly; tens of thousands died later of burns and wounds. On August 14, 1945, Japan surrendered.

An Uneasy Postwar Settlement, pp. 1090–1091

The Grand Alliance was composed of nations with vastly different political and economic systems and agendas, and wartime agreements reflected continuing differences concerning the shape of postwar Europe. In 1941, Roosevelt and Churchill forged the Atlantic Charter, which condemned aggression, reaffirmed the idea of collective security, and endorsed the right of all peoples to choose their governments. In October 1944, Churchill and Stalin planned the postwar distribution and occupation of territories. In an agreement that went against Roosevelt's faith in collective security and threatened the principle of self-determination, Churchill and Stalin decided that the Soviets would control Romania and Bulgaria, while Britain would control Greece and, together, they would oversee Hungary and Yugoslavia. Roosevelt, Churchill, and Stalin met in the Crimean town of Yalta in February 1945, where Roosevelt advocated the establishment of the United Nations, and supported Soviet influence in Korea, Manchuria, and the Sakhalin and Kurile islands in exchange for Stalin's promise of help against any future Japanese aggression. At the final meeting in Potsdam, Germany, in the summer of 1945, the leaders of the Soviet Union and the Allied leaders agreed to give the Soviets control of eastern Poland, to cede a large stretch of eastern Germany to Poland, and to adopt a temporary four-way occupation of Germany that included France among the supervising nations. However, as victory unfolded, the Allies scrambled to outmaneuver each other.

Key Events *For each question, select the most appropriate response from the choices provided.*

1929 The U.S. stock market crashes; global depression begins; Soviet leadership initiates war against prosperous farmers, the kulaks; German Thomas Mann wins the Nobel Prize for literature

1933 Hitler comes to power in Germany

1936 Show trials begin in the USSR; Stalin purges top Communist Party officials and military leaders; the Spanish Civil War begins

1938 Virginia Woolf publishes *Three Guineas*

1939 Germany invades Poland; World War II begins; the Spanish Civil War ends

1940 France falls to the German army

1940–1941 The British air force fends off German attacks in the battle of Britain

1941 Germany invades the Soviet Union; Japan attacks Pearl Harbor; the U.S. enters the war

1941–1945 The Holocaust

1944 Allied forces land at Normandy, France

1945 The fall of Berlin; U.S. drops atomic bombs on Hiroshima & Nagasaki; World War II ends

1. Which of the following was a prominent cause of the stock market crash in 1929?
   a. An accounting error
   b. A drop in purchases of new technologies
   c. Reckless investment using borrowed money
   d. The Federal Reserve Bank loosening the availability of credit

2. Which of the following was *not* a factor in Hitler's rise to power in 1933?
   a. His effective use of media to criticize the Weimar government
   b. Concerns among conservative elites of the growing Communist influence in Germany
   c. The view among several political elites that Hitler could be easily manipulated
   d. The majority of the Nazi Party membership being over age forty

3. Which of the following did *not* participate in the Spanish Civil War (1936–1939)?
   a. Great Britain
   b. Germany
   c. Italy
   d. Russia

4. Which country invaded Poland with Germany in 1939?
   a. Italy
   b. Czechoslovakia
   c. Russia
   d. Spain

5. Which of the following was a consequence of the German invasion of Russia in 1941?
   a. The United States entered the war
   b. Russian army was severely weakened and unable to fight for much of the remainder of the war
   c. Harsh winter prevented a quick victory and hampered the overall war effort for Germany
   d. Stalin discredited for having made an alliance with Germany and sent into exile

6. Which of the following did *not* occur after World War II ended?
   a. Refugees quickly found housing vacated by those killed during the war.
   b. Colonized peoples no longer exhibited deference to their European dominators.
   c. Western values changed drastically.
   d. New competition for territory arose among the Allied powers.

Key Terms   *Match each key term to its definition.*

A. **Appeasement** (p. 1075)
B. **Blitzkrieg** (p. 1077)
C. **civil disobedience** (p. 1054)
D. **Enabling Act** (p. 1062)
E. **family allowance** (p. 1066)
F. **five-year plans** (p. 1055)
G. **Lebensraum** (p. 1072)
H. **Nazi-Soviet Pact** (p. 1077)
I. **Nuremberg Laws** (p. 1064)
J. **Popular Front** (p. 1067)
K. **pump priming** (p. 1063)
L. **purges** (p. 1058)

1. _____ Deliberately but peacefully breaking the law, a tactic used by Mohandas Gandhi in India and earlier by British suffragists to protest oppression and obtain political change.

2. _____ Centralized programs for long-range economic development first used by Joseph Stalin and copied by Adolf Hitler; these plans set production priorities and give production targets for individual industries and agriculture.

3. _____ The series of attacks instituted by Joseph Stalin on citizens of the USSR in the 1930s and later. The victims were accused of being "wreckers," or saboteurs of communism, while the public grew hysterical and pliable because of its fear.

4. _____ The legislation passed in 1933 suspending constitutional government for four years in order to meet the crisis in the German economy.

5. _____ An economic policy used by governments to stimulate the economy through public works programs and other infusions of funds to the public.

6. _____ Legislation in 1935 that deprived Jewish Germans of their citizenship and imposed many other hardships on them.

7. _____ Government funds given to families with children in order to boost the birthrate in totalitarian and democratic countries alike.

8. _____ An alliance of political parties that joined together in the 1930s despite deep philosophical differences to resist fascism.

9. _____ Literally, "living space"; the land that Adolf Hitler proposed to conquer so that true Aryans might have sufficient space to live their noble lives.

10. _____ The strategy of preventing a war by making concessions for legitimate grievances.

11. _____ The agreement reached in 1939 by Germany and the Soviet Union in which both agreed not to attack the other in case of war. The agreement secretly divided up territory that would later be conquered.

12. _____ Literally, "lightning war"; a strategy for the conduct of war in which motorized firepower quickly and overwhelmingly attacks the enemy, leaving it in a state of shock and awe and unable to resist psychologically or militarily.

Identification   *This activity tests your recall of significant people, places, and events from this chapter. Fill in the blank with the correct answer.*

1. Between early October and mid-November _____, the American stock market collapsed as the value of listed companies dropped from $87 billion to $30 billion.

2. Trained in England as a lawyer, _____ later embraced a lifestyle of self-denial and advocated civil disobedience to nonviolently resist imperial rule.

3. In the 1930s, Persia forced the renegotiation of oil contracts that had allowed Western countries to take oil virtually cost-free and, in 1935, changed its name to _____.

4. In 1936, the British agreed to end its military occupation of _____, although not the Suez Canal.

5. In 1930, the _____ brutally crushed a peasant uprising in Indochina led by the Indochinese Communist Party.

6. In _____, Stalin ended Lenin's New Economic Policy and introduced the first of his Five Year Plans that radically transformed the Soviet Union's economy.

7. As part of Stalin's attempts to transform the Soviet economy, he confiscated land held by independent farmers called _____, and formed collective farms.

8. Media mogul _____ was one of Hitler's early supporters, and he used his press to slam the Weimar government for Germany's economic problems and wounded German pride.

9. The Enabling Act passed by the intimidated delegates of the German Reichstag, in _____, essentially gave Hitler's Nazi Party complete control over the German government unencumbered by representational government.

10. The _____ of the late 1930s used carbon monoxide poisoning and other means to kill large numbers of handicapped and elderly persons who were believed to be "inferior," which helped to pave the way for later mass exterminations.

11. The _____ of 1935 established a fund in the United States to which both employers and employees contributed, and which provided retirement benefits and unemployment insurance.

12. As Popular Front premier of France, _____ enacted social reforms that included family subsidies, welfare benefits, and guaranteed vacations.

13. The film _____ contrasted a woman's power to the ineffectuality of an impractical professor, and showed how a vital, modern woman could destroy men and civilization.

14. Astronomer _____ determined, in the 1930s, that the universe was an expanding entity.

15. Swiss theologian _____ encouraged opposition to the Nazis by teaching that the faithful should take scriptural justifications of resistance to oppression seriously.

16. In 1937, Japan launched a major attack on China that became known as the _____ because of its brutal nature.

17. In 1935, Mussolini decided to invade _____, one of the few African states that had not been overwhelmed by European imperialism.

18. Pablo Picasso's mural _____ memorialized the dead of a Spanish town that had been attacked by German planes.

19. In 1938, British prime minister _____ met with Hitler, Mussolini, and the French premier and consented to Germany's claims to the Sudetenland region of Czechoslovakia.

20. In 1939, Hitler annexed _____ and declared it a German province called the Ostmark.

21. The German invasion of _____, in 1939, began World War II.

22. After the surrender of France, in 1940, the Germans ruled the northern half of the country, while the elderly hero of World War I, _____, was allowed to govern the southern half from Vichy.

23. Escaping from France to London, in 1940, _____ directed a mixed organization of troops of colonized Asians and Africans, and other escaped soldiers in the Free French government.

24. In 1944, under the command of _____, Allied forces invaded the French beaches of Normandy in an offensive that eventually brought down Nazi Germany.

25. In February 1945, Roosevelt, Churchill, and Stalin met at _____ and agreed on the formation of the United Nations to replace the League of Nations.

CHAPTER REVIEW

Self-Test and Analytical Exercises

Multiple Choice *Select the best answer from the four choices provided.*

1. The Great Depression was triggered by
   a. Germany's invasion of Poland.
   b. fears of rising totalitarianism in Europe.
   c. the collapse of the American stock market.
   d. a reduction in international trade caused by Germany's debt crisis.

2. During the Great Depression, gender relations
   a. became more traditional as a defense against the uncertainty of difficult times.
   b. were unsettled because men were often unable to find work to support their families and the low-paying jobs for women became the family's main source of income.
   c. were on a more equal footing in the cities, but in rural areas patriarchal authority remained steady.
   d. were characterized in rural areas by spousal partnerships, but reverted to more traditional forms in the cities.

3. During the Great Depression, the birthrate in many countries
   a. declined.
   b. remained essentially unchanged.
   c. increased.
   d. ceased to be a matter of national concern.

4. The effects of declining purchasing power and unavailability of ready credit
   a. were mainly confined to Europe.
   b. added to colonial grievances and discontent.
   c. helped to diminish discontent among European colonies.
   d. had little impact outside of the West.

5. Stalin's primary method of industrialization was a wartime policy called
   a. democratic planning.
   b. central economic planning.
   c. economic incentives.
   d. democratic centralism.

6. What were collective farms called in the Soviet Union?
   a. *Kolkhoz*
   b. Kulak
   c. Gulag
   d. NEP

7. Which of the following is *true* regarding the Soviet Union under Stalin?
   a. Sexual relationships became freer and traditional forms of marriage were rejected as too bourgeois.
   b. An effort to increase the birthrate witnessed the return and enforcement of traditional gender relations, marriages, and attitudes toward sex.
   c. Birth control information, abortions, and contraceptive devices were readily available.
   d. The state tried to limit the birthrate in order to reduce the economic pressures caused by scarce resources.

8. The Enabling Act, passed in 1933,
   a. suspended the constitution and virtually ended democratic government.
   b. outlawed all other political parties.
   c. forced all non-Aryans to leave Germany.
   d. declared that Germany would no longer abide by the Versailles Treaty.

9. What was President Herbert Hoover's initial reaction to the Great Depression?
   a. Hoover instituted a massive program of government-sponsored assistance programs.
   b. Hoover devised an arms buildup that stimulated American productivity.
   c. Hoover encouraged the adoption of socialist-styled economic management modeled after European methods.
   d. Hoover believed that the economic problems were temporary and refused to undertake any direct governmental assistance.

10. Which of the following is *not true* of the Popular Front in France?
    a. Included Communists who were allowed to participate due to a reversal by Stalin of his opposition of Communist collaboration with Liberals and Socialists
    b. Extended governmental benefits and introduced reform policies similar to those engaged by Sweden and laid out in FDR's New Deal
    c. Maintained widespread support among the upper classes, who preferred the Popular Front to fascism
    d. Made republicanism responsive to the masses by offering a youthful, but democratic political culture

11. Who starred in the film *Modern Times*, which presented the hard times of the industrial age with humor and sympathy?
    a. Gracie Fields
    b. Charlie Chaplin
    c. Marlene Dietrich
    d. René Clair

12. Which British writer described experiences among the poor of Paris and London, wrote investigative pieces about the unemployed in the north of England, and published an account of the Spanish Civil War?
    a. Ernest Hemingway
    b. Thomas Mann
    c. George Orwell
    d. Edwin Hubble

13. In 1931, Japan embarked upon an expansionist military policy by invading
    a. China.
    b. Indonesia.
    c. Korea.
    d. India.

14. In 1935, Mussolini asserted Italian power by invading
    a. Montenegro.
    b. Libya.
    c. Ethiopia.
    d. Egypt.

15. Which of the following provided assistance to the Spanish republicans in order to fight fascism?
    a. Britain and France
    b. The Soviet Union
    c. Germany and Italy
    d. The United States

16. From which country did Hitler demand autonomy for the German-populated region called the Sudentenland?
    a. Austria
    b. Hungary
    c. Czechoslovakia
    d. Poland

17. Which wartime leader rallied the British people in part through his radio-broadcasted speeches?
    a. Winston Churchill
    b. Franklin Delano Roosevelt
    c. Neville Chamberlain
    d. Ramsay MacDonald

18. Concentration camps were
    a. always designed purely for the extermination of their inmates.
    b. both work camps established to drive the Nazi war machine and extermination camps developed specifically for the purpose of mass murder.
    c. the only places in which the mass murder of Jews and others took place.
    d. located outside of Germany only.

19. During the war, propaganda
    a. employed stereotypical depictions of wartime enemies to promote racist thinking.
    b. was mainly used by the Allied powers.
    c. was mainly used by the Axis powers.
    d. had little impact on the civilian populations of the Allied powers, who were accustomed to film and radio messages.

20. The final meeting of the Allied leaders, during which it was decided that the Soviets would control Eastern Poland, that part of eastern Germany would be given to Poland, and that Germany would be divided into four occupied zones was held at
    a. Yalta.
    b. Newfoundland.
    c. Tehran.
    d. Potsdam.

21. One of the factors that caused the stock market collapse was
    a. the fact that many people were investing in the market with money borrowed on margin.
    b. the way the Federal Reserve Bank loosened the availability of credit.
    c. the refusal of European debtors to pay their American creditors.
    d. a sudden panic about the possibility of war in Europe.

22. During the Great Depression,
    a. the majority of Europeans and Americans were unemployed.
    b. there was no industrial growth in any European country.
    c. prosperity did continue in some regions and economic sectors.
    d. municipal building and governmental building projects ended.

23. Governmental policies that contributed to a longer-lasting, more severe depression
    a. increased spending and promoted more free trade.
    b. forced unprofitable businesses to close.
    c. provided immediate, comprehensive, unemployment benefits.
    d. cut spending and enacted huge tariffs on imports.

24. Mahatma Gandhi advocated a policy of
    a. violent revolution.
    b. civil disobedience.
    c. peaceful and lawful demonstrations.
    d. continued deference toward British rulers.

25. *Totalitarianism* refers to
    a. governments that enforce economic discipline while allowing basic civil rights.
    b. centralized systems of government that control society and ensure conformity through a single party and police terrorist activities.
    c. the domination of society by the most wealthy.
    d. constitutional governments characterized by widespread or "total" political freedom.

26. Stalin's efforts at industrialization
    a. failed and the Soviet Union remained economically backward.
    b. succeeded in making the Soviet Union a leading industrial nation, but also had great social costs.
    c. became the model for Western economic regeneration.
    d. succeeded without causing much suffering among the Soviet peoples.

27. Hitler first became chancellor of Germany in 1933
    a. after winning a clear and overwhelming majority in the election of 1932.
    b. by staging a coup in which Nazi supporters violently seized power.
    c. when the president, at the urging of social elites, invited him to take office.
    d. by murdering his political opponents and taking power.

28. The term *Volksgemeinschaft* refers to
    a. a series of laws limiting Jewish rights.
    b. revoked German civil rights and employed by Hitler's opponents to critique his seizure of power.
    c. the Nazi goal of a "peoples' community" of racially pure Germans.
    d. the Nazi policy of burning books and banning "deviant" authors.

29. What name was applied to the series of economic and social programs instituted by FDR to ease the effects of the Great Depression?
    a. Fair Deal
    b. Socialist Solution
    c. Welfare State
    d. New Deal

30. Who was the leader of the French Popular Front?
    a. Léon Blum
    b. Engelbert Dolfuss
    c. René Clair
    d. Ramsay MacDonald

31. Religious leaders during this period,
    a. felt helpless in the face of the rise of dictatorships and withdrew from active intervention in politics.
    b. spurred many to recommit to activism and attempted to fight secularization and dictatorship.
    c. endorsed the rise of dictatorship because it represented an opportunity for the churches to fight secularization.
    d. were successful in stopping the rise of dictatorships in several countries.

32. Who developed the "indeterminacy" principle in physics, the theory that precise formulations were impossible because scientific observation disturbs the natural state of atoms?
    a. Ludwig Wittgenstein
    b. Kurt Gödel
    c. Edwin Hubble
    d. Werner Heisenberg

33. The Nazis claimed that Germany's requirement for sufficient living space to thrive as economy, was called
    a. Lebensraum.
    b. Blitzkrieg.
    c. Anschluss.
    d. Volksraum.

34. In 1931, Spanish revolutionaries
    a. overthrew their king and set up a republic.
    b. established a fascist dictatorship.
    c. established a Soviet-styled, Communist state.
    d. failed to overthrow the Spanish monarchy.

35. Who won the civil war in Spain?
    a. Falangists
    b. Loyalists
    c. Volunteer armies from democratic countries
    d. Soviet Union

36. The policy of "appeasement"
    a. was based on the democratic powers' belief that Germany had legitimate grievances.
    b. reflected widespread support for Hitler in Britain and France.
    c. eased the fear of Soviet power.
    d. was employed only because Britain and France did not possess the military force necessary oppose it.

37. During the World War II,
    a. Axis powers had the advantage of being able to outproduce the Allies.
    b. the Axis powers' control of Central and Eastern Europe gave them an advantage in the production of war matériel.
    c. Allied powers were able to produce more war matériel than Axis powers, especially as the war progressed.
    d. German efficiency outpaced Allied strategies for production.

38. The failed German siege of which city was a major turning point of World War II?
    a. Paris
    b. Helsinki
    c. London
    d. Stalingrad

39. In 1941, which of the following condemned aggression, reaffirmed the ideal of collective security, and endorsed the right of peoples to choose their governments—all issues that would become focal points for the Allies after the war?
    a. Lend-Lease Act
    b. Atlantic Charter
    c. Tripartite Agreement
    d. Newfoundland Agreement

40. Which of the following reflects colonialist reactions to World War II?
    a. Stifled independence movements by colonized peoples
    b. Increased the deference that colonized peoples showed toward Europeans
    c. Undermined European domination of colonized peoples who more and more refused to show deference to their imperial rulers
    d. Brought European dominance of colonies to an immediate end

Short Answer   *Answer each question in three or four sentences.*

The Great Depression

1. What main events triggered the Great Depression?

2. What were some of the economic and social effects of the Great Depression?

3. What were the effects of the Great Depression on non-Western countries?

Totalitarian Triumph

4. Why did totalitarianism triumph in several European countries?

5. Describe Joseph Stalin's program of economic transformation for the Soviet Union in the 1930s.

6. Which policies did Adolf Hitler follow after taking power in Germany?

Democracies on the Defensive

7. What challenge was posed to democracies by the apparent success of totalitarianism? How did democratic governments respond?

8. What was offered to the citizenry by those countries experimenting with the establishment of the welfare state?

9. What were some of the intellectual and artistic responses to the economic, social, and political issues of the 1930s?

The Road to Global War

10. What were the steps leading toward war in Asia?

11. Outline the significance of both the open and close of the Spanish Civil War.

12. What led to war in Europe?

World War II, 1939–1945

13. Describe the war against civilians and its intended effects.

14. Which factors contributed to the Allied victory over the Axis powers?

15. Which agreements made between Allies helped to shape the postwar world?

BUILDING HISTORICAL SKILLS

Reading Maps *Write a brief, paragraph-length response to each of the following questions based on* **Map 27.3: The Growth of Nazi Germany, 1933–1939** *(p. 1076).*

1. Why did Hitler need to enter into an agreement with the Soviet Union to continue his eastward expansion?

2. Looking at the map of Germany as it was in 1933, and paying special attention to its shape, why do you think Hitler might have targeted the territories he did?

Reading Illustrations *Write a brief, paragraph-length response to each of the following questions based on the illustration* **Nazis on Parade** *(p. 944).*

1. At first glance, what is happening in this picture? What might be the symbolic significance of these orderly troops?

2. Why did the Nazis fly so many flags and include so many swastikas? Wouldn't one have been sufficient, or was there a message they were trying to send?

3. The Nazis retained power through coercion and fear. Do any aspects of this picture appear menacing to you? Might it have seemed menacing to a German citizen in 1933?

Reading Historical Documents *Write a brief, paragraph-length response to each of the following questions based on the documents in your book.*

Dolgikh: The War on Kulaks *(p. 1058)*

1. Why were families like Elena Trofimovna Dolgikh's targeted by Stalin's government?

2. Was the oppression of the kulaks beneficial or detrimental to Stalin's plans to transform the economy?

The Greater East Asia Co-Prosperity Sphere *(p. 1072)*

3. What does this document reveal about Japan's ambitions?

4. How did the Japanese government portray itself and its goals?

New Sources, New Perspectives: Museums and Memory *(pp. 1082–1083)*

5. Why have historians begun to focus on historical monuments and museums?

6. What problems might historians face when using memorials or museums as sources of information about the past?

7. Do museums and memorials tell the "truth" about the past?

Remaking Europe in the Shadow of Cold War
c. 1945–1965

CHAPTER OVERVIEW

Chapter Questions *Keep these questions in mind as you go through the study guide chapter.*

1. How did the United States and Soviet Union use their superpower status after World War II?

2. What were the major factors in Europe's economic recovery?

3. Why did Western countries abandon colonialization?

4. How did the possibility and fear of nuclear war change society during the cold war?

5. What was the general sentiment in Europe at the end of World War II?

Chapter Summary

World Politics Transformed

World War II ended the global leadership of Europe as many countries lay in ruins and were unable to feed their populations. In contrast, the United States emerged as the world's sole economic giant and the Soviet Union maintained formidable military strength despite the immense losses it suffered during the war. With Europe divided into two spheres of influence under the dominance of either the USSR or the United States, the age of bipolar world politics had begun.

Europe Prostrate, pp. 1099–1101

In contrast to World War I, armies in World War II fought a war that leveled thousands of square miles of territory, leaving cities in shambles and millions of people suffering. People were so exhausted by the struggle for bare survival that, unlike after World War I, there were no uprisings. The tens of millions of refugees suf-

fered the most. Many had been inmates of prisons and death camps; others, especially ethnic Germans, had fled westward to escape the Soviet Red Army as it pushed toward Berlin. Survivors of the concentration camps continued to suffer after the war. Many had no home to return to because property had been confiscated and entire communities destroyed. Many Jews eventually went to Palestine; however, the British were reluctant to promote a vast Jewish migration to the Middle East, fearing it might hurt their interests by increasing conflict with the Arabs.

New Superpowers: The United States and the Soviet Union, pp. 1101–1102

Only two powerful countries remained in 1945: the United States and the Soviet Union. The United States was now the richest country in the world, and a confident mood swept throughout the country. A wave of suburban housing developments and high consumer spending kept the economy buoyant. Population soared with the "baby boom" that lasted from the late 1940s to the early 1960s. In a departure from U.S. isolationist attitudes before the war, Americans embraced their country's position as a global leader, expressing confidence in their ability to guide the rest of the world. The Soviets also came out of the war with a sense of accomplishment, and expected equality in decision making with the United States rather than the imposed international isolation of the prewar period. Citizens of the USSR expected hardship to end because they believed that the defeat of Hitler proved that goals concerning industrialization and defense had been met. Stalin, however, increased repression in order to increase his control; mobilization for total war had encouraged individual responsibility while relaxing Communist oversight. Stalin announced a new Five Year Plan (1946) that set increased production goals and mandated stricter collectivization of agriculture. To increase the birthrate, Stalin intensified propaganda emphasizing that working women should also fulfill their true nature by having many children.

Origins of the Cold War, pp. 1102–1106

Because no peace treaty officially ended the conflict with Germany, the origins of the cold war remain a matter of debate. After the war, Stalin wanted a buffer zone of friendly states to prevent what he perceived as aggression from Western Europe. To create this buffer zone, the USSR repressed democratic government in Central and Eastern Europe between 1945 and 1948, imposing Communist rule in Bulgaria, Romania, Hungary, Czechoslovakia, and Poland. As Western leaders witnessed the Soviets intervening in Eastern Europe, they worried about further Communist expansion. In March 1947, Truman reacted to the threat by announcing economic and military aid to regions threatened by communism, a policy that came to be known as the Truman Doctrine. Citing the deterioration of economic exchange during World War II as a threat to political stability, the United States also announced the Marshall Plan, a program of massive economic aid to Europe, under which the United States sent more than $12 billion in food, equipment, and services to Europe by the early 1950s. Stalin considered the Marshall Plan a political ploy that found him unable to supply similar economic aid to Eastern Europe, and his reaction was to suppress the remaining coalitions in Central and Eastern Europe. The only exception to the imposition of Soviet control came in Yugoslavia, ruled by the Communist leader Tito (Josip Broz [1892–1980]). Tito wished to see Yugoslavia develop industrially, but not in order to satisfy Soviet needs. Under Tito's strong leadership, the various ethnic groups that made up Yugoslavia's federation of six republics and two independent provinces remained at peace.

The Division of Germany, pp. 1106–1107

The agreements reached at Yalta provided for Germany's occupation by troops divided into four zones, each of which was controlled by one of the four principal victors of the war: the United States, the Soviet Union, Great Britain, and France. American leaders hoped for economic coordination among the four zones that would benefit the occupying countries and also support Germany, whereas the Soviets planned to use the economic output of their zone to help repair the Soviet economy. Amidst these tensions, the three Western allies agreed to merge their zones into a West German state instead of continuing to curtail German power as wartime agreements had stated. The United States began an economic buildup under the Marshall Plan to make the western zone a buffer against the Soviets. Stalin struck back at the Marshall Plan on July 24, 1948, when Soviet troops blockaded Germany's capital, Berlin. Although the city was deep in Soviet territory, it too had been divided into four occupation zones. The Soviets refused to allow vehicles from the west to travel through their zone. The United States responded by air shipping millions of tons of provisions to Berlin during the winter of 1948–1949, an operation known as the Berlin airlift. With this crisis, many Westerners began to view the conflict as a moral crusade. By the time the Soviet blockade ended (May 12, 1949), a divided Berlin had become the symbol of the cold war; this conflict created competing military alliances. The United States, Canada, and their European allies formed the North Atlantic Treaty Organization (NATO). The Soviet Union in turn established a military organization known as the Warsaw Pact, which included Albania, Bulgaria, Czechoslovakia, East Germany, Hungary, Poland, and Romania.

Political and Economic Recovery in Europe

The ideological clash between the United States and the USSR served as a backdrop to the remarkable economic and political recovery that occurred in Europe as the cold war unfolded. While eradicating the Nazi past, Western Europe revived democratic political structures, its individualistic culture, and its productive capabilities. Eastern Europe had a far less prosperous and far more repressive existence under Stalinism. Yet, by 1960, people across the continent had escaped the poverty of the depression and war to enjoy a standard of living higher than it ever had been.

Dealing with the Nazi Past, pp. 1108–1109

Confusion reigned in May 1945, as Europeans lived under a complex system of political jurisdictions including those of local resistance leaders, Allied armies of occupation, international relief workers, and the remnants of bureaucracies. Occupying armies often operated independent of any law. While some helped by distributing food and clothing, others—particularly the Soviet army—raped and robbed. With the discovery of the death camps, desire for revenge against the Nazis grew. Civilians perpetrated vigilante justice, shaving the heads of women suspected of collaborating or associating with Germans and making them parade naked through the streets. Members of the resistance conducted on-the-spot executions of tens of thousands of Nazi officers and collaborators. Governmental officials and Allied representatives undertook a more systematic "denazification." In the trials conducted at Nuremberg, Germany (fall of 1945), the Allies used Nazi documents to provide a horrifying image of Nazi crimes. As hardship continued in Germany, the Germans began to believe that they were the main victims of the war. Allied officials themselves often relied on high-ranking fascists and Nazis whose expertise was necessary for restoring governmental services, and many Nazi bureaucrats kept their jobs in the new West Germany to help wage the cold war more effectively.

Rebirth of the West, pp. 1109–1113

Resistance leaders had the first claim to offices in post-fascist Western Europe. The French approved a constitution in 1946 that established the Fourth Republic and finally granted women the vote. Italy replaced its constitutional monarchy with a full parliamentary system that allowed women the vote for the first time as well. Throughout Western Europe, the Communist Party attracted the most vocal loyalty of a consistently large sector of the population. People still remembered the common man's plight in the 1930s, and the Communists advocated his welfare most forcefully. In flourishing West Germany, however, communism had no appeal. In 1949, centrist politicians helped create a new state: the German Federal Republic. Its first chancellor was Catholic, anti-Communist Konrad Adenauer (1876–1967). It was in the United States that democracy was most threatened after the war. In 1949, fear caused by the detonation of a Soviet-built atomic bomb and a Communist revolution in China brought to the fore Joseph McCarthy (1908–1957), a senator from Wisconsin, who announced that Communists were infiltrating American institutions.

Up to 95 percent of major cities in Western Europe had been destroyed by bombing, and rebuilding was a priority in the months following the end of the war. As Marshall Plan funds began to have an impact, food and consumer goods became more plentiful, and demand for automobiles, washing machines, and vacuum cleaners boosted economies. The postwar recovery also featured continued military spending and the adaptation of wartime technology to consumer industry. In 1951, Italy, France, Germany, Belgium, Luxembourg, and the Netherlands formed the European Coal and Steel Community (ECSC). This organization would manage coal and steel production and prices, and, through creating common economic interests, prevent France and Germany from going to war. In 1957, ECSC members signed the Treaty of Rome, which provided for the sharing of atomic resources through a commission called EURO-COM and created a trading partnership called the European Economic Community (EEC), known as the Common Market. The EEC reduced tariffs among its members that led to increased cooperation and produced great economic rewards. Government experts, called "technocrats" after 1945, based decisions regarding economic policy on expertise rather than political interest, while those working for the Common Market were to disregard the self-interest of any one nation.

The Welfare State: Common Ground East and West, pp. 1113–1115

On both sides of the cold war, governments intervened forcefully to ameliorate social conditions. This policy of intervention became known as the welfare state, something that had been gradually building for almost a century. The welfare state encouraged population growth with direct financial aid, imitating the Swedish programs of the 1930s that had created family allowances, health care and medical benefits, and programs for pregnant women and new mothers. Nearly everywhere except the United States, state-funded medical insurance and subsidized medical care covered health-care needs. The combination of better material conditions and state provision of health care dramatically extended life expectancy and lowered rates of infant mortality. Vaccines for diseases such as tuberculosis, diphtheria, measles, and polio made an enormous difference. As people lived longer, governments began to establish programs for the elderly. Governments sponsored a postwar housing boom; in Western Europe, governments provided incentives to private builders as well as sponsored building projects. New cities arose around the edges of major urban areas in both East and West.

Recovery in the East, pp. 1116–1118

As he had done in the Soviet Union before the war, Stalin collectivized agriculture and industrialized Eastern European countries by nationalizing private property. The Soviet Union formed regional organizations, instituting the Council for Mutual Economic Assistance (COMECON) to coordinate economic relations among the satellite countries and Moscow. The terms of the COMECON relationship thwarted development in the satellite states because the USSR was allowed to buy goods from its clients at bargain prices and reap profits by selling these goods at exorbitant prices. These formerly peasant states did, however, become oriented toward technology and bureaucratically directed industrial economies. People moved to cities where they received better education, health care, and jobs. Repression accompanied the drive for modernization, and the Soviet Union dominated its alliances through physical coercion along with state-instituted programs to build loyalty to the regime. After Stalin's death in 1953, Nikita Khrushchev (1894–1971) emerged as the undisputed leader of the Soviet Union in 1955. Khrushchev denounced the "cult of personality" that Stalin had surrounded himself with, and announced that Stalinism did *not* equal socialism. In this climate of uncertainty, protest erupted in the summer of 1956, most notably in Poland and Hungary. As these rebellions were brutally suppressed, the United States refused to intervene, demonstrating that it would not risk another world war by militarily challenging the Soviets in their sphere of influence. The failure of Eastern European uprisings overshadowed significant changes in Soviet policy. Khrushchev ended the Stalinist purges, reformed the courts, and set a policy of more limited sentences for political offenders and criminals. These reforms came to be known as a "thaw." In 1957, the Soviets successfully launched the first artificial Earth satellite, *Sputnik,* and, in 1961, sent the first cosmonaut, Yuri Gagarin (1934–1968), into orbit around earth. The Soviets' edge in space technology shocked the Western bloc and motivated the creation of the U.S. National Aeronautics and Space Administration (NASA).

Decolonization in a Cold War Climate

World War II was the final blow to the ability of European powers to maintain their vast empires. The war had further disillusioned colonized peoples about the concept of European superiority, and fostered even greater resentment because of how colonial powers had treated them. This process of achieving independence, called "decolonization," was fraught with difficulties such as religious, ethnic, and cultural differences, which worked against political unity in the former colonies.

The End of Empire in Asia, pp. 1119–1120

By the end of World War II, leaders in Asia had begun to mobilize the mass discontent that had intensified during the war. The British had promised to grant India its independence in the 1930s, but postponed it when war broke out. After the war, the British Labour government, presiding over the end of the British Empire in India, decreed that because distrust was so great between the Indian National Congress and the Muslim League, two countries should be created. China experienced a Communist takeover (1949) led by Mao Zedong (1893–1976). Mao instituted social reforms such as civil equality for women, but also copied Soviet collectivization, rapid industrialization, and the brutal repression of the privileged classes. The Communist victory in China spurred both the United States and the USSR to increase their involvement in Asian politics. In 1950, the North Koreans, supported by the Soviet Union, invaded U.S.-backed South Korea. The United States maneuvered the UN Security Council into approving a "police action" against North Korea but, after two and a half years of stalemate, the opposing sides agreed to a settlement (1953) that reestablished the border between North Korea and South Korea at the thirty-eighth parallel. The cold war spread to Indochina after the war as well, where nationalists had been struggling against the renewal of French imperialism. The French fought all efforts at independence, but peasant guerrillas forced them to withdraw after the bloody battle of Dien Bien Phu (1954). The Geneva Convention of 1954 carved out an independent Laos and divided Vietnam into North Vietnam and South Vietnam, each free from French control. In its fight to prevent the spread of communism in Asia, the United States acquired a reputation as an "imperialist" power of the old school.

The Struggle for Identity in the Middle East, pp. 1120–1121

Middle Eastern peoples also renewed their commitment to independence and resisted attempts by the major powers to regain imperial control. The cold war gave Middle Eastern leaders an opening to bargain with the superpowers, playing them off one another, especially over resources (such as oil) to repair war-torn economies. The Western powers' commitment to secure a Jewish homeland in the Middle East made Arabs more determined to regain economic and political control of the region. Great Britain ceded Palestine to the United Nations, in 1947, to work out a settlement between the Jews and the Arabs. The UN voted to partition Palestine into an Arab region and a Jewish region. Conflicting claims led to war, and the Jewish military forces prevailed; Israel was established on May 14, 1948. Egypt had gained its independence from Britain at the end of the war. However, Britain retained its control of the Suez Canal, which was owned by a British-run company. In 1952, Colonel Gamal Abdel Nasser (1918–1970) became Egypt's president and, in July 1956, he nationalized the canal. The British called on the United States, which refused to help in order to avoid military conflict with the Soviet Union. American opposition to their plans caused the British to back down; Nasser's triumph inspired confidence that the Middle East could confront the West and win.

New Nations in Africa, pp. 1122–1123

In sub-Saharan Africa, nationalist leaders roused their people to challenge Europe's increasing demands for resources and labor, which resulted in poverty for African peoples. Kwame Nkrumah (1909–1972) led the diverse inhabitants of the relatively prosperous, British-controlled West African Gold Coast in passive resistance, in imitation of Gandhian methods. After years of such resistance, the British withdrew, allowing the state of Ghana to come into being in 1957. Nigeria, the most populous African region, became independent in 1960. The eastern coast and southern and central areas of Africa contained numerous European settlers who violently resisted independence movements. France easily granted certain demands for independence, such as those of Tunisia, Morocco, and West Africa, where there were fewer settlers, more limited economic stakes, and less military involvement. When Algerian nationalists rebelled against the restoration of French rule in the final days of World War II, the French army massacred tens of thousands of protesters. The Algerian Front for National Liberation, formed in 1954, attacked European settlers and their Arab supporters. The French fought back savagely, sending in more than 400,000 soldiers. The Algerian war threatened French stability as protests in Paris greeted reports of the army's barbarous practices, and the Fourth Republic eventually collapsed over the issue. In 1958, Charles de Gaulle, supported by the army and approved by the Chamber of Deputies, returned to power. In return for leading France out of its Algerian quagmire, de Gaulle demanded the creation of the Fifth Republic, a new republican government with a strong president who could exercise emergency power. As these new nations emerged, the United Nations was formed as a mechanism to promote international security. From its beginning, both the United States and the Soviet Union were active members of the United Nations. The charter of the UN outlined a collective, global authority that would adjudicate conflicts, provide military protection, and oversee the fate of nonindependent states.

The Arrival of New Europeans, pp. 1123–1125

In a reversal of the nineteenth-century trend of emigration out of Europe, people from former colonies began immigrating to Europe after the war. As European economies recovered, labor was in short supply, so immigrants were invited as temporary residents who would work in Europe as "guest workers" for a fixed period and then return home. Initially, immigrants were housed in barracks-like dormitories where they formed their own enclaves rather than assimilate into the population. These guest workers were welcomed because they availed themselves of few social services and, because they came as adults, they did not even require public education. Most worked in less desirable jobs such as collecting garbage, building roads, and cleaning homes. Former colonials came to view Europe as a land of opportunity and illegal immigration increased. As empires collapsed, the composition of the European population in terms of race, religion, ethnicity, and social life began to change, becoming more multicultural and diverse than ever before in modern times.

Cultural Life on the Brink of Nuclear War

Both World War II and the cold war shaped postwar leisure and political culture. Individuals engaged in heated debates over the responsibility for Nazism, the cause of ethnic and racial justice, and the merits of the two superpowers. Accompanying the influx of American dollars into Western Europe were consumer goods and cultural media, which caused many to wonder if they were becoming too materialistic. As Europeans examined their warlike past and the prosperity of the present, the cold war menaced hopes for peace and stability.

Restoring "Western" Values, pp. 1125–1127

After the depravity and inhumanity of Nazism, cultural currents in Europe and the United States reemphasized universal values, spiritual renewal, and political choice. Some saw the churches as central to the restoration of values. Their success was only partial, however, as the trend toward a more secular culture continued. Instead, people emphasized the triumph of a Western heritage, a Western civilization, and Western values over fascism. Literature called for a new commitment to tolerance and pluralism. Governments erected permanent plaques at locations where resisters had been killed; their biographies filled magazines and bookstalls; organizations of resisters commemorated their role in winning the war. By the end of the 1940s, existential philosophy became the rage among the cultural elite and students. It explored the meaning of human existence in a world where evil flourished, and attempted to define *being* in the absence of God and in the midst of the breakdown of morality. In 1949, Simone de Beauvoir (1908–1986) published *The Second Sex*, in which she argues that most women failed to take the kind of action necessary to create an authentic "self" through considered action. In the 1950s and 1960s, the immensely influential writings of Frantz Fanon (1925–1961), a black psychiatrist from the French colony of Martinique, began analyzing liberation movements. Fanon wrote that the mental functioning of the colonized person was "traumatized" by the violence and the brutal imposition of another culture as the only standard of value. Ruled by guns, the colonized person would decolonize through violence. In the United States, blacks who had fought in the war to defeat the Nazi idea of white racial supremacy, intensified their commitment to the civil rights culture as embodied in such long-standing organizations as the National Association for the Advancement of Colored People (NAACP, founded 1909). In 1954, the U.S. Supreme Court declared segregated education unconstitutional in *Brown v. Board of Education*, a case initiated by the NAACP. Foremost among the many talented leaders of civil rights groups that emerged was Martin Luther King Jr. (1929–1968).

Rising Consumerism and Shifting Gender Norms, pp. 1127–1130

Governmental spending on reconstruction, productivity, and welfare helped prevent the kind of social, political, and economic upheaval that had followed World War I. Nonetheless, the war affected men's roles and their sense of themselves. Young men who had missed World War II adopted the violent style of soldiers. Young men also took cues from pop culture. The leader of rock-and-roll style and substance was the American singer Elvis Presley (1935–1977), while film stars James Dean (1931–1955) in *Rebel Without a Cause* and Marlon Brando (1924–2004) in *The Wild One* inspired American and European youths alike. The rebellious and rough masculine style also appeared in literature. The American "Beat" poets critiqued traditional ideals of the upright and rational male achiever. In 1953, the inaugural issue of the magazine *Playboy* ushered in a widely imitated depiction of a changed male identity. The new man was depicted as sexually aggressive and independent of dull, domestic life—just as he had been during the war. The notion of men's liberty had come to include not just political and economic rights but also freedom of sexual expression. In contrast, postwar women were made to symbolize a return to normalcy by returning to the domestic sphere and no longer working outside the home. In the late 1940s, the fashion house of Christian Dior (1905–1957) launched a clothing style called the "new look," which was essentially a return to the nineteenth-century female silhouette. New look propaganda did not, however, mesh with reality. European women continued to work outside the home after the war; indeed, mature women and mothers were working more than ever before. The advertising business presided over the creation of new cultural messages. Guided by marketing experts, Western Europeans were imitating Americans, driving some forty million motorized vehicles, including motorbikes, cars, buses, and trucks.

The Culture of Cold War, pp. 1130–1133

Radio broadcasts were at the center of the cold war. During the late 1940s and early 1950s, the Voice of America, with its main studio in Washington, D.C., broadcast in thirty-eight languages from one hundred transmitters and provided an alternative source of news for peoples in Eastern Europe. The Soviet counterpart broadcast in Russian around the clock, although it initially spent much of its wattage jamming U.S. programming. News reports also kept the cold war alive, featuring stories about nuclear testing, military buildups, and hostile diplomatic incidents. In school, children rehearsed for nuclear war, and some families built personal bomb shelters. Popular culture centered on the cold war. Ray Bradbury's (b. 1920) popular *Fahrenheit 451*, whose title indicated the temperature at which books would burn, condemned the cold war curtailment of intellectual freedom. Consumer culture as a whole came under the cold war banner, as people debated the "Americanization" they witnessed taking place in Europe. The Communist Party in France led a successful campaign to ban Coca-Cola for a time in the 1950s. Leadership of the art world passed to the United States when art became part of the cold war. Abstract expressionism, practiced by American artists such as Jackson Pollock (1912–1956), departed completely from realism. Abstract expressionism spoke of the artist's self-discovery, spiritual growth, and physical sensations in the process of painting. Their canvases were said to exemplify Western "freedom." In Italy, the neorealist technique was developed by filmmakers such as Roberto Rossellini (1906–1977) in *Open City* (1945) and Vittorio De Sica (1902–1974) in *The Bicycle Thief*

(1948). Such works challenged Hollywood-style sets and costumes by using ordinary characters living in devastated, impoverished cities.

Kennedy, Khrushchev, and the Atomic Brink, pp. 1133–1135

John Fitzgerald Kennedy (1917–1963) became president of the United States in 1960. A war hero and early fan of the fictional cold war spy James Bond, Kennedy intensified the arms race and escalated the cold war. In 1959, a revolution in Cuba brought Fidel Castro (b. 1927) to power, who allied his government with the Soviet Union. In the spring of 1961, Kennedy, assured by the Central Intelligence Agency (CIA) of success, launched an invasion of Cuba at the Bay of Pigs to overthrow Castro. The invasion failed miserably. A few months later, Khrushchev threatened nuclear holocaust over the continuing U.S. presence in Berlin. In the summer of 1961, East German workers, supervised by police, began construction of a wall on the city's east-west border. The wall blocked movement between east and west, and increased superpower tensions. The matter came to a head when the CIA reported, in October 1962, that the Soviets were installing medium-range missiles in Cuba. Kennedy called for a blockade of ships headed for Cuba and threatened nuclear war. After a few tense days, the two leaders negotiated an end to the crisis. Following this scare, both Kennedy and Khrushchev worked to improve nuclear diplomacy.

Key Events   *For each question, select the most appropriate response from the choices provided.*

1945 Cold war begins

1947 India and Pakistan win independence from Britain

1948 State of Israel established

1949 Mao Zedong leads Communist revolution in China; Simone de Beauvoir publishes *The Second Sex*

1950 Korean War begins

1953 Stalin dies; Korean War ends

1954 *Brown v. Board of Education* prohibits segregated schools in the United States; Vietnamese forces defeat the French at Dien Bien Phu

1956 Egyptian leader General Abdel Nasser nationalizes the Suez Canal; uprising in Hungary against USSR

1957 Boris Pasternak publishes *Doctor Zhivago*; USSR launches *Sputnik*; Treaty of Rome establishes the European Economic Community (Common Market)

1958 Fifth Republic begins in France

1962 The United States and USSR face off in the Cuban missile crisis

1. All of the following were factors in the origin of the Cold War *except*
   a. Stalin's belief that Roosevelt and Stalin were deliberately allowing the USSR to bear the brunt of casualties in World War II.
   b. hostility toward the Soviets that originated as far back as the Bolshevik Revolution of 1917.
   c. early efforts to exclude the Soviet Union from the United Nations.
   d. Stalin's perceived need for a buffer zone to protect the Soviet Union from a western menace.

2. Why did two countries, India and Pakistan, emerge from the British colony of India in 1947?
   a. Natural barriers made it too difficult for the two regions to remain united.
   b. There was mistrust and hostility between the National Congress and the Muslim League.
   c. The two regions gained their independence at different times of the year.
   d. There was a language barrier between the Pakistanis and Indians.

3. Before World War II, who controlled the area that became the State of Israel in 1948?
   a. Turkey
   b. Germany
   c. Great Britain
   d. Palestine

4. What was the main argument of Simone de Beauvoir's *The Second Sex*?
   a. Homosexuality was a separate personality type.
   b. Women comprised an important element in the workplace.
   c. A greater feminine influence in government might prevent future global wars.
   d. Most women were not leading authentic lives.

5. Which of the following occurred in the wake of Stalin's death in 1953?
   a. The Soviet Union normalized its relations with the west.
   b. The Soviet Union ended its backing of the communist movement in Korea.
   c. The production of consumer goods increased in response to public protests.
   d. Arrests of political prisoners dramatically increased.

6. All of the following were consequences of the Hungarian Revolution in 1956 *except*
   a. U.S. refusal to intervene showed that it would not militarily challenge the Soviet sphere of influence.
   b. protesters briefly succeeded in returning Imre Nagy, a popular hero, to power.
   c. hundreds of thousands fled Hungary for the West.
   d. Hungary was expelled from the Warsaw Pact.

7. Which of the following brought about the collapse of the Fourth Republic of France in 1958?
   a. A communist revolution in Paris
   b. Political fallout from the defeat at Dien Bien Phu four years earlier
   c. The conflict in Algeria
   d. A military coup led by General de Gaulle

8. In 1949, a successful communist revolution occurred in what country?
   a. Greece
   b. China
   c. Vietnam
   d. Cuba

9. In 1962, United States intelligence warned that which country was installing missiles in Cuba?
   a. Iran
   b. Russia
   c. Japan
   d. Germany

Key Terms *Match each key term to its definition.*

A. **Christian Democrats** (p. 1110)
B. **cold war** (p. 1098)
C. **Cuban missile crisis** (p. 1133)
D. **decolonization** (p. 1118)
E. **economic miracle** (p. 1108)
F. **European Economic Community (EEC or Common Market)** (p. 1112)
G. **existentialism** (p. 1126)
H. **Marshall Plan** (p. 1103)
I. **NATO (North Atlantic Treaty Organization)** (p. 1107)
J. **thaw** (p. 1117)
K. **third world** (p. 1098)
L. **Truman Doctrine** (p. 1103)
M. **United Nations (UN)** (p. 1123)
N. **welfare state** (p. 1113)

1. _____ Rivalry between the United States and the Soviet Union following World War II that led to massive growth in nuclear weapons on both sides.

2. _____ A term devised after World War II to designate those countries outside either the capitalist world of the U.S. bloc and the socialist world of the Soviet bloc—most of them emerging from imperial domination.

3. _____ The United States' policy to limit communism after World War II by countering political crises with economic and military aid.

4. _____ A post–World War II program funded by the United States to get Europe back on its feet economically and thereby reduce the appeal of communism. It played an important role in the rebirth of European prosperity in the 1950s.

5. _____ Security alliance formed in 1949 to provide a unified military force for the United States, Canada and their allies in Western Europe and Scandinavia. The corresponding alliance of the Soviet Union and its allies was known as the Warsaw Pact.

6. _____ Europe's rapid recovery from the devastation in World War II and the striking prosperity of Germany in particular.

7. _____ Powerful center to center-right political parties that evolved in the late 1940s from former Catholic parties of the pre–World War II period.

8. _____ A consortium of six European countries established to promote free trade and economic co-operation among its members. Since its founding in 1957 it has expanded its membership and also its sphere of activity.

9. _____ A system comprising state-sponsored programs for citizens, including veterans' pensions, social security, health care, family allowances, and disability insurance. Most highly developed after World War II, this state intervened in society to bring economic democracy (to supplement political democracy) by setting a minimum standard of well-being.

10. _____ The climate of relative toleration for free expression in the Soviet bloc after the death of Joseph Stalin, in 1953. This climate alternated with periods when the government returned to repression.

11. _____ The process—both violent and peaceful—by which colonies gained their independence from the imperial powers after World War II.

12. _____ An organization for collective security and deliberation set up as World War II closed; it replaced the ineffective League of Nations and has proved active in resolving international conflicts both through negotiation and by the use of force.

13. _____ A philosophy prominent after World War II that stressed the importance of action in the creation of an authentic self.

14. _____ The confrontation in 1962 between the United States and the USSR over Soviet installation of missiles off the American coast; both John F. Kennedy and Nikita Khrushchev backed down from using nuclear weapons to resolve the situation.

Identification   *This activity tests your recall of significant people, places, and events from this chapter. Fill in the blank with the correct answer.*

1. The _____ proposed to contain the spread of communism by countering political crises with economic and military aid.

2. Hoping to alleviate some of the economic hardships that might make communism seem attractive to ordinary Europeans, the United States devised the _____ as a program of massive aid.

3. Drawing on the support of several different ethnic groups, Tito mounted a Communist revolution in _____, which kept itself independent from Soviet influence.

4. One of the early confrontations of the Cold War was the Soviet blockade of _____ in 1948.

5. In retaliation for the formation of a military alliance among Western powers, the Soviet Union established its own military organization called the _____.

6. Between 1949 and 1954, _____ sparked a wave of hysteria about a Communist conspiracy against the U.S. government.

7. In 1957, Italy, France, Germany, Belgium, Luxembourg, and the Netherlands signed the _____, which provided for a trading partnership called the European Economic Community (EEC).

8. To coordinate economic relations among the satellite countries of the Soviet Union and Moscow, the _____ was formed in 1949.

9. After the death of Stalin, _____ outmaneuvered his rivals to become the leader of the Soviet Union in 1955.

10. In the "golden" October of 1956, the people of _____ rebelled against forced collectivization.

11. In _____, a Communist takeover in China brought Mao Zedong to power.

12. The bloody defeat at Dien Bien Phu (1954) forced the _____ to withdraw from Indochina.

13. In 1952, _____ seized control of the Suez Canal from the British.

14. The *pieds noirs*, or "black feet" were French colonists from _____.

15. Using the same style of passive resistance as Gandhi, _____ forced the British to withdraw from Ghana in 1957.

16. In such novels as *The Stranger* and *The Plague*, _____ pondered questions of human responsibility in a corrupt political order.

17. In *The Second Sex*, _____ argues that most women lived in a world of biological necessity and did not create an authentic "self."

18. The character played by _____ in *The Wild One* created the beginnings of a conspicuous postwar youth culture.

19. British author _____'s book, *Casino Royale*, introduced James Bond as a spy who tested his wit and physical prowess against political villains.

20. *Open City*, by filmmaker _____, challenged Hollywood-style sets and costumes by using ordinary characters living in impoverished cities.

CHAPTER REVIEW

Self-Test and Analytical Exercises

Multiple Choice   *Select the best answer from the four choices provided.*

1. After World War II, the United States
   a. suffered an economic depression, leading to pessimism about its superpower status.
   b. maintained a reasonably stable economy, but experienced a sharp drop in its birthrate.
   c. focused on reviving a strong economy and retreated into its prewar policy of isolationism and nonintervention.
   d. maintained a strong economy, exhibited a growing birthrate, and embraced its position as a global leader.

2. Following World War II, how did Stalin view the West?
   a. Stalin's wary perception of the West had been transformed during wartime cooperation with Britain and the United States, and he continued to view the West as friendly.
   b. Stalin believed, initially, that the Soviet Union did *not* require a buffer zone of European states as a safeguard to its survival because he trusted its wartime allies.
   c. Stalin perceived the West to be a menace to the Soviet Union and believed that Churchill and Roosevelt had conspired to allow his country to bear the brunt of Hitler's attack as part of their anti-Communist policies.
   d. Stalin felt no threat from the West and therefore felt free to usurp Eastern-bloc nations as part of his goal of global domination.

3. What was the Truman Doctrine?
   a. It declared the American policy to counter international political crises with economic and military aid.
   b. It created dictatorships friendly to the United States in order to prevent the spread of communism.
   c. It was a U.S. program of massive economic aid to Europe.
   d. It stated Truman's denial of any legitimate role for Soviet power in the postwar world.

4. The division of which of the following established the border between the Eastern and Western superpowers?
   a. Czechoslovakia
   b. Germany
   c. Poland
   d. Berlin

5. The trials that focused on holding Nazi leaders responsible for atrocities committed during the war, and have impacted notions of human rights and international law ever since, were held at
   a. Berlin.
   b. London.
   c. Nuremberg.
   d. Munich.

6. The political party that descended from traditional Catholic centrist parties, and became influential in postwar politics, was which of the following?
   a. Social Democratic Party
   b. Christian Democratic Party
   c. Conservative Party
   d. Liberal Party

7. In which countries were women given the right to vote after the war?
   a. Great Britain and France
   b. Germany and France
   c. Germany and Italy
   d. France and Italy

8. After World War II, governments in both the East and West
   a. increased the role of the free market in spurring economic growth.
   b. developed more comprehensive welfare states.
   c. reduced their bureaucratic roles in shaping society and the economy.
   d. took less active roles in the lives of their citizens.

9. Who led the Communist army that overthrew the Chinese government in 1949?
   a. Ho Chi Minh
   b. Mao Zedong
   c. Jiang Jieshi
   d. Viet Minh

10. Who led a resistance movement in Indochina that forced the French to withdraw their colonial control?
    a. Ho Chi Minh
    b. Mao Zedong
    c. Jiang Jieshi
    d. Viet Minh

11. Who led the independence movement in Ghana emphasizing Gandhian methods of passive resistance?
    a. Colonel Gamal Abdel Nasser
    b. The Afrikaners
    c. Achmed Sukarno
    d. Kwame Nkrumah

12. Independence for Algeria was negotiated by
    a. Charles de Gaulle.
    b. Clement Attlee.
    c. Dwight D. Eisenhower.
    d. John Foster Dulles.

13. Who wrote *The Stranger* (1942) and *The Plague* (1947), which dissected the evils of a corrupt political order and pondered human responsibility in such situations?
    a. Albert Camus
    b. Simone de Beauvoir
    c. Jean-Paul Sartre
    d. Martin Heidegger

14. The Supreme Court's 1954 decision in *Brown v. Board of Education* declared that
    a. African Americans did not have to sit at the rear of buses.
    b. segregated education was unconstitutional in the United States.
    c. businesses were not allowed to discriminate on the basis of color.
    d. all forms of discrimination were illegal.

15. The development of which artistic style involved abstract paintings that ceased to reflect any element of realism?
    a. Existentialism
    b. New wave
    c. Abstract expressionism
    d. Neorealism

16. Whose writings suggested that colonized peoples had been traumatized by violence and the brutal imposition of an alien culture and posed the question of how to "decolonize" one's mind?
    a. Simone de Beauvoir
    b. James Watson
    c. Frantz Fanon
    d. Albert Camus

17. Of all the combatants in World War II, which two countries remained the most powerful in 1945?
    a. The United States and Great Britain
    b. Italy and France
    c. The United States and France
    d. The United States and the Soviet Union

18. In several Eastern European countries,
    a. spontaneous support for the Communist Party grew tremendously, without influence from the Soviet Union.
    b. Stalin imposed Communist rule and removed coalition-type governments that included liberals, socialists, and peasant party leaders.
    c. the Soviet Union approved of the traditional leadership and involved itself only in an advisory capacity.
    d. the Soviet Union initially increased political freedom and popular participation in government as a method of gaining the support of the masses.

19. The United States provided massive economic aid to Europe via the
    a. Truman Doctrine.
    b. Mutual Aid Plan.
    c. Marshall Plan.
    d. American Doctrine.

20. Which Western military alliance was formed in 1949?
    a. Mutual Aid Plan
    b. Warsaw Pact
    c. North Atlantic Treaty Organization
    d. United Nations

21. In the United States, who aroused anti-Communist hysteria and called people to testify on behalf of their political beliefs in an effort to identify and persecute Communist sympathizers?
    a. Konrad Adenauer
    b. Joseph McCarthy
    c. Harry Truman
    d. Dwight D. Eisenhower

22. The Treaty of Rome, in an effort to reduce tariffs among some European nations and to develop common trade policies, established the
    a. International Monetary Fund.
    b. European Economic Community (EEC).
    c. World Bank.
    d. newly arranged British Commonwealth.

23. Who became leader of the Soviet Union after Stalin's death, initiating a period of modernization and relative openness in Soviet life known as a climate of "thaw"?
    a. Yuri Gagarin
    b. Imre Nagy
    c. Nikita Khrushchev
    d. Wladislaw Gomulka

24. Which country decided *not* to join the European Economic Community?
    a. France
    b. West Germany
    c. Italy
    d. Great Britain

25. The Land Freedom Army, also known as Mau Mau, achieved independence for
    a. Kenya.
    b. Nigeria.
    c. Ghana.
    d. South Africa.

26. The superpowers faced off, indirectly, in the early 1950s during the
    a. Vietnam War.
    b. Chinese War.
    c. Indochinese War.
    d. Korean War.

27. Who nationalized the Suez Canal in 1956, sparking an unsuccessful Western invasion?
    a. Golda Meir
    b. Kwame Nkrumah
    c. Gamal Abdel Nasser
    d. Achmed Sukarno

28. In 1955, which of the following, sponsored by Achmed Sukarno, began working toward a common policy for nonaligned, postcolonial nations to achieve modernization?
    a. League of Nations
    b. Geneva Convention
    c. Bandung Convention
    d. United Nations

29. Which philosophical movement became popular among the cultural elite and students?
    a. Positivism
    b. Existentialism
    c. Essentialism
    d. Neorealism

30. Who wrote, *The Second Sex* (1960), which argued that women, defined as a passive "other" in society, had accepted this male-defined role?
    a. Nelly Sachs
    b. Jean-Paul Sartre
    c. Franz Fanon
    d. Simone de Beauvoir

31. In the 1950s, what was the dominant form of media for spreading entertainment and information?
    a. Newspapers
    b. Radio
    c. Television
    d. Movie theaters

32. In 1961, U.S. president John F. Kennedy launched a secret invasion of which country?
    a. North Korea
    b. Vietnam
    c. East Germany
    d. Cuba

Short Answer   *Answer each question in three or four sentences.*

World Politics Transformed

1. Describe the conditions in Europe after World War II.

2. How did the role and status of the United States change after World War II?

3. What were the origins of the cold war?

Political and Economic Recovery in Europe

4. What was "denazification"? Why was it not entirely successful?

5. Which factors led to Europe's economic recovery?

6. How did the Soviet Union reshape Eastern European states?

Decolonization in a Cold War Climate

7. What was the general impact of World War II on European colonialism?

8. How did the cold war affect the process of decolonization?

9. How did decolonization affect European society?

Cultural Life on the Brink of Nuclear War

10. What was the dominant philosophical movement in the postwar cultural world?

11. Which gender role model did Western society offer to women in the postwar period?

12. How was mass media affected by the cold war?

BUILDING HISTORICAL SKILLS

Reading Maps   *Write a brief, paragraph-length response to each of the following questions based on* **Map 28.3: European NATO Members and the Warsaw Pact in the 1950s** *(p. 1107).*

1. Why did cold war tensions center on Germany?

2. Why did Stalin permit Yugoslavia avoid Soviet control, but not Hungary or Poland?

Reading Illustrations   *Write a brief, paragraph-length response to each of the following questions based on the photo* **Women Clearing Berlin** *(p. 1111).*

1. During World War II, Allied propaganda was designed to strengthen American resolve to defeat Germany. Following the war and as the cold war began, propaganda had to convince Americans to protect Germany from the Soviet Union. How might this photograph contribute to making Americans more likely willing to aid Germany?

2. How are these women dressed? Does their dress contribute to the impact of the photograph?

3. The women are shown carrying something as a group. Would the photograph have been as effective if they had been shown picking through the rubble individually?

Reading Historical Documents   *Write a brief, paragraph-length response to each of the following questions based on the documents in your book.*

Consumerism, Youth, and the Birth of the Generation Gap (p. 1129)

1. What types of cultural changes and tensions are described here?

2. What were some of the important changes in Western society that contributed to these changes?

The Schuman Declaration (p. 1114)

3. How did Schuman propose to end the longstanding rivalry between Germany and France?

4. In which ways were unions such as the one Schuman was proposing products of the postwar era?

New Sources, New Perspectives:
Government Archives and the
Truth about the Cold War (pp. 1104–1105)

5. How did access to new archival materials change the United States' understanding of the USSR?

6. How did access to these archival materials change Americans understanding of the United States?

Postindustrial Society and the End of the Cold War Order

1965–1989

CHAPTER OVERVIEW

Chapter Questions   *Keep these questions in mind as you go through the study guide chapter.*

1. Which major advancements in technology occurred between 1960–1990?

2. What defines *postindustrial society*?

3. What sorts of causes did people protest, and why was protest so widespread?

4. How did the cold war begin to wane following the Cuban missile crisis?

5. Which areas of the world were involved in major crises following détente?

Chapter Summary

The Revolution in Technology

Advances in technology steadily boosted prosperity and changed daily life in the West, where people awoke to instantaneous news, worked on computers, and used revolutionary contraceptives to control reproduction. Technology seemed to be everywhere, from satellites orbiting the earth to household appliances. Human reliance on machines led one philosopher to insist that people were no longer self-sufficient, but had come to depend on machines to sustain ordinary life.

The Information Age: Television and Computers, pp. 1140–1143

Information technology catalyzed social change, as television, computers, and telecommunications increased the speed and range for conveying knowledge, culture, and politics globally. These media continued the trend begun by mass journalism, film, and radio, of forming a more homogeneous society. Between the mid-1950s and mid-1970s, Europeans rapidly adopted television. As with radio, European governments owned and controlled television stations and their programming, which they funded with tax revenues. In the belief that this medium should be used to preserve and enhance the humanist tradition, programming featured drama, ballet, concerts, variety shows, and news. The emergence of communications satellites and video recorders in the 1960s introduced competition to state-sponsored television because sports broadcasts could be diffused globally and television stations could purchase feature films on videocassette. In the Eastern-bloc countries, governments held complete control. News and educational programming were staples; travel shows were popular with an audience for whom travel was either impossible or forbidden. In both East and West, heads of state could and did preempt regular programming. In the West, electoral success increasingly depended on cultivating a successful media image. Computers were another important innovation. From the size of a gymnasium in the 1940s, computers shrank to the size of a briefcase by the 1980s and changed the pace and procedures of work by speeding up and easing tasks. Computers also made possible a revival of "cottage industry," allowing individuals to work from their homes.

The Space Age, pp. 1143–1144

In 1957, the Soviet Union launched the world's first satellite, *Sputnik,* into orbit, beginning a competition with the United States that was quickly labeled the "space race." U.S. president John F. Kennedy, obsessed with "beating" the Soviets in space, declared that America aimed to put a man on the moon by the end of the 1960s—a goal that was met in July 1969. Astronauts and cosmonauts were the era's most admired heroes. The space race spawned a new fantasy world in the West, influencing children's toys and games, and popularizing science-fiction novels, films (such as Stanley Kubrick's [1928–1999] *2001: A Space Odyssey* [1968]), and television shows (such as the *Star Trek* series). Similarly, Polish writer Stanislaw Lem's (b. 1921) novel *Solaris* (1971) portrayed space-age individuals engaged in personal quests. An international consortium headed by the United States launched the first commercial communications satellite, *Intelsat I*, in 1965, and by the 1970s, global satellite communication was a reality. Space exploration advanced pure science, as data regarding cosmic radiation, magnetic fields, and infrared sources was gathered by unmanned spacecraft. This information reinforced the "big bang" theory of the universe's origins, first posited in the 1930s by American astronomer Edwin Hubble (1889–1953).

Revolutions in Biology, Reproductive Technology, and Sexual Behavior, pp. 1144–1146

In 1952, scientists Francis Crick (b. 1916) and James Watson (b. 1928) discovered the configuration of deoxyribonucleic acid (DNA), the material in a cell's chromosomes that carries hereditary information. Beginning in the 1960s, genetics and the new field of molecular biology progressed rapidly, and a broader understanding of nucleic acids and proteins made possible new vaccines to combat polio and other deadly diseases. Understanding how DNA worked allowed scientists to bypass natural reproduction by a process called "cloning." As Western societies industrialized and urbanized, traditional constraints on sexuality began to weaken. By 1970, the widespread distribution of a new birth-control device, "the pill," provided the most reliable, temporary means of preventing pregnancy. Popular use of birth control led people to separate sexuality from reproduction, and Western society became saturated with highly sexualized music, literature, and journalism, without a corresponding rise in the birthrate. Pregnancy and childbirth were also transformed, as new medical procedures and equipment allowed closer monitoring of mother and child and childbirth increasingly took place in hospitals. New technologies, such as in vitro fertilization, also allowed couples who might otherwise be childless to reproduce. While sexuality became more open in what people were calling the "sexual revolution," efforts to decriminalize homosexual behavior also increased.

Postindustrial Society and Culture

In the 1960s, social scientists began to speak of a postindustrial society, one centered on intellectual work in services such as health care and education, rather than on manual labor in manufacturing and heavy industry. The service sector had become the leading force in the economy, which required soaring investment costs in science and the spread of technology.

Multinational Corporations, pp. 1146–1148

One aspect of this postindustrial society was the rise of multinational corporations. These companies produced for a global market and conducted business worldwide but, unlike older international firms, they also established major factories in countries other than their home base. Some multinational corporations had revenues greater than entire nations, and their interests reached beyond a national or local outlook. In the 1960s, multinationals repositioned more of their operations from Europe to the emerging economies of formerly colonized states or third world countries. Although these corporations provided jobs to third world inhabitants, profits mostly enriched foreign stockholders. Critics initially denounced multinationals as a new form of imperialism; however, multinational firms believed global expansion was necessary to remain competitive. In Europe, huge conglomerates were formed in sectors such as construction, and contributed to Europe's continuing economic growth. European firms were often closely tied to their nations' governments.

The New Worker, pp. 1148–1150

In both Eastern-bloc and Western countries, a new working class emerged, consisting of white-collar, service personnel. The relationship of workers to their bosses shifted as workers adopted attitudes and gained responsibilities that had once been managerial prerogatives. Economic distinctions based on the way one worked were also undermined. In the Eastern bloc in the 1960s, Communist leaders announced a program of "advanced socialism," meaning more social leveling, greater equality of salaries, and nearly complete absence of private production. In both the Western and Eastern-bloc countries, gender shaped the workforce. In the East, women held less prestigious, lower-paying jobs than men. In the West, farm life was modernized and became "agribusiness." To run a modern farm, one needed the newest technology and chemical products, and producers tailored their crops to global markets. Governments, farmers' cooperatives, and planning agencies took over decision making from the individual farmer, setting production quotas and handling market transactions.

The Boom in Education and Research,
pp. 1150–1151

Because research was necessary to economic growth, the United States funneled more than 20 percent of its gross national product (GNP) into research in the 1960s, siphoning off many of Europe's leading intellectuals and technicians in what came to be known as the "brain drain." In Eastern-bloc countries, on the other hand, having to navigate through enormous bureaucratic red tape often meant that scientific findings became obsolete before they received governmental approval and be applied to technology. In the West, the new criteria for success fostered an unprecedented growth in education, especially in universities and scientific institutes. Great Britain established a new network of polytechnics and universities to encourage technical research; France set up administrative schools to train future high-level bureaucrats. In principle, education increased social mobility, but, in fact, social leveling did not occur in most European universities, and education remained rigid and old-fashioned.

A Refined Family and a Generation Gap,
pp. 1151–1152

In the 1960s, the family appeared in many forms: single-parent households; "blended" households of two previously married persons, each with their own children; unmarried couples of the same sex or opposite sexes cohabiting; and traditionally married couples with fewer children. As the marriage rate was falling, the divorce rate was rising and, by the mid-1960s, the birthrate was falling as well. At the same time, however, the percentage of out-of-wedlock children soared. Daily life within the family changed, as radio and television filled a family's leisure time. Household appliances made housework less taxing, but also raised standards of cleanliness. More women worked outside the home, in part because children were going on to schools of higher education, which meant they stayed in school longer and therefore cost couples more money for their education. Whereas the early modern family organized labor, taught craft skills, and monitored reproductive behavior, the modern family seemed to have a primarily psychological function: to nurture the child while he or she learned intellectual skills in school. Psychologists, social workers, and social service agencies offered additional aid, if necessary, in providing this emotional support, while television programs about family life gave viewers the opportunity to observe how others—even fictitious others—dealt with the tensions of modern life. Even though young people stayed in school longer and were thus more financially dependent upon their parents than before, the development of a youth culture gave them an alternative emotional focus. This youth culture was char-

acterized by rebelliousness expressed through the music of heavily marketed and wildly successful bands like the Beatles. The cultural divide between parents and their children gave rise to a "generation gap" during the 1960s.

Art, Ideas, and Religion in a Technocratic Society,
pp. 1152–1155

A new artistic movement, "pop art," featured images from everyday life and employed the glossy techniques and products of a mass-consumer society, what its practitioners called "admass." Artists parodied modern commercialism and depicted grotesque aspects of ordinary consumer products, as in Swedish-born artist Claes Oldenburg's (b. 1929) *Giant Hamburger with Pickle Attached* (1962). Artists also drew on other sources such as folk traditions of the Caribbean and Africa for inspiration. In music, American composer John Cage (1912–1992) added sounds produced by everyday items to his musical scores. Other composers, called "minimalists," simplified music by scoring repeated and sustained notes. Some, like Karlheinz Stockhausen (b. 1928), emphasized modern technology and introduced electronic music into classical compositions in 1953.

The social sciences were at the peak of their prestige during these decades, often because of social scientists' increasing use of statistical models and predictions made possible by advanced, electronic computations. In anthropology, Claude Lévi-Strauss (b. 1908) developed structuralism, a theory that maintained that all societies functioned within controlling structures (such as kinship or exchange) that operated according to coercive rules. Amidst rapid social change, the Catholic church voiced concerns over the crisis of faith caused by affluence and secularism, and moved to modernize the liturgy, democratize church procedure, and renounce the long-standing doctrine that the Jews had killed Jesus. These changes took place in a series of meetings between 1962 and 1965 known as the Second Vatican Council, or Vatican II. In the United States, Protestant revivalism drew many people to join sects that believed in the literal truth of the Scriptures. In Western Europe, churchgoing remained low. Throughout the West, the religious landscape became more diverse as Muslims, Hindus, and Jews emigrated in search of economic opportunity and an escape from the hardships of decolonization.

Protesting Cold War Conditions

With their affluence, scientific sophistication, and military strength, the United States and the Soviet Union were at the peak of their power in the 1960s. Yet, by 1965, the six nations of the Common Market had surpassed the United States as the leader in worldwide trade, and often acted in their own interests across the U.S.-Soviet divide and, along with emerging nations, refused to become pliable allies to the superpowers. Rising citizen discontent formed another serious challenge to the cold war order.

Cracks in the Cold War Order, pp. 1155–1158

Across the social and political spectrum there were calls for at least softening the effects of the cold war, and many nations struck out on their own political course that was independent from the superpowers. Willy Brandt (1913–1992), the Socialist mayor of West Berlin, became foreign minister (1966) and pursued a policy of reconciliation with Communist East Germany known as Ostpolitik. In France, president Charles de Gaulle (1890–1970) steered a middle course between the United States and the Soviet Union, pulling France out of NATO, and signing trade agreements with Soviet-bloc countries. Following de Gaulle's lead, Western Europe began to reassert itself.

In Eastern Europe, Nikita Khrushchev (1894–1971) continued the process of de-Stalinization; however, his failure in the Cuban missile crisis, among other factors, led to his removal from office. In 1964, reform continued under new leaders: Leonid Brezhnev (1906–1982) and Alexei Kosygin (1904–1980). The relationship between the Soviet Union and its satellites changed as well, as members of COMECON (the Soviet bloc's economic organization) began to follow their own models. Poland allowed private farmers greater freedom to earn profits, and Hungary introduced elements of the market system into its national economy. In the arts, Ukrainian poet Yevgeny Yevtushenko (b. 1933) exposed Soviet complicity in the Holocaust in *Babi Yar* (1961). In East Berlin, Christa Wolf (b. 1929) wrote about a couple tragically divided by the Berlin Wall in *Divided Heaven* (1965). Repression returned later in the 1960s, and visual artists began holding secret exhibitions in their apartments.

In the United States, violent racism was a weak link in the American claim to moral superiority in the cold war. Civil rights activists, like Reverend Martin Luther King Jr. (1929–1968), pressed for reform. Lyndon B. Johnson (1908–1973; president 1963–1969), who became president when Kennedy was assassinated, steered the Civil Rights Act through Congress in 1964. This legislation forbade segregation in public facilities and created the Equal Employment Opportunity Commission (EEOC) to fight job discrimination. At the same time, the United States was becoming increasingly embroiled beyond its borders in Vietnam, where it supported non-Communist South Vietnamese leaders against a Communist uprising backed by the Soviet Union and China. The seemingly endless conflict created domestic tension and led to Johnson's decision in 1968 not to seek the presidency in the next election.

The Explosion of Civic Activism, pp. 1155–1163

In the midst of continued conflict, a new social activism emerged in the West. A broad cross section of Americans embraced the civil rights movement in the United States and transformed it. In 1965, César Chávez (1927–1993) led Mexican American migrant workers in the California grape agribusiness in a strike for better wages and working conditions. Meanwhile, the African American civil rights movement took a dramatic turn when riots erupted across the United States in 1965, and in subsequent summers. Some activists transformed their struggle into a militant affirmation of racial differences. They argued that blacks should celebrate their African heritage and work for "black power" by asserting and claiming the rights they were constitutionally entitled to instead of begging for them nonviolently. As the emphasis shifted in the civil rights movement, white, American university students who had participated in the early stages of the civil rights movement found themselves excluded from leadership positions among black activists. Many turned instead to the growing protest against technological change, consumerism, sexual repression, the educational establishment, and the Vietnam War. European youths also rebelled in Rome, Prague, and Poland. Students attacked the traditional university curriculum, and turned the defiant rebelliousness of 1950s youth culture into a politically activist style. In their personal lives, they rejected middle-class values concerning fashion, personal hygiene, living arrangements, and sexuality. Businesses made billions of dollars selling blue jeans, dolls dressed as hippies, natural foods, and drugs, as well as packaging and managing the superstars of the counterculture. Women active in the civil rights and student movements soon realized that protest organizations devalued women just as much as society at large did. They therefore began focusing their efforts on reforming women's status in society. More conventionally political middle-class women responded positively to the international best-seller *The Feminine Mystique* (1963), written by American journalist Betty Friedan (b. 1921). In the United States, the National Organization for Women (NOW) was formed in 1966 to bring about full female participation in American society. Some middle-class women joined street activists on behalf of such issues as abortion rights or the decriminalization of homosexuality. Many women of color went further, speaking out against the "double jeopardy" of being both black and female.

1968: Year of Crisis, pp. 1163–1166

In January 1968, on the first day of the Vietnamese New Year, or Tet, the Vietcong and the North Vietnamese attacked more than one hundred South Vietnamese towns and American bases, inflicting heavy casualties. The so-called Tet offensive caused many Americans to conclude that the war might be unwinnable. The antiwar movement gained crucial momentum, and protest escalated. Adding to the unstable situation was the assassination of Martin Luther King Jr. on April 4, 1968. More than a hundred cities across the United States erupted in violence as a result. In France, students at Nanterre University had gone on strike in January, demanding a say in university governance. Students at the Sorbonne showed solidarity, and the police responded by assaulting and arresting student demonstrators. The Parisian middle classes were sympathetic to the students, sharing their resentment of bureaucracy and horrified by police violence. By May, the protests had become outright revolt, and workers joined in. In June, President Charles de Gaulle announced a pay raise for workers, and businesses offered them a stronger voice in decision making. De Gaulle then sent tanks into Paris, and shut down the student movement. Protest erupted in Czechoslovakia as well. In autumn 1967, at a Czechoslovak Communist Party congress, Alexander Dubček (1921–1992), head of the Slovak branch of the party, called for more social and political openness. Dubček thus began the "Prague Spring." As the Czechs and Slovaks experimented with their newfound freedom of expression, Poland, East Germany, and the Soviet Union threatened Dubček's government daily. When Dubček failed to attend a meeting of Warsaw Pact leaders, Soviet threats became intensified. On the night of August 20–21, 1968, Soviet tanks rolled into Prague and put an end to the reform movement. Soviet determination to retain control over its Eastern-bloc countries was expressed in the Brezhnev Doctrine, announced in November 1968, which made clear that further moves toward change would meet similar repression. Governments as a whole generally turned to conservative solutions to these social uprisings.

The Erosion of Superpower Mastery Ends the Cold War

The 1970s brought an era of détente; that is, a lessening of cold war tensions. Despite this relaxation in the cold war, the superpowers and their allies faced further challenges by internal corruption, terrorism, competition from oil-producing nations, and continuing attempts to control the world beyond their borders. In the 1980s, as economic hard times set in, reformers began implementing drastic new policies to keep the economy moving forward; although, for the Soviets, postindustrial prosperity was not possible under the old system. Attempts at reform eventually led to the collapse of the Soviet system in 1989.

The West, the World, and the Politics of Energy, pp. 1166–1168

A shake-up of leadership occurred in the Soviet Union as well, where Brezhnev eclipsed Kosygin and began clamping down on critics. In 1974, Brezhnev expelled Aleksandr Solzhenitsyn (b. 1918) from the USSR after the publication of the first volume of his *Gulag Archipelago* (1973–1976) in the West. The Kremlin persecuted many ordinary people as well. Dissidents, falsely certified as mentally ill, were held as virtual prisoners in mental institutions. Anti-Semitism increased, and Jews were subjected to educational restrictions, severe job discrimination, and constant assaults on their religious practices. As attacks intensified in the 1970s, Soviet Jews protested and sought to emigrate to Israel or the United States, but the government severely restricted emigration. Despite this crackdown, dissent persisted in satellite states. Throughout the 1970s, workers and intellectuals in Poland generated protest writings and formed activist groups. In 1977, playwright Václav Havel (b. 1936), along with a group of fellow intellectuals and workers, signed Charter 77, a public protest against the Communist regime. Repression increased the brain drain from the East, and the presence of these exiles and escapees in the United States and Western Europe helped erode any lingering support for communism. Communist parties in the West broke their last remaining ties to the Soviet Union as a result.

After being tested by protest at home, the great powers confronted the world. In 1972, the United States pulled off a foreign policy triumph over the USSR when it opened relations with China, the other Communist giant. The Soviet Union reacted to this possible rapprochement between China and the United States by making overtures to the West. In 1972, the superpowers signed the Strategic Arms Limitation Treaty (SALT I), which set a cap on the number of antimissile and antiballistic weapons each country could own and position. In 1975, in the Helsinki accords on human rights, the Western nations officially acknowledged Soviet territorial gains in World War II in exchange for the Soviet-bloc countries' guarantee of basic human rights. Despite these successes, rising purchases of military and imported goods made the United States a debtor nation that owed billions of U.S. dollars to other countries. In the meantime, U.S. president Richard Nixon's (1913–1994; president, 1969–1974) administration was rocked by the Watergate scandal, and he resigned in disgrace in the summer of 1974.

The Middle East provided a new challenge to Western global dominance. In June 1967, Israeli forces responded to Palestinian guerrilla attacks by seizing Gaza and the Sinai peninsula from Egypt, the Golan Heights from Syria, and the West Bank from Jordan. In 1973, Egypt and Syria attacked Israel on Yom Kippur and, with military assistance from the United States, Israel successfully turned back the invasion. After their defeat, the Arab nations established in the Organization of Petroleum Exporting Countries (OPEC), quadrupled the price of oil, and imposed an embargo on oil exports to the United States in retaliation for its support of Israel. The oil embargo caused unemployment to rise by more than 50 percent in Europe and the United States. Whereas previous recessions had brought falling prices because goods remained unsold, the oil shortage created a recession that was accompanied by inflation. Rising interest rates discouraged industrial investment and consumer buying. The simultaneous rise in prices, unemployment, and interest rates was dubbed "stagflation." Encouraged by OPEC's successful stand against the West, many ordinary persons in the Middle East called for reform and, at the end of the 1970s, an uprising in Iran overthrew the U.S.-backed government and created an Islamic society.

The Western Bloc Meets Challenges with Reform, pp. 1168–1173

In Europe in the 1970s, the restoration of political order was met with terrorism as disaffected youths perpetrated kidnappings, bank robberies, bombings, and assassinations in West Germany and Italy. In Ireland, nationalist and religious violence pitted Catholics against Protestants in the north. In Britain, Margaret Thatcher's (b. 1925) Conservative Party came to power amidst stagflation and violence in Ireland, and instituted a package of economic policies known as "neoliberalism," based on the monetarist or supply-side economic theory, that the only way to ensure prosperity was in a business-friendly environment. Low taxes on businesses and the wealthy encouraged reinvestment, which created more employment, which made the welfare state unnecessary. Consequently, Thatcher began dismantling the welfare state, and her example was followed by Ronald Reagan (1911–2004) in the United States, and Helmut Kohl (b. 1930) in West Germany. In France, president François Mitterrand (1916–1996) took a different approach by increasing wages and social spending to stimulate the economy, although his successor Jacques Chirac (b. 1932) adopted neoliberal policies. Only Sweden maintained a full array of social programs for everyone, although high taxes and a huge influx of immigrants caused many to wonder if the welfare state had become too extreme.

Collapse of Communism in the Soviet Bloc, pp. 1173–1179

Reform was also begun in the Soviet Union but, instead of strengthening the economy, it provoked further rebellion and the eventual collapse of Communist rule in the USSR. A deteriorating economy, a corrupt system of political and economic management, and a deteriorating standard of living brought the need for reform to the forefront. In 1985, Mikhail Gorbachev (b. 1931) opened an era of change with a program of economic reform called "perestroika," and a policy of greater freedom of speech and openness in government called "glasnost." Gorbachev also scaled back the expensive arms production program and withdrew from the debilitating war in Afghanistan. Glasnost brought many of the Soviet Union's social and economic problems into the public arena and fostered increasing dissent.

In Poland, Lech Walesa (b. 1943) and Anna Walentynowicz (b. 1929) formed the independent labor movement called "Solidarity," which rivaled the influence of the Communist Party. In a reversal of the Brezhnev Doctrine, Gorbachev refused to interfere in the political course of another nation, and Walesa became president of Poland in 1990. Communism next collapsed in Hungary. In the summer of 1989, the Berlin Wall—the most potent and obvious symbol of a divided Europe—fell as crowds of East Germans flooded the borders of the crumbling Soviet bloc. In the "velvet revolution" of Czechoslovakia, dissident playwright Václav Havel was elected to the presidency. In Romania, the brutal Communist dictator Nicolae Ceauşescu (1918–1989) was tried by a military court in 1989, and executed. His death signaled that the very worst of communism was over.

Key Events   *For each question, select the most appropriate response from the choices provided.*

1962–1965 Vatican II reforms Catholic ritual and dogma

1963 Betty Friedan publishes *The Feminine Mystique*

1966 Willy Brandt becomes West German foreign minister and develops Ostpolitik, a policy designed to bridge tensions between the two Germanies

1967 South Africa's Dr. Christiaan Barnard performs first successful human heart transplant

1968 Revolution in Czechoslovakia against communism; student uprisings throughout Europe and the United States

1969 U.S. astronauts walk on the moon's surface

1972 SALT I treaty between the United States and Soviet Union

1973 North Vietnam and the United States sign treaty ending war in Vietnam; OPEC raises price of oil and imposes oil embargo on the West

1973–1976 Aleksandr Solzhenitsyn publishes *Gulag Archipelago*

1977 Feminists gather in Houston to mark the first International Year of Women

1978 The first test-tube baby is born in England

1978–1979 Islamic revolution in Iran; hostages taken at U.S. embassy in Teheran

1980 An independent trade union, Solidarity, organizes resistance to Polish communism; Prime Minister Margaret Thatcher begins dismantling the welfare state in Britain

Early 1980s AIDS epidemic strikes the West

1981 Ronald Reagan becomes U.S. president

1985 Mikhail Gorbachev comes to power in the USSR

1986 Explosion at Soviet nuclear plant at Chernobyl; Spain joins the Common Market

1989 Chinese students revolt in Tiananmen Square and government suppresses them; communist governments ousted in eastern Europe; fall of the Berlin Wall

1. Which of the following changes to Catholic policy did *not* occur during the period of Vatican II (1962–1965)?
    a. Jews were no longer blamed for the death of Jesus.
    b. New technologies in birth control were approved.
    c. Many church procedures were democratized.
    d. Mutual cooperation among the world's faiths was encouraged.

2. Which of the following resulted from the uprising in Czechoslovakia in 1968?
    a. Alexander Dubček gained control of the Czech government.
    b. Czechoslovakia gained its independence from the Soviet Union.
    c. The Soviet Union reversed its economic and social policies in Czechoslovakia.
    d. The uprising was harshly repressed.

3. What did the SALT I treaty between the United States and the Soviet Union entail?
    a. More open exchange between Eastern and Western artists and scientists
    b. Official recognition of Soviet sovereignty over territories it gained after World War II
    c. Limitation of nuclear arsenals in both countries
    d. Relaxing of American trade embargoes levied on Soviet Union goods

4. Which of the following was a consequence of OPEC's oil embargo on the West in 1973?
    a. Western powers invaded OPEC nations.
    b. Western powers persuaded Israel to return territories it had gained in the Six Day War.
    c. The embargo sparked a recession in the West marked by inflation and unemployment.
    d. Western powers looked to other sources of energy and eliminated their need for oil.

5. Which of the following *did not* immediately follow Margaret Thatcher's dismantling of the welfare state in Britain?
    a. Rioting in major cities
    b. Departure of leading scientists and scholars from the country
    c. Decrease in the quality of universities and hospitals
    d. Increased intervention in the British economy

6. Which of the following was a leader of the Solidarity movement in Poland?
    a. Lech Walesa
    b. Wojciech Jaruzelski
    c. Aleksandr Solzhenitsyn
    d. Gyorgy Ligeti

7. Which European leader did U.S. president Ronald Reagan most closely model his policies after?
    a. Margaret Thatcher
    b. François Mitterrand
    c. Mikhail Gorbachev
    d. Nicolae Ceauşescu

8. Which of the following leaders was ousted from power in 1989?
    a. Václav Havel
    b. Alexander Dubček
    c. Boris Yeltsin
    d. Nicolae Ceauşescu

Key Terms   *Match each key term to its definition.*

A. **DNA** (p. 1144)
B. **glasnost** (p. 1174)
C. **in vitro fertilization** (p. 1146)
D. **multinational corporation** (p. 1146)
E. **neoliberalism** (p. 1171)
F. **OPEC** (p. 1167)
G. **Ostpolitik** (p. 1156)
H. **perestroika** (p. 1174)
I. **pop art** (p. 1152)
J. **samizdat** (p. 1156)
K. **Solidarity** (p. 1176)
L. **stagflation** (p. 1168)
M. **terrorism** (p. 1168)
N. **Vatican II** (p. 1154)

1. _____ The genetic material that forms the basis of each cell; the discovery of its structure in 1952 revolutionized genetics, molecular biology, and other scientific and medical fields.

2. _____ A process developed in the 1970s by which eggs are fertilized by sperm outside the human body and then implanted in a woman's uterus.

3. _____ A business that operates in many foreign countries by sending large segments of its manufacturing, finance, sales, and other business components abroad.

4. _____ A style in the visual arts that mimicked advertising and consumerism and that used ordinary objects as part of paintings and other compositions.

5. _____ A Catholic Council held between 1962 and 1965 to modernize some aspects of church teachings (such as condemnation of Jews), to update the liturgy, and to promote cooperation among the faiths (i.e., ecumenism).

6. _____ A policy initiated by Willy Brandt in the late 1960s in which West Germany sought better economic relations with the Communist countries of eastern Europe.

7. _____ A consortium that regulated the supply and export of oil and that acted with more unanimity after the United States supported Israel against the Arabs in the wars of the late 1960s and early 1970s.

8. _____ The combination of a stagnant economy and soaring inflation; a period of this occurred in the West in the 1970s as a result of an OPEC embargo on oil.

9. _____ Coordinated and targeted political violence by opposition groups.

10. _____ A theory promoted by Margaret Thatcher, Britain's prime minister from 1979 to 1990, and those who followed her calling for a return to liberal principles of the nineteenth century, including the reduction of welfare-state programs and the cutting of taxes on wealthy people in order to promote economic growth.

11. _____ An outlawed Polish labor union of the 1980s that contested Communist Party programs and eventually succeeded in ousting the party from the Polish government.

12. _____ Literally, "openness" or "publicity"; a policy instituted in the 1980s by Soviet premier Mikhail Gorbachev calling for greater openness in speech and in thinking, which translated to the reduction of censorship in publishing, radio, television, and other media.

13. _____ Literally, "restructuring"; an economic policy instituted in the 1980s by Soviet premier Mikhail Gorbachev calling for the introduction of market mechanisms and the achievement of greater efficiency in manufacturing, agriculture, and services.

14. _____ A key form of dissident activity in the Soviet Union and its satellite countries of eastern Europe in the 1960s and 1970s; individuals reproduced uncensored publications by hand and passed them from reader to reader, thus building a foundation for the successful resistance of the 1980s.

Identification

This activity tests your recall of significant people, places, and events from this chapter. Fill in the blank with the correct answer.

1. Francis Crick and James Watson _____ in 1952.

2. In _____, the Soviets launched the first artificial satellite into orbit.

3. In 1978, _____, the first "test-tube baby," was born to an English couple.

4. One of the first electronic computers was _____, which the British had used to decode Nazi messages.

5. In July _____, U.S. astronauts Neil Armstrong and Edwin "Buzz" Aldrin became the first humans to walk on the moon's surface.

6. In 1976, the _____ completed its first flight from London to New York in less than four hours.

7. Advancing the parody of modern commercialism in art, _____ sold paintings of Campbell's soup cans as elite, artistic creations.

8. Continuing the trend away from classical melody, _____ incorporated silence into his music and composed by randomly tossing coins.

9. Anthropologist _____ developed the theory of structuralism, which insisted that all societies function within controlling structures that operate according to coercive rules similar to the conventions of language.

10. In 1962, Pope _____ convened the Second Vatican Council in response to what he saw as a crisis in faith brought on by affluence and secularism.

11. As foreign minister of West Germany, Willy Brandt began a policy known as _____, which pursued an end to cold relations with Communist East Germany.

12. In the wake of a relaxed Soviet posture on economic policy, Hungarian leader _____ introduced elements of a market system into the national economy.

13. In her book *Divided Heaven*, _____ depicted a couple tragically separated by the Berlin Wall.

14. In 1964, _____ steered the Civil Rights Act through the U.S. Congress, which forbade segregation in public facilities and set up a commission to fight job discrimination.

15. In 1963, journalist _____ published *The Feminine Mystique*, which became an international best-seller.

16. In 1972, American Secretary of State _____ arranged for President Nixon to visit China to take advantage of the rivalry between China and the USSR.

17. Following the scandal created by the break-in at the Democratic Party headquarters, Richard Nixon resigned from the presidency in _____.

18. In the late 1970s, Muslim religious leader Ayatollah Ruhollah Khomeini overthrew the American-backed government of _____.

19. The economic theories of _____, which contended that the economy benefits most when businesses prosper, were the basis of the neoliberal policies of Margaret Thatcher and other leaders of the 1980s.

20. Taking an opposite approach to Margaret Thatcher, _____ nationalized banks in his country and stimulated the economy with wage increases and social spending.

CHAPTER REVIEW

Self-Test and Analytical Exercises

Multiple Choice *Select the best answer from the four choices provided.*

1. Between the mid-1950s and the mid-1970s, Europeans overwhelmingly adopted which of the following as a major entertainment and communications medium?
   a. Computers
   b. Radio
   c. Cinema
   d. Television

2. The development of computer technology
   a. outmoded "cottage industries" as work was concentrated into centralized factories.
   b. saw traditional forms of skilled labor become more important because computers could not replicate the skills and efficiency of human workers.
   c. changed the pace and patterns of work, and allowed individuals to work in the physical isolation of their homes.
   d. never affected the labor force.

3. Which country launched the first satellite into an orbit around Earth?
   a. Great Britain
   b. The United States
   c. The Soviet Union
   d. China

4. Who was the first man to walk on the moon?
   a. John Glenn
   b. Yuri Gagarin
   c. Neil Armstrong
   d. John Cage

5. Postindustrial societies
   a. centered around manufacturing and heavy industry.
   b. placed their focus on manufacturing work, the leading sector of the economy.
   c. saw capitalist-style production undermined by socialist forms of economic management.
   d. emphasized the distribution of services, and intellectual rather than manufacturing work.

6. European companies
   a. avoided mergers and remained small, leaving them ill equipped to compete with American companies.
   b. were frequently denied government funding.
   c. jointly pursued technological and productive innovations and formed conglomerates in order to compete effectively.
   d. were able to completely dominate American multinational firms.

7. Which art form featured images from everyday life and employed the techniques of mass advertising?
   a. Abstract expressionism
   b. Minimalism
   c. Pop art
   d. Commercialism

8. Which of the following is *not true* regarding religion in the 1960s and 1970s?
   a. Church officials began to see merit in other cultures and promoted toleration.
   b. Church attendance remained low in Western Europe.
   c. The Catholic Church remained uninvolved with affairs in the Soviet-bloc countries.
   d. Immigrants from former colonies increased religious diversity in European cities.

9. Who promoted the policy of Ostpolitik?
   a. Charles de Gaulle
   b. Harold Wilson
   c. Willy Brandt
   d. Ludwig Erhard

10. Who tried to reform Soviet society but because he committed serious blunders, was ousted as leader in 1964?
    a. Aleksandr Solzhenitsyn
    b. Leonid Brezhnev
    c. Alexei Kosygin
    d. Nikita Khrushchev

11. Which year saw a vast explosion in protest movements in Europe, America, and in both Eastern and Western blocs?
    a. 1966
    b. 1967
    c. 1968
    d. 1969

12. Which of the following was a consequence of the Tet offensive in January 1968?
    a. American forces won a decisive victory over the North Vietnamese.
    b. America launched an attack on North Vietnamese bases in China.

c. Angered by the Soviet backing of the North Vietnamese, America went to the brink of war with the USSR.
   d. Antiwar movement gained new momentum as many began to conclude that the war in Vietnam was not winnable.

13. What does *détente* refer to?
    a. Escalation in cold war tensions
    b. Europe's pursuit of an independent position in the cold war
    c. Period of lessening cold war tensions
    d. End of the Vietnam War

14. What was the Yom Kippur War?
    a. Failed attack on Israel by Egypt and Syria
    b. Israeli attack on Jordan in response to Palestinian guerrilla attacks
    c. Brief civil war in Israel between conservatives and social reformers
    d. Series of Palestinian guerrilla attacks on Israel

15. Islamic revolt in which Middle Eastern country challenged Western dominance in the late 1970s?
    a. Iraq
    b. Saudi Arabia
    c. Egypt
    d. Iran

16. Which event became known as "Bloody Sunday"?
    a. The killing of several college students by the National Guard at Kent State University in 1970
    b. The killing of thirteen Irish protestors by British troops in 1972
    c. The beginning of the Tet offensive in Vietnam in 1968
    d. The takeover of the American embassy in Iran in 1979

17. Which of the following *best* describes television in Europe?
    a. Governments funded and controlled television programming to avoid what they saw as substandard American programming.
    b. Governments avoided involvement in television programming, letting private companies control funding and content.
    c. Governments funded and controlled programming, enthusiastically adopting American broadcasts as part of the cold war resistance to Soviet influence.
    d. American companies, owning large shares in European television firms, dominated television.

32. Which of the following statements regarding immigrant women is *not* true?
    a. Immigrant women suffer from unstable working conditions.
    b. Immigrant women are more likely than migrant men to be granted political asylum.
    c. Immigrant women are often victims of rape and other violent crimes.
    d. Immigrant women often face questions of identity and are torn between two cultures.

Short Answer   *Answer each question in three or four sentences.*

Soviet Collapse Releases Global Forces

1. How did the collapse of communism lead to civil war in Yugoslavia?

2. What economic problems continued to plague Russia after the collapse of communism?

3. What impact did the collapse of the Soviet Union have on the states of central Asia?

Global Opportunities Transcend the Nation-State

4. Describe some of the ways in which Europe has moved beyond the traditional nation-state.

5. In which ways did the European Union (EU) serve to unite Eastern and Western Europe?

6. What are some of the supranational organizations that globalization has spawned, and what effects do these have on developing nations?

Global Challenges and Discontents

7. What are some of the most prominent environmental concerns of the past two decades?

8. What was the significance of the growth of pan-Arabic Islam?

9. What caused Asian economic growth in the 1980s and 1990s? What global impacts did this growth have?

Global Culture and Society in the New Millennium

10. What was the influence of global migration in the late twentieth century?

11. How has the Internet affected Western society?

12. How has globalization affected Western culture?

BUILDING HISTORICAL SKILLS

Reading Maps   *Write a brief, paragraph-length response to each of the following questions based on* **Map 30.3: Countries of the Former Soviet Union, c. 2000** *(p. 1194).*

1. Why are the areas where violent ethnic conflicts occurred located in areas that broke away from the Soviet Union, and not, for example, within Russia to the east?

2. Why was the capital of the CIS placed in Minsk, a city in Belarus, and not in Moscow?

Reading Illustrations   *Write a brief, paragraph-length response to each of the following questions based on the illustration* **Europeans React to 9/11 Terror** *(p. 1209).*

1. What elements of a global culture are apparent in this picture?

2. In what ways are terrorist attacks, such as the one depicted here, unique to the late twentieth and early twenty-first century?

Reading Historical Documents   *Write a brief, paragraph-length response to each of the following questions based on the documents in your book.*

Petra Kelly, Activist for the Green Party (p. 1203)

1. How does the Green Party represent a departure from earlier forms of political activism?

2. How does the Green Party reaffirm older notions of the European Enlightenment?

Václav Havel, "Czechoslovakia Is Returning to Europe" (p. 1199)

3. What argument does Václav Havel make against claims that the lack of prosperity in Czechoslovakia would drag the European Union down?

4. What special insight does Czechoslovakia possess that Havel believes would be beneficial to the European Union?

Contrasting Views: The Debate over Globalization (pp. 1212–1213)

5. What are some of the various pros and cons of globalization presented here?

6. From what you have read here, who seems to benefit the most from globalization, and who seems to be at a disadvantage?

Answer Key

Chapter 14: Renaissance Europe, 1400–1500

CHAPTER OVERVIEW

Key Events

1. b; Portugal
2. d; The king of France gained more control of the church in his realm.
3. b; Germany
4. a; a revival of the crusading movement
5. a; A balance of power was established among the various Italian states.
6. b; The Tudor
7. c; Granada
8. c; The Atlantic world was divided between Spain and Portugal.
9. d; Portugal
10. b; The Medici

Key Terms

1. F; Renaissance (p. 505)
2. E; humanism (p. 507)
3. C; duchy (p. 523)
4. B; *conversos* (p. 528)
5. A; auto a fé (p. 528)
6. D; Gallicanism (p. 528)
7. G; tsar (p. 530)

Identification

1. Marsilio Ficino
2. China
3. 1000
4. Frankfurt-am-Main
5. the Bible
6. Sandro Botticelli
7. Jan van Eyck
8. Giovanni Pico della Mirandola
9. Leon Battista Alberti
10. Guillaume Dufay
11. Florence
12. Arno
13. Dowry Fund
14. abandoned children
15. government brothels
16. Visconti
17. Cesare Borgia
18. Charles the Bold
19. Louis XI
20. Constantinople
21. Calicut
22. 1512
23. Pedro Alvares Cabral
24. Aztec
25. Jacques Cartier

CHAPTER REVIEW

Multiple Choice

1. b	15. b	28. b
2. c	16. d	29. b
3. d	17. d	30. c
4. b	18. b	31. a
5. b	19. a	32. b
6. c	20. a	33. c
7. b	21. d	34. a
8. a	22. c	35. c
9. b	23. b	36. c
10. d	24. a	37. c
11. b	25. d	38. c
12. c	26. d	39. b
13. b	27. d	40. a
14. a		

Short Answer

Answers will vary.

1. Humanism expanded interest in human achievements and glory, both classical and contemporary. Humanists studied and supported the liberal arts or humanities. Rejecting the intricate logic and abstract language of scholastic philosophy, humanists advocated eloquence and style in their discourse, giving new vigor to the humanist curriculum of grammar, rhetoric, poetry, history, and moral philosophy. Humanists were a varied, largely middle-class group of professional scholars, high-ranking civil servants, rich patricians, notaries, and government officials. Humanist writers focused on classical history and literature in an attempt to emulate the glories of the ancient world. Humanist philosophers sought to harmonize the disciplines of Christian faith with ancient learning, such as with the philosophy of Plato.

2. The industrial production of paper and the commercial production of manuscripts were essential to the advent of printing. Papermaking came to Europe from China via Arab intermediaries. By the fourteenth century, paper mills operating in Italy were producing paper that was more fragile but much cheaper than parchment or vellum, the traditional surfaces used for writing in Europe. Consequently, the increase in paper production in the fourteenth and fifteenth centuries enabled a brisk industry in manuscript books to flourish in the university towns and major cities of Europe. Stationers organized *scriptoria*, workshops where manuscripts were copied by hand, bound as books, and sold. Generally, bookmaking remained slow and expensive, but the overall reduction in costs and the increased availability of books led Gutenberg to develop movable type.

3. In the 1440s, Johannes Gutenberg (c. 1400–1470), a German goldsmith, invented printing with movable type. Using durable metal molds, Gutenberg cast the letters of the alphabet individually; these letters were then arranged to represent the text of a page. Movable type allowed

entire manuscripts to be printed, since the imprint of each page was pressed on numerous sheets of paper with only a small amount of effort. This kind of printing spread rapidly from Germany to other European countries. Two German printers established the first press in Rome in 1467, and many other Italian cities had their own presses by 1480. The printing industry created a communications revolution, as the mass production of books and pamphlets made the world of letters more accessible to a literate audience.

4. Once perceived as artisans or hired workers, the best artists were recognized in the Renaissance as individuals with innate talents who created art according to their imaginations; they had "genius." As was the case in previous centuries, most artists of the fifteenth century relied on wealthy patrons for support, patrons who often directed or restricted the artists' work. Over the course of the fifteenth century, though, artists who gained great prestige negotiated with patrons to work without interference. Renaissance artists generally worked under any of three conditions: long-term service at princely courts; commissioned piecework; or production for the market. The commercial market for art began in the Low Countries and developed into a major force for artistic creativity because it gave artists greater freedom and the opportunity to work in an open and highly competitive public domain.

5. Renaissance art evoked classical works, but also saw the creation of new forms, as artists developed a more naturalistic style, especially in regard to the human body, and employed visual perspective, which united artistic creativity with scientific knowledge. Renaissance artists learned to depict ever more expressively human emotions and movements, and portraiture became increasingly popular, as Renaissance painting reflected a new, elevated view of human existence. Italian artists mastered perspective, which created an illusory three-dimensional space on a two-dimensional surface and the ordered arrangement of painted objects from one viewpoint. Renaissance artists strove to be "imitators of nature" and to achieve detail and reality theretofore unsurpassed.

6. During the Renaissance the northern European countries set the standards for musical styles. Guillaume Dufay (1400–1474) of the Low Countries was the leader in polyphonic composition, enjoying a successful career that took him to all the cultural centers of the Renaissance. His younger counterpart Johannes Ockeghem (c. 1420–1495) worked almost exclusively at the French court, but a mobile career was more common of polyphonic composers at this time. Josquin des Prez (1440–1521), another Netherlander, also traveled widely, writing music in Milan, Ferrar, Florence, and Paris. Within Renaissance polyphony there were three main musical genres: the canon of the Catholic Mass; the motet, which used both sacred and secular texts; and the secular *chanson*, which often used the tunes of folk dances. Human voices rather than musical instruments were generally used to express religious feeling in the more sacred compositions, whereas the tambourine and lute were indispensable for dances.

7. The data collected in the census reveal that Tuscany was one of the most urbanized regions of Europe. The capital city, Florence, contained 14 percent of the population and 67 percent of the state's wealth. The wealth was divided mostly between the "little people" (workers, artisans, and small merchants), who accounted for 60 percent of the households, and the "fat people" (wealthier merchants, leading artisans, notaries, doctors, and other professionals), who represented 30 percent of the households. A small number of slaves and domestic servants, both usually female, were at the very bottom of Florence's social hierarchy, while at the top, a tiny elite of patricians, bankers, and wool merchants controlled the state with their enormous wealth. According to the official survey, each household usually contained at least six inhabitants, with the form of the family unit (nuclear or extended) varying, generally according to wealth. Urban patricians and landowning peasants tended to live with their extended family. Wealthier families also had more children. It was also found that men outnumbered women in the Florentine state, but that statistical abnormality may have been a result of underreporting of women on the census.

8. Upper-class Florentine society traced descent and determining inheritance through the male line. Women were distinctly subordinate to men, and a daughter was able to claim inheritance only through her dowry. Italian marriages forged alliances between wealthy and prestigious families and were generally arranged by the male head of the household, and usually involved a young woman and an older man. This disparity in years left many Mediterranean women widowed at a young age, and those with children faced a difficult choice: to remarry at the request of their families and form new alliances or remain widows, as women could not bring their children to new marriages because children belonged to the families of their fathers. Marriage patterns were very different in northern Europe, where marital partners were much closer in age. Northern European women also had more authority over their own lives. They shared inheritances with their brothers, retained control of their dowries, and had the right to represent themselves before the law.

9. Sex in the fifteenth century often resulted in unwanted children, which created serious social problems. In 1445 the Florentine government opened the Ospedale degli Innocenti to help deal with the large number of abandoned children. These children, primarily girls, usually came from either poor families unable to feed another mouth or women who had given birth out of wedlock, often domestic slaves or servants impregnated by their masters. Although illegitimacy did not carry a social stigma for the man, it usually destroyed the woman's ability to marry, driving some mothers to infanticide in order to avoid public shame. Italian governments also addressed prostitution and homosexuality. A 1415 statute in Florence established government-regulated brothels. Homosexuality was not tolerated, and the government set fines for homosexual acts, even carrying out death sentences on men who had sex with young boys. Sexual violence against women was punished, although sentencing varied, with magistrates often treating noblemen with greater leniency and handling rape cases according to class distinctions between the attacker and the victim.

10. The four most powerful states in Renaissance Italy were the republics of Venice and Florence, and the principalities of Milan and Naples. Venice, a formidable sea power, enjoyed social tranquility internally, earning it the title of the "Most Serene Republic," but externally it was threatened by the duchy of Milan overland and the Ottoman Turks at sea. The republic of Florence was constantly engaged in civic strife as social classes and political factions created turbulence. Cosimo de Medici (1388–1464) and his family wielded enormous political influence in Florence by 1434. After being repeatedly driven from Florence in the late fifteenth and early sixteenth centuries, the Medici seized control of the republic in 1530 and declared Florence a duchy. Milan, the most powerful Italian principality, was a military state, dominated until 1447 by the Visconti dynasty. Their goal was to unify all of northern and central Italy, but they were opposed by the combined forces of Venice, Florence, and other Italian powers. The last Visconti duke died without a male heir, and the nobility proclaimed Milan a republic, but rebellion plagued this short-lived state, and Francesco Sforza entered Milan in triumph in 1450. His dynasty ruled Milan until 1494, when France invaded Italy. Between 1435 and 1494, the kingdoms of Naples and Sicily were ruled by the Aragonese Alfonso I and Ferante I. This dynasty struggled to dominate their powerful and often rebellious barons, but the greatest threat to the predominately rural kingdom of Naples was external: the Ottoman Turks from the east and France from the northwest. In 1480 Ottoman forces captured the Adriatic port of Otranto, massacring the entire male population; the French invasion of 1494 put an end to Aragonese rule entirely.

11. The most significant changes to shape the political and ethnic composition of the Iberian peninsula were the marriage of Isabella of Castile and Ferdinand of Aragon in 1469, the introduction of the Inquisition to Spain in 1478, the defeat of the Iberian Muslim state of Granada in 1492, and the expulsion of the Jews from Spain, also in 1492. The marriage of Isabella and Ferdinand was the first step in creating a unified Spain; the two monarchs retained their separate titles and the traditional laws and privileges of their regions, but they ruled jointly. In 1478, after more than a century of peace, war broke out between the Catholic royal forces and Muslim Granada, which finally fell in 1492, an event that forced many Moors to convert to Christianity or resettle elsewhere. Named "Catholic monarchs" by the pope, Ferdinand and Isabella made religion an instrument of state authority. Royal jurisdiction introduced the Inquisition to Spain in 1478, primarily as a means to control the *conversos*, Jewish converts to Christianity. In 1492 Ferdinand and Isabella ordered all Jews in their kingdoms to convert or be exiled. This expulsion from Spain dispersed the largest and most vibrant Jewish communities in Europe, creating thousands of Jewish refugees.

12. With the collapse of Mongol power, Ivan III (r. 1462–1505) expanded his territory and his power and claimed the imperial title *tsar* (or *czar*, from the name *Caesar*). In 1471, he defeated the northern Russian city-state of Novgorod with its vast territories, later abolishing its local civic government to consolidate his autocratic rule. He further expanded his territory to the south and east, forcing the Mongols back to the Volga River and claiming absolute property rights over all lands and subjects. The expansionist Muscovite state owed a spiritual and political debt to both the Byzantine Empire and the empire of the Mongols. After the fall of Byzantium, the tsar defended the Russian Orthodox Church against Islam and Catholicism, and Orthodox propaganda proclaimed Moscow to be the "Third Rome." The Mongol system of service to rulers, by which the prince's subjects were bound to him by life and blood and not by a contract of loyalty, greatly influenced Muscovite statecraft. In terms of fifteenth-century state building, the Muscovite princes created a state more in the despotic political tradition of the central Asian steppes and the Ottoman Empire than of western Europe.

13. The Portuguese focused their efforts on reaching India by sailing around Africa. In 1433 they began to explore the west African coast systematically. Bartholomeu Dias reached the Cape of Good Hope by 1478–1488, and Vasco da Gama led an expedition between 1497 and 1499 that rounded the cape and reached Calicut, India. By 1517 a chain of Portuguese forts dotted both the Indian Ocean and the west African coast. In 1455, Pope Nicholas V (r. 1447–1455) sanctioned Portuguese overseas expansion, commending the crusading spirit of King John II (r. 1481–1495) and granting him and his successors the monopoly on trade with the inhabitants of the newly "discovered" regions. Following the voyages of Christopher Columbus, however, Portuguese and Spanish interests clashed, so Pope Alexander VI mediated. The resulting Treaty of Tordesillas in 1494 divided the Atlantic world between the two royal houses, creating a demarcation line 370 leagues west of the Cape Verde Islands. The arrangement reserved the west African coast and the route to India for Portugal, giving Spain the oceans and lands to the west—except Brazil, which was claimed by Portugal in 1500.

14. Christopher Columbus (1451–1506) reached the Bahamas on October 12, 1492, believing he had reached the East Indies. He and his crew of ninety men established peaceful relations with the Arawak Indian communities they encountered, exchanging gifts of beads and broken glass for Arawak gold, and awing the Indians with their appearance and military technology. Despite Columbus's personal goodwill toward the Indians, evident from entries written in the ship's log, the Europeans' objectives were clear: find gold, subjugate the Indians, and propagate Christianity. When the second voyage of Columbus failed to find the anticipated gold mines and spices, the enterprise quickly switched its focus to finding slaves. Columbus and his crews of 1,200 to 1,500 men first enslaved the Caribs, the enemies of the Arawaks. In 1494 Columbus proposed a regular slave trade based in Hispaniola. Enslaved Indians were exported to Spain and sold, but the Spanish soon began importing sugarcane and forcing large numbers of Indians to work on plantations in Madeira, edging Columbus out of this new enterprise and the vast potential for material gain it offered.

15. The Aztecs, the Incas, and the Mayans were highly sophisticated societies native to the Americas, and all were subdued by the Spaniards as they built an empire that stretched from Mexico to Chile. The Aztecs and the Incas,

the largest political and social organizations of sedentary Indians, lived in the Mexican and Peruvian highlands, respectively. The Aztec civilization was based in a large, urban capital, Tenochtitlán, which was captured by Hernan Cortés (1485–1547) in 1519 with the help of other natives who had been subjugated by the Aztecs. Francisco Pizarro (c. 1475–1541), exploiting a civil war between rival Incan kings, conquered the Incas in the Andean highlands. The Mayans, located on the Yucatan peninsula, possessed a sophisticated knowledge of cosmology and arithmetic, but they too were subdued by the Spanish in the European conquest of the Americas.

BUILDING HISTORICAL SKILLS

Reading Maps

Answers will vary.

1. Europeans were familiar with Europe, the Middle East, and the North African coast. They were aware of, but less familiar with, parts of Asia, Iceland, Greenland, and a small portion of North America.

2. The only way that Europeans knew how to get to Asia was through the Middle East. With an enemy controlling this territory, trade was effectively blocked.

3. Although maritime exploration had begun with the goal of finding an alternate route to the East, it soon became evident that the Europeans were not aware of a large part of the earth's territory. Successive ocean voyages progressively revealed a larger and larger world. With the advent of better charts and navigational equipment as well as more technologically advanced vessels, long sea voyages became more feasible.

Reading Illustrations

Answers will vary.

1. When looking at this picture, the eye is drawn to the building in the background.

2. Although you may look at the religious procession in the foreground first, the slowly converging vertical lines in the pavement of the piazza pull the eyes back toward the building. The successive arches of the building lead the eyes even further back, toward the interior of the building.

3. The artist, Gentile Bellini, has used visual perspective and has gradually diminished the size of the human figures from the foreground to the background to create a sense of depth. Although painted on a two-dimensional canvas, the image gives the illusion of being a three-dimensional space. The painter has depicted this scene as the eye would see it; the figures are realistic and they "move" naturally across the Piazza San Marco, gracefully reflecting a myriad of human expressions and actions.

Reading Historical Documents

Answers will vary.

1. Rucellai tells his sons that "a true honor is one which is appreciated by all citizens," meaning that power should be used for the benefit of everyone. Although he does not mention the Medici by name, he says that "they" form

alliances, factions, and conspiracies, and "administer the state as if it were one's shop." According to Rucellai, desiring a political position in order to appropriate the wealth of a state is dishonest.

2. Compared to Machiavelli's view of power, Rucellai is more traditional. He values the common good, peace, equality, honesty, and humility, while scorning avarice (greed). These ethical values were based on Christian morality. Machiavelli, on the other hand, did not base political power in Christian morality or an ethical end.

3. Columbus claims a sense of fairness, forbidding his crew to trade worthless items for gold. He also wants to establish good relations with the Native Americans so that they could be led to become Christian and so that they can become good and loyal subjects of the Spanish king and queen.

4. Columbus describes the naiveté of the Native Americans, who "bartered like idiots." He also mentioned that gold is easily acquired, as the Native Americans will happily part with it in exchange for other goods. Despite their being naïve, he describes them as intelligent and capable of quickly understanding the Spaniards, which suggests the possibility of conversion. The possibility of conversion is also implied in his claim that Native Americans do not worship idols, but already believe that all good things come from heaven; such a belief could serve as a blank slate on which the Catholic faith could be written.

5. The nautical tide calendar provided sailors some accuracy in determining the hour of high tides, a necessity for ships that would be traveling close to coastal areas. A large vessel would need to avoid low tides so as not to run aground, marooning its crew and losing its cargo. The nautical solar guide provided a significant degree of accuracy to maritime navigation, enabling explorers to travel across wide expanses of water and still gauge their location with some assurance no matter the season or hemisphere.

6. Traditionally, the Portuguese have viewed their voyages of discovery on the Atlantic as glorious expeditions made by national heroes. They celebrate the technical innovations of Portuguese seamanship that made maritime exploration possible. Scholars have criticized this view because it overlooks the legacy of Portuguese colonialism, the conflicts between Portuguese explorers and the peoples they conquered and enslaved. By focusing only on the glory of Portuguese maritime exploration and the bravery and innovativeness of Portuguese mariners, the traditional view ignores the mistreatment of native inhabitants of the "discovered" lands and the plundering of resources and riches.

7. Historians are revising their view of Portuguese colonialism by looking more critically at historical evidence, with an aim to understanding the viewpoints of colonized peoples in Africa, Asia, and the Americas. For example, Sanjay Subrahmanyam, an Indian scholar, is examining the new level of violence that the maritime voyages of Vasco da Gama brought to the Indian Ocean with his attacks on Muslim shipping. The Scientific Committee of the Discoveries, headed by António Manuel Hespanha, is reveal-

ing the complex, multicultural aspects of colonialism that reach beyond the conventional, oversimplified, and narrowly conceived heroic interpretation traditionally held by the Portuguese.

Chapter 15: The Struggle for Reformation Europe, 1500–1560

CHAPTER OVERVIEW

Key Events

1. c; More's *Utopia*
2. d; 8 years
3. c; 29 years
4. c; 28 years
5. d; 18 years
6. c; 65 years
7. d; The sale of indulgences and church office
8. d; Luther's and Zwingli's
9. b; John Calvin
10. d; The papacy would not allow him to divorce.
11. d; The Jesuits
12. c; The Catholic church reconciled itself with the Protestant church.
13. a; The Habsburgs and Valois

Key Terms

1. C; Evangelicals (p. 548)
2. H; Protestants (p. 548)
3. D; indulgence (p. 549)
4. B; Christian humanists (p. 550)
5. G; predestination (p. 558)
6. A; Anabaptists (p. 561)
7. I; Vulgate (p. 562)
8. F; parish (p. 563)
9. E; infidel (p. 567)

Identification

1. Thomas More
2. Desiderius Erasmus
3. Charles V
4. Basel
5. indulgences
6. Worms
7. Zurich
8. Marburg
9. John Calvin
10. 1534
11. Thomas Müntzer
12. 1522
13. Juan Luis Vives
14. Henry VIII
15. Pieruigi da Palestrina
16. Titian
17. Vienna
18. Jakob Fugger
19. Catherine of Aragon
20. 1555
21. Pope Paul III
22. 1563
23. Ignatius Loyola
24. Japan
25. Mesican Ecclesiastical Provincial Council

CHAPTER REVIEW

Multiple Choice

1.	d	15.	c	28.	c
2.	c	16.	d	29.	a
3.	b	17.	c	30.	a
4.	d	18.	b	31.	d
5.	c	19.	d	32.	a
6.	d	20.	a	33.	a
7.	c	21.	c	34.	c
8.	a	22.	b	35.	a
9.	c	23.	a	36.	b
10.	c	24.	c	37.	a
11.	a	25.	c	38.	d
12.	b	26.	b	39.	a
13.	c	27.	a	40.	b
14.	c				

Short Answer

Answers will vary.

1. In the early sixteenth century, Muslim Turks were advancing on Christian Europe; Christian princes were fighting among themselves; and corruption and abuse existed within the church itself. The sanctity of the priestly office was compromised by clergy who sold indulgences, demanded sexual or monetary favors in return for forgiveness, and concocted "miracles." All of this led many to believe that the Last Judgment was imminent. In the face of widespread uncertainty and intense spiritual anxiety, many people intensified their search for religious comfort. Such religious fervor popularized pilgrimages, personal acts of devotion, the publishing of vernacular prayer books, and the building of new shrines. Critical of the Catholic church and its leaders, certain bishops and intellectuals led reform efforts, but their results were generally limited to specific monastic houses and dioceses. Laypeople yearned for a religion more meaningful to their daily lives and for a more responsive and moral clergy. They donated money to establish new preacherships for university-trained clerics who were schooled in Christian humanism and critical of the established church. Yet, even though these Christian humanists called for reforms, their appeals went mostly unheeded and the European crisis of faith continued to grow, setting the stage for the Reformation.

2. Desiderius Erasmus (c. 1466–1536) was a renowned humanist on intimate terms with kings and popes. Dedicating his life to scholarship, he believed that individuals could reform themselves and society only through education. Many of his books offered critiques and criticisms of contemporary society. In *Adages* (1500), a collection of quotations from ancient literature, he offered his witty and wise commentaries on the human experience. In the *Colloquies* (1523), a compilation of Latin dialogues, he exerted his wit to criticize the morals of his time, lamenting poor table manners, and mocking the corruption of the clergy and the ambitions of Christian princes. In his *Handbook of the Militant Christian* (1503), Erasmus made an eloquent plea for a unified, peaceful Christendom and a simple religion devoid of greed and the lust for power. In *The Praise*

of Folly (1509), he satirized contemporary values of pomposity, power, and wealth and encouraged a return to the true Christian virtues of modesty, humility, and poverty. He spent years translating a new Latin edition of the New Testament from the original Greek. Erasmus also instructed the future emperor Charles V. Challenged by angry, younger men with radical ideas during the Reformation, Erasmus chose Christian unity over reform and schism. He lived his last years isolated from the Protestant community, with his writings condemned in Rome and ignored by many leaders of the Catholic church.

3. Thomas More (1478–1535) believed that social injustice bred crime and warfare and that politics, property, and war fueled human misery. His work, *Utopia*, describes an imaginary land and was intended as a critique of English society. A just, equitable, and hard-working community, Utopia was the opposite of England. There was no need for money, and greed and private property disappeared as everyone worked the land for two years. Utopians enjoyed public schools, communal kitchens, hospitals, and nurseries. There was neither crime nor war in Utopia, although Utopians, when pressed, would protect their way of life fiercely. The community had few laws, goods being equally distributed, and people dedicated to the pursuit of knowledge and natural religion. More's idealized community sought to resolve many of the problems facing sixteenth-century English society. His narrative envisioned a better future, offering solutions and alternatives to the mounting troubles and turmoil of contemporary life.

4. In 1520, Martin Luther composed three treatises criticizing the church and calling for reform. The first, *Freedom of a Christian*, was written in Latin and addressed to Pope Leo X. Luther argued that faith alone, not good works, would save sinners, and sharply distinguished between the Gospel's teachings and invented church doctrines. Luther wrote of "the priesthood of all believers," arguing that the Bible held all the doctrines necessary for Christians, who did not, therefore, need professional priests. *Freedom of a Christian* made "by faith alone," "by Scripture alone," and "the priesthood of all believers" central tenets of the Reformation. Luther's second treatise, *To the Nobility of the German Nation,* was written in German and had a nationalistic appeal: he condemned the Roman church's corruption and called on the German princes to defend their nation and reform the church. His third major treatise, *On the Babylonian Captivity of the Church*, was composed in Latin and was intended for a mainly clerical audience; it condemned the papacy as the embodiment of the Antichrist.

5. While Luther provided the religious leadership for the German reform movement, the chief preacher of the Swiss city of Zurich, Huldrych Zwingli (1484–1531), led the Swiss reform movement. In 1520, criticizing Switzerland's export of mercenary soldiers Zwingli openly declared himself a reformer; attacked church rituals and the corruption of the ecclesiastical hierarchy; and condemned his superior, Cardinal Matthew Schinner, for sending Switzerland's young men off to serve in papal armies. Deeply influenced by Erasmus, Zwingli adopted the Dutch humanist's vision of social renewal through education. Zwingli made education part of the theocratic society that he set up and ruled in Zurich, uniting religion, politics, and morality. Zwingli did not tolerate opposition, neither did he stop short of execution to root out dissent. Unlike Luther, Zwingli equated the ideal citizen with the perfect Christian. Luther and Zwingli also differed in their views of the role of the Eucharist since Zwingli perceived the Holy Communion as simply a symbol of Christ's union with believers. Troubled by these differences, evangelical princes and magistrates assembled the major reformers at Marburg in 1529. After several days, the north German and Swiss reformers resolved many issues, but still disagreed on the nature of the Eucharist, so the two movements continued on separate paths.

6. John Calvin (1509–1564) had been converted to the Reformation through the influence of the leading French humanists. Fleeing France following the Affair of the Placards, Calvin was convinced by the local reformer Guillaume Farel to remain in Geneva. Under Calvin's leadership, Geneva became a strict Christian theocratic republic. Calvin published *The Institutes of the Christian Religion* in 1536, the first reformer to organize and codify the doctrines, organization, history, and practices of a reformation Christianity. Calvin advanced the idea that if God is almighty and humans cannot earn their salvation by good works, then no Christian can be certain of salvation. This doctrine of predestination argued that God had ordained every man, woman, and child to salvation or damnation even before the creation of the world. Despite the only few "elect" preordained for salvation, Calvin demanded rigorous discipline of all. Calvin's Geneva fused church and society into what followers named the "Reformed church." With a very low rate of extramarital births and less crime than other cities, supporters praised the community, but critics noted Calvin's despotism; for instance, having no toleration for dissenters, Calvin arranged the execution of his critic, Michael Servetus, in 1553. Nonetheless, Calvinism spread across Europe, becoming the established form of the Reformation in many countries.

7. Both the Peasants' War of 1525 and the Anabaptist movement challenged the social order of the Holy Roman Empire and were eventually crushed by political and religious authorities. After 1520, many city governments, under intense popular pressure or in sympathy, allowed reformers to sweep away established church authority but, in 1525, the erosion of traditional authority exploded in a massive rural uprising that threatened the entire social order. In recognition of Luther's anticlerical message, many peasants in southern and central Germany, joined by some urban workers and artisans, rose in rebellion, plundering monasteries and refusing to pay church taxes. They demanded village autonomy, the abolition of serfdom, and the right to appoint their own pastors. Some even called for the destruction of the entire ruling class. In response to this anticlerical fervor, German princes fought and defeated peasant armies all over the empire. Even Luther, who originally had tried to mediate the conflict, eventually advocated killing the rebels in order to restore social order. In Zurich, the Anabaptists, a pacifist group wanting to create a community of true Christians modeled after the first Christians of the Bible, challenged Zwingli. The Anabaptists believed in adult baptism and

rejected the authority of courts and magistrates. Zwingli attacked them for their refusal to bear arms and swear oaths of allegiance and, unable to convert the group, urged Zurich magistrates to put Anabaptists to death. Nevertheless, the Anabaptist movement spread quickly to many cities in southern Germany. Although defeated at Münster, the Anabaptist movement was maintained in northwestern Europe by the determined pacifist leadership of the Dutch reformer Menno Simons (1469–1561).

8. By the latter Middle Ages, two new social trends had emerged: a new work ethic arose simultaneously with a growing hostility toward the poor and the widespread poverty brought about by population growth and spiraling inflation. Rejecting the traditional notions that the poor played a central role in the Christian moral economy and that charity and prayers united the rich and the poor, sixteenth-century moralists decried the crime and sloth of vagabonds, distinguishing them from the genuine poor, or "God's Poor." The new work ethic acquired a distinctly Protestant flavor, equating laziness and poverty with a lack of moral worth and linking hard work and prosperity with piety and divine providence. By the sixteenth century, most secular governments—whether Catholic or Protestant—began to take over institutions of public charity from the church, restructuring relief for the poor on the local and national levels. Instead of using decentralized, public initiative, magistrates appointed officials to head urban agencies that would certify the genuine poor and distribute welfare funds to them. Public relief became a permanent feature of Protestant governments because private charity ceased to be one of the good works that were once thought necessary to earn salvation. In Catholic lands, however, collective charity persisted, supported by a theology of good works, by societies more sharply divided between the noble rich and the poor, and by the elites' sense of social responsibility.

9. In their effort to establish social order and discipline, Protestant reformers decried sexual immorality and glorified the family. Protestant magistrates established marital courts, passed new marriage laws, closed brothels, and gave harsher punishments for sexual deviance. In order to suppress common-law marriages, which were common practice before the Reformation, they declared that a marriage was legitimate only if it had been registered by an official and a pastor and, in many Protestant countries, parental consent was required as well. Although favoring reconciliation to preserve the integrity of the family, Protestant law stipulated that women could seek divorce for desertion, impotence, and flagrant abuse. For Protestant women, the Reformation brought limitations. The closure of convents meant that their only option was marriage, and as wives in a patriarchal family they were expected to be obedient, helpful companions; loving mothers; and God-fearing Christians. The Catholic church also sought to reinforce the institution of marriage, especially after the Council of Trent. As in Protestant communities, Catholic common-law marriages were suppressed and marriages were required to be registered by a parish priest. Unlike with Protestantism, Catholic doctrine condemned divorce. Catholic women, despite the increased control over marriage, could still avail themselves of lives of authority and relative independence as nuns and abbesses in convents.

10. French claims over Italian territories lit the fuse that began the Italian Wars, starting a conflict between the Valois dynasty (ruling France) and the Habsburg dynasty (ruling various lands, including the Holy Roman Empire and Spain). The fighting began in 1494 when France invaded Italy and lasted until 1559. The Habsburgs seemed triumphant during the 1520s, crushing the French army at Pavia in 1525 and capturing their king, Francis I (r. 1515–1547). Francis signed a treaty renouncing all claims to Italy to gain his freedom, but he quickly repudiated the agreement once released, which renewed the fighting. Scandalizing many Christians, Francis I formed an alliance with Turkish Sultan Suleiman I (r. 1530–1566) and the Ottomans, a new political strategy that saw religion as but one factor in power politics. Emperor Charles V (r. 1520–1558), angered by the pope's allegiance with France, went so far as to capture Rome in 1527. The 1530s and 1540s saw more indecisive and expensive battles, and Charles V was increasingly distracted by problems with the German Protestants. Eventually, years of fighting drained the treasuries of all monarchs involved, and the ensuing financial crises forced Spain and France to sign the Treaty of Cateau-Cambrésis in 1559. Other European powers were drawn into this Franco-Spanish struggle. Some, such as England, sought power, first siding with France and then with Spain; the papacy and the Italian states fought for independence; and the Protestant princes in Germany chose sides for religious reasons and exploited the conflict to extract liberties from the emperor. The Ottoman Turks used the Italian Wars to expand their territory.

11. England and Scotland both had a small minority of Protestants in the early sixteenth century, but Protestants would come to dominate both by about 1560; England due to the leadership of its monarchs, and Scotland through the will of powerful noble clans. In England, Henry VIII (r. 1509–1547) firmly opposed and suppressed the Reformation until 1527, when his request for a papal dispensation to annul his marriage to Catherine of Aragon and marry Anne Boleyn was denied. Needing a male heir, Henry allied with the small but influential noble faction of Protestants, appointing two of them, Cromwell and Cranmer, as chancellor and archbishop of Canterbury, respectively. From 1529 to 1536, Parliament passed a number of acts, including the Act of Supremacy, effectively severing ties between the English church and Rome. This reformed Church of England retained much of the traditional Catholic doctrine and ritual, but the principle of royal supremacy in religious matters would remain a lasting feature of Henry's reforms. Although Henry's son Edward VI (r. 1547–1553) furthered the Reformation, his first daughter (by Catherine of Aragon), Mary Tudor, restored Catholicism and persecuted English Protestants. Only with the long reign of Henry's other daughter (by Anne Boelyn), Elizabeth I, who succeeded Mary to the throne in 1558, did the Protestant cause gain momentum once again, eventually defining the character of England. In Scotland, the Protestants were a small minority until the 1550s, when their cause gained support in opposition to the queen regent, Mary of Guise, who cultivated a pro-French, Catholic atmosphere after

the death of her husband James V in 1542. In so doing, she alienated many Scottish noblemen, who joined the pro-English, anti-French, Protestant cause. John Knox (1514–1572), the most prominent Scottish reformer, contributed further to Mary's problems, publishing a diatribe against the "monstrous" rule of women in 1558. In 1560, the Protestants assumed control of the Scottish Parliament and Mary of Guise fled to England.

12. Repeatedly challenged by German Protestant princes, Charles V made numerous efforts to resolve the religious conflicts within the Holy Roman Empire. In 1541, Charles convened the Imperial Diet at Regensburg in the hope of patching up the theological differences between Protestants and Catholics, but negotiations broke down rapidly. War broke out between the Schmalkaldic League, a group of Protestant princes and cities, and the Emperor in 1547. Quickly defeating the league and capturing the leading Lutheran princes, Charles proclaimed the "Interim," which restored Catholics' right to worship in Protestant lands while permitting Lutherans to practice their own religious rites. While Protestant resistance to the Interim was strong, imperial power also frightened some Catholics, including Pope Julius III, who feared the imperial subjugation of Rome. Protestant princes rebelled against Charles again in 1552, this time joining a former imperial ally, Duke Maurice of Saxony. Practically bankrupt and unprepared for this new confrontation, Charles agreed to the Peace of Augsburg in 1555, which recognized the Evangelical (Lutheran) church, accepted the secularization of church lands while "reserving" the existent ecclesiastical territories for Catholics and, most important, established the principle that all princes—whether Catholic or Lutheran—enjoyed the sole right to determine the religion of their lands and subjects. Resigning his thrones in 1555 and 1556, Charles retired to a monastery, and the Augsburg settlement preserved a fragile peace in central Europe until 1618, but the exclusion of Calvinists planted the seeds for future conflict.

13. The Council of Trent (1545 to 1563) was convened by Pope Paul III and Emperor Charles V and met sporadically from 1545 to 1563. The council reasserted the supremacy of clerical authority over the laity, and provided for a more competent and responsive clergy by requiring bishops to reside in their dioceses and that seminaries be established in each diocese to train priests. It also reaffirmed church doctrine such as the sacrament of the Eucharist, confirming that the bread actually becomes Christ's body during the Mass. Concerning marriage, the council stipulated that all weddings must henceforth take place in churches and be registered by the parish clergy. It further declared that all marriages remain valid, explicitly rejecting the Protestant allowance for divorce. By refusing to compromise with Protestant positions on issues such as the Eucharist and divorce, the Council of Trent marked a permanent the schism between Protestantism and Catholicism.

14. The Society of Jesus, or the Jesuits, was founded by Ignatius of Loyola (1491–1556), a Spanish nobleman who, after being injured in battle, gave up his quest for military glory in 1521 in favor of service to the church. Young men gravitated to this charismatic figure, attracted by his austerity and piety. Due in part to his noble background and the intercession of a cardinal, Ignatius gained a hearing before the pope in 1540 and the church officially recognized his small band of followers as a new religious order. The Jesuits became the most vigorous defenders of papal authority and quickly expanded. They established hundreds of colleges throughout the Catholic world, educating generations of future leaders. Jesuits also served as missionaries, playing a key role in the global Portuguese maritime empire and bringing Roman Catholicism to Africans, Asians, and native Americans. The Jesuits and other new religious orders helped to restore the confidence of the faithful in the dedication and power of the Catholic church in the face of Protestantism.

15. Successful missionary efforts, seen as proof of the truth of Roman Catholicism and a sign of divine favor, were achieved by different methods in different parts of the world. Most missionaries focused on winning over local elites—the native lords of the Americas, African nobles, the Confucian scholar-officials in China, and the Japanese samurai (the warrior aristocracy). The Portuguese, to ensure rapid Christianization, were willing to train indigenous peoples as missionaries; young African nobles, like Dom Henry (son of King Afonso I of Kongo), actually went to Portugal to be trained in theology. Despite this example, however, Christian missionaries in the Americas and Africa were commonly inclined to preach "with the sword," an attitude criticized by individuals like the Dominican Bartolome de Las Casas (1474–1566), and the Catholic church in Spanish America remained overwhelmingly European in its clerical staffing. Unfortunately, after an initial period of relatively little racial discrimination, the Catholic church in the Americas and Africa adopted strict rules based on color. The first Mexican Ecclesiastical Provincial Council in 1555 declared that holy orders were not to be conferred on Indians, mestizos, and mulattoes or on descendants of Moors, Jews, and those who had been sentenced by the Spanish Inquisition. Missionaries in Asia, lacking immediate military backing, used the sermon rather than the sword to win converts, and the success of people like Francis Xavier prepared the ground for future missionary successes in Japan and China.

BUILDING HISTORICAL SKILLS

Reading Maps

Answers will vary.

1. England, Scotland, Norway, Sweden, and Denmark were predominantly Protestant by 1560 as was much of the northeastern part of the Holy Roman Empire and the northern part of the Swiss Confederation. Protestantism was also growing in Poland, parts of Hungary, and had made inroads into Bohemia. Spain and the Italian states were untouched by the Protestant Reformation as was much of the southern and central region of the Holy Roman Empire. Most of France was also unaffected, although large parts of the south and east were influenced by Calvinism.

2. England, although mostly Anglican, contained scattered pockets where Calvinist influences were strong and it was also bordered by largely Catholic Ireland. Likewise, although France was mostly Catholic, large areas, especially in the south, were strongly influenced by Calvinism, making a future struggle over religion likely. Finally, eastern Europe possessed a large mixed area; inhabitants of Austria, Hungary, Poland, Bohemia, and Lithuania could suffer religious strife as demographics shifted and established authorities exerted more spiritual control.

Reading Illustrations

Answers will vary.

1. The engraving shows an armor-clad, solemn-faced knight riding on horseback through a desolate forest; in the background rises a castle, or perhaps a cathedral. A dog accompanies him, his horse's stride is steady and majestic, and he is armed with a mighty lance and a fearsome sword; he seems a formidable opponent. But, even so, he is confronted by a devil wielding a pike and a second, mounted, demonic figure holding an hourglass.

2. The demonic figure on horseback with the hourglass is meant to represent death. The shifting sands of the hourglass symbolize the passage of time. Traditionally, death comes to an individual when his or her "sands of time" run out.

3. Regardless of the religious conflicts caused by the Reformation, all Christians believed that the reward for true religious faith and a righteous Christian life was the everlasting salvation of heaven. If the knight were interpreted as a pious and devoted Christian traveling through the desolate and dangerous wasteland that is life, beset by demons of worldly temptation and always facing the inevitability of his own death, then the castle in the background might be construed as eternal salvation, the knight's ultimate destination. To stay true to his goal and not be unnecessarily waylaid in his journey toward salvation, the knight must not be distracted by temptations confronting him along the way because these are only obstacles to his attaining true religious faith and, therefore, salvation.

Reading Historical Documents

Answers will vary.

1. Erasmus views Luther as a "brother of Christ" who possesses a "clarity of intellect" and whose letters "breathe with a Christian spirit." He seems to view Luther as a humanist ally against the university theologians for whom theology is "more important than Christ."

2. Erasmus is being blamed for being the "standard-bearer" of Luther's party and is concerned that his association with Luther might ruin his reputation. More important, he is concerned with "humane letters," which the theologians might now have a handle to destroy.

3. Erasmus states that the theologians should first read Luther's work before passing judgment on it. He says that such matters should not be solved by the common herd, but by learned men in published books. This reflects Erasmus's belief in the free exchange of ideas and the importance of learning in public debate.

4. Utopia is a patriarchal society in which the father is the head of the household. Equality and fairness are also important values. The towns are divided into equal districts, so no neighborhood is better than another, and everyone has equal access to the necessities of life.

5. More claims that no living creature, including humans, is naturally greedy except from fear of want. Thus the unequal distribution of the necessities of life creates greed in people. Greed is also created by vanity, which lets one believe he or she is better than others if that person can display superfluous property.

6. Effective popular propaganda in sixteenth-century Europe consisted of pamphlets, woodcuts, and broadsheets that often had prominent visual images.

7. The printing press made it possible for large numbers of pamphlets, woodcuts, and broadsheets to be produced cheaply, thus allowing them to be more widely distributed to and read by a larger audience.

8. Images played an important role in making propaganda appealing and meaningful to a largely illiterate or semi-literate society. Those who could not read Latin, or even German, could easily understand the symbolism of images and clearly identify with the causes that they had inspired. Representations of Martin Luther standing in victory over his Catholic opponent—depicted as the biblical Leviathan in Matthias Gnidias's 1521 woodcut, and as a holy monk guided by divine inspiration, represented by a dove, in the anonymous 1521 woodcut—presented positive images of Luther and the work of reformers, and were accessible and comprehensible as such to a wide audience. The seven-headed Luther, on the other hand, portrayed a negative image.

Chapter 16: A Century of Crisis, 1560–1648

CHAPTER OVERVIEW

Key Events

1. c; The battle of Lepanto
2. b; Huguenots
3. d; Allow limited religious freedoms to French Huguenots
4. d; It encouraged rebellion against unjust governments.
5. b; His belief that the Earth revolved around the sun
6. b; English Puritans
7. c; The Peace of Westphalia

Key Terms

1. C; Huguenot (p. 582)
2. F; *politiques* (p. 585)
3. E; Moriscos (p. 587)
4. G; Puritans (p. 589)
5. H; *raison d'êtat* (p. 597)
6. K; tithe (p. 601)
7. J; secularization (p. 606)
8. D; mannerism (p. 607)
9. A; baroque (p. 607)
10. B; heliocentrism (p. 612)
11. I; scientific method (p. 611)

Identification

1. Henry II
2. Guise
3. Gaspard Coligny
4. Philip II of Spain
5. Lepanto
6. Prague
7. Christian IV
8. Cardinal Richelieu
9. Gustavus Adolphus
10. Edict of Restitution
11. Virginia
12. Dutch
13. French
14. Muscovy
15. Mediterranean
16. El Greco
17. Jean Bodin
18. Hugo Grotius
19. Tycho Brahe
20. Paracelsus

CHAPTER REVIEW

Multiple Choice

1.	c	12.	c	23.	b
2.	b	13.	c	24.	c
3.	c	14.	c	25.	a
4.	c	15.	b	26.	b
5.	d	16.	c	27.	c
6.	d	17.	a	28.	b
7.	d	18.	a	29.	d
8.	d	19.	c	30.	d
9.	b	20.	a	31.	a
10.	a	21.	c	32.	a
11.	c	22.	a		

Short Answer

Answers will vary.

1. Because political power and religion were closely intertwined, political motives and religious beliefs were almost inseparable. In France, the battle between Huguenots and Catholics reflected political disputes among noble families—especially the Bourbon and Guise families—for influence over the French monarchy. The French Wars of Religion contained distinctly political elements and the opposing sides of the war mirrored both religious and political ties among the nobility. Religion also inspired independence movements such as in the Netherlands, where Protestants challenged the political dominance of their Catholic rulers. In England, Elizabeth I had her Catholic cousin Mary, Queen of Scots, executed for fomenting plots against her. In response, Mary's ally, Philip II of Spain, launched an invasion of England that was characterized as a Catholic crusade. In eastern Europe, the struggle between Ottoman Turks and Spain was, in part, a battle between Islam and Christianity and, in part, a battle for dominance over the Mediterranean.

2. As a result of the wars over religion, power began to shift from southern and eastern Europe toward the north and west. Alliances were formed between states that shared the same religious outlook, as when the Netherlands used its wealth and power to support Protestants in other countries and Catholics worked together to defeat Protestantism such as Philip II's support of the Catholic League in France and Mary, Queen of Scots in England. Religion also provided new justifications to challenge political authority as French Protestants proclaimed that they had a right to resist a tyrant who worshiped idols. This notion of "constitutionalism" was tied to the idea of a contract that bound the ruler with his subjects, which required the ruler, among other things, to uphold the true religion.

3. Religious toleration strengthened countries by preserving them from costly civil wars. Elizabeth I avoided the extremes of Protestantism and Catholicism and was able to pass on a strong and unified state to her successor, James I. The Edict of Nantes helped Henry IV create a strong French state by pacifying a significant minority. Religious toleration in the Dutch Republic went hand in hand with its widespread trading and cooperative system of government and made it a leader in intellectual and scientific achievement. Poland-Lithuania avoided debilitating religious wars that would have left it open to invasion like its neighbor the Holy Roman Empire. By contrast, the expense and social strife caused by Philip II's constant wars against non-Catholics was one element causing the dimming of Spanish power by the beginning of the sixteenth century.

4. The Thirty Years' War accelerated the growth of governments by increasing the size of armies and the bureaucracies that ran them. States required more revenue to support their armies; thus they needed more people to supervise tax collection, supply their soldiers, and to repress the uprisings that resulted from higher taxation. Many of these new professional bureaucrats had university education in law. As bureaucracies increased, power was centralized, and monarchs increased the size of their courts and palaces in order to present an image of great royal power. Like maintaining armies, these courts also required a vast sum of tax money, thereby further increasing the power of the bureaucracy. Increasingly massive governmental bureaucracies required managers, so government ministers—like Cardinal Richelieu in France—became extremely powerful.

5. The Thirty Years' War was the last major European war ignited by a religious conflict. During the war, the governments involved shifted decisively from fighting over religion to fighting over state power. This shift is visible in the way that the Catholic French government gave money to Swedish Protestant Gustavus Adolphus to support him against the Catholic armies of the Habsburgs. Similarly, the French also supported the Calvinist Dutch in their war for independence from France's political enemy Spain. Political power, or the *raison d'état* (meaning the state's interests were more important than any other), replaced religion as the main motivation for European wars.

6. The Thirty Years' War devastated the world of ordinary people, especially those who were caught between rival armies. These armies were often mercenary, and the states they fought for sometimes left them unpaid and poorly supplied; they therefore ransacked the countryside to support themselves. There were many sieges and numerous incidents of towns being repeatedly sacked as first one side, then the other took control. Ordinary Europeans were victims and witnesses of destruction and horrific brutality. Some of this brutality is recounted in one of the earliest German novels, *Adventures of a Simpleton*, by Hans Grimmelshausen, which describes the horrors of the war inflicted on the peasants of Europe. Even those who were not directly in the path of the warring armies suffered

from the back-breaking taxes that states collected from them in order to finance the war.

7. Several converging factors caused the European recession of the early 1600s. Among them were a stagnating or declining population, a leveling off and dropping of prices, the slowing of the influx of precious metals from the New World after 1625, and declining agricultural yields. A change in the climate toward colder weather contributed to the decline in agriculture. The demands of the Thirty Years' War also had an impact, with the high taxation demanded by the states participating in the war causing even greater burden on the economy and particularly on the peasantry. The devastation and dislocation brought by the war also affected the economy. An estimated one-fourth of the inhabitants of the Holy Roman Empire died in the 1630s and 1640s, which created a loss in both labor and demand.

8. As a result of the economic crisis, the balance of power shifted from the southern Mediterranean economies to the northern countries of Europe. The negative impact of declining imports of precious metals did not affect northern countries like England and the Dutch Republic as much as it did Spain, since they were not as dependent upon these resources. England remained unscathed by the Thirty Years' War, whereas many of the regions of the south took decades to recover from the devastation. The Dutch Republic also benefited from having the most efficient agricultural system in Europe, which shielded them from the agricultural decline that affected other regions. Overall, the French, English, and Dutch began to dominate trade and overtook the Italian and Spanish cities that had previously dominated the European economy.

9. The economic recession created a great deal of suffering for the majority of ordinary people in Europe. It increased the likelihood of food shortages and thereby the prevalence of malnutrition, famine, and disease. Food shortages and recession caused people to limit the number of children they had, mainly through delaying marriage. Women lost some of their economic independence and many people left their homes to look for better conditions or charity. Over the long term, the economic crisis increased the division between prosperous and poor peasants.

10. Secularization was a long-term process that occurred in the countries that progressed economically during this period—England, the Dutch Republic and, to some extent France—in which religion became a matter of private conscience rather than public policy. Although it did not entail a loss of religious faith, it prompted a search for nonreligious explanations for political authority and natural phenomena. Nonreligious subjects were depicted more frequently in the visual arts, and scientists such as Kepler and Galileo sought laws in nature to explain movements in the heavens and on Earth. Political theorists such as Jean Bodin discussed types of governments in the abstract, which implied that they might be subject to choice rather than divinely ordained, while Hugo Grotius argued for a natural law of government that stood beyond secular or divine authority.

11. The new trends in scientific thought emphasized systematic experimentation and rational deduction over a reliance on ancient learning and church theology. While religion and the supernatural were still important, they were no longer the central explanation for natural phenomena. The advance of scientific thought eventually led to the end of witchcraft trials, as the evidence used for them was called into question and authorities began to suspect that accusations were based more on peasant superstitions. These breakthroughs in scientific thought did not, however, completely replace beliefs in magic. Many scientists, such as Paracelsus who helped establish the modern science of pharmacology, continued to practice magic, alchemy, and astrology. Overall, the new trends in scientific thought occurred alongside religion and beliefs in magic.

12. Two new forms of artistic expression developed to express secular values during this period: professional theater and opera. The plays of William Shakespeare did not refer to religious disputes, but reflected on contemporary concerns on the nature of power by setting them in faraway times and places. Opera combined music, drama, dance, and scenery usually with themes chosen to please the ruler and aristocracy. These themes were sometimes religious but were often drawn from familiar stories. The visual arts also reflected trends in political and religious thought. Dutch painters such as Rembrandt van Rijn occasionally used biblical subjects but more often depicted scenes from everyday life. Baroque art, which was preeminent in Catholic countries, was a sensationalistic style that featured exaggerated curves and lighting, and a release from restraint to reaffirm dramatically the Catholic faith and the monarchy.

BUILDING HISTORICAL SKILLS

Reading Maps

Answers will vary.

1. Philip controlled much of the western Mediterranean. He ruled Spain and Portugal, southern Italy and parts of the North African coastline. He also ruled much of the eastern, southern, and northwestern parts of the Holy Roman Empire. In addition, he had several colonies in North and South America, on the east and west coasts of Africa, in India, and in Asia.

2. Part of Spain's possessions included the Dutch Republic, which had a large Protestant population. This would have caused conflict as the devoutly Catholic Spanish monarchy tried to limit Protestantism there. Countries like France, which were largely surrounded by the Spanish, would have viewed them as a threat. Spain's vast overseas empire would have fostered rivalries with other European powers.

Reading Illustrations

Answers will vary.

1. The fact that a prayerbook shows the monarch praying shows a unity between religion and the state. There are several royal emblems here, such as the sword, the scepter, and the crown. The crown is placed higher than the prayerbook, symbolizing the fact that the state was above the church.

2. This picture shows the queen as a pious person. She is dressed in rich clothing, and surrounded by symbols of power.

Reading Historical Documents

Answers will vary.

1. Galileo states that too few people seek the truth and that most people follow mistaken methods. He complains that he has observed many natural phenomena that cannot be explained by accepted theory. He also expresses concern over the fact that many individuals who introduce new ideas and theories suffer a bad end, such as Copernicus, who was being mocked for his ideas.

2. Scientists like Galileo and Kepler established personal friendships and exchanged gifts such as books. They kept in contact by writing letters over long distances.

3. Grimmelshausen's description emphasizes the senselessness of the violence, characterizing the destruction as being purposeless to the soldiers and even detrimental to them because they were destroying things that they would have been able to use. The horrific crimes of rape and torture were also described as senseless, since the peasants did not have any information or possessions the soldiers could use.

4. Grimmelshausen seems to find religious warfare to be senseless. He shows how innocent people suffered during this war who probably did not care one way or another about the religious issues at stake, but would rather have lived in peace. Like the sacking of the village, the Thirty Years' War caused a lot of unnecessary havoc and devastation that, in the long run, did not resolve anything. By the end of the war, religion had ceased to be a factor in war.

5. Some of the evidence comes from letters written during the seventeenth century that describe glaciers burying villages. Other evidence includes the dates of wine harvests; grapes are harvested later when the weather is cooler. More recently, scientists have studied ice cores from Greenland and tree rings, which are thinner during cold summers. All of this evidence suggests that global temperatures dropped significantly during the seventeenth century.

6. Historians rely on written texts, so the evidence from the ice cores and tree rings is not as typical for them as the letters and records of wine harvests. Historians find such atypical evidence helpful in confirming or explaining what is contained in written records. People living during the seventeenth century may not have been aware that they were living in a period of global cooling, so the evidence from ice cores and tree rings helps to explain the events described in the written record.

Chapter 17: State Building and the Search for Order, 1648–1690

CHAPTER OVERVIEW

Key Events

1. a; Charles I
2. d; The Fronde
3. c; *Levithan*
4. b; A slave code
5. b; Tsar Alexei's
6. c; The Thirty Years' War
7. d; The Edict of Nantes
8. c; *Principia Mathematica*
9. c; England
10. a; John Locke

Key Terms

1. A; Absolutism (p. 621)
2. D; constitutionalism (p. 622)
3. E; Fronde (p. 623)
4. K; parlements (p. 623)
5. B; bureaucracy (p. 627)
6. I; mercantilism (p. 628)
7. J; Old Believers (p. 635)
8. H; Levellers (p. 639)
9. F; Glorious Revolution (p. 644)
10. L; social contract (p. 650)
11. G; law of universal gravitation (p. 651)
12. C; classicism (p. 654)

Identification

1. Cardinal Mazarin
2. Apollo
3. Jean-Baptiste Lully
4. the marquise de Maintenon
5. Augsburg
6. Frederick I
7. Vienna
8. Stenka Razin
9. Jan Sobeiski
10. Hungary
11. Charles I
12. Archbishop William Laud
13. Charles II
14. James II
15. Bill of Rights
16. Orange
17. Benedict Spinoza
18. Dutch
19. Louis XIV
20. Benedict Spinoza
21. John Locke
22. Sir Isaac Newton
23. John Milton
24. Molière
25. Hannah Wooley

CHAPTER REVIEW

Multiple Choice

1.	b	15.	d	28.	a
2.	c	16.	c	29.	b
3.	d	17.	b	30.	c
4.	b	18.	c	31.	d
5.	b	19.	c	32.	d
6.	c	20.	a	33.	d
7.	c	21.	c	34.	a
8.	c	22.	c	35.	d
9.	c	23.	d	36.	d
10.	d	24.	c	37.	a
11.	b	25.	b	38.	b
12.	b	26.	a	39.	d
13.	b	27.	b	40.	c
14.	c				

Short Answer

Answers will vary.

1. Absolutism was the claim of a ruler to sole and incontestable state power. To build his version of absolutism, Louis XIV domesticated the nobility by replacing their violent disputes with court rituals and by making their presence at court necessary for gaining rank, money, and privileges so they did not cause trouble in the provinces. He elevated to positions of power middle-class men who owed him their personal loyalty, and built up the size and influence of the bureaucracy. Louis used a variety of methods including art, music, architecture, and literature to glorify his rule, labeling himself the "Sun King" and declaring that all state power resided in him personally.

2. From the beginning, Louis believed he ruled by divine right, which made him ordained by God to rule like a father over his people and, like a father, he was responsible for seeing his subjects were instructed in religion. Intolerant of any form of dissent, he believed that he must defend Catholicism against both Protestants and dissident Catholics. As a result, he repressed the Jansenists, Catholics who valued individual conscience over conformity to church authority. In 1685, Louis ended religious toleration in France by revoking the Edict of Nantes, stripping all Protestants of the right to worship according to their faith.

3. Louis XIV waged almost constant warfare between 1667 and 1713 to extend French territory and power throughout Europe. As a result, he needed to build up a huge army, which required both the expansion of government bureaucracy and an increase in taxes. In this way, expanding government power and war fed each other. Louis used much of his skill and success as a military leader to justify his absolute rule. Ultimately, his territorial conquests—with the exception of Strasbourg—were all regained by his enemies. Moreover, constant warfare eroded the state's resources and prevented administrative and legal reforms such as ending the sale of offices and lowering taxes.

4. Central and eastern European leaders studied Louis's model of absolutism, but adapted this model to the peculiarities of their own political and social situations. For example, Frederick William of Prussia made a deal with his nobility that provided him with a stable income in order to rebuild a land devastated by the Thirty Years' War in return for exemption of taxes and allowing them complete control over their enserfed peasants. The Habsburgs under Leopold I had to adapt absolutism to a kingdom composed of numerous ethnicities and threatened by the Ottoman Turks. He created a new, loyal multi-ethnic nobility in Bohemia to replace the native aristocracy that had revolted against Austrian authority in 1618, and in Hungary he revived the parliamentary diet, which formed the core of a pro-Habsburg Hungarian aristocracy. In Russia, Tsar Alexei created a strict and stable hierarchy with the code of 1649, which increased the oppression of peasants by merging them with the serfs. Nobles owed absolute obedience to the tsar and were required to serve in the army.

5. Decades of war in Poland-Lithuania had weakened the monarchy and made the nobles into virtually autonomous warlords. They used the Sejm (parliament) to hinder monarchical power and demand constitutional rights for themselves. Each noble wielded an absolute veto power, which deadlocked parliamentary government and left the monarchy without room to maneuver. Even a talented and ambitious king like Jan Sobieski failed to rebuild the monarchy and halt Poland-Lithuania's decline into powerlessness. The weakened monarchy and political disarray left Poland-Lithuania vulnerable to its neighbors. A revolt of Ukrainian Cossacks in 1648 sparked two decades of chaos known as the Deluge in which Russia, Sweden, Brandenburg-Prussia, and Transylvania all sent armies to seize territory.

6. In the seventeenth century, the cooperation of the nobility was crucial to absolutism. In the absolutism of Louis XIV, the creation of an absolutist state depended on the monarch taming the power of his nobility by making them his satellites at court. Frequently in central and eastern Europe, cooperation was accomplished through negotiation; for example, Frederick William came to an agreement with his Junkers, and Tsar Alexei granted special rights to his nobles under the code of 1649. In these cases, the nobles were turned into loyal servants of the monarch, exchanging, for instance, exemptions from taxation for obedience to the ruler. The case of Poland-Lithuania tells us that absolutism or even effective central government was impossible so long as the nobility refused to yield power to a monarch or to each other.

7. Charles I had attempted to introduce various kinds of absolutist policies. Hoping to avoid interference from an increasingly assertive Parliament, he refused to call it into session between 1629 and 1640. He collected taxes without the consent of Parliament, and his Archbishop of Canterbury, William Laud, attempted to introduce ceremonies into the Anglican church that Puritans thought were too close to Catholicism. When discontent over Laud's religious reforms caused a Scottish invasion, Charles had to call Parliament in 1640 in order to raise an army. Parliament sought to reverse many of Charles's policies and removed Laud from office. In 1642, Charles attempted to arrest the leaders for Parliament who had challenged his power but was unsuccessful and forced to flee from London.

8. Although Puritans dominated the Parliament, they were divided over the proper form of church government. The Presbyterians wanted a Calvinist church with some central authority. The Independents favored entirely autonomous congregations that were free from any other church government. During the civil war, these factions put aside their differences and united under the leadership of Oliver Cromwell. When Parliament sought to disband Cromwell's army after the war, disgruntled soldiers protested. These were called Levellers because they insisted on leveling social differences, demanding that common people be allowed to participate in Parliament and that the male head of every household be allowed to vote.

9. Two years after Oliver Cromwell's death left England with no strong government, Parliament voted to reinstate the monarchy in order to restore social order and state power. Charles II was sympathetic to Catholicism, and his brother James II had openly converted. Both tried to push the English monarchy toward absolutism. Despite parliamentary efforts to block a Catholic from the throne, James II succeeded his brother in 1685, and when his Catholic wife gave birth to a male heir who would take precedence over his two older Protestant daughters, it seemed that a new Catholic and absolutist dynasty would govern England. In response, Parliament ousted James II and replaced him with his oldest daughter Mary and her husband William of Orange, who agreed to a constitutionalist form of government, including provisions for a strong Parliament in the Bill of Rights.

10. The Dutch Republic had a decentralized constitutional state. The individual provinces gave much of their power over foreign affairs to an assembly known as the Estates General; however, internal affairs were directed by rich merchants called regents. Through the Estates General, the regents would elect an executive officer known as the stadholder, who was responsible for defense and for representing the state at all ceremonial occasions. The stadholder was usually a prince of the house of Orange, but the Prince of Orange was more like a president than a king.

11. Because their decentralized state and religious toleration encouraged and protected trade, the Dutch Republic became the trading and financial capital of Europe. Dutch people became known for their prosperity, education, cleanliness, and industriousness, characteristics that were mirrored in their art, which reflected scenes of everyday life and business. Women were expected to focus their energies on the maintenance of the home—which defined and protected moral character—while their husbands managed the commercial and public affairs of the family. Although prosperous and successful, the Dutch increasingly came to depend on other countries, particularly England, to defend them in international wars.

12. The English colonies in North America took advantage of the political upheavals in mid-century England to develop representative government and resist the control of royal authority. Even more strikingly, the countries that were most advanced in developing constitutionalist ideas of freedom (the English and Dutch) were those most involved with the slave trade, which expanded dramatically during the seventeenth century. The Dutch West India Company was the most successful trafficker in African slaves during the seventeenth century. While they were elaborating constitutionalist notions of liberty, they stripped African slaves of their rights. In 1661, for example, Barbados instituted a slave code that stripped Africans of their rights under English law and codified slavery as an inherited status that applied only to blacks.

13. While Hobbes and Locke both argued that political authority derived from a "social contract" among citizens, Hobbes believed in absolute rule and Locke in constitutionalism. Hobbes believed that human nature was deeply self-centered and the state of nature tended toward disorder, which made life miserable—"solitary, nasty, poor, brutish and short." The only way to prevent disorder was to surrender personal liberty to an absolute power invested either in a king or parliament in return for collective security from the defects of human nature. Locke had a more optimistic view of human nature, seeing it as reasonable and the state of nature as peaceful. In Locke's view, authority rested in the will of a majority of property-owning men, with government being the limited goal of protecting life, liberty, and property. Governments that failed in this protective role could be justly overthrown. Locke's writings held significant importance to American revolutionaries and abolitionists.

14. Absolutist rulers quickly saw the potential of new science for enhancing their prestige and glory. Frederick William of Brandenburg-Prussia set up agricultural experiments in front of his palace, and various other German princes supported scientific societies in their states. Government support of the sciences was greatest in France, where it became an arm of Colbert's mercantilist policy. The Royal Academy of Sciences provided stipends to scientists who met in the king's library. Constitutional states such as England gave more informal support, but provided an environment that encouraged the spread of scientific knowledge. The Royal Society of London had a royal charter but maintained complete independence from the monarchy.

15. The cultivation of manners served two main purposes: they taught people how to act in more self-controlled, pleasing ways and began to distinguish elites from common people, who came to be seen as disgusting by the aristocracy. The art of pleasing through proper manners became an essential part of political advancement, as aristocrats were required to please their monarch or patron. The nobility also began to set itself apart from the masses by disdaining popular festivals and fairs in favor of private theaters where behavior was more formal.

BUILDING HISTORICAL SKILLS

Reading Maps

Answers will vary.

1. The Dutch Republic traded with other parts of Europe, with North and South America, and with Africa. It also had ports in India and in southeast Asia, and traded with China and Japan.

2. The Dutch traded in numerous commodities including tobacco, sugar, tea, timber, wool, spices, exotic woods, silk,

and porcelain. They also brought African slaves to the New World. Some of these commodities—especially exotic woods, silk, and porcelain—were luxury items that would have been destined mainly for the upper class and would further distinctions between rich and poor. Items like sugar, tea, and tobacco would have been more widely available. All of this gave Europeans access to goods that had previously been extremely rare and expensive or unavailable, and would have changed their lifestyles.

Reading Illustrations

Answers will vary.

1. The people in the painting are the baker Arent Oostward and his wife. They are putting baked goods on a tray.

2. Arent Oostward and his wife are wearing modest and clean clothing. Their expressions are calm and smiling, and their postures appear relaxed and active.

3. The attitude of Dutch painter Jan Steen as revealed in *The Baker Arent Oostward and His Wife* presents daily life as industrious but happy and relaxed. The painting hints that ordinary people are in charge of their own lives by presenting the baker and his wife in respectable clothing, making bread, and happy.

Reading Historical Documents

Answers will vary.

1. Milton describes books as living things, and an "image of God." Because they contain knowledge that lasts past the lifetime of individuals, they are immortal. They are also essential to civilization because a "rejected truth" is impossible to recover, which makes "whole nations fare the worse."

2. According to Milton, there is no virtue in never facing vice "with all her baits and seeming pleasures." Virtue comes with facing vice and resisting it; "that which purifies us is trial, and trial is by what is contrary." If all vice were to be eliminated, then virtue would no longer exist.

3. Oroonoko is set apart from other Africans by his knowledge of world events, his fluency in European languages, and his physical characteristics. He had a "graceful mien," good skin, and white eyes and teeth. His nose was "rising and Roman, instead of African and flat," and his lips were also well shaped. In other words, it is his Europeanness that sets him apart.

4. Aphra Behn's description shows that Europeans did not have positive attitudes about Africans in the seventeenth century. She implies that it is only Oroonoko's European features that make him exceptional: the "civility of a well-bred great man," his knowledge of European languages and history, and his European facial features. By emphasizing that he is an exception to other Africans, she reflects the attitude that Africans are generally uncivilized, ignorant, and without good physical features.

5. The Levellers were a reform-minded political group and so represented interests that were mainly political. Lucy Hutchinson was the wife of a Puritan who had been imprisoned upon the restoration of the monarchy. She was defending religious interests, but also expressing social concerns as seen in her comments on the "griping of the poor" and "swarms of needy Scots." She also had a personal interest because her husband was in prison. Thomas Hobbes wasn't representing a particular interest except that people "may nourish themselves and live contentedly." He was speaking about politics in a more theoretical and less personal way.

6. In the first two documents, the authors identify the enemies or the problems they face and then argue, often in emotional or personal terms, that their interpretation of the nature of political power is correct. The Levellers and Lady Hutchinson appeal to a sense of injustice and oppression. Whereas the first two documents are meant to appeal to the emotions, Hobbes's treatise is presented as a logical and reasoned argument for the importance of strong government: Hobbes avoids direct appeal to the emotional, and speaks instead in general and hypothetical terms so as to make his argument appear more objective.

Chapter 18: The Atlantic System and Its Consequences, 1690–1740

CHAPTER OVERVIEW

Key Events

1. a; Sugar
2. d; Louis XIV's restrictions on French Protestants
3. c; The loosening of restrictions on serfs
4. a; France
5. b; To block the succession of a Catholic, in particular the son of the deposed James II
6. d; Sweden
7. a; The province of Lorraine

Key Terms

1. B; Atlantic system (p. 666)
2. I; plantation (p. 667)
3. G; mestizo (p. 674)
4. C; buccaneers (p. 674)
5. D; consumer revolution (p. 676)
6. A; agricultural revolution (p. 676)
7. J; rococo (p. 681)
8. H; Pietism (p. 683)
9. F; Jacobitism (p. 686)
10. K; Westernization (p. 688)
11. E; Enlightenment (p. 695)

Identification

1. Brazil	11. Charles II
2. the Caribbean	12. John Law
3. sugar	13. Robert Walpole
4. mestizos	14. William Petty
5. calico	15. Edward Jenner
6. *Spectator*	16. Pierre Bayle
7. Rococo	17. Voltaire
8. George Frederick Handel	18. Montesquieu
9. Eliza Haywood	19. Mary Astell
10. Jansenists	20. Elizabeth Elstob

CHAPTER REVIEW

Multiple Choice

1.	c	12.	a	23.	b
2.	d	13.	b	24.	b
3.	d	14.	c	25.	b
4.	c	15.	b	26.	d
5.	b	16.	d	27.	b
6.	b	17.	c	28.	d
7.	b	18.	c	29.	d
8.	b	19.	d	30.	d
9.	c	20.	d	31.	a
10.	a	21.	d	32.	a
11.	c	22.	c		

Short Answer

Answers will vary.

1. Coffee was one of the products of the Atlantic system that came to Europe from the Caribbean, where it was grown on plantations worked by slaves transported from Africa. Coffee became a staple among Europeans, particularly western Europeans, whose economy was growing and had more money to spend on items previously considered luxuries. People got together in coffeehouses not only to drink coffee but also to exchange ideas and share newspapers. Coffeehouses were important alternatives to the court, university, and church as sources for the dissemination of information—information that provided the foundation for an informed public opinion.

2. As the supplies of precious metals from the New World dwindled in the seventeenth century, Europeans discovered that they could make fabulous profits by producing crops that couldn't be grown in Europe, such as sugar, cotton, tobacco, or coffee. To work the large, profitable plantations, Europeans imported African slaves, who suffered from harsh living conditions and the brutal treatment they received from Europeans. While the owners at first justified this treatment on the grounds that it maintained discipline and order, by the eighteenth century they claimed that Africans were no better than beasts and didn't merit the same treatment as whites.

3. In China, Europeans were viewed with disdain and suspicion, and the Chinese emperors were secure and powerful enough to restrict European trading entirely to the city of Guangzhou (Canton), where only about 1,000 Europeans lived by 1720. Europeans had far greater scope in India, where Muslim rulers struggled for control against Hindu princes, Sikh rebels, Persian invaders, and even their own officials. French and British traders in particular took advantage of this confusion to extend their power in various places throughout the territory, and, while Europeans living in India by the early eighteenth century numbered only in the thousands, there were many more soldiers stationed there to protect them, further increasing European influence.

4. One part of the Agricultural Revolution called for smaller parcels of land to be gathered into larger and more efficient holdings. In England, cottagers lost their land to big landowners through enclosure or through forced sale, and those who stayed in the countryside became salaried agricultural workers or tenant farmers who rented from the big landlords. In Prussia, Russia, and Poland, however, while aristocratic landholders also forced peasants off their common or privately owned land, these peasants did not become paid employees or renters; rather, peasants were pushed further into serfdom as landowners demanded even more compulsory labor to work the enlarged estates.

5. Novels like *Robinson Crusoe* provided a glimpse into the workings of the Atlantic system and also promoted the values of hard work, ingenuity, and self-reliance that were important to middle-class men. Moreover, the presence of the black man Friday showed how the lives of blacks and whites intertwined in the new colonies. Women characters were particularly important in novels, and women writers excelled in the genre. The question of women's proper place in a changing world was examined in novels like Eliza Haywood's moralistic *Persecuted Virtue* or Daniel Defoe's exuberant *Moll Flanders*. Readers of both sexes valued the novel's emphasis on social relations and realities and on individual psychology.

6. Many of the religious revival movements of the late seventeenth and early eighteenth centuries sought a more intensely emotional or even ecstatic religion with an emphasis on mysticism and a personal connection with God. The Pietists in Protestant states believed in a mystical religion of the heart, but also encouraged bible study and attended prayer meetings and church services frequently. Offshoots of the movement, such as the Philadelphians founded by Jane Leade, studied mysticism and believed in visions from God. Leade herself advocated a universal, nondogmatic church. Jeanne Marie Guyon started Quietism, a Catholic version of Pietism that stressed prayer and simple devotion, in France; she also claimed to have miraculous visions and prophesy. In the 1720s the Jansenists, who were originally an austere sect of Catholics, also took a mystical and highly popular turn after miracles were reported at the grave of a Jansenist priest.

7. In 1700, shortly before his death, the childless king Charles II of Spain named the duke of Anjou, a grandson of Louis XIV, to succeed him. The Austrian Habsburgs—long the enemies of France—contested this deathbed will and other countries joined in to prevent the union of Spain and France under a single monarch. After a war that lasted from 1701–1713, the Peace of Utrecht gave the throne to Philip of Anjou, but he had to renounce his claims to the French throne, thus barring the unification of the two kingdoms. Both Spain and France lost territories to the war's victors. This stopped France's plans for European expansion and reflected the changing balance of power in Europe—no one country would be able to dominate the continent militarily.

8. Peter the Great instituted the Table of Ranks in 1722 to replace social status based on birth with status bestowed as recognition for service to the state. This not only forced nobles into compulsory state service and made social and material advantages dependent upon serving the crown, but it also undermined the independence of the nobles, making them less able to resist the centralization of royal control. To increase his power over the church, Peter

allowed the office of patriarch or supreme head to remain vacant, and replaced it with a bureaucracy of laymen under his supervision called the Holy Synod.

9. Medicine was very poor during this period. Most people still practiced household cures and trained physicians competed with quacks, midwives, bonesetters, and "cunning women" for patients. There was no licensing of physicians, and there was a fine line between competent practitioners and dangerous quacks. But the scientific revolution, which encouraged observation, experimentation, and rational thought, improved the practice of medicine. In hospitals (originally charitable institutions rather than places where diseases were studied and cured), surgeons began to dissect cadavers and categorize their knowledge regarding the body and its illnesses using specialized Latin words. The new terminology made diagnosis easier. Physicians also began to practice inoculation against smallpox, an innovation introduced from the Middle East largely through the efforts of Lady Mary Wortley Montagu and popularized in a safer technique by Edward Jenner.

10. The Scientific Revolution introduced the scientific method that emphasized the importance of observation, experimentation, and rational thought. During the late seventeenth and early eighteenth centuries, science became increasingly popular because Enlightenment writers like Fontenelle and Voltaire wrote works in which the ideas of Copernicus and Newton were made accessible to a growing literate public. While scientists had used the scientific method to examine natural phenomena, Enlightenment writers applied that same method to social and political institutions.

11. Montesquieu's satire presents the fictional letters of two Persian gentlemen who travel to France to gain knowledge. They constantly contrast Persia and France, usually to France's detriment. Although it was a fictional work and involved travelers to rather than from Europe, the *Persian Letters* nevertheless reflected eighteenth-century travel literature's impact on political commentary; many authors used descriptions of foreign cultures to contrast them with (and criticize) their own culture.

12. Mary Astell was an English author who drew comparisons between the state and the family as a basis for arguing that men and women should be equal partners in marriage. She pointed out that since the state did not need an absolute monarch in order to function well, it made no sense to argue that the much smaller and less complex family unit had to be dominated by a husband with the power of a despot over his wife. She further pointed out that all men were born free, but when women were under the control of their husbands, they lost that freedom, and this was inconsistent with English political principles and practices.

BUILDING HISTORICAL SKILLS

Reading Maps

Answers will vary.

1. During this period slaves were mainly being imported into the Spanish and Portuguese colonies in Central and South America, although there were small French and Dutch colonies in these regions that also imported slaves. Slaves were exported primarily from the west coast of Africa, but some were also exported from Portuguese territories on the east coast of Africa as well.

2. Europeans imported precious metals from Central and South America. From the West Indies they imported sugar, and from the colonies in North America they imported timber, fish, and tobacco.

3. The triangular trade system was a network in which Europe, Africa, and the Americas were joined together in an interconnected economic relationship. Africa and the Americas both provided markets for manufactured goods from Europe. Africa provided slaves, which were brought to the Americas, where their labor produced the raw materials that were sent back to Europe to make more manufactured goods. Thus Europe depended on Africa and America both as markets for the goods it produced and for the labor and raw materials needed to produce them.

Reading Illustrations

Answers will vary.

1. There are many ways to interpret a painting, and no one particular reading is necessarily the "correct" one. The first thing this image tells us is that Europeans' perceptions of Africa and Africans was not gained first-hand but depended on the accounts of travelers, writers, and artists like Carriera. Second, it is reasonable to think that the symbolism and imagery used by Carriera corresponded to a general idea of Africa that her audience would recognize. Carriera sought to portray Africa as a strange and exciting continent, full of wealth but not without a certain element of danger. Africa's exoticism is apparent from her feathered and jeweled turban and brightly colored garment, while her precious necklaces and earrings evoke its riches. The wriggling snakes, clutched in her left hand, might symbolize the perils that await the unwary foreign visitor to that continent.

2. Overall, the image is attractive and emphatically feminine: Africa is beautiful and beautifully dressed—a far cry from a brutalized victim of slavery and racism. Carriera has also chosen to highlight her sexuality: the string of red beads moves down toward her breasts, her lips are parted, her cheeks are flushed pink, and her neck and ears are decorated. The snakes in her hand suggest male sexuality, as can the scorpion. At the same time Carriera creates an impression of innocence. Pearls were a symbol of virginity, and Africa's turban is white, the color of purity. Moreover, covering the hair was a sign of female modesty. And while snakes suggest male sexuality, the snakes here are held harmlessly in Africa's hand, and the scorpion is an ornament and chained to her necklace. Carriera seems to be an advocate of Africa, having given her both attraction and self-control.

Reading Historical Documents

Answers will vary.

1. Voltaire says that even Christian philosophers knew that faith and reason were two different matters and that philosophers would never form a religious sect because their writings were not meant for everyone. Too few

people read, and too few of those who did read philosophy. Past philosophers like Montaigne, Bayle, or Spinoza created less of a stir than religious divines did. Philosophy did not reach a wide enough audience to challenge the status quo.

2. Voltaire estimates that the vast majority of humanity is illiterate and incapable of understanding much more than the ambition of religious divines. Those who are literate would sooner amuse themselves with romance novels than read anything philosophical. Voltaire pessimistically estimates that the thinking portion of humanity is infinitesimal.

3. Lady Montagu is admiring of Turkish culture and their innovations in medicine; however, she describes some of the Greeks who also live there as superstitious because they inoculate themselves in the shape of a cross. In Montagu's description the Turks are presented more favorably than the English, because she states that British doctors value the profits they make from smallpox over the lives that could be saved by introducing the vaccine to Europe.

4. The fact that Lady Montagu's letters were published suggests an interest in travel and foreign places. It also shows that people like Lady Montagu were relatively open-minded to foreign innovations. Her desire to bring the smallpox vaccine to Europe reflects the new interest in public health and hygiene. Her interest in medicine and contempt for superstition indicate that she shared the upper-class taste for scientific knowledge. The fact that a woman found a publisher for her writing indicates an "enlightened" attitude toward women writers and women in general.

5. Because slaves were not literate, oral histories provide the only information available about what the experience of slavery must have been like for them. From the oral histories, historians are able to gain insight into how slaves thought about being enslaved, being punished, and their enslavers. Because the information has been handed down over many generations, there is a danger that inaccuracies have been introduced into the accounts. Lapses in memory may significantly alter an oral account of an event. Storytellers may have embellished the tales for a variety of reasons, attempting to portray actors in a particularly heroic or dramatic light according to the expectations of listeners or because of cultural traditions about storytelling.

6. The slave narratives seem to have different purposes—one to transmit a sense of justice, the other to transmit a sense of pride. The description of Providence Plantation emphasizes the slaves' suffering and leads to a moral evaluation and a claim of divine protection: "And the gods told them that this is no way for human beings to live. They would help them." The oral history from Cassewinica Plantation lays more stress on the slaves knowledge, courage, and careful planning. It mentions "a great council meeting" and that "they knew all about this plantation from slavery times" and that they conducted a successful night raid. The whipping of Lanu is mentioned but only to distinguish Lanu's plantation from Cassewinica. The killing of the white plantation head gets a similar matter-of-fact treatment. The "moral" comes at the end: "They took all the things, everything they needed."

Chapter 19: The Promise of Enlightenment, 1740–1789

CHAPTER OVERVIEW

Key Events

1. a; Denis Diderot
2. c; Austria
3. d; The *Philosophical Dictionary*
4. b; Sweden
5. d; The rebellion was brutally suppressed and nobles tightened their control over their serfs.
6. a; Weaving cloth
7. c; Elections for major state offices
8. d; some philosophical questions were unanswerable by reason alone.

Key Terms

1. J; philosophes (p. 708)
2. L; salons (p. 711)
3. B; atheist (p. 712)
4. C; deist (p. 712)
5. A; abolitionists (p. 713)
6. H; laissez-faire (p. 716)
7. K; romanticism (p. 720)
8. F; Hasidim (p. 721)
9. I; Methodism (p. 721)
10. E; Freemasons (p. 723)
11. G; industrialization (p. 728)
12. D; enlightened despots (p. 729)

Identification

1. Madame Tharie Thérese Geoffrin
2. Émile du Châtelet
3. David Hume
4. Adam Smith
5. John Wesley
6. Josiah Wedgwood
7. Ludwig van Beethoven
8. Frederick II of Prussia
9. James Watt
10. mechanized loom
11. Maria Theresa
12. Peter III
13. Paris
14. Leopold II
15. Jacques Turgot
16. Flour War
17. Peter III
18. Gustavus III of Sweden
19. Pierre de Beaumarchais
20. Tea Act

CHAPTER REVIEW

Multiple Choice

1.	d	12.	d	23.	b
2.	a	13.	a	24.	d
3.	c	14.	d	25.	c
4.	b	15.	b	26.	c
5.	d	16.	b	27.	d
6.	b	17.	c	28.	a
7.	d	18.	c	29.	d
8.	b	19.	a	30.	c
9.	b	20.	b	31.	a
10.	b	21.	c	32.	b
11.	d	22.	c	33.	b

Short Answer

Answers will vary.

1. The philosophes were writers and philosophers, mainly from the upper classes, although some were of more modest origins. They sought to reform society through the application of "reason," which referred to critical, informed, and scientific thinking about social issues and problems. They wrote about all aspects of social life and believed that through the spread of knowledge and reason, social elites and governments could undertake all sorts of reforms. The philosophes did not advocate revolution because, for the most part, they distrusted the lower classes. Rather, they believed that published criticism could bring about reform.

2. Because the philosophes often challenged the religious and political ideas of the time, they often found it difficult to become published and were often opposed by church-run universities. They thus spread their ideas primarily through personal contacts, particularly by letter writing and at salons, often organized by women, where philosophes and their followers met for discussion. These networks of personal contacts transcended national boundaries and formed an international "republic of letters." In countries with strong constitutionalist governments, such as the Dutch Republic and Great Britain, the philosophes found it easier to spread their ideas through publication and were not always banned from universities. As the Enlightenment gained strength and censorship eased, philosophes wrote and published in a diversity of genres including encyclopedias, novels, and newspapers.

3. The most directly opposed views were those of Adam Smith and Jean-Jacques Rousseau. Adam Smith wrote that individual interests naturally harmonized with those of the entire society and advocated an economic policy known as laissez-faire, in which governments took as small a role in economic life freeing the individual to pursue personal advantage. Jean-Jacques Rousseau argued, on the contrary, that individuals must subject their individual wills to what he called the "general will," or the good of the community as a whole. Rousseau argued that a "social contract" between the various inhabitants of a state would make everyone equally free and equally moral because they lived under a law to which they all had consented.

4. During this period, upper-class youths went on "Grand Tours" of Europe where they often saw the newly discovered ruins of Pompeii and Herculaneum in Italy, arousing an enthusiasm for a neoclassical style in architecture and painting that emphasized the purity and clarity of forms. In painting there was a growing taste for moralistic family scenes that reflected the middle-class preoccupation with the emotions of ordinary private life that was related in novels. Music was performed more and more for paying audiences rather than private patrons, so composers created works that could be played repeatedly as part of a classical repertory.

5. The Enlightenment's emphasis on reason rather than birth and tradition opened new doors to the middle class. The Enlightenment offered social, intellectual, and cultural advancement. The middle class or bourgeoisie mingled with enlightened aristocrats at salons; joined learned societies, academies, and Masonic lodges; and imitated or adopted upper-class tastes in travel, architecture, and the arts. The Enlightenment combined with the growing prosperity and numbers of the middle class established them as a dominant part of the new audience for books and music influenced by Enlightenment thought.

6. The population increase led many villagers to move to the city where greater opportunities existed. As they moved to the city sexual behavior changed, as is evidenced in the dramatic increase in the number of out-of-wedlock births. The causes of this increase are debated among historians, with some arguing that the liberation of women from the control of their families allowed them to seek their own sexual fulfillment, whereas others argue that increased mobility allowed a man to move about freely to escape his responsibilities if he impregnated a woman. Although some reformers criticized the harshness of laws against infanticide, which were often acts of desperation, homosexuals continued to be persecuted. The emphasis on reason and self-control during the Enlightenment caused parents concern about their children's sexuality, especially masturbation.

7. Many of the sovereigns of this period were "enlightened despots" or "enlightened absolutists" who aimed to combine Enlightenment reforms with absolutist powers. Every European ruler tried to introduce reforms during this period. For example, Frederick II of Prussia instituted a uniform civil justice code, creating the most consistently administered laws and efficient judiciary of the era. Joseph II of Austria granted religious freedom of worship to Protestants, Orthodox Christians, and Jews in 1781. However, groups such as the nobility, who feared that the reforms undermined their power, resisted.

8. Governments, especially those in western Europe, had to become more responsive to public opinion. A broader group of individuals informed both by Enlightenment ideals and a growing press held governments accountable for scandals and pressured governments for reform. Government actions reported and criticized in the press could provoke intensely hostile public opinion. For example, in 1760s when the British government arrested John Wilkes, a popular opponent of the king and Parliament, the British faced an international backlash. Governments attempting reform, such as the monarchy of Gustavus III of Sweden, could also work through the press to mobilize

public opinion in their favor so that they could use it to counter opposition from the nobility.

9. Rulers everywhere wanted more control over church affairs and used Enlightenment criticisms of religion to extend their powers. For example, European rulers pressured Pope Clement XIV to disband the influential Jesuits. Joseph II of Austria required his bishops to swear loyalty to the state and supervised religious training. Religious tolerance was pursued by many rulers, such as Louis XVI, who granted Protestants civil rights, and Joseph II, who granted wide-ranging freedom of worship in 1781. Established churches often resisted enlightened reforms because these undermined their virtually unquestioned social authority.

10. The food supply became the main focus of popular discontent and popular resistance took the form of rioting. The common people had a long-held belief that governments should ensure a supply of food. Some governments, however, were deregulating the grain market. Deregulation allowed farmers to earn higher profits by shipping grain out of their local areas during times of scarcity. Threatened with starvation, peasants and townspeople rioted. Food riots were highly structured and often led by women. They involved an appeal to local authorities to regulate the price of grain and, at times, rioters would take grain themselves, paying what they believed to be a "just" price.

11. The American War of Independence was driven by public opinion propelled by Enlightenment ideals of rational government and liberty. American leaders used the Declaration of Independence to justify their break with Britain by appealing to European public opinion in the language of the Enlightenment. The war was not motivated by religion or dynastic disputes, but by the Enlightenment ideas that government power derived from the people and that the people had natural rights no government could take away. Tradition did play a part in that the American colonists protested that Britain, by denying them the traditional rights of British subjects, was not governing according to reason. But the colonists changed the rules of the game when they claimed this violation of traditional freedom and reason gave them the right to rebel against their government.

12. The Wilkes affair raised the issues of freedom of the press, the right of citizens to criticize the government, and the need to reform Parliament. In 1763, a member of Parliament named John Wilkes attacked the government in his newspaper. He was arrested, sued the government, won, and was reelected—but Parliament would not let him take his seat. All this made Wilkes a hero of popular freedom. All sorts of publications took up his cause. The middle class circulated petitions in his favor and demanded Parliamentary reform. The Wilkes affair was followed in America because Wilkes's problems so closely matched the colonists' grievances. Americans demonstrated for Wilkes and made donations to his supporters in Britain. But the Wilkes affair failed to produce concrete reforms, and this convinced many colonists that Parliament was hopelessly corrupt and that they would have to take matters into their own hands.

BUILDING HISTORICAL SKILLS

Reading Maps

Answers will vary.

1. The two main alliances were between France, Spain, Austria, Hungary, Russia, and Sweden on one side; and Prussia, Portugal, and Great Britain on the other.

2. During the Seven Years' War, fighting in Europe was mainly conducted in the German and Austrian territories of central Europe. However, there were also hostilities in Portugal and in European colonies in North America, the West Indies, and India. This suggests that colonial interests had become a factor in European power politics.

Reading Illustrations

Answers will vary.

1. During the eighteenth century, there was a new emphasis on emotion and family life, especially among the middle class, which was becoming increasingly active in the art world. This was a change from the intimate sensuality of rococo and the monumental baroque style.

2. Sexual behavior was changing during this time, as out-of-wedlock births rose to 20 percent from 5 percent the century before. There was also increased mobility among villagers, which would have allowed a man to avoid responsibility for impregnating a woman. This man is obviously just being confronted and, if the child is his, he has clearly been away for an extended period of time.

Reading Historical Documents

Answers will vary.

1. Rousseau emphasized the "general will" of human societies, by virtue of which all are both citizens and free. By living in a society, a person consents to live according to the vote of the majority. Because this is a voluntary arrangement, it is not contradictory to human freedom.

2. According to Rousseau, government is not a relationship between a ruler and his or her subjects, but between the citizens of a society. Rousseau does not mention God, religion, or tradition in any way as a legitimization of government. These notions differed greatly from previous theories of government.

3. The Declaration of Independence justifies the actions of the revolutionaries with an appeal to the laws of nature rather than on tradition or religion. It claims that governments are "instituted among Men, deriving their just powers from the consent of the governed." It also states that a "respect to the opinions of mankind" requires them to declare the reasons why they are separating from their sovereign. The secular justification of the American Revolution, the idea that government derives from the governed, and the value of public opinion were all derived from the Enlightenment.

4. Most Enlightenment thinkers did not believe that revolution was the best way to bring about reform. They typically did not trust the lower classes, who they viewed as superstitious, ignorant, and violent, and would not have approved of government being placed in their hands.

They generally believed that published criticism was the best way of bringing about change.

5. The education of women is the main issue at stake here. Madame de Beaumer says that her journal educates women by guiding them toward virtue, which is compatible with the traditional view of women's educational needs, but her last sentence also suggests that men cannot simultaneously withhold scientific education from women and blame women for not knowing the sciences. Catherine Macaulay supports the idea that women should be educated because the lack of education can "debilitate both the powers of the mind and the body." Macaulay takes issue with Jean-Jacques Rousseau who claims that the role that nature has given women as child-bearers requires them to live a quiet and sedentary life in order to raise and nurture their offspring. This is not a human institution according to Rousseau, but a natural condition that could not be changed.

6. The Enlightenment claimed to apply reason to all aspects of society—politics, religion, laws, traditions—that obstructed social reform. But when women or men applied reason to patriarchy, Enlightened men like Rousseau used their reason to obstruct reform. The focus of debate was education because the Enlightenment idea that society must be based on reason demanded that society be educated. Giving men and women the same education would open the door for women to be recognized as men's equals. To deny women an intellectual education on "rational" grounds would put them back in their traditional place permanently.

Chapter 20: The Cataclysm of Revolution, 1789–1800

CHAPTER OVERVIEW

Key Events

1. c; Political reforms
2. b; There were too many internal divisions among its participants
3. a; Haiti
4. d. The overthrow of the monarchy
5. b; Treason
6. c; Slavery
7. b; Maximilien Robespierre
8. d; Poland
9. a; Napoleon Bonaparte's coming to power

Key Terms

1. A; Atlantic revolutions (p. 749)
2. D; Estates General (p. 753)
3. F; Great Fear (p. 757)
4. C; Declaration of the Rights of Man and Citizen (p. 757)
5. H; sans-culottes (p.761)
6. G; Jacobin Club (p. 761)
7. I; Terror (p. 763)
8. B; de-Christianization (p. 766)
9. J; Thermidorian Reaction (p. 770)
10. E; First Consul (p. 781)

Identification

1. Protestants
2. Americans
3. Marie-Antoinette
4. 1615
5. National Assembly
6. Civil Constitution of the Clergy
7. Varennes
8. Austria
9. Jacobin Club
10. Mountain
11. Jean-Paul Marat
12. general maximum
13. Georges-Jacques Danton
14. September 22, 1792
15. Maximilien Robespierre
16. Helvetic Republic
17. Catherine the Great
18. Gustavus IV
19. François Dominique Toussaint L'Ouverture
20. François Dominique Toussaint L'Ouverture

CHAPTER REVIEW

Multiple Choice

1. a	12. b	23. b
2. d	13. b	24. b
3. c	14. c	25. b
4. a	15. a	26. a
5. b	16. d	27. c
6. d	17. b	28. b
7. d	18. a	29. c
8. d	19. a	30. b
9. c	20. a	31. d
10. b	21. b	32. b
11. d	22. b	33. a

Short Answer

Answers will vary.

1. As a whole, the Atlantic revolutions of the late eighteenth century were the product of long-term prosperity and high expectations, as Europeans were generally wealthier, more numerous, healthier, and better educated than ever before. However, individually, these revolutions had differing causes and long-term consequences. The Dutch Patriot revolt of 1787 was a consequence of middle-class support for the American Revolution, while the stadholder was closely allied with Britain. The Belgian Independence movement was a result of the attempted reforms of the Austrian emperor Joseph II, which would have eliminated many offices that belonged to nobles and lawyers. The Polish Patriot movement began when reform-minded Poles tried to overhaul the weak commonwealth along modern western European lines. Several of these revolutions, especially the Belgian Independence Movement, were inspired by the American example. To an extent, they all used Enlightenment principles in their push to implement modern reforms.

2. The Estates General were called in response to a serious fiscal crisis in the French nation. Due to an outdated and

inefficient taxation system, the lack of a national bank, and the debts incurred in supporting American independence, the French nation was in dire financial straits. In 1787, Louis XVI called an Assembly of Notables to consider various royal reform proposals, but the Assembly refused to cooperate, wanting reform only on their own terms. Pressure from the nobles in parlement and the Assembly of Notables forced Louis to call the Estates General into session. The Estates General, last having met 175 years before, was a body of deputies divided into three estates representing each social order in France: noble, clergy, and commoners.

3. The unwillingness of the Third Estate (representing over 95 percent of the general population) to accept the traditional voting rules of the Estates General, which gave dominance to the nobles and clergy, led them to establish a new assembly, the National Assembly, in which each deputy had individual voting privileges. Two days later, the clergy (the First Estate) voted to join them. Louis XVI ordered thousands of troops to march on Paris. Fearing a plot by the king and nobles to disperse the assembly and arrest its members, citizens began to arm themselves and attack grain and munitions stockpiles. These events culminated in the attack of the Bastille, a symbol of royal authority, and the brutal execution of its governor.

4. In response to a potential peasant insurrection in 1789, the National Assembly abolished feudal rights and obligations, including the last remnants of serfdom and special tax privileges for nobles. They also passed the Declaration of the Rights of Man and Citizen granting all men equality, freedom of religion, freedom of the press, equality of taxation, and equality before the law. The declaration also established the principle of national sovereignty with the assertion that the king derived his authority from the nation, and therefore the people, rather than from tradition or divine right. The National Assembly also established the first written constitution in French history, which created a constitutional monarchy with a one-house legislature, severely limited the powers of the king, and granted voting rights to white men who possessed a suitable amount of wealth.

5. Motivated partly by an ongoing financial crisis, the National Assembly confiscated all of the church's property and in return promised to pay clerical salaries. In July 1790, it passed a Civil Constitution of the Clergy that set pay scales for the clergy and allowed voters to elect their own parish priests and bishops. Believing monastic life encouraged idleness and a decline in population, the taking of monastic vows was outlawed, and existing monks and nuns were pushed to return to private life. Half of the clergy refused to swear allegiance to this new constitutional arrangement, which caused an enduring rift between French Catholics—those loyal to the old church and those committed to the Revolution and the new "constitutional" church.

6. The war with Austria and Prussia brought hope to both Louis XVI and the revolutionaries. Louis hoped the Revolution would be crushed, and many revolutionaries hoped the war would lead to the king's downfall and the establishment of a French republic. However, because numerous aristocratic army officers had emigrated to Austria to join Leopold's counterrevolutionary army, the remaining French troops were ill-prepared for battle. With the Austrians advancing on Paris, the authority of the newly elected Legislative Assembly in question, and the king and the remaining army officers fueling the distrust and panic of the revolutionaries, the sans-culottes, or ordinary people of Paris, organized an insurrection against the royal family and the Legislative Assembly. They forced new elections for a National Convention that would write another constitution. The National Convention abolished the monarchy on September 22, 1792, and established a French republic. Then, in December 1792, despite internal disagreements, the convention found the king guilty of treason and voted for his execution.

7. The execution of the king did not bring peace and contentment to the new French republic. The moderate Girondin and the radical Mountain factions of the Jacobins engaged in increasing amounts of vicious political infighting. At the same time, the crisis caused by the early defeats of the French army against Austria contributed to a general atmosphere of fear, confusion, and distrust. The introduction of a national draft and the need for more war funds provoked resistance in some French regions. In response, the National Convention established the Committee of Public Safety, which, under the leadership of Maximilien Robespierre, introduced the use of terror to better reorganize French society to fight the war and to stamp out dissent.

8. The Republic of Virtue was the brainchild of Robespierre. He aimed to use the government to teach, or force, citizens to become virtuous republicans through a massive program of political reeducation. He politicized all aspects of French life in a cultural revolution meant to transform the old subjects of the monarchy into ideal republican citizens. It involved a wide variety of cultural changes: the sponsorship of republican works of art, changes in patterns of speech, a revolutionary calendar, the organization of civic celebrations and festivals, and the introduction of a new metric system of measurements. Some revolutionaries also pursued a campaign of de-Christianization to supplant the influence of the Catholic church with new forms of enlightened worship or civic religion. Successive revolutionary legislatures also effected change in traditional family life, making marriage a civic concern rather than a church issue, legalizing divorce, and instituting a series of laws that created equal inheritance among all children in a family, including females. Unfortunately, the invasiveness of the Republic of Virtue into the cultural, spiritual, and private lives of French citizens provoked massive resistance and widespread discontent.

9. As resistance to the republican government grew, the Terror became increasingly repressive, particularly in response to counterrevolutionary rebellions on the part of the peasantry. Countless revolutionaries, counterrevolutionaries, clerics, and civilians were killed in rebellions or executed as participants in suspected conspiracies. In an atmosphere of fear and paranoia, revolutionary leaders began plotting against one another; they, too, were often arrested and executed. The final crisis of the Terror came in July 1794 when Robespierre accused yet another group

of officials for actions against the state. Afraid for their lives, the National Convention turned on Robespierre. Their actions, termed the Thermidorian reaction, resulted in the arrest and execution of Robespierre and the creation of a new constitution in 1795, which ended the programs of Terror and placed the republic's future in the hands of a two-house legislature and an executive body— the Directory—headed by five directors.

10. The French army, fueled by revolutionary fervor, swept beyond the borders of France and brought revolutionary principles to many of the countries it occupied. "Sister republics" were set up in places like Switzerland and the Austrian Netherlands, and French legislation was introduced to these semi-independent states, including the abolition of seigneurial dues. The French occupation of Egypt, although short-lived, was long enough for Enlightenment-inspired legal reforms to be introduced to Egyptian law: the abolition of torture, equality before the law, the elimination of religious taxes, and the proclamation of religious tolerance. However, the French revolutionaries' abolishment of monarchy and nobility and their encouragement of popular participation in politics made many heads of European states quite wary. The threat of the French army and its agitating effect on commoners often resulted in severe repression of the peasantry by those in power in countries fighting against France.

11. In a number of European countries, such as Great Britain, the beginning of the Revolution was optimistically seen as a positive application of the principles of the Enlightenment, especially among liberal-minded thinkers. As the Revolution became more radical and violent, however, some European states feared that the spread of revolutionary ideals might undermine the traditional hierarchical arrangement of their societies. The British government, for instance, alarmed at the French abolition of monarchy, quickly suppressed constitutional and reform societies claiming these were institutions that bred sedition. Not surprisingly, pro-French sentiment ran high in both Ireland and Poland, which were under the tight rule of Britain and Russia respectively, as well as in the French colonies, where the Revolution inspired revolts in the name of the Enlightenment principles of liberty and independence.

12. Napoleon Bonaparte rose through the ranks of the French army very quickly due to his military prowess and his political connections in Paris. He was named commander of the French army in Italy in 1796 where his successful Italian campaign established his reputation and power. He established client republics dependent upon his authority, personally navigated through successful diplomatic negotiations with other European powers, won the loyalty of his troops by paying them in cash drawn from the tributary funds of conquered territories, and appeased the Directory government with artworks confiscated from Italian museums. Despite an unsuccessful Egyptian campaign, Napoleon remained popular. He led a coup against the Directory with the support of the army on November 10, 1799, demanding changes in the Constitution. With the aid of his brother, the president of the lower legislative house, Napoleon's rump legislature abolished the Directory and replaced it with a new constitution and a three-man executive government called the Consulate. Bonaparte served as First Consul, a title harking back to the Roman republic.

BUILDING HISTORICAL SKILLS

Reading Maps

Answers will vary.

1. By 1799, France had annexed Nice, Savoy, the Austrian Netherlands, and the papal territories in southern France just north of Marseilles. France had also occupied Piedmont and Tuscany on the Italian peninsula.

2. By 1799, France had established the Batavian Republic by the North Sea, and a series of states on the Italian peninsula including the Neapolitan Republic, the Roman Republic, the Ligurian Republic, and the Cisalpine Republic. France had also established the Helvetic Republic in modern-day Switzerland.

3. French expansion would have been perceived as a threat to the German states, Prussia, and the Austrian empire to the east. Great Britain would have also felt threatened, as would Spain to the south.

Reading Illustrations

Answers will vary.

1. The noble and the clergyman (representing the Second and First Estates respectively) are standing together, displaying similar expressions of alarm. The clergyman has his hand on the shoulder of the noble, thus reinforcing the close tie between the two.

2. When we look at the noble and clergyman, our gaze is drawn by theirs to the member of the Third Estate because we want to see what they are looking at. When we look at the member of the Third Estate, however, our eyes can rest upon him because he is looking at a rifle, which is relatively close to him and can thus be encompassed by our view of him. The effect on the viewer is to constantly draw the attention back to the member of the Third Estate.

3. The lack of effective defense on the part of the noble and the clergyman and their slightly comic stance and expressions make them seem weak and lacking any power. The member of the Third Estate seems strong (having just broken his chains) and determined, so many viewers would likely see this positive portrayal of the Third Estate as supporting its actions. However, for those who feared what course the Revolution might take, the presence of arms in the foreground and the Bastille and National Guard in the background might raise some concern.

Reading Historical Documents

Answers will vary.

1. According to Clermont Tonnerre, adversaries of the Jews argue that Jews are not sociable, are commanded to loan money at usurious rates, cannot be joined to the French by marriage or social interchange, the armies would not have them serving in the defense of the country, and Jews have their own judges and laws. Clermont Tonnerre proposes that Jews be treated and handled as individuals, not

as a separate nation, and that their separate judges and laws should be removed so that they can become integrated into France. If they refuse, then they should be banished.

2. One of the key ideals of the Enlightenment that this speech represents is that Jews, or any other group, should not be oppressed or denied civil rights based on their religion. He argues that the only test a creed should pass in regard to the social body is that of morals. The idea that citizenship should be based on secular rather than religious qualifications is one of the hallmarks of the Enlightenment.

3. In the fourth paragraph the society alludes to the notion that slavery should eventually end, although not yet because an immediate end to slavery would create chaos in the colonies and the slaves themselves are not ready for their freedom. Immediate freedom would be a "deadly gift" tantamount to abandoning "without assistance children in the cradle or mutilated and impotent beings."

4. Although the society condemns the mistreatment of black slaves on the plantations and the "prostitution" of the slave trade, it seems to be more from a concern with preserving the image of France than with the slaves themselves. The pamphlet even suggests keeping the institution of slavery, but treating slaves more kindly so that they might reproduce and make the slave trade unnecessary. According to the pamphlet, it is how slaves are mistreated rather than the institution of slavery itself that is the main problem.

5. The debate between Edmund Burke and Thomas Paine revolves around whether or not a government can be founded on the abstract principles of natural rights. Burke argues that experience and not theory is the most important part of constructing a government, whereas Paine argues that governments are based on constitutions, which really do exist.

6. Both these writers had the benefit of hindsight. Joseph de Maistre was writing later in the Revolution (1797), and Madame de Staël after the Revolution (1818). They both focus on the violence of the Revolution and the Terror. De Maistre pays particular attention to the affects of the Revolution on religion, such as the desecration of objects of worship and the apostasy of the clergy. He gives the Revolution an almost mystical quality, saying that it "seems to belong to another world." De Staël is less critical of the Revolution, and blames its excesses on the oppression of the nobles and clergy of the old regime.

Chapter 21: Napoleon and the Revolutionary Legacy, 1800–1830

CHAPTER OVERVIEW

Key Events

1. b; Napoleon Bonaparte
2. d; The decade-long conflict between the church and France came to an end.
3. b; Slavery was abolished.
4. c; Supply problems and the weather forced Napoleon to withdraw, which began his eventual downfall.
5. d; The rebellion was crushed by an invading French Army
6. a; Bavaria

Key Terms

1. C; consuls (p. 789)
2. A; Civil Code (p. 792)
3. D; Continental System (p. 801)
4. H; restoration (p. 808)
5. B; conservatism (p. 808)
6. K; working class (p. 811)
7. E; ideology (p. 812)
8. F; liberalism (p. 812)
9. J; socialism (p. 813)
10. G; nationalism (p. 814)
11. I; romanticism (p. 815)

Identification

1. Joseph Fouché
2. neoclassical
3. Josephine
4. Legion of Honor
5. François-René de Chateaubriand
6. the Louisiana Territory
7. Austerlitz
8. Frederick William III
9. Borodino
10. St. Helena
11. Klemens von Metternich
12. Charles Maurice de Talleyrand
13. Alexander I
14. Edmund Burke
15. George Stephenson
16. Lord Byron
17. William Wordsworth
18. Eugène Delacroix
19. Caspar David Friedrich
20. Nicholas I
21. Otto I
22. Simon Bolivar
23. Louis-Philippe
24. George IV

CHAPTER REVIEW

Multiple Choice

1.	d	15.	d	28.	b
2.	c	16.	b	29.	b
3.	b	17.	d	30.	a
4.	d	18.	a	31.	b
5.	d	19.	b	32.	d
6.	c	20.	b	33.	a
7.	b	21.	b	34.	b
8.	c	22.	b	35.	a
9.	c	23.	c	36.	b
10.	c	24.	b	37.	c
11.	d	25.	c	38.	c
12.	d	26.	b	39.	d
13.	b	27.	d	40.	a
14.	b				

Short Answer

Answers will vary.

1. Although Napoleon did not hold any deep religious convictions, he reconciled France with the Catholic church because be believed it was an important institution for upholding authority and because he wanted to gain the support of Catholics who had been alienated by the policies of the Revolution. In 1801, he entered into a concordat with Pope Pius VII in which the pope would accept to the sale of all church lands that had occurred during the Revolution, and the government would pay the salaries of bishops and priests who swore loyalty to the state. Catholicism was officially recognized as the religion of "the great majority of French citizens."

2. The Civil Code sharply curtailed women's rights in almost every aspect of public and private life. Even those revolutionary laws that had been favorable to women were modified, and rights held by women under the monarchy were revoked. Napoleon firmly believed women possessed inherent weaknesses, both mental and physical, requiring their restriction to the domestic sphere. Thus, the law obligated husbands to support their wives, but only husbands could control any property held in common. Divorce was possible, but severely restricted, especially for women, and a wife's infidelity was more reprehensible than a husband's. The state believed that the imposition of the Civil Code would reinforce the family and make women responsible for private virtue, while leaving public decisions to men.

3. Napoleon attributed his military successes mainly to morale; years of revolutionary ideology had taught soldiers to identify the army with the French nation, greatly contributing to the passionate loyalty and vigor of Napoleon's troops. Also significant, Napoleon had opened the way for middle-class citizens to become officers, making military service a means to social mobility. In addition, due to nationwide conscription, Napoleon's army was very large, significantly larger than other continental armies. Napoleon also owed much of his success to his style of leadership and his military tactics. He fought alongside his soldiers in many of his battles, and had a pragmatic and direct approach to strategy in which he attacked the main body of the opposing army and tried to crush it in a lightning campaign. This formidable French force, united into one Grand Army, was personally commanded by Napoleon, a brilliant strategist who, until the Russian campaign, consistently outmaneuvered his opponents on the battlefield.

4. Whenever the Grand Army was victorious, Napoleon annexed territories and set up satellite kingdoms with French-appointed rulers. He tried to impose standardized, central government based on the model of the French Empire and he forced French-style reforms on the territories he annexed or ruled indirectly. In Germany and Italy, for instance, Napoleon consolidated the disparate, small territories in order to rule more effectively. He abolished serfdom and seigneurial dues, introduced the Napoleonic Code, and extended religious toleration and some civil rights to religious minorities such as the Jews. Reactions to Napoleon's influence were mixed; his rule often brought about real improvements to public works, legal systems, trade, and education, but tax increases and imposed conscription fomented discontent. Resistance to Napoleonic rule saw the development of nationalist sentiment in many European countries.

5. In 1812, Napoleon ruled over a vast empire despite growing resistance in some annexed territories. In that same year, however, Napoleon made a tactical error and invaded Russia. Exhaustion, hunger, failing morale, disease, and a growing dead-body count resulted in Napoleon's eventual retreat. The Russian campaign, a massive and humiliating defeat for Napoleon, had been compromised by Napoleon's military involvement on two distant fronts—Spain and Russia—simultaneously. This defeat was followed by the organization of a British–Russian coalition against Napoleon. His control over Europe crumbled as revolts against him spread and military defeats followed one after another. The allied powers invaded France and marched toward Paris. The Senate deposed Napoleon in 1814 and he was sent into exile on the island of Elba. Although he soon returned and attempted to regain power, he was decisively defeated at Waterloo by a British coalition and the Prussian army and sent into exile for the rest of his life on the West African island of St. Helena.

6. The overall aim of the Congress of Vienna was to establish a balance of power in Europe that relied on cooperation among the major powers while guaranteeing the status of smaller states. The congress sought to restore to their former rulers as many regimes as possible, but this was not always feasible because so much had changed in the twenty-five years between the beginning of the Revolution and the fall of Napoleon. In these cases, territories were rearranged in a way such that balanced the competing interests of the great powers. This produced a new diplomatic order in which the legitimacy of states depended on the treaty system, not on divine right.

7. Conservatism was a political ideology that developed as a reaction to the rapid changes of the Revolution and Napoleonic wars. Many conservatives were inspired by Edmund Burke, an outspoken critic of the French Revolution. They rejected the Enlightenment and the Revolution, and believed that religious and other major traditions were an essential foundation for any society. The church, the state, and the patriarchal family would provide an enduring social order; while faith, history, and tradition should fill the vacuum left by the failure of reason. This ideology benefited greatly from the atmosphere of disillusionment in potential of reason that resulted from the violence excesses of the Revolution.

8. The religious revivals in post-Napoleonic Europe were spawned largely by the experience of revolutionary upheaval and decades of nearly constant European warfare. Although these often challenged the status quo, especially in Protestant countries, revivalist movements usually avoided open criticism of the government. In their hostility to rigid doctrine, and their encouragement of popular preaching, some revivalists fostered a sense of democratic community and even a rudimentary sexual equality because there were many women preachers. They

also worked on improving literacy among the poor. Revivalist movements also sent missionaries to other parts of the globe, which eventually became one of the arms of European imperialism and cultural influence in the nineteenth century.

9. The Industrial Revolution is a term used to describe the set of changes that brought steam-driven machinery, large factories, and a new working class to Great Britain, and then to the rest of Europe. Its influence spread slowly, but its impact was dramatic. The Industrial Revolution first transformed the textile industry, as new steam-driven machines brought workers together in urban factories. A surge in eighteenth-century urban populations fed workers into the new factory system, leading to the gradual development of a new socioeconomic class made up of factory laborers: the working class. Although the European Industrial Revolution threatened the survival of some artisans as well as local and foreign industries, it allowed for economic growth and spurred various political reforms and the development of labor unions.

10. Liberalism was derived from the writings of John Locke and the philosophy of the Enlightenment; liberals defined themselves in opposition to conservatives on one side of the political spectrum and revolutionaries on the other. It advocated constitutional guarantees of personal liberty and free trade in economics, believing that greater liberty in politics and economic matters would promote social improvement and economic growth. Liberals were thus also supportive of industrialization and the social and economic changes it produced, and many joined the abolitionist, antislavery movements. Liberalism denounced the violence and excessive state power promoted by the French Revolution. This ideology appealed mainly to the middle class.

11. Nationalism holds that all peoples derive their identities from their nations, which are defined by common language, shared cultural traditions, and sometimes religion. Nationalists could also be liberals, socialists, or conservatives. Nationalists were particularly disruptive in the Austrian Empire, which included a variety of peoples united only by their enforced allegiance to the Habsburg emperor. The domestic policy of Metternich, the chief minister to the Habsburg emperor Francis I, aroused nationalist sentiments. Secret nationalist societies, like the *carbonari* and the *Burschenschaften*, supported political rights and national self-determination. Similarly, in Russia when Tsar Alexander began revoking various constitutional rights, Polish students and military officers responded by forming secret nationalist societies to plot for change. In the small states of the Germanic Confederation and Italy, nationalism led to a push toward national unity.

12. The Congress of Vienna crushed the hopes of liberals and nationalists for constitutional freedoms and national unity and autonomy because the influence of the great powers was often insurmountable. Although isolated revolts threatened the hold of some conservative governments, most insurrections were quickly crushed. The great powers often combined to deal with such uprisings and often intervened to defeat them. For example, great power foreign intervention ended a liberal revolt in Spain and the nationalist uprisings in the Italian kingdoms of Naples and Piedmont. A notable exception was that great power intervention in support of Greek independence was the decisive factor in the success of the Greek revolt against the Ottoman Turks. Turkey was defeated by a combined force of British, French, and Russian armies and navies, and Greece was declared an independent kingdom in 1830.

13. Upon his accession to the throne, the new French king Charles X instituted a series of increasingly repressive policies in the 1820s. Compensating nobles who had lost property during the French Revolution, passing strict laws defending the church, dissolving the legislature, and imposing strict censorship, enraged liberals and led to insurrection. In response to mass demonstrations and street fighting, a group of liberal leaders, afraid of the reestablishment of a republic, offered the throne to Louis-Philippe, duke of Orléans. Charles X went into exile, and the new king extended political liberties and voting rights. These limited reforms had very little effect on the indigent and working classes, though. Despite further revolts by more radical groups, the 1830 revolution only managed to install a more liberal, constitutional monarchy.

14. The 1820s was a period of liberal reform in Britain under the leadership of Robert Peel and the Duke of Wellington. Nevertheless, when the Whig Party introduced legislation to expand the right to vote, enough members of the Tory Party resisted its passage. In response to mass demonstrations and the threatened intervention of the king, the bill was passed. Although not revolutionary, the Reform Bill gave representation to the new industrial cities in the north for the first time and set a precedent for the further extension of voting rights.

15. The new paternalism was an assertion of a patriarchal model of power in the Napoleonic state. Napoleon's personal version of paternalism was applied to many aspects of public and private life. For example, the Civil Code not only established a system of male domination over women, but also that of a father over his children, as absolute obedience was expected of children and financial support for children was expected of fathers. On a grander scale, the state saw itself obligated to impose similar patriarchal authority over its citizens as well as provide succor to those in need, like indigent mothers, foundlings, and poor citizens deserving of aid. The new paternalism also affected the employer–employee relationship with the state prohibiting union organizing and closely monitoring the conduct of workers.

BUILDING HISTORICAL SKILLS

Reading Maps

Answers will vary.

1. Wherever possible, the delegates at the Congress restored pre-Napoleonic monarchs to their thrones, such as the king of Spain. France had to surrender all the territories it had gained after 1790, but still kept its status as a major power to balance other European powers. However, not everything was returned to the way it was. The Austrian Netherlands and the Dutch Republic were united to form the kingdom of the Netherlands, the German states were

made into a German Confederation, and the Grand Duchy of Warsaw became the kingdom of Poland with the Russian tsar as its ruler.

2. France lost its territories in Savoy, central Italy, the Netherlands, and on the east coast of the Adriatic Sea as a result of the Congress of Vienna. Some of Napoleon's satellite states, such as Spain, returned to their prerevolutionary rulers. The Grand Duchy of Warsaw was absorbed by Russia and Prussia. Some of the Confederation of the Rhine was given to the Austrian Empire, whereas the remainder became the German Confederation. Napoleon's satellite kingdoms in Italy were formed into a series of small kingdoms.

Reading Illustrations

Answers will vary.

1. The scene depicted in *The Coronation of Napoleon and Josephine* is one of grandeur and respectfulness. The elegant and large room, the noblemen, the ladies-in-waiting, and the orderliness of the scene all suggest grandeur and respectfulness.

2. An upstart who seized power in a military coup, Napoleon was concerned with placing his rule on a continuum of the long tradition of French rulers. David's painting shows a crowd of people watching Napoleon's coronation, which could be taken as a statement regarding popular approval concerning this event. The painting shows a court scene, with richly dressed people and impressive surroundings, which give the impression that Napoleon's coronation was legitimate.

3. Napoleon's belief that he was the master of his destiny came across in his decision to crown himself, rather than have the pope crown him, as was traditional. While some may have admired this act, others may have seen it as the action of an upstart with no respect for tradition or the church. It was much safer for David to depict Napoleon's crowning of his wife, especially because this action seemed consonant with beliefs concerning women's subordination to men that were codified in the Civil Code and widely accepted at the time.

Reading Historical Documents

Answers will vary.

1. Although they defeated the Russian army when they confronted it, the march into Russia was slowed by the scorched-earth strategy employed by the retreating Russian army. The French were further slowed by the need to clear downed trees and barricades left behind by the Russians to impede the French. Napoleon's army also faced serious morale problems, as suggested in Walter's memoir. Because the countryside had been so completely devastated, the French army could not forage for food, and so was weakened by supply problems.

2. Napoleon preferred to face the enemy in a decisive battle and then overwhelm it with superior numbers. He also recognized the importance of soldier morale. The army he brought into Russia was enormous (over 600,000) but the Russians never met him in a decisive battle. As a result, Napoleon was forced deeper and deeper into Russia, and supply problems eroded the army's morale.

3. Wordsworth writes about his nostalgic recollection of his childhood "when first I came among these hills." He also writes about the beauty of nature with its deep rivers, lonely streams, tall rocks, and gloomy woods. He has a melancholic sense of regret for the past and the sense of union he felt with nature as a child.

4. Wordsworth's emphasis on emotion, melancholy, and nostalgia is in sharp contrast with the Enlightenment emphasis on reason. This poem is about an escape from human society, whereas the Enlightenment sought to apply reason to solve social problems.

5. Benjamin Constant gives the more thorough of the two criticisms of Napoleon. He blames Napoleon for stifling intellectual life in France, and extorts the nation for its support of the man who struck terror into the hearts of people and plunged the nation into war. Constant argues that constant war was the only way Napoleon was able to remain in power. Victor Hugo portrays Napoleon as an almost supernatural villain who suffers divine punishment for "all the tears he caused mankind to shed, and all the blood he caused to flow."

6. Napoleon states that all the good he accomplished outweighs all the faults he committed. He claims that his rise to power was unparalleled because he did not achieve it through crime. He also argues that his real legacy will be the Civil Code he helped institute, and the fact that he replaced the traditional oligarchies with a system based more on merit. In Napoleon's mind, his wars were a small price to pay for these benefits, and the only reason why he will be criticized is because he did not ultimately succeed.

Chapter 22: Industralism, Urbanization, and Revolution, 1830–1850

CHAPTER OVERVIEW

Key Events

1. c; Polluted water
2. d; Alcohol abuse
3. b; There was little immediate effect, and the slave trade continued, peaking in the early 1840s
4. c; An economic alliance in the German Confederation
5. c; The United States
6. d; Great Britain and Russia
7. a; An exhibition hall for displays of modern industry

Key Terms

1. B; cholera (p. 829)
2. H; lithograph (p. 829)
3. I; opium (p. 830)
4. J; social question (p. 840)
5. E; daguerreotype (p. 843)
6. K; temperance movement (p. 845)
7. F; domesticity (p. 847)
8. G; imperialism (p. 848)
9. D; Corn Laws (p. 853)
10. C; communists (p. 855)
11. A; Chartism (p. 855)

Identification

1. Belgium
2. 5
3. women and girls
4. tuberculosis
5. Central Short Time Committee
6. Thomas Cole
7. Gothic
8. Elizabeth Fry
9. opium
10. Nicholas I
11. Adam Mickiewicz
12. Ireland
13. Corn Laws
14. Flora Tristan
15. Thomas Macaulay's
16. Alphonse de Lamartine
17. 1852
18. Frankfurt
19. Hungarian
20. Crystal Palace

CHAPTER REVIEW

Multiple Choice

1. d	12. a	23. b
2. a	13. c	24. a
3. a	14. d	25. b
4. a	15. a	26. a
5. d	16. a	27. d
6. c	17. b	28. c
7. b	18. b	29. b
8. c	19. c	30. c
9. b	20. d	31. c
10. a	21. b	32. b
11. c	22. c	

Short Answer

Answers will vary.

1. Railroads and steam were the two most important technological developments of the Industrial Revolution. Railroads created new, efficient transportation networks for raw materials and finished goods, which in turn spurred still more industrial development. The success of railroads is attributable, in large part, to the invention of the steam engine, the force driving the locomotive. The steam engine also provided power for textile factories, mining operations, and steamboats. Steam-powered engines made Britain the world leader in manufacturing, and generated enormous economic and industrial changes in Europe and elsewhere.

2. The factory system created huge gains in productivity and unheard-of wealth, but also new forms of toil and poverty. The promise of work attracted rural people facing hunger and poverty and, wherever factories were built, the populations of cities grew. As more people moved to cities, overcrowding, lack of sanitation, inadequate clean water, alcoholism, prostitution, child labor, a shrinking life expectancy, and other social problems became a concern for all authorities and all social classes. Although industri-

alization proceeded slowly on the European continent, factories began replacing the households of preindustrial artisans laboring in cottage industries. In rural areas, where factory work did not dominate, new forms of the putting-out system emerged: labor was divided into piecework and farmed out to women paid low wages.

3. Rapid urbanization created serious social problems. Surging population far exceeded the capacity of the urban sanitation systems. Garbage littered streets; raw sewage collected in cesspools; dirt and smoke polluted the atmosphere; and the availability of clean drinking water was limited. Available housing fell far behind demand, and overcrowding was severe. Under these conditions, disease spread rampantly. Epidemics of cholera were particularly terrifying and deadly. Municipal authorities were not capable of accommodating the population growth or combating its ill effects. As pollution worsened and disease spread, governments began to investigate and ameliorate some urban woes. Middle-class reformers somewhat improved the deplorable working conditions in mines and factories, but urban life strained traditional family life, particularly in the lower classes. Fear and resentment between the middle and lower classes also led to unfounded accusations that the working class was morally degenerate.

4. The social question referred to concerns about the changes brought to European society by industrialization and urbanization. Romanticism, the dominant artistic movement of the period, had always idealized nature and took a dim view of the changes industrialization brought. Many romantics looked to the preindustrial past and unspoiled nature; others, like Joseph M. W. Turner, explored the contrast between past and present. Novelists began writing about the working classes and their associated social problems. In particular, Charles Dickens and Honoré de Balzac depicted everyone from the most elite gentlemen and ladies to the least presentable vagabonds and whores. Artists Gustave Doré and Honoré Daumier produced thousands of drawings and lithographs that exposed and satirized contemporary problems. Art that reflected society and social relations attracted the European masses, who flocked to cultural events, leading to an explosion of culture. Museums opened to the public, mass media expanded, and reading material of all genres was made readily available.

5. Social reforms, generally instigated by religious-minded members of the middle and upper classes, were devised to instill morality and respectability in the working classes. Religious organizations worked to overcome working-class indifference to religion and, in both Catholic and Protestant countries, women took an active role in fighting prostitution and excessive drinking. Sunday schools and Bible groups promoted education and literacy as vehicles to promote moral conduct for the working classes. The European elite used religion to impose discipline and order on those they perceived as wayward and potentially destructive to the moral health of society. In addition, believing that the enslavement of human beings was detestable and utterly unchristian, religious reformers of the 1830s and 1840s were vital to the cessation of European involvement in the Atlantic slave trade.

6. In the first half of the nineteenth century, European colonialism underwent a subtle but momentous transformation. Colonialism became imperialism. Imperialism involved both a geographical shift—as attention turned away from the plantation colonies of the Caribbean and focused on new colonies in Asia and Africa—and a change in the way that colonies were administered. Rather than eliminating indigenous peoples and creating settler colonies ruled directly by Europeans who often imported slave labor, imperialism involved more indirect forms of economic exploitation of and political rule over the native population. Europeans still profited from their colonies, but they now also aimed to reform colonial peoples in their own image, often enforcing their economic interests through the use of military force.

7. Nationalists sought political autonomy for their ethnic group, usually defined as a people linked by language and shared traditions. Channeling the revolutionary spirit of the preceding century into ethnic pride, nationalism became a major determinant of personal and political identity. Although Poles, Italians, Germans, Irish, and Russians all pursued nationalist goals, ethnic clashes were especially explosive within the Austrian Empire, which ruled over many different nationalities, such as Magyars, Czech, Slovaks, Serbs, Croats, Romanians, Poles, and Italians. Each of these peoples produced leaders who called not only for political rights but also for a cultural revival in language, literature, and education. Disagreements over less sweeping issues and ethnic rivalries caused nationalistic revolts to splinter and fail, and rarely did differing ethnic groups form a united front against their opponents. An exception was the German customs union known as the *Zollverein*, which was established in 1834 to advance the economic unification of the German states, arguing for external tariffs to promote industrialization and cooperation across German borders in order that Germany might compete with the rest of Europe.

8. There were two major types of liberalism in the 1830s and 1840s: British and continental. British liberals, having already achieved many constitutional reforms and political rights, focused on economic issues. Because Britain was the dominant industrial power, the political program of British liberals pressed for free trade and less governmental intervention in the economy. British liberals wanted the Corn Laws and high tariffs on low-cost imported grain repealed. Continental liberals focused mainly on achieving political and constitutional reforms. Unlike the British, they were opposed to international free trade, which would have given the British an overwhelming advantage; rather, continental liberals favored governmental intervention in the hope that free internal trade and tariffs against imports would protect their small but growing industries. Before 1848, continental liberals failed to achieve significant constitutional reform, and that led to insurrections by working-class and republican radicals.

9. Socialists saw the positive potential of industrialization and hoped that economic planning and working-class organization would solve the problems caused by industrial growth. Believing that liberalism did not go far enough to correct social inequalities, socialists aimed at completely reconstructing social relationships along a more equal basis. Socialists decried class inequality and criticized the theft of workers' profits by industrialists, financiers, and factory owners and managers. They perceived workers as the only productive part of the economy and pressed for an economic future where all citizens were workers, sharing a cooperative and prosperous life in a classless society. Because of their collectivist vision, socialists were increasingly known as communists.

10. The revolutions of 1848 were impelled by ideological turmoil combined with large-scale unemployment, inflation, and famine. Throughout Europe, poor harvests caused food shortages; the resulting famine jeopardized social relations as rural desperation grew and crowds rioted in markets and bakeries demanding government action to ensure fair prices. With officials unable to feed the hungry and starving, financial tensions escalated and governments came under harsh criticism. The crop failures and rising rates of poverty in rural areas damaged the industrial economy as well. Rural people could no longer afford to buy industrial goods, which caused urban workers to lose their jobs to factory closures and decreased production. Class conflict was open and sometimes violent. These revolutions were further fueled by political ideologies such as nationalism and socialism, which were opposed to the conservative policies of many European governments.

11. The inaction of the government of Louis-Philippe in the face of famine plus its continuing resistance to electoral reform, brought together working- and middle-class opposition. Their combined pressure forced the creation of a liberal republic. The government of the Second Republic introduced reforms that satisfied the middle classes, but the workers wanted further action and pressed for the creation of national workshops to provide them with employment and minimal wages. The workshops were established, but the government drastically underestimated the number of workers who would seek relief from them. The workshops' growing costs and the increasing radicalism of workers frightened middle-class liberals and the workshops were closed, an event that led to street fighting and disorder. The workers' revolt was crushed and stability was reestablished through the widely supported election of Louis-Napoleon Bonaparte as president. Like his uncle before him, Bonaparte eventually ended the republic and declared himself emperor.

12. Although the revolutionaries of 1848 failed to achieve most of their goals, their efforts left a profound mark on the political and social landscape of Europe. No revolutionary nationalist or constitutionalist governments survived, yet the way was paved for both these political trends in the future. In France, despite the swing toward the conservative Louis-Napoleon, it was recognized that no future government could rule without extensive popular consultation. The failure of Italian states to unify did not stop the spread of nationalist ideas, neither did it stop demands for democratic participation. In Austria, Prussia, and Germany, nationalism was taken up with enormous popular enthusiasm and became a practical reality. The participation of artisans, workers, and journeymen in democratic clubs increased popular political awareness and helped prepare the lower classes for broader political participation.

BUILDING HISTORICAL SKILLS

Reading Maps

Answers will vary.

1. Great Britain was by far the most industrialized nation in Europe by 1850, with the greatest concentration of railroads, and heavily industrialized regions around Liverpool and Manchester, Birmingham, and Glasgow. France and northern Italy also had some industrialized areas along with Belgium. There were also several pockets of industrialization in the German Confederation.

2. Spain, Sweden and Norway, the Ottoman Empire, Italy, and Russia were the least industrialized parts of Europe, although some of these areas did have some railroad development, usually around major cities.

3. Countries like Spain, Sweden, and Norway were not very industrialized, but had important deposits of iron ore and coal. These raw materials were extremely important for the Industrial Revolution. Areas of France that were not industrialized also had large amounts of coal and iron.

Reading Illustrations

Answers will vary.

1. This painting is about change and the passing of old ways. New industrial technologies are changing the older ways of life.

2. The emphasis on nature, which takes more of the canvas than human activity, is typical for romanticism. There is also a sense of nostalgia for the passing of the old ways. Even on its final voyage, the *Téméraire* is a beautiful ship.

Reading Historical Documents

Answers will vary.

1. Heine writes about how "the rich man's king" was unmoved by the suffering of the workers and how he allowed them to be shot by his soldiers. He also writes that nothing but disgrace and shame thrives in Germany, which is rotting and molding.

2. Like other romantic poetry, Heine's poem uses natural imagery and decries the changes brought about by industrialization. However, there is more of a political and ideological edge to this poem.

3. Like proponents of other political ideologies, Marx and Engels offered their own reading of history that supported their political position. They summarize all of history as a constant class struggle between "oppressor" and "oppressed." Despite the rapid changes of the nineteenth century and the fall of feudalism, class antagonisms continued.

4. Marx and Engels believed that industrialization would bring about the final downfall of the bourgeoisie. By bringing together the proletariat, who were previously isolated from one another, industry would unite them as a single class that would inevitably overtake the bourgeoisie.

5. Scholars who focus on the positive impact of industrialization emphasize higher paying jobs in factories, work opportunities for women, and a greater availability of lower priced consumer goods. Scholars who emphasize the negative effects point out that artisans and weavers lost jobs to factory workers, families suffered from women's absence, and pollution from factories damaged the environment and lowered life expectancies.

6. The numbers in the left-hand column represent the year, and the numbers in the right-hand column represent the difference between the average of nonfarm unskilled wages and farm wages. In the first year, the difference is zero —nonfarm and farm wages were equal; in 1805, nonfarm wages were only 86.6 percent of farm wages. Similarly, in 1810, farm wages were higher than nonfarm wages. This began to change in 1815, when nonfarm wages began to exceed farm wages.

7. One might look at the cost of living in cities to see if it was high enough to cancel out the higher wages nonfarm workers received. One could also look at quality-of-life issues, such as health, leisure, sanitation, and diet. If nonfarm workers were worse off in these categories, then that might suggest that higher wages alone do not indicate a higher standard of living.

Chapter 23: Politics and Culture of the Nation-State, c. 1850–1870

CHAPTER OVERVIEW

Key Events

1. b; The idea that careful study of facts would generate accurate laws of society
2. d; A sense of disillusionment with commercial values and the expanding reach of the nation-state
3. c; The concert of Europe, which had lasted since 1815, came to an end.
4. a; The British government began to rule India directly.
5. c; Russia's defeat in the Crimean War
6. c; A move to turn Japan into a modern, technologically powerful state
7. d; They were blamed for causing violence and disorder in the Commune.

Key Terms

1. M; Realpolitik (p. 873)
2. G; mir (p. 880)
3. O; zemstvos (p. 880)
4. N; Russification (p. 881)
5. H; nation-state (p. 881)
6. B; dual monarchy (p. 887)
7. I; Pan-Slavism (p. 888)
8. C; Haussmannization (p. 891)
9. F; Meiji Restoration (p. 898)
10. L; realism (p. 899)
11. D; Kulturkampf (p. 903)
12. J; positivism (p. 905)
13. A; anarchism (p. 907)
14. E; Marxism (p. 907)
15. K; proletariat (p. 907)

Identification

1. Corps legislative
2. Eugénie
3. Suez Canal
4. France
5. Romania
6. Piedmont-Sardinia
7. 1861
8. William I
9. Hungary
10. Benjamin Disraeli
11. Georges-Eugène Haussmann
12. Louis Pasteur
13. Sweden
14. Prussia
15. China
16. George Eliot
17. Charles-Pierre Baudelaire
18. Fyodor Dostoevsky
19. Gustave Courbet
20. *Des Ring des Nibelungen*
21. Pierre-Joseph Proudhon
22. anarchism
23. Karl Marx
24. London
25. Prussians

CHAPTER REVIEW

Multiple Choice

1.	a	15.	c	28.	b
2.	b	16.	b	29.	b
3.	c	17.	d	30.	b
4.	c	18.	c	31.	a
5.	b	19.	c	32.	b
6.	b	20.	a	33.	b
7.	d	21.	b	34.	d
8.	c	22.	d	35.	c
9.	d	23.	b	36.	d
10.	b	24.	c	37.	d
11.	c	25.	d	38.	b
12.	b	26.	d	39.	c
13.	d	27.	c	40.	a
14.	b				

Short Answer

Answers will vary.

1. Louis-Napoleon Bonaparte encouraged the resurgence of French grandeur, and his nation-building policies were aimed at political stability and strong state authority. He reduced representative government to a mere façade, and replaced republican rituals with an opulent, imperialistic style. Also a modernizer, Napoleon III promoted a strong economy, public works programs, and jobs, all of which enticed the middle and working classes away from radical politics. Internationally, Napoleon III's goals were to free France from the containment imposed upon it by the Congress of Vienna, to realign continental politics to benefit France, and to increase national glory.

2. Spectacularly bloody, the Crimean War claimed three-quarters of a million lives, more than two-thirds of whom died due to disease and starvation. This war introduced new technologies to combat, such as the railroad, the shell-firing cannon, breech-loading rifles, and steam-powered ships. Increasing press coverage and innovations like the telegraph changed the relationship between the battlefield and the home front, as news of the wars was spread more rapidly and in far greater detail than ever before. Shock and dismay over news from the front lines led to universal criticism of how governments were conducting the war. Some civilians assumed an active role in the war, like Florence Nightingale, who organized a battlefield nursing service. At war's end, the alliance between Russia and Austria was broken, and their grip on European affairs was loosened, undermining their ability to contain the forces of liberalism and nationalism in each of their countries. In Russia, defeat of serf conscript armies forced Alexander II to emancipate the serfs and to promulgate other liberal reforms.

3. Tsar Alexander II began the age of Great Reforms after Russia's defeat in the Crimean War that came at the close of a decade of insurrections and acts of defiance by the serfs, which had alarmed the aristocracy. The failure of armies comprised of serf conscripts made emancipation of the serfs as necessary for national renewal as for the serfs themselves. Nearly fifty million people were freed. Other reforms included the relaxation of censorship and travel restrictions. The tsar created a new judicial system that offered access to modern civil courts and recognized equality of persons before the law. Military reforms improved the treatment of soldiers and decreased the period of conscription from twenty-five years to six. Unfortunately, the Great Reforms left Russian autocracy intact and burdened the former serfs with debts and restrictions that prevented them from becoming a truly free and mobile labor force.

4. The main architect of Italian unification, Camillo di Cavour, entered into an alliance with Napoleon III in order to secure the military forces necessary to defeat the Austrians and gain independence for the kingdom of Piedmont-Sardinia. As nationalist aspirations grew, other parts of Italy rallied to the cause, undermining maneuvers by Napoleon III to gain the upper hand; Italians everywhere ousted their rulers and stood behind Piedmont's leadership. Guiseppe Garibaldi, a committed republican and guerilla fighter, landed in southern Italy with an army of volunteers to help liberate Sicily. Together, the armed forces of the Piedmontese and Garibaldi defeated anti-unification forces. Laying aside his dream of an Italian republic, Garibaldi cooperated with Cavour to name Victor Emmanuel king of Italy. Thus, shrewd diplomacy, military force, and a united popular front combined to create a unified Italian state.

5. Otto von Bismarck of Prussia guided the process of German unification. Realizing that the Habsburg Empire would never allow the full flowering of a Prussian state, Bismarck outmaneuvered the liberals in the Prussian parliament and began a military buildup. Once assured of Prussia's military might, he instigated a series of wars to gather German territories into Prussia or into an alliance with her. According to plan, the wars also heightened nationalism among the Prussian people. Victorious in his

war with Austria, Bismarck drove Prussia's rival from the German confederation and created a North German confederation led by Prussia. Then, in 1870, Bismarck used diplomacy, German nationalism, and deception to ignite a war with France; Prussia won decisively and eliminated the ambitious Napoleon III as a potential roadblock to German unification. King William of Prussia was pronounced the kaiser of a new German Empire; the new German Reich was based on Prussian military might and intense German nationalism.

6. Britain was a country with a stable and respected monarchy and a parliamentary system that steadily introduced constitutional and economic reforms, making for a relatively contented citizenry. As a relatively independent and ethnically homogenous nation, Britain experienced very few of the conflicts of other nations during that period despite its vexatious relationship with Ireland. Parliament, which steadily admitted more men into the political process, was run predominantly by the Liberal and Conservative parties and presided over by a monarchy that united critics, activists, and differing social classes in national causes. Economic prosperity further fortified the island nation and resulted in relative social peace.

7. As national pride grew in importance and, at the same time, disease was rampant, governments resolved to renew and improve their capitals' cityscapes and attend to the welfare of their citizens. As many European cities, especially capital cities, became the backdrop for displays of state power and national solidarity, refurbished cities became symbols of national grandeur, sporting handsome parks, wide boulevards, impressive museums, and imposing buildings of state. These new features represented national wealth and power, stability, and order. Such construction, however, required the destruction of previously existing structures; old, poor, working-class neighborhoods were often destroyed and their inhabitants dislocated. New understanding of the transmission of disease inspired public works projects to enhance sewer systems and drainage; pave roads; build public toilets; and provide safe, clean water for drinking and bathing. Expanding cities also created new suburbs and public transportation to move workers to and from the city's center.

8. Expanding states required larger bureaucracies. In order for bureaucracies to run smoothly, citizens were expected to follow a growing catalog of state regulations and government authority reached further into the realm of everyday life. Routine censuses provided states with details of their citizens' personal lives; such information was used for planning, for example, to set quotas for military conscription or to predict the need for new prisons. Sweden imposed an income tax on its citizens. The state also regulated prostitution and matters of public health. States took a more active role in schooling—from kindergarten to university—in the belief that education would create a general population more fit for citizenship and useful in economic progress. Expanding bureaucracies also increased social upward mobility because competitive exams opened more jobs to middle-class candidates, rather than to those with only social rank and connections to recommend them. In this case, it was the citizens who forced the state to conform to their ideas of order and competence.

9. Before the 1850s, European nations welcomed the commercial opportunities afforded them by their colonies, but they were also slow to invest significant resources in colonial government. After midcentury, Great Britain, France, and Russia revised their colonial policies by instituting direct rule, expanding colonial bureaucracies and, in many cases, providing a wider array of social and cultural services such as schools. For example, in India, Great Britain had exercised control indirectly through the East India Company, benefiting from trading treaties and transactions and permitting regional rulers to maintain their thrones but moving into areas whose thrones fell vacant. Gradually, British institutions arose in India, bureaucratic and economic presence made themselves felt, and colonists began efforts to instill Indians with European values. Indian resistance and resentment grew, leading to the Indian mutiny. After the mutiny was put down, the British government took direct control of India.

10. Artists and writers of the 1850s and 1860s reacted against the expanding nation-state and its intrusion into the private lives of citizens. Bemoaning the failed revolutions of 1848, many artists and writers criticized the brutal repression of revolutionary activists and expressed real concerns about the effect of enfranchising working-class men. Unable to romanticize their work or recapture an ideal past, disenchanted midcentury artists and writers expressed themselves through a literary and artistic style called realism. Professing to depict ordinary reality, writers such as Charles Dickens, George Eliot, Gustave Flaubert, and Charles-Pierre Baudelaire portrayed characters from all parts of society, emphasized social problems, and attacked a range of social conventions from marriage to family, and work to sex. Visual artists, such as Gustave Courbet and Édouard Manet, portrayed their subjects realistically, choosing to hide neither the shabbiness nor the depravity of life. Many of these writers and artists were labeled unsettling and obscene by authorities.

11. While some saw religion as a source of social order, some nation builders, intellectuals, and economic liberals came to object to the competition for loyalty and to religious worldviews not always in harmony with their own. Bismarck mounted a *Kulturkampf* (culture war) against religion. The Roman Catholic Church, feeling its status threatened and its role usurped, explicitly attacked nineteenth-century visions of progress and reform, especially those embodied in such institutions as secular public schools. But, in 1878, a new pontiff began encouraging up-to-date scholarship in Catholic institutes and universities and accepted aspects of democracy. New Catholic doctrines, like papal infallibility and the Immaculate Conception, stirred popular religious sentiment. In the case of Bernadette Soubirous's visions of the Virgin Mary at Lourdes, the Catholic church showed that it could use railroads, medical verifications of miraculous cures, and journalism to make Lourdes a modern religious center. The Orthodox church's Pan-Slavic appeal fostered nationalism among oppressed Serbs. Many urban Jews abandoned religious practices. The social composition of people of faith no longer included everyone.

12. The entire Judeo-Christian tradition was called into question by Charles Lyell, a geologist who suggested that the

earth's structure was far older than the Bible's assertions, and Charles Darwin, who argued that life and human beings had taken shape over millions of years. Gradually, Darwin's findings and the subsequent work of other scientists went beyond affecting religious traditions and beliefs: biological research began influencing societal roles and relationships as well. The discovery of spontaneous ovulation led scientists to determine that women were passive in reproduction, lacking all of the sexual drives present in men. Darwin's theory of natural selection was used to explain the social order; although Darwin pointed to a common ancestor for all races, he maintained that white European men dominated the nineteenth century because they were more highly evolved than women and people of color. Scientific approaches to nature also pressed for a new understanding of social order that led to positivism, which claimed that the careful study of facts would generate accurate laws of society and thereby promote progress and order.

13. After a period of repression in the 1850s, workers' organizations slowly reemerged as a political force. These were part of a developing pattern of horizontal rather than vertical allegiances, stressing similarity and equality rather than hierarchy and subordination. A variety of unions existed, their outlook shaped by many different sorts of political theories, but they all challenged the established political order. For example, Pierre-Joseph Proudhon opposed centralized states and proposed that society be organized around groupings of men in artisans' workshops, something he defined as a mutualist social organization. Mikhail Bakhunin argued that the existence of the state was the root of social injustice and advocated anarchy—the destruction of all state power.

14. Marx held that human existence was defined by the basic need to work and that the fundamental organization of any society, including its politics and culture, was based on the relationships arising out of work and production, theories known as dialectical and historical materialism. This meant that the foundation of a society rested on class relationships. The type of relationship—feudal, capitalist, etc.—was what Marx called "the mode of production." Rejecting the liberal focus on individual rights, Marx emphasized the unequal class relations imposed on workers by the upper classes: lords, slaveholders, capitalists, and the bourgeoisie. He believed that social organization and productive life were in conflict rather than in harmony. For Marx, a working-class revolt against capitalism and the abolition of private property would end class struggle and lead to a true socialist society.

15. The defeat of France in the Franco-Prussian War and the economic hardship resulting from the war left the people of Paris discontented and bitter. Suffering through a harsh winter and a Prussian siege that cut off the supply of food, Parisians demanded to elect their own local government. The interim French government attempted to repress the Parisians with French troops; the Parisians condemned the utter despotism of the centralized state and declared Paris a self-governing commune. The Commune sought liberal political equality and the liberation of the worker through social revolution. The Communards, however, disagreed on specific policies and methods for achieving their vision of social justice. After two months of existence, the Commune was crushed by the French army engaged in bitter and bloody street fighting with the citizens; following their victory, the army executed tens of thousands of citizens perceived as traitors.

BUILDING HISTORICAL SKILLS

Reading Maps

Answers will vary.

1. The Ottoman Empire controlled the Dardanelles Straits. These connected the Black Sea (and Russia) to the Mediterranean Sea. The weakening of the Ottoman Empire opened the possibility for the Russia and the Austrian Empire to gain new territories.

2. France helped orchestrate the war to fracture the conservative alliance between Russia and the Austrian Empire that had kept French ambitions in check since the Congress of Vienna. Great Britain was drawn in because it needed to protect its Mediterranean trade routes to East Asia, which would have been threatened if the Russians gained dominance over that region.

Reading Illustrations

Answers will vary.

1. Darwin argued that all species developed through the process of evolution, a process whereby species responded to their environments in ways that enhanced their ability to reproduce; as species evolved, they got stronger. The illustrator is demonstrating the principle of evolution by showing the similarities between humans and monkeys. Darwin and the monkey both have similarly shaped, hairy bodies; similar hands and feet; and both have high, bald foreheads, large ears, and long chins.

2. Although both have human expressions on their faces, Darwin's face is more recognizably human, whereas the monkey's face still looks like that of a monkey. Darwin seems to be older than the monkey, and is more active, holding out the mirror into which they both gaze.

3. Darwin seems to have more authority because he is older and active, holding out the mirror in an authoritative manner. Social Darwinists believed that evolution had created a natural social hierarchy whereby more evolved groups, viewed as superior to less evolved groups, were justified in their claims to more power and more wealth. By depicting the monkey and Darwin as similar, and yet not equal, the illustration reflects Social Darwinist assumptions about the consequences of evolution and perceived social roles.

Reading Historical Documents

Answers will vary.

1. Mary Seacole's activities as a nurse were an extension of the domestic role of women. She talks about bringing the comforts of home to sick soldiers, and providing them with nourishing food. She performs these tasks with modesty, and not for her own reputation.

2. Mary Seacole was performing these services at a time when medicine was becoming more professionalized, and persons without official training and certification—especially women—were being forced out. The fact that a

woman of minority descent was able to participate in the Crimean War in this capacity is also unconventional.

3. Bismarck justifies his actions by arguing that avoiding war will cost Prussia its honor and national confidence in her. Maintaining national honor is the highest priority, and without honor there would be no confidence in the state, which could lead to disorder.

4. The most important condition that allowed Bismarck to trick the public into going to war was a literate public that read newspapers. The political importance of public opinion was another condition, as were nationalist sentiments about the honor and pride of the state.

5. Governments issued photographs of wars, such as the Crimean War, to gain the support and loyalty of their citizens. Governmental figures issued photographs of themselves so as to appear more familiar to their subjects. Governments could use photographs to promote advances made under their administration, or even to promote a false image of their reign, as had Queen Isabella II of Spain. Individuals might use photographs to support a cult of celebrity for themselves, such as the professors who sold pictures of themselves outside their classrooms, or merely to send to relatives. Photographs also had commercial uses, such as photographs of merchandise that salesmen used to advertise their wares.

6. Although photographs can show the past more vividly, they can also be tampered with. Details can reveal everyday life and let us see the faces of persons from the past; but touched-up or altered photos are manipulative. Battlefield photos have been found to be staged after the fact.

Chapter 24: Industry, Empire, and Everyday Life, 1870–1890

CHAPTER OVERVIEW

Key Events

1. c; Camera
2. b; A thirty-year period of economic fluctuations that featured sharp downturns, the severity of which varied from country to country
3. c; Russia
4. d; Italy had an imperial rivalry with France
5. c; The aristocracy lost its traditional influence in the countryside
6. a; Anarchists

Key Terms

1. G; outwork (p. 918)
2. A; capital-intensive industry (p. 920)
3. E; limited liability corporation (p. 921)
4. D; impressionism (p. 944)
5. F; new unionism (p. 946)
6. I; Second International (p. 946)
7. H; Reform Act of 1884 (p. 948)
8. C; home rule (p. 948)
9. J; Third Republic (p. 949)
10. B; Dual Alliance (p. 953)

Identification

1.	Karl Benz	11.	1903
2.	Andrew Carnegie	12.	Fabian Society
3.	Sergei Witte	13.	Aletta Jacobs
4.	1873	14.	Thomas Hardy's
5.	John Wanamaker	15.	William Morris
6.	Egypt	16.	1889
7.	Congo	17.	*Pall Mall Gazette*
8.	Cecil Rhodes	18.	William Gladstone
9.	1885	19.	Charles Parnell
10.	Tokyo	20.	Georges Boulanger

CHAPTER REVIEW

Multiple Choice

1.	b	12.	c	23.	a
2.	d	13.	d	24.	d
3.	d	14.	b	25.	c
4.	c	15.	c	26.	d
5.	d	16.	d	27.	c
6.	d	17.	d	28.	c
7.	d	18.	c	29.	c
8.	b	19.	a	30.	a
9.	a	20.	b	31.	b
10.	c	21.	b	32.	d
11.	a	22.	c		

Short Answer

Answers will vary.

1. The decades from the 1870s through the 1890s were characterized by industrial, technological, and commercial innovations. New products, like the bicycle, typewriter, telephone, and the gasoline engine, provided proof of industrial progress. Industrial developments also affected agriculture as farm and chemical fertilizers diversified and increased Europe's food supply. The invention of refrigeration and commercial canning made many foods available year round. Expectedly, industrialization led to the decline of cottage production, but home industry, or outwork, persisted in certain trades. During these decades, Germany and the United States began to surpass Britain in research, technical education, innovation, and rate of growth, but industrialization remained a slow process in other countries, particularly Russia.

2. Two years after the Franco-Prussian War, many industrial countries experienced severe economic depression. The subsequent decades were characterized by economic fluctuations and a series of sharp downturns the severity of which varied from country to country. Because economic ties bound industrialized western Europe to international markets, effects of the recession were felt broadly. Entrepreneurs suffered as the start-up costs of new enterprises skyrocketed and industrialization became capital intensive rather than labor intensive. Increased productivity in both agriculture and industry led to rapidly declining prices, which brought about wage deflation and unemployment. Markets were also limited leaving entrepreneurs to refocus their attention on finding ways to enhance sales and distribution.

3. In an attempt to minimize the damage of economic downturns, industrialists revolutionized the everyday conduct of their businesses. Industrial production increasingly focused on consumer items, such as bicycles, typewriters, and cameras. Shopping changed dramatically with the introduction of department stores, which made many items conveniently available in one large and elegantly appointed emporium. Enticing displays and new advertising techniques, like "sales," enticed women shoppers, stimulating the household economy as well as that of the nation. Industrial production also offered new items from imperial territories to consumers. Industrial production thus catered to consumers and came to shape everyday life as the appetites of Europeans were whetted for more diverse goods.

4. As business rivalry fueled the contest for territory in Asia and Africa, the new imperialism, unlike the trader-based domination of preceding centuries, saw European states extend direct rule over these two continents. For Europeans, imperial expansion came to be identified with nation building, and industrial prosperity derived from imperial territories elicited national pride. For indigenous peoples, new imperialism and direct European rule dramatically impacted (and debilitated) native agricultural systems, economies, politics, and autonomy. Europeans imposed new social hierarchies on their conquered territories, and European-style cultural innovations were introduced to replace traditional native customs and beliefs. In certain instances, European influences improved the lives of indigenous peoples by providing innovations in sanitation and medicine, western education, and bureaucratic jobs.

5. As European industrialization progressed, Japan encouraged foreign trade and industry. Japanese officials visited Europe and the United States in the 1870s to study technological developments. Western dress became the norm at the Japanese imperial court, and western architectural styles were readily adopted. By 1894, Japan had gained enough influence on the international scene to force traders to accept its terms for commerce and diplomatic relations. Japan's rapid transformation into a modern, industrial nation with its own agenda allowed it to escape the clutches of the new European imperialism.

6. Although it was meant to stabilize great-power status, imperialism intensified distrust and competition in world politics as countries vied for ever-increasing international influence. Economically, imperialism was both costly and profitable: different sections of European society benefited from and paid for imperialist ventures. The high costs of maintaining an army and a bureaucracy in the colonies often outweighed the economic benefit for an imperial nation; however, imperialism created many jobs at home and abroad. Finally, the motives for imperialism—to spread Christianity, to foster national pride, and to improve the lives of indigenous populations—conflicted with the dominant imperative of exploiting these foreign markets and redirecting Asian and African societies to suit European needs.

7. Soccer, rugby, and cricket began to draw mass audiences during this period that united lower and higher classes in a common culture. Competitive sports were seen as valuable to national power and spirit; as such, team strategy and sportsmanship was used to mold the strength and character of young men. Sports also helped to reinforce male and female spheres, thus promoting a social order based on distinction between the sexes: men were encouraged to participate in team sports, and women were directed toward individual sports and leisure activities. Reformers rejected the idea of women's frailty, though, and introduced exercise and gymnastics in schools for girls. The middle classes, always trying to better themselves and increase their opportunity for advancement, believed their leisure pursuits should be edifying as well as fun, and so entertained pastimes such as mountain climbing. Working-class individuals hoped for social mobility as well and adopted middle-class habits by joining clubs for pursuits such as bicycling, touring, and hiking. The new emphasis on physical fitness and recreation gave individuals and, therefore, nations, a new sense of power and national pride.

8. Often lacking the possibility for social mobility, many working-class persons emigrated to find new work and opportunities. Some emigrated from rural areas to urban areas in the hope of a more secure future, especially in the most urbanized countries like Great Britain and Belgium, while others emigrated internationally. For working-class citizens of countries with imperial territories, new colonies provided land, posts for soldiers and administrators, and the possibility of wealth. Foreign countries also beckoned with the promise of future prosperity. Immigrants frequently contributed to the family economy in their native lands by sending money home. Unfortunately, however, adjustment to their new countries often undermined their traditional beliefs and cultures, alienating them from their homelands and even from each other as the experiences of husbands and wives, parents and children differed.

9. Changes in technology and management practices eliminated outmoded jobs and often made the tasks of those who survived job cuts more difficult. Unfortunately, old skills, based upon preindustrial types of production, became unnecessary or were replaced by machine labor; new skills, including knowledge of machinery, grew in importance. The rate of industry far outpaced the traditional labors of artisans. Many work processes were broken down into discrete tasks so that labor could be doled out more efficiently. Individuals who developed particular types of knowledge or were able to direct workers became managers. It was the manager's job to ensure that production ran smoothly, from the least-skilled workers—women and children earning paltry wages—to the most specialized machinists. Despite the steady loss of traditional skills, the urban working class benefited from their labors and their nineteenth-century environment by being better informed, more visible, and more invested in the progression of industry and empire.

10. At the end of the nineteenth century, political consciousness continued to grow among workers, leading to the organization of formal unions. These unions, attracting the allegiance of millions, demanded a say in working conditions and various wage guarantees. In contrast to the small, craft-based unions common in the early part of the century, a new unionism attracted a wider array of

workers, from miners to dockworkers. These new unions formed nationwide groups with salaried managers who could plan massive general strikes across trades, with most strikes addressing the conditions of everyday life for workers and not aiming at political revolution. New political parties also engaged the masses in political life by focusing on working-class issues; the socialist- and labor-oriented parties had wide influence, attracting members with the promise of collective power in national elections.

11. The rise of mass journalism after 1880 gave Europeans ready access to information about politics and world events, creating an informed European community. As the franchise was extended, popular political participation meant that a politician's election depended on those informed masses rather than on the power of small, influential cliques. Mass politics was born. In Great Britain, for instance, William Gladstone, leader of the British Liberals, waged an experimental campaign in northern England and Scotland for a seat in the House of Commons. He organized a speaking tour, addressing thousands of workingmen and -women and praising middle-class work ethics. News reports of his campaign and organized mass meetings fueled public interest in the political scene. Despite Queen Victoria's denunciation of his tactics, Gladstone won and eventually became prime minister.

12. In Germany, Austria-Hungary, and Russia, political liberalism was thwarted by agrarian, conservative political forces. In Germany, for example, Bismarck attacked the Catholic church and the socialist parties through laws and the support of more conservative political factions. He outlawed the Social Democratic Party in 1878, and attempted to wean the working class from socialism by sponsoring an accident and disability program—the first of its kind in Europe and an important step in broadening the mandate of government to encompass social welfare. In Austria-Hungary, Emperor Francis Joseph and his ministers, resolutely monarchist and authoritarian, were able to play their country's ethnic minorities against each other to maintain the monarchy's predominance as the central mechanism for holding competing interest groups together. Austrian Prime Minister Taaffe also built a coalition of clergy, conservatives, and Slavic parties and used its power to weaken the Liberals, most of whom were ethnic Germans. Although Russia had many active political groups, they were effectively (and often brutally) repressed by the tsars. In addition, liberals failed to win the support of the populous Russian peasantry, who criticized the murder of Tsar Alexander II in a bomb attack by revolutionaries.

BUILDING HISTORICAL SKILLS

Reading Maps

Answers will vary.

1. Colonial expansion into Africa generally began along the coastlines in places where European powers had established colonies and then penetrated inward. The French and the British were the two main powers that expanded into the interior, with France moving from its territories in Algeria and Senegal, and the British moving into Egypt and northward from Cape Colony.

2. The borders of the Congo Free State were rather linear and did not correspond with any natural boundaries. It encompassed parts of several different indigenous political territories, such as Tippu Tib's Domain, Msiri's Kingdom, and Chokwi Domain. In some cases, the boundaries actually divided indigenous territories and did not correspond with any indigenous political boundaries.

Reading Illustrations

Answers will vary.

1. This painting is not as realistic as earlier artwork and shows a distorted version of reality. The subject is also different. This is not a portrait of a woman, but a glimpse of a fleeting moment of life.

2. This is a scene of a middle-class woman at home, which reflects the emphasis on domesticity for women. The clothing she is wearing shows the influence of foreign cultures on European fashions. One could imagine that she bought them at one of the new department stores that were appearing at the time. The style, technique, and palate of the painting itself also show the impact of foreign cultures in Europe.

Reading Historical Documents

Answers will vary.

1. Imperial expeditions are portrayed as "fun" adventures to exciting new locales. This song definitely portrays Stanley as having the advantage over his African adversary.

2. The song suggests that Europeans did not have much sense of the consequences of their actions for indigenous civilization. Africa is presented as an almost empty continent where anyone with trinkets to sell and a gun could take whatever he or she wanted.

3. The central conflict is a woman's duty. Helmer claims that a wife's "sacred duty" is to her husband and children. Nora claims that she has an equally sacred duty toward herself.

4. Darwinistic anxieties about the health of nation led many to emphasize the role of women as mothers whose primary focus was the household. This was particularly true for the middle class, where the potential for women to earn income was not as crucial. However, there were new opportunities for middle-class women to work in the service industry or in department stores. Women were also becoming more politically active, some joining workers' parties. Thus, there was a tension between what many considered to be the ideal for women and the other options available to them.

5. All of the sources that give a clear indication of who was migrating stress that the people migrating were the poor. Through migration, they sought better economic opportunities and to escape some of the hardships of life in Europe at the time.

6. Migration provided better economic opportunities and, as the Swedish poem suggests, perhaps a sense of greater freedom. Migrants still had to work hard, as document four suggests, for although jobs may have been plentiful, the work was still physically demanding and even dangerous. Migrants also faced loneliness when they left their families behind; those left behind were also lonely, as

document two indicates, and may have faced greater economic hardship.

7. Migration, linked to economic dislocation and the problem of poverty, was an indicator of a nation's economic problems; thus, many believed migrants should be allowed to seek opportunities elsewhere. Migration was also linked to a lack of patriotism, with critics believing that migrants did not love their country. The Swedish poem also suggests that some migrants resented being worker bees for rulers who got "drunk [with the] nectar" that the worker bees collected. Governments, however, fearing that poverty might create social unrest, were often relieved to see the poor leave, even though a loss of population might reduce the strength of the nation.

Chapter 25: Modernity and the Road to War, c. 1890–1914

CHAPTER OVERVIEW

Key Events

1. c; Were alarmed at Japan's victory and forced it to relinquish other imperial gains it made.
2. c; Cecil Rhodes was forced to resign in disgrace.
3. a; There is a repressed part of the human psyche where all sorts of desires are more or less hidden.
4. d; Violent attacks on public and private property
5. c; Little changed because the tsar could dismiss the Duma and force new elections.
6. c; Russia's victory in the Russo-Japanese War
7. d; Austria-Hungary

Key Terms

1. G; new woman (p. 965)
2. H; psychoanalysis (p. 967)
3. F; Modernism (p. 970)
4. A; art nouveau (p. 974)
5. I; suffragists (p. 977)
6. J; Zionism (p. 984)
7. B; Boer War (p. 985)
8. C; Duma (p. 989)
9. D; Entente Cordíale (p. 993)
10. E; Mitteleuropa (p. 993)

Identification

1. Havelock Ellis
2. eugenics
3. Oscar Wilde
4. Ivan Pavlov
5. Sigmund Freud
6. Max Weber
7. Friedrich Nietzsche
8. Max Planck
9. Isadora Duncan
10. Vaslav Nijinsky
11. revisionism
12. Mensheviks
13. Millicent Garret Fawcett
14. Nicholas II
15. Émile Zola
16. 1898
17. 1894
18. Soviets
19. Boxers
20. India
21. Agadir
22. 1912
23. Alfred Nobel
24. Alfred Thayer Mahan
25. Gavrilo Princip

CHAPTER REVIEW

Multiple Choice

1.	b	15.	c	28.	a
2.	d	16.	d	29.	a
3.	b	17.	a	30.	b
4.	b	18.	d	31.	d
5.	c	19.	a	32.	b
6.	c	20.	c	33.	c
7.	a	21.	a	34.	c
8.	b	22.	c	35.	b
9.	c	23.	b	36.	c
10.	a	24.	c	37.	b
11.	b	25.	b	38.	b
12.	a	26.	d	39.	c
13.	c	27.	c	40.	d
14.	a				

Short Answer

Answers will vary.

1. The declining birthrate caused great anxiety in some countries as politicians worried over their nations' vitality and competitiveness. Birthrate issues turned into anxieties over class and race, and raised the concern that too few of the "fittest" people in society were having children while the lower classes, often seen as "less fit," were having too many children. This fear of one's nation or race being polluted or overrun by the perceived degenerates of society was a characteristic of eugenics, a pseudoscience that wrongly applied Darwin's idea of the survival of the fittest to human society. Eugenicists favored increasing the fertility of the "fittest" and limiting the fertility of the "unfit" by sterilization, if necessary. Several European countries looked to alternate social solutions to the declining birthrate and granted wives more legal rights in order to make marriage and motherhood more appealing.

2. With the availability of white-collar jobs, middle-class women were able to achieve more independent lives than ever before. Termed "new women," they rejected the traditional roles prescribed for women. In comparison to previous generations of women, they took advantage of increasing educational opportunities, dressed more practically, lived apart from their families, and sometimes lived more openly sexual lives.

3. Unlike previous theorists, Freud believed that human nature was driven by irrational forces and that human behavior reflected motivations repressed in the unconscious. His theory that the human psyche was divided into three competing parts—the id, the ego, and the super ego—challenged the accepted liberal belief in a unified, rational self that acted in its own interest. Freud held that the human maturation process was intimately tied to sexual drives, many of which needed to be repressed in order for children to attain maturity and for society to remain civilized. His ideas asserted that gender was less fixed than anatomy would suggest, and flew in the face of long-held theories by maintaining that girls and women possessed powerful sexual feelings.

4. Positivism, which was based on Enlightenment rationalism, held that with science one could discover enduring social laws based on rationally determined principles. It emphasized the permanent nature of fundamental laws and motivated reformers to perfect legislation through the study of society. In the late nineteenth century, however, new theories rejected positivism and any belief in the innate rationality of humanity and society, arguing that because experience is ever-changing, theories and standards could not be constant or enduring; human understanding was, therefore, founded on the conditions of day-to-day existence. For example, Max Weber questioned the extent to which a governmental bureaucracy, once perceived as a rational alternative to monarchy, could manage modern society and all its variables.

5. In the late nineteenth century, several new discoveries in science radically changed long-standing scientific views of the universe. The research that Antoine Becquerel and Marie and Pierre Curie conducted with radioactivity changed the way that atoms were understood, just as Planck's experiments in the transmission of energy revolutionized quantum physics. In 1905, Albert Einstein published his Special Theory of Relativity, proclaiming that space and time are not absolutes but, instead, vary according to the vantage point of the observer; only the speed of light is constant. Einstein also proposed that mass and energy are not two, distinct physical properties, but connected forces. This theory undercut Newtonian physics and time-honored scholarship.

6. Some modern artists tried both to challenge and to comfort Europeans amid the rush of modern life. Talents like Henri Matisse abandoned impressionism and pioneered the movement called fauvism, creating canvases covered in intense colors. Some artists explored styles that reflected the mathematical and scientific nature of the late nineteenth century; Paul Cézanne used structure in his compositions, employing rectangular daubs of paint to break down his subjects into geometric patterns and shades of color. Pablo Picasso made a radical departure from artistic traditions with cubism, which featured distorted, angular forms. Expressionism attempted to capture the inner reality of humanity and the anguish of modern life, as exemplified by Edvard Munch's *The Scream*. Many of these styles were unsettling to viewers. However, the style called "art nouveau" boasted beautiful, comforting designs and was an immediate, commercial success.

7. Labor and socialist politics became more influential in this period as more workingmen received the vote, but the immediate and long-term goals of political activists and their methodology were, however, at odds. Workingpersons' voices had never been so powerful, and the middle and upper classes were duly anxious. Unions greatly expanded their working-class membership and Socialist and Labor parties won seats in parliaments, but electoral victory raised new questions for Socialists: Should they pursue reformist policies from within government or continue to seek power through revolutionary means? Bolsheviks and Menshevik—both advocating forms of Russian Marxism—struggled to suppress each other. Syndicalists—advocating the use of direct action such as general strikes and sabotage to control government and industry, and anarchists often acted in concert to antagonize the Marxists by committing acts of terrorism.

8. Despite the expanding liberties granted to men at the turn of the century, women continued to be without the vote; without parliamentary representation; and without legal rights to property, free speech, and free press. Many countries prohibited women's membership or participation in political groups. Despite such repression, however, many women contributed to political activism; they agitated to reform education, monitored the regulation of prostitution, advocated pacifism, and launched a suffrage movement in order to reduce male privilege by gaining for women an equal say in society. In the 1890s, major suffrage organizations with paid officials and permanent offices emerged. More radical women, namely Emmeline Pankhurst, believed that suffragettes could accomplish nothing without attacking male property, and so began campaigns of violence that shocked society and the political world.

9. A direct result of state-building, nationalism was a powerful force in turn-of-the-century politics. Politicians used the concept of nationalism to bolster their campaigns, to maintain interest-group support, and to direct hostility away from themselves. As industrialization took its toll on traditional ways of life, politics and economies, and many Europeans sought scapegoats for their woes. Thus, the complex issues and problems raised by modernity were often too easily blamed on the Jewish influence in society, leading to an explosion of anti-Semitic sentiment throughout Europe. Anti-Semitism was particularly harsh in the east, where Tsar Nicholas II persecuted the Jews in vicious attacks called pogroms and severely restricted Jewish life. Anti-Semitism was also present in the West, the most sensational case being the Dreyfus Affair, in which a Jewish officer in the French army was framed by the government on charges of espionage. In Germany, right-wing nationalists who were invested in the agrarian politics of rural areas blamed Jews as the root of German social problems, while Austro-Hungarian nationalists increased hostility toward Jews by ascribing to their influence the growing discontentment of Hungarian ethnic minorities —Czechs, Serbs, and other Slavic groups.

10. The late nineteenth century witnessed nationalism spreading to European colonies. Imperialism was called into question as colonized peoples began challenging European control and conflicts arose between European powers. The British, accustomed to crushing any resistance to their imperial ambitions, encountered harsh criticism as a result of its bloody Boer War in southern Africa. The result of British expansionist efforts, the war ended in the British annexation of Boer territories, but its costs— in money, lives, and destruction—led many Britons to begin questioning the value of imperialism. The United States became an imperialist power after its victory in the Spanish American War of 1898, gaining the territories of Cuba, Puerto Rico, and the Philippines; Filipino resistance to yet another imperial oppressor, however, resulted in a brutal war. In Asia, the Boxer rebellion in China arose against Western influences. Japan became an imperial power in its own right when it inflicted a humiliating defeat on Russia in 1905, the first victory by a non-European nation over a European great power.

11. At the turn of the eighteenth century, the Russian government, an autocracy, continued to resist constitutional and social reform, leading to greater popular unrest. The Russian Revolution of 1905 began when Tsar Nicholas II's troops killed and injured hundreds of demonstrating workers on Bloody Sunday outside his Winter Palace. In the aftermath, a year-long period of political and social turmoil swept across Russia. Workers organized soviets (councils) and political violence continued and escalated to include the assassination of governmental officials, and the spread of strikes and mutinies. To quell the revolutionaries, Nicholas reluctantly instituted minor reforms, including the creation of a legislative assembly known as the Duma. Under the direction of Prime Minister Pyotr Stolypin, a series of land reforms were introduced to pacify the peasants. In general, however, the lack of a substantial response from Russia's rulers to the revolution of 1905 only heightened social tensions, bringing about an even greater revolution in 1917.

12. The defeat of Russia by Japan and the success of the Russian people in gaining some reforms from their government, a great European power, inspired nationalist resistance to European rule in Asia. The Chinese, for example, were humiliated both by their defeat in a war against Japan and continuing European domination. In response, peasants organized secret societies to restore Chinese integrity and confront foreign influences. One group, known as the Boxers, massacred Western missionaries and Chinese Christians. Despite its defeat, the Boxer Rebellion discredited the Qing dynasty, leading to its demise and the declaration of a Chinese republic by Sun Yat-Sen in 1911. Subsequent economic and social reforms instituted by Sun Yat-Sen weakened the stranglehold of Western imperialism in China. In India, radical Hindu nationalism and the Indian National Congress pressed for greater independence from Britain and a revival of Eastern culture. The British countered by supporting the Muslim League, a rival nationalist group that exhibited more restraint than the Hindus.

13. German leader William II was dissatisfied with Germany's international and diplomatic status. Encouraged by Germany's growing economic strength and convinced of hostilities between Britain and France, he twice challenged French rule in Morocco, thinking he would garner British support. After achieving little in these efforts, the German statesman turned his attentions toward the European continent; he envisioned the creation of a Mitteleuropa, a region controlled by Germany that included Central Europe, the Balkans, and Turkey. Then, Austria-Hungary, with German backing, sought reprieve from conflicting ethnic demands in the Dual Monarchy and determined that their expansion into the Balkans, and the resulting addition of even more ethnic groups, would weaken the claims of any single ethnic minority under Habsburg control. The Russians, too, had territorial ambitions in the Balkans, appointing their nation as the rightful protector of the widely dispersed Slavic peoples. Thus, the imperialistic aims of the great powers, along with the nationalistic conflicts among the smaller powers of the Balkans themselves, dramatically increased European tensions and laid the groundwork for full-scale war.

14. In the decades before World War I, European countries developed new ways of organizing their military forces and new technologies of warfare. Heightened imperialistic tensions placed European nations on a war alert. Regular conscription and large standing armies became the norm and, between 1890 and 1914, all of the major powers dramatically increased military spending. The modernization of weaponry also transformed the nature of warfare. The invention of dynamite and smokeless gunpowder changed the face of land warfare, while innovative new artillery improved the accuracy and increased the range of military firepower. Military leaders responded by devising new strategies to protect their armies, such as the use of the trench and barbed wire. At sea, developments in naval construction saw ships, like the British warship *Dreadnought*, constructed of metal instead of wood.

15. After the Austrian Archduke Francis Ferdinand and his wife were assassinated by a Serbian nationalist, evidence showed that the shooter had received help from Serbian officials. The Serbs were conciliatory in dealing with subsequent Austrian demands; however, their resistance on one point served as the pretext for the Austrian declaration of war on July 28. With the war still localized, the diplomatic alliances established in prior decades held fast, as the Germans displayed support for Austria, the British and the French restrained themselves, and the Russians mobilized in order to protect their Slavic allies, the Serbs. However, the Germany's Schlieffen Plan, devised by Alfred von Schlieffen to combat antagonists on two fronts—in this case, the allied nations of France and Russia—was undermined when the Belgiums denied the Germans passage through their country in order to attack the French. The Germans, determined to violate Belgian neutrality anyway, attacked France to the west, and then deployed troops to the east to confront Russia. The German invasion of Belgium convinced the British to join with the French and the Russians against the Triple Alliance: Germany, Austria-Hungary, and Italy.

BUILDING HISTORICAL SKILLS

Reading Maps

Answers will vary.

1. The British controlled territory stretching from Egypt in the northeast, to southern Africa, to portions of the eastern coast. They wished to create a united north-south block encompassing most of eastern and central Africa. The French controlled much of the northwestern corner of Africa as well as portions of central Africa and French Somaliland on the eastern coast. They wished to push eastward from central Africa to unite the western and central territories to French Somaliland.

2. France and Great Britain control large portions of Africa, Germany controls relatively little territory. Because the possession of colonies was increasingly considered necessary for great power status, Germany's lack of possessions fueled the country's feelings of insecurity. Germany's desire for colonies at any cost led to the 1905 and 1911 Moroccan crises in which Germany unsuccessfully challenged France for control of Morocco.

3. With the exception of the insurrection in German East Africa, the uprisings were located along the central and southern western coast of Africa, suggesting that each was influenced by the other. The uprisings on the Gold Coast and in German southwest Africa occurred during or immediately following the Boer War, whereas most other rebellions occurred following the Russo-Japanese War. In both cases, outside conflicts kept the Europeans occupied, which encouraged opponents of colonialism to resist their European conquerors.

Reading Illustrations

Answers will vary.

1. Both foreigners and those who adopt foreign ways are portrayed as animals and less than human. The foreign missionary is portrayed as a pig; the Chinese converts are depicted as goats. The foreigner suffers a worse fate, being killed with arrows; the Chinese converts are beheaded. Because the Chinese converts are depicted as goats, which are passive animals and easily led astray, they are considered less guilty than the missionary pig.

2. The depiction of the Boxers in traditional Chinese garb, and the depiction of the cross, a symbol of foreign religion, presents the Boxers as upholding Chinese culture and protecting it from foreign influence. The violence they are committing is not random, but is being carried out in an orderly fashion by the man behind the desk. His magisterial appearance suggests that the killings are even lawful, and the Boxers were in fact encouraged by the Qing Dowager Empress Tz'u-hsi.

Reading Historical Documents

Answers will vary.

1. Pinsker begins by saying that Jews are a "distinctive element" within the nations they live in, and that they cannot be assimilated into any nation. He also mentions the long history of hostility toward Jews, arguing that because Jews have no nation, they are defenseless against aggression. A Jewish nation would allow Jews to live in security.

2. Pinsker is much aware of the mounting anti-Semitism that was spreading throughout Europe at the time and led to great violence perpetrated against the Jews—particularly in Russia—where Pinsker was from. Another trend is nationalism, both in the sense that nationalism contributed to the exclusion of Jews in European society, and in the sense among Jews that they themselves comprised a nation.

3. Von Treitschke argues that the protection of its members is a state's primary task. As long as there are multiple states, each with the duty of protecting its members, there will be war. War is a natural part of the human psyche that cannot be changed.

4. Von Treitschke argues that every state in history has come into being through war. He also speaks of the "laws of human thought and of human nature."

5. History in the nineteenth century focused on the workings of public officials, religious institutions, and dynasties. It was fact-based, recounting the details of events, laws, and treaties. It ascribed the actions of historical fig-

ures to clear motives such as self-interest, ambition, greed, or hate. Psychohistory, on the other hand, focused on the inner workings of an individual's or group's psyche to address historical phenomena that were less rational, such as intense nationalism or persons blindly following vicious dictators.

6. Psychohistory draws attention to the way in which individuals and groups are motivated by fears, desires, and perceptions that may not always appear rational, but that may be rooted in emotional traumas or a feeling of being threatened. Psychohistory emphasizes the way in which events take on form and meaning for human beings in unexpected ways, and teaches that emotions, fears, and anxieties, however irrational they may appear, should be taken into account when studying the past.

7. Critics of psychohistory claim that it can be formulaic because it fits the behavior of historical individuals into Freud's schema, which is in itself controversial. Other critics find psychohistory to be too imprecise because it is more theoretical and not based on the same kinds of documentary evidence that historians usually use.

Chapter 26: War, Revolution, and Reconstruction, 1914–1929

CHAPTER OVERVIEW

Key Events

1. a; France
2. c; Uprising was quickly defeated
3. c; Provisional Government
4. a; V. I. Lenin
5. a; Austria-Hungary
6. c; King Victor Emmanuel III
7. c; Economic disaster circled the globe making militarism and authoritarianism seem appealing to many.

Key Terms

1. L; total war (p. 1003)
2. B; cult of the offensive (p. 1006)
3. J; Schlieffen Plan (p. 1006)
4. I; Provisional Government (p.1016)
5. K; soviets (p. 1016)
6. A; Bolshevik Revolution (p. 1017)
7. N; Weimar Republic (p. 1021)
8. D; Fourteen Points (p. 1022)
9. H; Peace of Paris (p. 1022)
10. M; war guilt clause (p. 1022)
11. E; League of Nations (p. 1023)
12. F; mandate system (p. 1026)
13. G; march on Rome (p. 1041)
14. C; Fascism (p. 1041)

Identification

1. Alfred von Schlieffen	14. Rapallo
2. *Britannia*	15. Young Plan
3. *Lusitania*	16. Erich Ludendorff
4. Italy	17. Amritsar
5. Jutland	18. Marie Stopes
6. Aleksandr Kerensky	19. Ernest Hemingway
7. Lavr Kornilov	20. Frederick Taylor
8. Comintern	21. Sergei Eisenstein
9. Leon Trotsky	22. George Grosz
10. November 11, 1918	23. Erich Maria Remarque
11. Friedrich Ebert	24. Marcel Proust
12. Freikorps	25. Josephine Baker
13. David Lloyd George	

CHAPTER REVIEW

Multiple Choice

1.	b	15.	d	28.	c
2.	b	16.	a	29.	d
3.	b	17.	b	30.	d
4.	b	18.	b	31.	b
5.	d	19.	b	32.	c
6.	d	20.	c	33.	b
7.	b	21.	c	34.	d
8.	a	22.	c	35.	b
9.	d	23.	c	36.	b
10.	c	24.	d	37.	d
11.	d	25.	c	38.	c
12.	c	26.	c	39.	d
13.	b	27.	a	40.	a
14.	b				

Short Answer

Answers will vary.

1. The opposing sides in World War I arose from the prewar alliances that had evolved during the preceding fifty years of European diplomacy and imperial tension. Austria-Hungary and Germany formed the Central Powers, joined later by Turkey. Great Britain, France, and Russia were known as the Allies. Japan, interested in increasing power in Asia, also joined the Allies. After the Treaty of London (1915), which promised territory in Africa, Asia Minor, and the Balkans, Italy also joined the Allied powers. The United States maintained a policy of neutrality until April 1917, when it joined the Allies after German submarine warfare had sunk several American ships.

2. Each side in World War I expected a fast and decisive victory. However, because of innovations in military technology, like the machine gun and chemical weapons, the expected rapid offensive war became a stationary, defensive, impasse. The Central Powers and the Allies faced each other in a stalemate on all fronts, which resulted in trench warfare. Millions of soldiers lived their daily lives in a maze of trenches. Soldiers often fraternized with the enemy: meals were eaten in peace, holidays were celebrated jointly, and troops on both sides secretly arranged with their "enemies" to avoid battles. Trench life forged new bonds of male camaraderie; often, traditional class distinctions were overlooked and racial barriers fell as men shared the hardships and danger of death.

3. Total war meant the indispensable involvement of civilians in war industry, achieved by the unprecedented and overwhelming intervention of governments into their citizens' economic, social, and political lives. Economically, the vast needs of the front-line soldiers for equipment and supplies required the planned reorganization of society in order to guarantee the heightened levels of production necessary for warfare. As more and more men left home for the trenches, women took over jobs in industry and other traditionally "male" occupations formerly unavailable to them. The widespread rationing of food, which eventually resulted in severe shortages, as well as other consumer goods, also affected people's daily lives. Normal politics were suspended as nearly all political parties joined the patriotic war effort. In order to maintain morale, sedition laws limited free speech and, therefore, any blatant criticism of the government.

4. By 1917, living conditions in Europe had deteriorated so drastically that civilian support of the war was waning dramatically. Food shortages in cities in Italy, Russia, Germany, and Austria-Hungary provoked riots. As inflation mounted, tenants conducted rent strikes, factory hands and white-collar workers walked off the job, and women protested the cost of living and their fatigue from overwork. Nationalist movements came to the fore on the political scene and led to instability, as was the case in Austria-Hungary where the new emperor tried to consolidate his control by negotiating a secret peace with the Allies. In Russia, which had suffered the greatest number of casualties in the war and had experienced the most serious political protests, social and political breakdown saw wartime protest erupt in outright revolution. As a result, the tsar was forced to abdicate and Russia pulled out of the war.

5. In the midst of widespread social breakdown and discontent following the abdication of the tsar, the new ruling entity in Russia, called the Provisional Government, tried to pursue the war successfully, better manage internal affairs, and establish the government on a firm constitutional footing. Germany, however, in an attempt to further destabilize Russia, provided safe rail transport to the exiled Russian and Bolshevik leader V. I. Lenin from Switzerland though German territory. Shortly thereafter, Lenin issued the April Theses, which called for Russia to withdraw from the war, for the soviets to seize power on behalf of workers and poor peasants, and for all private land to be nationalized. As Bolshevik popularity rose, the Provisional Government was discredited. The Bolsheviks seized power and awaited the upcoming elections. When elections were finally held, the Bolsheviks fared worse than their rivals, the Socialist Revolutionaries. Consequently, Lenin led a coup in which Bolsheviks took over the government by force.

6. Resistance to Bolshevik policies initiated a civil war. The fighting between pro- and anti-Bolshevik forces shaped communism as well as economic and social policies in Russia. Leon Trotsky, Bolshevik commissar of war, was instrumental in building a Communist state. He put an end to democratic procedures in the army and increased the autocratic authority of the state. Trotsky and Lenin introduced the policy of war communism, which involved the forced requisitioning of food for the army and workers

from the peasantry. The secret police, known as the Cheka, were also part of the expanding bureaucratic state, setting up detention camps and stamping out political dissent. As the Bolsheviks clamped down on their opponents, they organized their supporters to foster revolutionary Marxism throughout Europe. Although the Russian Revolution had successfully removed the privileged aristocracy from power, the ravages of civil war and the way the Bolsheviks stamped out any and all opposition to their rule ushered in a political style at odds with earlier socialist goals.

7. Following its defeat in the war, Germany was politically and socially unstable, especially after Kaiser William II fled the country in 1918. The moderate Social Democratic leader, Friedrich Ebert, headed the new government and advocated the formation of a parliamentary republic. In the midst of this political uncertainty, Ebert called on the German army and the Freikorps—a roving paramilitary band of students, demobilized soldiers, and others—to suppress workers' councils and radical demonstrators. Subsequently, a constituent assembly met in the city of Weimar, where it approved a constitution and founded a parliamentary government known as the Weimar Republic. Despite the support of moderates, however, the republic continued to face opposition from the left and the right—including an attempted right-wing coup known as the Kapp Putsch—that undermined its stability.

8. The Peace of Paris treated the defeated Central Powers, especially Germany, very severely. Despite the urgings of the United States for a conciliatory settlement, Britain and France sought to satisfy their angry citizens' desire for revenge against Germany. The treaties separated Austria from Hungary, reduced Hungary by almost two-thirds of its inhabitants and three-quarters of its territory, and broke up the Ottoman Empire. The Habsburg Empire was replaced by a group of small, internally divided, and relatively weak states: Czechoslovakia, Poland, and the Kingdom of the Serbs, Croats, and Slovenes, later renamed Yugoslavia. The settlement expressly forbade a union between Austria and Germany. Poland was reconstructed from parts of Russia, Germany, and Austria-Hungary. By the terms of the Treaty of Versailles, Germany was occupied, obliged to pay heavy war reparations, forced to limit the size of its military, required to give up its colonies, and expected to accept blame for starting the war. The Peace of Paris also set up the League of Nations, an international conference for maintaining collective, global security and managing imperial colonies.

9. Issues like the economic recovery of Europe, the paying of war debts, the conditions of international trade, the strain of German reparations, and the ensuring of future peace in Europe occupied politicians in the 1920s. The fragile Weimar Republic, suffering inflation, continued to renegotiate German debts. In an attempt to ease their economic woes, the Germans printed huge quantities of nearly worthless currency. The result was a massive economic crisis in Germany, which threatened the international economy. New treaties were negotiated: the Dawes Plan (1924) and the Young Plan (1929) reduced the war reparations of Germany and restored the value of German currency. A treaty at the city of Locarno provided Germany with a seat in the League of Nations, an attempt at

increasing the collective security of all European nations. The publicity and planning that yielded the international agreements during the 1920s sharply contrasted with old-style diplomacy, which was conducted in secret and subjected to little public scrutiny or democratic influence. The new openness suggested a diplomatic revolution and promised a peaceful age in international relations.

10. Postwar political and social developments reflected democratic ideals, but the existence of extremist groups, revolutionary trends, and nationalistic forces revealed the instability of and the popular unrest within 1920s Europe. The League of Nations, in its attempt to secure peace, had created new nations either by dividing or reconsolidating old ones; in any case, these countries, like Poland, Yugoslavia, and Austria, struggled with their new political situations. In Poland, for example, economic hardship, class tensions, and ethnic divisions saw reunification threatened by growing nationalism (defined in ethnic terms) and revolution. Despite the formation of a constitutional government, the economy failed to prosper, leading to a coup in 1926 by Jozef Pilsudski, whose strong-arm economic and political policies brought some relief as a result of class and ethnic divisions. There were tensions, too, in countries with more established parliamentary traditions, like Germany's Weimar Republic, where extremists protested the government and many citizens had contempt for parliamentary politics and blamed the weak wills of democratic politicians for Germany's defeat in the war. In France and Britain, postwar extremism had less of an impact, but tensions were still present. For instance, Britain faced a nationalistic revolt in Ireland by Irish Republicans pressing for home rule and a general miners' strike that, although unsuccessful, showed the potential nationwide power of unions.

11. Following the war, the ability of European nations to compete in the worldwide economy became an enormous challenge. During the war, the European economy had lost many of its international markets to India, Canada, Australia, Japan, and the United States. Conveniently, however, the war had also made European manufacturing more efficient and production more diversified as the demand for consumer goods grew. The 1920s saw a resumption in the growth of mergers and cartels and, therefore, in the growth of large conglomerates. The United States had become a model of economic modernization. There, assembly-line production was pioneered by Henry Ford, and scientific management involving the streamlining of workers' tasks and the timing of their movements increased production. Industrialists, looking to quell revolutionary voices, worked to increase productivity with the hiring of managers and decrease worker discontent with higher wages and shorter hours. Union bureaucracies grew in size and political influence despite their attempt to exclude women.

12. Brutalized and often incapacitated by war, veterans of World War I found it difficult to reenter civilian life. Old European lifestyles had changed dramatically while they had been at the front, particularly gender roles and standards of morality. Many veterans felt hostility toward those who had not taken part in the war, blaming civilians for their own sense of alienation. Used to lives of violence

and depravation, they also had difficulty resuming their old jobs. Civilians, especially women, often felt estranged from these returning warriors who had maimed and killed and lived in squalor and decay. Many feminist activists turned their efforts away from achieving gender equality in public life and toward creating a protected female space in the home aided by family welfare programs. Despite these and other attempts to restore traditional family values, however, women retained much of their newfound independence and sex and sexuality were discussed more openly.

13. Radio, film, and print media—the purveyors of mass culture—all expanded their influence in the 1920s after having been used in World War I to inform citizenry, spread propaganda, and enhance political party lines. Filmmaking became an international business in this period and gave rise to specialized experts, film stars, and studios. A powerful form of expression as well as a political tool, films reflected the sentiments of postwar life, were used by some governments for propaganda purposes, and helped to create both a national and an international culture. Radios and radio broadcasts, had an enormous impact on the public, especially because they quickly became inexpensive and their purchase brought entertainment, news, and propaganda directly into the private space of one's home. As for print media, postwar novels and poetry reflected the widely varying sentiments of the European masses, from the glory of war to the futility of life, the hopelessness of modern society to the haunted inner life of the individual.

14. While some cultural leaders in the 1920s were obsessed by the horrendous experiences of war and modernity, others celebrated the possibilities of a peaceful, technologically advanced future. The Dada movement attracted artists who were filled with postwar rage and revulsion at the carnage society had inflicted upon itself. They produced works punctuated by nonsense, incongruity, and blatant expressions of alienation. Other artists held high hopes for creating a fresh, utopian future that would differ from the past. A group of German artists, called the Bauhaus, celebrating the promise of technology, designed streamlined office buildings and functional furniture, utensils, and decorative objects. Many artists were fascinated by technology and machinery and were drawn to the most modern of all countries, the United States, particularly New York, for inspiration. New York City stood as a potent example of avant-garde expression that rejected a terrifying past and boldly shaped the future.

15. Political chaos and postwar discontent brought Fascist leader Benito Mussolini to power in Italy. Economic problems, contempt for the apparent ineffectiveness of parliamentary government, and the refusal of the Allies to honor the territorial promises of the Treaty of London enraged the Italian populace. Italians therefore responded positively to Mussolini and his army of Black Shirts because they promised to increase Italy's glory and to remake the country. Using force to take over the government, Mussolini used mass communication methods, such as radio, to spread Fascist propaganda and maintain support for his regime.

BUILDING HISTORICAL SKILLS

Reading Maps

Answers will vary.

1. Austria-Hungary was a multiethnic country, whose various ethnic groups were calling for increased recognition, and eventually independence, before and during the war. At the end of the war, a number of smaller countries were created out of Austro-Hungarian territory to meet the demands of these various groups.

2. Because it had a mostly ethnic German population, the partition of Germany would have raised an enormous outcry, so the only territorial losses were Alsace and Lorraine, taken from France in 1870, and an area in eastern Germany that was made part of Poland. After the quick French defeat in 1870 and the bloody carnage of World War I, however, France was enormously concerned with security on its eastern border; the demilitarized zone was a concession to French concerns for security.

3. The territorial settlement created more problems than it solved. Despite Wilson's proclamation of national self-determination—the idea that a people should be able to determine their own futures—those who lost the war were not given choices as to how the postwar map would redraw boundaries. Such heavy-handed tactics created enormous resentment, and territorial settlements would continue to be a source of instability.

Reading Illustrations

Answers will vary.

1. This picture suggests that the economy was in such poor shape that German currency had become a plaything during the 1920s. However, the fact that these children are obviously not living in poverty suggests that at least some people were able to manage. The worthlessness of the German mark at this time did, however, cause the ruination of many individuals' life savings.

2. Images such as this might have stirred up resentment among the German people toward the countries they were being forced to pay reparations to, as well as toward their own government's leaders. Germans might have become more willing to listen to leaders who presented themselves as strong enough to stand up their nation.

Reading Historical Documents

Answers will vary.

1. The narrative of this passage relies on the mental thoughts of the characters to propel the story, which is similar to the "stream of consciousness" style used by James Joyce and Marcel Proust. The style is also fragmented, indicating how the World War I had dissolved the solid society upon which stories were once based. The idea of reincarnation in the story demonstrates how Eastern culture had influenced the West.

2. This story partly an expression of the breakdown in traditional gender roles that accelerated at the end of the World War I as more and more women began to work outside the home live independently. Woolf's reflections on the ease with which the main character turned from a man

into a woman implies a certain degree of interchangeability between the sexes, something that was becoming more apparent in Western society at that time.

3. The crowd was in an almost "festive" mood, and strangers embraced and kissed in the streets. The mood was relatively peaceful, and there was no mob violence.

4. In both cases, the authors wish to establish that the governments do not serve European interests, but instead serve the interests of the people who live under them; both documents state that the eventual goal of people in both Africa and the Middle East is independence. Colonized peoples, by coming to the peace talks to voice their demands for greater autonomy and eventual independence, reveal that they had lost much of their deference to or fear of Europeans. However, the authors of these documents imply that the natives of Africa and the Middle East must experience further development before their eventual independence, and that European society, to some extent, would serve as the model to which they would aspire.

5. These documents indicate that people believed that the end of the war provided an opportunity for making major changes in European and colonial society. The experience of the war, particularly on the battlefront, but also on the home front where women gained new opportunities, broke down race, class, and gender barriers. The war had disrupted life in Europe and the colonies to such an enormous extent that the end of the war seemed like a new beginning. These documents reflect this willingness, indeed eagerness, to create a new world.

6. These documents reveal that, although many people saw the end of the war as an opportunity for change, old hatreds and resentments, such as anti-Semitism, still existed, and were merely reapplied to new situations. The postwar period would be characterized by conflict between different ethnic and religious groups in the newly created nations of Central Europe, conflict between Europeans and colonized peoples, and class conflicts.

Chapter 27: An Age of Catastrophes, 1929–1945

CHAPTER OVERVIEW

Key Events

1. c; Reckless investment using borrowed money
2. d; The majority of the Nazi Party membership being over age forty
3. a; Great Britain
4. c; Russia
5. c; Harsh winter prevented a quick victory and hampered the overall war effort for Germany
6. a; Refugees quickly found housing vacated by those killed during the war.

Key Terms

1. C; civil disobedience (p. 1054)
2. F; five-year plans (p. 1055)
3. L; purges (p. 1058)
4. D; Enabling Act (p. 1062)
5. K; pump priming (p. 1063)
6. I; Nuremberg laws (p. 1064)
7. E; family allowance (p. 1066)
8. J; Popular Front (p. 1067)
9. G; Lebensraum (p. 1072)
10. A; Appeasement (p. 1075)
11. H; Nazi-Soviet Pact (p. 1077)
12. B; Blitzkrieg (p. 1077)

Identification

1. 1929
2. Mohandas Gandhi
3. Iran
4. Egypt
5. French
6. 1929
7. kulaks
8. Alfred Hugenberg
9. 1933
10. T4 project
11. Social Security Act
12. Léon Blum
13. *The Blue Angel*
14. Edwin Hubble
15. Karl Barth
16. Rape of Nanjing
17. Ethiopia
18. *Guernica*
19. Neville Chamberlain
20. Austria
21. Poland
22. Henri Philippe Pétain
23. Charles de Gaulle
24. Dwight Eisenhower
25. Yalta

CHAPTER REVIEW

Multiple Choice

1.	c	15.	b	28.	c
2.	b	16.	c	29.	d
3.	a	17.	a	30.	a
4.	b	18.	b	31.	b
5.	b	19.	a	32.	d
6.	a	20.	d	33.	a
7.	b	21.	a	34.	a
8.	a	22.	c	35.	a
9.	d	23.	d	36.	a
10.	c	24.	b	37.	c
11.	b	25.	b	38.	d
12.	c	26.	b	39.	b
13.	a	27.	c	40.	c
14.	c				

Short Answer

Answers will vary.

1. In the 1920s, in a period of economic growth, many investors in the American stock market—including U.S. corporations, banks, and individual investors—had borrowed money on margin to increase their holdings in the stock market. These investors bought shares in popular new companies with readily available credit. In an attempt to stabilize the market, the Federal Reserve Bank tightened available credit. Becoming anxious, brokerage firms demanded the immediate repayment of loans that had been used to buy stock. The large-scale sell-off of stocks by investors in order to pay back their debts resulted in the collapse of the market. Because the United States had become the leading international lender, the crisis spread globally as American investments abroad shrank.

2. The depression's main social impact was widespread unemployment. Still, the majority of Europeans and Americans held jobs throughout the 1930s, and the global

economic situation was not uniformly disastrous. Some sectors of Western economies continued to flourish, particularly in new industries. Postwar advances in infrastructure continued unabated and consumer goods remained in high demand, particularly by those workers who sustained employment. Socially, gender relations were upset as unemployed men lost the ability to support their families and lower-paid women's work became crucial for survival. The economic hardship of the depression also contributed to a declining birthrate that struck nearly all industrial countries as couples chose to have fewer children. This population crisis, as interpreted by Social Darwinists, foretold of social deterioration as "superior" persons failed to breed, while "inferior" persons—the poor, certain ethnicities, and Jews—continued to overbreed. Population issues coupled with economic misery fueled ethnic hatred and anti-Semitism.

3. The collapse of European economic activity meant that, in some economic sectors, non-Western countries were able to gain ground against their European rivals. Important examples include Japan, which developed into a formidable industrial rival; and India, where the textile industry largely freed itself from British domination. In non-Western countries that had been forced to grow a single, cash crop, the price drop of various foodstuffs, like rice and coffee, proved disastrous. Economic distress also fed into other colonial grievances, increasing resistance to European rule, particularly as the example set by Japan showed that non-European nations could be economically powerful. Countries in the Middle East, Africa, and Asia also pressed for independence, or at least reform.

4. After 1929, Italy, the Soviet Union, and Germany saw the rise of highly centralized systems of government that attempted to control society and ensure conformity through a single party and police terrorist acts. These regimes, although violent, received significant popular support for their vision of a powerful state. Postwar social, economic, and political crises led many Europeans to perceive representative government as weak and ineffectual; totalitarian states offered strength, national glory, and economic recovery. Conditioned to accept the military directives of wartime, Italians, Russians, and Germans overlooked the brutality of their totalitarian states because they admired the discipline that Mussolini, Stalin, and Hitler brought to social and economic life.

5. Under Joseph Stalin's direction, the USSR was transformed from a largely illiterate, peasant society to an industrial power in a decade. His vision was achieved by way of centralized planning and political terrorism. In a series of Five Year Plans, Stalin set goals for industrial production; the first, for example, established a program of massive increases in the output of coal, iron ore, steel, and industrial goods. Communist Party managers, supervisors, and workers were expected to meet very specific and often unrealistic production quotas. Although central planning proved enormously successful and the USSR became a formidable industrial nation, almost everyone falsified production figures to protect their jobs (and their lives), thereby introducing official lying and corruption into the Soviet economic system. National pride and utopian hopes, however, saw Soviets tolerate the vast suf-

fering caused by Stalin, his use of terrorist tactics such as purges, and his policies instituting the forced collectivization of land.

6. In 1933, under Hitler's direction, the Nazi Party undermined the control of the Reichstag and managed to pass the Enabling Act, which suspended the constitution for four years and allowed subsequent Nazi laws to take effect without parliamentary approval. Hitler then set about creating a *Volksgemeinschaft* ("people's community") of like-minded and racially "pure" Germans. Obedience to the state was enforced via terrorist tactics. To build popular support, the Nazi government pursued economic pump-priming programs—the stimulation of the economy through government spending—focusing such spending on armaments and infrastructure. Social policies were also implemented: German couples were rewarded for having children; labor unions were closed and all workers were compelled to join the Nazi-controlled German Labor Front; and membership in the Hitler Youth organizations became mandatory for all boys and girls over age ten. German cultural life was also affected as books by "deviant" authors were burned and/or banned and the works by artists in disfavor were destroyed.

7. Nazism, communism, and fascism offered bold, new approaches to modern politics and new kinds of economic and social policies. The apparent success of these totalitarian regimes in resolving the economic crises of the Great Depression and their denunciation of representative governments and democratic values as outdated, ineffectual, and weak, placed democracies on the defensive economically, politically, and culturally. Thus, democratic governments had to find innovative ways to deal with economic depression and sustain faith in democratic rights and popular government. The result was a reconceptualization of government's role in promoting social welfare and economic democracy. Nations like Sweden, Britain, and the United States, all advanced the trend toward the welfare state, which guaranteed a certain level of economic well-being for individuals and businesses in order to reduce social suffering and the appeal of totalitarian solutions.

8. The spectrum of solutions to economic and social woes provided by the emerging welfare states—Sweden, the United States, and Great Britain—was frequently inspired by the central control of the economy achieved during World War I. In the United States, President Roosevelt created a variety of innovative, but moderate, social welfare programs and increased governmental planning in the economy: relief for businesses and instructions to firms on how to cooperate in stabilizing prices, price supports for hard-pressed farmers, public works programs for unemployed youths, and refinancing agencies for homeowners' mortgages. Social Security provided retirement benefits for workers, unemployment insurance, and payments to mothers with dependent children, and persons with disabling physical conditions. Far more comprehensive welfare states were created in Europe, notably in Sweden, which instituted central planning of the economy and social welfare programs. Then, in 1937, the government began a loan program for married couples and introduced prenatal care, free childbirth in a hospital, a food relief program, and subsidized housing for large families. In Britain

and France, steps were taken to increase the government's investment in infrastructure and to provide minimal health benefits to many workers.

9. In response to the Great Depression, writers and artists of the 1930s became deeply engaged with public life and drew attention to economic suffering and the confrontation between totalitarianism and democracy. The day-to-day grind of workers, the plight of the unemployed, and fluctuating gender roles motivated filmmakers and authors to depict economic deprivation, the absurdities of industrial society, and both the decay and redemption of modern civilization. Some intellectuals returned to realistic portrayals in order to drive home their antifascist, pacifist, or pro-worker messages, as art became increasingly politicized. Scientists explored the limits of human knowledge, casting doubt on the absolutist proclamations of totalitarianism, while many religious thinkers devoted themselves to expanding the reach of religious activism and fighting injustice.

10. Tired of Western interference and competition, and desiring new markets and resources for their recovering industries, Japan's military leaders believed their country was destined to be the dominant power in Asia, and saw military expansion as key to their empire's prosperity. Japan, acting on its vision, invaded the Chinese province of Manchuria, set up a puppet government, and then further invaded Chinese territory to push its goal of political and economic penetration of the Asian continent. The League of Nations, requested by China to adjudicate the question of Manchuria, took little action other than to condemn the attack. This Western rebuff offended the Japanese and drove them to form a closer alliance with Italy and Germany. In 1937, Japan again attacked China, which resulted in the massacre of hundreds of thousands of Chinese in what became known as the "Rape of Nanjing." This act led to a series of economic sanctions imposed by the United States and warranted by heightened Japanese-American hostilities, setting the two countries on a path toward war.

11. The seizure of power by Spanish revolutionaries from their king, in 1931, and their establishment of a republic went against the trend of rising totalitarianism in Europe and reflected widespread popular support for the cause of democracy. In the face of centuries of economic and political decline, republicans hoped to modernize Spain by promoting industry and efficient, independent farming. Their government failed to enact land distribution, however, which left rural peasants dissatisfied and large, anti-republican landlords too powerful. Due to internal strife, the republican revolutionaries, or Loyalists, had difficulty maintaining a united front, opening the way for a military coup by right-wing and fascist forces under the leadership of General Francisco Franco. Hitler and Mussolini supported the fascist side, giving Franco military technology and using the conflict to test new weapons and new military tactics, including terror bombing of civilians. Deaf to Loyalist pleas, no democratic country provided official support to the revolutionaries, and Soviet assistance proved unable to stop fascist victory in 1939, which reinforced the European trend toward authoritarian government.

12. World War II began with the fall of central Europe to Nazi forces. Hitler's 1938 Anschluss of Austria was welcomed by many Austrians as a unification of "Aryan" people; as such, Hitler was able to present the annexation as justifiable and the democratic world did nothing in response. Hitler also usurped a part of Czechoslovakia that was inhabited by German-speaking people. The Munich Pact, signed by Britain, France, and Germany, granted the legitimacy of Hitler's claim to Czechoslovakia's Sudetenland and managed to avoid war. The strategy of preventing a war by making concessions for legitimate grievances (in this case, the alleged affront to Germans in the Peace of Paris) was called "appeasement." The following year, after Hitler sent troops into Czechoslovakia once again, Britain and France promised military support to Poland, Romania, Greece, and Turkey in case of Nazi invasion in their lands. This a precaution failed to curtail Hitler's advances. Because Britain and France had been so cautious in their dealings with Nazi Germany, Hitler did not feel sufficiently threatened and invaded Poland in 1939, after which Britain and France declared war on Germany.

13. World War II killed far more civilians than soldiers because everyone was a target. Both sides bombed cities to destroy civilian morale and their will to resist. As the German army swept through Eastern Europe, it murdered millions whom Nazi ideology deemed as racially "inferior" or politically unacceptable, such as Jews, Slavs, Communists, and the literate. The Japanese likewise killed millions of Chinese civilians. These tactics were intended to stifle resistance, purge undesirable elements from the population, and destroy the public's will to resist.

14. Throughout the war, the Allies successfully outproduced and outstrategized the Axis powers, leaving the Axis countries at a distinct disadvantage. The vast conquests by the Germans and Japanese during the war committed them to fighting on unfamiliar terrain. Colonial powers, such as Britain, were wiser and avoided this error. Allied governments were also overwhelmingly successful in generating civilian participation, especially among women. Allies took advantage of colonized peoples, drawing them into the war through conscription and forced labor. The armed forces ultimately defeated the Axis powers, but civilian resistance in Nazi-occupied areas, such as the *maquis* in France, also contributed to the Allies' triumph.

15. In 1941, the Atlantic Charter signed by the United States and Britain condemned aggression, reaffirmed the notion of collective security, and endorsed the right of all peoples to choose their governments. In 1944, Churchill and Stalin divided control of Eastern and Central Europe: the Soviet Union would control Romania and Bulgaria, Britain would control Greece, and they would jointly oversee Hungary and Yugoslavia. In 1945, Churchill, Roosevelt, and Stalin met at Yalta, where Roosevelt advocated the creation of the United Nations as a global peace mechanism and agreed to Soviet influence in parts of Asia in return for Stalin's promise of assistance against any future Japanese aggression. In Potsdam, in 1945, at the final meeting of the Allied leaders, the United States and Britain agreed to give the Soviets control of eastern Poland, to give part of eastern Germany to Poland, and to adopt a temporary four-way occupation of Germany.

BUILDING HISTORICAL SKILLS

Reading Maps

Answers will vary.

1. Hitler was conquering and annexing territories in the east, and was thus coming dangerously close to the Soviet Union. Only by signing an agreement with the Soviets could Hitler hope to continue his eastward expansion without provoking a war on Germany's eastern front during the initial phases of his expansion.

2. Germany in 1933 looked as if it has been carved up: it has a slice taken off its western border, a big hole cut out of its southeastern corner, and its northeastern corner is divided from the rest of the country. Issues of territorial integrity were certainly a motivation in Hitler's expansion plan. The larger Germany created by 1939 is a far more unified geographical entity, a nation well on its way to achieving Lebensraum ("living space") in Central Europe.

Reading Illustrations

Answers will vary.

1. The picture seems to show a military parade with crowds of people watching and Nazi flags flying. The Nazi troops, with their military bearing and uniforms, signify a restoration of Germany's military might—a historical reversal of fortunes because one of the great complaints of the Nazis and their supporters was that the German military had been betrayed following World War I. One of the promises the Nazis made was to restore order, and the troops certainly give the impression of order.

2. The endless flags, banners, and other insignia serve to place the Nazi icon anywhere one might look. The Nazis wanted to create a total reality, in which all aspects of each function would be controlled and defined by the Nazis. From whatever angle one observed this parade, one could not miss that this was a Nazi event.

3. The towering Nazi eagle and the profusion of black flags and black uniforms seem to give this photo a menacing air. However, our hindsight of what occurred in Germany under the Nazis allows us to interpret this photo in a way that most German citizens in 1933 could not. They would have seen the large crowd, the impressive decorations, and the strong military presence, and perhaps believe that Germany was on the road to recovery.

Reading Historical Documents

Answers will vary.

1. Families like Elena Trofimovna Dolgikh's were targeted by Stalin's government because they resisted his demands for more grain to feed the urban workforce and to export to finance industrialization. Because they were relatively well-off, they also made easy targets among the resentful poorer peasants, who were very willing to buy the Dolgikhs' property.

2. The forced labor of kulak prisoners might have helped Stalin's plans somewhat because they worked on the construction of industrial complexes such as coal mines and metallurgical plants. However, it seems that his plan to collectivize the farms seized from the kulaks was less suc-cessful because the farms were poorly managed and many of the products on these farms that might have made a profit were allowed to die.

3. This document shows that Japan had intended to occupy or "emancipate" Siberia, China, Indochina, Australia, the South Seas, and India. Japan also planned to eliminate any competing influences from the region and create a single state under totalitarian rule.

4. The Japanese government portrayed itself as a liberator that would rescue the region from aggressive British, American, and Russian influences. It also viewed itself as bringing superior values to the region.

5. Historical monuments and museums are of interest to historians because they are testimonials to historic events. They provide records of information concerning these events, and also show how people felt about them.

6. Museums or memorials may not tell the whole story about an event. In order to create a sense of consensus, museums may exclude the voices of those who experienced the event differently and, because they are designed for the general public, they may not contain the detail or nuance that a historian needs to fully understand an event. A memorial, often created by one individual, reflects a highly personal experience of an event, and might be difficult for a historian to interpret.

7. The design and content of a museum or memorial may not reflect the whole truth about what happened in the past and why, but these do relate a partial, incomplete truth about the past. Museums and memorials reflect the feelings and reactions of certain people toward an event—sometimes immediately afterward, and sometimes years later. These are assigned meaning by their makers and contributors.

Chapter 28: Remaking Europe in the Shadow of Cold War, c. 1945–1965

CHAPTER OVERVIEW

Key Events

1. c; early efforts to exclude the Soviet Union from the United Nations.
2. b; There was mistrust and hostility between the National Congress and the Muslim League.
3. c; Great Britain
4. d; Most women were not leading authentic lives.
5. c; The production of consumer goods increased in response to public protests.
6. d; Hungary was expelled from the Warsaw Pact.
7. c; The conflict in Algeria
8. b; China
9. b; Russia

Key Terms

1. B; cold war (p. 1098)
2. K; third world (p. 1098)
3. L; Truman Doctrine (p. 1103)
4. H; Marshall Plan (p. 1103)

5. I; NATO (North American Treaty Organization) (p. 1107)
6. E; economic miracle (p. 1108)
7. A; Christian Democrats (p. 1110)
8. F; European Economic Community (EEC or Common Market) (p. 1112)
9. N; welfare state (p. 1113)
10. J; thaw (p. 1117)
11. D; decolonization (p. 1118)
12. M; United Nations (UN) (p. 1123)
13. G; existentialism (p. 1126)
14. C; Cuban missile crisis (p. 1133)

Identification

1. Truman Doctrine
2. Marshall Plan
3. Yugoslavia
4. Berlin
5. Warsaw Pact
6. Joseph McCarthy
7. Treaty of Rome
8. Council for Mutual Economic Assistance
9. Nikita Khrushchev
10. Hungary
11. 1949
12. French
13. Gamal Abdel Nasser
14. Algeria
15. Kwame Nkrumah
16. Albert Camus
17. Simone de Beauvoir
18. Marlon Brando
19. Ian Fleming
20. Roberto Rossellini

CHAPTER REVIEW

Multiple Choice

1. d	12. a	23. c
2. c	13. a	24. d
3. a	14. b	25. a
4. b	15. c	26. d
5. c	16. c	27. c
6. b	17. d	28. c
7. d	18. b	29. b
8. b	19. c	30. d
9. b	20. c	31. b
10. a	21. b	32. d
11. d	22. b	

Short Answer

Answers will vary.

1. Europe was physically devastated by the war; its cities destroyed, refugees numbered in the tens of millions, and its infrastructure was inoperative. There were shortages of food, shelter, and fuel; and brutality by occupying armies was widespread, particularly in the areas controlled by the Soviet Union. Refugees faced hostility and violence as they competed for scarce resources, and Jews in particular endured further suffering, confronted by anti-Semitism and violence, especially in Eastern Europe. On the other hand, the defeat of Nazism inspired an upsurge of hope, a revival of religious feeling, and a new commitment to humanitarian goals.

2. After the war, the United States was the richest country in the world. It had amassed great wealth during the war and its strong economy was characterized by continued industrial and military research, a wave of suburban housing development, strong consumer spending, and a "baby boom"—all symbols of its singular prosperity. The United States also began to embrace its role as a global leader, shedding much of its prewar tendency toward isolationism and assuming a leading role in shaping the postwar world.

3. The cold war emerged from an atmosphere of mutual mistrust between the United States and the USSR: Stalin perceived his country threatened by the West and its anti-Communist policies and believed that the USSR required a permanent "buffer zone" of loyal, Communist, European states as a blockade against a Western menace. Similarly, the United States perceived Soviet efforts to occupy Eastern Europe as the heralding of a new era of Communist expansion, an attempt at world domination. As the United States and the Soviet Union faced off against one another over the partition of postwar Europe, the formation of opposing military alliances, the West's North Atlantic Treaty Organization (NATO), and Stalin's Warsaw Pact, solidified the political outline of the cold war.

4. *Denazification* refers to the systematic process by which occupying Allied armies and resistance fighters removed former Nazi officers and Nazi collaborators from positions of influence and forcing German civilians to own up to Nazi atrocities. Members of the resistance did not wait for courtroom justice but executed tens of thousands of Nazi officers and collaborators on the spot. Allied representatives, on the other hand, conducted numerous investigations in order to identify collaborators. However, denazification was not entirely successful. Some of the leaders most responsible for war crimes managed to escape detection. German civilians interpreted the trials of Nazis as the characteristic retribution of victors rather than the well-deserved punishment of the guilty, and also believed that the real victims were the German prisoners of war still being held in Soviet camps.

5. The influx of American dollars under the Marshall Plan combined with determined rebuilding efforts by Europe saw the depravation and misery of the late forties transformed into astonishing economic growth during the 1950s. The U.S. Marshall Plan sustained the initial recovery with American financing; food and consumer goods became more plentiful. The demand for automobiles, washing machines, and vacuum cleaners boosted economies, and growth in all types of production eradicated most unemployment. Recovery was also assisted by international economic cooperation such as the formation of the International Monetary Fund to stabilize the international economy, and the formation of the European Economic Community (EEC, also known as the Common Market), which reduced tariffs on trade between several European countries and began taking steps toward European economic integration.

6. In Eastern Europe after the war, Stalin reshaped the economy using the same methods he had employed to industrialize the Soviet Union in the 1930s. Agriculture was forcibly collectivized, private property was nationalized, and a series of centrally planned economic directives pushed Soviet industry throughout the eastern bloc to match U.S. productivity. A Soviet-dominated agency, COMECON, coordinated Eastern European development to benefit the Soviet Union. Repression accompanied the drive for modernization: the Catholic clergy was squelched; and agrarian elites, professionals, intellectuals, and other members of the middle class were discriminated against, imprisoned, or executed. Stalin's Communist policies did, however, manage to transform the Eastern-bloc states from peasant economies into technological and bureaucratically directed industrial economies.

7. World War II accelerated anticolonial tendencies that had taken root before the war. During the war, Allied imperial powers relied heavily on Asian and African troops and encouraged anti-Axis independence movements. Now, at the close of the war, the European powers were unable to maintain their vast empires or their global influence. The exposure of colonized peoples to European barbarism led to doubts about purported European superiority. The mass discontent that had intensified during the war was mobilized and foreign rulers driven out.

8. In the cold war, as countries in Asia and Africa achieved their independence, they were subjected to superpower rivalry. The threat of nuclear war kept the United States and the Soviet Union from engaging in direct confrontation; instead, they supported different movements and countries in the decolonizing third world. The United States and the USSR sought to impress upon newly emerging nations the advantages of capitalism and communism, respectively, and supported regimes that subscribed to their political ideologies and agendas.

9. As empires collapsed, many colonized peoples emigrated to Europe to take advantage of opportunities presented by the labor shortage after the war. Initially, these new immigrants were only given temporary, or "guest" visas to live and work in Europe, then they were supposed to return home. However, illegal immigrants formed the vast majority of new arrivals. By 1980, 8 percent of the European population was foreign-born, making Europe more diverse in terms of race, religion, ethnicity, and culture than it had ever been before.

10. By the end of the 1940s, a philosophy known as existentialism had become popular, particularly among academics, intellectuals, and students. Existentialists confronted the question of what "being" involved in the face of an increasingly secular society and the twentieth-century breakdown of morality. Authors and intellectuals, like Albert Camus and Jean-Paul Sartre, concluded that "being" was not the automatic process either of God's creation or of birth into the natural world. Instead, one created an "authentic" existence through individual choices and defining actions.

11. The postwar model for women emphasized a return to a domestic, nonworking norm, a far cry from their experiences as wartime laborers and family heads. This return to a restricted version of femininity was reflected in fashion; the "new look" style reintroduced mass culture to images of nineteenth-century, middle-class femininity. New household products, like refrigerators and washing machines, raised expectations for women's accomplishments in the home.

12. As the two superpowers negotiated through numerous conflicts, the power of radio and television was recognized and mass media became a tool of communism and capitalism. Conveyed by radio and other media, the cold war had a far-reaching impact on Western and Eastern nations. The U.S. dominance of mass media and consumer production saw American culture become very influential throughout the world. Radio was the primary means of disseminating cold war propaganda. When its programming was not being jammed by Soviet broadcasts, the Voice of America—based in Washington, D.C., and broadcasting in thirty-eight languages—provided an alternative source of information for peoples in Eastern Europe. Russian programs stressed a uniform Communist culture and values; the United States by contrast, emphasized diverse programming and promoted debate about current affairs. Then, as television grew in popularity, mostly in the West, governments began to recognize the power of visual media as well.

BUILDING HISTORICAL SKILLS

Reading Maps

Answers will vary.

1. After World War II, Germany was divided by the Allies into East and West. With the exception of the border between West Germany and Czechoslovakia, the border within Germany was the only place where East and West met in Europe. For both superpowers, the future of this historically powerful country seemed vital to ensure their national security and international interests.

2. One of Stalin's primary concerns after World War II, along with bringing about the economic recovery of the Soviet Union, was creating a buffer zone of states that could protect the Soviet Union from future Western aggression. Whereas the inclusion of Yugoslavia in the Warsaw Pact would have increased the size of that buffer zone, its borders do not touch those of the Soviet Union. Hungary and Poland's borders, on the other hand, touch directly to the Soviet Union; they could not therefore be allowed to leave the Soviet sphere.

Reading Illustrations

Answers will vary.

1. The photograph shows the tremendous devastation of Berlin from Allied bombing attacks. We see the enormous task facing these women as they try to clean up the rubble. The viewer identifies with the hardship these women are facing and feels sympathy experiences empathy toward them.

2. These women are dressed in everyday clothing: simple dresses and skirts. They lack gloves or any other sort of protective clothing. Their simple attire helps the viewers identify these women as ordinary women, while their

lack of protective clothing makes them appear more vulnerable.

3. The fact that these women are all carrying something as a group draws our attention to the differences between them (for example, the age differences) and underscores the significance of their united effort for recovery. This effort implies the existence of a united society, able to overcome its differences and work together to clear the devastation left by World War II. Americans, who considered themselves part of a "melting pot" society, may have been reassured by the impression that divisions among differing groups in society seemed unlikely to cause the conflicts they had in the past.

Reading Historical Documents

Answers will vary.

1. This woman's description of her youth shows that new styles of clothing, hairdos, and music were coming into fashion among Austria's youth. Sex and sexuality also appears to have been talked about more openly among the young, although, as the woman explains, they never discussed these topics among their elders. These changes in values and fashion created tensions between the young and the old, and the woman describes her mother's opposition to her choice in clothing, and her boss's opposition to her hairstyle.

2. American culture was being introduced into Europe at the time, both as a result of America's increased participation in world affairs, and of the expansion of the consumer market after World War II. More young people were working outside the home, especially after Europe's dramatic economic recovery from the war, and would have had more of their own money to spend on items such as records and fashionable clothing.

3. Schuman appealed to the economic interests of these two countries by proposing an economic union between the two so that war would be "not only unthinkable, but materially impossible." Such a union would counter nationalist impulses, and create an interdependence among member nations so that war would be counterproductive and against their interests.

4. The destruction wrought by World War II made clear the importance of avoiding another catastrophic war and maintaining world peace. Such unions were also important for the recovery of Europe, and for maintaining independence from the superpowers that had emerged after the war.

5. When the USSR made public its archives in the 1980s and 1990s, it was revealed that Stalin was not solely responsible for the violent repression the Soviet Union had experienced from the 1930s on as Khrushchev's public statements had suggested. Rather, Lenin and his contemporaries had begun the pattern of using violence to silence opposition. The almost universal condemnation of Stalin acting alone is, therefore, misguided. Russian archives also revealed that both Stalin and Khrushchev were usually eager to negotiate with the United States to avoid nuclear war.

6. American archives reveal that the United States did not solely use the atomic bomb to bring about a quick conclusion to the war; it was also used to intimidate the Soviets. Documents also show that Kennedy was not a "cold warrior," he had been characterized as. In fact, the material suggests that the superpowers never came as close to nuclear war as many had previously assumed.

Chapter 29: Postindustrial Society and the End of the Cold War Order, 1965–1989

CHAPTER OVERVIEW

Key Events

1. b; New technologies in birth control were approved.
2. d; The uprising was harshly repressed.
3. c; Limitation of nuclear arsenals in both countries
4. c; The embargo sparked a recession in the West marked by inflation and unemployment.
5. d; Increased intervention in the British economy
6. a; Lech Walesa
7. a; Margaret Thatcher
8. d; Nicolae Ceausescu

Key Terms

1. A; DNA (p. 1144)
2. C; in vitro fertilization (p. 1146)
3. D; multinational corporation (p. 1146)
4. I; pop art (p. 1152)
5. N; Vatican II (p. 1154)
6. G; Ostpolitik (p. 1156)
7. F; OPEC (p. 1167)
8. L; stagflation (p. 1168)
9. M; terrorism (p. 1168)
10. E; neoliberalism (p. 1171)
11. K; Solidarity (p. 1176)
12. B; glasnost (p. 1174)
13. H; perestroika (p. 1174)
14. J; samizdat (p. 1156)

Identification

1. discovered the configuration of DNA
2. 1957
3. Louise Brown
4. Colossus
5. 1969
6. Concorde
7. Andy Warhol
8. John Cage
9. Claude Lévi-Strauss
10. John XXIII
11. Ostpolitik
12. János Kádár
13. Christa Wolf
14. Lyndon B. Johnson
15. Betty Friedan
16. Henry Kissinger
17. 1974
18. Iran
19. Milton Friedman
20. François Mitterrand

CHAPTER REVIEW

Multiple Choice

1. d	12. d	23. b
2. c	13. c	24. b
3. c	14. a	25. b
4. c	15. d	26. b
5. d	16. b	27. b
6. c	17. a	28. a
7. c	18. b	29. d
8. c	19. b	30. a
9. c	20. a	31. a
10. d	21. a	32. b
11. c	22. a	

Short Answer

Answers will vary.

1. Although America had led television ownership, Europeans rapidly adopted television in the decades spanning the mid-1950s to the mid-1970s. Useful in advancing various ideological platforms, television spread propaganda, relayed information, and provided entertainment, but its influence also affected postwar culture and united far-flung viewing audiences with standardized programming. Some argued that TV broadcasting made culture too standardized and less accomplished. As such, European governments, fearing Americanization and believing this new medium should be used to preserve and promote the humanist tradition, funded television broadcasting with tax dollars and limited programming to feature drama, ballet, concerts, variety shows, and news. Television also made it increasingly important for politicians to cultivate a successful media image.

2. Beginning with the launching of the first satellite, *Sputnik*, by the Soviet Union in 1957, the United States and the Soviet Union competed to develop space technology in order to both win international prestige and prevent the other from gaining any significant advantages. Large amounts of money were invested in these new technologies, and missions into space made heroes of astronauts and cosmonauts. The space race also drove Western cultural developments: science-fiction writing became wildly popular as authors raised concerns about human morality, spiritual belief, and extraterrestrial life; films and TV drew viewers into a technological and futuristic fantasy. Although the space race grew out of cold war hostilities and involved national rivalries, it, along with other interlocking space, computer, and information technology systems, depended on a great deal of international cooperation. This helped to counter virulent nationalism (even if it failed to ease cold war tensions).

3. In Western societies, a combination of new technologies, uninhibited experimentation and changing social mores had a great impact on sexuality. The community and family norms of traditional societies no longer possessed the influence they once did, and the growing availability of effective birth control devices—particularly the birth control pill—meant that young people were sexually active earlier with less risk of pregnancy. The popular use of birth control allowed Western culture to be saturated with highly sexualized music, literature, and journalism without a corresponding rise in the birthrate, proof of the increasing separation of sexuality from reproduction. In a climate of increased publicity of sexuality, more open homosexual behavior became apparent, along with continued efforts to decriminalize it in the West.

4. The label *postindustrial* refers to the shift from manufacturing and heavy industry to an emphasis on the distribution of services that began in the 1960s. Because the service sector had become the leading force in the economy, intellectual rather than industrial work became primary in creating jobs and profits. One of the major innovations of postindustrial society was the growing number of multinational corporations, which produced goods and services for a worldwide market and conducted business on a global level. A new kind of white-collar working class replaced the older manufacturing worker, and even farming was transformed as bureaucracies took over the decision-making process from farmers. Heavy investments in education and research were key to running postindustrial society.

5. In the 1960s, the family appeared in many new forms: households were now headed by a single parent, by remarried parents merging two sets of unrelated children, by unmarried couples cohabiting, or by traditionally married parents who had fewer children. Households of same-sex partners also became more common. At the end of the 1970s, the marriage rate had fallen and the divorce rate had risen. After almost two decades of a "baby boom," the birthrate dropped significantly. Radio and television filled a family's leisure time and often formed the basis of its common social life. More women worked outside the home during these years to pay for the prolonged economic dependence of children who attended school into their twenties. Whereas the early modern family organized labor, taught craft skills, and monitored reproductive behavior, the modern family seemed to have a primary psychological mission: to provide emotional nurturing while their children learned intellectual skills in school.

6. Cultural trends evolved with the march of consumer society. Rock music replaced romantic ballads and celebrated youthful rebellion against adult culture. Bands such as the Beatles were themselves products of marketing for mass consumption. Visual artists, particularly those in the pop art trend, employed some of the same techniques used by advertisers, often as a parody of modern commercialism. Others focused on the grotesque aspects of consumer products or incorporated ordinary objects such as scraps of metal or dirt into their works. Composers likewise incorporated sounds produced by ordinary objects into their music, continuing the trend away from the classical melody.

7. In Europe and Asia, some countries sought ways to undermine the strict cold war division of the world. Willy Brandt, the Socialist mayor of West Berlin, became the foreign minister of West Germany and pursued a policy, Ostpolitik, which ended frigid relations with the Soviet bloc and pursued reconciliation and trade with East Germany. In France, Charles de Gaulle also moved to break the cold war stranglehold on Europe by advocating a cooperative

Europe in opposition to the superpowers. He withdrew French forces from NATO, and signed trade agreements with the Soviet bloc, thereby offering an alternative to passive obedience to the superpowers. In the Soviet Union, Khrushchev pushed de-Stalinization further by reducing the privileges of Communist officials, although he was ousted in 1964. His successors loosened cultural restrictions, allowing Soviet scientists to participate in meetings with Westerners and tolerating dissident artists.

8. A new social activism emerged in the West as a wide variety of social groups attempted to transform society to fit their ideals. Minorities increasingly celebrated their cultural heritage and, in some cases, turned to violent means to promote social equality and attract attention to their causes. Opposition to the Vietnam War and the advocacy of civil rights became the most popular rallying points for movements, especially among students. Women, finding that protest organizations often devalued them as much as dominant cultures, began fighting more vigorously, and separately, in their struggles to overturn traditional patterns of femininity and restrictions on women's work and social lives. In the Eastern bloc, dissident movements demanded political democratization and social change.

9. A variety of social protests exploded worldwide in 1968, changing the style and direction of political activism in Western societies. The Tet offensive saw the antiwar movement gain momentum, and the assassination of Martin Luther King Jr. caused American cities to erupt into violence as African Americans vented their rage at the faltering civil rights movement. As expected, activist confrontations with authority grew. In France, student protests paralyzed French society until the French government used a combination of shrewd political maneuvering and military force to crush the student movement. In the Eastern bloc, attempts at reforming Communism in Czechoslovakia, under the leadership of Alexander Dubček during the so-called Prague Spring, were brutally crushed by a Soviet invasion and a clear renunciation by the Soviets of reform movements throughout the Eastern bloc. These movements challenged the political direction of Western society, yet little turned out as reformers had hoped. Many governments turned to conservative solutions and, in some cases, violent repression.

10. Détente was a period of lessening cold war tensions between the United States and the Soviet Union in the 1970s. It was shaped by the withdrawal of the United States from the Vietnam War and increasing negotiation between the superpowers. The United States and USSR began to negotiate limits on their nuclear arsenals in the SALT I treaty. In the Helsinki accords (1975), the West officially acknowledged Soviet territorial gains in World War II in exchange for the Soviet's guarantee of basic human rights.

11. Tensions between Israel and the Arab world provided the catalyst for an oil crisis when Israeli forces delivered a humiliating defeat to Egypt, Syria, and Jordan during the Six-Day War (1967). In response, the Arab states formed a common political and economic strategy through the Organization of Petroleum Exporting Countries (OPEC). OPEC increased the price of oil and imposed an oil embargo on the United States in retaliation for its support of Israel. This upset the balance of economic power because the oil-producing nations provoked a recession in the West that was marked by increased unemployment and inflation. It also demonstrated that the Middle East could successfully stand up against the West.

12. Neoliberalism is an economic policy based on the theory that the economy as a whole benefits when businesses grow and their prosperity "trickles down" through the rest of society. Such monetarist or supply-side theories are associated most prominently with American economist Milton Friedman who contended that inflation results when governments pump money into an economy at a faster rate than the nation's economic growth. Thus, in order to keep prices from rising rapidly, governments were urged to tighten the money supply, usually by cutting back on social services, and spur new investment in business by reducing income taxes on the wealthy. In some cases, neoliberalism had a moral component: supporters of these economic policies claimed that social service programs made people lazy.

BUILDING HISTORICAL SKILLS

Reading Maps

Answers will vary.

1. Seeking improved economic opportunities, East Germans flooded soviet bloc countries hoping for eventual passage into West Germany which willingly took in all East German immigrants. When Hungary opened its borders, a flood of East Germans circumvented the wall. Finally, as crowds reached fever pitch in East Berlin, the government of East Germany released an ambiguous statement about allowing passage into West Berlin. East Germans immediately flowed into West Germans, unabated by border guards.

2. These countries served as an effective border between the USSR and Western Europe. Following Russia's terrible losses during World War II, losing some 25 million of its citizens, Stalin believed he had much to fear from the West. Truman, the new American president, fearing Soviet expansionism, immediately cut off aid to Russia at the end of the war. Stalin, ever more suspicious, engineered not just a temporary military occupation, but a permanent "buffer zone" of European states loyal to the USSR. Russia imposed Communist rule on Bulgaria and Romania, as well as provided support to the communist regimes in Hungary, Poland, and elsewhere. The countries colored here in orange are part of that "buffer zone."

Reading Illustrations

Answers will vary.

1. The children have either drastically shrunken or missing arms. The children are playing and seem very happy. Even the boy in the front, who appears pensive, is smiling slightly.

2. The photograph is heart-wrenching in its depiction of these children with birth defects. Although they look happy, one might assume that they have faced, and will continue to face, numerous difficulties in life. The

juxtaposition of the trees and the tire-like objects could be seen as emphasizing the ways in which science and technology encroach on natural environments and processes, like the womb or childbirth, respectively.

3. Despite the birth defects, the children are smiling. The companies might wish to send a message that they care about the children affected by the drug, and that even though the drug had terrible consequences, the children still appear to be able to live normal lives.

Reading Historical Documents

Answers will vary.

1. Thatcher's economic policies were to cut back on government spending, particularly in social programs, and then use the savings to reduce taxes for businesses. She hoped that this would stimulate the economy by easing the pressure on businesses, which would consequently create more jobs for the unemployed. This would in turn contribute to a more prosperous, "independent" Great Britain.

2. When this document was produced, Great Britain, like most of Western Europe, was deep in a recession that had been largely brought about by the dramatic increase in oil prices. The days of prosperity and economic confidence were over, and Great Britain was faced with high inflation, high unemployment, as well as the revolt in Northern Ireland.

3. Gorbachev continually remarks that the economic difficulties the Soviet Union is facing are "alien to socialism" and that his proposed reforms are "fully based on the principle of more socialism." Gorbachev repeatedly emphasizes the vitality of socialism, dispelling rumors from the West that it is dead.

4. Gorbachev criticizes the situation in the USSR in which wasteful and inefficient uses of steel, raw materials, fuel, energy, and grain produces shortfalls in what should actually be a plentiful supply. He also points to ideological problems that prevented objective scrutiny of the problems the Soviet Union was facing and ignored the opinions of the public at large. His call for more democracy, and a turn away from the dominant environment of "eulogizing and servility," represent a turn away from the direction things had been taking in the Soviet Union up to that point.

5. Feminism was united by a belief that women's issues were important and needed to be addressed, and that sexist attitudes and discrimination against women needed to be reformed. However, the ways in which these points were made varied greatly, from calls for equality in the workplace to pleas for healthy environments. Regardless of the arena, feminists were not afraid to voice their concerns, but they may have made greater strides had they been more cohesive.

6. Feminism focused on women in relation to larger issues, such as the environment, racism, sexuality, and the organization of work. Above all, women fought to make the point that women's experiences were not separate from these other issues, but were intimately tied to them.

Chapter 30: The New Globalism: Opportunities and Dilemmas, 1989 to the Present

CHAPTER OVERVIEW

Key Events

1. c; Because war with Iran had ruined the Iraqi economy and Kuwait's oil would help rebuild it
2. c; Serbia
3. b; Boris Yeltsin
4. c; extraordinarily wealthy Russians
5. b; Nelson Mandela

Key Terms

1. B; euro (p. 1185)
2. A; ethnic cleansing (p. 1189)
3. C; European Union (EU) (p. 1198)
4. I; World Bank (p. 1201)
5. F; Nongovernmental organizations (NGOs) (p. 1201)
6. D; global warming (p. 1202)
7. G; Pacific tigers (p. 1210)
8. H; postmodernism (p. 1219)
9. E; Maastricht Treaty (p. 1198)

Identification

1. Croatia
2. Bosnia-Herzegovina
3. 1991
4. Chechnya
5. Vladimir Putin
6. 1994
7. 1999
8. Turkey
9. International Monetary Fund
10. Association for the Taxation of Financial Transactions
11. Chernobyl
12. Central Africa
13. Nelson Mandela
14. Afghanistan
15. Saddam Hussein
16. 1989
17. Nawal el-Saadawi
18. Toni Morrison
19. Mikhail Bulgakov
20. Michel Foucault

CHAPTER REVIEW

Multiple Choice

1. c		12. b		23. a	
2. a		13. b		24. b	
3. b		14. a		25. c	
4. c		15. c		26. c	
5. c		16. c		27. b	
6. a		17. c		28. c	
7. d		18. d		29. d	
8. c		19. b		30. a	
9. b		20. c		31. c	
10. c		21. c		32. b	
11. c		22. b			

Short Answer

Answers will vary.

1. Before its collapse in the early 1990s, communism had enforced a unity among several religious and ethnic groups and attempted to instill common ideals among them. When it collapsed, ambitious politicians, most notably Slobodan Milosevic, used ethnicity to assert the dominance of the Serbs over the Yugoslav federation. When other ethnic groups resisted Milosevic's pro-Serb nationalism and seceded, Milosevic resorted to military force and genocide, sparking a civil war that lasted throughout much of the decade.

2. The attempts to develop a free market in Russia created several problems as salaries went unpaid, food remained in short supply, and essential services disintegrated. The opening of Russia's borders permitted many talented workers to leave the country, which made recovery even more difficult. Much of the country's industrial infrastructure had grown outdated after being removed from global development for decades, and many officials were selling state property for personal gain.

3. As the Soviet Union collapsed, central Asian states such as Chechnya, Kazakhstan, and Uzbekistan began to assert their independence and influence. The oil-rich state of Chechnya tried to secede from the USSR in 1991, and the following year it gained control over a large stockpile of Russian weaponry. In 1994, Boris Yeltsin, partly to prop up his sagging authority in Russia, invaded Chechnya. Other Central European states became involved in issues of terrorism and the global economy, particularly centered around issues of oil. Uzbekistan allowed anti-Western terrorists to train in their territory, while Kazakhstan has been using its vast oil reserved to play Western oil companies off against Muslim interests in the region.

4. For decades, European nations had been working to eliminate national distinctions that had hindered commerce and transportation. In 1992, the twelve countries participating in the Common Market ended passport controls on many borders and agreed that all of the member nations' firms be treated the same by every government. In 1994, the European Community was transformed into the European Union and, five years later, a common currency, the euro, began to replace individual national currencies. Common policies standardized such things as pollution controls, while a central bank guided interest rates and economic policy. In this way, economies and many social policies were no longer determined by an individual nation-state, but by a union of several nation-states.

5. Membership in the European Union was very attractive to poorer countries in the east as the infusion of EU funds and economic relationships improved their economies. After the collapse of the Soviet Union, several Soviet states privatized industry, often selling them to Western businesses. Many Western businesses also viewed Eastern Europe as a promising new market and extended their businesses into these states. In 2002, the EU voted to admit ten new members, many of which were from Eastern Europe.

6. Globalization has brought about many new supranational organizations for a variety of purposes such as regulating international finance and addressing social issues. Organizations such as the World Bank and International Monetary Fund provide loans to developing nations on condition that they restructure their economies on neoliberal principles. Other charitable organizations that are not affiliated with a government, such as Doctors Without Borders, provide medical and other social services in poorer or wartorn regions. Although developing nations often benefit from loans and charity, they are often forced to adopt policies that are detrimental to them. Free trade often prevents them from being competitive on a global market because more powerful nations enact tariffs and subsidies that keep out foreign products.

7. Technological development, rapid population increases (primarily in less-industrialized nations) and the corresponding drain on natural resources continued to threaten ecological systems around the globe. Nuclear proliferation led to concerns about exposure to high levels of radioactivity, a danger made all too real with the explosion of a nuclear plant in Chernobyl, USSR. Fossil-fuel pollutants—from natural gas, coal, and oil-mixed with atmospheric moisture to produce acid rain poisoned forests in industrialized areas. The public's use of chlorofluorocarbons had opened up a hole in the ozone layer. Automobile and industrial emissions accumulated in the ozone layer, which led to an increase in the temperature of Earth's lower atmosphere in a process known as global warming. Changes in temperature and dramatic weather cycles of drought or drenching rain indicated that a greenhouse effect might be permanently warming Earth.

8. Led by charismatic and ambitious leaders, and using oil as a powerful bargaining tool, the combined forces of religion and nationalism in the Middle East challenged the dominance of the West. Ayatollah Khomeini successfully created a religious republic in Iran that rejected earlier strides toward Westernization and capitalism. His program— "Neither East, nor West, only the Islamic Republic"—had wide appeal. Similar pan-Islamic movements in other countries were also influential, including Afghanistan, where Islam provided a center of resistance against the invading Soviet army. Despite pan-Arabism, power in the Middle East remained dispersed and Islamic leaders did not achieve their unifying goals. War plagued the region as Iraq tried to make itself the dominant force via a lengthy war with Iran and by invading Kuwait. Some leaders used international terrorism to advance their causes; terrorism did much to reshape international politics of the twentieth century.

9. Asian economic growth was fueled by explosive technologically based productivity as well as low labor costs in the "tiger" economies of the Pacific Rim countries. Japan led Asia's economic development, basing its growth on massive investment in high-tech production methods. Japanese companies turned out high-quality consumer products that found an eager international market. As the profits rolled in, Asian-Pacific funds were used to purchase U.S. government bonds, thereby financing America's ballooning national debt. However, low-paid workers did not generally benefit from the national financial success for which

they labored. Nonetheless, many Pacific Rim countries have seen educational standards rise, along with access to birth control and medical care.

10. As a result of uneven economic development, political persecution, and warfare, millions of people migrated in the latter few decades of the twentieth century to seek work in countries with more opportunity. There they contributed to a nation's wealth and often sent money home to their native lands, providing much-needed funds to their less mobile family members. In many instances, these funds have become a substantial portion of non-Western nations' national income. Immigrants often experience difficulties, and are frequently discriminated against or exploited. In some cases, they have become scapegoats for native Europeans who suffer from economic hardship and unemployment.

11. The rapid growth of the Internet after the mid-1990s created a global community based on business needs, shared cultural interests, and other factors that transcend common citizenship in a particular nation-state. The Internet allows users to escape governmental regulations and censorship, and has contributed to the further globalization of the marketplace. There are mixed opinions as to the benefits of this because, although the Internet might help promote world democracy, it only benefits those who have access to computers and the necessary computer skills. The Internet has contributed to "outsourcing" whereby service jobs are exported to non-Western nations with cheaper labor, thereby allowing the service industry to globalize much like the manufacturing sector had done.

12. Remarkable innovations in communications, and the breakdown of national borders, have created a global culture that maintains a distinctly Western flavor. The economic and political power of the United States and the legacy of British imperialism have made English an international language of culture, and the power of American and European media corporations has filled the world with Western styles. Simultaneously, however, Western culture has also absorbed elements from other cultures. Through modern technology, music, literature, and film from non-Western societies can now reach a worldwide audience, although these styles are sometimes modified in order to appeal to a wider Western audience. The mixing of a variety of international styles has become common, and when this hypermixing takes place without a central unifying theme or privileged canon, the resulting style is sometimes referred to as postmodernism.

BUILDING HISTORICAL SKILLS

Reading Maps

Answers will vary.

1. When these territories broke away from the Soviet Union, they were free to establish their own identities and create their own political, social, and cultural systems. Without the uniformity imposed by communism, ethnic differences became more important, as diverse groups struggled to make their voices heard. Thus it is not surprising that these new republics experienced violent, ethnic conflict.

2. Moscow was the capital of the Soviet Union. By locating the capital elsewhere, the CIS demonstrated its desire to break its ties with the Soviet past. At the same time, Minsk is relatively close to Moscow, which retains enormous economic, cultural, and political clout in the region.

Reading Illustrations

Answers will vary.

1. This person is reading a British newspaper in Italy about an event that took place in the United States. The availability of foreign-language newspapers in Italy attests to a more global marketplace, while the fact that a British newspaper has this headline shows that news such as this had international implications. Presumably, the person reading this newspaper is not Italian, which shows that people travel a lot, either as tourists or for business.

2. Terrorist attacks such as those on September 11 were motivated by a desire to wreak retribution on the West for its role in geopolitical affairs. The nature of the attacks themselves had an international aspect because the hijackers were trained in Afghanistan in camps established by a wealthy Saudi Arabian. The destruction of the World Trade Center had an important symbolic value for the hijackers, while their method was made possible through modern technology and the commonality of air travel.

Reading Historical Documents

Answers will vary.

1. The Green Party defines itself here as "half [political] party, half local action group," meaning that they try to work both from within and without the political system. Rather than protest against the government from the outside, or trying to gain power in the same way as established parties, the Green Party proposes to work within the government not according to party politics, but according to what they assert are the best interests of humanity in general.

2. The Green Party is concerned with more than just the environment; it also promotes the protection of human rights. They propose to build a better society through the protection of individual human rights and a more rational use of natural resources.

3. Havel argues that Czechoslovakia's unsuitability for the European Union are not due to its innate inadequacies, but is a legacy of Soviet subjugation. He also argues that Czechoslovakians are like "wayward children" of Europe who were unnaturally cut off during Soviet rule.

4. Havel argues that years of living under Soviet rule have given Czechoslovakia a special introspection into human nature and moral responsibility. He claims that people are still unable "to put morality ahead of politics, science, and economics." Czechoslovakia's experience living under an oppressive regime has taught it the importance of moral responsibility that would benefit the European Union.

5. Globalization forms alliances and partnerships that are potentially beneficial to smaller enterprises because it links them to a global network thereby giving them greater purchasing power or market clout. However, it imposes regulations on local economic systems that are

often incompatible and can facilitate terrorist activity. The migration that goes along with globalization also has the potential to provoke ethnic tension.

6. Businesses seem to benefit the most from globalization because it ties them into networks that promote their growth. Local communities, such as the farmers in India, are at a disadvantage because new rules can interfere with their traditional modes of agriculture. Globalization has mixed advantages for others. While it gives many migrant workers the opportunity to find work outside their own country, it also creates an environment for terrorist activity that did not exist before.